THE DEVELOPMENT OF DRAMATIC ART

BY

Donald Clive Stuart, Ph.D.

This new Dover edition, first published in 1960, is an unabridged and unaltered republication of the work first published by D. Appleton-Century Company in 1928.

DOVER PUBLICATIONS, INC.
NEW YORK

792.09
St 9d

42,238
December, 1961

Manufactured in the United States of America

Dover Publications, Inc.
180 Varick Street
New York 14, N. Y.

To
REED STUART

PREFACE

The aim of this book is to trace the development of dramatic art from its origin to the present day. Therefore it includes within its scope only those forms of drama which contributed directly or indirectly to the development of the art as it appears on the modern stage. No play is discussed merely because it is a fine example of dramatic art. Certain plays that are mediocre have been analyzed because they have contributed in some degree to the development of the art. The omission of a play is not to be construed as a tacit criticism of its artistic value. Oriental drama, English and American drama of the nineteenth century and even plays of such dramatists as Jonson, Beaumont and Fletcher, Congreve, Sheridan, Alfieri, Calderon and others are not treated because modern dramatic art would not be essentially different had they never been written.

The ultimate origin of modern drama is found in certain primitive Greek rituals. These ritualistic practices developed into Greek tragedy and Aristophanic comedy. New Comedy was an outgrowth of these two forms and it was preserved in the plays of Plautus and Terence. The so-called Senecan tragedies were the only serious plays by a Roman playwright to survive the downfall of the Roman Empire.

About the tenth century a new form of drama developed from the Christian rituals. The classical drama remained in manuscript form, while medieval drama developed as the living form of the art. During the Renaissance the classical form was rediscovered and revived in Italy. Its influence then spread to France, Spain and England where it combined with the medieval form and produced drama more or less classical in proportion as its influence was operative.

With the closing of the theatres in England in 1642 and with the decay of the vitality of Spain, the French theatre assumed the leadership of dramatic art and held it for many generations. By the middle of the eighteenth century, sentimental comedy and domestic tragedy began to demand a place on the European stage which had been dominated by neo-classical ideals. Steele, Cibber, Lillo and Moore in England, Diderot and Sedaine in France, Lessing and Schiller in Germany were exponents of these new forms. But the Shakespearean revival brought forth romantic tragedy in the late eighteenth and early nineteenth centuries in Germany and France and delayed the natural development of bourgeois drama into the problem play, which finally took place after the middle of the nineteenth century.

French dramatic craftsmanship always tended to stress construction according to rules. The well-made play was the result of the classical ideals of dramatic art combined with the innate clarity, orderliness and logic of the French. Towards the end of the nineteenth century the Germans, the Russians and the French naturalists attacked the well-made problem play. At the same time symbolism began to permeate the plays of Ibsen and of Maeterlinck. Strindberg, inspired by Maeterlinck's symbolism, introduced expressionism into drama.

The expressionistic dramatists have cast aside all rules, all conventions. The modern theatre is open to every known form of dramatic art. The dramatist who has something to say has only to choose the form in which he wishes to say it. All the arts and much of the mechanics of the modern world are at his command. Whatever synthesis he employs, he will be heard, provided he knows how to play upon the delicate mechanism of the human mind.

Such is the development in brief outline which this book aims to trace in detail. Emphasis has been laid upon that form of drama which was preparing for the advance, or was actually progressing, or was the dominant influence in the theatre in any given period. Hence an apparent lack of proportion in the treatment of the respective dramatic epochs was unavoidable. The book is not a history of dramatic art; but it is hoped that the reader who follows the discussion to the end may obtain a clearer understanding of how and why dramatic art arose at the altar of Dionysus and developed into the many forms which thousands of people are witnessing at this moment.

D. C. S.

THE DEVELOPMENT
OF DRAMATIC ART

CHAPTER I

THE ORIGIN OF GREEK TRAGEDY. ÆSCHYLUS

DRAMA exists when a human being pretends, for artistic reasons, that he is something or someone else. Drama is more than imitation. A portrait is an imitation, an artistic likeness. Drama is an artistic illusion, although it is not a perfect illusion of reality by which we are entirely deceived.

Drama could spring from the play of a child who imagines, for the time being, that he is someone else; or it could arise from theriomorphic dances in which a childlike man pretends that he is an animal. Modern dramatic art developed from pagan and Christian rituals in which the celebrants began to impersonate the divine beings or forces of nature they were worshipping.

Rituals are devised to celebrate an important event of the past, such as the birth or death of a god or hero, or of the present, such as the return of spring or the annual resurrection of a god. In the first case, the ritual is retrospective. It is an evocation of the past. In the second case, the ritual is the celebration of some event that is supposedly taking place. Celebrants of a ritual usually wear some insignia such as a mask, or some special article of clothing. Drama is more than persons in costume reciting a ritual; but the insignia sets them apart from others. Drama hovers on the threshold of existence when, under the stress of religious emotion, the celebrant unconsciously loses his own identity and begins to feel that he is the god or hero or someone closely connected with the god or hero in whose honor the ritual is being performed. An audience is in process of creation when any onlooker, not taking an active part in the ritual, feels that the celebrant is no longer a priest but is a character in the event which is being celebrated. No matter how fleeting such impressions may be, drama is potentially existent so long as they last.

Drama exists when these impressions are the result, not merely of religious inspiration, but also of artistic inspiration. A dramatic ritual is not drama; but it sometimes gives birth to ritualistic drama.

In connection with the worship of Dionysus, there was the celebration of his birth in the form of a dithyramb. Plato believed that the original meaning of the term was a song in celebration of the birth of Dionysus. At first the dithyramb was improvisational. It was probably a performance in which a chorus, disguised as caprine satyrs, rendered a ritualistic chant in connection with improvisations sung or spoken by a leader. It was a wild, orgiastic rite. The tone of the dithyramb was undignified, the language was ludicrous. The revelry was obscene.

Whether or not there was impersonation on the part of the celebrants in these extemporaneous performances, no one knows. The fact that they were extemporaneous would not militate against impersonation or imitation. The actors of the Italian *commedia dell' arte* extemporized their dialogue. The mental condition of the worshippers of Dionysus would be favorable to impersonation. If there was impersonation, the result was a dramatic ritual and not drama, for drama is the result of an artistic impulse.

Aristotle states that tragedy was "improvisational by origin" and that it was derived "from the leaders of the dithyramb." A fragment of Archilochus says that he "knows how, when his heart is crazed with wine, to lead lord Dionysus' dithyramb." Leading a dithyramb does not mean writing it; but it might mean enacting it. Aristotle does not imply that the leaders of the dithyramb were the first authors of a form of drama which developed into tragedy, but were the first actors of a ritualistic mimesis which became tragedy.

When did the dithyrambic ritual in honor of Dionysus become a form of drama as a result of an impulse not wholly religious but, in part, artistic? Solon of Athens is said to have made the statement in his *Elegies* that "Arion introduced the first drama of tragedy." Herodotus says: "Arion was second to none of the harpists of that time and was the first of the men known to us to compose a dithyramb and to give it a name and to represent it at Corinth." Whether Arion was really the first or not, at least we know that, by the middle of the seventh century, B.C., the dithyramb was not merely an improvised religious ritual but was a form of art with titles, composed as the result of an impulse which was artistic as well as religious.

We cannot be certain that impersonation was an element in the dithyramb at this period; but it is probable that such was the case. The phrase "drama of tragedy" may mean a mimetic choral ritual. As Aristotle said: "Imitation is one instinct of our nature." Impersonation would naturally arise under the stimulus of orgiastic rites when the dithyramb was purely an act of emotional celebration in honor of the god of wine. We know that impersonation arose in connection with the Christian rituals commemorating the death and resurrection of Christ. Since it could arise in such circumstances of a solemn, retrospective ritual, it could develop all the more easily in the Greek orgiastic revelry.

It has been suggested by a modern critic that even at an advanced stage the dithyramb "was probably much like a sacred oratorio of modern times in which the performers may sing words which are appropriate to characters and yet make no attempt by costume, gesture or action to represent those characters." But the chorus in the dithyramb were in costume; and because of this costume, they made a very different impression from that of the oratorio singers in ordinary dress. Also, the celebrants of a ritual usually make gestures which are at least symbolic, if not imitative. It is probable that these Greek worshippers were no exception to the rule. An uncostumed, sacred oratorio is more undramatic than a ritual, and we are concerned with an orgiastic rite in which costume was worn by the priests.

Tragedy was originally joyous in its tone. Aristotle describes its development as follows: "Tragedy acquired also its magnitude. Discarding short stories and a ludicrous diction, through its passing out of its satyric stage, it assumed, though only at a late point in its progress, a tone of dignity." When Aristotle defines the form of tragedy which he treats in the *Poetics,* his first statement is that "tragedy, then, is the imitation of an action that is serious." Of all the differences between early tragedy and the tragedy of his age, the difference in tone is the most striking, the most important. Aristotle gives the time of this development as "late." Professor Flickinger would place it, by implication, as post-Thespian, since he believes that Thespian tragedy was ludicrous. Professor Bywater conjectures that it refers to the period of Phrynichus. What Aristotle meant by "late" we shall probably never know.

The reason of this momentous change in tone seems rarely to have interested classical scholars of the past or present. To consider this evolution as a natural development is to avoid the question. Usually the serious tone of tragedy is ascribed to the influence of epic poetry on dramatic art. Classical scholars have been prone to exaggerate the influence of epic poetry and to make assumptions that have no basis of historical facts, so far as we know them, nor any validity whatsoever so far as the art of drama is concerned.

Professor Flickinger represents correctly the consensus of opinion of classical scholars when he says: "The indebtedness of tragedy to epic poetry for subject matter, dignity of treatment and of diction, and development of plot, including such technical devices as recognition and reversal of situation, is too well established to require argument." It is true that these views are held tenaciously; but the indebtedness of tragedy to the epic, so patent as to require no argument, is that of subject matter and diction. Even this indebtedness seems to have been incurred in the Æschylean period or but slightly prior to it.

Recognition and reversal of situation are not really technical devices inherent in dramatic art. Aristotle's theories and his discussions concerning them have greatly exaggerated their importance. They are not a necessary part of drama or of the epic. Their presence in a drama or their absence does not automatically increase or decrease the dramatic value of the piece. They are, at times, excellent means of arousing certain emotions in both drama and epic. They are a means to an end, but not an end in themselves, as Aristotle believed.

Unless the evidence furnished by extant plays is entirely misleading, development of plot occurred in the Æschylean period. His *Persians, Suppliants* and *Prometheus Bound* have little plot. The *Phœnician Women* by Phrynichus seems to have had almost none at all. The Æschylean plays require two actors and a chorus. Phrynichus had to compose his early dramas for one actor, or one individual character and a chorus. Naturally they could not have much plot. There is no reason to believe that the development of plot on the part of Æschylus and Sophocles was the result of their study of the epic. It was rather due to an increasing skill on their part as dramatists who realized that the Greek audience enjoyed the complications which they introduced gradually. It was also due to the fact that Æschylus could employ two speaking actors and finally three speaking actors to play scenes in these more developed plots. Sophocles' *Electra* is much more developed in plot than the *Libation-Bearers* of Æschylus. Surely this difference between the two plays on the same theme is not due to the influence of epic poetry on Sophocles as a dramatist.

In the development of any art, the reasons for the changes are to be sought in the art itself rather than in any other form of art. To ascribe the narrative speeches in tragedy to the influence of the structure of the epic, to ascribe the dignity of tragedy to the influence of the tone of the epic, is to assume a close relationship which does not exist between these two arts. Epic poets treated certain stories. Dramatists also treated them. Æschylus dramatized the Homeric epics; but Æschylus did not learn his art of playmaking from Homer.

We are naturally led to seek some form of dramatic ritual or even ritualistic drama which would influence primitive joyous tragedy and which would cause it to develop into the serious tragedy written by Æschylus. The serious drama of the Middle

Ages developed from a solemn, retrospective ritual dealing with the death and resurrection of Christ. The Greeks performed similar rituals in honor of their dead heroes. Herodotus is our authority for the existence among the Sicyonians of such a ritual in honor of their dead king, Adrastus. He says: "Besides other ceremonies, it has been their wont to honor Adrastus with tragic choruses, which they assigned to him rather than Dionysus, on account of his calamities" (v. 67). The question arises whether these choruses would have performed joyous rituals had they been assigned to Dionysus first. Probably such would have been the case. But the dramatic ritual performed by a chorus in honor of Adrastus "on account of his calamities" was serious and dignified, not orgiastic and ludicrous. Herodotus makes the additional statement that "Clisthenes now gave the choruses to Dionysus, transferring to Melanippus the rest of the sacred rites." This transfer of choruses is evidence of the close association of different forms of choral worship.

The evolution of tragedy may now be traced. From the leaders of the dithyramb—whom I would identify with the leaders of the choruses—arose impersonation and mimesis as they performed an orgiastic, joyous rite in honor of the birth of Dionysus. This impersonation and mimesis caused the dramatic ritual to evolve into ritualistic drama performed by a chorus dressed as caprine satyrs. From the goat-like appearance of the chorus was derived the word tragedy or goat-song. At Sicyon, the choruses, which Herodotus implies might have been assigned to Dionysus, were assigned to Adrastus. They performed solemn rites and introduced into this ritual the elements of impersonation and mimesis, which had sprung from the leaders of the dithyramb and which caused these solemn rites to evolve into a ritualistic drama in honor of the dead hero. It was then that serious tragedy became an offshoot of joyous tragedy. The original joyous form of dramatic art did not disappear, but developed into the satyr play. When the chorus at Sicyon was assigned to Dionysus, the construction and serious tone of the ritualistic drama in honor of Adrastus was, to some extent, superimposed upon the dithyramb in honor of Dionysus. The joyous tragedy continued to exist side by side with serious tragedy. A new form of drama does not instantly supplant an older form; but the elements which are acceptable innovations develop gradually.

According to a tradition handed down by Suidas, Epigenes of Sicyon was the first tragic poet. It was also a tradition that the Greek proverb, "nothing to do with Dionysus," arose "when Epigenes had composed a tragedy in honor of Dionysus." Professor Flickinger gives a very simple and highly credible explanation of the origin of the proverb. "We have no information," he says, "as to the costume which the choreutæ wore honoring the sorrows of Adrastus. There was, of course, no reason for their appearing as satyrs. But were satyric choreutæ introduced at the same time that the dances were given over to Dionysus? If we answer this question in the negative, the situation becomes clear. The audience, or part of it, was sufficiently acquainted with the performances instituted by Arion at Corinth to expect a chorus of satyrs in the Sicyonian dances after they were transferred to Dionysus. And when Epigenes brought on his choreutæ in the same (non-satyric) costume they naturally manifested their surprise with the ejaculation: οὐδὲν πρὸς Διόνυσον (nothing to do with Dionysus). By this they meant: 'Why, these choreutæ are just what we have had all the time; there is nothing of the satyr about them. They have nothing to do with Dionysus.' "

At least we have the tradition that some non-Dionysiac element had been introduced by Epigenes at Sicyon into the ritualistic drama. The influence of the ritual in honor of the dead hero accounts for the serious tone of tragedy, and the same ritual explains the construction of tragedy as we know it. Therefore, it seems that this influence was operative; and in view of the statements of Herodotus in regard to what happened at Sicyon, the reciprocal influence of these two rituals was operating at that place and in the sixth century. The dramatic element of mimesis was furnished by the Dionysiac dithyramb. The serious element and the general construction of tragedy sprang from the ceremonies in honor of Adrastus.

Surely Epigenes had at least seen the rites in honor of the dead hero. Furthermore, it is quite possible that Epigenes had composed the choral songs in honor of Adrastus before he began to compose tragedies in honor of Dionysus when Clisthenes transferred the chorus to that god. In either case, what could be more natural for him than to introduce not only the non-satyric choreutæ, but also the tone and construction of the ritual of the dead hero into the ritualistic drama in honor of Dionysus?

Also this theory furnishes us with the probable reason for the non-satyric choreutæ in the "tragedy of Dionysus" composed by Epigenes: a chorus of caprine satyrs would be out of place in tragedy of serious tone. The chorus in the ritual performed in honor of the dead hero would naturally be composed of citizens in sympathy with the hero. Such a chorus is exactly the chorus of Æschylean tragedy.

We have, then, a more serious form of tragedy, with a non-satyric chorus. The subject of the tragedy may well have been Dionysiac. The joyous tragedy—resembling the satyr-play or satyr-like poetry—still existed; but, with the introduction of this solemn dignified tone and the non-satyric chorus, tragedy must have begun the development which Aristotle calls "its passing out of the satyric stage." The joyous tragedy continued both at Sicyon and elsewhere to develop into the satyr play.

In 534 B.C. Pisistratus established at Athens the City Dionysia, a festival in honor of Dionysus Eleuthereus. Thespis, a native of the Attic village, Icaria, was the first to win the prize in this tragic contest. Perhaps because he was the first successful contestant, he was called by the ancients "the father of Attic tragedy." Certain innovations in the art of tragedy are ascribed to him. Diogenes Laertius says that "in ancient times the chorus alone carried on the action, but Thespis invented the single actor." But this statement cannot be accepted as literally true. The single actor or individual rôle evolved from the leader of the dithyramb. Indeed, the functions of the author, leader, and actor were originally performed by the same individual. Even down to the time of Sophocles, authors acted in their own tragedies. It may be that Thespis developed the individual rôle in length and importance, and that in this manner the function of the cory-phæus became more distinctly that of an actor.

According to Themistius, Thespis was the first to add a pro-logue and spoken statement to the song of the chorus. But improvised spoken statements had been part of the dithyramb. The prologue—that part of the tragedy before the first choral entrance—may have been the invention of Thespis. As there was only one speaking actor in any given scene, it must have been a monologue. At least, it seems safe to assume from the state-ments of Diogenes Laertius and Themistius that Thespis de-veloped to some extent that part of the tragedy played by indi-vidual characters.

Describing the development of primitive tragedy, Aristotle says: "Another change was the plurality of episodes" or as they would be called today, scenes. This development would hardly be possible until more than one individual character was intro-duced into the play. When this innovation was made a "plurality of episodes" would be inevitable because two individual char-acters did not appear together in any one scene until the Æschy-lean period.

Aristotle also states that tragedy did not originally confine its action to a single "revolution of the sun." Only when tragedy had acquired a plurality of episodes, would the duration of the action naturally be prolonged. So long as there was but one episode and one individual character, the duration of the action would tend to correspond to the duration of the performance.

Such innovations are important and would be additional reasons for calling Thespis the father of Attic tragedy. We know that they were introduced by someone before the time of Æschylus. They could hardly have been made by Arion or Epigenes. What evidence we have—tenuous and conjectural as it is—points to Thespis as the innovator. The only other possibility would be

Phrynichus. But if he was the first to make these changes, upon what does the traditional fame of Thespis rest?

Suidas gives *Phorbas or the Prizes of Pelias, Priests, Youths* and *Pentheus* as the titles of four Thespian plays. Were they crude, coarse and ludicrous, as has been conjectured by modern scholars? Was tragedy so close in time to Æschylean drama still totally without its serious tone? It seems improbable. Thespian plays may well have had a happy dénouement. The tragedy with an unhappy ending was considered the best form by Aristotle, but such an ending was not the *sine qua non* of Greek tragedy either in theory or in practice.

Was Phrynichus the first to compose serious tragedy? That possibility also seems improbable. But even if he was, why did he alter the tone of this form of drama? It would be difficult to believe that this innovation was the result of the influence of the narrative epic, either in manuscript form or chanted by a bard, on choral drama. It is much more probable that the change in tone was due to the influence of the commemorative choral in honor of the dead hero, which was similar to primitive tragedy in that it, too, was performed by a chorus and was originally an act of worship. Somewhere and sometime, if not at Sicyon in the sixth century, the development of choral tragedy must have undergone the influence of this form of choral performance. The second oldest extant tragedy, the *Persians,* is a solemn lamentation at the tomb of a dead hero. It is almost wholly retrospective, solemn, heroic, full of elegiac lamentation and often close to an act of worship. Did Æschylean tragedy assume these characteristics because of the influence of narrative epic, or because of the influence of a retrospective, solemn, religious worship of a hero performed by a chorus and its leader, lamenting his calamities and voicing their own resultant sorrow and woe as the chorus does in the *Persians?*

Those who believe that Greek tragedy was modified to that extent by a form of art so dissimilar as the epic, might just as well hold the theory that the medieval *Passion Play* owes its dignity and tragic tone to the influence of the medieval epic.

Luckily, in this case, we know from irrefutable documents that the serious drama of the *Passion* and *Resurrection* sprang from the ritual performed at Easter in honor of the dead God and that the epic had no influence whatever. We know that the ritual in honor of the birth of Christ gave rise to joyous drama in which such comic episodes as the *Shepherds' Play* were introduced. That is one more reason for believing that the dithyramb celebrating the birth of Dionysus produced joyous tragedy. If the parallel is exact in the latter case, why may it not be so in the former?

There were two kinds of lamentation for the dead. In one the leader sang the lament and the chorus sang the refrain. The composition of the oldest extant tragedies is similar to this form. The other form consisted of antiphonal choral song, of which examples are found in the *Seven Against Thebes,* the *Libation-Bearers* and the *Persians.*

Commemorative rites were performed at the tomb of the dead hero. Naturally his heroic deeds would be recalled to mind in the song. The manner of his death would be recounted. Perhaps we may also assume that, towards the close of the ritual, there was the foreshadowing of future peace or future ill, which occurs in so many Greek tragedies just before the end, and which is a feature peculiar to Greek tragedy. It would be natural for the chorus, having sung of the deeds and of the death or triumph of the hero, to think of the future and what it holds for those who are so closely bound to him.

Such a ritual could have been performed by a chorus without a leader. No individual characters are needed. According to Professor Bywater, when Aristotle said that tragedy began with improvisations, he meant that the author (leader) of the dithyramb came forward with an improvisation or spoken statement, which he intercalated between the separate choral songs—that being the origin of the important constituents of a Greek drama: a spoken part and sung part, an actor and a chorus. Aristotle was not speaking of a chorus worshipping a dead hero; but since improvisation took place in the choral rites to which Aristotle refers, it seems quite probable that the same development would occur in the choral worship of the dead, especially since we know that in one form, though perhaps a late form, the lament was actually carried on between the chorus and a leader. It is probable that the *genre* of the choral ode developed as a whole; and if the leaders of the choral odes connected with the worship of Dionysus began to improvise between the songs of the chorus, a parallel development was likely to take place in the choral odes connected with the worship of the dead hero. It is not without significance that the origin of the Greek prose encomium of the dead and the Roman *laudatio*, delivered by one person, is to be sought in the *threnos* sung by a chorus.

A chorus with a leader, therefore, sang of a dead hero at his tomb. The fact that the hero of the ritual was dead explains much of the construction of serious tragedy. The great deeds and all that was important in the life of the hero would necessarily be recounted in narrative form, because the beginning or point of attack of a ritual performed for a dead hero is naturally placed after the death of the hero. The retrospective, narrative element, which remains in great degree even in the most highly developed Greek tragedy, is very effective when skillfully handled; but it is contrary to the normal procedure of dramatic art which is to represent events in the present and not to narrate events of the past. Aristophanic comedy, in which there is no retrospection or narration, except as a burlesque of tragedy, is a more normal form of drama in this respect. In the whole history of drama down to the present, retrospection and narration appear only as the result of the direct or indirect influence of Greek tragedy. This procedure, which we take for granted because it is effective and has become common, calls for explanation and finds it in the ritual in honor of the dead.

The original function of the leader of the chorus was that of narrator. He was the herald or messenger who recounted the calamities and the death of the hero. Such scenes of narration and lamentation were the nucleus about which other scenes were to be grouped in later tragedies. The chorus lamented and sympathized with the hero. Thus the chorus became the principal character, not in the myth or historical event, but in the ritualistic drama. We see a survival of this not only in the preponderance of the choral element in tragedy, but also in the fact that the chorus is always most interested in the hero when he finally appears upon the Greek stage. Its fate is linked with his. We follow the action in the *Seven Against Thebes* and in the *Persians* by the reaction of the emotions of the chorus to the different events.

Other characters in addition to the messenger developed by what may be called the individualization of choral functions, *i.e.*, the introduction of individual characters to perform functions that originally belonged to the chorus. Thus in the *Persians* the character of Atossa, the wife and mother, is the individualization of a function of the chorus with the maternal interest added. Her rôle could revert to the chorus and the play would still exist. A development has taken place in which, out of the chorus interested in the fate of the hero, has evolved an individual much more vitally interested in his fate. A still further individualization of a collective rôle is to be found in such characters as Chrysothemis and Ismene, the respective foils of their sisters Electra and Antigone. These characters fulfill the somewhat pale rôle of prudent counsellor, which is distinctly a rôle of the chorus transferred to an individual.

To be dogmatic in regard to the exact chronological order of the successive steps in the evolution of this ritualistic drama would be dangerous; but it is evident that the point of attack (the point in the story where the play begins) had to be pushed back to include the hero within the play itself. It would be natural for a band of worshippers, stimulated by religious ecstasy and deep emotions, to feel the presence of the departed spirit. In early tragedy, after the process of individualization had progressed far enough to create the type of character represented by Atossa, the next step would naturally be the embodiment of the spirit of the hero. Examples of such scenes are found in the *Persians* when the spirit of the dead Darius appears, and in the *Eumenides* when the shade of Clytemnestra calls for vengeance. We know that medieval drama underwent a parallel development. In one of the earliest liturgical plays an angel, acting as messenger, announces the resurrection of Christ. In another play, the spirit of Christ appears and announces the resurrection.

The fact that the same actor-leader of the Greek chorus could essay such a rôle should hardly be offered as evidence that the leader of the chorus first impersonated the hero. We must distinguish carefully between the actor and the rôle itself. The leader had assumed the rôle of the messenger or narrator before the hero could have possibly appeared in the play. In the ritual and in the primitive drama influenced by the ritual, before the rôle of the hero was introduced, the chorus must have been practically the hero in the tragedy itself. The choral rôle was the sympathetic rôle to the spectators. In the *Suppliants*, for example, the chorus is, let us say, the heroine. Thus the chorus, which was at first not the chief character of the story but only the principal character in the enacting of the ritual, became the heroine of the tragedy. That is a natural development which would almost inevitably take place if the choral worship of a dead hero began to influence dramatic art.

However, this was not the sole way in which a hero or heroine was introduced on the Greek stage. Once the spirit of the individual hero had appeared, the next step was to place the point of attack back far enough to include the hero in the drama just before the hour of his death or the climactic event of his life. This is the usual point of attack even in highly developed Greek tragedy. It is perhaps not without significance that Polynices, one of the heroes in the *Seven Against Thebes*, does not appear on the stage alive, but that his body is brought on and the conventional lament or *threnos* is sung over it and over the body of Eteocles. In *Agamemnon*, the hero, the character with whom the chorus and the spectators sympathize, is on the stage but once during the whole play. It seems that the individual hero had great difficulty in playing an important part on the stage, and had to force his way before the spectators, because in the ritual he played no part at all before the eyes of the worshippers.

Since the hero in Greek tragedy had difficulty in getting on the stage and in staying on for any length of time, his adversary or antagonist had at least as much difficulty in this respect. So long as there was but one individual actor in any one scene, there could be no agon or contest between two individual characters on the stage. Even in the early plays of Æschylus, when two actors were employed, there is no agon on the stage between two individuals. In the *Persians*, the agon has taken place before the play begins. In the *Seven Against Thebes*, the agon is behind the scenes. In the *Suppliants*, the agon is between the chorus and an individual, a herald who represents in a rather pale manner the real antagonists, the sons of Ægyptus. Indeed, it is not until three actors are employed that we find a real antagonist and a clash between two individuals on the stage. Eteocles, in the *Seven Against Thebes*, is hardly to be considered an antagonist, for the chorus, through whose eyes we watch the action unfold, laments for him as well as for his brother. However, the scene in which his mood clashes with the emotions of the chorus is, perhaps, a primitive form of agon—a form which may have existed before the appearance of an antagonist who remains actively hostile to the hero throughout the play. The *Suppliants* illustrates the next step, in which the active antagonist is vicariously represented on the stage. Finally, in *Agamemnon* the two contestants, Clytemnestra and Agamemnon, face each other on the stage in an obligatory scene.

Again, the reason for the non-appearance of the antagonist on the stage can be found in the influence of the worship of the *dead* hero on early Greek tragedy. If the hero had to be brought to life and then put upon the stage, naturally the antagonist and the clash of contending forces in the agon would be introduced slowly, almost haltingly, as the framework of Greek tragedy became larger. Thus there are comparatively few scenes of any kind between individuals in the early dramas of Æschylus, and he learns how to handle the agon only after the introduction of the third actor. Indeed, in order to explain the construction even of highly developed Greek tragedy, we must postulate the influence of a ritualistic drama in which neither the hero nor his enemy appeared.

In this connection it is significant that in early extant tragedies there is a preponderance of choral and female rôles, over the short rôle of the hero himself. Also, in the lament over the dead body of Hector in the *Iliad*, it is the women who carry on the *threnos*, while Priam, although he is present, does not take part in the lament. Thus perhaps in the preponderance of the choral and female rôles in early tragedy we may have the survival of the traditional lament sung by women. Suidas asserts that Phrynichus was the first to represent female rôles; but this statement may well mean that Phrynichus was the first to introduce individual female rôles of the Atossa type, not the first to have a female choral rôle.

When the point of attack had been set back and the hero was brought on the stage, his rôle slowly but surely increased in importance and length, and the rôle of those interested in his fate became less important. But it is a striking fact that rarely in Greek tragedy do we see the fault of the hero committed and expiated in the same play. Old tradition evidently held the point of attack close to the death of the hero. As tragedy evolved, the dramatic emphasis and the sympathy of the spectator were shifted from the chorus to persons interested in the hero and finally to the hero himself who had, as it were, risen from the tomb to enact before the eyes of the audience many if not all the events that the ritual had presented in narrative form.

In the interval of about thirty years between the careers of Thespis and Æschylus, many dramatists flourished; but only three names, Chœrilus, Pratinas and Phrynichus have come down to us. Chœrilus began to compete between the years 534 and 521. One of the titles of his tragedies, *Alope*, is preserved. Pratinas is said to have competed with Æschylus and Chœrilus in the seventieth Olympiad (500-497 B.C.). He was known best as the writer of satyr-plays, and even the title of one of his tragedies, the *Caryatids,* is rather uncertain. The third of this group of tragic poets, Phrynichus, is said by Suidas to have won his first victory in the sixty-seventh Olympiad (512-509 B.C.). The following titles of nine of his plays are known to us: the *Egyptians, Alcestis, Antæus or the Libyans,* the *Danaides,* the *Capture of Miletus,* the *Women of Pleuron, Tantalus, Troilus,* the *Phœnician Women.*

The place where the primitive dramatic rituals were enacted by the cyclic chorus consisted of an orchestra or circular dancing place for the chorus in the centre of which was an altar. This altar constituted the "scenery" of the Greek stage, in the earliest period, and even in the time of Æschylus it was a very important property. In the *Suppliants,* the daughters of Danaus cling to the altar. It is on this altar, or the steps of this altar, that Danaus mounts when he descries Pelasgus from afar. In the *Persians,* this altar becomes the tomb of Darius. In *Prometheus Bound* it represents the rock to which Prometheus is chained.

The primitive orchestra was circular and without a scenic background. At first, the spectators may have been on all sides. From the beginning of the fifth century until about 465 B.C., the theatre in Athens in which the plays of Æschylus and Phrynichus were produced consisted of an orchestra about ninety feet in diameter. The audience occupied rows of wooden seats extending around two-thirds of the circumference of the circle. On the other side of the orchestra, the ground fell off sharply for about six feet. There was no back-scene or stage-building. The performers entered the orchestra on two opposite passage-ways or *parodoi* between the end of the seats and the declivity. If there was a *skene* or dressing-room for the performers, it was not visible to the audience and was not used as an exit or as a scenic background. The early plays of Æschylus need no other scenic accessories than a place for choral evolutions and the altar or tomb.

The plays preceding the time of the introduction of the second actor by Æschylus must have contained little real dramatic action. The choral rôle was preponderant. The custom of naming Greek tragedy after the chorus is evidence that whoever was the hero in the story, the chorus was the principal character in the play; but, since certain of the tragedies of Phrynichus are given the name of the individual hero in the story, we are safe in assuming that by his time the individual hero had appeared on the stage. His adversary also could have appeared; but so long as there was only one actor in any one scene, the hero and villain could not enact the agon or struggle on the stage. If we may judge from the fact that it is only in the extant plays of Æschylus written for three actors that the individual adversary of the hero makes his appearance on the stage in person, it is probable that the individual rôles in these tragedies were usually restricted to the messenger whose function is to narrate, the hero or his ghost, and characters of the type of Atossa which are individualizations of the sympathetic chorus interested in the fate of the hero. The Herald in the *Suppliants* represents the adversary or villain embodied in the collective rôle of the fifty sons of Ægyptus who do not appear. The individual villain may also have been represented vicariously by a herald or messenger. Phrynichus seems to have introduced a eunuch in the *Phœnician Women*.

In these circumstances tragedy was naturally elegiac, lyric, and narrative. Action, as in the *Persians*, must have been kept at the minimum. Not only had the one event in the *Phœnician Women* taken place when the play began, but even this bit of dramatic action made possible by the announcement of this incident during the play was precluded by the fact that the defeat of Xerxes was reported in the prologue. There was little if any opportunity for anything but elegiac lamentation. The point of attack was after the climax. Some of the early plays may have opened with a prologue—an exposition of the cause for lamentation—given by an individual character, but the fact that Æschylus begins the *Suppliants* and the *Persians* with the chorus shows that the prologue was neither the absolute rule nor was considered the best opening. In the foreground is the chorus singing pathetic, emotional laments. Foreshadowing, fingerposts, suspense, surprise, struggle, climax, could hardly exist in these circumstances. The dramatic action in these tragedies must have been either in the past or behind the scenes. The events in the plot served as the dim background for the lyric lamentations. These plays, like the *Persians,* were the vivid representations of the one great emotion called forth by tragedy: pathos. They were not the dramatizations of a plot, or a dramatic struggle, but a dramatization of the effect of a great struggle on the mind of sympathetic onlookers. The interest did not lie in what was done. Aristophanes bestows high praise upon the choral odes of Phrynichus which, he says, were like the song of the nightingale "from whom, like a bee, Phrynichus sipped the fruit of heavenly melodies, ever bearing away the load of sweetest music." And perhaps Aristotle had these very dramatists in mind when he affirmed that the interest in early drama lay more in their diction and delineation of character than in the plot. Beginners in the art of playwriting, he says, "succeed earlier with the Diction and Character than with the construction of the story; and the same may be said of nearly all early dramatists." This statement is strikingly true throughout the history of dramatic art.

By the time that Æschylus was born in 525 B.C., drama had become an important art in Greece. Dramatic representations were held yearly and a prize was bestowed upon the author of the play adjudged the most worthy example of dramatic art. The first tragic contest at Athens was probably held in 534 B.C. and Thespis won the prize. The Greeks had become fully conscious of the art of dramatic technique. Had there not grown up certain definite artistic criteria by which the Greeks thought they could judge the merits of a play, they would not have instituted a contest in playwriting and the production of plays in which the artistic excellence of the different dramas was weighed by specially constituted judges. Just what these criteria were, we do not know; but the critical faculty of the Greeks is too apparent in their whole life and literature to doubt that these judges, even in the earliest times, were able to give reasons for their opinion. Undoubtedly Æschylus did not know, just as no genius knows, all the technical excellencies of his tragedies; but the statement ascribed to Sophocles, and from which too much has been deduced by modern critics, that "Æschylus does what is good but he does it without knowing it" must be utterly false if it is taken to mean that Æschylus was wholly unconscious of certain rules and traditions in the construction of tragedy.

The art of plotting and the depiction of character were rudimentary; but the art of drama was ready for a period of splendid development. Greece was awakened to full national consciousness and pride at Salamis and Marathon. Greek myths and legends and history were filled with potential dramatic situations awaiting the touch of a master hand. The people, under the stimulus of great events, were mentally alive. They were sensitive to beauty; and they were highstrung, emotionally. Rarely if ever in the history of mankind has there been a people of such intellectual power and yet capable of such great emotion. Religious ecstasy was practically a part of their life. Plato condemns drama because it arouses dangerous emotions. Aristotle defends drama on the grounds that it is the cure for painful emotions. Also, the Greeks loved a contest. The great athletic games, the literary and musical contests, and the Hellenic interest in law suits, all bear witness that this people constantly indulged in the emotions called forth by a struggle or debate. The emotions evoked by a contest are the emotions aroused by drama, such as suspense, surprise, sympathy, exultation, sorrow. In these circumstances, so favorable for a man who has something to say in the theatre, Æschylus, in about his twenty-fifth year, began to compete for the tragic prize.

Aristotle's statement in regard to the number of actors has generally been interpreted as meaning that in early Æschylean tragedy two men played all the speaking rôles and, after Sophocles added the third actor, three persons handled all the spoken lines by doubling in several parts. There is no evidence to support this view; and in certain tragedies it would be a physical impossibility for three actors to impersonate all the characters that speak lines. Aristotle was evidently discussing the number of speaking rôles in any one scene in different periods of the development of Greek drama. The two earliest extant plays of Æschylus, the *Suppliants* and the *Persians,* were composed so that only two individual speaking rôles appear in any one scene, although three or four separate characters appear in the casts. The *Suppliants* was produced about 491 B.C. Thus the date of the introduction of the second actor or second speaking rôle falls probably within the first decade of the fifth century.

The *Suppliants* is a dramatized story, but the *Persians* is a precious example of a play founded upon an event which had not become crystallized in legend or history. The plot is not entirely invented, but Æschylus composed the drama with practically a free hand. His ideas and especially his choice of technical details, such as point of attack and exposition, were untrammelled by incidents preconceived in his own mind or in the mind of his audience. From events leading up to and culminating in the defeat of the Persians at Salamis, he was free to select that part of history which seemed best fitted for tragic representation in a Greek theatre in 472 B.C. Of all these events Æschylus chose merely the dénouement of the story. The point of attack is placed after the climax, the battle and defeat of Xerxes. Even this event is narrated by a messenger; but whereas Phrynichus had this event announced in the exposition of his play, Æschylus shows an instinct for dramatic suspense by withholding the announcement of the incident until the audience has become interested in the characters of the story.

The play opens, not with a speech by an individual, but with the entrance of the chorus of Persian Elders. This is the opening of primitive Greek tragedy before the actor was introduced. The chorus gives the exposition, telling how Xerxes has set forth to Hellas' strand to conquer the Greeks. Even in this early play, however, Æschylus employs foreshadowing. A spirit of gloom and suspense is created by the lines:

Wherefore my heart is shrouded in gloom and is racked with fear (woe!) for our Persian armament, lest the State learn that the mighty capital of the Susuan land is made desolate of its sons. . . .

The foreshadowing is continued when Atossa enters and recounts a dream and tells of an omen, both of which foreshadow the catastrophe, but vaguely enough not to rob the moment of a ray of hope necessary to produce dramatic suspense: a combination of hope and fear. Atossa speaks of Xerxes as one who is alive, but she has dreamed of his being thrown from a chariot. The chorus give hopeful reply: "In our interpretation of these portents, the issue will in all things prove prosperous to thee." Although this play is a dramatization of a dénouement, Æschylus has produced dramatic suspense for the moment by withholding the announcement of the defeat. There is actual dramatic progression of action.

The Messenger arrives with the news that the whole barbaric host has perished. The first part of this scene, in which the messenger narrates the one event to the chorus and the chorus breaks out into wails of lamentation, must be a survival of many a similar scene in primitive Greek tragedy in which the leader of the chorus told of the misfortunes of the hero to those vitally interested in the hero's fate. This scene between the bearer of ill-tidings and the queen-mother would have been staged between the messenger and the chorus when only one actor was available. The introduction of the second actor gave Æschylus the opportunity of intensifying the pathos of the situation by having the audience witness the sorrow of Atossa, the mother, who is far more affected by the defeat of Xerxes than are the Persian Elders.

Atossa, grief-stricken, withdraws while the chorus chants a canonical threnody, a survival of the ancient ritual of lamentation, although the hero, Xerxes, is not dead. The next scene, however, in which Atossa returns with the elders, pours libations upon the tomb of her husband, and invokes his shade with pious supplication, is an example of the influence of the ritualistic worship of the dead hero on the construction of Greek tragedy. While the ritual was purely a religious act of worship, probably the presence of the spirit of the dead hero was only felt, not seen, by the devout; but when this ritual became an art, the shade of the dead hero appeared as does the shade of Darius in this tragedy.

Darius rebukes the Persians, telling them that this misfortune is a just punishment for their pride, and he warns them of future defeats. This scene has been called theatrical and episodic, but it is actually dramatic and by no means episodic if one considers it in connection with the ritual underlying tragedy. In introducing it, Æschylus was not seeking an easy means of holding the attention of an audience by a ghostly personage, he was following tradition. The scene is perfectly logical and explicable on the ground that it is a step in the progression of the pathetic, tragic situation. At first there is the gloomy foreboding of the Elders. This suspense, this feeling of impending doom, is intensified by the more individual, human touch of the queen-mother with her dreams. Then even this dénouement reaches a kind of crisis when the news comes that all is lost. The tragic note is intensified when the spirit of Darius points to the ultimate cause of the calamity:

For presumptuous pride, when it is burgeoned, bears as its fruit a crop of calamity, whence it reaps a plenteous harvest of tears.

The entrance of the ill-starred Xerxes, regretting that he did not die with the brave when Destiny overtook them, adds the final touch. The play ends with a heart-rending threnody sung by Xerxes and the chorus.

However slight the plot may be, however little the story may progress, there is dramatic progression and intensification of the pathetic, tragic emotion. Had Æschylus kept Atossa on the stage and shown us the meeting of the mother and son, the emotion would have been more personal and hence deeper. However, one does not have to explain the interest in any scene or play in which the pathos is gradually but so strongly intensified.

The *Persians* is the dramatization of a dénouement; and it is the dramatization of grief. Although most critics insist upon the superhumanity of the characters of Æschylus, this grief is very human.

The *Suppliants*, Æschylus' earliest extant play, is constructed on somewhat different lines; but it furnishes examples of certain survivals of the older dramatic form. The chorus has developed from those interested in the fate of the hero into the principal rôle. The play opens with the entrance of the suppliant maidens, the daughters of Danaus, who explain in their choral chant that they are fleeing from the marriage with their cousins, the sons of Ægyptus, and have arrived on Grecian soil. The exposition is continued in a scene of dialogue between Danaus and his daughters. The king of Argos visits these strangers and they implore him for protection. This scene contains a certain amount of suspense, as the king hesitates to promise to defend them. The situation reaches a kind of climax when the Danaides, almost in despair, vow to hang themselves with their girdles unless protection is granted. The king is won over but must go to the city to consult the will of his people. After a choral ode, Danaus returns with the glad tidings that his daughters shall be held inviolate. This news is greeted with a hymn of rejoicing; but at its close, Danaus descries the fleet bearing their pursuers, the sons of Ægyptus, approaching the shore. Danaus withdraws. The chorus raises a cry of fear and the climactic scene of the play begins as the Herald comes to drive them to the ships. Here is the first extant example of a dramatic clash between two hostile forces on the Greek stage. The heroine is the chorus, and the villain is only vicariously represented. Yet the handling of the situation may be regarded as a very primitive attempt at the representation, instead of the narration by a messenger, of an obligatory scene. The dénouement of the play is brought about by the arrival of the king, who drives the Herald away to the ships. The play ends with a scene of rejoicing between Danaus and his daughters and with a hymn of praise as the chorus wends its way to Argos.

Although the play is earlier than the *Persians*, it shows in some respects a less primitive form of construction; but in the evolution of every art, especially drama, innovations are adopted slowly and many examples of reversion to type are found. Thus both plays begin with the earlier choral opening notwithstanding the fact that Phrynichus had employed the prologue form of exposition. The point of attack in the *Suppliants* is farther away from the dénouement and there are more events in the development of the situation, more dramatic progression of the plot, more suspense caused by situations arousing alternate hope and fear, and more of a clash of contending forces than in the *Persians*. There is much narration and retrospection in the *Suppliants*, yet the later *Persians* contains more of the elements handed down to tragedy from the form and content of the ritual. However, the *Persians* is noteworthy because the one step forward that is made in the progression of the story is caused by disclosing the fact that Xerxes has met with defeat: an event which took place before the play begins. The development of the action through the unveiling of the past is strikingly characteristic of the technique of Greek tragedy. The dramatic elements in both plays are overshadowed by the lyric, elegiac, narrative and spectacular elements. Exposition, foreshadowing, suspense and the obligatory scene exist in rudimentary form. The characters in the *Persians* are more clearly drawn and show more distinctive personality than do the more lay figures of the *Suppliants*.

An examination of the functions of the chorus and the characters in these plays may serve to throw light on the question of the construction of still earlier dramas. In the *Persians*, the chorus plays its primitive rôle of those interested in the fate of the hero. The handling of the character of Darius, or rather of his ghost, illustrates one way in which the hero made his way onto the stage. In other words, the spirit of the dead hero appears. Furthermore, although Xerxes may seem to be an unheroic figure, yet the entrance of this important character at the end of the play is another example of the hesitating manner in which the hero of older tragedies was introduced on the stage.

In the *Suppliants*, a different development of the choral rôle has taken place, in that the chorus, the chief character on the stage in primitive drama, has become the chief character in the plot; but, with the development of the individual hero, this function of the chorus naturally fell into disuse. It was from the Xerxes-Darius type that the hero developed; and the Herald in the *Suppliants* is the first pale impersonation of the antagonist preserved to us in Greek tragedy.

With the growth of interest in the individual characters such as Atossa—offsprings of the chorus—and with increased emphasis laid upon the hero, the function of the collective and hence vaguer character of the chorus will become less important. Since Æschylus curtailed the business of the chorus and made the dialogue take the leading part in the play, earlier tragedies must have contained very little dialogue, for more than two-thirds of the lines of the *Suppliants* are sung by the chorus. Since it takes much longer to sing lines than to speak them, much more than two-thirds of the actual time of representation is given over to the choral part. Since this was the case when Æschylus had two actors at his disposal, it is easy to realize the overwhelming preponderance of the choral rôle when there was but one actor. The spoken portion must have been more or less in the nature of an interlude, just as the choral song itself finally became an interlude in later tragedies.

The changes wrought by the introduction of the second actor tended to be more potential than actual. The *Suppliants* could be adapted for representation by a chorus and one actor by altering only two scenes comprising only seventy lines. The first of these passages is the one in which Danaus, directly addressing the king, asks for attendants to conduct him to the temples. The passage could be excised without affecting the action. The second passage is far more important, as it is a part of the obligatory scene in which Pelasgus defies the Herald; but it would have been possible to have this scene narrated with Danaus acting as messenger. Such would have been the procedure of earlier dramatists. According to A. E. Haigh, whose opinion has been generally accepted, "Æschylus was the first to conceive the possibility of depicting in dramatic form the central incidents of the story, and he effected his purpose by the employment of a second actor. By this expedient he was enabled for the first time to bring the chief antagonists face to face, and to expose them to view in the very act of contention; thus imparting to the drama that energy and vitality in which it had previously been deficient." Significant as this statement is, one must not be led to believe that, after the introduction of the second actor, Greek tragedy became a series of scenes between the two chief antagonists. Even the rôle of the individual hero was in a rudimentary form at this period; and the rôle of the individual antagonist of the hero seems to have been even less developed. Even when scenes with three speaking characters had been introduced and the rôle of the hero had reached a higher stage of development, Æschylus did not avail himself of the opportunity of bringing the chief antagonists face to face on the stage in the very act of contention in *Prometheus Bound* or the *Seven Against Thebes*.

The *Persians* shows that the actual change wrought by the introduction of the second actor was the possibility of representing such scenes as those between Atossa and the Messenger, Atossa and Darius. The two actors made it possible to increase the tension of the situation by allowing a more human, sympathetic character of the type of Atossa to listen to the narration by a messenger of the misfortunes of the hero. And this was no small advance in the art of tragedy. To adapt the *Persians* for presentation by one actor and the chorus, it is only necessary to allow the rôle of Atossa to revert to the chorus when the Messenger and Darius are on the stage. The story would unfold just as it does in its present form; but the loss in the emotional effect on the audience, no longer listening through the ears of the mother to the downfall of a son, would be almost immeasurable. The dialogue between individuals is dramatically more important in every way in the *Persians* than in the *Suppliants*.

Mr. Haigh has pointed out the potential changes in dramatic technique made possible by the employment of a second actor— changes seen in embryonic form in the *Suppliants*. The actual influence of the second actor seems rather to have been exerted in giving more opportunity for emotional effects and in allowing the audience to see the few events and hear of many events in a play through the eyes and ears of more concrete characters, such as messengers, heralds, and servants. Secondary rôles were more prominent on the stage than the important characters in the plot.

At this period of its development, tragedy was a synthesis of the several arts. Aristotle believed that every tragedy must have six parts and that these parts determined its quality. Arranged in order of relative importance they were plot, character, thought, diction, song and spectacle. However correct this order may be for tragedy of Aristotle's time, it must be exactly reversed to apply to early Æschylean drama. Æschylus was least concerned with plot and character. The singing and dancing chorus of fifty dominated his synthesis.

Greek dancing was a mimetic art. It was a system of eurhythmics, expressing and harmonizing with the events and mood of the drama, just as orchestral music in modern opera accompanies and expresses the dramatic action. The inner meaning of the tragedy came through the eye as well as through the ear. We may be sure that the colorful, rhythmic chorus made complete use of the large circular dancing place, and swept back and forth over it in the manifold figures of their joyous or solemn dances and their triumphal or sorrowful processions. Phrynichus boasted that he had invented "as many figures of the dance as the billows on the sea under a dread night of storm." Æschylus could not have been far behind his rival as a mimetic ballet-master or he would not have won the prize in a dramatic art which must have resembled the modern Russian ballet in its effects.

Since plot and character were to develop into the dominating elements of the tragic synthesis, we must deal with them at length. But one must never forget that Greek tragedy was a music-drama in which wonderful spectacular effects of human beings in motion emphasized and even revealed the inner soul of the play.

Since their theatre had no lighting equipment beyond that of the sun, the Greeks could not control the light, or flood the scene with color in a manner befitting the mood of the tragedy. At first the chorus was the sole scenic background.

About 465 B.C. a scene-building was erected on the declivity on the open side of the orchestra of the Athenian theatre. It was probably a simple structure consisting of one story with two projecting wings or parascenia. In the centre was a large door serving as entrance and exit for individual characters in the play. Two smaller doorways flanking the main entrance were added later. This building served as a dressing-room for the actors and as a scenic back drop for the spectators. The interior became that very important locality known as "behind the scenes." There may have been a few steps leading up to this building. If such was the case, the setting was more effective according to modern ideas, for steps permit a more artistic grouping of actors and chorus, than a flat stage. In either case, there was no insurmountable gulf between the orchestra, where the chorus danced, and an elevated stage just in front of the scene-building, until long after Greek tragedy had passed the heyday of its glory.

Such a setting formed a simple, fitting background for Greek tragedy. It kept the eye from wandering beyond the domain of the action, but it did not distract the attention of the spectator from the human actors in front of it. Even when the façade was ornamented with pillars, the effect was not so ornate as to detract from the color and ever-changing form of the plastic chorus.

The point of attack in the earlier *Persians* was after the battle which forms the climax of the story. In the *Seven Against Thebes* the point of attack is before the battle which brings about the climax. This is an example of the normal development of playwriting. Æschylus reduced the great amount of narration made necessary by the primitive form of Greek tragedy in which the play began even after the dénouement of the story. The opening scene between Eteocles and the Messenger is the first extant example of a scene of dialogue occurring before the parodos or entrance of the chorus. Moreover, this scene is not a mere recital of preceding events and an explanation of the situation in narrative form as in the *Persians*. It is a scene of exposition in dramatic form. Eteocles, the hero of the play, is addressing the men of Thebes and exhorting them to mount the battlements and defend the city against the Argive army. The citizens were undoubtedly represented on the stage, although they do not compose the chorus nor do they speak during the play. Their presence on the stage not only keeps the first speech of Eteocles from being a narrative monologue but also sheds an interesting and dramatic atmosphere over the situation and immediately causes the story to unfold through the action. This is an excellent procedure to employ in the exposition of any drama. The audience is thus more aroused both mentally and emotionally than by mere narration.

A spy, in the rôle of messenger, increases the tenseness of the situation by announcing to Eteocles that seven Argive chiefs are preparing to march against the seven gates of Thebes. Eteocles offers a short prayer to the gods for victory, and then withdraws. For all this exposition Æschylus employs only three speeches. Then comes the long elegiac and epic portion of the play. The chorus of Theban maidens enters giving utterance to lamentations. Eteocles returns to the scene and chides them for their unbridled fear, since they may unnerve the warriors. The messenger returns and describes each of the seven Argive chiefs posted at each gate; and, after each description, Eteocles names a champion to defend the gate while the chorus breaks in with eager prayers for victory. Æschylus shows a feeling for climax in saving the disclosure of the fact that Polynices, the brother of Eteocles, is stationed before the last gate and that Eteocles will oppose him. Even in this narrative passage there is a cumu-

lative suspense and emotion rising to a climax. The choral hymn
following this scene gives the whole story of Laius and Œdipus
and the causes leading up to the present situation. The dramatic
value of this procedure of unveiling the past at this moment
cannot be denied. Of course, the audience was in possession of
the facts in the story not only because of its knowledge of the
myth but from the preceding plays in the trilogy of which
the *Seven Against Thebes* is the last; but his vivid *résumé* of
the events leading up to the present condition of affairs drives
the situation home with dramatic poignancy and considerably increases the emotional effect of the following scene. When the
messenger reënters, his first words are:

Be of good cheer, mother-bred-children, that ye are. Our city
has escaped the yoke of servitude.

The reassurance of the first lines makes the news of the death
of the brothers "by mutual slaughter slain" even more of a dramatic shock. Such technical excellencies are not the result of
blind chance nor of any indefinite factor called genius or inspiration. They are the touches of a conscious artist.

During the next choral hymn the bodies of Polynices and
Eteocles attended by their sisters, Antigone and Ismene, are
brought upon the stage. Then begins the canonical wail of
lamentation over the dead heroes—a survival of the primitive
ritual. Bury the heroes in a tomb and the scene would be a
perfect example of ritualistic worship of the dead hero. Also, it
seems plain that Æschylus is aiming to foreshadow a final well-
known detail of the story. To call the scene inartistic because
it breaks the unity of action—a theory of which Æschylus probably knew nothing—and because it foreshadows the unlawful
burial of Polynices and the resultant situation in *Antigone,* is
to apply standards of criticism unknown at this period and to
forget that at the end of almost every Greek tragedy, whether
it belongs to a trilogy or not, the playwright foreshadows future
events which happen after the play is ended. This is not the

case with modern playwrights who invent their plots; but it was a natural procedure on the part of the Greeks. The dramatist and the audience both know the ultimate fate of the characters in these plays. It would be strange if the playwright did not refer to them just as Shakespeare in most of his historical plays calls attention to the result of the events in the future and sounds a note of peace and thanksgiving.

The Herald brings the news that Polynices shall not be buried and Antigone bids defiance to the decree. However, there is absolutely nothing in the lines to inform the audience that a struggle will inevitably arise from the performance of Antigone's pious duty. Thus it can be categorically denied that Æschylus is inartistic enough to foreshadow a dramatic question that he leaves unanswered. It is our knowledge of the rest of the story which raises the question; and, in this case, our pre-knowledge cannot be made the basis of just criticism of the play and ought not to serve as a basis for argument that the scene is a later interpolation. The scene as it stands is explicable from every point of view.

The rôle of the hero in this tragedy shows a marked development. Eteocles holds the centre of the stage during much of the play. The plot revolves about him and his will is directly responsible for the events leading up to his death. But, although the rôle of the hero has increased in length and significance and he has become the central figure in the play, the rôle of the chorus has not lost its important functions and attributes. While the fate of the Theban maidens is not entirely dependent upon the fate of the hero, since they are saved from danger finally, yet during the first part of the play the audience is in sympathy with them in their evident peril, perhaps at times more in sympathy with them than with the overbearing, violent hero. During many passages the audience beholds the play through the emotions of the chorus instead of interpreting the action in the light of the character of the hero. This is partially due to the fact that Æschylus has not thrown the character of Eteocles into high relief by his failure to introduce the living Polynices, the antagonist, on the stage. Only one side of the struggle is presented. Had there been scenes between Eteocles and his sisters, had the mother, Jocasta, been introduced, had Polynices been shown alive, the effect of the situations would have been much stronger. But the playwrights of the period evidently had not learned the full dramatic value of such procedures. Thus these plays present only small, one-sided parts of the whole problem which forms the basis of the plot.

It would have been very easy for Æschylus to have Antigone and Ismene enact in a far more personal way the functions and emotions of the much vaguer character, the chorus. This would have enhanced the whole tragic atmosphere. The last scene in the play would have been far more touching, for the audience would have been more in sympathy with the sisters if Antigone and Ismene had already lived through the crisis in view of the spectators. If the whole situation had reached the heart of the audience through these characters, they would have become very vivid. But Antigone and Ismene enter for the first time, unannounced and unprepared for, almost at the end of the play. The traditional function of the chorus was still too strong to allow individual characters to replace it entirely; but the fact that Æschylus does introduce the sisters at all, instead of allowing the chorus to carry on the lamentation alone, is evidence that the value of the individual character is beginning to be felt.

Prometheus Bound, composed after 475 B.C., shows a distinct advance in many ways over the *Seven Against Thebes*. The hero has at last come to his own. He is a distinct personality, a character commanding attention, admiration and sympathy unshared by the chorus. The plot revolves entirely about the heroic figure of Prometheus. The rôle of the chorus has consequently diminished in importance. The Oceanides are not concerned with the plot, but simply fill the rôle of confidant. One cannot think of the *Suppliants,* the *Persians* or the *Seven Against Thebes* without thinking of the chorus; but when *Prometheus Bound* is recalled to mind, one of the last things remembered is the chorus.

It is the only extant Greek tragedy in which the individual hero is on the stage during the whole play.

The opening of the play is in dialogue form. Hephæstus, accompanied by Power and Force, the latter being a mute character, lead in Prometheus and in a striking scene chain the Fire-Bringer to a rock. The *Seven Against Thebes* opens with a scene of dialogue and the exposition is accompanied by an incident; but, while the first scene of the *Seven Against Thebes* is short and two of the speeches are strongly tinged with narration, this scene portrays, at sufficient length, the incident before our eyes. We do not have to be told, as in the *Seven Against Thebes,* what is happening behind the scenes. As the attention of the audience is caught and held by the event on the stage, swiftly moving dialogue between Power and Hephæstus unfolds both sides of the story. The contrast between the harsh, unfeeling attitude of Power and the pitying attitude of Hephæstus, who does his duty with regret, gives Æschylus an excellent opportunity not only to explain how Prometheus stole the fire for men and incurred the wrath of Zeus, but also to win full sympathy for his stoical, silent hero, the benefactor of mankind. The art of exposition has developed under the hand of Æschylus.

Having placed this situation before the audience, Æschylus presents it under different aspects, without developing much dramatic action. Prometheus, when left alone, breaks his proud silence; and the entrance of the chorus and subsequently the presence of Oceanus furnish the opportunity for the usual lyric lamentation and narration of past events leading up to the present. At this period of the evolution of Greek tragedy, however, the dramatist cannot harp monotonously on one string. In order to vary the tone, Æschylus introduces the character of Io. The character of Io has a special significance because she is the destined ancestress of Heracles who will finally destroy the vultures gnawing at the hero's vitals and deliver Prometheus. The past and future career of Io is then unfolded. At the close of the play, Hermes tries to break the hero's pride and silence in a scene of dramatic struggle of opposed wills. But Prometheus refuses to disclose the secret of the marriage which will over-throw Zeus, his arch enemy. As in the *Suppliants,* the real antagonist is only vicariously represented, but Hermes is far more a real personality than the nameless Herald of the older play. The clash in the *Suppliants* depends on physical force. Here it is a clash of mighty wills. The choral odes fall into the background with the chorus. The individual characters are not mere personifications of the collective rôle. The action develops very little; but the individual characters are distinct entities, and the play could not exist without dialogue between two indi-viduals, as could the *Persians.* In the earlier tragedies the spoken dialogue seems but the primitive interlude between the more important parts of choral song; but in *Prometheus Bound* it is the choral song which makes the effect of being an interlude.

In these four plays we have pointed out dramatic scenes and situations; but the art of plotting is in an embryonic stage of development. Dramatic action is still overshadowed by lyric, elegiac and narrative passages. The interest is by no means centred on a dramatic representation of a clash of opposing forces or wills. There is exposition, foreshadowing, crisis and dénouement. There are one or two obligatory scenes of con-flict. However, none of these elements of plotting stands out boldly. It is not the scenes of conflict, such as between Antigone and the Herald in the *Seven Against Thebes,* Pelasgus and the Herald in the *Suppliants,* or between Prometheus and Hermes, which remain impressed on our memory. One is not conscious of any sustained suspense. The crisis in the plays is treated hurriedly. With the exception of *Prometheus Bound,* a rela-tively late play, the opening scene of exposition is summarily handled.

Æschylus did not make the most of the dramatic situations in these plays. He was striving for other effects. He had other means of holding his audience such as the spectacular element, the music and the dancing. He was not trying to unfold an intricate situation but to give a representation of an emotional situation suffused with a religious atmosphere. His plot is subordinate to the development of an emotional situation, such as a disastrous defeat (*Persians*); the punishment of a hero (*Prometheus Bound*); the death of brothers, mutually slain (*Seven Against Thebes*). The defeat, the punishment, the fratricidal conflict, and even the underlying causes are of less importance to Æschylus than the resultant emotion aroused in the hearts of the hero and those who hold the hero dear. Events and the plot itself are necessarily of secondary importance. The tragedies are the representations of the emotions aroused in the hearts of the spectators of a struggle, rather than the representation of the dramatic struggle itself. They are a psychological study of what a sensitive, imaginative human being would feel if he had been told of the defeat of his king, or of two brothers in mortal combat, or if he saw his benefactor chained to a rock. The simple plot is a picturesque background.

And all this is the more explicable if one remembers that the effect of these tragedies is exactly the effect of the worship of the dead hero. Not only in construction but in psychological effect does early Greek tragedy seem to be the outgrowth of a band of worshippers analyzing their emotions as they recall the deeds and death of a hero. The religious, the analytical, the emotional, the narrative, the heroic elements are thus explained. The emotions represented in these plays are rather reflective lamentations for what has happened in the unalterable past than dramatic emotions which force the hero of a drama to act in order to control the changing present and mould the unformed future. They are the passive emotions of elegy, not the active emotion of drama. While there are dramatic scenes and instances of a hero with an active will, the general effect and lasting impression of these four plays is tragic in the sense of pathetic, not tragic in the sense of dramatic.

Æschylus poured the whole richness of his art into his last plays, the trilogy, consisting of *Agamemnon,* the *Libation-Bearers* and the *Eumenides,* produced in 458 B.C., two years before his death. How much he had learned from Sophocles, who began to compete in the dramatic contests in 468 B.C., we do not know; but great development in the art of playwriting had taken place. While tragedies will be written which revert to the older forms, yet each play of this trilogy is a drama in the modern sense of the word. Many of the scenes recall situations of the older plays both in spirit and construction; but the dramatic element at last is paramount. The final impression is dramatic, not pathetic. One follows the unfolding plots with suspense. The interest lies in the present action and its possible results, not in the achieved results of a past action.

When *Agamemnon* opens, the Watchman is waiting wearily for the dawn, as he has waited year after year hoping that in the long night, the torch announcing the fall of Troy would gleam forth. He is sleepless, "for fear doth sit in slumber's chair," and he weeps the misfortunes of his master's house. Suddenly the beacon is seen shining. He is ready to dance the prelude of Troy's fall. Soon will he carry his dear lord and master's hand in his own. Then in foreboding contrast to this joyous outburst come the significant lines, foreshadowing calamity to one who knows the situation:

For the rest, I'm dumb; a great ox stands upon my tongue— yet the house itself, could it but speak, might tell a tale full plain.

The suspense aroused by this dramatic opening scene is made possible only by assuming a knowledge of former events in the story; but this knowledge granted, it is a scene of undeniable power. It is exposition brought about by a striking bit of action very vital to the plot of the play. Here is no lifeless messenger announcing the fall of Troy, but the fact is conveyed to the audience by an exceedingly clever piece of stage business.

The point of attack is not only much farther away from the dénouement than in the earlier plays, but it is also placed at the correct point in the story. Agamemnon, in order to sail for Troy, has had to sacrifice his daughter Iphigenia; and although this act was performed at the command of the gods, the mother, Clytemnestra, cannot forgive the deed. Clytemnestra has been faithless to her lord and has accepted Ægisthus as a paramour. In these circumstances the return of Agamemnon is the incident from which dramatic action arises inevitably. Thus the point of attack correctly allows the initial cause to be included in the action. When an incident gives rise to such a question or problem, the material for drama is at hand.

After the dramatic opening scene, the chorus enters and, as is usual, gives more details in regard to events leading up to the present. Stress is placed on the sacrifice of Iphigenia; but, while the recollection of the deed of Agamemnon helps to state the problem of the plot and arouses suspense, it does not break down the sympathy for the hero which has been won for him in the opening speech of the Watchman by presenting him to the audience as a victorious hero, as a "dear loved master" who is returning to something which may not even be whispered.

When Clytemnestra enters, a real antagonist appears for the first time in any extant Æschylean tragedy. Here is no pale, indefinite character representing vicariously the force opposed to the hero, but a well-defined antagonist. She is a relatively subtle, complex, forceful personality, the greatest of all Æschylean creations.

After the two preceding scenes of foreboding which shed the correct atmosphere of gloom upon the situation, the note of hope and victory is stressed in the scene between Clytemnestra and the chorus; but at the end she pronounces the fateful foreshadowing lines:

But even if, void of such offense towards the gods, our host should reach home, the grievous suffering of the dead might still prove wakeful—so be it fresh mischance do not befall. These are my woman's words but may the good prevail and that right clearly!

Thus, in this play with a tragic outcome, the opening is joyous, but with a touch of foreboding to arouse suspense. The audience awaits the obligatory scene, the meeting of this husband and wife, with mingled emotions of hope and fear.

After a hymn to the gods the Herald enters and prepares for the coming of Agamemnon. This scene, however, is a reversion in part to the earlier type of drama. Much of it is narration. Clytemnestra inquires concerning the fate of Menelaus, and the narrative passage which follows is entirely episodic so far as the plot is concerned. The playwright cannot yet allow an opportunity for poetic narrative to escape. The action, however, begins to unfold again as Clytemnestra describes how she "raised a shout of triumph in joy erewhile, when the first flaming messenger arrived by night telling that Ilium was captured and overthrown." Even here we have an example of the tenacity of the narrative element in Greek tragedy. The audience would have been more interested in beholding her emotions when this news came to her, than in hearing her recount her feelings, especially since she is actually dissembling. Had the dramatist allowed us to see the real effect on Clytemnestra of the news of Agamemnon's return, the subtle dissembling would have been far more effective.

Again there is a choral hymn and Agamemnon enters. For the first time in an extant Æschylean play the hero and the real antagonist are face to face in an obligatory scene which has been prepared in dramatic fashion from the first line in the play. Externally here is a wife welcoming home her victorious lord; but underneath this joyous exterior lurks death, for in reality a faithless wife stands before the husband who sacrificed her daughter, and near her husband stands his captive mistress, Cassandra. Clytemnestra bids the maids spread a purple carpet where the hero treads, and on this purple carpet the husband and wife enter their home; but in reality the carpet is deep blood-red and Agamemnon, the victorious hero, walks to his death. The chorus is suddenly haunted by shapes of fear and inexplicable portents hover over the scene. Clytemnestra returns and bids Cassandra enter; but Cassandra remains motionless and dramatically silent. Clytemnestra enters the palace once more. At this intense moment, Cassandra suddenly breaks the silence with a wild cry of woe, and there ensues one of the most remarkable scenes ever constructed.

The violent death of one person at the hands of another was not represented in view of the Greek audience. Either the victim was forced off the stage by his slayer and the shriek betokened the death blow, or else a messenger reported the fact in traditional form; but Æschylus cleverly devised still another means of handling the death scene. Cassandra is gifted with the power of prophecy and divination, but she is never believed. Æschylus has her employ these powers to describe what is going on behind the scenes in a manner that must arouse any audience to the highest pitch of dramatic emotion. With slow but perfect gradation she works her prophecy to the climax, recalling the causes leading up to the situation. "The house reeks with blood-dripping slaughter. . . . Enough of life," she cries as she goes into the palace to her death. As her words are not believed by the chorus, they make no move to save Agamemnon. His death shriek confirms her prophecy. Thus Æschylus conforms to the custom of concealing the actual murder; but, instead of a cold narration of the incident, he builds up a scene of complete suspense and nerve-racking emotion, leading to the climax of the action. Centuries will roll by before dramatic art will produce similar scenes in which the death is actually messengered but messengered in such a way that no one would prefer to have them enacted. Sometimes things heard are more dramatic than things seen, even in drama.

At this moment of the action the chorus of old men breaks up into twelve parts. Mr. Haigh is of the opinion that "the sententious ineptitude of the old men, in the presence of the crisis, is one of those passages of semi-comedy with which Æschylus occasionally relieves the tension of the feelings." The theory of comic relief, however, is entirely an English invention and it cannot be admitted that this scene, in which these old men show confusion and hesitation, exists for the sake of comedy. If these speeches were given in quick succession, the effect would be much like that of the clamorous mob scenes in Shakespeare.

Instead of being inartistically comic, the scene gives the right atmosphere of tumultuous excitement which prepares for the disclosure of Clytemnestra standing over the dead bodies of Agamemnon and Cassandra, for it is Clytemnestra, no indefinite messenger, whom the dramatist brings before us. The tragic self-possession of Clytemnestra reflected in the almost brutal calmness with which she describes, defends, and even boasts of her deed forms an excellent contrast to the preceding disordered exclamations. Such changes in tone and tempo in drama are as effective as they are in music. The scene is intense and would be a fitting close to the vivid action of this drama; but Æschylus does not end his tragedy here nor with the lamentation of the chorus, the threnody for the dead hero. He introduces Ægisthus who exults over the slaying of Agamemnon and even threatens the entirely hostile chorus. Daggers are drawn on both sides but Clytemnestra holds Ægisthus back, saying: "Not so, best beloved! there needeth no enlargement of our ills."

Playwriting has been defined as the art of preparation. Æschylus has shown that he knew the value of preparation and foreshadowing events throughout this play; but he did not recognize the necessity of introducing all principal characters early in the play and allowing the audience to become acquainted with them. The entrance of Ægisthus is perhaps more unexpected at this moment than at any other. He should have intensified the situation by appearing before Agamemnon arrived, especially as his presence is the secret to which the Watchman refers with such subtlety in the opening scene. The character is vital to the plot; and, while Æschylus may have taken it for granted that the knowledge of the myth on the part of the audience was sufficient to make the presence of Ægisthus felt even if he did not appear in person until the end, the poignancy of the situation would have been greatly increased had the audience beheld Ægisthus earlier in the play. Drama has reached a stage in development in which certain chief dramatic scenes are well represented but many scenes of importance are omitted.

As *Prometheus Bound* shows the ever-increasing importance

of the protagonist, so the rôle of Clytemnestra in *Agamemnon* is an example of a fully developed antagonist, who remains on the stage much of the time and carries on the action. The rôles of Cassandra, Ægisthus and even of the Watchman are evidence of growing skill in the delineation of distinct personalities and in the differentiation of character. These people are not mere lay figures like Danaus, or Pelasgus. While the chorus is no longer a vital character in the plot, its rôle is long and it serves as interlocutor throughout most of the play. In spite of the development of the individual rôles there are only two scenes in which the single characters carry on the dialogue. All other scenes of dialogue are carried on between a person and the chorus. The hero appears alive only once. Æschylus did not feel it necessary to have individuals carry on the action, although in the next play the single characters have more scenes together. The choral rôle is still an important element in his scheme of play construction, for much of the exposition and foreshadowing is given by the chorus, while at the end there is a clash between the chorus and the antagonists, Clytemnestra and Ægisthus. Although the dramatic interest in the plot is at last paramount and the individual characters are well handled, the choral rôle retains its usual length and most of its primitive functions.

The opening scene of the *Libation-Bearers*, the next play of the trilogy, contains the initial cause, the event which causes the action to develop. In this case it is the return of Orestes, seeking vengeance, foreshadowed at the end of *Agamemnon*. As a general rule the point of attack should be placed so as to allow the initial cause to be included in the play. Æschylus has learned to place dramatic scenes on the stage. Orestes and Pylades approach the altar in the centre of the orchestra or dancing place, which now represents the tomb of the dead hero, Agamemnon. Orestes invokes his father's spirit and places a lock of hair on the tomb as a votive offering. As they stand there, they perceive "a sad procession of marshaled maids in sable mantles clad" issuing from the palace to pour libations on the tomb. Electra leads this band. Orestes and Pylades go aside "to learn the purpose of the murky pomp." The scene which follows is evidently a survival of the ritual of the worship in honor of the dead hero; but it fulfills a dramatic purpose in that it gives exposition accompanied by an event. Electra prays for the return of Orestes, that he may claim his father's sceptre. The knowledge of the presence of the concealed Orestes arouses suspense in the minds of the spectators, who await the probable meeting with pleasant impatience. One desires to see the unexpected joy of the recognition. Again Æschylus has created suspense very early in the play.

Suddenly Electra recognizes the lock of hair as belonging to her brother and the further proof of the presence of Orestes is furnished naïvely by the fact that Electra's foot fits the footprints by the tomb. Orestes discloses himself; and the touching recognition of the brother and sister sheds an atmosphere of happiness over the situation which forms a dramatic contrast to the preceding gloomy lamentation and the coming tragedy of which the germ lies in this very meeting. Such contrasts are extremely valuable in that they throw the audience quickly from one mood to another and, by changing the emotions, arouse the sepectator to a high degree of excitement.

The action does not stagnate for a moment, for Orestes immediately tells of the oracle which bids him avenge his father's death; and the chorus joins 'n a hymn of lamentation and vengeance. Electra tells how Clytemnestra, haunted by foreshadowing dreams, sent her with the maidens bearing funeral gifts. Clytemnestra dares not come herself to her murdered husband's tomb. This passage narrates a part of the story which might well have been included in the action. Had Æschylus opened his play with the appearance of Clytemnestra, a prey to her conscience-stricken dreams, sending forth Electra on this pious mission, the whole situation would have been explained in action, and the dramatic intensity of the sudden appearance of Orestes would have been increased. Æschylus has learned to place dramatic scenes on the stage; but he has not acquired the ability to represent situations which are stronger when acted than narrated. The narrative passages were evidently so acceptable to the audience that, while certain obligatory scenes are represented on the stage, those of secondary importance are likely to be narrated. While the point of attack in these later plays includes the initial cause, it has not been placed far enough back to include situations just preceding this incident. Thus there is still a fair amount of exposition which must be narrated, although this amount decreases as the point of attack is placed farther towards the beginning of the story.

However, as the point of attack recedes from the climax, there is more opportunity for the dramatist to employ the art of preparation, so important in creating suspense. Thus at the end of this scene Orestes lays his plan to knock at the door with Pylades as any stranger might, and if no one greets them, to chide some passing servant for inhospitality and to enter. Then when he sees Ægisthus seated on his father's throne, before there is time for the question: "Whence is the stranger?" Orestes will slay him. Although events do not turn out as he plans, just enough is told to foreshadow what is to happen, but not enough to anticipate the outcome too plainly. Thus suspense is created. After a choral hymn, Orestes knocks at the door. Does Æschylus anticipate in a way, the suspense aroused by the knocking in the Porter's scene in *Macbeth* by having no answer given until the third time Orestes knocks? Did the dramatist recognize the value of suppressed excitement aroused by this device centuries before Maeterlinck consciously employs it? It would be rash to ascribe this procedure to mere chance. Such devices are evidence, rather, of the increasing care to arouse suspense whenever possible.

When the servant appears, Orestes bids him announce that a bearer of tidings has arrived. Clytemnestra enters, and there is an obligatory scene between the protagonist and the antagonist. As the mother faces the son whom she sent away as a child, there is suspense as to whether she will recognize him or not; but Orestes tells her that her son is dead, and Electra, cleverly seconding the ruse, pours forth her hopeless grief, with subtle dissembling. Clytemnestra, no less cunningly, invites Orestes in and tells him he shall not fare the worse for his bad news. Nor is this all the crafty stratagem, so interesting in such situations, displayed at this point in the action. When the guilty Clytemnestra and her children have entered the palace, she sends the Nurse of Orestes to summon Ægisthus. The Nurse is fully alive to the perfidy of Clytemnestra who, she says, "hid her laughter behind eyes that made sham gloom." The chorus, hearing that the Nurse is to summon Ægisthus, artfully asks whether he shall come alone, or with his guards. The Nurse replies that Clytemnestra bids his spearmen attend him. Again Æschylus has seized the opportunity to produce suspense in a minor scene. Craftily the chorus bids the Nurse make Ægisthus come unprotected to his doom and hints that Orestes lives. The situation has reached its climax. Suspense is perfect. Ægisthus appears for a moment on his way to the palace. His entrance in the play is late; but at least Æschylus realized that this character must appear even for a moment. This entrance of Ægisthus is not merely an obvious procedure which would occur to any Greek playwright. Euripides, a much more sophisticated dramatist, fails to have Ægisthus appear in his play based on this story.

Once more the chorus refers vividly to what is about to take place within the palace. The death shriek is heard. A servant rushes forth wildly to warn Clytemnestra, who suddenly appears and grasps in an instant the whole situation as Orestes and Pylades drag in the body of Ægisthus. She calls for a weapon to defend herself.

In *Agamemnon* there is an obligatory scene between the protagonist and the antagonist; but, while that scene is dramatic, the present situation is more powerful because now there is no dissembling. Both characters know the deep tragedy of the situation. The son is going to slay his mother to avenge her murder of his father. It would be difficult to construct a more intense moment of climax; and, having reached this obligatory scene, Æschylus does not rush through it with primitive haste. He arouses alternate hope and fear. The struggle is psychological as well as physical. He holds the situation as long as possible. Clytemnestra's first cry of grief is: "Ah me! Dead, valiant Ægisthus, my beloved." Orestes answers: "Thou lovest this man? Then in the same grave shalt thou lie." Clytemnestra recalls to Orestes how she nursed him as a child with slumbrous eyes. The blow strikes home and Orestes wavers. He turns to Pylades, but his friend warns him of the wrath of the gods if the oracle bidding him avenge Agamemnon be not fulfilled. Clytemnestra uses every argument and appeal: her motherhood, the faults of Agamemnon, the threat of avenging Furies; but Orestes answers all with the telling lines: "Thou slewest what thou shouldst not; so suffer what should not be." He drags her within the palace. Æschylus has learned not only to put the obligatory scene on the stage but to show all sides of the problem, to arouse and sustain suspense and bring a strong climax.

The chorus intones an ode which ends with the peaceful refrain: "So the light hath come"; but suddenly with dramatic contrast and change of emotion, Orestes is disclosed standing over the dead body of Clytemnestra grimly defending his deed. He is about to go to the oracle of Apollo where refuge is promised. He seems to behold in terror the Gorgons, avenging Furies, haunting him. In vain the maidens of the chorus assure him they are but phantoms. He flees in awful horror. Thus Æschylus foreshadows and prepares for the ensuing action of the last play of the trilogy.

The analysis of this play shows how the individual characters have increased in importance. Their wills are active. They guide the action. The interest lies in the development of the action, not in the poetic element. Suspense and climax are well handled. The situations are both powerful and carefully worked out. Instead of being merely passed over with haste, the obligatory clash is sustained. The dialogue is full of telling lines and is more dramatic than elegiac.

The opening of the next play, the *Eumenides,* is notable for a succession of theatrical scenes and stage pictures. The arrangement of the characters on the stage forms a tableau which silently performs the function of exposition. The play begins with a scene before the temple of Apollo at Delphi. The Prophetess, after a prayer, enters the temple but returns suddenly in fear at what she has seen within. A man "defiled before Heaven" is clinging to the altar and holding in his bloody hands a sword, while before him on thrones are the horrible Eumenides. With this preparation, the doors of the temple are opened and we behold the stage picture. Orestes is clinging to the altar and near him is Hermes. The Eumenides are sleeping. Apollo appears. No further words are needed.

With the audience in possession of the fact that Orestes, still pursued by the Furies, has reached the temple, the action begins to develop. Apollo still promises protection and sends Orestes with Hermes as a guide to stand trial at Athens. As they retire, the shade of Clytemnestra rises and arouses the sleeping Furies, who moan in their horrid slumber and finally awake with shrill cries. Clytemnestra's shade goads the Furies to pursue Orestes. The snaky-locked women then intone a wild choral hymn and Apollo drives them from the temple in a spirited scene in which he defends the deed of Orestes while the Furies defy the god. This rapid succession of incidents and stage pictures forms the most striking opening of all the Æschylean tragedies. Scenes in which the shade of a murdered being cries for vengeance, or in which Furies arise were to become favorite openings of later Senecan tragedies. This is the first extant example of this kind of opening scene, which will be so well handled centuries later by Shakespeare in *Hamlet*.

The Furies who form the chorus are the antagonist in the plot. This is entirely a new development in the function of the chorus from those interested in the fate of the hero to those opposing the hero. Indeed, this is the only extant tragedy in which the chorus is hostile to the sympathetic character. This is so contrary to the tradition and spirit of Greek tragedy that it must be regarded as anomalous. It is evident at this time in the development of drama that departures from old customs are quite possible provided they suit the purpose of the playwright.

The first part of this tragedy serves as a kind of prologue, in the sense of an opening act, leading up to the main problem of the play and to the dénouement of the trilogy. The problem to be solved is whether Orestes, having slain his mother at the command of Apollo, shall be freed from guilt. Contrary to general practice, a considerable interval of time elapses between the two episodes. In order to represent these opening scenes in action, Æschylus has deliberately placed the point of attack much farther away from the dénouement than perhaps it had ever been before. With these scenes of exposition enacted instead of narrated, the amount of narration in the play is greatly reduced. This procedure is a good example of the increasing amount of dramatic action and the consequent diminution of narrative and descriptive poetry. This change in the point of attack, the dramatic representation of what would have been narrated in earlier plays, and the resultant increase of the dramatic element constitute the most important changes made by Æschylus in the art of exposition.

The place of the action changes from the temple of Apollo to the temple of Pallas in Athens. The action recommences as Orestes throws himself upon the shrine of Pallas and, clasping her image, asks for protection. The chorus has plainly not left the stage, there being no choral chant for an exodus. It is simply taken for granted that the scene has changed and the Furies have overtaken their quarry. They threaten Orestes and he implores the aid of Athena in a scene of considerable excitement. The Goddess appears and there is a clash between her and the Furies. She bids a Herald summon the Areopagites to act as judges during a formal trial of Orestes. This is the first extant example of a trial scene, a situation which always furnishes suspense and leads to a climax. The handling of this situation does not differ in its broad aspect from similar scenes in modern drama. Orestes is cross-examined by the Furies and defended by Apollo. Both sides of the problem of his guilt are dramatically presented in this obligatory scene. As the Areopagites advance to cast their votes, both the Furies and Apollo plead their causes in alternate couplets. Æschylus sustains the suspense as long as possible. The votes are equal, but Athena casts the deciding vote for the accused hero. The Furies rebel against the verdict and threaten dire vengeance; but after a rather long scene their wrath is finally appeased by Athena, who leads them into a subterranean temple to become guardians of Athens' future power. This episode is probably introduced in order to glorify the city before the Athenian audience. It is far less closely connected with the plot of the trilogy than the episode of Antigone is with the plot of the *Seven Against Thebes*, but both scenes are explicable unless critics insist upon applying as standards later theories of playwriting.

While each play of the trilogy stands as a separate entity, if one considers the whole trilogy as a three-act play, certain technical excellencies in the Æschylean form of drama appear. Æschylus manifested a breadth of view, the ability to lead a plot through many incidents, a fine skill in foreshadowing and preparation, and at the same time a dramatic recalling of past events vital to the present. The drama gives a general impression of unity of action, and reflects unerring selection of most of the important scenes to be represented in action. Suspense and a progression of the action toward climaxes are present. Of course, there is narrative and lyric poetry in the choral odes, and the chorus itself still plays an important rôle; but the individual characters are well sustained. They are active and present more than one side of their nature.

Thus Clytemnestra becomes a well-rounded character. At first, the calm, subtle, self-possessed queen, scoffing at significant dreams, she shifts to the woman fearing dreams, wishing to appease her husband's spirit, but afraid to approach his tomb; she sinks to the level of a human being at bay, pleading with her son for life, and lastly fades into the spirit calling upon the Furies for vengeance. This development of character is made possible by the trilogy.

These are the general impressions left by the trilogy and they bear witness of conscious dramatic skill. The Æschylus who wrote the *Suppliants* and the *Persians* had learned much about the art of drama. He made the work of his successors much easier.

One of the strongest proofs of his understanding of dramaturgic art appears in his ability to devise striking theatrical effects. Even in a period when dramatic art was slowly emerging from a chrysalis of narration, and when the poetical element was so strong, Æschylus knew the dramatic value of silence on the stage. In the *Persians,* Æschylus purposely keeps Atossa mute as the chorus bewails the news of the defeat. Prometheus is haughty and proudly silent under the torture of being bound to the rock. In a lost play, Niobe clings silently to the tomb of her children during two scenes. Cassandra is an auditor dumb to the questions of Clytemnestra. Electra does not speak until the chorus reaches Agamemnon's tomb. It is superfluous to point out the emotional effectiveness of silence maintained by a character whom the audience desires to hear speak, and the dramatic contrast attained when the silence is broken. An impression of reserve power, of unsounded depth, of unknown possibility is created when a character keeps silent in these circumstances. This device became famous as "the silence of Æschylus," and in the *Frogs,* Euripides accuses Æschylus of "cajoling the spectators" by such tricks so that "the spectator by this quackery might sit expecting, when his Niobe would utter something." Thus Aristophanes makes Euripides give the true explanation of the dramatic effect of silence, provided one grasps the full meaning of these words. The expectation or suspense aroused in the spectator is exactly the effect which the dramatist aims to produce by silence. Many procedures of playwrights are tricks which "cajole" the spectator. An artistic *coup de théâtre* is often produced by technical tricks. The difference between a technical trick and a *coup de théâtre* is that the former is a bit of thimble-rigging which has not the deep emotional and psychological significance necessary to produce true art. Did Cassandra keep silent merely to arouse suspense, the procedure would be a mere theatrical trick; but, since her silence is due to the fact that she knows that the woman questioning her is going to slay Agamemnon, her dumbness and the breaking of her silence become a legitimate *coup de théâtre*.

It is the effect, not the means which must be judged. Had Aristophanes made Euripides criticize the effect of the silence of Æschylus, one would be forced to question the procedure. As it is, we do not need to cite the approval of Longinus who refers to Æschylus in pointing out "the eloquence of silence." If it is strange that so early a playwright employed this means of producing dramatic effect, it is still more strange that it was not until the eighteenth century that another dramatist, Diderot, made conscious use of "the great art of silence," as Voltaire called it.

Although the scenery was still rudimentary, Æschylus was remarkably successful in devising striking theatrical effects and stage pictures. The chaining of Prometheus to the rock, the lonely Watchman in *Agamemnon*, the symbolistic, blood-red carpet over which Agamemnon walks to his death, Orestes clinging to the altar, with the Furies sleeping about him, are pictorially dramatic and leave a vivid impression on the mind. They are further evidence of the decrease in importance of the narrative element in drama, since they tell the story and make an emotional impression. The ear was not the only channel through which these tragedies reached the mind. At times the eye was called upon to act as medium. Early dramatist as he was, Æschylus laid the solid foundation upon which Sophocles and Euripides could build. To ascribe this development of dramatic art to a man who did not analyze what he was doing but who worked by inspiration alone, is to disregard the plain traces of conscious artistry.

CHAPTER II

SOPHOCLES

ACCORDING to Aristotle, Sophocles introduced scenery on the Greek stage. The statement probably means that Sophocles was the first to have the stage-building, which served in place of the modern back drop, decorated in some way to represent more distinctly the different scenes required, such as a temple, a palace, a forest, the seashore, etc. The façade was adorned with a row of columns. It is possible that the Æschylean *skene* was built in this manner and would therefore resemble the Hellenistic *proskenion*. In the Sophoclean period, the *proskenion* or colonnade was roofed over, and the *skene* rose behind it, forming a second story. The scenery introduced by Sophocles probably consisted of flats painted to represent the scene of the action and placed between the columns of the architectural background. Such an arrangement would not seem incongruous to an audience accustomed to vase paintings in which a single tree symbolized a whole forest or four pillars with a roof represented a palace or a temple. Painted scenery is indicative of a slight trend toward realism and of the diminution of the imaginative, religious atmosphere pervading the earlier tragedies, in which the action revolves so much of the time about the altar or tomb in the centre of the orchestra. Yet in spite of this realistic trend, which gained more ground, Greek scenery was more a suggestion than a representation of a locality.

The roof of the *proskenion* was practicable. In *Orestes* it represented the roof of Orestes' dwelling, on which he stood with his sword at Hermione's breast, and threatened Menelaus on the stage proper, which represented the street. About 428 B.C. a crane or "machine" was introduced by means of which characters could be swung through air or lifted from the stage to the roof of the stage-building. This contrivance was employed in the entrance of divine characters, especially when a god appeared at the end of a play to give an oracular decree. The expression *deus ex machina* (god from a machine) arose from this practice and was finally applied to any character or incident which brings a plot to a somewhat forced or illogical conclusion.

There are few interior scenes in Greek drama. They may have been effected by opening the large double doors in the stage-building. A device called the *eccyclema* seems to have been employed in connection with interior scenes. The *eccyclema* was probably a platform, resembling a section of a modern wagon-stage, which could be wheeled through a door and revolved. Possibly such scenes as the interior of the shrine in the opening of the *Eumenides* were disclosed in this manner, when the stage was equipped with such scenic devices towards the close of the fifth century. The Greeks did not hesitate to put any scene on the stage because of scenic limitations. They changed the scene, when necessary, during the play; and they indicated the change by altering the setting in a simple way. The usual practice of observing the unity of place did not arise from inability to change the scenery; nor was the practice due to the continuous presence of a chorus on the stage. The scene did not change usually because the first serious tragedies had but one scene—the tomb of the hero.

Another innovation ascribed by Aristotle to Sophocles was the introduction of the third actor or third speaking rôle. In primitive tragedy only one individual character appeared in each scene. In early Æschylean tragedy two individual actors or characters carried on the dialogue, although mute characters might be present on the stage as in the first scene of *Prometheus Bound*. The first extant tragedy requiring three speaking actors in one scene is the *Seven Against Thebes*, which was produced in 467 B.C. As Sophocles began to present plays in 468 B.C., the third speaking rôle would seem to have been introduced by him in that year. After the introduction of the third actor, a fourth and even a fifth silent character were permitted to appear in scenes in which three interlocutors carried on the dialogue. Thus in the last scene of *Orestes*, Menelaus, Electra and Orestes are the speaking characters, while Pylades and Hermione are mute rôles.

The introduction of the third actor or third speaking rôle did not immediately cause important modifications in the construction of tragedy. Although all the extant plays of Sophocles are relatively late productions, few scenes in *Ajax, Antigone* and the *Women of Trachis* require three actors. However, there are eight to nine characters in these plays as against five to seven in the Æschylean tragedies requiring three actors in certain scenes. Euripidean tragedies contain seven to eleven rôles. Whether the wider range of characters caused the introduction of the third actor or the third actor gave opportunity for more characters is a matter of conjecture. In either case, dramatic art became richer as more important characters were introduced in the play and could appear in different combinations on the stage. The playwrights gradually learned how to construct plays in which three speaking actors were employed in most of the scenes.

Æschylus had employed the device of opening a play with an incident connected with the plot; but with the exception of the *Libation-Bearers*, in which Orestes and Pylades appear, at least one of the individual characters was either a messenger or a protatic character, that is, a character which appears for the purpose of exposition and then disappears entirely. Power, Force, Hephæstus in *Prometheus Bound;* the Watchman in *Agamemnon;* the Prophetess in the *Eumenides* are all protatic rôles. *Antigone,* however, opens not merely with an incident but with a dramatic clash between Antigone and Ismene, two characters vital to the plot. Evidence of an attempt on the part of the playwright to avoid the fault, common in expository scenes, of having one character inform another person of circumstances already known by the second character is furnished by the fact that Sophocles represents Ismene as ignorant of the decree that no one shall bury the body of Polynices. Antigone asks Ismene to aid her in paying the last pious honor to their brother but Ismene tries to dissuade her. A dramatic conflict ensues between the sisters; and in the end Antigone goes forth to carry out her purpose.

A modern playwright would hesitate to place such a vital situation in the very opening scene of his play. He would fear that the audience, with its attention distracted in many ways, would not grasp the full significance or feel the full emotional effect of such an important scene. The modern dramatist prefers to gain the attention of the audience slowly, to create the atmosphere by which he wishes to surround his situation, to work up to great moments by degrees. The Greek dramatist often opened his play with a scene which, as in *Antigone,* would form the climax of the first act in modern drama. The evidence furnished by this play and by the later dramas of Æschylus indicates that the practice of the Greeks was to seize the attention of the audience with an effective first scene, then after the introduction of the chorus, to begin to build up the situation and create the correct atmosphere. Shakespeare follows this practice in certain of his plays, *Macbeth* and *Hamlet,* for instance, although he would not open a play with such an important scene as Sophocles would choose, because the usual point of attack in Elizabethan drama was so far removed from the dénouement that a vital scene would come well along in the plot.

The distinct advance over earlier dramas to be noted in the opening of *Antigone* is that the first scene is a dramatic clash of wills of two important persons in the plot. Had a conversation between two protatic characters or even one protatic character and either Ismene or Antigone conveyed the information to the audience, the spectators would have been far less interested and far less emotionally aroused. With the more prudent sister serving as foil for Antigone, both sides of the problem are presented, and the audience lives through the situation with Antigone. In this way, Sophocles wins sympathy immediately for the heroine. The Greek playwrights were learning the art of allowing the audience to see the problem through the eyes of the principal characters instead of through the eyes of a secondary character or a chorus.

When Antigone and Ismene have left the stage, the chorus of Theban Elders enters and, as is usual, gives more of the exposition of events which preceded the first event of the play. The ode deals with the battle of the seven chiefs in which Eteocles and Polynices were mutually slain. With the entrance of Creon the edict is reiterated that the body of Polynices shall be left "unburied, a corpse for birds and dogs to eat, a ghastly sight of shame." Hardly have the words been spoken when a man who was supposed to guard the body brings the news that someone—he knows not whom—has buried it.

The technical skill of Sophocles is striking at this point. He has allowed the audience to know who has buried the body; and thus, when Creon threatens the guard with death unless he discover the person who has performed the last rites over Polynices, suspense, already aroused, is greatly increased. A less skilful dramatist might have had a messenger announce that Antigone had performed the act and so have removed all doubt that she would be seized. Also, it is not a characterless messenger, a mere mouthpiece for narration, but a guard who brings the news, a character who is vitally concerned in discovering the person who has broken the law. Slight as the point may be, it shows an increasing skill in making use of every event in the complication of the plot, and making every rôle in the play a character that acts, not merely a person who narrates events.

In order to obtain this effect Sophocles has practically departed from the chronological order of events. A strictly chronological sequence would place the scene in which Creon announces his decree forbidding the burial of Polynices before the scene between Antigone and Ismene. It is true that the decree has been promulgated before this scene takes place; but we are simply told by Antigone that such is the case. After she has gone to bury the body, Sophocles shows us the scene in which Creon actually threatens with death anyone who buries Polynices. Had this scene come first we would be mildly interested but no suspense would be aroused, since to our knowledge no one would intend to break the law. But since we now know that Antigone is burying the body, every word that Creon speaks is significant and arouses suspense.

The chorus at the end of its song is overwhelmed with sorrow at seeing Antigone led in as a prisoner. Antigone defends her deed before Creon and the situation is dramatically complicated by the appearance of Ismene who, though guiltless, swears she shares the blame. A further complication is brought out in spirited dialogue by the disclosure of the mutual love of Antigone and Hæmon, Creon's son. The scene ends with Creon sentencing Antigone to death. In no earlier extant Greek tragedy is there such a complication of plot and situation. Also, more events and more dramatic action have taken place already than in Æschylean tragedy, and yet the play is only half done.

After a choral ode, which is practically an interlude, Hæmon pleads with his father for Antigone's life. His plea is based upon a desire to save his father's reputation. Already the citizens are murmuring against the brutal sentence. The scene rises to a climax when Hæmon's plea is scorned by Creon as the mere pleading of a lover; and Hæmon leaves with the foreshadowing line:

> My face thou never shall behold again.

The Elder who speaks for the chorus in the scenes of dialogue persuades Creon to pardon Ismene, but Antigone is condemned to be buried alive in a rock-hewn cave.

Antigone and the chorus sing a threnody in alternate song; and when Creon orders her to be led away to the tomb, she once more defends herself with touching dignity and goes forth to death. Still the play does not end. On the contrary, when all hope seems gone, Sophocles is able to arouse suspense once more by bringing Tiresias, the blind seer, before Creon. The prophet tells of evil omens. Creon is obdurate and rashly accuses Tiresias of speaking falsely for the sake of gain. Tiresias warns him, seemingly in vain, that he will pay for the death of

Antigone with the death of his son. But when Tiresias has gone, Creon begins to reflect; and the chorus through its spokesman bids him free the maiden from the tomb, for never did Tiresias speak falsely. Creon at last gives in and goes to save Antigone. A song of joy puts the final touch on this reversal of the situation from hopeless gloom to promised light. In no tragedy thus far, has the pendulum-like swing of the action been so pronounced. A joyous scene of reassurance just before the catastrophe is always effective. Especially in a Greek tragedy, where so much of the atmosphere is sombre, the introduction of this hyporcheme or dancing-song serves to deepen the approaching tragic gloom.

The rest of the play is in narrative and elegiac form, but Sophocles has been careful to make even the narrative and elegy as dramatic as possible. A messenger brings the news to the chorus that Antigone and Hæmon are dead. The scene is short and only that fact is reported. Sophocles then introduces Eurydice, the mother of Hæmon. The intensity of the situation is increased by having the mother listen to the detailed recital of how Creon first buried the body of Polynices and then, going to the living tomb of Antigone, found she had hanged herself and that Hæmon was clinging to the body of his lifeless bride. Finally the audience hears through the mother's ears, not the ears of the chorus, how Hæmon first attempted to slay his father and then turned the sword upon himself. Eurydice has spoken only once, as she entered. In stunned silence she reënters the palace. Creon comes with the body of his son and his wail of lamentation is interrupted by the news that Eurydice is dead. The palace doors open, her body is disclosed, and the play ends with this tragic picture and lamentation.

Antigone is one of the earliest plays in which a problem of human life is emphasized. It is the conflict between duty to the family, represented by Antigone, and duty to the State, represented by Creon. There is no such problem in the Persians, the Suppliants or the Seven Against Thebes. Having witnessed a performance of any of these plays, one would not feel impelled to discuss the amount of right or wrong involved in the situation. The intellectual element is stronger in *Prometheus Bound;* but, whatever problem there is in that play, it touches human life indirectly. Few men are fire-bringers. In *Antigone,* however, the problem, which arises from the conflict between duty and man-made law, governs the selection and the conduct of the scenes. An audience at a performance of the *Persians* need only feel emotion. An audience at a production of *Antigone* must not only feel but also think. It must weigh the question in the scales of reason as well as in the scales of emotion. Greek tragedy was still a work of art appealing to the emotions through the senses; but the intellectual element has appeared in drama. In the nineteenth century is found the so-called "drama of ideas." *Antigone* foreshadows from afar that development of dramatic art.

The plot of this play is more complicated and passes through many more incidents than has been the case heretofore. The drama seems to be more in the present and less in the past. The principal characters carry on the action and there are more characters which are vitally concerned with the story. The messenger alone is the only person in the play who is unaffected by any turn the situation may take, for even the sentinel is in danger of his life unless he discovers who buried the body. The chorus is individualized. During the dialogue one member of the chorus speaks for all. The choral odes tend to assume more the character of interludes. While the chorus is never hostile to Antigone, it begins by passively assenting to Creon's wishes but ends by taking an active part in winning him over to clemency. Suspense is not only well sustained from the first moment, but also there is a fine intermingling of hope and fear. The entrance of Eurydice, however, totally unprepared for and so late in the play, recalls a questionable practice of earlier tragedy.

The most striking difference between *Antigone* and modern tragedies founded on similar situations lies in the fact that the young lovers, Antigone and Hæmon, never meet on the stage. Modern versions of the story centre almost the entire interest

on the love of the two young people. Indeed, the lost Euripidean version ended with the marriage of the pair. Thus perhaps even a Greek audience might have been more impressed
had Sophocles made more use of the love motive, or at least
had heightened the pathos of the narrative of their death together by having allowed the audience to see them alive together.

Ajax and the *Women of Trachis* exemplify the tendency to
introduce more action in Greek tragedy and to place the events
on the stage. As a result, the scene of *Ajax* changes during the
play, and the events of the *Women of Trachis* cannot happen
during "one revolution of the sun." The death of Ajax occurs
on the stage, contrary to the usual practice. Heracles endures
his mortal agony of the poisoned robe in a long scene and is
borne forth just before his actual death. The Greek playwright
was not bound by rules; and Sophocles was not allowing tradition or convention to hinder him from complicating the plot
and staging scenes which were originally narrated just as
Æschylus had narrated the suicide of Ajax in his play on this
theme.

The Sophoclean version is the first extant tragedy containing
a monologue on suicide. Such meditations on death were imitated by Seneca. The playwrights of the Renaissance were inspired to introduce similar passages in their tragedies. Hamlet's
soliloquy is indirectly derived from such monologues as the one
spoken by Ajax.

In dealing with the subject of the vengeance wreaked upon
Clytemnestra by her children Electra and Orestes, a theme which
Æschylus had already dramatized, Sophocles was confronted by
a problem which resulted from the fact that the Greeks gradually discarded the custom of writing three plays on one subject.
As the framework of the single play was enlarged and more
of the story was represented in action, the form of the trilogy
on one subject became less necessary. At the same time, the
dramatist had not yet enlarged the scope of the single play so
that all of the material used in the trilogy could be included

in one tragedy. A compromise had to be effected between the older tragedy with few events and the trilogy with many events. The problem which Sophocles had to solve in writing a play on this subject was how to include more events in the plot in response to the demand for more action and yet avoid leaving unanswered the question of the fate of a matricide —a question which Æschylus had been able to dispose of in the third play of his trilogy. Since he chose the identical point of attack which Æschylus had selected and since the dénouement is fixed by the death of Clytemnestra, the greatest change in the construction of the play had to take place in the scenes leading up to the climax.

Sophocles opens his play, as does Æschylus, with the return of Orestes, accompanied by Pylades, but he has introduced as a third character the old Guardian. They plan that the old Guardian shall bring the false news of how Orestes has been killed by a fall from his chariot. They hear a cry of woe from Electra within the palace, and Sophocles is careful to remove these characters from the stage instead of allowing Orestes to see and recognize Electra when she enters, as does Æschylus. Electra, herself, then recalls the murder of her father and prays for the return of Orestes. The chorus of Mycenæan women and Electra in a long scene give the complete exposition by no means in plain narrative but in a dialogue in which the chorus begs Electra to be calm, to endure, and not to heap ill upon ill. Electra paints a vivid picture of the sufferings she endures. She lives like a stranger in her father's hall, reviled by Clytemnestra, with Ægisthus on her father's throne. The chorus in the Æschylean play has the same hostile attitude that Electra has; but Sophocles has made his situation somewhat more dramatic and has heightened the uncompromising character of Electra by conceiving the chorus as more conservative and as counselling patience and even forbearance.

Sophocles has thus far followed the *Libation-Bearers* on broad lines. He has caught the attention of the audience by an important event and then allows the dialogue between Electra and the chorus to give the exposition; but Sophocles dwells longer upon the exposition and gives more details because he cannot rely upon any preceding tragedy of *Agamemnon* to create the correct atmosphere or to explain the situation. Also, he must paint Clytemnestra as darkly as possible, since his audience has not actually seen her murder her husband and especially since he must justify entirely the coming matricide. He cannot allow the question of Orestes' guilt to arise since he has no third play in which to solve the question.

From this point until the meeting of Electra and Orestes, Sophocles devises wholly new material in order to introduce more dramatic action. In the *Libation-Bearers*, Electra has been sent by Clytemnestra to pour libations on her father's tomb; but Sophocles introduces the character of Chrysothemis, the sister of Electra, to perform this act. In *Antigone* Sophocles has built up a strong scene by differentiating the rôles of Antigone and Ismene, which in Æschylus' *Seven Against Thebes* were quite similar. As is so often the case with playwrights of all times, Sophocles employs a situation which he had previously found to be effective. The situation in *Antigone* is practically transferred to *Electra*. Chrysothemis, like Ismene, tries to win over her uncompromising sister to a calmer and more obedient frame of mind. Electra scorns her sister and ranges her among her enemies. The clash of wills is even more violent than in the parallel scene in *Antigone* and seems to heighten our impression of the stronger sister, firm in her purpose of vengeance. Finally Electra persuades Chrysothemis not to bear the appeasing gifts from her mother, troubled by dreams, to Agamemnon's tomb.

In the Æschylean tragedy the rôle of Clytemnestra consisted of but forty-six lines and she did not appear until after the meeting of Electra and Orestes. Sophocles, however, brings her on the stage at this point and, in a scene of mutual denunciation between mother and daughter, he drives home the impression of the unnatural wife and mother. This scene serves the purpose of representing vividly to the audience the picture that Æschylus had given them in *Agamemnon*. This is a second scene of dramatic action added by Sophocles to his plot.

The Guardian thereupon brings the false news of the death of Orestes which he describes at length. With the exception of the exposition this is practically the only narrative passage in the play, and it is plain that the dramatic element has become far more important than the narrative element. Yet, at the same time, this passage is evidence that playwrights still considered that opportunities for rhetorical description and narration could not be allowed to escape. Although the audience knows that every detail of this description of Orestes' death is false, and although it is only necessary so far as the plot is concerned to give enough circumstantial evidence of his death to convince Electra and Clytemnestra, this description goes into minute detail and is eighty-three lines long—almost twice as long as Clytemnestra's rôle in the Æschylean tragedy.

This device of reporting that Orestes is dead is one of the most important elements in the Sophoclean play, and it seems to have been suggested to Sophocles in a curious way. In the Æschylean tragedy Orestes plans to enter the palace and, pretending to be a Phocian stranger, to slay Ægisthus before the king can ask "Whence is this stranger?" There is no idea of giving false news of Orestes' death until Orestes unexpectedly faces his mother instead of Ægisthus. It is then on the spur of the moment that he tells of his own death and Æschylus does not explain why, although one may infer that it is to disarm suspicion, but it is mere inference. Sophocles builds up the plan of the false news from the start and bases much of his action on it; but the only explanation that he gives is that Orestes expects, out of this report, to blaze forth star-like, living on his foes, since men who falsely pretended death, when they came back home have been more prized than ever. Thus Sophocles seems to have appreciated the theatrical effect of this device, but, while he makes more use of it than does Æschylus, he has not sufficiently motivated it.

Also, Sophocles has made Electra, who is of secondary importance, in the *Libation-Bearers,* the central figure of his play. He develops her character and her will to act. At first Electra is indulging in lamentation but finally the chorus feels it necessary to try to restrain her rising anger. The sight of Chrysothemis bearing offerings at her mother's request to Agamemnon's tomb increases her righteous wrath. Unlike Hamlet in a similar situation, hers is no hesitating melancholy. Then, as Clytemnestra taunts her, degree by degree the will to act grows stronger. Through ever-rising intensity, not abruptly, the situation passes from the *pianissimo* of the first lamentation, to the *mezzo forte* of the scene with Chrysothemis to the *forte* of the open defiance of Clytemnestra. Such dramatic crescendo is only in embryonic form before Sophocles. Finally it is with great art that Sophocles delays the appearance of Orestes and the recognition until Electra has passed through all these emotions and we have beheld her intense though heroic suffering at the news of Orestes' death. The great improvement over Æschylus is manifest in this conscious art of deftly handling the emotions of his heroine.

It is by innuendo and suggestion in Æschylus' play that the audience becomes conscious of the brutal satisfaction of Clytemnestra at the news of her son's death; but Sophocles, in order to justify the matricide, has Clytemnestra rejoice openly. Electra is left alone with the chorus, but their lamentation is interrupted by Chrysothemis who rushes to her with the glad tidings that Orestes must live, since she has discovered his votive lock of hair on their father's tomb; but Electra turns her joy to grief by telling her the news of Orestes' death. In a passionate scene Electra vows to wreak vengeance on the guilty pair. Chrysothemis tells her such a vow is madness and leaves Electra to act alone.

The entrance of Orestes after these new situations marks the point at which Sophocles' plot begins to run parallel to the older plot; but a comparison of the two recognition scenes shows how much more careful the later dramatist has been to employ every means of complicating the situation and prolonging the suspense. In the *Libation-Bearers* Orestes recognizes Electra as she issues from the palace and, on hearing her filial lamentation, discloses his identity. In *Electra* Sophocles has been careful to remove Orestes from the stage so that he cannot recognize his sister by overhearing her words of sorrow. Thus the scene of recognition is artistically and logically prolonged. Furthermore, the striking theatrical trick of having Orestes place in Electra's hands an urn supposed to contain his own ashes, has enabled Sophocles to devise an opportunity for arousing deep sympathy, as Electra weeps over the urn. This leads to the recognition of Electra by Orestes; and then, still making the most of the situation, Sophocles prolongs the scene by having Orestes gradually prepare her mind for the discovery of his identity leading her through surprise, conjecture, and hope to conviction. The art of prolonging suspense and of arousing sympathy, has developed greatly since Æschylus constructed his scene of recognition.

The Guardian, who has been keeping watch, now bids the brother and sister go within, where Clytemnestra is alone. The song of the chorus, as the women wait in suspense, creates an effective tension. From this moment the action fairly rushes to the dénouement. Instead of messengering the death, Sophocles has Electra suddenly come forth and the following dialogue depicts dramatically the murder without having it committed on the stage.

ELECTRA

A cry goes up within:—hear ye not, friends?

CHORUS

I heard, ah me, sounds dire to hear, and shuddered.

CLYTEMNESTRA (*behind the scenes*)

O hapless that I am! Ægisthus, where art thou?

ELECTRA

Hark, once more a voice resounds.

CLYTEMNESTRA (*within*)

My son, my son, have pity on thy mother!

ELECTRA

Thou hast none for him, nor for the father that begat him.

CHORUS

Ill-fated realm and race, now the fate that hath pursued thee day by day is dying—is dying.

Clytemnestra cries out again and then silence falls.

Orestes and Pylades appear for a moment and Orestes says: "In the house all is well if Apollo's oracle spake well." Thus does Sophocles once more successfully palliate the matricide by placing the blame, if blame there be, on Apollo. At the approach of Ægisthus, Orestes and Pylades retire, leaving Electra to face Ægisthus, who comes with sinister joy to hear the confirmation of the news of Orestes' death. Electra answers his questions with fine irony and dissembling, and he commands that the gates of the palace be opened. The doors swing back and a shrouded body is disclosed. Thinking he will see the dead Orestes, Ægisthus removes the shroud and beholds the face of Clytemnestra.

It is scarcely necessary to call attention to this remarkable *coup de théâtre* with its attendant emotions of suspense and surprise. It would be impossible for a modern dramatist versed in every theatrical trick to devise a more effective scene.

The play ends at the climax as Orestes, pouring forth his wrath, drives the miserable Ægisthus within and slays him; and in four lines the chorus justifies the whole procedure. There is no thought of punishment of Orestes; no foreshadowing of a trial of the hero.

Although *Electra* is longer than the *Libation-Bearers,* the greater length is not due to narration or lyric passages but to a greater number of events and dramatic situations placed between the point of attack and the climax. The action of the *Libation-Bearers* gives one the impression of jumping from one situation to another. Then the situation is held stationary. In *Electra* the action develops gradually but surely and one situation blends into another. The characters appear and reappear in *Electra* with more motivation. Sophocles, like Æschylus, fails to introduce Ægisthus before the very end of the play, yet he motivates the late entrance by supposing that Ægisthus is away from the palace. A modern dramatist would construct a scene in which Clytemnestra and Ægisthus would be together on the stage; but in the three Greek plays on this subject there is no scene between these important characters. While the playwrights were gradually learning to place the principal characters together in some obligatory scenes, they still made their pictures somewhat one-sided by failing to represent all obligatory scenes.

Aristotle considered *Œdipus Rex* a masterpiece of Greek tragedy, although, according to tradition, it failed to receive first prize when it was produced. It is difficult to point to a finer piece of dramatic art, especially in respect to the construction of the plot which is based upon the following story.

Laius asked the oracle of Apollo whether a child would be born to him and his wife, Jocasta. The reply was given that a son would be given to him but that he would be slain by the child. When the babe was born, Jocasta gave it to a servant with orders to expose it so that the oracle would not be fulfilled. The man gave the child to a Corinthian herdsman who took it to Corinth and bestowed it upon the king, Polybus. The king reared the boy as his own son and named him Œdipus. Having grown to manhood, Œdipus was taunted by a young man with not being the true son of Polybus. Œdipus consulted the oracle of Apollo; and, when the answer came that he would slay his father and marry his mother, he resolved not to return to Corinth. Travelling in the opposite direction, he met a man at a crossroad. The right of way was disputed. Œdipus slew the man and all but one of his retainers. He came to Thebes, solved the riddle of the Sphinx, was proclaimed king and married Jocasta. A plague fell upon the city. An oracle declared that the plague would abate only when the slayer of Laius was discovered and driven from Thebes. Œdipus discovered that the man he had slain was Laius, his father, and that Jocasta was his mother. Jocasta hanged herself. Œdipus punished himself by self-inflicted blindness and went into exile.

Such is the tissue of improbability, murder, suicide, torture and incest which Sophocles transformed into lofty tragedy, appalling in its inevitability.

Æschylus had dramatized the myth in the form of a trilogy consisting of *Laius, Œdipus* and the extant *Seven Against Thebes*. By employing the trilogy he had produced a work which is comparable to a Shakespearean play in the amount of action included within the three plays. The Shakespearean point of attack, however, would probably have been a scene in which Laius asks the question of the oracle at Delphi and would have been much farther back than the Æschylean point of attack which was probably placed to include only the murder of Laius.

Sophocles, however, had a delicate and difficult task to perform since he discarded the trilogy dealing with one subject and had to include this story in one tragedy. Furthermore, the Athenian audience was evidently no longer content to have a play consist mainly of narration. Action was necessary, and yet the story contains many details to be explained. Action could be furnished by compressing into one tragedy the material which Æschylus had employed for two plays; but tradition held the point of attack so close to the dénouement that Sophocles begins his action with the promise of Œdipus to do all in his power to abate the plague. Any playwright, except a Greek or one who is master of the technique of Greek drama, would find it very difficult to choose this point of attack and write a play which would consist of anything but exposition. Even if most of the play were given up to exposition, it would be difficult to make the audience understand the whole situation, since a spectator is rarely capable of fully comprehending many details unless they are represented before his eyes instead of being narrated without action.

In *Œdipus Rex* every event is the result of withdrawing a veil from the past and almost every event turns out contrary to the hope and expectation of the audience. These events are disclosed in almost complete inverse order to that of the temporal sequence. For these reasons, this tragedy is one of the most remarkable pieces of dramatic construction in existence.

Exposition consists of making the audience acquainted with past events which lead up to a dramatic problem. Exposition may be carried on by means of narration or by representation of the incidents which cause the dramatic problem to arise. Critics are likely to make the mistake of believing that any narration of an event which precedes the initial cause is exposition provided it is merely explanatory, but if the narration or representation of an incident in the past causes a development of the present situation, it becomes dramatic action. Since every disclosure of the past in *Œdipus Rex* causes a development of the plot, exposition is reduced to a minimum. What would normally be exposition becomes action.

The opening scene of the play is a striking tableau in which Œdipus receives the band of suppliants, moaning citizens of all ages. Only the first eighty-six lines can be called exposition and even in this first scene the narrative element is rendered entirely unobtrusive because of the interest in the expressive, massive stage picture, and because the details of the present situation are brought out through the incident of the people of the stricken city begging Œdipus to find some means to alleviate the plague which is upon them. Attention is immediately fastened upon the question of what Œdipus can do. An atmosphere of suspense and of tragedy pervades the scene; but Œdipus wins our sympathy and arouses hope when he tells the plague-tormented citizens how his heart bleeds for the people and that he has sent Creon to the Delphian oracle to ask by what act or word he can deliver the city. From the moment that Creon arrives the unveiling of the past begins. The oracle has said that the murderer of Laius must be punished in order to purge the land of its misfortunes. In these circumstances it is not only natural but essentially dramatic for Creon and Œdipus to begin the investigation of the murder of Laius, in regard to which the principal known facts are disclosed. Since this constitutes the first step in solving the problem upon which the plot rests, it is action.

Exposition consists in stating a dramatic problem. Action consists in solving the problem.

The whole development of the plot depends upon the discovery of the murderer of Laius. Sophocles discloses the truth gradually, leading us from conjecture, through suspicion, to certainty. He carefully avoids letting the audience penetrate the mystery until towards the close of the play. Yet almost every Greek spectator must have known that Œdipus was the slayer of his father Laius. The question arises, therefore, whether the audience felt any suspense in regard to the ultimate discovery or any surprise when the horrible fact is disclosed. In all probability, however, Sophocles felt that if he did not state this fact plainly, he could rely upon the rapidity of his action and upon his constant insistence on the hopeful aspect of the situation to create a conflict of emotions in the audience. No matter how well the spectator may know the sad outcome of any tragedy, while the tragedy is being enacted he shares every ray of hope which comes to the sympathetic character. He views the tragedy, for the most part, through the eyes of the hero. He hopes with the hero; he despairs with the hero. But at times his knowledge of the unhappy ending breaks in upon him with a vague but nevertheless awful irony. This conflict of emotion arises during a representation of *Œdipus Rex;* but it would have been destroyed, in a great measure, had Sophocles informed the audience at the beginning of the play that Œdipus had slain Laius. Had he done so, the tragic irony of beholding Œdipus trying to discover the murderer of Laius would still remain, and the audience would still feel suspense. By not directly informing the audience, he preserves tragic irony, since the audience is vaguely conscious of the horrible discovery that Œdipus will make. Since this consciousness is vague, a greater amount of suspense and surprise still remain as the plot unfolds. The effect of this play on the stage would be far less dramatic had Sophocles called attention directly to the fact that Œdipus had slain Laius. The master hand is betrayed by the handling of such apparently minor considerations which in reality are of prime importance.

It is difficult to find a play in which there is more poignant irony in the situation; and Sophocles makes the most of it, first in having Œdipus promise the senators to do all in his power to aid the suffering people, secondly in having Œdipus swear to discover the guilty man, not knowing that he is directing the violent imprecations against himself.

With consummate skill, the dramatist has involved the three principals in the plot and has made Œdipus the character who takes every step to solve the mystery and brings about his own doom as he tries to save the city. Œdipus may be haughty and guilty of rashness, but his faults are overshadowed by his bravery and sense of justice, for when the unbelievable truth begins to dawn he goes heroically on, in spite of every entreaty to give up the attempt to solve the mystery. Tiresias, Jocasta, the old shepherd, implore him in vain to seek no farther. Such heroism is awful in its grandeur.

Sophocles unfolds the plot with careful selection of scenes. One of his greatest problems in the construction of the play must have been to find incidents to keep the action developing inevitably, but slowly. The first step towards the solution of the problem is the summoning of Tiresias. The blind seer does not wish to answer the question. Œdipus' calmness gives way and his mood becomes angry and threatening. After creating suspense by refusing to answer, Tiresias accuses Œdipus of being the abominable contaminator of the land and he hints at the horrible relationship in which Œdipus lives with Jocasta.

It is daring on the part of the playwright to have the actual truth in regard to the situation come out so early in the play; but Sophocles has been unerring in his order of scenes. Tiresias' knowledge springs from his second sight, and no concrete evidence has been offered by him or anyone else thus far to make one give credence to his words. The results of his accusation are to make Œdipus impress the audience with the seeming preposterousness of the idea and with his innocence, and also to make him accuse Creon of having invented the tale to ruin him. This development brings a new complication to the plot and furnishes opportunity for an obligatory scene between Œdipus and Creon and Jocasta. Had the accusation of Tiresias been placed by Sophocles after the slightest suspicion of the truth had entered the mind of Œdipus, the whole delicate mechanism of the plot would have been thrown out of gear. This is just the right kind of incident to retard dramatically the development of the plot which otherwise might have come to a rather hurried ending unless it were held back by undramatic means such as choral odes or situations drawn out at length.

One hesitates to call Sophocles clever in connection with this titanic tragedy; but the manner in which he sheds an atmosphere of hopeful reassurance over every situation up to the end and makes every act of Œdipus when he seems about to prove his innocence bring his own doom nearer, must be sheer conscious cleverness on the part of the playwright. The play opens with a majestic but gloomy scene of prayer for release from the horror brooding over the people, but Œdipus promises his aid. Already he has sent to Apollo for help. When Creon arrives from Delphi and is asked concerning the answer of the god, he says the reply is favorable. The Priest's last words in this scene and indeed the whole choral ode following it sound a note of hope. Œdipus summons Tiresias as the man who can aid them. Then the pendulum swings back to fear as Tiresias accuses him; but Œdipus' anger and finally Jocasta's words that nothing in human life turns on the soothsayers' art give a reassuring touch. Then Jocasta tries to dispel any possible fear by telling what she knows of the murder and her words of reassurance create the first shadow of doubt in the mind of Œdipus. Jocasta assures him that the old herdsman, the only surviving witness, said that "robbers," not a single man, slew Laius. Then comes the messenger with the news that Polybus, the supposed father of Œdipus, is dead and with intense relief Jocasta summons Œdipus to hear the news that frees him from the fear of slaying his father as the oracle foretold he would. Œdipus, however, expresses the fear that the rest of the oracle, that he would marry his mother, might be fulfilled. Again come words intended to reassure him. He is not the son of Merope but a foundling, whom the old herdsman gave to the messenger. It is then that the incredible truth dawns on Jocasta and she implores him to delve no further into the mystery of his birth. Then comes the herdsman and he is tortured until he speaks the unspeakable: Œdipus is Jocasta's son. With consummate art Sophocles reaches one of the greatest climaxes of all drama.

Let the undramatic critic analyze the narrative story and he can prove that the whole plot is a tissue of improbabilities. Why, he asks, did not Œdipus inquire whether Jocasta was older than he before he married? Or he may ask, with Œdipus, why Tiresias, with his second sight, did not expose the deed of Œdipus long before. But only the meticulous critic in his study is capable of such hopeless comments. An audience feels that the whole development of the story is crushingly inevitable. Aristotle indicates how Sophocles has produced this effect when he says that there should be nothing improbable among the actual incidents but that if the improbability be unavoidable it should be outside the tragedy, as in *Œdipus Rex* of Sophocles. No matter how unbelievable any incident may be, if the audience knows that the incident has taken place before the play begins, whatever action arises from it seems perfectly probable. All the events upon which the action turns have happened in the past. Hence these events are unchangeable. The action consists of the discovery of unalterable facts. Therefore, the action seems inevitable. One may escape fate; but there is no escape from the past. Thus does Sophocles transform the improbable into the inevitable; and we have in *Œdipus Rex* a brilliant example of the development of a plot by the withdrawal of veils from the past. This procedure is inherent in primitive Greek tragedy because of the influence of the ritual of the worship of dead heroes. This play shows the artistic culmination of the procedure and not until Ibsen shall we find the same method so successfully employed to produce the effect of the inevitability of the action.

Sophocles was unerring in his choice of characters; and the

principal characters are on the stage whenever they ought to be. Œdipus is before our eyes almost all the time. The hero has come to his own. It is the will of Œdipus which sets the action in motion and every event of the present is the result of his mental attitude. The choral rôle is short but the odes are not mere interludes. They give the finishing touch to the preceding scene, accentuating the supplication, hope, suspense or despair as the case may be. They are dramatic and not mere lyric embroidery of the theme as they become in later plays.

Both Æschylus and Euripides had dramatized the story of Philoctetes before Sophocles chose it as the subject of one of his last tragedies, produced in 410 B.C. According to the epic legend Philoctetes, suffering from a noisome wound, had been abandoned by the Greeks and left on the island of Lemnos as they sailed to the siege of Troy. After ten years of undecisive struggle, the chieftains of the Greek hosts learned from a soothsayer that Troy could not be captured until Philoctetes was brought to Troy with the death-dealing arrows of Heracles and until Neoptolemus came from Scyros and received Achilles' armor. Diomedes performed the task of inducing Philoctetes to come with his arrows; and Odysseus succeeded in bringing Neoptolemus to Troy.

Æschylus substituted Odysseus, Philoctetes' worst enemy, for Diomedes and thus created a dramatic situation. Euripides introduced a dramatic struggle by having two rival embassies, one Greek and the other Trojan, visit Philoctetes and try to win the support of the hero. From Dion Chrysostomus' account of the play, the inference may be drawn that the climactic scene was characteristically Euripidean in that the rivals argued their case in the oratorical style of a court of law or a public debate.

With the sure touch of a master craftsman, Sophocles combined the two episodes of the underlying myth by introducing Neoptolemus into his play. As Professor Jebb has pointed out, "It is no longer only a critical episode in the Trojan wars, turning on the question whether the envoys of the Greeks can conciliate the master of their fate. It acquires the larger significance of a pathetic study in human character—a typical illustration of generous fortitude under suffering and of struggle between good and evil in an ambitious but loyal mind." This tragedy is by no means lacking in suspense or in unexpected turns of the plot. Yet the chief interest lies in the psychological reactions of the three principal characters. Philoctetes, basely wronged by Odysseus, holds the fate of the Greeks in his quiver. Neoptolemus, loyal as a friend, loyal as a Greek, must bring Philoctetes by deceit to Troy. Odysseus, loyal to the State, will sacrifice all for victory.

Euripides opened his play with a formal prologue spoken by Odysseus, but Sophocles, by the introduction of Neoptolemus, is able to place two important characters on the stage for the exposition. They have arrived at the cave in which the unfortunate Philoctetes lives. Odysseus tells Neoptolemus in a few words that they are at Lemnos where Philoctetes was abandoned. The rest of the expository scene is combined with the incident in which Neoptolemus discovers the cave and the bed of leaves and the rough-hewn cup of Philoctetes. When Odysseus lays his plan before Neoptolemus, the exposition glides unconsciously into action and skilful preparation for the scenes to come. Neoptolemus is to win the friendship of Philoctetes by saying that he, Achilles' son, is deserting the Achæans who have wronged him by bestowing Achilles' armor on Odysseus. The hesitation of Neoptolemus to practice such guile on an innocent man foreshadows the development of the plot; but he consents at last. Finally Odysseus says that, should it seem that Neoptolemus is wasting time, he will send one of their followers disguised as a sea captain from whom Neoptolemus must gather the meaning of his words though he speak in parables.

One of the important elements in constructing plays is to arouse the curiosity of the audience so that they are anxious to see what will happen; and certainly in this planning, foreshadowing, and preparation Sophocles has accomplished this task of arousing the interest in the first scene without giving any hint of the ultimate outcome of the play. Since the plan by which

Neoptolemus hopes to gain the arrows of Philoctetes has already been laid, their meeting in the first obligatory scene is full of suspense. Philoctetes tells Neoptolemus the story of the wrongs done him by the Greeks; and Neoptolemus unfolds his lying stratagem, which seems likely to succeed, as Philoctetes is willing to go with him.

Then comes the follower of Odysseus disguised as a ship captain bringing the news, at once both false and true, that Odysseus has sailed for Lemnos to bring Philoctetes to Troy and that others have gone in search of Neoptolemus. In justifying this part of the play, which has been called episodic, Professor Jebb points out that this story quickens the impatience of Philoctetes to leave Lemnos, while it also strengthens his sympathy for the son of Achilles and supplies the motive for the transfer of the bow to Neoptolemus.

Philoctetes, knowing that he will fall asleep after the paroxysm of pain that visits him, gives the bow and arrows to Neoptolemus, who swears to keep them safe. The suffering of Philoctetes is no sentimental bid for sympathy on the part of the audience but is dynamically dramatic. Neoptolemus has gained possession of the arrows, and apparently nothing remains for him but to hand them over to Odysseus; but the frankness of Philoctetes, his perfect trust in his new-found friend, the covenanted pledge cause a conflict in the heart of the son of Achilles. Neoptolemus can no longer bear the deceit he is practicing on this man and dramatically tells him the truth. Suddenly Odysseus enters as Neoptolemus is about to give back the bow and arrows. The action rises still higher as Philoctetes, pouring out his wild wrath upon the cold, calm Odysseus, attempts to throw himself into the sea but is held by the attendants. Odysseus bids Neoptolemus follow him as he leaves for the ship, and the youth reluctantly obeys, but orders the sailors to stay and try to prevail upon the wretched Philoctetes to accompany them to Troy.

The scene which follows between the hero and the chorus is no mere lament but a dramatic struggle in which Philoctetes refuses to follow them and begs for death. Thus does Sophocles turn the choral scenes into dramatic action. The plot quickly develops into a new phase as Neoptolemus returns with Odysseus dogging his footsteps; and another obligatory scene of clashing wills takes place when Neoptolemus, deaf to threats and entreaties, avows his purpose of restoring the bow to its luckless owner. As Odysseus departs to summon the army to punish Neoptolemus, the latter calls forth Philoctetes and gives him back his arrows. Then occurs a *coup de théâtre* which would be merely melodramatic were the tragedy not so psychologically intense. Odysseus steps forth and Philoctetes aims a death-dealing arrow at him. The moment is a strong climax. Neoptolemus holds Philoctetes' arm, and Odysseus escapes death. The final obligatory scene begins as Neoptolemus entreats Philoctetes to come freely with him to Ilium, but although Philoctetes dramatically wavers for a moment and seems about to give in to the prayers of his new-found friend, he at last bids Neoptolemus fulfill the promise to take him home and they set forth.

Up to this point the treatment of the theme is masterful. The principal characters have been on the stage constantly; and the pendulum of the action has swung back and forth in dramatic suspense. The *coups de théâtre* have produced moments of intense psychological interest without which the plot would be merely theatrical, not tragic and dramatic. The tragedy has taken place in the souls of the young heroes. But Sophocles was faced with a dilemma. The playwright could not alter the events of the fall of Troy by not having Philoctetes sail to Ilium. That would be doing too much violence even to pseudo-history. He solved the problem by introducing Heracles, as a *deus ex machina*, who gives the oracular decree that Philoctetes shall go to Troy. Philoctetes bows to the divine mandate.

It has been said that Sophocles employed the *deus ex machina* in imitation of Euripides, who often called upon supernatural aid to untie his Gordian knots. The appearance of a god, whether logical or illogical, is thrilling and theatrically effective. So long as such a theme is given a mythological and supernatural setting, any audience will accept such a solution for that particular play. We would not, however, feel satisfied with such a solution of the problem of *A Doll's House,* of Galsworthy's *Loyalties,* or even of Corneille's *Cid.* Sophocles has made his conflict in this tragedy so entirely human and so purely psychological that many of his modern admirers have sought to prove that the appearance of Heracles is a logical, psychological dénouement. Heracles has been explained as the personification of the conscience of Philoctetes. His appearance has been compared to the appearance of Christ in the *Quo Vadis* legend. Such explanations are brilliant, perhaps logical deductions; but they are deductions from reactions of modern minds, not from the Sophoclean text.

The purely human problem of *Philoctetes* is not solved if the plot is stripped of its setting and analyzed abstractly. Aristophanes answers his problems more clearly than do the tragic dramatists. Greek tragedies contain problems but they are not problem plays, in the modern sense, in which a dramatist aims to demonstrate a thesis. *Philoctetes* resembles a modern *pièce à thèse* because finally all the characters are in full possession of all facts, but Sophocles did not care to answer the problem by showing the reaction of the human mind to these facts. Nevertheless, *Philoctetes* is the finest example in all Greek tragedy of the inter-reaction of events and character. In this respect it marks an advance in playwriting over *Œdipus Rex* in which the characters do not understand the situation until the very end. *Philoctetes* is Sophocles' greatest achievement as a dramatist of the conflict in the souls of men, conscious of their duty to individuals and to society.

CHAPTER III

EURIPIDES

EURIPIDES (484-406 B.C.) was a contemporary of Sophocles and yet his principles of playwriting differ in so many ways from those of Sophocles and prepare so plainly for the future development of the art of constructing plays that he seems to mark a new period in the history of the drama. The history of dramatic art shows a constant struggle between the spectacular and narrative elements on the one hand and the dramatic element on the other. Drama generally begins with the spectacular and narrative elements in the ascendancy. The dramatic element slowly emerges, and growing more and more important, finally becomes paramount, with a corresponding diminution of the spectacular and narrative interest. Then through various influences, the spectacular and narrative elements begin once more to overshadow dramatic action. The development is not a closed circle, but dramatic art in its decadence comes close to the point from which it started. First, poets write plays. Then the poets become dramatists who are willing to sacrifice the poetical and literary element to dramatic action. Finally the writer of plays becomes a poet who will not sacrifice literary excellence to dramatic excellence. The art of plot construction reached its highest point among the Greeks with Sophocles. Euripides, though a great artist, marks the beginning of a decline which culminates, so far as extant tragedies are concerned, with Seneca. Certain elements in Euripides' principles of play-making coalesced with a few elements of Aristophanic comedy and produced that form of drama known as New Comedy. While Euripides makes certain innovations, his dramatic art shows reversions to a more primitive form.

It is probable that Euripides was the last of the three playwrights to compose his tragedy on the subject of the vengeance wreaked on Clytemnestra by her children. Since Sophocles had followed the Æschylean version in its main outlines and had made his effects by expanding and developing scenes and situations in the older play, it was incumbent upon Euripides to strike out on new lines in composing his *Electra* about 413 B.C. Both in this play and in his *Helen,* Euripides departs from the well-known versions of the myths; and in exercising his powers of invention he prepares for the wholly invented plots of later tragedies such as Agathon's *Flower.* Naturally a time came when so many plays had been composed on the well-known myths that in order to produce any new effects the dramatist would have to rely upon his own imagination. Euripides, therefore, changes the situation treated by Æschylus and Sophocles by supposing that Electra had been married by Ægisthus to a farmer who is poor but of noble birth. Æschylus had placed the scene of his play at the tomb of Agamemnon. Sophocles represents the action as taking place before the royal palace. Euripides sets his scene before the humble cottage of the Farmer. Perhaps in these settings is reflected respectively the religious atmosphere of Æschylean tragedy, the heroic atmosphere of the Sophoclean superman and the more vivid humanity of the Euripidean men and women. The Euripidean setting needs little alteration to become the setting for New Comedy. While the Farmer is not a comic character, his station in life and the fact that he is married to a woman to whom he is husband in name only, leads one to think of the worthy citizens whom Menander will put upon the stage. The dividing line between comedy and tragedy is very faint and the amount of seriousness in a situation depends upon our point of view. The lofty and tragic atmosphere of Æschylus and Sophocles constantly gives way to pathos verging on sentimentality in Euripides. Because of this closer approach of the tragedies of Euripides to the sentimental plays of today, modern audiences generally prefer the tragedies of Euripides to the more austere tragedies of Sophocles. Æschylus and Sophocles employ human suffering and situations which

arouse pity either as a background or a point of departure
for their plot; but many scenes and situations are introduced by
Euripides for no other purpose than to call into play the emotion
of pity, and pity rather than sympathy. The idea of having
Electra dressed in rags, doing menial work, married to a poverty-
stricken man, and a little ashamed to invite strangers into her
humble home is dangerously close to a bid for tears. The situation may enhance the pathetic value of the play, but it detracts
somewhat from the tragic value of the situation and is wholly
unnecessary so far as the plot is concerned. If Euripides introduced this situation in order to motivate Electra's longing
for vengeance, he cheapened the tragic effect by shifting the
attention for one moment from the one great motive which inspired Electra: the murder of her father. The substitution of
the pathetic for the tragic is as sure a sign of decadence as the
similar procedure of substituting the horrible for the tragic, of
which traces will be found in certain Euripidean plays.

Electra opens with a speech of Auturgus in which he explains
both the well-known facts of the situation and the new circumstances of Electra's marriage. The passage is entirely narrative,
formal exposition. It is a prologue in the modern sense of the
word, for the information is given directly to the audience, not
to a character in the play. Electra issues from the cottage, and
in a few words of dialogue between her and Auturgus, certain
facts of the set prologue are reiterated. The purpose of the
scene is to arouse pity for Electra, clad in rags and going about
menial tasks, not to arouse tragic sympathy for a heroine. The
tone of the scene is distinctly Euripidean. When the pair has
withdrawn, Orestes and Pylades enter; then when Orestes has
told how he has come to seek his sister and learn what has
happened, they see Electra, whom they believe to be a slave,
approaching. They draw aside with the intention of questioning
her later. From her lamentation Orestes learns that she is
Electra. The chorus then enters, and the lyric passage which
follows does not advance the situation. Orestes comes forward;
and, pretending that he has come as an emissary of her brother,

he questions her at length but does not disclose his identity even after he has every reason to be satisfied with her attitude of mind. Euripides did not miss the opportunity of holding the suspense of the recognition scene as long as possible. He keeps Orestes silent in regard to his identity. Auturgus appears, invites the strangers to his house, and then goes to seek an old man, Agamemnon's ancient guardian. When the old tutor arrives after a choral interlude, he recognizes Orestes by the scar above his eyebrow. This makes a very leisurely beginning of the real action; and the suspense of the recognition scene has been so prolonged as to lose some of its effect. There is much less action up to this point in the plot than in the Sophoclean version.

The action now begins to unfold as plans are laid for vengeance. Orestes is to seek out Ægisthus who is performing a sacrifice. Electra is to entice Clytemnestra to her house on the pretence that a child has been born to her. After a choral ode which recalls the origin of the misfortunes of the house of Atreus, a messenger reports at length how Orestes slew Ægisthus. This is a reversion to more primitive technique which keeps both the protagonist and the antagonist off the stage. Indeed, the living Ægisthus does not appear during the whole play, and Clytemnestra enters late in the development of the action. Orestes drags in the body of Ægisthus. Electra pours forth the vials of her wrath in triumph over the dead Ægisthus. As she incites the hesitating Orestes to slay his mother, the question of the matricide emerges in the rapid alternate lines. One is reminded of the scene in which Lady Macbeth, the woman, bids the man to screw his courage to the sticking point. Thus Electra exhorts Orestes not to "sink unmanned to weak and timorous thoughts." Such scenes are unquestionably dramatic; but, while Electra's outburst over the body of Ægisthus leads up to this and arouses Orestes to action, the scene is highly sensational. Nor is it the only example of sensationalism in Euripides.

The play reaches the climax when Clytemnestra comes in royal state, and the obligatory scene takes place between her and

Electra. In the Æschylean version there is no scene between the mother and daughter. In Sophocles' *Electra* the scene between them comes rather early in the play, before the recognition scene. Euripides, however, is inclined to make a climax in which his characters discuss both sides of the question in a manner which resembles an oratorical contest, so enjoyed by Athenians in real life. This scene is more argumentative than the corresponding scene in Sophocles. The theatrical effectiveness of such scenes is undeniable, provided the question at issue is the vital problem of the play as in this case; but this type of situation becomes merely rhetorical in the hands of Seneca, who strives to imitate Euripides but makes the mistake of discussing side issues or abstract questions which have nothing to do with the plot.

Clytemnestra enters the cottage and a choral song serves to prolong the suspense, since we know that Orestes is waiting for her with drawn sword. Her death shriek resounds. Orestes and Pylades come forth, and Orestes describes the murder which has just occurred behind the scenes but which in Æschylus' play was on the stage. This is further evidence that dramatic action, having emerged from behind the scenes in the later plays of Æschylus and in the tragedies of Sophocles, is now beginning to return whence it had issued.

Æschylus was able to answer the question of matricide in the third play of his trilogy, and Sophocles carefully avoided raising the question. Euripides, however, has brought up the problem; and he introduces the *deus ex machina* in the shape of Castor and Pollux, who throw the blame upon Apollo and bid Orestes marry Electra to Pylades and then go to Athens where he will find absolution. Such a procedure is as typical of Euripides as it is inartistic. It destroys the impression of the inevitable sequence of cause and effect in the development of the plot. The proposed marriage between Electra and Pylades, wholly unmotivated and coming suddenly at the end of the play, foreshadows the ending of later comedy by a marriage. The play, therefore, shows some of the forces at work which will cause the disintegration of dramatic technique in tragedy, but which will develop dramatic art along the lines of New Comedy.

Euripides' *Medea* (431 B.C.) is a fascinating and even baffling study of a strange woman, a barbarian enchantress, who murders her children. We are not concerned with the problem of the justice of her act nor with the question of the dramaturgic skill displayed in this tragedy. Medea remains one of the great feminine rôles of all times; but it is our somewhat thankless task to point out certain elements in the play which were to become inartistic manifestations of a degenerate art of tragedy in the Renaissance.

Jason owed everything to Medea; but Creon said to him: "Lo, I will give thee my daughter to wife, and thou shalt reign after me, if thou wilt put away thy wife Medea; but her and her two sons will I banish from the land." Jason consented. The play opens at this point. Medea sends a poisoned robe and diadem to the bride who dies in agony after donning the fatal gifts. Creon also becomes a victim when he throws himself on his daughter's body and is consumed by the fiery venom. Medea kills her own children and escapes in a chariot drawn by dragons to Athens where Ægeus has promised her asylum.

Vengeance as the motivating cause of an action appears in other Greek dramas such as the *Eumenides* and Sophocles' *Electra*. Medea is so skilfully drawn that her deeds do not make a horrible impression on an audience. She arouses a baffling sympathy and admiration. The crime committed against her by Jason in his complacent stupidity seems almost to merit such punishment. It is not strange that Seneca and his imitators in the sixteenth century were impressed by this tragic rôle; but it was unfortunate that they sought to emulate Euripides by producing plays in which a heinous villain becomes the hero whose every act is motivated by a desire for revenge often totally unjustifiable. Medea acts in part through motives of anger and vengeance; but she remains a tragic heroine. Yet the "revenge play" and the phenomenon of the villain becoming the hero in

Italian and Elizabethan drama are due to *Medea* primarily. Nothing is more dangerous to art than a masterpiece.

Exposition of the facts necessary to make intelligible the unfolding of the plot had not been difficult so long as the point of attack in Greek drama remained close to the dénouement. With very little of the action taking place in the present and with the very few events and the quite uninvolved plots of the typical Æschylean play, the playwright had no difficulty in making the situation clear. He had to hark back to the past for his material. When the point of attack receded from the dénouement and, as a result of the natural development of dramatic art, more events and greater complication of the plot appeared between the point of attack and the dénouement, exposition became difficult. This would not have been the case had the point of attack receded temporally, as it were, from the dénouement far enough to include more events of the past in the play. In that case there would not have been so much of the past to explain in the exposition. Also, the trilogy on one subject, which had been employed by Æschylus in order to include more of the underlying myth in the action of the drama, was discarded by the later dramatists, who, therefore, had to treat the whole story in one play. Although they did not represent the action of the past within the limits of their play, they had to unveil the past. The three plays dealing with Electra's vengeance begin with the return of Orestes; but there is more action in the versions of Sophocles and of Euripides than there is in the *Libation-Bearers*. Although the same amount of explanation of the past is necessary in all three plays, Sophocles and Euripides have to deal much more with the present action, and hence they have to dispose of the exposition far more quickly than does Æschylus.

Euripides aimed to produce the tragic effect upon his audience, not so much by unveiling the past, as by representing a series of tragic or pathetic scenes of the present. For this reason it was necessary for Euripides to state immediately the problem of his plot and the antecedent events which lead up to its unfolding in order that he might have plenty of time to represent this series of pity-compelling situations. In *Hecuba*, for example, there is enough material that deals with the present for two Æschylean tragedies. A troublesome problem of exposition had been created by the fact that the point of attack remained temporally in the same place but actually had receded from the dénouement, so far as the amount of action represented in the present is concerned. Euripides solved the problem by introducing a formal prologue addressed to the audience, in which the facts necessary to understand the play are set forth. From Aristophanes' time down to the present day, Euripides has been criticized for this procedure which has been branded as dull, inartistic and undramatic.

In only two of the Euripidean plays is a prologue indispensable to the full understanding of the action. In *Ion* the spectator must know from the beginning the fact set forth in the prologue that Ion is the son of Creusa. In the *Bacchantes* the identity of Dionysus, the speaker of the opening monologue, must be made known immediately in order to create suspense in the highest degree. But the artistic value of a prologue is not to be judged by the question as to whether the ensuing action can be understood without it or not. As Aristophanes pointed out in the *Frogs,* these formal monologues are too full of genealogical details in which Euripides delighted exeessively. From the point of view of artistry and technical excellence, this formal opening is not to be compared with the opening of *Agamemnon* or *Œdipus Rex*. So far as the expository part of the prologue is concerned, it is doubtless somewhat inartistic. The events of the past, the present situation of the characters in the play, the names of the characters and the places of the action are set forth in a clear but summary fashion; but the function of the Euripidean prologue is not merely to supply necessary information to the audience.

The difficulty besetting the dramatist in constructing the opening scenes of a play exists because he must acquaint the audience with certain facts and because he must arouse interest in the plot by creating suspense as quickly as possible. At least he must put the spectators in such a frame of mind that they would not willingly leave the theatre until the play is over and curiosity is satisfied. Euripides does this by means of the prologue which always contains lines that arouse suspense. generally by foreshadowing events more or less truly, rarely by plainly foretelling. Sometimes these lines purposely mislead the spectator, or foreshadow events that do not take place, or arouse hope or fear, as the situation may demand, in order that the spectator may be held in doubt as to the final issue. They never forestall suspense. Only in *Hippolytus* does the prologue plainly foretell an event, the death of Phædra, without casting doubt as to whether it will really take place or not. In all the other prologues there is foreshadowing, not of what will take place, but of what may take place.

In the prologue to *Alcestis*, Apollo informs the audience that Alcestis is dying and that Thanatos is coming to conduct her to the halls of Hades. Any normal spectator will immediately infer that this is the end of Alcestis, if not of the play. Unless one takes into consideration pre-knowledge of the myth on the part of the audience—which is manifestly unjust in such a discussion—the possibility of the resurrection of Alcestis and of a happy outcome of the situation could not occur to anyone. In the next scene Apollo pleads with Thanatos to spare Alcestis; but the messenger of death is obdurate. Finally, Apollo says that someone will come to take Alcestis from Thanatos. The ray of hope dawns; but does not the spectator believe that Alcestis must be rescued while she is still alive? Otherwise, if Apollo knows that she can be saved even after death, why does he plead with Thanatos? But Alcestis dies, and her resurrection comes as a surprising *coup de théâtre*. Euripides has indulged in false foreshadowing in the prologue in order to arouse suspense.

The prologue to *Ion* deliberately misleads, when Hermes foreshadows the outcome. Hermes says:

He [Apollo] shall give Xuthus, when he entereth,
His own [Apollo's] child, saying to him, "Lo, thy son,"
That the lad, coming home, made known may be
Unto Creusa, and Loxias' deed abide
Unknown . . .

It is true that Apollo bestows Ion upon Xuthus as if Xuthus were the father of Ion, as is foretold in the prologue; but Creusa does not for this reason accept Ion as her son. Indeed, she arouses great suspense by planning to slay this supposed son of Xuthus; and the manner in which she is saved from this terrible act is wholly surprising. In order to bring about the recognition between the mother and the son, Loxias' deed has to be made known in spite of the fact that Hermes foretold that the amour between Creusa and Apollo would remain secret. This is more than false foreshadowing. It is false foretelling. At the end of the play Athena says that the divine seer meant to keep this secret until the truth could be proclaimed at Athens; but evidently the intention of a god must give way to the desire of the playwright to arouse suspense and surprise.

Euripides' skill in foreshadowing appears to excellent advantage in the formal prologue to the *Mad Heracles*. Amphitryon tells us that Heracles does not return from the house of Pluto, that the children have no hope of safety save to cling to the altar of Zeus, since Lycus aims to slay the children, their mother, and even Amphitryon himself. Thus suspense is immediately aroused. One gains the impression that almost all hope is gone. Since Heracles is in the realm of the dead, one hardly expects him to return. Therefore, when he does appear wholly unexpectedly just at the moment when he alone can save the children, the suspense caused by the knowledge that Lycus seeks to slay them is ended by a dramatic *coup de théâtre*. Again Euripides has employed false foreshadowing, as the event foreshadowed in the prologue does not take place. Had the playwright foretold or even foreshadowed the arrival of Heracles, the suspense and surprise would have been immeasurably reduced. On the other hand, the speech of Iris, which serves in effect as a prologue to the second part of the tragedy, correctly foretells the murder of the children by Heracles. If we were not given to believe that the children would be slain by him, the action of the play at this point would wander on in an aimless manner. There would be no suspense but only surprise; and when one of these elements must be sacrificed to the other, it is almost always, and certainly in this case, surprise which must be given up even though suspense is reduced to fear.

The foreshadowing and preparation were not confined by Euripides to the prologue; but, like Æschylus and Sophocles, he was careful to introduce scenes which look towards the ensuing development of the action in such a way as to keep the interest of the spectator alive. Thus the chorus in *Hippolytus* foreshadows Phædra's state of mind and prepares for her entrance in a very dramatic manner. The foreshadowing dream, which was used effectively by Æschylus and was to become one of the most frequently employed means of foreshadowing in modern imitations of classic tragedy, is used by Euripides. The loss of Hecuba's children, foretold in the prologue of *Hecuba*, is foreshadowed later in a cryptic dream. Oracles and the prophecy of seers, the other canonical means of foreshadowing in classical tragedy, also appear. In the *Phœnician Women*, Tiresias foretells the death of the two brothers; and in *Ion*, Trophonius is reported as having said in a manner to arouse curiosity that neither Xuthus nor Creusa shall return from the temple of Apollo destitute of children. There was always enough doubt of veracity of dreams, oracles, and prophecies to supply the mingled hope and fear necessary to arouse suspense.

Euripides also paves the way for much of his action by having his principal characters lay plans for their future deeds. Thus Dionysus in the *Bacchantes* tells how he is sending Pentheus to death at his mother's hands. Medea plans to slay her children and Jason's wife. Helen and Menelaus in *Helen*, and Iphigenia and Orestes in the *Iphigenia in Tauris*, tell how they will attempt to escape. Helen says that one of two things is certain: either

Menelaus and she will escape or die. Doubt is created; and, throughout the rest of this play with a happy ending, Euripides has carefully stressed the note of fear. The scene prepares for the dénouement but does not assure a happy outcome. This foreshadows but by no means forestalls the action as many critics have believed. The difficulty and the danger attendant upon the successful accomplishment of these plans are insisted upon to such an extent that the audience cannot be sure that the plans will be consummated.

An audience always wants to know, in a more or less vague way, what the characters intend to do. The dramatist must simply avoid giving the impression during the play that the whole action is cut-and-dried, that the plot will develop in the way it unfolds and in no other. When the play is ended, the development of the action must seem to have been inevitable.

It is this impression of inevitableness which the tragedies of Euripides fail to produce. One does not feel that the incidents in his plays are the necessary result of a preceding cause. He does not take a situation and show what events arise from it in necessary sequence. His aim is rather to take a situation and show what pathetic events arise from it as in the *Trojan Women;* or he may take a character such as Hecuba and represent the different pitiable situations in which she finds herself. The development of his plot is more likely to be a gradation of increasingly pathetic episodes rather than the careful working out of a problem. For this reason many of his plots, such as those of the *Trojan Women, Hecuba, Andromache,* the *Children of Heracles,* lack the unity of necessary sequence of events. The unity may consist only of a fictitious unity furnished by the fact that the same character undergoes these pathetic emotions, as in *Hecuba* or the *Trojan Women.* He may even introduce a second set of characters not so interesting as the first, as in the *Children of Heracles.* His aim is to portray as many theatrical and emotional scenes as possible; and, in order to do so, he is willing to construct his plot so loosely that the episodes are connected by a very tenuous thread. The interest in the unfolding of the plot is sometimes overshadowed by emotional effects arising from the situation.

This is not always the case, however, for there is a very strong plot interest in *Ion* and in the romantic *Helen*. But even in these plays and in *Orestes*, Euripides sacrifices psychology and true depiction of character to theatrical effects. "Thus in *Ion*," as Mr. Haigh points out, "the character of Creusa, which at first arouses our sympathy, is sacrificed for the sake of a powerful situation; and her atrocious resolve to murder Ion, though it leads to interesting complications, lowers her in the eyes of the spectator. In *Orestes*, in the same way, the brutal design on Helen, while giving a new direction to the plot extinguishes our compassion for the sufferings of the brother and sister."

Orestes is an example of tragedy turned into melodrama which is more theatric than tragic. In the prologue, Electra stands by the bedside of the feverish Orestes and explains that they have been deserted by their friends and are awaiting probably a death sentence as matricides. The one vague hope lies in the arrival of Menelaus for whom she watches. Helen, not daring to venture among the fathers whose sons died at Troy, sends her daughter to the tomb of Clytemnestra with propitiatory offerings. The Argive maidens enter; and, in a realistic scene which must have been effective on the stage, Orestes tosses on his bed and awakes, sick in mind and body, a prey to visions of the avenging Furies, while Electra tries to quiet him. The lines are practically stage directions and prove how vividly Euripides must have imagined the action as he wrote. Menelaus arrives; and, as Orestes appeals to him, Tyndarus, the father of Clytemnestra, enters and vows vengeance. Orestes knows that Menelaus is deserting him in spite of his dissembling promise to try to soften Tyndarus and to ask the Greeks to use their power with gentleness. Even hope forsakes him, but Pylades urges him to try one more chance: to appear before the Greeks and plead his cause. They go to the trial and a messenger soon brings the dire news to Electra that she and her brother are condemned to commit suicide. In a scene portraying intense human suffering, Electra begs Orestes to slay her; and Pylades, faithful friend, vows to share their suffering. But the desire comes to them for vengeance, and they swear to punish Menelaus by killing Helen before they die. If Menelaus in turn attempts revenge, they plan to hold the sword over Hermione and to threaten to slay her. They believe they have carried out their brutal design on Helen. The play sinks from the lofty Greek plane of tragedy to a Senecan play on revenge and finally to melodrama. They lay hold of Hermione as she returns from the tomb, and, holding a sword at her breast, threaten to plunge it home as Menelaus appears. Nor can this present tangle be straightened out without a Euripidean god from the machine to give the play a happy ending. Apollo bids Menelaus marry another wife, but tells how he has actually saved Helen from death. Orestes is to be acquitted at Athens. Pylades is to marry Electra and—crowning touch— Menelaus bestows Hermione on Orestes as his bride. Thus ends the play with the marriages of comedy! There can be no doubt that Euripides aimed at variety and attained his goal.

No one play of Euripides equals Æschylus' *Agamemnon* or Sophocles' *Œdipus Rex* in technical excellence, but neither of the other playwrights employs such a wide range of effects as does Euripides. Because he was fully aware that a series of pathetic scenes is emotionally effective on the stage, he cared less for the well-constructed plot. Thus the plot of the *Trojan Women* arouses little interest; but after seeing the play one never forgets the heart-rending scenes in which the child Astyanax is torn from his mother and is brought back dead to the grief-stricken woman.

The plot of the *Suppliants* is very slight, but the play is typical of one method of Euripides. It begins with a band of suppliants kneeling about an altar. There is a debate on forms of government; pathetic lamentation; a theatrical episode, as Evadne throws herself from a cliff; a description of a battle; glorification of Athens; a *deus ex machina* foretelling the future. The causal sequence of events hardly exists. The play is a succession of events following an incident of the past.

On the other hand, Euripides shows in *Ion* how successfully he can handle a complex plot without breaking the unity of action. *Medea, Iphigenia in Aulis* and the *Bacchantes* are excellent evidence that he could observe as strict a unity of action as did Sophocles, and could guide his plot to one great climax when he wished, or could arrive at two climaxes, as in *Mad Heracles* and *Andromache*.

As a rule, however, Euripidean technique does not aim to produce what is known as the well-made play. It is for this reason that Aristotle says Euripides was not always happy in the conduct of his plots. Looking back on his work as a whole, one is impressed by the great variety of single effective scenes. Greek tragedy becomes more human, more realistic with Euripides who, as Aristotle says, paints men as they are. Realistic details, found sparingly in Sophoclean tragedy, abound in Euripides. He introduced domestic affairs into tragedy as Aristophanes has him say in the *Frogs*. Thus he shows us Electra drawing water; Clytemnestra stepping from her chariot; Ion sweeping the steps of the temple. The chorus in *Hippolytus* has learned of Phædra's illness from a friend who has been washing clothes. Orestes tosses on his bed of fever in a scene which a modern realist might envy. In addition to the pathetic scenes already mentioned, there is Alcestis dying on the stage and taking leave of her husband and her child. In the *Suppliants* there is the episode of Menœceus, who throws himself from the battlements in order that the prophecy of Tiresias may be fulfilled; and in the *Children of Heracles,* Macaria goes forth to death voluntarily to save her brothers and sisters. These episodes are introduced for the sake of pathos. Neither one of them alters the development of the action. Indeed, we lose sight of Macaria entirely after her exit. Euripides often employs children in his plays to arouse the softer human emotions, while Æschylus seems not to have brought them on the stage at all, and Sophocles only in *Ajax* and in *Œdipus Rex*.

There are such striking scenes as Hecuba enticing Polymestor within the tent in order to put out his eyes; Menelaus enticing

Andromache from her refuge by telling her she must die to save her son and then seizing her; Orestes with his sword at the breast of Hermione threatening to slay her before the eyes of her father; Orestes confronted with the father of Clytemnestra; Medea taking leave of her children before she slays them; Agave discovering the body of her son slain by her own hands; Hecuba, thinking to see the body of her daughter, beholding the body of her son, a scene which reminds one of Sophocles' Ægisthus, who, thinking to uncover the body of Orestes, discovers the body of Clytemnestra. One remembers vividly such theatrical effects as Medea wailing within the palace; Medea in her car defying her husband; the suicide of Evadne; the earthquake and lightning in the *Bacchantes;* the appearance of Iris and Lyssa on the roof of the palace in the *Mad Heracles;* Alcestis veiled and silent brought in by Heracles and suddenly disclosed to her husband who believes she is dead. There is the stage picture of Theseus brandishing over the body of Phædra the incriminating tablets and falsely accusing Hippolytus of having made love to her; there is the suppressed letter which warns Clytemnestra not to bring Iphigenia to the camp at Aulis; there is the sudden and unexpected arrival of Heracles in time to save his children. All these devices make plots; but they are too palpable devices and give a touch of theatricalism. Tragedy begins to be a series of incidents often depending on chance instead of being the inexorable and inevitable working out of a problem. The conduct of the plot seems often to be arbitrary, fortuitous, for theatrical not tragic effect.

The principal characters are on the stage most of the time in the tragedies of Euripides. Few obligatory scenes are omitted. Since Euripides' aim was to put pathetic situations on the stage, he had to place the characters undergoing the emotion before the eyes of the spectators. Yet it is curious that in *Medea* Jason's bride does not appear on the stage although she is one of the principal characters in the story and meets her death during the play. In the extant version of *Hippolytus,* Phædra and Hippolytus, although they appear on the stage together, never address each other. It is probable that in the first version of the tragedy, Phædra confessed her love to Hippolytus, but that Euripides changed the scene because it shocked the Attic sense of propriety. Euripides, however, handles the situation in his extant play with finesse and overcomes the limitations placed upon him by the psychology of the Attic audience. He has the nurse begin to tell Hippolytus of Phædra's love off the stage, but within Phædra's hearing. Then Hippolytus and the nurse enter and the interview is continued. In this way the emotions of Phædra are represented almost as powerfully as if she had confessed her passion to her step-son.

Although obligatory scenes are portrayed upon the stage by principal characters as a rule, the messenger overshadows the principals in the *Phœnician Women*. The two brothers, Polynices and Eteocles, appear but once; and the whole play is a succession of pathetic scenes in which the principal characters are bewailing instead of acting. At the same time that Euripides was placing theatrical scenes and *coups de théâtre* on the stage and was appealing to the eye as well as to the ear, he actually began to increase the oratorical element in tragedy and to restore to the rôle of the messenger the importance it possessed in earlier plays. The Greeks loved a debate and Euripides often appeals to this desire for oratorical effect even though he may have to hold up the action of the play to do so. Theseus and the Herald debate on forms of government in the *Suppliants*. In *Orestes* there is an oratorical contest on the question of the love of a son for his father and mother. The obligatory scene in *Medea* between Jason and Medea in which Jason defends, like a lawyer, his marriage with Creon's daughter, and the scene in *Hippolytus* between Theseus and Hippolytus show only too plainly oratorical effects encroaching upon the drama. Euripides divides his dialogue symmetrically now into prolonged harangues and then into rapid replies in which maxim is answer to maxim. Although he derides the length of the Æschylean description of the seven chiefs before Thebes, he indulges in long narrative passages full of minute description of details hardly necessary to the action.

Especially is this true of his description of battles. The Greek audience enjoyed rhetorical effects and stylistic flowers. The ubiquity of rhetoricians and orators in real life is ample evidence of Athenian taste for rhetorical argumentation and haranguing. Having freed itself of such undramatic elements, tragedy began to follow a road which was to reach the undramatic goal of Seneca. Tragedy was to become rhetorical poetry.

As Euripides is noted for opening his plays with formal prologues, so he differs from Æschylus and Sophocles in his frequent use of a god from the machine in order to end his plays. Also, just as he has been criticized adversely by both ancients and moderns for employing the formal prologue, so he has often been called to account by critics, from Plato and Antiphanes down to the present writers on Greek tragedy, for introducing a *deus ex machina* at the end of so many of his plays. Again it is difficult to discover why Euripides chose this manner of ending plays, for only two or three of his plots actually need divine intervention to cut the Gordian knot. In *Orestes*, Euripides has so entangled his principal characters that there is no chance of extricating them from the situation without at least divine intervention if not inartistic intervention. Indeed, Apollo's announcement of the fact that he has saved Helen, whom Orestes and Electra believe to have killed, shows that Euripides has been indulging in legerdemain worthy of a Scribe. He has excited the emotions of the audience over an event that he later admits did not take place. There is no justification for the supposed murder of Helen or the scene in which Orestes threatens to kill Hermione. These episodes are introduced for theatrical purposes and, as a result, the happy ending of the play is entirely forced. In *Hippolytus*, Artemis appears in order to prove the innocence of Hippolytus, and in the first version of *Iphigenia in Aulis*, Artemis came to Clytemnestra and told her of the substitution of a deer for Iphigenia on the sacrificial altar.

Thus Euripides must have had other motives for introducing the god from the machine than the necessity of ending the play. The entrance was an effective spectacle. Also, it gave an opportunity to foretell events of the future. In this way, together with the recital of events of the past which took place in the prologue, Euripides was able to include in one play much of the story which formerly constituted the basis of the trilogy. Euripides seems to have invented the episode of the adverse wind in *Iphigenia in Tauris,* an event which certainly is not in causal sequence with the rest of the plot, merely to introduce a god from the machine. As in the case of the prologue, Euripides did not introduce the god from the machine out of sheer ineptitude as a dramatist. Both procedures were a part of the practice of a very clever, sophisticated dramatist who, as Aristophanes says in the *Frogs,* "contrived all things cunningly," who even in his faults gives evidence that he knew what his public wanted and gave it to them in many varied forms.

The Greek chorus, which had originally consisted of fifty, was reduced in number to fifteen. The reduction may have been gradual; or it is possible that about 487 B.C. the original unit of fifty was transformed into four choruses of twelve, one group being assigned to each play of the tetralogy. Sophocles and Euripides both employed choruses of fifteen. The average choral part in the tragedies of Æschylus is about two-fifths of the whole play. In Sophoclean and Euripidean tragedy it averages only one-fifth of the whole. The number and length of conversations between the individual characters and the chorus were reduced by Euripides.

Commenting upon the function of the chorus, Aristotle says: "The chorus too should be regarded as one of the actors (characters); it should be an integral part of the whole and take a share in the action, that which it has in Sophocles rather than in Euripides." In early tragedy the chorus had played the whole tragedy. Then scenes of dialogue had been interspersed in the choral performance. Such is the impression left by Æschylus' *Suppliants.* In his later plays the individual characters begin to overshadow the chorus so far as the plot is concerned. The Sophoclean chorus also has a share in the action. His chorus began to assume also a function described as that of the "ideal spectator." It expressed in words the thoughts and emotions of the real audience. This function was inherent in the original chorus of early tragedy; but it developed clearly when the interest of the audience was shifted from the choral rôle to the rôle of the individual. The chorus then changed from subjective sufferers into more objective observers. But they were not passive ideal spectators. Their songs guided the real audience in its emotions and subconscious thoughts much as an orchestral accompaniment guides the audience at a Wagnerian opera. Their dancing was expressionistic as scenery and plastic color are expressionistic in the modern theatre. They were "an integral part of the whole," even though in certain tragedies of Euripides they did not "take a share in the action" throughout the play.

The chorus plays the rôle of a character in certain episodes of Euripides' tragedies. It informs Hecuba of the decision of the Greeks to sacrifice her daughter Polyxena which constitutes the initial cause of the plot of *Hecuba*. Later in the action, it arouses suspense during the scene in which Hecuba is putting out Polymestor's eyes within the tent and hence behind the scenes. The chorus in *Ion* informs Creusa that Xuthus has apparently found his son, although they have been threatened with death if they report this supposed fact. This information changes the whole course of the action, for Creusa resolves to slay Ion who is really her own child. In the *Suppliants*, the chorus is practically the heroine of the play as it is in the *Suppliants* of Æschylus, although the later dramatist has introduced Æthra as the spokeswoman for the chorus. The chorus is indispensable in the *Bacchantes*.

In other Euripidean dramas, such as *Iphigenia in Aulis* and *Electra*, the choral rôle is not vital to the plot. The chorus in the *Phœnician Women*, although it imparts certain information to Creon, occupies the pauses in the action and does not enter into the plot as does Æschylus' chorus in the *Seven Against Thebes*. Such choral odes as that which glorifies Athens in *Medea*, the recital of the labors of Heracles in the *Mad Heracles*, the description of the shield of Achilles in *Electra* have a subtle but very tenuous connection with the plot. There is that tendency toward irrelevancy which will culminate in the development of the ode described by Aristotle when he says: "With the later poets, however, the songs in a play of theirs have no more to do with the plot of that than of any other tragedy. Hence it is that they are now singing intercalary pieces, a practice first introduced by Agathon."

But Euripides did not reach this point in the decadence of the choral element of tragedy. No matter how tenuous the connection of this element with the plot may have been, his chorus and their songs are an integral part of the whole drama. They cannot be transferred from one play to another without destroying the unity of impression. The audience may not have been fully conscious of the real meaning of certain odes but the songs expressed the spirit of the play. Like an orchestral interlude, which weaves together the motifs of a modern opera, they held the audience within the spiritual domain of the tragedy.

If standards of realism are applied, the Euripidean chorus is found at times to be an obtrusive character in the scene. It is hard to explain why the chorus of women would allow Hippolytus to be punished for a crime of which he was innocent, as they knew. In *Iphigenia in Tauris*, the chorus overhear Orestes and Pylades carry on their generous conflict as to which of them is to deliver the letter of Iphigenia; and, unless the chorus were very inattentive, they learned then and there the identity of Orestes which they are supposed to discover later with Iphigenia. Also, Iphigenia lays the plan to steal the image of Artemis within hearing of these guardians of the temple. Such episodes are illogical, if judged from the point of view of a realist; but standards of realism should not be invoked. To the Greek audience the chorus could become a pure abstraction. It could be theoretically as non-existent as the real spectators. Probably only modern critics feel that such procedures are illogical and unreal. Either Euripides was a childish bungler at such moments or else theatrical conventions removed the chorus from the domain of the action, although it was present on the stage. The Euripidean chorus was still an essential part of Greek drama, not merely a poetical embellishment, although it could cease to be a character in the plot. It furnished legitimate psychological spectacle and, at times, action. It guided the emotional mood of the audience.

Greek tragedy was still an harmonious synthesis of all the arts. Aristotle recognized the synthetic quality of drama. He considered plot and character the most important, music and spectacle the least important of the elements of the synthesis. His theory was prophetic of the development of dramatic art. Plot and character became the chief aim of playwrights. Music disappeared from drama and spectacle was regarded as a questionable means of making an impression. Not until centuries passed was the synthetic quality of dramatic art to be recognized once more. Not until the twentieth century have the potentialities attainable by synthesis been realized and developed in dramatic art. In the space of one hundred years, the Greeks had created and brought to full bloom an art from which all the beauty of the modern theatre is derived. Every great play, serious or comic, every valid theory of dramatic art owes its existence directly or indirectly to Greek tragedy. Remove Euripides, and the modern theatre ceases to exist.

CHAPTER IV

THE ORIGIN OF GREEK COMEDY.
ARISTOPHANES. MENANDER

BOTH tragedy and comedy were originally joyous and ludicrous. Tragedy became serious. Comedy remained humorous. The only difference between these two forms of drama which has survived throughout the ages is precisely this difference in tone which did not exist originally. All other differences insisted upon in certain periods, such as the social status of the characters and the dénouement, have disappeared. Tragedy may end happily. Comedy must end happily, otherwise it would become serious. Both forms may deal with the same problems and situations of human life. Either form may depict men as better or worse than they are in real life, although Aristotle held that tragedy represented them as better, and comedy, as worse. Even the difference in tone is often so faint in modern drama that the terms tragedy and comedy are of dubious value as descriptive of a play. One can only be sure that a play is a play.

In the fifth century in Greece, however, many technical differences existed between tragedy and comedy, in addition to that of tone. In tragedy, the point of attack is closer to the dénouement than in comedy. There is much more narration of past events and of events behind the scenes in tragedy. The rôle of the messenger, so important in tragedy, occurs in comedy only as a burlesque of tragedy. Every event of any importance is represented on the comic stage with the exception of the canonical feast, which may be a survival of an act of worship, hidden from all but the initiate, in the ritual from which comedy developed. In this respect comedy is the more normal form of dramatic art which by its very nature represents, not narrates an action. Scenes of violence and death are generally banished from view in tragedy, while in comedy scenes of violence are portrayed on the stage. The agon or contest in comedy is enacted on the stage and is carried on by the individual hero and villain; but in certain tragedies the principal agon occurs behind the scenes, or, if it is on the stage, takes place between an individual and the chorus. In early Æschylean tragedy, both hero and villain are relatively unimportant figures, seldom issuing from behind the scenes, and the rôle of the villain never became extremely important. In comedy, both these parts attained a fuller development and the chorus became a relatively less important factor in the play. There is a stricter unity of action and the plot is more important in tragedy than in comedy. Tragedy is so retrospective that one can almost say it is in the past tense, while comedy is prospective and is in the present and future tense. Both forms are similar in that they employ a chorus. But the comic chorus is very partisan. At the beginning of the agon it is more or less violently on the side of one of the adversaries; or it may be divided against itself in two hostile groups; but it always ends on the victorious side. In only one tragedy (*Eumenides*) does the tragic chorus take sides against the hero; and it never changes its allegiance and never divides into hostile half-choruses. We follow the action of tragedy through the eyes and the emotions of the chorus; but in comedy we follow the action through the hero rather than through the reactions of a possibly hostile chorus.

This wide divergence in tone and construction existed when the history of tragedy and comedy actually begins for us and when both forms were being presented in the same theatre during the same festivals in honor of Dionysus. Aristophanic comedy was influenced in certain respects by contemporary tragedy; and the construction of comedy, as it developed into New Comedy, became more and more similar to the technique of Euripidean tragedy until the two forms became practically identical except in tone. Even that difference was less marked as New Comedy became less boisterously humorous and tragedy, as in

Helen and *Alcestis*, became less solemn and began to contain humorous scenes, or, at least, episodes lacking in tragic dignity. In the last part of the *Symposium*, Socrates was insisting to Aristophanes and Agathon "that the genius of comedy was the same as that of tragedy and that the writer of tragedy ought to be a writer of comedy also." The idea was doubtless novel but is perfectly sound. The passage is evidence that at least one Greek had discovered that these two forms of art are not so dissimilar as they had seemed. Unfortunately, we do not know surely the opinion of Aristophanes and Agathon even as reported by Plato. They were "compelled to assent, being sleepy, and not quite understanding his meaning."

Since tragedy and comedy coalesced when brought into contact, since they were both joyous in tone at the beginning, since they both owed their origin to rituals of the cult of Dionysus, the cause for the wide divergence in tone and construction, relatively temporary though it was, must lie in the influence of the ritual in honor of the hero on primitive tragedy. Primitive comedy developed independently.

According to Aristotle, comedy had its origin in the comus which was a combination of religious hymn, scurrilous jesting, and mockery. It was evidently a part of a ritual performed to insure fertility. The *Acharnians* contains a scene in which Dicæopolis, his family and slaves are represented as. celebrating a part of this Dionysiac rite while Dicæopolis intones the song.

The ritual was not commemorative of past events. It dealt with the present and was performed in order to insure fertility in the future. It was essentially an agon or contest between the good and evil, Summer against Winter, Light against Darkness. Good triumphed over evil in the end. Since comedy sprang from such a ritual, it is joyous with a happy ending, the action is before the eyes of the spectators, there is no retrospection or unveiling of the past, and a physical or verbal contest, such as the long debate between Cleon and the sausage-seller in the *Knights*, is an important element in the play. There are individual agonists and antagonists, and the chorus of twenty-four may be divided into hostile semi-choruses of twelve. Perhaps in the agon in the ritual, both the agonist and antagonist, representing respectively the forces of good and evil, were originally leaders of a half-chorus. Thus the original ritualistic form may be preserved in *Lysistrata*, in which the chorus is divided into two hostile groups. Also in the *Acharnians*, Dicæopolis desires to make peace with Sparta. He harangues the hostile chorus and wins half of them to his views. The other half-chorus calls for Lamachus. Dicæopolis and Lamachus indulge in a physical and verbal agon in which Lamachus is worsted. The whole chorus decides that Dicæopolis "prevails with his arguments."

Thus, since in the ritual underlying comedy there was a well-defined agon, the chorus would naturally be divided, some siding with the hero, some siding with the villain. In the end, since there must be a joyful outcome, the whole chorus would be on the side of the victor—the new god. On the other hand, since there was no enacted agon in the worship of the dead hero, the whole tragic chorus would be immutably in sympathy with the hero as soon as this ritual became the dominating factor in tragic dramas. Indeed, before the hero was portrayed in tragedy on the stage, the chorus was what is technically known as the sympathetic character. There would be no possibility for divided allegiance in such circumstances.

This situation explains the relative unimportance of the chorus and the relative importance of the rôles of hero and villain in comedy in comparison with early tragedy. These two rôles in comedy probably developed from the leaders of hostile semi-choruses in the ritual. The rôle of the messenger, indispensable in tragedy, was totally unnecessary in the comic ritual. From the earliest times, the interest of the worshipper or the spectator must have been centred on the individual agonist and antagonist, instead of on those merely beholding the struggle. In the ritual in honor of the dead hero, the hero was present in spirit. In the ritual underlying comedy, the hero and villain were present in flesh and blood.

The point of attack in the ritualistic tragic drama was necessarily close to the dénouement; and even in highly developed tragedy, it remained late in the story. The most important result of this selection of the opening scene is what Aristotle calls the unity of action. Whatever may be narrated in a play thus constructed, little can be enacted that is episodic. In the comic ritual, the point of attack was at the beginning of the story, because the ritual was not retrospective. It was a magic rite performed in the present. Hence the point of attack in comedy is at the beginning of the story.

The compression of the action caused by placing the point of attack close to the dénouement in serious drama, made it natural for the action of tragedy to run its course during "one revolution of the sun." The hero had but little time to live even when he had been resurrected. The element of time in comedy is indefinite and unimportant because the question of lapse of time did not enter into the magic rites.

The original scene of the worship of the dead hero was the tomb. Because there are few events in the last hours of a hero's life, they are likely to happen in one place. Thus the single scene is natural in Greek tragedy and changes of scene are rare even in the highly developed form. The ease with which the scene shifts in such comedies as the *Frogs* and the *Acharnians* must be due to the indefiniteness and unimportance of the locality of the ritual underlying comedy.

The continuous presence of the chorus in tragedy has been adduced as the reason for the unity of time and the unity of place. To shift them from one place to another and to think of them as remaining for a long time without food or slumber, it is said, would be an absurdity. This theory originated among Renaissance scholars and is held by many modern critics. It is the result of applying standards of realism totally foreign to the spirit of Greek tragedy. If the continuous presence of the chorus had this effect on tragedy, it would have had a similar effect on comedy. Such is not the case. Comedy was freer in this respect than tragedy because of different circumstances in their early development. Also, to ascribe the freedom of comedy to the fact that the Greeks did not take Aristophanic comedy seriously is merely to beg the question.

A curious element of Aristophanic comedy is the parabasis, during which the chorus and the leader lay aside temporarily their assumed character and address the audience directly. Professor Navarre has suggested that the parabasis is a survival of a practice of the maskers of the primitive comus who momentarily removed their disguise in order to disclose their real identity to their fellow townspeople in a diverting manner. At the same time the chief of the troup would profit by the moment to praise the spectacle, and to give his opinion on public affairs, and to lampoon his noted fellow citizens. There was naturally a parodus, or noisy entrance of the chorus, and an exodus, a kind of final triumphant ballet of the revelers, of which examples are found in Aristophanic comedy. The structural elements which sprang from the comus as it was performed in Attica are, therefore, parodus, agon, parabasis, exodus. Between the parabasis and the exodus there were scenes or references to a ritualistic sacrifice, feast, and marriage. The feast was evidently not represented, as it is behind the scenes in almost every Aristophanic comedy. The marriage was a symbol of the fertility which the ritual was to insure.

In the Peloponnesus were bands of actors, variously called phlyakes, autokabdaloi, phallophori, which also traced their origin to the cult of Dionysus. In Megara, about 581 B.C., a kind of farce played by peasants and satirizing the wealthier classes came into existence. This farce was transported by Susarion from Megara, about 570 B.C., into the Attic deme of Icaria where it was evidently combined with the comus, by intercalating satiric scenes between the parts of the comus. At first there was probably little if any connection between the comic scenes of the farces and the spectacular comus; but the two disconnected elements were welded together, probably by making the chorus and the leader (or leaders) play a part in the comic plot. Continuity, if not unity, would be attained.

Unity in comedy is not very noticeable until the later plays of Aristophanes and even then is not perfect.

The Dorian farces did not contain a real plot, but rather a situation. According to Athenæus, the stealing of a fruit or a satire of a foreign doctor and his outlandish jargon were subjects of these plays. Megarian comedy was political in tone. As produced by Susarion, it was evidently a series of more or less isolated scenes in verse and was about three hundred lines long. These farces may be compared in structure to the series of scenes, with little connection with the plot, found after the parabasis in the *Acharnians*. According to Aristotle, "the invented fable or plot, however, originated in Sicily, with Epicharmus and Phormis."

Epicharmus began to present comedies at Syracuse by 486 B.C. Therefore the introduction of an invented plot into Attic comedy took place some time after the writers of tragedy had become relatively expert in the handling of what may be designated as a real plot, simple as it must have been. Comedy, by nature, can make its effect and arouse laughter by mere buffoonery and lampooning. Tragedy, on the other hand, deals with episodes in the lives of heroes and gods; and these episodes even in narrative form contain the germ of dramatic action, whereas the lampooning and satirizing of individuals or classes of society, which form the basis of Dorian and Megarian farces, lacked the element of dramatic plot. The modern vaudeville sketch entertains the audience without containing the vestige of a plot, in the modern sense of the word. Although the ritual to insure fertility offered a framework for dramatic action and for the development of plot before the eyes of the spectator and contained a certain embryonic dramatic plot in itself, the influence of tragedy, with its well-defined though simple plot, had to be brought to bear on comedy before this latter form of dramatic art could actually be said to contain a plot with all the elements of a developing action and story implied by that term. The special influence of the ritual to insure fertility was to cause the plot to develop in the present and to keep the action before the eyes of the spectator, when the plot and action were introduced; whereas the influence of the ritual of the worship of the dead hero had kept the action more in the past and behind the scenes in tragedy.

Aristotle assures us, however, that comedy had "certain definite forms at the time when the record of those termed comic poets begins." Thus it seems highly probable that when Aristotle ascribes the introduction of the plot to Epicharmus, he is referring to a fairly well-developed plot with an exposition, a climax and a dénouement. The twenty-nine titles of the comedies or *dramata* of Epicharmus may be divided into two classes: those on realistic subjects, such as the *Peasant* and the *Megarian Woman*, and those on mythological subjects which correspond to the subjects of the Athenian tragedy and satyr-play, such as *Busiris* and the *Marriage of Hebe*. It is possible that Epicharmus was composing such plays under the influence of Attic tragedy and that the element of plot was injected in this way into plays of a strictly comic nature. How much farther this possible influence worked is a matter of conjecture. Some fragments seem to point to a prologue. On the other hand, these *dramata* lacked a chorus, although there were ensemble scenes and songs. The individual characters must have been more important than those in contemporary Attic drama. The action was doubtless on the stage, since there was no reason why it should be behind the scenes. Yet since the plot of contemporary tragedy was simple and since comedy had amused the spectators without plot, the action in his plays must have developed quickly and with few complications. Epicharmus could depend upon brilliant wit, dialectics, clever reasoning, and juggling of words. He possessed ability for dialogue: the fundamental requisite for the comic playwright.

His comedy had no apparent connection with the ritualistic worship of Dionysus, but had reached a point where it might have developed easily and quickly into a form resembling New Comedy. Indeed, Plautus did imitate him. Epicharmus employed the characters of the drunken man, the boor, and the parasite which will appear in New Comedy. So far as we know, he was the first to put them on the stage. The title *Megarian Woman* sounds more like the title of a New Comedy than of an Aristophanic comedy.

Although Epicharmus introduced plot into comedy, the choral tradition in Attic drama was so strong that the structure of his plays was not accepted as a whole. Attic comedy retained the chorus and tried to harmonize the new element of plot with its original spectacular, choral and musical elements. The first attempts were probably not very successful, for, according to Tzetzes, it was Cratinus who made a more regular arrangement of the scenes of comedy and began to model the structure of his comedies on the technique of Æschylean tragedy. It would be natural for comedy to undergo the influence of tragedy at this time in the middle of the fifth century when tragic drama was reaching a high degree of technical excellence.

A chorus was first granted comedy by the archon in 486 B.C. Before that date the chorus had been formed of volunteers. "Who it was who supplied it with characters or prologues or a plurality of speaking rôles and the like has remained unknown," says Aristotle. This remained unknown because comedy had characters and a plurality of speaking rôles either from the early days of the ritual or of the non-choral comedies of the Peloponnesus. The prologue was either imitated from early tragedy or was due to the influence of non-choral comedy. Fantastic animal disguises for the comic chorus were certainly in vogue by about 460 B.C. when Magnes was writing such plays as the *Birds* and the *Frogs;* and such costumes are probably due to the influence of old theriomorphic dances.

Crates, who had acted in the plays of Cratinus, "was the first of Athenian poets to drop the comedy of invective," according to Aristotle, "and to frame stories of a general and non-personal nature, in other words fables or plots." Thus in his *Beasts*, two people dream of a time when men will no longer be in need of slaves but will be served by animals or even by utensils endowed with intelligence. Aristotle's statement does not mean that Crates introduced a well-knit plot with a "beginning, a middle, and an end," but that he used situations which were not actual events, and abstract, rather than real persons, as his characters. The satire and lampooning were at least veiled. Such an act of the imagination means inventing a fable or plot, but it does not mean the introduction of a plot in the sense of an action developed to an end.

Cratinus, however, was known to the ancients as "the people's lash." He spared neither persons nor ideas. Even Pericles did not escape his lampooning. Fragments of Crates and of his imitator Pherecrates point to a comedy like the less personal plays of the fourth century; but Cratinus and Aristophanes held to the older tradition of coarser wit. Aristophanes, with his unbridled imagination, found the older comedy a more fitting medium in which to deliver his sledgehammer blows of humor and to lampoon his fellow citizens under a very thin veil. He was not an innovator in regard to the construction of comedy at the beginning of his career.

The plot of Aristophanic comedy is uninvolved. It is a situation which allows two sides of a question to be argued. The interest consists in looking at the situation from various angles. It is a *pièce à thèse*. The point of attack is not late in the simple story or plot, as it is in tragedy. The action is almost entirely on the stage. Few if any past events need explanation. There are no concealed identities or intricate relationships among the characters such as occur in tragedy and in New Comedy and which need explanation. In these circumstances, exposition is a simple and easy task; whereas in contemporary tragedy it was more difficult. The audience listening to tragedy was sometimes aided in grasping the situation by pre-knowledge of the myth which formed the basis of the plot; but in comedy the situation was known to the audience because it involved a contemporary political or social question such as the value of peace (*Acharnians* and *Lysistrata*); democracy (*Knights*); new and old education (*Clouds*). In the *Knights* the audience merely has to identify the two slaves as Nicias and Demosthenes. Through the satirical but thin mask of the Paphlagonian, the spectator must perceive Cleon. There is nothing else to be explained to the contemporary audience. The action can develop freely; or rather Aristophanes can present the question of the value of democracy from all sides in a series of burlesque scenes. Because the audience was perfectly familiar with the political or social situation, it followed the series of scenes with ease. It was not a question of following an intricately developing plot. There is less plot in a comedy of Aristophanes than there is in any comedy of Bernard Shaw.

Of the eleven extant comedies of Aristophanes only two of them, *Acharnians* and *Women in Council,* begin with an extended monologue. Both these opening speeches are plainly parodies of the opening monologue of tragedy. The exposition of the *Acharnians* is a parody of *Telephus* of Euripides. The speech of Praxagora in the *Women in Council,* in which she apostrophizes the lamp, is a burlesque of poetic invocations of the opening of tragedies, which survive in Senecan drama. Thus we find an influence, through burlesque, of the technique of tragedy on the construction of comedy.

The first speech in *Lysistrata* is a short monologue, but the real exposition is in dialogue. In the *Clouds,* Strepsiades begins with a monologue, but only because his son is sleeping. There are two characters on the stage. The usual opening of Aristophanic comedy is a scene of dialogue. Very often two slaves, as in New Comedy, are discoursing; and, when the attention of the audience is caught, one of them directly addresses the spectators and explains the situation in a few words. Thus it is in the *Knights, Wasps* and *Peace,* while in the *Birds* one of the principal characters sets forth the simple fact necessary to understand the situation. These explanations are not so involved as they are in the Euripidean prologue or in the prologues of later comedy. They are simple and direct. Probably, as in the case of the parabasis in which the audience is directly addressed, these words of explanation are a survival of conditions in primitive comedies in which the bands of revellers had scarcely become actors and when there was little line of demarcation between merrymakers and onlookers, as jests were bandied back and forth between them. In the *Knights*, Demosthenes says:

> Would you I told the story to the audience?

and Nicias replies:

> Not a bad plan; but let us ask them first
> To show us plainly by their looks and cheers
> If they take pleasure in our words and acts.

Then Demosthenes commences his explanation of the burlesque situation. We find that Demosthenes and Nicias are slaves of the bean-fed, crabbed, somewhat deaf old man Demus, or, in other words, the Athenian people. Demus has lately bought a most villainous and calumniating slave, a tanner of Paphlagonia, or Cleon. The question is how can Nicias and Demosthenes (the aristocrats) escape from the power of Cleon (the democratic demagogue). Nicias steals the oracles of the Paphlagonian, and the oracles disclose the prophecy that a sausage-seller will destroy the Paphlagonian leather-seller and of course the sausage-seller enters immediately. Here again the comedy burlesques the technique of tragedy, for the plot depends upon the fulfilment of the oracle, just as did many a dignified tragic plot. For this reason the action of the *Knights*, unlike many other Aristophanic comedies, develops to the end, as do the plots of tragedy.

Since practically all the scenes in Aristophanic comedy are the result of a riotous imagination, it is not strange to find that the opening of most of the comedies is theatrically effective. In the *Acharnians*, there is the turbulent meeting of the assembly. The hero of *Peace* enters on the back of a huge beetle. In the *Clouds*, the sleepless Strepsiades bewails the debts brought upon him by his snoring son who lies in the bed next to his. In the opening scenes of the *Wasps*, Xanthias and Sosias are watching the house of Philocleon with Bdelycleon on guard on the roof, to circumvent the old man as he tries to escape when his friends, the jurymen, bearing lanterns to light their way, summon him before dawn to the law courts. At the opening of the *Frogs,* Dionysus and Xanthias are asking the road to Hades; and then Dionysus is ferried across the dark, swampy waters to the song of the Frogs. Throughout almost all the plays, similar remarkable scenes form the background for burlesque and satire; and such situations are effective in gaining the attention of an audience immediately.

The exposition, though plain and handled quickly, never discloses the course the action will take; nor does Aristophanes find it necessary to employ foreshadowing except as a burlesque of tragedy, as in the oracles in the *Knights* or the dreams of the slaves in the *Wasps,* which are modelled on the dignified tragic framework. Foreshadowing and suspense are necessarily negligible quantities in comedies which depend for their interest on spectacle, satire, and burlesque rather than on plots of intricate construction or actions which develop through surprising incidents. The construction of Aristophanic comedy, therefore, is conditioned by the fact that it is a *pièce à thèse.* A question is set up. It is solved; and, finally, the effects of the solution are represented.

In the *Acharnians* (425 B.C.) the peace question forms the basis of the plot. The play opens with Dicæopolis at the Pnyx waiting for the Assembly to convene. This worthy citizen is tired of war and informs the audience in a monologue that he is "thoroughly prepared to riot, wrangle, interrupt the speakers whene'er they speak of anything but peace." The Assembly meets; and when the several ambassadors make their reports, Dicæopolis constantly interrupts, derides and exposes the precious humbugs. Since the question of peace with Sparta is farthest removed from the thoughts of the presidents, he bids Amphitheus set out to the Lacedemonian kingdom and make a private peace for him.

Since comedy does not pretend as yet to observe any verisimilitude in regard to lapse of time or change of scene, as soon as the Assembly is dissolved, Amphitheus is seen returning from

Lacedemonia bringing samples of peace in the shape of treaties of five, ten, and thirty years' duration. Dicæopolis finds the thirty-year brand delectable and chooses it joyfully.

The prologue is over, for Amphitheus enters pursued by a band of enraged old men. They are the Acharnians who form the chorus of the play and make their entrance, noisy and turbulent, in striking contrast to the dignified entrance of the tragic chorus. These Acharnians, whose vineyards have been destroyed by the long war, are infuriated at the idea of any peace with Sparta which does not provide them with indemnities for their losses. They pelt Amphitheus with stones until they hear Dicæopolis crying from within to keep a holy silence; and, realizing that he is the man they really seek, the irate old men stand aside as Dicæopolis enters to celebrate the rites of the Rural Dionysia.

Unlike the tragic chorus, which is rarely if ever out of full sympathy with the hero, the Acharnians are distinctly hostile to Dicæopolis, and they interrupt the ceremony by hurling stones at the hero of this play. A fight ensues in which we may see a survival of the old ritual. Dicæopolis, however, finally makes himself heard in the uproar, and proposes to argue the justice of his conclusion of a separate peace while laying his head on the chopping-block. The chorus refuses to hear him. Thereupon, he threatens to slay a hostage dear to the Acharnians and he withdraws, leaving the chorus alarmed and anxious.

Here is dramatic suspense of a kind which recalls tragic situations and it is not surprising to find that Aristophanes is burlesquing Euripides' *Telephus* in this part of his play and in the following scenes. In Euripides' tragedy, Telephus is only successful in gaining a hearing from the Greeks by playing a very melodramatic trick, characteristic of Euripidean dramaturgy. He seizes Orestes, the infant son of Agamemnon, and threatens to kill him unless the Greeks hear his plea. So Dicæopolis comes forth from his house bearing a "child" of the Acharnians, in the shape of a basket of charcoal, which he threatens to slay unless he is allowed to argue his case. He asks permission to dress like many of the heroes of Euripides and especially like Telephus, in the rags of a beggar. He straightway betakes himself to the house of Euripides; and, in a scene of lively satire on the penchant of that poet to attempt to arouse sympathy for his characters by their ragged and pitiable condition, he borrows the costume of Telephus.

Then begins the important scene in which Dicæopolis, defending his course in making a private peace, discusses the whole problem of the play. It is the verbal struggle without which no Aristophanic comedy is complete. This scene contributes the canonical agon which is evidently a survival of the old ritual performed to insure fertility. Dicæopolis converts half of the chorus to his view, and again we find a phenomenon impossible in Greek tragedy: a chorus divided against itself. The first half-chorus, however, calls upon Lamachus for aid and he enters, crested and in panoply of war, as the individual villain or antagonist of the hero who practically personifies peace. The agon is continued between these two characters; but Lamachus is worsted in the wordy debate and the rest of the chorus is won over by the "plea of truce so ably set forth by Dicæopolis."

The problem is solved and a modern play would end here; but it is not the Aristophanic procedure to end the play with the solution of the problem. He demonstrates the result of the solution. Here, as in other comedies, occur a few lines of transition after the agon which foreshadow the ensuing scenes to be represented after the parabasis. Dicæopolis announces that he is going to install a private market. Megarians and Bœotians may trade with him—but not Lamachus, that is, not the militarists.

Then occurs the parabasis in which the chorus doffs its costume and directly addresses the audience on subjects which do not concern the plot of the play.

When Dicæopolis sets up his market, the second part of the play begins with a series of scenes demonstrating the value of peace. Such scenes are generally in groups of two parallel situations. Thus in this play, a Megarian comes to sell his two daughters as little pigs for sacrifice. A sycophant arrives and denounces the goods as contraband. He is beaten for his pains. Then in a similar scene, a Bœotian comes to take advantage of the joys of peace by selling his game to Dicæopolis. He, in turn, is denounced by an informer; but the informer is seized and carried away to Bœotia as a curiosity. The "horrors" of war are shown by a scene in which a servant of Lamachus is refused a share of Dicæopolis' purchases. Warriors shall go hungry at the great Pitcher-feast, to which all citizens must bring their share of provisions. After a second parabasis, preparations for the feast continue; but Lamachus is summoned to go to battle, while Dicæopolis is invited to a feast. As the soldier takes his weapon, Dicæopolis picks up his precious basket of food.

When they enter once more, Lamachus, groaning and wounded, is limping along between two slaves; while in humorous contrast, Dicæopolis enters joyously and triumphantly between two amorous courtezans. He has drained the pitcher all alone and is riotously shouting victory and caressing his darlings. Thus the relative value of peace and war is fully demonstrated and the play ends with a procession and a pæan as the chorus escorts Dicæopolis off the stage in triumph.

Aristophanes, in the *Knights* (424 B.C.), made a slight step forward in regard to the unity of his plot. The oracle, announced at the beginning and fulfilled at the end of the play in imitation of tragedy, at least gives the plot the appearance of developing until the end instead of stopping in the middle of the comedy. If the *Knights* is carefully analyzed, however, it will be seen that the plot is practically static from the moment that the Paphlagonian and the Sausage-seller meet and begin to threaten each other.

The *Clouds* (423 B.C.) contains a plot which has, as Aristotle would say, "a beginning, a middle and an end." It presents many events and they follow each other in logical sequence. They are the result of the idiosyncrasies in the character of Strepsiades. The unity of action arises from the interplay of character and event and not from burlesquing the technique of tragedy, as in the *Knights*. Strepsiades and Phidippides are individuals of flesh and blood. Socrates, though a travesty on the real man, is a character, not a mere rôle. Nicias, Demosthenes and Cleon in the *Knights* are but figures with a comic mask in comparison to Socrates in the *Clouds*.

But the *Clouds* was not successful. In the *Wasps* (422 B.C.) Aristophanes complains that his efforts were not appreciated. While he is not going to revert to the older vulgar comedy, yet this play will not be more clever than the spectators. It is idle to speculate just how serious Aristophanes was in this attitude. Nevertheless, the *Wasps* is a reversion to the earlier type of play. After the parabasis, occurs a series of scenes rather than a train of events. The broad humor and the buffoonery of the trial of the dog, the decking out of Philocleon for the feast and his boisterous drunken return from the banquet were provocative of Homeric laughter. Low comedy and slapstick humor were not wanting in the *Clouds*, yet the *Wasps* may have made a greater appeal to the audience than satirical comedy of character with a developing plot, such as the *Clouds*. There is little evidence that the audience cared much for the story or plot in comedy.

Aristophanes, therefore, returned to the older form in the *Wasps, Peace* (421 B.C.), and *Birds* (414 B.C.) in which plot or story is relegated once more to the background. *Lysistrata* (411 B.C.) and *Women Celebrating the Thesmophoria* (411 B.C.) both contain interesting plots and foreshadow later comedy which, under further influence of tragedy, will introduce a story furnishing some curiosity, suspense, and a bit of sentiment. These elements were almost wholly lacking in Aristophanic comedy. The *Frogs* (405 B.C.) is later, but is a reversion to the formless, almost plotless type of play. Aristophanes did not march steadily toward a carefully developed action, nor did he go far in that direction, because he could hold his audience through spectacle, fancy, humor, satire, burlesque, and the discussion of his thesis. The situation had to be striking. The story could be a background. One does not remember easily the plots of Old Comedy. One never forgets the thesis demonstrated by a series of amazing scenes devised by an unbridled imagination. The six elements of the Aristotelian synthesis in the order of importance in Aristophanic comedy would be: thought, diction, spectacle, character, plot, music.

Old Comedy was militant. It used, indeed abused the weapon of personal satire. It was political, not social. It dealt with local public life. There was personal satire in later comedy and in New Comedy; but personal satire was not their end and aim as was the case in Old Comedy. The younger contemporaries of Aristophanes, such as Theopompus, Strattis and Sannyrion still dealt in personalities; but they seem to have been less violent in their attacks. The fierce polemics of Aristophanes and Cratinus were more and more avoided by this younger generation. The tone of comedy swung back to that of the comedy of Crates and Pherecrates. Comedy became allegorical and mythological and hence more general, such as it had been in the hands of the Sicilians, Phormis and Epicharmus. Because of his great genius in handling the older comedy, Aristophanes had delayed the development of that art towards the goal towards which it was tending when he began to write, which it neared perceptibly in his last extant play, *Plutus,* and which it finally reached in New Comedy.

These younger men began to write between 415 and 405 B.C.; and most of them continued to produce after 388 B.C. when the choral songs and the parabasis had disappeared. No law was promulgated against the representation of living personages on the stage or forbidding personal satire. Yet a change was creeping over the tone and spirit of comedy and more general problems were being presented in dramatic form. Times had changed. The prominent men against whom Aristophanes hurled his thunderbolts were gone. The disastrous Peloponnesian War had dimmed the glory of Athens for ever. The national pride was broken; and public affairs that are admittedly bad are not fitted for· successful satire in the theatre. Travesty of tragic heroes and of the gods began to take the place in the theatre of the lampooning of generals, statesmen, and poets who were forgotten. In parodying tragic themes once more, comedy returned to an old source of amusement which had existed in the earlier period. Strattis wrote at least six parodies of well-known tragedies among which are the *Myrmidons* of Æschylus, *Troilus* of Sophocles, and *Medea* of Euripides. Aristophanes had burlesqued the foreshadowing dream, the oracles of tragedy, and the messenger's speech. In the *Acharnians* he had burlesqued melodramatic and sentimental scenes of Euripides' *Telephus*. But these parodies, which retain the name of the original, were burlesques which probably followed the original play closely. The result would be a comedy constructed according to the technique of tragedy. The deep significance of such a procedure can be appreciated when it is remembered that New Comedy will resemble the construction of Euripidean tragedy far more than Aristophanic comedy, except in so far as Aristophanes imitated the technique of the tragedy, which he seems to have done, to some extent, in his last play, *Cocalus*. According to the author of the Greek *Life* of Aristophanes, *Cocalus* contained a recognition scene; and the recognition scene is a device employed primarily by tragedy.

This development of comedy from personal satire towards the refutation of general error and the transformation of the technique of Old Comedy into New Comedy can be seen in the second version of *Plutus*, Aristophanes' last extant comedy, produced in 388 B.C. In this play there is still a thesis demonstrated. Aristophanes postulates the idea that the God of Wealth is blind and then shows by a series of scenes what happens when Plutus regains his sight. The first part of the play contains the few events of the developing action. The second part is a demonstration. The unity of the play depends upon the fact that all the scenes are grouped around one idea, and not upon a developing action as in *Lysistrata* or the *Clouds*. The situation is allegorical, but the scenes are less fantastic and seem less the result of giving a wild imagination free play. While it is not the best Aristophanic comedy, it is the one which would most easily be understood by the modern audience without an intimate knowledge of Greek life and Athenian political conditions. In so far as it deals with a general situation, it differs from Old Comedy which dealt with actualities.

The scene of action is in a street in front of the house of Chremylus and the only lapse of time is the passing of one night. In other Aristophanic plays the scene changes and the audience may be suddenly transported from one part of the city to another or to some fantastic region as in the *Birds*, or to the abode of Zeus as in *Peace*, or across the Styx to Hades as in the *Frogs*. But this exterior street scene, which does not change, is the usual setting of later comedy. While there was no rule for the unity of place or time, yet it was the general practice of tragedy and of later comedy to retain the same scene and to have the action take place in "one revolution of the sun."

The opening scene consists of a dialogue between the old Chremylus and his slave. The conversation of an old man and a slave is later a characteristic opening of Latin comedy. The old man informs the slave that he has consulted the oracle as to whether his son should become a rogue in order to succeed and has been told to follow the first man he meets and win him, in friendship, to his home. Thus the point of attack fails to include an event intimately connected with the plot and this event must be narrated after the play begins. The consulting of the oracle and the position of the point of attack after an important event in the plot recall the technique of Greek tragedy and look forward to the technique of later comedy. The exposition is more detailed and longer than in the comedies in which the point of attack includes all events connected with the plot.

This man whom Chremylus is following turns out to be the blind God of Wealth. Chremylus finally persuades Plutus to come and dwell in his house. This is a carefully developed bit of action ending with a peripeteia; and such a scene in the prologue is not characteristic of Old Comedy.

When Plutus has gone with Chremylus, Cario, the slave, summons the Farmers who form the chorus, and tells them that Chremylus will make their life luxurious. After a dance by the chorus, Blepsidemus, a neighbor of Chremylus, enters. He has learned of the good fortune of Chremylus, but he suspects that the old man has acquired it by theft. He is finally convinced, however, that this guest of Chremylus is Plutus, or Wealth himself. The tone and the handling of the situation remind one far more of scenes which we shall find in New Comedy rather than the burlesque, boisterous scenes of Old Comedy.

They are making arrangements to take Plutus to the temple of Asclepius to have him cured of his blindness, when Poverty stops them, objecting strongly to such a procedure; and she offers to prove that she is the source of every good to men and that men live through her. This leads to the agon in which she argues that all virtues and arts spring from her; but she is driven away with curses. Plutus is taken to the temple. A night is supposed to elapse during which the sight of Plutus is restored.

There are a few examples in earlier Aristophanic comedy of action taking place off the stage in order to introduce a burlesque messenger speech. In *Plutus* this important incident is simply related by Cario to the Wife and not in a burlesque manner. Perhaps Aristophanes did not wish to change the scene even in order to keep the action on the stage. Whatever the reason was, comedy was approaching tragedy in construction by not representing certain scenes, especially those which do not take place in the street. Tragedy does not usually represent interior scenes. New Comedy will be similar to tragedy in this respect.

The play continues without a parabasis which would naturally occur here or just after the return of Chremylus and Plutus from the temple. The restoration of the sight of the god is the important event of which the results are demonstrated in the usual episodic, parallel scenes.

Not only is the parabasis lacking in this play, but also there are no choral songs. Indeed, one of the plainest signs of the transformation which the technique of comedy was undergoing is found in the diminishing importance of the choral rôle about 388 B.C. when *Plutus* was produced in the extant version. In the first part of *Peace*, the rôle of the chorus is almost as important as the rôle of Trygæus. In the *Knights,* the chorus fight and beat the Paphlagonian. In the first part of Aristophanic comedy the chorus plays an active rôle and one connected with the plot; but in the second part its connection with the play is very slight. This is true even of the earliest comedies, such as the *Acharnians,* the *Knights,* the *Wasps,* the *Birds.* The chorus furnished spectacle; but the spectacular is not always dramatic, and sooner or later the chorus was bound to disappear. In *Lysistrata* the double chorus seems to be necessary to the plot, but in reality it is merely an auxiliary of the chief characters. The passive quality of its rôle, exemplified in the second part of this play, began to extend over the whole play. The chorus plays no part in the action of the *Frogs.* It began to become a mere spectator. Its songs, like some choral songs in the tragedies of Euripides, are tenuously connected with the situation.

The chorus is of little importance even in the first part of *Plutus.* It is a mere onlooker. It recites no parabasis with bitter invective and satire. There is but one choricon. At the time of the second version of *Plutus,* the archon still furnished a chorus; but the choregus, under the pretext of poverty, refused to have the comic chorus instructed, and the chorus entered only into the dialogue. With the parabasis and choral songs removed, there was less reason to retain the chorus itself. Its part in the dialogue and its rôle were finally given to a single actor. Just how long the chorus remained as an integral part of the play is not known; but probably Antiphanes and his contemporaries constructed their plays with a chorus appearing only between the acts. It would be natural for the later poets in view of these circumstances to allow this element, which had become undramatic in comedy, to fall into disuse.

In order to replace the gaps left by dropping the parabasis

and choral songs, the dialogue had to be extended; and in *Plutus* we find the juggling with words, especially on the part of the slaves, which will appear in Latin comedy. Indeed, the growing importance of the slaves in the *Frogs* and *Plutus*, comedies in which the chorus is relatively insignificant, may well be due to an elaboration of these rôles by the playwright to offset the disappearing choral rôle. At any rate, Xanthias and Cario are direct ancestors of the slaves of Plautus and Terence.

When the parabasis and choral songs had disappeared, the only technical element belonging to Old Comedy exclusively was the agon. It still remained in *Plutus;* but instead of being an essential scene, it seems more episodic than any other scene in the play, although the plot is not an important factor. The character of Poverty is introduced to argue for the thesis that an unequal distribution of wealth is to be desired and that virtue and the arts exist because of her. The rest of the play is hardly a demonstration of this thesis. This part of the technical structure of Old Comedy, which already seems to be somewhat out of place in *Plutus*, probably disappeared very soon. Its place may have been filled with descriptions in dialogue form of banquets, of the blandishments of courtezans and coquettes, and of the feats of gourmands. Comedy in the early part of the fourth century resembled *Plutus*, with the scene of the agon removed.

Lucian's dialogue, *Timon the Misanthrope*, probably follows the construction of Antiphanes' comedy *Timon* fairly closely. Timon begins by upbraiding Zeus because he closes his eyes to the wrongdoing of mortals and to the lack of respect shown him by men. This passage would correspond to a monologue in the play. The point of attack is after Timon has lost his money by pouring out his wealth in floods to his friends. Shakespeare, writing under a medieval system of playmaking, places his point of attack before Timon has become poverty-stricken. Shakespeare is telling a story. Lucian and Antiphanes are demonstrating a thesis.

Zeus orders Hermes to take Wealth and visit Timon. Wealth

objects that he was badly treated by Timon, but finally is persuaded to go. On the journey, a long conversation takes place between Hermes and Wealth in regard to riches and why Wealth is lame and blind. They arrive and drive Poverty away from Timon who finds Treasure, who has accompanied Wealth. Then a series of scenes occurs in which Timon's old friends, who cast him out when they had ruined him, try to wheedle themselves back into his good graces. They are all received by Timon with blows of his pick and driven away, as are the sycophants and informers and imposters in the second part of Old Comedy.

Antiphanes' *Timon* evidently did not differ greatly from Aristophanes' *Plutus* in construction. There is the same movement of the point of attack toward the dénouement in both plays. The exposition is given in the opening monologue. There is not much action; but there is a peripeteia, and the second part of the play is a series of scenes demonstrating the result of this peripeteia. There are long scenes in which the interest lies in allegorical discussions. The boisterous element in Old Comedy has given way to a more refined, almost rhetorical humor. Comedy of this period seems to have undergone the influence of the rhetoricians and sophists as did tragedy.

In comparison with *Plutus*, however, there is more of a plot in *Timon*, for the characters introduced at the end of the play actually suffer retribution for their former sins towards Timon. In *Plutus*, the other characters do not have any special connection with Chremylus. In *Timon*, the last scenes have been prepared by previous events in the story. They represent the retribution visited upon the very persons who had contributed to Timon's ruin by accepting his largess before the play begins. That their desertion of Timon in his hour of need is in the story, but not within the limits of the play, is significant. The influence of tragedy was operative in placing the point of attack of comedy closer to the dénouement.

These scenes constitute a dénouement of comedy in which the virtuous are rewarded and the wicked are punished. The similar scenes in *Plutus* end the play, but they do not constitute a real dénouement. One event in *Plutus,* the consultation of the oracle, takes place before the play begins; but in no Aristophanic comedy is the dénouement prepared by events which precede the point of attack. This procedure is characteristic of tragedy. From now on, it will be found in both comedy and tragedy. Finally, the appearance of Poverty in *Timon* is motivated by the action. In *Plutus,* Poverty is introduced merely to make the agon or debate possible.

In comparison with New Comedy, the plot of *Timon* is still unimportant and not interesting enough to carry the play. The chief interest lies in the episodic humor of monologues of cooks and parasites, in the allegory, in debates. Insistence upon such elements precluded the more careful treatment which the plot was to receive from Menander. His plots, like those of Greek tragedies, are interesting stories in themselves.

The *Persian Woman* by Plautus is an adaptation of a play or plays belonging to the period of transition. In the first act, Toxilus, a slave, asks Sagaristio, another slave, for money to purchase the freedom of his mistress, Lemniselenis, from Dordalus, the procurer. Sagaristio promises to try to obtain the necessary amount. Toxilus bribes the parasite, Saturio, by the promise of a dinner, to dress his daughter as a foreigner and allow her to be sold to the procurer as a slave. Thus Toxilus will obtain money and the parasite can appear and claim the girl as his daughter. Act II. Lemniselenis appears with her maid for an instant, saying: "Wretched is the person that is in love," and exits. Toxilus gives a boy a letter for Lemniselenis. The boy meets Sophoclidisca, the maid, who has a letter for Toxilus. After a scene of much bantering, they go to deliver the letters. Sagaristio returns with the money which his master has given him to buy oxen but which he intends to hand over to Toxilus. After a scene of abuse between Sagaristio and the boy, Toxilus enters and receives the money with much bandying back and forth of jokes. Act III. The parasite and his daughter are ready for the trick of the false sale. Toxilus gives the procurer the money furnished by his obliging friend. They abuse each other. The procurer goes to fetch Lemniselenis. Act IV. With Sagaristio and the parasite's daughter masquerading as Persians, the girl is sold to the procurer as a slave; but when Sagaristio has gone, the parasite enters, claims his daughter and drags the procurer to the magistrate. Act V. Toxilus, Lemniselenis, Sagaristio and the boy are enjoying a banquet. Dordalus appears. They scoff at him and make game of him. The boys beat him. They continue the feast.

The characteristics of New Comedy are conspicuously absent in this play. There is no real recognition scene, no real concealed identity so far as the audience is concerned. Circumstances prior to the beginning of the play do not bring about the dénouement. The play could exist in just this form, with the possible exception of the love story, had Euripides never written a word. Even the love motive is very unimportant. The whole plot is very slight and serves, as does the plot of Old Comedy, merely as a background for comic scenes. As in Old Comedy, the point of attack is at the beginning of the story. Nothing of importance has to be explained, and hence there is no formal prologue to unveil the past. The plot is simple, develops slowly, and comes to an end in the fourth act; but the action is all on the stage. There is a banquet with revellers who take the place of the Aristophanic chorus. There are whole scenes of abuse and a procurer who comes to interrupt the feast is beaten and scorned like the informer of Old Comedy.

All these characteristics are due to the influence of Old Comedy, not of tragedy. The parasite, however, is originally from Sicilian Comedy. The procurer has certainly not stepped from tragedy to comedy. The courtezan comes from Aristophanes; and she has learned to speak a few lines now and to appear momentarily at the beginning of the play. In Aristophanic comedy, the courtezan was mute and appeared only in the last part of the play. Finally, the banquet, which was behind the scenes in Old Comedy, is now on the stage in spite of the scene in the street.

In the middle period there was less buffoonery, less indecency, less grandiose burlesque and spectacle, less fantasy and play of the imagination. The Muse of Comedy, once wild and fearless, was becoming docile and circumspect. She no longer lashed mercilessly men in public life, but was content to burlesque ancient gods and heroes. She indulged in tirades against courtezans or made them heroines of the play, instead of boldly attacking demigogues or lampooning a Socrates. On the surface, comedy became more moral and weaker in intellectual content. No great political, moral, or, artistic questions were discussed with rapier-like satire or Rabelaisian humor, although, under the influence of the *Frogs,* literary criticism was still found at times. The element of personal satire became so unimportant that, according to Platonius, the masks, which in Old Comedy were made to resemble persons, now aimed only to excite laughter. The characters of Old Comedy, often drawn from life, were varied and individualistic. They now become stock types—a momentous change, and not a fortunate one. They turned into masks of different kinds but each kind was made from the same model, and the expression never changed.

Comedy became social and more realistic. Some plays bear the names of trades such as the *Goldsmith* and the *Painter.* The *Marriage of the Children of the Same Father* and the *Sisters* by Antiphanes are evidence that family relationships, as in tragedy but not in Old Comedy, formed the basis of the plot. Ephippus' play, the *Doubles,* recalls Euripides' *Helen* and foreshadows the *Menæchmi* in which mistaken identity through similarity of appearance was to furnish the humor.

Platonius says that the authors of comedy were beginning to construct their plots more carefully. The Greek *Life* of Aristophanes says that he introduced into *Cocalus* the dramatic "seduction and recognition and all the other things that Menander imitated." Unless that comedy is anomalous, the point of attack must have been after the seduction; and the concealed identity, revealed in the dénouement, furnished some suspense.

A fragment of the prologue to *Poetry* by Antiphanes contrasts tragedy and comedy as follows:

Tragedy is, in all respects, a fortunate literary form in as much as, in the first place, its plots are familiar to the spectator before anyone has spoken. As a result, the poet has only to recall them [the plots] to memory. Let me only name Œdipus and you know all the rest: his father, Laius, his mother, Jocasta, his daughters, his several sons, what he will suffer, what he has done. Again, if anyone mentions Alcmeon, even every child straightway says that he went mad and slew his mother and that Adrastus will straightway come and go away again. Furthermore, whenever the poets are able to say nothing more but are absolutely at the end of their powers, they raise a machine, as easily as one raises a finger. and the spectator is satisfied. These conditions do not hold good for us [comic poets] but we have to invent everything, new names, previous events, present circumstances, the dénouement, the opening. If some Chremes or Phedon omits any of these features, he is hissed off the stage. These liberties are only allowed Peleus and Teucer.

Aristophanes never felt any of these difficulties, at least until he began to write his last play, *Cocalus*. He invented a plot; but his plot was very simple and dealt with circumstances known to everyone in the audience. He only had to have an actor step out of his rôle for a moment and explain what circumstances and what situation he was treating and all was plain to the spectators. He did not have to devise or give an exposition of previous events except in *Plutus* and in *Cocalus*. The dénouement of his story often came in the middle of the play. He did not have to answer any questions except his one great thesis. His point of attack was the beginning of the action; and his opening scene did not have to explain intricate situations or relationships, or conceal certain identities. On the other hand, it is evident from this passage that the plot of comedy now carries an interest of curiosity. As in tragedy it rests upon previous events. The poet must decide upon the point in the story where his play must begin. He cannot take it for granted, as could the tragic poet, that the audience would know the identity or relationship of the characters as soon as they entered. In a general way, the masks and the costumes would furnish the information that the modern audience would glean from a program; but for the first time, so far as we know, a playwright complains of the difficulty of the art of exposition and of correctly placing the point of attack. The fact that Antiphanes complains that a dénouement must be invented shows that plots were becoming more intricate and more important. The play could not merely stop. It had to end. For this reason the recognition scene was introduced from tragedy to serve as dénouement and as a means of clearing up obstacles which disappear if true relationships are known.

The influence of Euripidean tragedy on the comedy of this period is plainly attested by the playwrights themselves. Diphilus speaks of "the golden Euripides"; while Philemon says: "If in truth the dead have consciousness, gentlemen, I would hang myself so as to see Euripides." In the life of Euripides by Satyrus we read "that reversals of fortune, violations of virgins, substitutions of children, recognition by means of rings and necklaces are the things which comprise the New Comedy and these were brought to perfection by Euripides." Suidas says of Anaxandrides that he introduced into comic art "love and the misfortunes of virgins." The source of these motives is found in such plays as *Ion.* Whole lines were borrowed by Menander from Euripides. Indeed, it is difficult to know whether to ascribe certain fragments to Euripides or to Menander.

Neither Aristophanic comedy nor Sophoclean tragedy can be regarded as realistic; but Euripidean tragedy and later comedy often present domestic and realistic scenes. In language and tone, Euripides drew nearer to comedy. The dénouements of *Orestes* and of his *Antigone* are endings of comedy with marriages. The plot of *Ion,* like that of *Cocalus* and of many other comedies, is based on a seduction and a recognition. The first extant long-lost child is Ion. He will have countless descendants in serious and comic drama down to the present whenever Greek and Latin influence is operative.

The plot of *Helen* borders on the comic. Let Helen and Menelaus be unmarried and the framework is that of comedy, for the plot of New Comedy depends upon mistaken identity through similarity of appearance and upon obstacles in the path of lovers. When the last obstacle is overcome the play ends happily. The Euripidean tragedy is based on the idea that a replica of Helen went to Troy. When Menelaus finds the real Helen he is so baffled that he does not recognize her. Helen has become twins; and twins are the basis of the *Menæchmi*. The play ends when Helen and Menelaus overcome the last obstacle separating them.

The plot of Plautus' *Captives,* adapted from a Greek comedy, borders on the tragic. Hegio, desirous of exchanging Elean prisoners for his son captured by the Eleans, has purchased two captives, one of whom is another son of his who was lost long ago and is now a servant. The two captives have changed stations in life. Hegio intended to send the master to Elis to effect the exchange of his other son; but through ignorance he sent the servant. When he finds out what he has done, he condemns to death the servant who is his own unrecognized son; but the recognition comes in time to save the boy. This situation is the best for the deed of horror in tragedy, according to Aristotle. Here we have "one meditating some deadly injury to another, in ignorance of his relation" but making "the discovery in time to draw back." It is the situation in the tragedy *Cresphontes,* where, Aristotle says, "Merope on the point of slaying her son recognizes him in time." One has only to compare this situation founded on human relationship with any Aristophanic comedy to realize how New Comedy differs from Old Comedy and sometimes resembles tragedy in tone, construction and emotional effect.

Alcestis has a comic touch in the drunken Heracles. The scene in which Admetus and Pheres upbraid each other for not being willing to die to save Alcestis contains humor that is hardly even grim. The comic effects in the *Bacchantes,* when old Cadmus and the blind Tiresias prepare for the Bacchic revels and rehearse a few dance steps, remind one of the scant respect with which old men are portrayed in comedy.

Under the influence of tragedy, the point of attack in comedy moved toward the dénouement. Many events were thrown into the past. Other events went behind the scenes. The plot was developed; but, after all, the plot of New Comedy is a background for humorous episodes on the stage. The plot in many Euripidean tragedies is a background for emotional scenes on the stage. In both cases the plot is a means, not an end, and the element of chance is so freely employed that the action is not always even plausible or probable.

The satyr-play helped to draw comedy into the framework of tragedy. This form of drama was cast entirely in the tragic mould. It contained no distinctive element, such as the parabasis, which differentiated it from tragedy. It differed only in tone and in the fact that the lyric element was materially reduced. It was unlike Old Comedy, however, because its principal characters, although amusing, inspired respect and the audience was in full sympathy with them. The Heracles in the satyr-play *Syleus* and in the tragedy *Alcestis* is amusing; but he is not merely amusing as he is in the comedy of the *Frogs.* In the *Cyclops,* the spectator would have a personal interest in the fate of Odysseus and a fellow feeling for him, which the principal character in an Aristophanic comedy could never arouse, no matter how much one might approve of his views and actions. The plot of the satyr-plays was constructed on recognitions, disguises, misunderstandings, miscomprehended oracles, all of which are the basis of many a Euripidean tragedy and of New Comedy.

New Comedy will accept the framework and, in certain respects, the tone of Euripidean tragedy. The satyr-play made this acceptance easier. For the most part, the stock characters of New Comedy, especially the mirth-provoking ones, will be drawn from Old Comedy. The sympathetic hero and heroine, the lovers in whose path obstacles are placed, will come from tragedy; and with them will come new emotions of sympathy and sentiment, wholly lacking in Old Comedy. In Sophocles' *Antigone*, the lovers were tragically separated. Euripides united them in his version. The comic playwrights will follow Euripides in marrying their heroes and heroines at the end of their plays. Thus a marriage became the canonical dénouement of comedy. Greek tragedy and comedy, originally similar, then widely divergent, have now joined hands once more. Even in Aristotle's time the poets were following "their public and writing as its wishes dictate" in giving tragedy a happy ending.

The direct influence of tragedy on New Comedy is illustrated by the plot of Menander's *Arbitrants,* for the situation is taken in part directly from Euripides' *Auge* and in part from his *Alope.* In *Auge,* Heracles violated Auge during a festival and left a ring in her possession. In later years Heracles recognizes their child by means of the ring. In *Alope,* the heroine, daughter of Cercyon, exposed her child of whom Poseidon was the father. A shepherd found it and took it to his house. Another shepherd asked him for the child and he gave it to him but refused to give the clothes in which the child was found. To settle their dispute, they bring the question to Cercyon. As in the *Arbitrants,* the judge is the grandfather of the child. In the tragedy, the grandfather recognizes the clothes as belonging to his daughter; but in the comedy, Smicrines does not recognize the ring which belongs to his son-in-law. The recognition scene, which performed so many functions in tragedy, became the usual dénouement of comedy through the influence of such plays as *Ion* and *Helen.* It is possible that in the *Hero,* Menander introduced the Hero as a divine personage to bring about the recognition scene. This would be the transference to comedy of the god from the machine who frequently intervenes in tragedy to solve the problem. Plautus employs a *deus ex machina* to bring the dénouement of *Amphitryo.* This is partially a burlesque of tragedy, but it is evidence that, by parodying tragedy, comedy assumed a new form.

The scene of the *Arbitrants* passes in a street or public square, around which are grouped the houses of Charisius, Smicrines and Chærestratus. The street scene, already found in Aristophanes' *Plutus*, is from now on the regular setting for plays of lighter vein. Comedy is played outdoors; and centuries will pass before it goes indoors.

Act I. Onesimus, a slave, enters with a cook whom he has hired for the day; and from their conversation it is found that Charisius, the slave's master, married recently Pamphila, the daughter of his neighbor, Smicrines. But the young husband has just bought the slave girl Habrotonon, a flute player, and has set aside his wife. When the cook has entered the house, Onesimus informs the audience in a monologue that the reason for this estrangement of the young couple is that Onesimus informed Charisius that Pamphila had given birth to a child during the absence of her husband and had exposed the infant. Smicrines, the father of Pamphila, enters and learns that a banquet is being prepared at the house of his son-in-law. He is scandalized at the action of Charisius, and decides to take his daughter home and reclaim her dowry. Davus, a slave, and Syriscus, a charcoal-burner, appear, accompanied by Syriscus' wife who is carrying a child. The two men ask Smicrines to act as arbitrator of a question. Davus tells how he found the child and first decided to rear it, but finally gave it to Syriscus, at the latter's repeated prayers. Syriscus, however, now demands certain trinkets found with the child but retained by Davus. Smicrines decides that they must be given up to Syriscus; but, as Syriscus and his wife, left alone, joyfully look them over, Onesimus appears and recognizes among them a ring belonging to his master. The slave finally persuades Syriscus to give him the ring; and his first plan is to turn it over to his master, but he decides to wait, because his master is banqueting.

Act II. Onesimus still hesitates to speak to Charisius of the ring. He fears his young master may become reconciled to

Pamphila. Habrotonon bursts out of the house. Charisius, who bought her three days before, will have nothing to do with her. Syriscus arrives, and, on inquiring about the ring, is told by Onesimus that Charisius lost it at a festival, that in all probability he had forcibly seduced a maiden and is the father of the child with whom it was found. Habrotonon then hits upon a plan by which she may be freed. She will take the ring, show it to Charisius and tell him she is the mother of his child. Then she will search for the mother whom she remembers seeing at the festival. Onesimus consents, after objecting that in this way she will be freed but he will remain a slave. Smicrines enters, and in a monologue explains how he has come to get his daughter. The cook comes out wailing that the whole banquet is a failure, while Smicrines pours out his anger at his son-in-law's prodigality. Smicrines goes into the house to see what he shall do with Charisius and a band of revellers enters dancing and singing.

Act III. Almost the whole act is lost but it is probable that Habrotonon follows out her plan. Charisius recognizes the ring but has no idea that the child is not Habrotonon's but his own wife's. He evidently consults a friend in regard to his predicament and is advised to keep silent. Charisius keeps the child; but Smicrines, believing that the child belongs to Habrotonon, takes his daughter back home, although it seems she is loath to leave her husband.

Act IV. Habrotonon enters carrying the child and meets Sophrona. Seeing Pamphila on the balcony, Habrotonon recognizes her as the mother of the child and informs Sophrona that Charisius is the father. They enter the house of Smicrines. Onesimus recounts how Charisius overheard a conversation between Pamphila and her father in which Pamphila defended her husband, and how Charisius is beside himself with grief and remorse for his treatment of his wife. Charisius enters, giving full play to his feelings. Habrotonon enlightens Charisius in regard to the real state of affairs; and he learns that his own wife is the mother of his child.

Act V. Charisius brings Pamphila back to his house without her father's knowledge. Smicrines is told by Sophrona that Pamphila is reconciled with her husband; but the full explanation for the reconciliation is withheld in order that Onesimus may ridicule the old man when he comes pounding at the door of Charisius' house. After worrying the old fellow by expounding a new theory of Providence, he tells him the truth, and the play ends.

After all allowance has been made for scenes which are conjecturally restored, enough of the original remains to show that the plot is complicated and the plot interest, so tenuous in Old Comedy as to be almost negligible, has become important.

Tragedy presents a serious situation which gives rise to a problem that must be solved in accordance with the moral laws that constitute the ideals of the particular audience before whom the tragedy is played. But when the same situation is given a humorous treatment, the situation is often falsified so that the question which arises from it cannot be treated seriously and cannot be answered logically, because the supposed situation does not really exist. The problem of the *Arbitrants* cannot be solved because the problem does not really exist. Neither the husband nor the wife has really sinned. The problem is not what shall the husband do with a wife who has borne an illegitimate child. If the situation were really true, a very different series of scenes would have been selected by the playwright to be enacted on the stage. Many events, which are behind the scenes and which happen before the play begins, would have been on the stage. Charisius would be informed of his wife's sin. We would see their interviews; but since this is comedy, the problem really is: how can the truth in regard to this situation be brought out? Plots of New Comedy are often plots of problem plays; but the problem does not exist. Hence we cannot expect a rigorous application of the law of cause and effect.

The complications in New Comedy constantly arise from concealed identity, mistaken identity, concealed relationships and mistaken relationships; and the slaves are so prone to indulge in prevarication that the spectator often does not know what is true and what is false. The action begins because of mistakes and misinformation. It develops through more mistakes and ends when the truth is found out. It would be very difficult to end the situation upon which the *Arbitrants* is built logically and happily, if that situation really existed. Were Charisius not the father of Pamphila's child and Pamphila not the mother, the logical ending is tragic. Even in *Ion,* the whole truth is never told to Xuthus who thinks he is the father of Ion.

In order to keep the comedy from being a tragedy, the situation had to be built upon mistakes. In order to keep the action developing, more mistakes had to be made, and the more mistakes there were the funnier the play was likely to be. The result was a plot far more complicated than the plot of tragedy. Not only must all be invented, but all must also be made plain to the audience in every detail. The comic playwright had a more difficult task than the tragic playwright, because his plot was now far more intricate than the plot of tragedy. The audience often had to know not only the real situation, which was complicated enough, but also what each character thought the situation was. When the point of attack in comedy was late in the story, the task of the comic playwright was made still more difficult than that of a tragic dramatist, because there were more events, as a rule, which were supposed to have taken place in comedy than in tragedy. Euripides had to explain few events in the prologue of *Ion* in comparison with the events set forth in the prologue of the *Lady with the Shorn Locks.* Antiphanes was correct in saying that the construction of tragedy was simpler than that of comedy of his time. Menander, according to Plutarch, considered his comedy practically finished when he had completed the scenario and had to write only the dialogue.

CHAPTER V

LATIN COMEDY

THERE were rudimentary theatrical performances from the earliest times in Italy. In 364 B.C., a temporary stage was erected, in connection with the Roman Games, upon which different kinds of buffoons, musicians and singers of ballads with no dialogue or plot performed. In the early days of the Atellan farce, appearance upon a public stage was looked upon as an occupation fit for only the lowest class of citizens and foreigners. In Greece, the poet and the actor had been honored; but in Rome, these professions were not respected in the early times. Drama cannot prosper in such conditions. Not until Greek art attained its full sway over the Roman conquerors of Hellas, did drama in Italy become worthy of notice. As in all other forms of art the Romans turned to the Greeks, so in drama they accepted the highly developed forms of Greek comedy and tragedy.

In 240 B.C. Livius Andronicus, a Greek captive later freed by his master, began to represent in Rome, comedies translated from the Greek. At that time Plautus was fourteen years old. When his *Stichus* was produced, the uncultured Roman audience, dull to the artistry of fine technique, was probably perfectly content with this loosely constructed play with its jerky plot which snapped in the middle. The audience doubtlessly took it at its face value as a series of more or less unconnected scenes each one of which brought a laugh to gaping mouths.

Stichus is a "contamination" or adaptation of two, possibly three, Greek plays. Menander's *Brothers* is the source of the first part of the play, in which two sisters are anxiously awaiting the return of their husbands who have been away for years. Their father, Antipho, is trying to persuade them to marry again; but the husbands arrive at the end of the second act, and the question is solved. A second play furnishes other scenes in which a parasite, who tries to fasten himself upon the returning husbands, is rebuffed. Antipho is reconciled to his sons-in-law and asks them to give him a music-girl whom they have brought home. The play ends with a scene of revelry and feasting carried on by Stichus, his friend, Sagarinus, and their mistresses.

The play is a mosaic of loosely connected episodes. The meagre plot ends in the middle of the play. The last scene of banqueting with courtezans is originally from Old Comedy, and was retained in later comedy which had no real plot to bring it to a solution. It is a mere closing scene, rather than a dénouement. The process of contamination will finally cause situations in Latin comedy to become very complex. It resulted merely in making this play episodic. Between *Stichus* and *Epidicus* are plots of all grades of complication.

The audience was aided in following these plots by the fact that the persons in the play were stock characters and the plots were founded on stock situations. The young spendthrift lover employs a tricky lying slave to beg, borrow or steal money from someone—often his father—to purchase his mistress from a procurer or a captain; and the mistress often turns out to be the long-lost child of some opulent neighbor. A parasite, who spouts monologues on his profession and his constant hunger, is employed to do some nefarious business. A cook wanders on and off the stage, but has little to do with the plot. A love story forms the framework of the action but is kept in the background or even behind the scenes. In order to overcome obstacles which bestrew the path of true love, plan after plan is laid within the hearing of the audience. The lover generally stands aside and the slave tries to carry out the plans. Or the young lover may unconsciously spoil the plan by some mistake. When some scheme is successful, the play ends or a recognition scene may remove the obstacles. The situation may be complicated by similarity of appearance (*Menæchmi*), by one character impersonating another (*Braggart Captain*), or by identical names (*Bacchides*).

Plautus realized that comedy contained these elements for he points out that his *Captives* departs from the usual form. It presents no "perjured pimp or unprincipled courtezan or braggart captain." In the epilogue he says: "Spectators, this play was composed with due regard to the proprieties. Here you have no vicious intrigues, no love affairs, no supposititious child, no getting money on false pretenses, no young spark setting a wench free without his father's knowledge."

Variety in the plays did not arise by presenting new situations, but by varying stock situations with different combinations of complications. Inventive power was turned in the direction of complication. Plautus was forced by his desire for intricate situations to introduce the element of chance into his action. As a result, neither his plots nor the development of the action will stand the Aristotelian test of the necessary or even probable sequence of events. He did not aim to produce such effects. Neither did the Greek dramatists from whom he drew his material, nor did Euripides from whom they, in turn, had learned much of their art of playwriting. Euripides constructed a plot which allowed him to stage tragic scenes. The writers of New Comedy constructed a plot which furnished an opportunity to stage comic scenes.

The intricate situation forced Plautus to use every possible means such as explanatory prologues, monologues, asides and repetitions, in order to have the play understood. He cast illusion to the four winds. The monologue and the aside were rare in Euripidean tragedy but had been employed more frequently by Aristophanes. In Plautine comedy, they serve as copious annotations to the dialogue. Sometimes one monologue follows another. Or they are practically simultaneous, as two characters speak on opposite sides of the stage but are not supposed to hear each other. Again, the action may turn on a monologue overheard by another character, as in *Rudens* when Labrax learns from Sceparnio's monologue that his two young women are in the temple. Once in a while, Plautus justifies the monologue, as in *Cistellaria* when the old courtezan addressing the audience, as characters sometimes do in Old Comedy, says: "I've got the same fault as most of the women in my profession. Once we get properly ballasted, our tongues loosen up at once and we talk too much." She then explains a part of the action of the play. In *Pseudolus*, Plautus avoids repetition by having Pseudolus refuse to answer a question because the audience knows the answer. He says: "This play is being performed for the sake of these spectators. They, who were present here, know. I'll tell you another time." The intimacy between audience and actor had diminished. It had arisen in the rituals underlying comedy in which jests were bandied back and forth between celebrant and onlooker. In tragedy, the line of demarcation between actor and spectator was never overstepped, probably because tragedy became solemn and dignified.

Most Plautine comedies founded upon mistaken identity open with a prologue which explains the plot of the play, especially the events in the past. The explanatory prologue may also open the second act, as in *Miles Gloriosus* (*Braggart Captain*). These explanatory prologues do not show the technical artistry of the Euripidean prologue. Sometimes they are too involved and long-winded. But, with their interlarded jests, they put the audience into a good humor and a receptive mood. They piqued curiosity. Plautus could have dispensed with them as Terence did later. Yet they helped the spectators grasp the situation in a theatre very different from modern playhouses in which the audience is supplied with programs, is quieter, is in a small auditorium, and looks at a stage which blazes with light and forms a hypnotic centre.

The opening scenes of Latin comedy are also frankly explanatory. Picturesque and striking scenes of exposition, found in Aristophanic comedy and Greek tragedy, occur only in *Rudens* which opens with a storm on the seashore. In this case, the original play by Diphilus which Plautus adapted was undoubtedly influenced by Euripides' *Alcmena*, which opened with or contained a similar scene, mentioned in the opening of *Rudens*. Indeed, the whole play is constructed on tragic lines; and, although it is comedy in the last analysis, the mood and atmosphere are often serious.

As the play begins, a storm has been raging all night. A ship has been wrecked. Palæstra and Ampelisca are being driven ashore. Palæstra enters with her clothes torn and wet. This theatrical situation becomes dramatic as we realize that she, the slave of a procurer, is unknowingly standing before her father's house in the very place her lover has just quitted. She cries out in tragic accents: "My parents, you know not of this, that I am thus wretched." For the moment, the comedy has become tragedy.

As Ampelisca enters and these two young women kneel as suppliants before the temple of Venus, whence comes the priestess, the scene, the stage setting, the atmosphere, the tone and situation are tragic. Suppliants clinging to an altar is a recurrent scene in Greek tragedy. An additional touch of tragic technique is found at the beginning of the third act when Dæmones, father of Palæstra, recounts a dream, which, humorous as it may be, is still a device of foreshadowing borrowed from tragedy.

When Labrax, the procurer, enters, he learns by overhearing a monologue of Sceparnio that his two young women are in the temple. He pursues them within; and Trachalio rushes forth from the sacred precinct imploring aid for the two damsels, who, attacked by Labrax, are clinging to the statue of Venus. This situation is even messengered in a way that recalls the procedure of tragedy, and messengering is rare in comedy up to this time. Finally the young women rush forth on the stage and kneel at the altar of Venus in prayer for protection. The scene has humorous touches; but the situation actually arouses our sympathy and for that reason differs widely from any scene in Old Comedy in which tragic scenes were burlesqued.

Dæmones and his slaves drag Labrax forth; beholding Palæstra, Dæmones is reminded of his long-lost child. Since the audience knows that she is his daughter, we have here the suspense and sympathy attendant upon the recognition scene in tragedy, although this scene becomes boisterously comic when Labrax is placed at the altar and is guarded by two slaves ready to use the slap stick, if he makes the slightest movement. When Plesidippus, the lover of Palæstra, drags Labrax to jail, the play seems to be ended except that the recognition of Palæstra and her father has not taken place. The rest of the action is concerned with the preparation and consummation of the recognition. As the fourth act begins, Gripus, a fisherman, has found in his net a wallet lost by Palæstra; but Trachalio, to whom he has shown it, disputes his right to keep it and they fight over it. Finally Gripus permits the question of ownership to be settled by arbitration and Dæmones is selected as judge. Of course the wallet contains tokens proving that Palæstra is the daughter of Dæmones. Here again, as in Menander's *Arbitrants*, is a scene drawn from Euripidean tragedy. Thus far the play is cast entirely in the tragic mould. The fifth act alone is purely comic. Gripus is offered a reward by the procurer if he will tell who has the wallet. He indicates Dæmones as the possessor. Dæmones receives the reward, while Gripus gets nothing.

In modern times, Terence has been considered the more serious of these two Roman playwrights. In this respect the critics have accepted the verdict of antiquity. The English and the French critics of the eighteenth century justified sentimental comedy on the ground that Terence had introduced sentiment and sympathetic characters into comedy. They failed to see that, while these elements are in the story of his plays, the sentimental situations and the sympathetic heroine are kept behind the scenes. No extant Terentian play is so close to sentimental, serious drama as *Rudens*. But Plautus was not destined to furnish the modern theatre with the model of sentimental drama. The playwrights of the Renaissance drew from him the situation of mistaken identity through similarity of appearance found in his *Bacchides*, *Amphitryo* and especially in his *Menæchmi*. He jokingly called his *Amphitryo* a tragi-comedy because it con-

tained both gods and slaves as characters. The term tragi-
comedy came to mean in the Renaissance a serious play with a
happy ending. In this sense of the word his *Rudens* is more a
tragi-comedy than any extant play by Terence.

Both *Amphitryo* and the *Menæchmi* are less episodic than most
Latin comedies. Once the hypothesis is admitted, the action
develops in a series of events, each one of which grows out of
the other. The order in which the scenes occur in the *Menæchmi*
cannot be altered without seriously disturbing the mechanism of
the plot. The Roman audience was evidently beginning to enjoy
a unified action in comedy. The episodic, loose construction of
earlier Latin comedy was disappearing.

The plot of Old Comedy was simple and contained a single
action. Euripides displayed a tendency to combine two actions.
New Comedy seems to have carried on this practice, and the
fabulæ duplices or double plots are probably of Greek origin.
Contamination as practiced by Plautus meant combining episodes of two or three plays into one play. At first these episodes
were merely juxtaposed and scarcely reacted upon each other.
Both the double plot and contamination tended to produce complex plays. In the Renaissance, complexity of plot was carried
still further. Thus Shakespeare introduces two pairs of twins in
the *Comedy of Errors*, founded on the *Menæchmi*, and adds
other complications by having the father of the twin brothers
condemned to death as a foreigner. The comic playwrights of
the Renaissance also practiced contamination. Hence we have
the *Merchant of Venice* with three, perhaps four plots.

Terence followed the technique of Plautine comedy in general,
but he introduced certain modifications. The loose construction,
the slapstick humor disappear almost entirely from Terentian
comedy. Like Plautus, Terence practiced contamination. He
constructed complicated stories; but he handled his plot material
more deftly. There are no loose ends and the action is easier to
follow than in many Plautine plays. His complications, however, are introduced primarily for purposes of humor and not
for dramatic effect. He builds a chain of circumstances which

will produce a happy ending but not in order to place on the stage surprising, emotional scenes. The recognition scene is employed to bring the dénouement, not as a sentimental climax.

Although his plots presuppose many events in the past and although he founds them on mistaken and concealed circumstances and identities, he dispenses with the explanatory prologue used by Plautus. At times, he introduces a protatic character—a person who appears only in the *protasis* or first part of a play. Aristophanes and Sophocles had both employed this device for the purpose of exposition. A protatic character is supposed to be ignorant of the situation, and the explanation given him is really directed to the audience. This procedure gives a stronger illusion of reality than does the monologue whether it be frankly addressed to the audience or considered as thinking aloud on part of the speaker. Terence was making a step in the direction of realism and was drawing a clearer line of demarcation between actor and audience than had existed heretofore in comedy. The Roman stage was elevated and the physical separation of actor and audience emphasized the mental separation. Many modern producers are attempting to bring the stage and the actor closer to the auditorium and to the spectator by abolishing the physical and mental lines of demarcation. But drama in Rome was becoming realistic.

The objection to the protatic character is that he is not vitally connected with the action. When information is given, he has little emotional reaction, and hence the spectator is not much interested in what is said. Illusion of reality may be preserved, but little dramatic effect is produced. Thus in the *Hecyra* (*Mother-in-Law*), two protatic characters and a secondary character give the exposition. Parmeno explains to Philotis that Pamphilus who has been emamored of Bacchis, a courtezan, has taken a wife, has become estranged from his former mistress, and has transferred his affections to his wife. Donatus says that Terence chose this method of exposition in preference to having a prologue or a god from a machine explain the situation. The scene is more realistic than a Plautine prologue would have been; but it is far from being dramatic because we hear about the emotions and actions of Pamphilus and his young wife in a second-hand manner from characters not vitally interested in the situation. As a result, we are as calm as the protatic characters. Had Pamphilus himself explained his feelings in a monologue, there would have been less realism and more dramatic emotion in the scene. The exposition in the *Eunuch* is more artistic because Thaïs explains to the hero, Phædria, why he is kept away from his mistress. Thus Terence does not always employ a protatic character; but his opening scenes are calm because, having dispensed with the explanatory prologue, he uses the first act for exposition rather than action. The Latin grammarians will tell us, and the critics of the Renaissance will echo them, that tragedy has a calm opening and a "turbulent" closing, and that the reverse is true of comedy. This statement is not borne out by the facts. In certain Greek tragedies the opening scenes have an external appearance of majestic calmness, and Aristophanic comedy often begins turbulently. But Greek tragedy sometimes closes calmly; and, with the exception of *Rudens*, Latin comedy begins calmly and becomes more "turbulent" as the action develops.

The position of the point of attack in comedies of Terence and the place where it would occur in other forms of drama may be illustrated by the argument of *Andria*.

Chremes and Phania were brothers, citizens of Athens. (Here would come the medieval point of attack.) Chremes, going to Asia, leaves his daughter, Pasibula, in the care of his brother, Phania, who, afterwards setting sail with Pasibula, is wrecked off the Isle of Andros. Escaping with their lives, they are kindly received by a native of the island; and Phania soon afterwards dies there. The Andrian changes the name of the girl to Glycerium, and brings her up as his own child, with his daughter, Chrysis. On his death, Chrysis and Glycerium sail for Athens to seek their fortune there. (Here would be the Elizabethan point of attack.) Chrysis being admired by several Athenian youths, Pamphilus, the son of Simo, an opulent citizen, chances to see

Glycerium and falls violently in love with her. She afterwards becomes pregnant by him, on which he makes her a promise of marriage. (A Bernard Shaw could take the situation at this point and brilliantly satirize our customs and ideas concerning marriage, family life, the bringing up of children.) In the meantime, Chremes, who is now living at Athens and is ignorant of the fate of Pasibula, agrees with Simo, the father of Pamphilus, to give Philumena, another daughter, in marriage to Pamphilus. While these arrangements are being made Chrysis dies. (The point of attack in a sentimental version of the eighteenth century might well occur here.) Simo accidentally discovers his son's connection with Glycerium. Chremes, also coming to hear of it, declines the match, having no idea that Glycerium is really his own daughter. (It is at this point that the Latin play begins.)

This synopsis also illustrates the large number of chance events which had to take place before the plot could exist; and the long arm of chance does not cease to operate throughout the whole plot.

This situation is treated by Terence as a comedy; and it can end happily because, in reality, no obstacle exists to keep the lovers apart. A catastrophic character appears just in time to prove that Glycerium is the daughter of Simo. Of course one asks what would happen if the situation really existed and were developed logically in accordance with ancient customs; but one asks in vain. Authors of New Comedy never allow such situations to exist in reality. We shall have to wait for Dumas and the nineteenth century before such a problem is solved on the stage; and then a pistol shot will put an end to the tragedy. Perhaps in the twentieth century the young couple would marry and go to seek a lovers' paradise in Australia or the Rocky Mountains where we believe that indiscreet innocence is sheltered from the heavy hand of conventionality.

Terence uses much plot material. The *Mother-in-Law* is his only extant play which does not contain a double plot. He introduces two pairs of lovers. Terentian comedy develops more smoothly and more convincingly than does the usual Plautine play in which the action may be held up at any moment for purposes of humor. Terence reveals his action and develops his story carefully, yet the action in his plays has a tendency to go behind the scenes as was the case in Euripidean tragedy. A note by Donatus on line 825 of the *Mother-in-Law* says that the incident narrated by Bacchis was represented in the original Greek play. It probably means the recognition of the ring by Myrrhina was enacted and not the event mentioned in line 825 which happened months before the usual point of attack in comedy. In either case, the action has gone behind the scenes in Terence's play.

In Plautine comedy, the action is generally on the stage, as in Aristophanic comedy, unless, like *Rudens*, the play is influenced by tragic technique. Plautus did not hesitate to represent on the stage any event which would naturally take place indoors and hence behind the scenes. The banquet in the *Bacchides* and women at their toilet are placed by Plautus in the street with utter disregard for realism. He was willing to sacrifice veri-similitude—the bogey of neo-classicists—in order to present all situations directly to the spectators. Such scenes as that in the *Braggart Captain,* in which the slave looking through the skylight beholds the lovers caressing each other, are narrated, because they cannot be represented out-of-doors; but the action in Plautine comedy is often on the stage, even at the expense of realism.

In the plays of Terence, there are no banquets or reclining courtezans on the stage. Undoubtedly a feeling for realism began to preclude the stretching of stage conventions to such a point as to have these scenes on the street. Tragedy dealt with life of the past. Because a Clytemnestra or an Œdipus was far away in time, it was not so strange to see them always in the open air. Old Comedy was anything but realistic. Fantasy was its very soul. New Comedy, however, dealt with the present and with everyday life. Inevitably it would become more and more realistic. The less realistic Plautine comedy perhaps represents more of the spirit of comedy of the fourth century when some of the easy conventions and fantasy of Old Comedy remained to smooth out the path of the dramatist.

The fact that Terence observes more carefully the conventionalities of the out-door setting may account, in part, for his tendency to place certain important situations behind the scenes; and it may have influenced his treatment of the rôle of heroine.

Euripides had developed the rôle of heroine and had even introduced the guiltless woman in his *Helen* and in *Alcestis*. In New Comedy the innocent heroine, although very important in the plot, appears on the stage with increasing infrequency, although the courtezan appears even more than she did in Aristophanic comedy. In Plautus, the respectable wife and the innocent maiden are on the stage far more than in Terence, although Plautus has a mute heroine in *Pseudolus*, and although he introduces no feminine characters either in the *Captives* or in *Trinummus*. In Terence's *Andria*, Pamphila appears once, but does not speak; and the recognition of Pamphila by her brother takes place behind the scenes. In the *Brothers*, the *Mother-in-Law* and *Phormio*, the heroines are kept within doors. Only in the *Self-Tormentor* is there a scene between an innocent heroine and her lover, in spite of the fact that obstacles in the path of lovers form the basis of the plots of the plays. The fragments of Menander's comedies contain few scenes in which the heroine figures on the stage. The evidence furnished by extant plays of Terence shows that he almost entirely banished from view this character who plays such an important part in his story, but who must wait until more modern times to enact her rôle on the stage.

Evidence that the infrequent appearance of the respectable woman was partially due to the out-door setting is furnished by Stobæus who quotes the following passage from Menander. A husband is upbraiding his wife who has appeared at the door. "Take care. You are crossing the boundaries of a married woman, when you come forth from the interior court, because the threshold of this court is looked upon as the limit of the house for an honest woman; but to come out-of-doors and run into the street, to cry out, that is the impudence of a dog."

Other considerations, however, tended to keep the heroine off the stage. Terence did not aim to produce romantic or sentimental comedy. The love story was a comic complication, not a problem to be treated for its own interest. The love of Antigone and Hæmon in *Antigone* is a tragic complication but not the subject of the play. The ancients did not produce either a *Romeo and Juliet* or an *As You Like It* because they did not care for love scenes. Love interest was a means not an end in classical drama. The lover easily becomes a comic character, especially when he is unsuccessful; but an innocent or wronged maiden is not very funny and never has been a satisfactory source of comic effect. Had Terence emphasized this rôle, his plays would have been romantic and more serious. These shy heroines arouse sympathy in us moderns. We regret their almost continuous absence; but we are thinking of them in terms of the modern theatre in which love plays a great part on the stage. The ancients were content to have the heroines of comedy out of sight and wasted no sympathy on them. Latin comedy is more humorous because the tricky slaves, parasites, courtezans and obstructive old fathers hold the stage than it would have been had the sympathetic heroine been the medium for developing the action and guiding the emotions of the audience.

The out-door setting and the absence of the heroine make these plays very different from what they would be if the same stories were dramatized by modern playwrights. The principal characters in the love story become secondary characters in the play. The action is carried on by slaves, parasites, courtezans, old men. The chief characters are constantly paired off in scenes with secondary characters. The recognition scene had been a dramatic event in tragedy. Now it has become unimportant. Either it is narrated, as in the *Eunuch* and the *Mother-in-Law*, or is staged between the wrong characters as in *Andria*, for Pasibula is not on the stage when Chremes discovers she is his long-lost daughter. The dramatic recognition has become a mere perfunctory means of bringing about a happy ending. It lacks even a sentimental interest when treated thus.

The late point of attack, the street-scene, and the absence of the heroine cause the plot to develop through secondary characters and in a second-hand manner. In comparison with modern plays, Terentian comedy seems to reach the spectator indirectly. Even comic incidents are sometimes narrated.

If the plays of Terence were produced on a revolving stage with the action taking place in the interiors as well as in the street, and if the stage were revolved halfway, we would witness the scenes which a modern dramatist would naturally place before our eyes; and we would only hear about the scenes which Terence placed before the Roman audience.

CHAPTER VI

THE ORIGIN OF MEDIEVAL DRAMA. FRENCH
MEDIEVAL DRAMA

I

IN the downfall of the Roman Empire the theatre came crashing to the ground. The great shows and spectacles of the period of decadence in Rome and in Byzantium passed into oblivion and nothing of them remained upon which to build. Only a faint spark of drama seems to have remained—kept alive by the mimes and *histriones;* and even these wandering mountebanks, ostracized and anathematized by the church fathers, have been held by certain scholars to have been merely jugglers, rope-walkers and acrobats. But if the desire to be someone else is natural, although impossible to fulfill, the desire to impersonate someone else is just as natural, and so easily fulfilled that peoples of all degrees of intelligence and civilization have indulged this human desire and created some sort of drama. Some form of worship of a higher power always exists among every race of human beings; and every ritual contains the germ of drama.

It is difficult to understand why the Church was so hostile to the mime if it consisted only of rope-walking and dances in the eighth and ninth centuries when we last hear of it before the rise of liturgical drama. The dramatic mime must have kept the spark of drama alive until it began to appear in church services. In 836, Agobert mentions the mime and in the tenth century the primitive drama of the adoration of the shepherds was being produced. Indeed, a late ninth or early tenth century manuscript of St. Gall preserves the earliest extant tropes interpolated into the Easter service. That a new kind of drama sprang from the Christian ritual is undoubted; but that there was a period in the history of Europe in the ninth and early tenth century when there was no mimetic representation of events or impersonation of characters is unbelievable in spite of the fact that these plays or shows of that period have all disappeared.

In a ritual of Gallican origin from the ninth century and used at the dedication of a church is found mimetic action and impersonation. Mr. Chambers describes the ritual as follows: "The bishop and his procession approach the closed doors of the church from without, but one of the clergy as if hiding (*quasi latens*) is placed inside. Three blows with a staff are given on the doors and the anthem is raised, *Tollite portas, principes, vestras et elevamini, portæ æternales, et introibit Rex gloriæ.* From within comes the question, *Quis est iste Rex gloriæ?* and the reply is given: *Dominus virtutum ipse est Rex gloriæ.* Then the doors are opened, and as the procession sweeps through, he who was concealed within slips out (*quasi fugiens*) to join the train. It is the dramatic expulsion of the spirit of evil" (*The Medieval Stage,* Vol. II, p. 4). Here is a play; and the spirit of evil is the character which will become the great antagonist or villain of medieval drama.

Just as serious Greek tragedy developed from the ritual performed in honor of the dead hero or god, so the tragic drama of the Middle Ages developed from the ritual performed in Holy Week in honor of the death and resurrection of Christ. The service readily lends itself to dramatic reading under the emotional exaltation of the moment. It became a practice to have the words of Christ chanted in a sweet low tone, the speeches of Judas and Pilate in a shrill treble tone, while the narrative version was in a tenor voice without much accentuation.

Antiphonal song had been introduced into the church service in the early part of the fourth century. The different parts of the ritual were rendered by half-choirs or a cantor answered by the whole choir. Real dialogue, however, arose from the practice of inserting lines, known as tropes, in certain portions of the mass. A manuscript of St. Gall contains the following tropes introduced into the Easter service about the year 900. Angels sing to persons or a choir representing for the moment the woman at the tomb of Christ:

> Whom seek ye in the tomb, O Christians?

The answer comes:

> Jesus of Nazareth, the crucified, O Heavenly Beings.

To this the angelic voices reply:

> He is not here; he has risen as he foretold.
> Go and announce that he has risen from the tomb.

The development of mimetic action, the introduction of costume and properties are illustrated by the following passage from the *Concordia Regularis* drawn up by Ethelwold, Bishop of Winchester, in the tenth century. This ritual is of English origin but was founded upon customs in vogue in continental monasteries.

"While the third lesson is being chanted, let four brethren vest themselves. Let one of these, vested in an alb, enter as though to take part in the service, and let him approach the sepulchre without attracting attention and sit there quietly with a palm in his hand."

This brother is to play the part of the angel. The sepulchre is represented by the altar. Then the unconscious dramatist, ultra-modern in his careful stage directions, describes how the brothers who are to play the rôles of the three Marys shall act.

While the third respond is chanted, let the remaining three follow and let them all, vested in copes, bearing in their hands thuribles with incense, and stepping delicately as those who seek something, approach the sepulchre. These things are done in imitation of the angel sitting in the monument, and the women with spices coming to anoint the body of Jesus. When therefore he who sits there beholds the three approaching him like folk lost and seeking something, let him begin in a dulcet voice of medium pitch to sing *Quem quæritis*. And when he has sung it to the end, let the three reply in unison, *Ihesu Nazarenum*. So he, *Non est hic, surrexit sicut prædixerat. Ite, nuntiate quia surrexit a mortuis.* At the word of bidding let those three turn to the choir and say, *Alleluia! resurrexit Dominus.* This said, let the one still sitting there and as if recalling them, say the anthem, *Venite et videte locum.* And saying this, let him rise and lift the veil, and show them the place bare of the cross, but only the cloths laid there in which the cross was wrapped. And when they have seen this, let them set down the thuribles which they bare in that same sepulchre, and take the cloth, and hold it up in the face of the clergy, and as if to demonstrate that the Lord has risen and is no longer wrapped therein, let them sing the anthem, *Surrexit Dominus de sepulchro,* and lay the cloth upon the altar. When the anthem is done, let the prior, sharing in their gladness at the triumph of our King, in that, having vanquished death, He rose again, begin the hymn, *Te Deum laudamus.* And this begun, all the bells chime out together (*The Medieval Stage*, Vol. I, p. 14).

The Greek ritual in honor of a dead hero was probably similar in tone and construction. Here we have a single voice answered by a chorus of three. In the Greek ritual a single leader was answered by a chorus of fifty. In order to turn this ritual into a miniature Greek tragedy one would only have to introduce a narrative description of the crucifixion.

Another scene, dramatized at Augsburg about 1100, is the visit of Peter and John to the tomb. They find the sepulchre empty and announce the resurrection.

The appearance of Christ as a gardener to Mary Magdalene is portrayed in the following liturgical drama of the thirteenth century. As in Greek tragedy, the spirit of the hero appeared before the live hero was portrayed.

MARY

My heart burns with the desire to behold my Lord. I seek and find not where they have placed Him.

In the meantime, let someone come in the likeness of a GARDENER *and standing at the head of the sepulchre, let him say:*
Woman, why weepest thou? Whom seekest thou?

MARY

Master, if thou hast taken Him away, tell me where thou hast placed him and I will carry Him away.

HE

Mary.

MARY (*throwing herself at His feet*)

Rabboni.

HE (*drawing back from her as if avoiding her touch*)

Touch me not, for I have not yet risen to my father and your father, my Lord and your Lord. (*Thus let the* GARDENER *withdraw.*)

MARY (*turning to the people*)

Congratulate me, all ye who cherish the Lord because He whom I was seeking appeared to me while I was weeping at the sepulchre. I have seen my Lord. Halleluia.

The serious plays of the Middle Ages developed by a steady process of adding scenes to such dramatized rituals. At first tropes were introduced. These tropes were given a dramatic background and setting and were delivered by monks or priests impersonating the different characters. Then as different scenes were added, the dramatized ritual became liturgical drama entirely detached from the Introit. While this phenomenon of accretion cannot be traced with absolute chronological exactness because the manuscripts of the extant plays date from different centuries, yet we shall probably not go far wrong in assuming that one of the next stages in the development of this episode is exemplified in the *Holy Women at the Tomb* preserved in a manuscript of the twelfth century. The point of attack has been pushed back so as to include a song of lamentation sung in alternate verses by the three Marys before they reach the tomb. In the *Three Marys* the women buy oil of a merchant as they go to the Holy Sepulchre; and in this play Christ himself appears to Mary Magdalene. In the *Resurrection* of the twelfth century the point of attack has gone back still farther. The librettist or dramatist wishes to prove the fact that Christ rose from the dead, so he begins his play by having Pilate send soldiers to guard the tomb. An angel strikes them down with a thunderbolt. The Marys enter and buy oil of the merchant. They find the tomb empty and the angel announces that Christ has risen. The soldiers report to Pilate what has happened. Mary Magdalene gives her lamentation. Christ appears to her. The other Marys come. Christ appears to the disciples. Thomas doubts. The other disciples behold the empty tomb and the chorus sing *Te Deum laudamus*.

The similarity of early Christian plays to early Greek drama again is striking. The lamentation for the dead hero or god, the spirit and tone of the drama, the point of attack close to the dénouement, the lack of conflict between hero and villain, the hero himself appearing only twice, all recall the Greek tragedy. At the end, there is a song of praise, almost joyous, which corresponds to the note of future peace sounded at the end of so many Greek plays. There is this difference: Christianity has made death a triumphant passage into glory, whereas with the Greeks death was the solemn fulfilment of a decree of Fate.

The differences between the two forms of tragedy are external. The Greeks were greater artists so far as form is concerned; and they soon fixed the mould into which their plays would be cast. The drama of the Middle Ages was to know no limits or bounds. It poured forth like a flood from the pen of the dramatist. The point of attack never became fixed. The "stage" itself grew to vast dimensions. The salutary Greek maxim "Nothing too much" was unknown to these child-like people who preferred exaggeration and vastness to restraint in their works of art.

Another influence, no less potent, which enlarged the framework of the medieval drama to huge proportions, sprang from the fact that Christianity not only celebrated the death and resurrection of its God but also his birth. A second series of scenes arose in connection with the ritual honoring the birth of Christ, and were given dramatic representation at the same time that the ritual concerning the Resurrection was developing into material for drama. The Christian ritual which was dramatized finally included the whole life of the hero. The Greek ritual which influenced early tragedy was in honor merely of the dead hero and was retrospective. The Christian ritual was not only prospective, but also the point of attack in the ritual was placed far away from the dénouement. Hence the same conditions prevailed in the drama which developed from these services at Christmas and in Holy Week.

At first there were these two groups of liturgical dramas: the one containing the scenes which grouped themselves about the Resurrection; the other embracing scenes related to the Nativity, such as the *Annunciation,* the *Three Kings,* and the *Massacre of the Innocents.* As years went on, the spoken drama developed and ceased to be intimately connected with the ritual. The point of attack in the Resurrection group was placed far enough back to include the Passion. This episode was one of the last to be portrayed. The dénouement included the Last Judgment. Scenes were added to the Nativity group and the events leading up to the Passion were finally dramatized. The point of attack in the Nativity plays went back to a scene in Heaven in which God decides to send his Son to earth as the Savior.

Thus plays of stupendous length, taking many days to perform, grew out of the practice of juxtaposing the two groups of scenes, of making additions of single scenes and of lengthening them. Versions were enlarged by learned clerks in different towns. This fact explains the similarity of many mystery plays.

The Maestricht *Passion,* of French origin and produced before 1350, contains the following scenes in a fragment of about fifteen hundred lines: Creation and Fall of the Angels; Creation and Fall of Man; Debate of Justice and Pity; Prophecies of the Birth of Christ; Annunciation; Nativity; Three Kings and Herod; Massacre of the Innocents; Flight into Egypt; Jesus in the Temple; Baptism; Temptation; Calling of Peter and Andrew; Wedding at Cana; Jesus at the House of Simon; Resurrection of Lazarus; Entrance into Jerusalem; Expulsion of the Money Lenders; Jesus at the House of Martha; Council of the

Synagogue; Betrayal; Garden of Olives; Arrival of Judas and the Soldiers.

The action fairly gallops. In later *Passion Plays* begins the process of addition of new episodes drawn from apocryphal sources; likewise, episodes already dramatized are lengthened. Thus Michel's *Passion* is an amplification of two *journées* or long acts of Greban's *Passion*. The "very eloquent and scientific doctor, Master Jehan Michel," adds but never cuts. He introduces many secondary scenes which make the action drag through thousands upon thousands of additional lines. Eloquent and scientific doctors should not write plays. Medieval drama began with three or four lines and attained epic proportions. The French *Mystery of the Old Testament* contains over fifty thousand lines.

The plays were built piecemeal as was the medieval cathedral. Different architects were employed and each generation added something to the cathedral: altar, transept, nave, chapel, tower. The edifice was never finished. It could always be embroidered with sacred, comic, grotesque or realistic scenes in stone or glass. The medieval cathedral has not the formal unity of a Greek temple. Yet it is an architectural unit. At times the eye prefers to dwell upon a chapel or a tower or a grotesque carving. So the mystery cycles have not the simple, formal unity of Greek tragedy. Pathetic episodes, such as Abraham and Isaac in the *Brome Play*, or the grotesque scenes between Noah and his wife, or the comic *Second Shepherds' Play* of the Towneley cycle offer the greatest delight to the modern spectator. Greek tragedy and architecture are unified in tone. The mystery cycle and the cathedral run the scale of all human emotions from the tragic and pathetic to the grotesque and comic. It is thus that Shakespeare was to build his plays, divided into scenes of great variety.

There is a striking similarity between the spirit and construction of Greek tragedy and plays of the Resurrection group. The Nativity plays are constructed on different lines. They are not tragic but joyous. Thus the whole medieval play was not entirely serious. There was a mixture of tone. The total effect was not tragic in a depressing sense, because even the death of Christ in the *Passion Play* or of a hero in a *Miracle Play* was followed by a triumphant apotheosis. When these groups had coalesced, the point of attack was placed even before the birth of the hero; and the play presented his birth, life, death and ascension into eternal life. In 1195 the *Creation of the World and the Fall of Lucifer* was given at Regensburg. In this play, the medieval point of attack at the beginning of the story is perfectly exemplified. It can recede no further from the dénouement. The retrospection, so effectively employed in Greek drama, was not only unnecessary but almost impossible in medieval drama. All the action is on the stage. It never occurred to the medieval playwright to have events in his story narrated. In the rare cases in which a messenger is introduced, he almost invariably reports incidents which have already been enacted before the spectators but which one of the characters is not supposed to know. The medieval dramatist therefore knew no rule or convention or practice of having the action represented as happening in one place or during a short period of time or even of limiting the length of his play.

The aim of medieval drama was primarily didactic. As is stated in the preface to the *Concordia Regularis*, the priests had instituted this custom of giving visual representations of certain ceremonies in order to "fortify unlearned people in their faith." The mimetic rituals and the medieval drama performed a function similar to that of the motion picture in visual education in modern schools. The drama began to flourish when many worshippers were unable to understand the service in Latin. Naturally the element of spectacle was important in such a drama and the action was kept before the eyes of the audience. Greek tragedy aroused emotions by representing emotional reactions of characters to events on or off the stage. That was its artistic aim and even its moral justification according to Aristotle. Medieval sacred drama taught a moral lesson by telling a story on the stage. It had relatively little artistic aim, for its moral justification weighed too heavily on its framework.

The system of simultaneous stage decoration was also a strong factor in the development of the technique of medieval drama. The Greek ritual was performed about the tomb of the dead hero; and, since it was a retrospective narrative of his life, the practice and convention of not changing the scene easily grew up. The tomb was the first "scenery" in Greek tragedy and it represented nothing but just what it was. Of course, the Greek stage finally had other scenery; but there was nothing in the primitive ritual to establish the custom of changing the scene.

In the ritual underlying medieval tragedy, the altar of a church was the first scenery; and it became scenery when it began to represent something other than itself, such as the Holy Sepulchre in the *Concordia Regularis* or the manger in the *Three Kings*. As other episodes were added to these plays, more scenery had to be devised. Thus in the *Massacre of the Innocents,* there is not only a stable but also Herod is seated on a throne. Chairs are employed in the *Conversion of Saint Paul* to represent Jerusalem and Damascus. A boy placed upon the pulpit represented an angel; and the choir in the lofts was supposed to be in the sky. When Heaven came to be represented in later years, it was placed on a level above the stage. Thus the ritual from which these plays developed demanded many scenes. Since different parts of the church were used to represent these scenes, the practice of setting all scenery on the stage grew up and was followed throughout the Middle Ages. In France the custom lasted well into the seventeenth century.

Since there was no convention of limit of time either of the action or of the actual representation itself, the dramatist was able to represent any scene at any moment. There was practically no such place as "behind the scenes." The material conditions of the medieval theatre were partially responsible for the loose construction of medieval drama. The stage setting, the lack of any fixed point of attack or dénouement, and the aim to present a visual lesson naturally led the playwright to represent everything in the story upon which his plot was founded. He followed his source closely. He began his play where the story began. He had everything enacted in temporal order. But if the art of selection, of compression, of the elimination of the non-essential was rarely practiced by the medieval playwright, at least he kept the action on the stage, where it generally belongs. He did represent non-essential scenes, but he never omitted an obligatory scene.

It has been said that the spectator in the Green theatre was in an "Olympic coign of vantage"; but this is truer of the spectator in the medieval theatre. His view extended from the beginning of time to the present and could rest upon any spot on Earth, in Heaven or Hell. Not only was there simultaneous scenery but simultaneous action. Those who have seen the simultaneous setting and action in the last act of *Aïda* can gain some impression of the emotions of the medieval audience when it beheld simultaneously the sufferings of tortured souls in Hell and the bliss of the saved souls in Heaven. Such dramatic contrast was a powerful factor in those bygone ages which can hardly be reproduced today. There is little wonder that the audience, which believed in the unbearably grim reality of Hell and the incomprehensibly beautiful reality of Heaven, would sit through prolix dialogue for days in order to behold this picture of the end of mortal life and the beginning of an immortality of torture, or of peace that passes understanding.

Yet medieval drama as a whole is formless and inartistic because the selective faculty of the artist, so essential to any dramatist, was never developed by the medieval playwright. He was content to follow his narrative source, or, if he were re-writing a play, to add, enlarge upon and emphasize certain episodes. Often these scenes were not vitally important and were given undue importance and length. For example, the scene of the forging of the nails for the crucifixion, often depicted in the fine arts, was given prominence in the *Passion Plays*. It is a scene of realism and grim cynicism, but it is generally far too long and not vital to the action. The trial scene in Heaven at the beginning of these plays finally became a long-winded debate. The rôle of the mother of Christ was given adequate treatment

for the first time in the Semur *Passion*. These theologians, trying to be dramatists, were blind to the tragic emotion in this
rôle. Not until 1485 did Michel produce a profoundly touching
scene in his *Passion* between Christ and his mother.

The Sainte Geneviève *Passion* illustrates the utter lack of proportion which became such a great fault in later plays and which
was so harmful to artistic construction. The rôle of Christ is
quite overshadowed by secondary rôles. He is kept silent. Realism drives out tragedy, for the scenes in which the ruffians are
preparing to capture Jesus and in which they seize him are
greatly prolonged in order to introduce realistic details, such
as Judas advising the thugs to take along lanterns. In the scene
of the Crucifixion, emphasis is placed again on the secondary
rôles of the ruffians, who nail Christ to the cross, instead of on
the tragic sufferings of the hero. The torture scenes are portrayed with minute detail. Throughout many medieval plays
realistic scenes of fishing, building, etc., are staged in a fashion
which delights the investigator of everyday life in the Middle
Ages but which is undramatic, so far as modern taste is concerned.

These playwrights were realists such as the realists of the nineteenth century never dreamed of being. Their unconscious
though literal interpretation of the idea that everything which is
in nature is in art is responsible for the introduction or development in detail of many scenes which are not in the narrative
source. They showed no desire to suppress unnecessary, commonplace details and much of their art consisted in making a
literal transcript of life. In the episode of the *Three Kings* in the
Sainte Geneviève *Passion,* the Kings feel the need of sleep and lie
down on the stage. Then Gabriel appears and warns them not
to return through Herod's realm. When the author of the Arras
Passion reaches this scene he cannot imagine being so unrealistic
as to allow Kings to sleep out-of-doors. Therefore he has them
send a servant to engage rooms in advance at an inn. When the
Kings arrive, supper is served and then they retire for the night.

Thus it is in life. Thus it is *not* in drama. As a result of this striving for realism, incidents entirely unnecessary so far as the dramatic action is concerned are constantly represented in minute detail. Every human action known to medieval man was enacted at one time or another on the stage. In comparison with the drama of the Middle Ages the modern plays of the Grand-Guignol type are suitable entertainment for puritans suffering from nervous prostration. Thrills, horrors, indecency, the commonplace, the comic, all are intermingled with the great theme of life, its meaning, its struggle, its temptations, and the judgment of God. The soul of a people is revealed in the way it constructs its plays.

In the development of medieval drama from the tenth century to the Renaissance, it was perhaps inevitable that one play would be produced which fulfills many of the conditions of what we believe dramatic art should be. This play is entitled *Adam* (1147-1174). It was written in French by an Anglo-Norman in England. The first episode, a complete drama in itself, requires no indulgence on the part of a modern theatre-goer. If modern censorship did not forbid the representation of God on the stage, the play could hold an audience on the modern stage.

The stage is the parvis of a cathedral. At one end of the stage are shown the gates of Hell. Earthly Paradise is filled with fruits and flowers. Adam is clad in a red robe and Eve is dressed in white. The author anticipates the request of many a modern playwright when he begs the actors to make gestures befitting what they say and to speak deliberately. They are not to add or leave out a syllable of the lines and are to speak them in the order in which they come. Also whoever speaks the word "Paradise" is to look at the scene and point to it. *"In the beginning God created Heaven and Earth"* is read. A choir sings an anthem and the play begins with God addressing Adam:

GOD
  I have formed thee
  From clay of the earth.

ADAM

I know it well.

GOD

I have given thee a living soul,
So have I formed thee in my semblance,
In my image have I made thee of earth,
Thou must never strive against me.

ADAM

So I shall not do, but I shall trust thee,
I shall obey my creator.

The point of attack is well placed. When mechanical spectacle enters medieval drama, such plays will show the actual creation of the world; but it is often the case that more primitive drama is better constructed than highly developed forms, because it is likely to be free from an overemphasis of the purely spectacular element, the literary and poetical element.

There is correct foreshadowing with the exposition. It is a question of obeying the commands of God. He bids Adam to love his wife, and Eve to hold Adam dear. Paradise is theirs so long as they do not eat the forbidden fruit. Then God withdraws into the church; and the action begins with a scene which is remarkable for psychology and dramatic effect.

The devils rush forth from Hell and in pantomime show the forbidden fruit to Eve "pursuasively that she may eat." Then the Devil addresses Adam, asking if all is well with him, insinuating that things could be better and arousing his curiosity. But Adam fears his Creator. He will not transgress his law. He will not touch the fruit. There is a pause while the Devil withdraws, and, with his companions, rushes through the audience, arousing laughter tempered by shivers. He returns to the temptation "merry and rejoicing." But Adam resists him. "With a sad and downcast expression," the Devil leaves Adam. After holding a council in pantomime with other devils at the gates of Hell, he comes to Eve "with a flattering expression." He gains her promise to keep a secret.

DEVIL

Thou hast been in a good school.
I have seen Adam, but he is very unreasonable.

EVE

He is a little hard.

DEVIL

He will be mild;
He is harder than hell.

EVE

He is very noble-minded.

DEVIL

But he is very servile.
If he will not take care of himself,
Let him at least take care of thee.
Thou art a delicate and tender thing,
And thou art fresher than the rose;
Thou art whiter than crystal,
Than snow which falls on ice in the valley;
The creator has made a bad match,
Thou art too tender and he too hard;
And yet thou art wiser.

Making sure that Adam does not overhear them, he explains that the fruit that God has given is worthless. The forbidden fruit has great virtue. It is the means of life, of power, of sovereignty, of knowledge. Its flavor is celestial. It is fitting for Eve, with her beautiful face and body, to be queen of the world. Thus he continues with promises and flattery to sow temptation in the woman's soul. She goes to Adam who warns her and upbraids her for listening to the Devil. In a scene in which no word is spoken, a serpent ascends a tree. Eve seems to listen to its council. At last she takes the fruit and hands it to Adam. The man hesitates. Eve tastes it and cries out in ecstasy:

Now my eyes are so clear-seeing
I am like God the Almighty;

> Whatever has been and whatever is to be
> I know fully. . . .

Adam yields to her command to eat; he recognizes his sin; he begins his lamentation: "Alas sinful one, what have I done."

These people are not one-sided figures which have stepped down from stained glass windows. The man, the woman and the tempter are real characters in this scene of suspense with hope and fear prevailing alternately. In the climax of this scene, the medieval audience beheld enacted the cause of human misery, the beginning of sin in the world.

The whole conception of this scene; the quiet, peaceful opening; the foreshadowing; the gradual rise of the action so artistically shaded in ever-increasing intensity of interest and emotion; the lyricism, not overshadowing the action and giving a touch of beauty; the insight into human nature; the tragic climax in which the woman is exalted by her sin and the man is crushed; the tenseness and power of the dialogue in the original language make this play worthy of production on any stage. There is that artistic restraint in its beauty and dramatic power that shows the touch of the real dramatist, whose name is lost to us. Medieval drama offering such scenes holds out fair hopes. But the promise of future beauty in dramatic art was not fulfilled, so far as we know from extant plays.

The first episode ends with the dramatic appearance of God before the sinners and with his curse for their crime. They are expelled from Paradise by the angel with the flaming sword. They cultivate the ground and sow it, often turning towards the lost Paradise with tears and beating their breasts. Weeds spring up and the sinners pour forth their lamentation. At last in a scene of pantomime the devils come and chain them and lead them to Hell whence issues smoke, an infernal din, and cries of demoniac joy.

The second episode represents the murder of Abel. It moves swiftly but not hurriedly. While it does not contain the keen psychology of the scene of the temptation, the situation is handled in a dramatic manner with dialogue which goes straight to the point. Pantomime again plays a large part in unfolding the action.

The last episode is a series of prophecies of the coming of a redeemer. As each prophet finishes, he is led away to Hell by the devils. Contrary to the general rule, this dramatist has practiced the art of selection of scenes to be represented. He did not wish to tell a story or to solve a problem. He represents the idea of the Fall of Man and the first shedding of blood; and he foreshadows the Redemption. There is no unity of action in the strict sense of the word, such as is found in Greek tragedy. The episodes do not follow each other in causal relation; but to the medieval mind the unity consisted in the idea of the Fall and the Redemption. The unity is not dramatic, but philosophic and religious. The first two scenes taken by themselves are not only the stuff that dramas are made of, but also they are dramatic and artistic. It is very doubtful, however, that a playwright of the twelfth century would have thought of presenting them alone as a work of dramatic art without adding the last episode of the prophets, which is not material suitable for the theatre. There is dramatic art of high quality in this play; but it is subordinate to the religious idea. It is not in accordance with canons of dramatic art but in accordance with the religious idea that the play has been constructed.

The Last Judgment—the most terrible and the most vital fact in the medieval conception of the universe—is the climax of many religious dramas. The literal interpretation of this event was never questioned. The idea was constantly held before the people by the clergy. Lives were regulated according to this belief. The Last Judgment was a fact as inevitable as death. Men heard it preached; they saw it depicted in stained glass windows and carved over the western portals of the cathedral. The passer-by merely had to raise his eyes and there broke in upon his vision the climax of his own personal drama depicted with all its tragic emotion. Whether he would be in the company of joyful souls singing as they ascended into eternal life or whether he would be in the tortured crowd of damned souls whipped by horrid devils into the jaws of Hell, what would be the dénouement of his own drama, he knew not. If the picture in glass, on canvas or in stone aroused tragic emotions, what must have been the effect of this scene enacted on the stage!

The playwright of the Middle Ages never had realized that drama often portrays the clash of two contending forces; but he constantly put the struggle between good and evil, God and the Devil, on the stage. By fortuitous circumstances, he could not escape treating the most dramatic of all themes and portraying the struggle, not of a manifestation of good and evil, but of the personification of Good and Evil. Almost every serious play of the Middle Ages presents the struggle of Heaven against Hell for the erring soul of weak human beings baffled by the enigma of life. The themes of Greek tragedy grow pale in comparison to the theme of medieval tragedy. And herein lies the weakness of medieval drama: the theme is too great, too mysterious. As art transcends nature, so certain thoughts and dreams of men transcend art. The mystery of life and of death and of the hereafter cannot be portrayed without losing much of the mystery.

II

The form of medieval drama which resembles the modern form most closely is the miracle play, which had come into existence by the beginning of the twelfth century. About 1100 a lost drama in honor of Saint Catherine was played at Dunstable. During this century Hilarius, probably an Englishman, wrote his *Miracle of Saint Nicholas* in Latin and French.

In this early play, a Barbarian King, according to the stage directions, gathers together his property and commends it to the care of the image of Saint Nicholas. He then speaks sixteen lines explaining what he is doing. Another pantomimic scene follows in which robbers, "finding the door open and no guard," steal the treasure. The Barbarian King returns. He discovers that his treasure is gone. Addressing the image, he expresses his rage and grief in a more or less comic manner. Saint Nicholas, himself, then goes to the robbers and threatens to announce their crime to the people. In pantomime once more, the robbers restore the treasure and the Barbarian King finds it. Thereupon, he breaks out in rejoicing and praise and gives thanks to the image. Saint Nicholas appears to him, and, in a few words, tells the Barbarian King to praise God, not him. The Barbarian King is converted to Christianity.

The situation is dramatic but the scenes lack development. They are finished before the audience can grasp their full significance. The medieval playwright rarely knew how to develop entirely the dramatic possibilities of his successive scenes. He is either summary or prolix in his treatment of the separate scenes.

About 1205, Bodel, a Frenchman, dramatized the same story. His *Saint Nicholas* opens with an account of the story by a preacher, which serves as a prologue, although the action of the play departs from the synopsis. A Pagan King captures in battle a Christian who possesses an image of Saint Nicholas. The Christian asserts that this image will safeguard all property. Thereupon, the King places it over his treasure to test its power. Robbers, hearing this fact advertised, promptly steal the treasure; but Saint Nicholas makes them give up their ill-gotten wealth and the pagans turn Christian.

Bodel invented scenes of gambling and drinking on the part of the robbers at an inn which are not found in the story as told in the prologue. These scenes are very long and show the influence of the medieval taste for realism and comedy. They are connected with the plot, since the inability of the robbers to pay their bill motivates the theft. But the scenes in which the pagan kings are summoned to battle, one after the other, have nothing to do with the plot. The episodes showing the preparation for battle and the battle itself are scarcely necessary even as exposition. Yet one would be sorry to lose the grotesque scene in which the King consults the pagan idol which laughs and then weeps, thereby foreshadowing, in a manner not unlike the cryptic oracles in Greek tragedy, the victory of the King and his conversion to Christianity.

The addition of all these scenes and the recession of the point of attack to the beginning of the story are indicative of the development which drama was undergoing. Bodel's version is much longer than the earlier play of Hilarius. The point of attack is too early; but, once Bodel's plot begins, there is more suspense, as he introduces the idea that the King will torture the Christian, if the treasure is stolen and if it is not restored. There is more dramatic action in the later play; but, as is so often the case in medieval drama, the secondary and even undramatic scenes are given more space than the scenes of dramatic conflict. The principal rôles are not well handled and all the interest latent in the plot is not aroused. Hilarius, even with his humorous touch, emphasized the miracle. Bodel overshadows the miracle with realistic scenes, humor and development of plot. Hilarius reduced the essential elements of the story to the simplest terms. Bodel expanded even non-essential elements.

Much more dramatic, from the modern point of view, is Rutebeuf's *Miracle de Théophile*. It is an early dramatization in the thirteenth century of the story of a man who, like Faust, sold his soul to the devil. The situation is undeniably dramatic.

The action actually plunges *in medias res* and has a quick exposition. Théophile, in a monologue, tells how he has given all his goods to the poor but is abandoned by his Bishop and by God. He goes to Salatin "who spoke to the devil when he wished." Salatin promises him aid, if he will renounce his allegiance to God. Théophile agrees. Salatin conjures up the Devil and arranges an interview between Théophile and him. Théophile sells his soul to Satan and gives him a written agreement. The Bishop immediately restores to Théophile his prebend; and Théophile boasts to his former colleagues of his return to power. Suddenly and without sufficient motivation, he repents and prays to Notre Dame. This is the longest scene in the play and was probably the climax for the medieval audience.

The modern spectator would be interested in the psychological reason for repentance. The medieval spectator was content with the repentance itself because it was the great factor in his conception of life and death. The scene between Notre Dame and the Devil, which would be carefully developed by a more modern playwright, is inartistically brief. Notre Dame utterly routs the defiant Satan by the one threat: "I will trample on thy belly." Satan gives her the letter. Théophile has the Bishop read the letter aloud so that "all people who have not perceived such trickery may not be deceived."

A further advance in the art of playwriting is evident in *Une Femme Que Notre Dame Garda d'Estre Arse* (*A Woman Whom Notre Dame Kept from Being Burned*), produced in the fourteenth century.

The play opens with a short scene in which Guillaume and his daughter set out to the harvest fields. The wife Guibour and her son-in-law Aubin start to go to the church. Their neighbors insinuate that Guibour is in love with Aubin, although their innocence is plain from their conversation. A friend informs Guibour of the scandalous gossip; and the poor woman, distracted, hires two harvesters to hide in the cellar and strangle Aubin when he goes down. Guibour pretends a sudden illness and sends the unlucky Aubin into the cellar for wine. The murder, contrary to usual medieval practice, takes place behind the scenes but the body is brought up by the murderers and laid in a bed. Her husband and daughter return for dinner. They make sport of the supposedly sleeping, lazy Aubin. This dramatist knows the tragic effect of grim comedy at such a moment. The daughter discovers her husband's death. The neighbors rush in at the outcries of grief; but the bailiff is suspicious when he hears of the sudden death. He comes just as the daughter is weeping over the coffin and begins a cross-examination. He orders the coffin opened and discovers marks on the neck. He immediately arrests the whole family. Guibour confesses to save her husband and daughter, swearing truthfully that her love for Aubin was a mother's love. The father and daughter are set free. Aubin's brother demands justice. Sentence is passed, the stake is ready, but Guibour prays to Notre Dame as she is bound to the stake. God sends Notre Dame to the rescue just as the flames spring up. In vain, Aubin's brother rages; the fire will not burn. Notre Dame forbids the flames to touch Guibour. The bailiff recognizes the miracle, and the woman is set free. This would be the end of a modern play, but the medieval playwright shows Guibour living a humble, charitable life. The play ends with a scene from a second narrative source, in which God and the saints appear to Guibour and celebrate mass. Guibour then enters a convent.

The playwright has learned how to handle his narrative source in order to construct a dramatic plot. Gautier de Coincy in the narrative merely says in two lines that the woman hears that she is accused of being her son-in-law's mistress; but these two lines are skilfully dramatized. The narrative version treats the action as taking place during several weeks; but the drama compresses the first scenes into a few hours. The arrest, the investigation, the confession all had to be developed from comparatively few lines.

It is almost unnecessary to point out the dramatic elements in this plot. The preparation is skilful and the careful arrangement of scenes produces an exciting climax. The dramatic contrast of the laughing daughter trying to awaken her dead husband; the prayer of Guibour interrupted by the bailiff hastening the execution; the anger of the brother when Notre Dame, invisible to him, quenches the flames; all show theatrical skill. For the medieval audience the arrival of Notre Dame, just at the climax, was a great *coup de théâtre*.

At first glance it seems as if the dénouement of the miracle play is merely an ending brought about by a god from a machine and is similar in this respect to the ending of certain Greek tragedies in which the Gordian knot of the plot is conveniently untied by a character of superhuman power. In Greek tragedies, such as *Philoctetes* and *Orestes,* and in New Comedy, the god or catastrophic character actually prevents an unhappy ending and changes the course of events, thereby keeping the plot, as it has been constructed, from becoming a blind-alley theme. This is not the case in the medieval drama. In many miracle plays the whole plot aims to bring about the appearance of the Virgin. Instead of being a mere catastrophic goddess from the machine to bring about the desired ending, her entrance is a *coup de théâtre*, the great dramatic climax. Many of these plots would be difficult to bring to an end. Our modern sense of justice is shocked by the fact that revolting crimes are pardoned because of repentant prayers offered by a criminal to the Virgin; but, just as it was a mark of greatest faith to believe the impossible, so in these scenes the greater the act of forgiveness, the more artistic and dramatic it seemed to the medieval audience. Aristotle considered the ending in which vice was punished and virtue rewarded as less tragic and hence less artistic than the unhappy ending. But the majority of theatre-goers in his time, as he admits, preferred a happy ending. The miracle play, by its very nature, had to satisfy this desire on the part of the medieval audience. The dramatist was relieved from having to devise a means to untie a knotty problem. The Greek god from a machine sometimes produced an illogical ending and broke the chain of cause and effect. The medieval goddess from the machine brought about a dénouement which was inevitable and logical to the mind of the faithful and to the believers in miracles. The importance attached to this scene is fully attested by the fact that the intervention of the Virgin is often brought into the play even though it is not necessary to the plot. Again, technique is subordinated to the religious idea; yet the French authors of miracle plays of the fourteenth century were learning a real art of playwrighting.

The climax of the miracles, however, is not always brought about by the intervention of the Virgin. In the miracle of the *Marquise de la Gaudine*, the heroine has been unjustly accused of infidelity to her husband; and she is saved from being burned by a champion who overcomes her accuser and forces him to confess the truth. The Virgin appears to the Marquise and tells her she will be vindicated, and also comes to assure her champion that the Marquise is innocent. No real miracle occurs.

The transition from such plays to the purely profane drama in which there is no divine intervention is easy. Thus in *Griseldis,* (1395) there is no supernatural power or divine character to alter the development of the plot. The story is dramatized in the usual medieval fashion. The early point of attack, unnecessary episodes, all the events, including the birth of two children, are found as usual on the stage. Yet when the dramatist keeps to his subject, the testing of the patience of Griseldis by her husband, the resulting conflict between two human wills produce an impression far more modern than that of medieval plays in which the dramatist calls upon divine intervention to solve his plot. In invoking such aid the medieval dramatist was devout. He was not inartistic through inability; but, inasmuch as he did not take the liberty to solve human problems in a human way, his mind was trammelled artistically. These plays in which divine intervention occurs are really nothing but representations of the idea that no matter what you do, if you repent, the wrong will be righted and you will be saved. The situation and setting are varied. The dramatist was not free to vary the ending to suit varying situation or character.

With the advent of the strictly profane drama, although the structure of drama remains the same and although the ending is still happy, the dramatist was free to work out his ending as he saw best. With this liberty came the opportunity to create the dénouement, although centuries will roll by before dramatists take much advantage of their liberty. Creative power as regards both plot and ending was practically lacking from the earliest times of the medieval period down to the seventeenth century. The playwright followed his narrative source as a rule. He only added dialogue. He expanded certain situations but he rarely invented them. At most he developed realistic scenes. This liberty gained by the writer of profane plays was almost entirely potential. His plays did not have the monotonous ending brought about by divine intervention. In the early sixteenth century the plays became more profane and the dénouements were varied in respect to the means by which they were affected; but the happy ending, which pointed a moral or illustrated the grace of God, still remained.

The *Empereur Qui Tua Son Nepveu* (*The Emperor Who Killed His Nephew*) is called a morality but is really a miracle play. The initial cause of the action presented an old emperor who gives up his power to his nephew. The nephew violates a young girl and the emperor kills him. One feels that a tragedy is inevitable but the emperor is the hero and the play does not have a tragic ending. The emperor is dying and is refused the sacrament. He is allowed only to see the chalice; but the host comes forth from the chalice and enters his mouth. All present recognize the miracle and the infinite grace of God who pardons the crime. Once more a playwright has written his play in order to arrive at a miracle as a happy climax.

In the morality of *Une Pauvre Fille Villageoise* (*A Poor Village Girl*) (1536) no divine miracle occurs; but, although the situation is tragic, a psychological miracle brings a completely happy ending. The lord of a village wants to possess a young girl. To save her chastity she bids her father cut off her head. He is about to do so, when the lord arrives and is so overcome by the spectacle that he places a wreath of flowers as a "crown of chastity" on the young girl's head, and makes the father his steward. His valet is also converted to a moral life. The potential tragedy becomes a morality. Such situations will have a tragic dénouement only after the revival of classical tragedy in France when the aim of drama will be more to arouse emotions and less to teach a moral. It is not until 1571 that Bretog will write the *Amour d'un Serviteur envers Sa Maîtres* (*Love of a Servant for His Mistress*) and produce realistic, non-classical tragedy.

These miracle plays cover a wide range of subjects, and their variety is in strong contrast to the monotony of the plays on Biblical stories. They contain many of the faults of medieval technique; but they are often strikingly similar to plays of the nineteenth century in the situations presented on the stage. The sources of Maeterlinck's *Sister Beatrice* and Reinhardt's *Miracle* are among them. Others, such as *Griseldis* and *The Woman Whom Notre Dame Kept from Being Burned*, have been produced in adaptations for the modern stage. Many other themes of these plays might have been presented in the theatre of the nineteenth century if they had been modernized by a Sardou or a Dumas; but the medieval synthesis was not revived until the twentieth century, when Reinhardt began to bring the audience and actor into closer relationship, in such productions as the *Miracle*, by abolishing the picture frame proscenium, enlarging the playing space, decorating the whole theatre to represent a cathedral, mingling the actors and spectators, and appealing to the emotions by spectacle.

III

The comic element soon developed in the serious, sacred drama as a result of the desire to make the plays a realistic transcript of life. Scenes such as the three Marys purchasing oil from the merchant and the dialogue of the soldiers guarding the cross offered an opportunity for the introduction of commonplace details even in liturgical plays. It is but a short step from the commonplace to the grotesque and from the grotesque to the comic. The same spirit which produced grotesque, comic, even indecent sculpture on the medieval cathedral introduced these elements into religious plays. Nothing was too sacred to escape burlesque in the Feast of the Innocents, the Feast of the Fools and the Feast of the Asses which consisted, in part, of processions, a kind of comic mumming and even a parody of the rituals and sermons. The Christmas Merrymakers were responsible for the *Second Shepherds' Play*. Elements of pagan festivals can be found in these Christian Saturnalia.

The comic element also made its appearance in the character of the ranting Herod and, one may even say, in the characters of the ass and other animals in the early nativity plays. Balaam's ass was likewise a source of humor. By 1170, Herrad of Lands-

berg, Abbess of Hohenburg, was denouncing the scenes of buf
foonery in the nativity plays.

The devil was first a serious antagonist, but the costume and
appearance of this character were grotesque and grimly humorous. The defeats suffered by this enemy of mankind began to
give an impression of stupidity. Flouted stupidity of an antagonist provokes scornful laughter. The comic element is an inevitable outgrowth of the character of a villain. He is a caricature of the ideal, and the grotesque humor inherent in a caricature
may rise to the surface in spite of the playwright. Barabas in
the *Jew of Malta* and Shylock in *The Merchant of Venice* are
rôles in which the tragic and comic elements are so inseparable
that the general effect depends upon the interpretation of the
actor and the mood of the audience. We moderns find less
humor in them than did the Elizabethans.

Because of the influence of the rôle of the devil in France and
of the vice in England and because of the development of
realistic scenes into comic scenes, tragedy and comedy are intermingled in most serious plays of the Middle Ages. The playwrights began to realize that their serious scenes of great length
had to be interspersed with humorous episodes, not in order to
relieve the artistic tragic tension or to produce dramatic contrast
or a conflict of emotions, but to arouse the flagging interest of
the audience. The author of the *Mystère de Sainte Geneviève*
introduces grotesque cripples, who complain of their ills and are
cured of them by the saint, for the distinct purpose of comic
relief in the true sense of the term, or, as he says, "in order
that the performance may be less boring and more pleasing."
The delightful *Second Shepherds' Play,* whatever its origin may
be, serves the same purpose in the Towneley cycle.

Thus the practice of introducing comic relief did not grow up
as the result of an artistic ideal. Shakespeare introduced comic
scenes into his tragedies because it was a medieval practice which
he inherited and accepted. In the late eighteenth and early nineteenth centuries, the false interpretation of this practice was
devised by admirers of Shakespeare in order to defend him from

the criticism of classicists for having mingled tragedy and comedy. The phrase "comic relief" was coined. It meant relieving tragic tension which would become too painful, if continued, by introducing scenes of comedy. Unfortunately for those who believe in this theory, certain scenes of so-called comic relief, such as the Porter's scene in *Macbeth,* are played not to relieve but to intensify the tragic tension. How Shakespeare intended this scene to be played is a matter for conjecture; but he certainly was not afraid of making his tragedies too tragic, although he introduced the Grave-diggers' scene in *Hamlet* to get a laugh—and for no other reason. Neither psychologically nor historically is there any justification for the theory of comic relief as interpreted by its modern exponents. Comic effects do not relieve but intensify tragedy. Otherwise they are as inartistic as is the scene of the Grave-diggers in *Hamlet.*

The pagan merrymakings and festivals celebrating the return of spring are probably the ultimate source of such plays as *Li Jus Adan ou de la Feuillée (The Play of Adam or of the Bower)* (1262) and *Robin et Marion* (1283-5?) probably written by Adam de la Hale, certainly written by a man also known as Adam le Bossu. *Adam or the Bower* is composed, by chance, in the general style and form of Aristophanic comedy, although there was no real atavistic influence since the works of Aristophanes were entirely unknown. *Robin et Marion* is a kind of charming opera. The plot deals with a pastoral love story and the action is interspersed with songs and dances. Written in the thirteenth century, when profane playwrights had learned how to handle a plot with a fair degree of artistry, these plays are by no means crude specimens of drama. They are the only extant examples of this form of humorous play and they did not exert any influence on the later development of comedy. To find one source of the dramaturgy of Molière one must go not to such plays as these or to the comic scenes of serious medieval dramas but rather to the farce.

It is possible that Roman comedy had an indirect influence on the farce. In the fourth century *Querolus or Aulularia* was composed containing passages from Plautus and Virgil; but the work was not intended for the stage. It cannot be proved that Hrowswitha's pious comedies of the tenth century were intended for the stage, although they were inspired by a desire to imitate in a moral manner the "immoral" plays of Terence. The two so-called comedies, *Amphitryo or Geta* and *Querolus or Aulularia,* of the twelfth century and ascribed to Vitalis Blesensis, are not plays but narratives. Medieval writers such as Chaucer and Dante accepted the definitions of tragedy and comedy based upon the kind of ending and the social status of the characters, but they applied these terms to narratives as well as to plays.

There were, however, monologues and dialogues in Latin, composed for recitation by one actor, such as *De Clericis et Rustico,* and the *Comœdia Babionis* which may have been played by several actors. This "comedy," whether recited by one or several actors or intended to be read, is not to be overlooked in the history of the farce. It is composed in verse; and, on the margin, the names of the character speaking and of the person to whom he is speaking are indicated. The play opens with Babio extolling the charms of his step-daughter Viola and bewailing the fact that the knight Croceus is seeking her hand. Viola pretends she cares naught for Croceus. Babio's servant Fodius is in love with Pecula, his master's wife. He hopes to get rid of Viola. Babio orders a feast grudgingly, in the manner of Plautine misers, for Croceus and his parasitical friends. When they arrive, Babio announces that Viola is not visible because she is ill. However, she appears and Croceus takes her away.

The second part of the play begins with Fame, an allegorical Virgilian character, telling Babio of the infidelity of his wife with Fodius. He accuses them but they deny the charge. Babio pretends to go away; and, when he returns unexpectedly, he is beaten as a thief. After a month he repeats the trick and undergoes even severer punishment. At last he becomes a monk.

The author of this work certainly knew Plautus, as is shown not only by his punning in Plautine fashion but also by the scene in which the feast is ordered. The plot, however, is not classical but medieval. It is a typical situation of the farce with the stupid husband and the unfaithful wife who outwits and beats him. The ending, showing the lovers triumphant, although one of them is married, is the usual outcome of such situations in medieval comedy and in such plays as Machiavelli's *Mandragola* and Molière's *George Dandin* which are highly developed medieval farces. The *Comœdia Babionis,* itself, is more complicated and more developed than farces in the vernacular. If this work is a real play, the author must have found his inspiration in Plautus or in narrative comedies founded upon Plautus.

There is little of classical comedy left in this *Comœdia,* for the author employs a medieval method in dealing with a medieval theme. Whether or not the play was played or intended to be played, at least the writers of farces in the vulgar tongue did not have to invent the form or material they employ. They only had to translate or imitate such works and have them acted. Not until the fifteenth century will farces be found showing a development in plot or technique beyond the *Comœdia Babionis*. The fact that there is no other extant work in Latin exactly similar to this comedy is by no means evidence that others did not exist. Manuscripts of medieval plays were extremely perishable. Liturgical dramas and mystery plays would be more likely to survive in the hands of pious monks, but profane comedy would survive almost by chance.

The farce is a short play in one act which deals with marriage, marital misadventures, politics, religion and social satire. *Li Garchons et li Aweules* (*The Boy and the Blind Man*) in Flemish of the thirteenth century is the earliest extant farce and presents an episode of a blind beggar robbed by a boy. It is amusing but very primitive in its construction. Many such plays must have been lost and not until the fifteenth century did a collection of farces survive. These plays represent all degrees of complication of situation from the humorous monologue of the *Franc Archier de Baignolet* (*Free Archer of Baignolet*), to the well-developed plot of *Maistre Pierre Pathelin* by Alécis. But the plot never attained the complexity of certain Latin comedies and later comedies of the Renaissance.

The later farces, however, bring new elements into medieval drama. As they are at least unmoral, their construction is unmodified by didactic or religious considerations. In comedy alone the medieval playwright was untrammelled. He shaped and developed the situations on lines which seemed to him to be artistic. So far as can be discovered, the writer of comedy was less inclined to dramatize narratives, whereas the serious playwright sought his plot and its development in scenes from sacred or semi-sacred narratives. The very nature of the farce precluded the introduction of long, rambling scenes. The principal characters are never crowded out of the action by voluble persons who have little or nothing to do with the plot. There are never more than six characters in French farces and everyone in the play is indispensable to the action. Not until the sixteenth century in England will Heywood introduce a larger number of rôles into the farce.

The exposition is swift, for the situation, at the beginning, is always very simple. No complicated relationships, previous events, concealed identities or long-lost children have to be explained as was the case in Latin comedy. The *Farce d'un Gentilhomme*, also known as *Naudet*, illustrates how quickly the exposition is given and how subtly the initial cause of the action is explained. Lison, the wife of Naudet, begins:

LISON

Am I not out of luck to have married such a man.

NAUDET

What? Is my shirt dirty? Well now, if it is, I am sorry. Do you know what I am laughing at? At the lord of our village who goes carousing around at night.

LISON

What do you know, you wicked fellow?

NAUDET

What do I know? Ha. That's a good one. What do I know? Who would know? I saw him.

LISON
  When, when?
NAUDET
  Last night.
LISON
  Where, where?
NAUDET
  Standing there, under the gable of our house, where he was with a girl.
LISON
  Do you know who she was?
NAUDET
  Oh yes. I knew them both.
LISON
  Do you mean it was me?
NAUDET
  Softly, softly! I'm not saying a word about it.
LISON
  I promise you, by my faith, that if he hears you, he'll have you put in prison.
NAUDET
  Well, I'm not talking about it, Lison.

The situation is sufficiently plain. The Gentleman arrives and sends Naudet away on several errands; but the troublesome husband always returns, inopportunely for the Gentleman. Finally he sends Naudet to the manor with a message for his Lady. When Naudet arrives, she is not loath to receive the advances of the rustic. The Gentleman grows suspicious at Naudet's absence. When he returns to the manor, Naudet informs him that sauce for the goose is sauce for the gander. In the circumstances, the dénouement is rather peaceful but is typical of the farce.

The farce of the *Poulailler* (*Hen-House*) shows a development in the art of complicating the plot, for the dramatist takes a similar situation and, by adding a second Gentleman and his wife, is able to introduce many more comic scenes. This play

opens with two Gentlemen discussing the question of receiving
the favors of the miller's wife. The second scene presents the
miller and his wife. They are involved in financial difficulties;
and, in order to get money, the wife proposes a scheme to extract
the needed sum from her two gallants. The miller is to pretend
to go on a journey and return and catch the two Gentlemen with
his wife. Thus the whole plot is motivated and an obligatory
scene is foreshadowed. Motivation and foreshadowing are rare
in medieval drama. Also, the dramatist does not rush immediately to the obligatory scene as is generally the case with the
farce. The action develops smoothly and gradually.

They hear the first Gentleman coming. The miller pretends
to sleep, while his wife makes the bargain. With difficulty they
awaken the miller and give him the money. The Gentleman
leaves. The second Gentleman arrives, and the same game is
played on him. The dramatist knew that in such scenes repetition is humorous. When the second gallant has departed to
await an hour propitious for his return, the miller hides. The
first Gentleman returns; but his tête-à-tête over the little supper
is interrupted by the arrival of the second lover; and he conceals
himself in the hen-house above the room, and dolefully watches
his friend supplant him at the table. When the husband thinks
that the comedy is about to turn into a tragedy for him, he
pretends to return and the second gallant hastily climbs the
ladder and joins his friend. The two shamefaced Gentlemen are
forced to witness the husband devour the supper they had provided.

But the dramatist has not yet exhausted the possibilities of
the situation. The miller is now in a merry mood. He sends
his wife to bring the spouse of the first Gentleman; and then he
sends for the wife of the second Gentleman. The miller proceeds
to make love to the wife of the first Gentleman, who looks on
from above and finally starts to climb down the ladder but is
restrained by his friend who has nothing to gain by being discovered. When the wife of the second Gentleman arrives, the
miller turns his amorous attention to her and now it is the turn

of the second Gentleman to rage and listen to the good advice he has just given his friend. At last the miller investigates the noise in the hen-house, and drags the unfortunate gallants down. He lets them sadly go their way when they promise to give him outright the money they have loaned him.

Whatever one may think of the morality of the play, the technique is undeniably clever. Not a word is wasted, not a possibility of comic effect is lost. It is not great art but it is artistic, and, on the whole, better constructed than most serious medieval plays. With the French playwrights of the Middle Ages able to handle a situation with such deftness and directness, there is little wonder that modern French dramatists became masters in the art of theatrical legerdemain.

Such is the medieval comedy of situation in its most highly developed form; but the *Maistre Pierre Pathelin* offers subtlety and wit in place of the broad humor of the usual farce. Also, the character of Pathelin, which dominates the action, is drawn with such clearness that his name has become a synonym for wheedling, flattering, sharp lawyers.

The play begins with a scene between Pathelin and Guillemette, his wife. They are out of money and their clothes are threadbare; but Pathelin boasts that he will get cloth for new outfits for both of them. He hies himself to the Draper's shop. They exchange polite greetings, and Pathelin begins his subtle attack by praising the Draper's father. "What a wise merchant he was! By God, your face is the very picture of his." The Draper immediately begs Pathelin to sit down. The lawyer continues his flattery, and, casually fingering a bit of cloth, says: "What a fine piece of cloth." He grows more and more enthusiastic; and with no little haggling, the cloth is bought—but not paid for. The merchant is wary about credit; but, when Pathelin invites him to come and collect the money and eat a roast goose, the Draper consents and says he will bring the cloth. Pathelin, protesting that he cannot burden the Draper with the package, marches off with the cloth under his arm, hinting to the audience that the merchant will never get a sou from him, while the Draper chuckles over the price he has obtained.

Pathelin reports to his wife what he has done. The audience is in delightful comic suspense, because the fingerposts are pointing to a real clash of wits between the two sharpers. A fine balance is kept between anticipatory curiosity and certain knowledge of what is going to happen, when as Pathelin says, the Draper comes "braying around" for his pay.

On the arrival of his guest, Pathelin jumps into bed; and his wife tells the dumbfounded Draper that the idea of Pathelin having bought any cloth is preposterous, for he has been sick unto death for weeks. The Draper cannot believe his ears or eyes; but, after going away once, he returns only to find Pathelin feigning a raving, staring madness. He finally believes that the devil himself tricked him, just as every one in the medieval audience would have believed had he been in the Draper's place.

The plot then takes a new, but perfectly logical turn. The Draper hales his shepherd into court for having eaten several of his sheep, whereupon the shepherd engages none other than Pathelin to defend him. Again one awaits with comic suspense the meeting of the two sharpers. When court convenes, Pathelin, feigning a toothache, covers his face. When the Draper is in the midst of his eloquent speech of accusation, Pathelin springs a *coup de théâtre* by disclosing his face, whereat the Draper looses his wits; and, forgetting the stolen sheep, he begins to accuse Pathelin of stealing cloth. The judge is stupefied and the situation becomes more and more entangled and absurdly humorous. The judge questions them all and begs for sanity as they talk first of sheep and then of cloth. Finally, when the shepherd, coached by Pathelin, responds to all questions by bleating like a sheep, the judge leaves in despair. Pathelin then denies absolutely to the Draper that he ever bought any cloth of him; and the poor Draper can only rush away, saying to Pathelin: "I am going to your house to see, by Heaven, if you are here or there." The clever Pathelin has won his game. But when he demands his fee from the shepherd, the rustic only replies by bleating, as this mad-cap comedy comes to a close.

Since the medieval Frenchman Guillaume Alécis could produce this play, there is little wonder that Molière wrote masterpieces and relied to a great extent on the technique of the farce.

CHAPTER VII

ENGLISH MEDIEVAL DRAMA. KYD.
MARLOWE. SHAKESPEARE

WHEN English drama emerged as a distinct national art in the fourteenth century it differed in certain respects from French drama. In England the miracle play, such as the French *Miracles de Notre Dame,* dealing with romantic concrete stories, was not popular. In spite of the *Second Shepherds' Play,* which is a delightful little comedy, the farce does not seem to have been either indigenous or even popular until Heywood adapted French originals to the English stage. The two native forces at work in shaping drama in the fourteenth, fifteenth and early sixteenth centuries are the cyclic plays on the Bible, and the morality presenting abstract plots and characters. The purely abstract morality play existed in France; but the French miracle play, with its wide range of situations and characters, over-shadowed the morality as a force in dramatic art. English drama, aside from certain episodes in the cycles, was tedious and monotonous in comparison with French plays until Continental influences crossed the channel and began to instill new life into the morality plays.

The origin of the plot and characters of the morality is found in such allegorical works as *Psychomachia* composed by Prudentius in the fifth century, and, in later times, in the *Romance of the Rose.* The allegorical machinery of the *Psychomachia,* dealing with a conflict between vices and virtues representing abstract characters, was taken over by the serious drama. Perhaps the lost *Paternoster Play* of York, "in which play" we are told, "all manner of vices and sins were held up to scorn and the virtues were held up to praise," represented the primitive type of the

morality in which, as in the work of Prudentius, there were con-
flicts between vices and virtues, without Man as the bone of
contention or hero. The second phase of the development would
be the introduction of the hero, and Mr. Chambers is probably
right in his conjecture that Vicious in a pageant given in 1469 at
Beverly was probably a typical representative of frail humanity.
Thus one of the vices may have furnished the necessary transition to a hero, if this pageant is at all reminiscent of earlier moral
plays.

When the history of the separate moral play actually begins
for us with the fragmentary *Pride of Life* (*ca.* 1410) and *The
Castle of Perseverance* (1400-1440), the form is highly developed;
and any future changes to be noted are developments away from
the abstract, religious morality towards secular, concrete situations and characters. There are three motives on which the plot
of the moral plays is based: the Conflict of Vices and Virtues;
the Coming of Death; the Debate either of the Heavenly Graces
or of the Soul and Body. The prologue of *The Pride of Life*
points to a debate of the latter type, but no example of this
motive has been preserved. These three elements of the moral
play are used in different combinations or alone as the basis of
the action. *The Castle of Perseverance* employs all of them.
The famous *Everyman,* a late translation from the Dutch,
dramatizes the Coming of Death. Indeed, this element and the
Debate are merely dénouements to the conflict. The Debate, in
which the soul of the sinner was saved, served as the required
happy ending of the medieval drama. The Coming of Death is
used only in *Everyman* as a tragic dénouement unrelieved by
any sense of a happier future. In *The Pride of Life,* the King
of Life, the hero of the play, is slain by Death; but the tragedy
of the episode is mitigated by a scene indicated in the prologue
in which Our Lady intercedes successfully for the soul of the
King. Tragedy with an unhappy ending was not a medieval
form of drama.

The Conflict of the Vices and Virtues became the mainspring
of the plot of moralities, especially after 1450. Professor Ramsey

has analyzed the normal form of the Conflict type of moralities as follows:

> Humanity or Mankind is presented surrounded on the one hand by certain Vices, on the other by certain Virtues. The Vices are assisted by the Devil or his agents or else combine in themselves the functions of Vices plus Devils or Tempters; and the Virtues are similarly assisted by God or divine agents, or themselves act as both Virtues and the agents of God. Humanity is innocent and usually inclines to the side of the Virtues. A conflict ensues between the parties of good and evil, which takes the form of strife for the favor of Humanity. The powers of evil successfully accomplish their temptation. Humanity joins their side, and lives in sin for a season. Another conflict arises; this time the powers of good advance to the attack by persuading Humanity to repentance. Humanity is convicted of sin, and, after exhibiting the proper marks of penitence, is reclaimed once more to the side of virtue. The plot was often doubled by depicting a renewed assault by the Vices, a renewed fall and life of sin by Humanity, and a renewed repentance; in this case one of the two battles might be made subordinate to the other, or turned into a mere skirmish.

This scenario, which with minor modifications would fit any English morality, has certain potential dramatic features. The action develops from an exposition showing the hero in a state of innocence through a conflict to a dénouement. There is dramatic progression and a peripeteia. The skeleton of a play exists. But the skeleton lacks life, just as the abstract characters representing Mankind, Perseverance, Gluttony, etc., are devoid of human qualities in the typical moral play. The personages are one-sided. The Virtues represent one virtue and the Vices but one vice. The plots and characters are monotonous. Although the imagination of the playwright was not hampered by historical or sacred sources, the writers of the moral plays showed little originality or variation of story and characters.

The earliest extant morality, *The Pride of Life*, has characters concrete enough to be designated as the Queen, the Bishop; but the later plays, such as *The Castle of Perseverance* and *Wisdom and Mankind,* contain only abstractions. Furthermore, the plots of these moralities are theological. The secularization of the morality came about when the characters ceased to be abstractions and became types of human beings. This development can be observed in Skelton's *Magnificence* (*ca.* 1516) in which the theme is the preservation of worldly prosperity instead of the usual theme of salvation of the soul. The hero is not an abstract Mankind or Man, but is a typical prince. The satire is directed at actual persons, not at mankind. Yet *Magnificence* still retains the construction of the morality in its plot.

In *Nice Wanton,* the scene in which Dalila begins her downward career by playing dice is represented; but, after a long interval of time has elapsed, Dalila enters in a deplorable condition of mind and body. The playwright has suppressed the realistic scenes in which her downfall is accomplished. Worldly Shame acts as messenger of the news of the death of Dalila and Ismael; and Barnabas reports the repentance of the two before their death.

The development of realism and of comedy in the morality was very slow. Such elements were really out of keeping with the aim of such plays; and it seems that the playwrights actually avoided realistic scenes by using the device of reporting and not representing certain scenes. This procedure is exceedingly rare in medieval drama and cannot be ascribed to any feeling for unity of place. In *Nature* and in *The Four Elements,* for example, the episodes in the tavern are kept behind the scenes and the audience is merely told what happens in each case. In the Mary Magdalene episode in the *Digby Plays,* the heroine is as real a person as one finds on the medieval stage; and, although she is tempted by abstract vices, there is a realistic scene in a tavern. However, this is not an example of realism introduced into a moral play, but the machinery of the morality employed in the more concrete Biblical play.

The avoidance of the scene in the tavern, which offered practically the sole opportunity for realism in the morality, also militated against the introduction of comedy which follows naturally in the wake of such realistic scenes. In *Mundus et Infans* the events of 'the hero's sinful career in London are kept off the stage, but Folly's narration of the life in London abounds in realistic and humorous details.

The play of *The Four Elements* also illustrates the growth of the comic element in the later morality. The author has constructed his play in scenes alternately "sad and mery," and makes the remark that "yf ye lyst ye may leve out much of the sad mater." The author of this play does not set a scene in a tavern, but at least he brings the real taverner on the stage to indulge in coarse humor with the abstract Experience, Humanity and others. In *Nature,* such concrete characters as the trull Margery and the taverner are carefully kept off the stage, although we hear of the comic scenes in which they play an important rôle.

The character of the vice, whether developed from an abstraction or from the rôle of the devil, became one of the chief funmakers as the morality turned more and more from serious religious teaching to philosophical subjects and finally into satirical comedy. From this character will spring the merry fools of Elizabethan comedy.

Yet the morality remained stereotyped in spite of these developments which are comparatively slight so far as technique is concerned. The range of characters, situations and scenes is very limited. The tendency toward comedy is marked; but foreign influence had to be brought to bear upon these plays before Elizabethan comedy could come forth from its abstract chrysalis and enmeshing web of allegory.

The morality, however, is important because it was not played by guilds at stated periods in certain districts, but was rather a professional performance taken on tour, unless *The Castle of Perseverance* is anomalous in this respect. This play was acted, according to the prologue, in different towns; and the actors were strolling players instead of worthy tradesmen or pious clerks. Also, these plays, which became more and more secular entertainments, steadily declined in length. Drama of the epic proportions it had assumed in Biblical plays began to be compressed into "the two hours traffic of our stage." Since the length of a play influences the whole construction, this tendency of the moral play toward brevity is important. The rise of the professional actor and the formation of an audience, which wished to be entertained and not merely edified, were contributary causes to the movement toward compactness in drama.

French influence on English drama has almost always been a factor to be taken into account from the earliest times down to the present. There are records of French actors who visited England in 1494 and 1495; and also of six "Mynstrells of France" who came about 1509. The repertory of these companies is unknown; but as the farce was at that time a popular form of entertainment in France, they probably produced some of these gay, cynical comedies in England. By 1535 the famous farce of *Pathelin* was known in England.

Heywood was the first English playwright to hold the sound theory that the aim of drama is to amuse and not to teach. Even his *Pardoner and the Friar* and *The Four P's,* in which there is little or no plot, are plainly written to make people laugh. His *Play of the Weather* shows the influence of the morality in the character of Merry-report, a humorous Vice; but it is comedy without a trace of the didacticism of the morality.

His *Johan Johan* (1533-1534), like the *Second Shepherds' Play,* is a gay farce; but, unlike the episode of the Towneley cycle, it has no connection with any religious play. It is comedy for the sake of comedy. This play is founded in part upon the French farce *Pernet*. It contains a typical farcical situation. Johan Johan opens the play with the boast that he will beat his wife Tyb because she visits the priest Syr Jhan too frequently and tarries too long. When Tyb arrives, Johan calms down very quickly; and it is easy to see who rules the household. Tyb bids her husband invite the priest to come and eat a pie with them. Johan sets out on his errand, grumbling and suspicious. Syr Jhan, however, disarms him by pretending that he is unwilling to accept the invitation because Tyb is angry at him, he alleges, for penances he has imposed upon her. When he has sufficiently duped the husband, the priest accompanies him home. Tyb sends Johan for water with a pail that has a hole in it. He returns with the empty pail in time to interrupt the usual love-making; and he is set to chafing wax to mend the pail, while the lovers sup. Finally, his patience gives way and "they fight by the ears a while, and then the priest and the wife go out of the place," soon to be pursued by the husband who wisely fears to leave them alone.

The technique is that of the highly developed French farce. If the extant version of *Pernet* is the only source of *Johan Johan,* Heywood has considerably improved upon his model. The scene of the supper is only suggested in the French version, and Heywood constructs a very humorous situation out of the idea. The scene between Johan and the priest is also added by the English dramatist. Both in dialogue and in the development of the plot, Heywood shows a skill beyond any of his English contemporaries. He must be given full credit for his ability to handle a situation; but he probably attained some of his skill from reading or seeing French farces. At any rate, English comedy had now freed itself from the unreal atmosphere of the morality. It was ready to develop into the lively realistic comedy of the Elizabethan age, although classical influence was also necessary to produce the finished products of Shakespeare and of Jonson.

The Spanish tragi-comedy entitled *Calisto y Melibea* but generally known as *Celestina* brought still another foreign influence on English drama about 1530 when the play *Calisto and Melibea* was published and perhaps written by Rastell. The original Spanish play, attributed to Fernando de Rojas, had been completed in 1502. It consists of twenty-one acts and is more a romance in dialogue than a play. Nevertheless, it had a wide influence in Europe during the sixteenth century especially in presenting the model of a bawd through the character of Celestina. This famous personage, as well as the situation, is drawn probably from the medieval Latin comedy entitled *Pamphilus,* and from similar characters of classical comedy.

The Spanish play, however, deals with the situation in a manner different from that of Plautus or Terence. The young lover appeals to a servant and through the servant to a bawd for the opportunity of meeting the object of his desires. While in Latin comedy the obstacles separating the lovers arise from extraneous circumstances, in this play it is the modesty of the heroine which must be overcome. Also, in the Spanish play, the love story is not a mere situation kept off the stage and devised for the purpose of creating humorous scenes. The romantic love between Calisto and Melibea is the main interest of the play and is given a tragic ending. Calisto is accidentally killed by a leap from a wall and the heroine commits suicide by throwing herself from a tower. This is romantic drama but designed to teach young people to guard against tricky servants and go-betweens. Celestina herself is killed by two servants who are executed for their crime. Thus little remains of Latin comedy except the initial situation. The tone of the play is romantic and tragic.

The English play *Calisto and Melibea* is drawn from the first four acts. Calisto meets Melibea and declares his love for her, but she repulses him. Through his servant, he enlists the bawd Celestina to plead for him and she gains access to the heroine. Melibea upbraids Celestina for presenting the suit of Calisto; but the old go-between makes her believe that Calisto merely desires Melibea's girdle, which has touched many relics, as a cure for a toothache. Having reached this point where romantic and tragic scenes would develop, the English playwright introduces Melibea's father. He recounts an allegorical dream to Melibea who is so impressed by the warning that she decides to stifle her growing love for Calisto and remain virtuous. Thus the didactic tendency of the Spanish play and of the English morality play brings a possible romantic tragedy to an end which is not tragic nor comic nor artistic, but simply moral. No better example can be cited of the blighting effect of didacticism in dramatic art. The playwright had before him in the Spanish play life-like characters in a dramatic situation, instead of the usual abstract characters in an allegorical situation of the moral plays. He needed only to condense the original in order to bring forth the first English romantic drama. But he failed, dismally.

Classical comedy reached England in translation before 1530 when *Andria* was printed by Rastell under the title *Terens in English*. Latin comedy had been acted in the original by 1520, when Henry VIII had "a goodly comedy of Plautus" staged for the entertainment of French hostages. In schools and colleges the acting of Latin plays was a frequent occurrence. In 1527 the *Menœchmi*, with its situation of mistaken identity, so popular in the Renaissance, was played by the boys of St. Paul's school. These performances were more than extra-curriculum activities, for a rule was passed at Cambridge in 1546 that any student who refused to play a rôle in a tragedy or comedy or who did not attend a performance would be expelled.

A secondary influence of Latin comedy also came from Holland where the humanist William de Volder, known as Gnaphæus, wrote *Acolastus* which was performed at The Hague in 1529. John Palsgrave translated this play and published both the Latin and English versions in 1540. *Acolastus* is the story of the prodigal son treated in the manner of Terence.

The English dramatists did not immediately adopt the complicated plot of Latin comedy. They still employed a simple situation of the medieval farce. In *Thersites* (1537), adapted probably by Heywood from one of Ravisius Textor's dialogues, the principal character is a loutish braggart captain; and the play deals, for the most part, with his cowardice when confronted with a snail and later with a soldier. It resembles the French farce of the *Free Archer of Baignolet* more than a comedy of Plautus or Terence. In *Jacke Jugeler* (1562), the servant Jacke makes Jenkin Careaway believe that he is not himself just as

Mercury tricks Sosia in *Amphitryo*. The play, however, is a mere farce without any of the complications of the original Plautine comedy.

A long-lost child brings about the dénouement of *Misogonus*. The wicked brother gives up his riotous life when the virtuous brother returns from Poland; but the play is much more of a farce and a morality in technique than a Latin comedy. The riotous scenes in the tavern, which were behind the scenes in moral plays, are represented with great realism. The wicked Misogonus is deserted by his boon companions, when he is disinherited; and he repents like the hero of the morality. There are scenes of revelry with courtezans in Plautine comedy, but the hero in Latin comedy is not left in the lurch by his friends nor does he have to mend his ways. It is the old father who relents or repents on the Roman stage; but in *Misogonus* the father is triumphant. *Misogonus* was inspired by *Acolastus* more than by the morality; but the moral play is the ultimate source for such situations and their development. The idea of the prodigal son is not Roman but Christian.

The plots of such plays, remotely connected with classical comedy, make a very different effect than do the plots of Plautus or Terence. Had *Misogonus* been written by a Roman playwright, the hero would have married the courtezan and she would have turned out to be the long-lost child of a worthy citizen. The other episodes in the play belong to the realm of the farce; and the priest, especially, recalls Heywood's Syr Jhan. As was the case in France, the farce was a form too sturdy to be driven off the stage at the first appearance of foreign importations.

These diverse elements, however, are handled with skill; and, while English comedy does not as yet accept the complicated plot, it shows a development in the plotting beyond the farces of Heywood. There are many more episodes in *Misogonus* than in *Johan Johan*, and none of the prolixity and formlessness of the medieval drama. Still more carefully constructed and more classical in its characters is Udall's *Ralph Roister-Doister* (1534-

1541). The play is divided into acts and scenes; and, following a frequent practice of classical comedy, each act begins with a monologue.

The situation, however, is more medieval than classical. Roister-Doister, a boastful coward, is enamored of Dame Custance. Through his parasite Matthew Merrygreeke, he woos her unsuccessfully, for she is faithful to Gawyn Goodluck who is away on a long voyage. When Roister-Doister presses his suit too violently, he and his servant are put to rout by Dame Custance in a rough-and-tumble fight. Gawyn Goodluck returns but not as a *deus ex machina*. His servant reports that he has seen the servant of Roister-Doister bearing gifts to Dame Custance and he suggests that Gawyn investigate the matter. Gawyn learns how the Dame has flouted Roister-Doister who is finally received by them as a friend once more.

In *Gammer Gurton's Needle,* there is naught of classical comedy save the division into acts. The characters are all from the medieval farcical interludes. Gammer Gurton has lost her needle. Diccon, the bedlam or fool, accuses Dame Chat of having taken it. He tells Dame Chat that Gammer Gurton suspects her of stealing her cock. The result is a slapstick fight between the two dames. By similar trickery, Dame Chat is led to beat the village priest in the dark, believing him to be Hodge, Gammer Gurton's servant, who is stealing hens. A trial takes place and it is discovered that Doctor Rat has the broken skull, not Hodge; and the needle is discovered sticking in Hodge's breeches.

In both plays there is just enough plot to carry the five acts but the plots are secondary. The humor lies in the lively characters and the dialogue. The didactic element has disappeared and the classical element is barely visible in the episode of the return of the husband of Dame Custance in *Ralph Roister-Doister*.

The complicated plot depending upon mistaken identity entered English drama when the students of Gray's Inn acted a translation of Aristo's *Suppositi* in 1566. This translation was the work of George Gascoigne and was called *The Supposes*. The whole machinery of Latin-Italianate comedy is contained in this play including the characters, the street-scene, the mistaken identity, the romantic love in the background, and the dénouement through a recognition scene. The heroine appears but once. The lovers do not meet before our eyes. The point of attack is late in the story. The play opens after Erostrato has changed places with his servant in order to be near his mistress in her father's house. Many of the scenes present the usual complications of mistaken identity.

The *Bugbears,* published in 1561, offers a still more complicated plot. This play is a free adaptation of Grazzini's *Spiritata*, together with ideas borrowed from *Gl' Ingannati* and *Andria*. The intricate plot is handled in the usual Italian fashion; and, because of the street-scene, the observance of the unities and the late point of attack, much of the action is off the stage. English playwrights, however, tend to keep the action on the stage when they have learned the art of building complicated plots. In spite of all this foreign influence the Elizabethan stage remains medieval. It represents events to the eye. Indeed, there are two comedies of the classical type in which the action is for the most part on the stage. Pasqualigo's *Fidele* (1575) is notable for the large part played by the lovers and the play was adapted, probably by Anthony Munday, as *The Comedy of Two Italian Gentlemen* (1584). The play is founded on a typically complicated plot dealing with two pairs of lovers and their servants. In the Italian play one of the women is married, and her husband is duped in the manner of the medieval farce. The English version drops out the character of the cuckold which was not so popular in England as on the Continent. A braggart captain, a pedant and a go-between of the Celestina type are the other characters. In spite of the street-scene, the heroines are often on the stage; and there are several scenes between the lovers which are normally off the stage in classical comedy. Mistaken identity through disguise and scenes of incantation are the chief sources of humor; yet the dénouement is not brought about by any discovery, but by the different pairs of lovers becoming reconciled.

Lyly's *Mother Bombie* (*ca.* 1590) offers a similar set of complications. Here there are three pairs of lovers, and they are often on the stage in spite of the presence in the cast of the usual servants and irate parents. A recognition scene clears up the identity of two of the couples and helps to solve the problems. Thus by 1590, the English dramatist was acquainted with all the situations and the characters of classical comedy; but the separation of tragedy and comedy was a theory which did not appeal to the English. Classical comedy and classical tragedy were both strongly modified by romantic drama. There is much less difference between the construction of comedy and that of tragedy in England than in France, where the two forms are kept rigorously distinct.

In his *Endimion* (*ca.* 1585), Lyly also employed the technique of classical comedy. The situation is one of love at cross purposes among pairs of lovers. The men have their usual servants and the ladies have their maids-in-waiting. Sir Tophas is a braggart captain. Several scenes are familiar ones of Italian comedy, such as the opening scene in which two young men in love give the exposition, the soliloquies of the lovelorn, the scene between Tellus and her confidant, the scenes between Sir Tophas and the pages. Even Dipsas the enchantress, an old hag, smacks of the Italian go-between and magician type.

But Lyly performed the same service for comedy in England that the writers of pastoral plays did for Italian comedy. His principal characters are decent young men and women. Also, instead of making them always shepherds and shepherdesses, he often created them as classical, mythological beings. Instead of removing them from the public square to Arcadia as in *Love's Metamorphosis,* he placed them generally in a classical fairyland, or in a classical country. His scenes are not restricted to a woodland. The same wide variety of scenes and situations, common to other forms of English drama, is found in Lyly's *Woman in the Moone.*

The situation and the plot are subservient to the dialogue. His main story gives just enough continuity to a series of graceful, charming scenes, such as Watteau painted in the eighteenth century. The lovers weave romantic filigrees against a background of pastel shades. The main story is often interrupted by another series of scenes in which rustics or pages discourse on a much lower scale of humor. The connection between these two series is tenuous. Some of his plots are simple, as in *Campaspe*. He never relies primarily on interest in his plot; but the tendency towards complication is manifest in his *Endimion, Love's Metamorphosis, The Woman in the Moone,* and *Mother Bombie.*

Even when Lyly turned to classical history in *Campaspe,* he did not produce a chronicle or a tragedy. The episode which attracted him in the life of Alexander the Great was not a conquest or a tragic deed, but his love for his beautiful captive and his renunciation of her to Apelles. He found romantic comedy wherever he looked; and he gave to Shakespeare, as models, witty people who find wooing a delightful experience.

The transition from the morality to tragedy took place as the plays began to lose their didactic purpose, as the characters became more concrete or historical, and as scenes were put on the stage for the sake of horror, or for dramatic rather than didactic reasons. *Everyman* with its tragic ending, effective even today, did not give rise to a series of plays tending toward tragedy. After 1530 the moralities were rarely entirely devoid of concrete characters and situations, yet the formula of the moral plot still persisted. The development from morality to drama treating seriously events in the lives of concrete characters was slow. Bale's *Kynge Johan* (*ca.* 1548) is a morality so far as its plot is concerned, although the hero is a historical character and he suffers death. Yet the play has a happy ending, for it does not end with his death but with the downfall of the Vices and the triumph of Virtue in the usual medieval fashion.

Nice Wanton is more dramatic, but its aim is moral. Certain scenes are not represented. The author, perhaps Thomas Ingeland, was not so interested in showing the events in the story or in portraying characters as in pointing a moral. The *Interlude of the Virtues and Godly Queen Hester* (1560-1561) and *King Darius* (*ca.* 1565) show that the playwrights were beginning once more to seek for plots in narrative sources, although characters of the morality appear.

There is almost nothing in the plays which discloses a conscious art of dramatic technique beyond the mere representation of a story on a stage and pointing a moral. The point of attack is the beginning of the story. There is little or no foreshadowing or preparation. The action wanders, and the reason why certain scenes are enacted and others are left out is not plain. The dénouement is the result of poetic justice. That is the one sure guide for the dramatist. The rest is confusion, so far as technique is concerned.

Latin humanistic dramas, such as had been produced in Italy and France, were known to English scholars; but it was not until after the middle of the sixteenth century that the classical influence began to be manifest in English drama. In 1559 Heywood published his translation of Seneca's *Troas*. Several of Seneca's plays were translated from that time until 1581 when the so-called *Tenne Tragedies* were published by Thomas Newton. The first play in English which shows the influence of classical technique is *Ferrex and Porrex*, or, as it is better known, *Gorboduc*. This five-act tragedy by Norton and Sackville was produced before Queen Elizabeth at Whitehall on January 18, 1561.

Having in mind Seneca's *Phœnissœ or Thebaïs*, the authors found in Goeffry of Monmouth's chronicle, *Historia Britonum*, a story which resembles the struggles of Polynices and Eteocles for the throne of Thebes. In this case, Gorboduc resolves to divide his kingdom between his sons, Ferrex and Porrex, with the result that jealousy causes Ferrex to move against Porrex only to be slain by him. Videna, mother of the two, slays her younger child for murdering her favorite son, and both she and Gorboduc are slain by the people. All these deaths, however, occur off the stage. A fifth act brings on a new set of characters in order to draw a moral for the royal spectator, Queen Elizabeth, on the woes of a state in which the succession is uncertain.

The play has some characteristics of Seneca's technique; but it does not observe the unities, and no ghost arises to demand vengeance. The point of attack is farther from the climax than in the usual Senecan tragedy; but the action is almost entirely off the stage. Spectacle was supplied between the acts by dumb shows, which foreshadowed the events of the play symbolically. The scenes are given over to interviews between principals and confidants, to councils and to messengers. There is no scene between the two warring brothers probably because there is no scene between Polynices and Eteocles in the Senecan model. The plot is badly handled; but there is a plot, with dramatic events in the background. Plot had been lacking in English drama. Whatever may be said of the technique of Senecan drama, all such plays are based upon a dramatic situation; and it was a great help for English playwrights to come into contact with these classical plots in the theatre or in book form. With all its faults, *Gorboduc* is far more dramatic than anything produced in England up to that time with the exception of *Everyman*. In comparison to *Horestes, Cambises, Appius and Virginia*, or any of the moralities in transition form, *Gorboduc* is the more dramatic. The spectator knows from the first scene what the play is about; the action is foreshadowed; there is suspense as to the outcome; and although the action is slow, the plot develops to an end. The play continues for another act, but the end is at least a "shocker" if not tragedy. These are virtues lacking in English drama uninfluenced by the technique of classical tragedy.

The personages of the play are eloquent in the wordy Senecan fashion, but they indulge in introspection and personal analysis of character. Senecan characters are one-sided and their range is limited, but the introspective, self-analysis of a Hamlet finds its origin in plays of this type. Unfortunately for the development of the art of character drawing in the classical drama of the Renaissance, the Aristotelian critics had laid down rules for depicting character. Basing their false deductions on Aristotle's discussion of character, they held that kings, queens, counsellors, etc., should represent types. Classicism pays less attention to the individual than does romanticism. Thus in spite of the introspection of Senecan characters and their analyses of their motives, the rôles in the tragedies are almost interchangeable. A character of any type in one play could be substituted for a person of the same type in any other play. Yet these typical personages are more human than the abstract automatons of the moralities. In the process of evolution they will become distinct entities such as Lear, Romeo, Hamlet, Othello.

Even plays such as *Horestes* (1567), founded on a classical plot, are more interesting than interludes like *Queen Hester* or *King Darius* (1565) drawn from Biblical sources, for *Horestes* contains more plot and the situation develops sooner. The play embraces much more of the story than does Greek tragedy. The Vice begins by introducing himself as Revenge which is plainly a Senecan influence. Horestes is presented as living at the court of Idumeus and plans to return to his home and slay his guilty mother. He carries out this project as in *Electra,* and the story continues along the lines of Euripides' *Orestes,* ending with the marriage of Horestes to Hermione.

Pickering, the author, was more interested in presenting hand-to-hand fights, battles and processions which are directed "to be long," than in sustaining the obligatory scenes with dramatic suspense. The scenes and characters from the moralities which still appear in these plays are excrescences to modern eyes, whatever may have been the effect of their curious combination of moralizing and slapstick comedy on the audience of the latter half of the sixteenth century. The presence of comic scenes in tragedy, frowned upon in France, was enjoyed by English audiences; but the time was soon to come when the abstract characters of the moralities and their monotonous scenes were to disappear. The mixture or rather mere juxtaposition of tragedy, comedy and morality found in such plays as *Horestes, Cambises* (1569-1570) and *Appius and Virginia* (1563) was too bewildering and artistically incongruous to last long, when the audiences had beheld purer forms of dramatic art. Historical and mythological characters, once introduced on the stage, drove the personifications of abstract vices and virtues out of the theatre.

The first true tragedy to be played in England was *Jocasta* (1566). This play is a translation by Gascoigne and Kinwelmersh of Dolce's *Giocasta,* founded in turn upon Euripides' *Phœnician Women.* Although the Italian play differs in certain details from the original, yet the English audience, which was present at Gray's Inn on this occasion, saw an example of Euripidean technique. Though *The Phœnician Women* is not one of Euripides' finest tragedies, yet even in this form, the play presents a dramatic situation with many phases. The action develops with clearness and calls forth sympathy and suspense in a measure undreamed of by English audiences up to this time. Sympathetic characters, such as Jocasta and Antigone, pass through dramatic events culminating in a tragic ending. Heroes, not merely villains, suffer death, unrelieved by any hope of an eternal life in Heaven. Here was a new sensation for the English spectator.

Roger Ascham proclaimed in *The Scholemaster* (1570) the superiority of the Greek playwrights over Seneca in technique and decorum. Greek tragedies were known both in the original and in translations. But the art of Æschylus, Sophocles and Euripides reached the English drama only in a distorted form in the plays of Seneca and of classic dramatists of France, such as Garnier, and of Italy, such as Dolce and Giraldi Cinthio.

In 1567-1568, *Gismond and Salerne* was acted at the Inner Temple. This tragedy is founded upon the first novel of the fourth day of Boccaccio's *Decameron.* It is possible that a stage version of the story of Romeo and Juliet had already been produced, for Brooke, the author of the poem *The Tragicall Historye of Romeus and Juliet,* says in his preface (1562) that he had seen the same plot lately set forth on the stage. However, *Gismond and Salerne* is the first extant tragedy in English founded upon an Italian novel in which the love of a young man and woman is the basis of the action.

The play is constructed on classical lines, but the point of attack is farther back in the story than in more strictly Senecan tragedies, and the unity of time is not observed. The play begins with a prologue spoken by Cupid, borrowed from Dolce's *Didone*. The fury, Megara, opens the fourth act in canonical Senecan fashion. There are five acts, a chorus, and a messenger's speech describing the death and disemboweling of the hero in the approved horrible fashion. The usual bloody heart of the lover is presented to the heroine who takes poison and dies, whereat her father, overcome with remorse, commits suicide. The action is often behind the scenes. The lovers never meet on the stage. The romance and poetry of *Romeo and Juliet* are supplanted by horror and wailing. The unlovely side of the situation is emphasized. Instead of the passionate love of a man and woman, a Cupid and Megara motivate the action. Yet in the background and behind the scenes are motives and situations which will develop under the hands of greater artists into romantic tragedies such as *Romeo and Juliet* and *Othello*.

The debt of Elizabethan tragedy to just such plays can be realized when one remembers that although medieval English drama might supply the broad framework and keep the action on the stage, plot and the orderly development of the action had to come from foreign sources. The problem before the English playwrights was to get rid of the Senecan elements; to emphasize the romance and the tragic beauty of such plots; and to make the audience love the hero and heroine instead of pitying them with feelings of horror.

This attempt to revivify the interlude by introducing classical plots was a natural result of the influence of Senecan and Italian drama. The abstract hero of the interlude was started on the downward path by some external Vice. The Senecan hero was animated by Revenge or a Fury or even by Cupid. Thus the transition from the interlude to plays of the type of *Appius and Virginia* and of *Cambises* was easy. The action, however, was kept on the stage. For instance, *Appius and Virginia* is founded upon a Senecan situation. Urged on by the Vice, Appius decides to get possession of the virtuous Virginia by force. Rather than lose her honor, Virginia accepts death from the hands of her father who beheads her and delivers the bloody head to Appius. Instead of being behind the scenes, the beheading takes place on the stage. While there is no act division and no chorus, the plot is Senecan in its simplicity, its horror, and its unhappy ending so far as the innocent victim is concerned. The villains, Haphazard and Appius, are punished; and, in so far as poetic justice is meted out, the play is somewhat medieval.

Had the extraneous slapstick comedy and other situations belonging distinctly to the interludes dropped out of such plays by the process of evolution, tragedies resembling those of the French and Italian Renaissance in their simplicity would have been produced in England, although the action would have remained on the stage. Indeed, the circle of Lady Mary Sidney, which included Kyd, admired Garnier's ultra-classical plays; and Lady Mary herself translated *Marc Antoine* in 1590; and in 1594 Kyd produced a version of *Cornélie*. The elegiac tragedy of France, however, was too refined, too lacking in action in both senses of the word, to appeal to the usual English audience. There were few critics in England who were whole-hearted classicists. Ascham and especially Sir Philip Sidney in his *Apologie for Poetrie* (*ca.* 1579) set forth the theories of classical drama; but they were accepted by the playwrights and the audiences only in a modified way. The classicists did not obtain control of the actual theatre in England. Kyd himself, though he belonged to the coterie surrounding Lady Mary and Sir Philip Sidney, produced his *Spanish Tragedy* (1587) which did much to point out the road midway between medieval and ultra-classical drama which the English playwrights were to follow.

Even in the universities, the seats of classical learning, the Senecan form began to be modified in the plays written and acted in Latin. Legge divided his *Richardus Tertius* into three parts, each one of which was acted on separate nights in 1579 at Cambridge. The result was a combination of Senecan technique and the construction of a chronicle play. The deaths are narrated and the messenger appears frequently; but the taste for spectacle inherent in the English theatre-goer of every class was satisfied by battles and parades. With the English humanists presenting such plays before students who were to become playgoers and even playwrights, such as young Marlowe, it is not strange that English drama of a decade later scarcely hesitated between the classical technique of *The Misfortunes of Arthur* and the broader construction of *Tamburlaine* or *The Spanish Tragedy*.

Not only was the popular audience out of sympathy with certain classical rules such as the observance of the three unities, but also the stage itself and the method of setting the scenes militated against the acceptance of the unity of place. In France the simultaneous stage decoration was in vogue when the question of the unities was under discussion even in the seventeenth century. Scenery representing places far distant from one another was juxtaposed on the stage and was visible to the spectators throughout the whole performance. To behold the proverbial "Rome and Constantinople" at the same moment on the stage was naturally a strain on the imagination of the realists in the French playhouse. But no such incongruity was produced by the Elizabethan stagecraft. The medieval system of simultaneous setting had been employed in England both in its movable form on floats or wagons, and in stationary form as in the elaborate setting for *The Castle of Perseverance*. But as travelling theatrical companies were formed and began to present plays in the inn-yards, the typical Elizabethan stage developed; and this stage was introduced into the permanent theatres as they were built.

The platform was divided into an inner and an outer stage. There was no curtain to the outer stage, which was probably twenty to thirty feet deep and twenty to twenty-five feet wide at the curtain which hung before the inner stage. A large portion of the outer stage, the apron, projected into the audience which surrounded it on three sides. On each side of the procenium there was a door with a window above it. The inner stage behind the curtain, which could be opened and closed at will, was about ten to twelve feet deep, twenty to twenty-five feet wide and twelve feet high. A gallery or balcony was built over the inner stage and could be hidden or disclosed by drawing a curtain.

This arrangement of the curtained stage made it possible to change not only the scene but also the scenery itself without incongruity. The outer stage was practically neutral ground representing any locality in the open air, such as a square, a courtyard, a field or very often no place in particular. By placing necessary properties on the inner stage behind the curtain, any indoor scene could be easily set or changed at will. The balcony was also at hand for any scene requiring the impression of height. Whereas in the French theatres the scenes were all set at once and were limited in number by physical conditions, in the English theatres there was no such restriction. Any scene could be revealed at any moment even with greater ease than on the modern stage, which, in spite of reforms, demands more scenery than the few properties used at that time. Certainly no better stage could have been devised for plays in which the unities of time, place and action were to be disregarded. Had the Elizabethans not possessed such a flexible stage, many a drama of that period might have been written so that it could be produced today with success, instead of failing because of a lack of continuity of impression. Even though the use of drop curtains, the revolving stage and modifications of the Elizabethan stage have made it possible to change scenery quickly, the modern audience is somewhat baffled and confused by the swift succession of scenes and impressions in a Shakespearean play. It is not the modern stage but the modern mind which refuses to absorb completely an action passing through many phases, in many places, in many hours.

The lack of scenery and of lighting effects was counterbalanced by descriptive lines sometimes of great beauty. The very bareness of the stage made the spoken word of great importance. Mob scenes, processions and reviews of armies were the only spectacular appeal to the eye. Beyond this there is no evidence of the use of stage pictures either as a psychological or purely æsthetic appeal. On the modern stage, scenery and lighting supply the elements of pictorial beauty and are employed to interpret the mood as well as the atmosphere of the play. The spoken word is thus less important so far as descriptions are concerned, but modern dramatic art is producing plastic pictures of great beauty and significance.

Such a stage was only too convenient for playwrights who did not know, as Sidney said, "the difference betwixt reporting and representing." The chronicle play naturally flourished in such surroundings. Some book of history was selected by the dramatist; and the period that offered the most spectacular events and cruel murders was dramatized in a series of scenes arranged chronologically. The aim was scarcely to tell a story but rather to juxtapose events which happened, not because one developed from another, but because they occurred in the same period of time.

One valuable asset of dramatic art resulted from this system of playmaking and also from the use of histories and stories of many lands and ages as sources. English drama presents an astonishing variety of scenes on the stage. No other drama in any like period is so rich. Only the frequenter of modern motion picture theatres finds unrolled before his eyes a view of so many episodes and situations entering into the life of man. This variety had come in a relatively short time to a theatre in which the monotonous and repetitious morality had held the stage; and, as years went on, the range of subjects and scenes increased, until Shakespeare gave his dramatic portrayal of all human life.

But how were these episodes to be welded into a single unified framework? How was the "historie play" to become less of a history and more of a play? The pure Senecan drama was not accepted by the public; but in this form of dramatic art and in the influence of the Italian novella there were certain factors which were acceptable to the theatre-goers and which worked favorably upon the technique of popular drama. The Senecan motive of vengeance tends toward unification and was effectively operative in Kyd's *Spanish Tragedy*. The importance of a central figure had also been illustrated by classical drama, and this was a strong factor in giving a broad unity of action to the plays of Marlowe. Finally, the Italian novella offered dramatic situations stripped of non-essential details and of episodes which obscured such moments in contemporary prosy chronicles. To make an effective dramatization of the story of *Romeo and Juliet* or of *Othello* requires much less skill and artistic insight than to discover and dig out the tragedy of *Macbeth* from the clay of Holinshed's *Chronicles*.

About 1587, Kyd composed *The Spanish Tragedy*. It achieved a deserved success, for it is the best example of theatrical art in England up to the time of Shakespeare, who was indebted to Kyd for much of his technique. The plot is based upon the Senecan motive of revenge represented by an abstract character which enters with the ghost of Andrea in a prologue inspired by *Thyestes*. These two characters act as a chorus; and, at the end of the play, they pronounce an epilogue. Their presence gives the whole series of scenes a kind of fictitious unity, for the plot purports to represent the retribution for the death of Andrea in a battle which has already occurred before the play begins. Unfortunately for the dramatic value of the device, the spectator has little interest in the death of Andrea and cares not at all whether his death on the field of battle is avenged or not. Andrea was loved by Bel-Imperia, the heroine; but she, immediately and with no artistic motivation, turns her affections to Horatio who monopolizes the sympathy of the audience, so far as the character of the young lover is concerned. His murder at the hands of Lorenzo, Bel-Imperia's brother, is the death which the spectators wish to see avenged by his father Hieronimo. The motive of revenge in the case of Andrea is purely external. In regard to Horatio, it springs from the father's heart. The theatrical Senecan motive thus becomes dramatic. Kyd wished to open the play with a ghost. He could have chosen the ghost of Horatio; but he also wished to place many events on the stage in conformity to English taste. He therefore selected an early point of attack and introduced the ghost of Andrea. But the point of attack is too late, if we are to be interested in Andrea, and too early, if our sympathy for Horatio is to be the point of departure. The interest of the spectator in the dramatic possibilities is fully assured when Bel-Imperia has fallen in love with Horatio and is loved by the captured prince, Balthazar, who is seconded in his unrequited passion by Lorenzo.

These circumstances cause the spectator to look forward, at least; and when Horatio is murdered, Hieronimo's vow to discover and punish the assassins of his son arouses suspense in a manner and to a degree hitherto unknown in English drama. The vengeance is delayed; but as Professor Boas points out: "The cardinal weakness in the play which prevents it ranking among dramatic masterpieces, is Kyd's failure in an adequate psychological analysis of the Marshal's motives for this delay. Inaction only becomes dramatic material when, as in the case of the Shakespearean *Hamlet*, it is shown to be rooted in some disease of character or will." But the delay is theatrically effective. At first it is caused by the fact that Hieronimo does not know, hardly suspects the identity of the murderers. Then he distrusts Bel-Imperia's letter in which she denounces the guilty men. When the intercepted letter from one of the accomplices confirms his suspicions, he is on the point of demanding justice in plain terms, but is evidently cowed by Lorenzo. At last come sickness of heart and mind and self-upbraiding for his delay. It is a first sketch of the original portrait of Hamlet, drawn probably by Kyd, to which Shakespeare added the strokes of dramatic genius. In these progressive steps there is a sweep of climactic action which culminates in the play within the play. Kyd foreshadows the tragedy but does not anticipate the successive *coups de théâtre* in which the feigned avenging murders and suicide turn out to be real.

Although much of the exposition is in narrative form and the battle in which Andrea was killed is described in classical fashion, most of the action is represented. There are several scenes—notably those at the Portuguese court—which do not even deserve reporting, much less actual representation. But in the succession of scenes, there are many situations handled with deftness and melodramatic power. The love scene between Bel-Imperia and Horatio in the bower shows that Lyly's graceful dialogue was not falling in vain upon Kyd's ears. It is a scene in which sympathy goes out to innocent lovers—a rare situation in tragedy up to that time, be it Greek or Senecan, English or French. The ensuing murder of the lover in the presence of his mistress by her brother and her jealous admirer, the finding of the body of his son by Hieronimo plucked from his "naked bed," the entrance of the mother, form a series of effective scenes. Throughout the rest of the play there are too many surprising *coups de théâtre;* Hieronimo takes a handkerchief from his pocket and finds it to be a cloth stained with Horatio's blood; he suddenly discloses the body of his son to show why he has slain the prince and Lorenzo; he makes a sign for a knife to mend his pen when he has bitten out his tongue, and stabs the Duke and himself with the weapon. Theatrical and sensational as they may be, it was from such striking tricks that Shakespeare learned to handle such dramatic actions as the suicide of Othello.

Kyd skilfully combined a secondary action with the main plot. Pedringano, Bel-Imperia's servant, betrays to Lorenzo the secret of her love and her tryst with Horatio. He also is an accomplice, together with Serberine, in the murder. Lest these wretches betray him, Lorenzo incites Pedringano to slay Serberine; Pedringano does so, is captured and condemned to die by Hieronimo himself. Lorenzo has no desire to save him but pretends to send him a pardon in a box. The grisly jesting on the part of Pedringano, who thinks his life is safe just before he is hanged, foreshadows such scenes as the Porter's ghastly joking in *Macbeth.* The effect is not comic relief but grotesque intensification of horror. Finally, the letter of Pedringano to Lorenzo discloses the truth. In no serious play up to this time had such artistry been employed. The sub-plot in Lyly's plays had only a tenuous connection, if any, with the main story. The moralities and chronicles were most inept in this respect. To Kyd belongs the credit of showing future playwrights how to handle striking situations and construct a plot which arouses suspense and sympathy.

His depiction of characters is not so successful; yet even in this respect he shows an advance over his predecessors. The hero is Hieronimo. He becomes prominent too late in the play; but he is a real personality in comparison to the stock characters of earlier plays. He develops into a different being through a crisis which he himself directs and plans. He suffers, where other heroes merely wail or rage. He is opposed by a somewhat Machiavellian villain in the person of Lorenzo and a lesser villain in Balthazar, neither of whom is drawn with the subtlety of Iago. However, they serve their purpose of actively opposing the protagonist in obligatory scenes, not developed to the utmost, but of a kind rarely represented in Senecan drama. Bel-Imperia and Horatio enlist our sympathy, not merely pity. The mother of Horatio is only sketched. Kyd did not realize the finer shades of psychology inherent in these rôles nor did he make character the keystone of his dramatic structure. That important contribution to dramatic art in England was made by Christopher Marlowe.

Such plays as Preston's *Cambises* purport to be the representation of the life of a hero. The title page of the printed version describes the play with surprising accuracy, as follows: *"A Lamentable Tragedy mixed full of pleasant mirth containing the Life of Cambises King of Percia from the beginning of his kingdom unto his Death, his one good deede of execution, after that, many wicked deeds and tyrannous murders committed by and through him, and last of all, his odious death by God's Justice appointed, Done in such order as foloweth."*

It is not clear why these deeds were "done in such order." Any other order would have been just as ineffective. The play is no more dramatic than is real life unrefined by art. Even the death of Cambises lacks a gleam of tragedy, for he dies from a wound received when his sword jumps out of its scabbard as he is mounting a horse. The other incidents of the story are equally unrelated to each other. It seems actually curious that one should follow the other, even though they happen to one man. There is no unity or climactic action. The sole advance in technique over the diffuse plays of the strictly medieval period lies in the tendency to drop out scenes which are absolutely trivial. The writers of serious plays still juxtaposed scenes of unrelated slapstick, vulgar comedy and supposedly tragic events; but, under the influence of Seneca, they tended to select for representation shocking deeds and to leave out minor events. The interest was not focussed on any one crisis. Rigorous selection of scenes according to set rules or traditions was never practiced by popular English playwrights.

Marlowe's university education was not without effect upon him as a playwright. He dramatized, perhaps as his first play, the story of Dido and Æneas, a popular theme among classicists. In spite of the non-observance of the unities of time and place, his *Dido* is classical in so far as it deals with one action: the love of Dido and Æneas. Marlowe follows strictly the development of a plot which reaches a climax and a conclusion. Structurally, the play is closer to the usual modern form of drama than any other Elizabethan play. With the exception of the passages in which the fall of Troy is narrated, the play could almost be classed as well made.

Whether it was too well made to be popular with the audience or not, history does not record. At any rate, Marlowe chose the looser form of the chronicle play for his other dramatic writings. But instead of putting into dialogue a series of events which happened in temporal order, he selected a hero and showed how these events were caused by his ruling passion. In *Tamburlaine*, it is the hero's lust for power and victory; in *The Jew of Malta*, the greed of gold together with desire for revenge; in *Edward II*, the guilty passion of Edward for Gaveston. His heroes are often exaggerated beyond the limits of artistry. Their fault lies not in being inhuman but unhuman.

Yet Marlowe's method gave these plays a kind of unity. One knows what to expect from his heroes. At last, in English drama, the character and not the author is the motive power of the action. The difference in general between Marlowe's heroes and those of Greek tragedy lies in the fact that his characters are always governed by the same emotions and shape events in response to one or two primitive, brutal passions. The Greek heroes are victims of some error of judgment which starts an avalanche of inescapable consequences. When a Greek hero makes the initial decision, he becomes a human being struggling, often in vain, with adversity. The Marlovian hero has a very active will. He does things, many things; but his deeds have a monotonous similarity because he is a criminal, and while his crimes may be various they are not varied. He increases his passion in a climactic manner, but he is too much of a villain to be subtle. His character does not take on different shades in the face of various events. He causes events; but the reciprocal influence of events and character is lacking in Marlowe's plays. His heroes are practically interchangeable. Tamburlaine, Guise, Barabas, Faustus could all perform each other's deeds with the same efficiency. The soliloquies express the same sentiments in the same manner; but to interchange Romeo, Hamlet, Iago, Macbeth or Othello would destroy the whole framework and dialogue of the plays. To put Romeo in Hamlet's situation in the first act of *Hamlet* would make a wholly different tragedy; but Tamburlaine in the situation of Barabas would scarcely alter the action of *The Jew of Malta*.

One reason for the one-sidedness of Marlowe's characters lies in the frequent use of soliloquies and asides, in which the character thinks aloud, but is not overheard. Such a procedure is not to be criticized on the ground that it is unlifelike. There are certain thoughts which no one speaks just as he thinks them. Either drama will admit the convention of the soliloquy or else it will not represent certain states of the human soul.

There is no theatrical reason why Hamlet should not speak his soliloquy on death in the presence of another character; but it would be psychologically false for Hamlet to discuss suicide in this way with anyone. To all except a few belated realists, a soliloquy is legitimate or illegitimate in proportion as it is psychologically fitting and dramatically effective.

On the other hand, just as a character can be disclosed in relation to events, it can be still more clearly and delicately revealed in relation to other personalities affected by the same events. The scenes between Clytemnestra and Agamemnon, Othello and Iago, Hamlet and his mother, Phèdre and her nurse would be irreparable losses if they were replaced by alternate soliloquies. Fine shades of emotion and character are brought out by the fact that the dramatist must rely upon delicate impressions and sensations. We do not know so much about a character who announces in a monologue or an aside that he is a wicked person, as we do from seeing that character give the impression or sensation of wickedness in his relation to other characters in certain situations. Such scenes are lacking in Marlowe's plays. He depends too much upon direct information given in soliloquies and asides. He has antagonists in his plays but he does not show the protagonists in relation to the antagonists as does Shakespeare in *Othello* or *Hamlet*. Marlowe tends to present only one side of the conflict at one time; whereas in *Othello*, Shakespeare presents both sides of the conflict in the scene between Othello and Iago.

In a scene between Barabas and Lodovick in the second act of *The Jew of Malta*, Barabas constantly explains his real emotions and purpose in asides to the audience. Most of the irony inherent in the situation is lost. There is no subtlety in the dialogue. The scene is undramatically clear. Instead of receiving delicate impressions and sensations, the audience is told plain facts.

Marlowe's contribution to English dramatic art, however, is the unification of events into a plot which develops in relation to a great personality who goes down to defeat. Marlowe accepted the structure of the chronicle play. He did not show merely the downfall of a superman. He placed his point of attack so that we see the protagonist in a state of prosperity. We watch him succeed in his undertakings because of his all-powerful passion for power, and then behold his downfall because of this same passion. The hero does not arouse sympathy; but he does command admiration accompanied by shudders.

The writer of a chronicle play sought for a series of striking events to present on the stage. He did not seek for a great character or a plot. Marlowe became interested in a man preeminent because of some ruling passion and wrote a play about him. Kyd was evidently moved to dramatize the story of *The Spanish Tragedy* because of the melodramatic plot. The Italian novella was attractive to dramatists not primarily because of characters, but because it contained a plot. The novella was short. Unlike histories or chronicles, it did not contain a vast amount of material either non-essential or unsuitable for dramatic treatment. The novella aimed to give artistic pleasure, not to inform or to teach or even to moralize to any unfortunate extent. Whether the novelist had based his story on fact or myth, he had already discarded non-essentials and had compressed the incidents into a unified story. He had performed a task which many an English playwright often failed to perform.

The growing skill in plotting is noticeable in Greene's *Friar Bacon and Friar Bungay* (*ca.* 1589) and in his *James IV* (*ca.* 1590). His plot begins to unfold immediately; and, by means of foreshadowing, he is able to project the mind of the spectator forward and create suspense. He excels both Kyd and Marlowe in this respect. Greene places on the stage some unnecessary scenes such as that of the Lawyer, the Merchant and the Divine in the fifth act of *James IV*; but most of his scenes are effective. He does not emulate Kyd in describing battles. The influence of the technique of classical tragedy is scarcely discernible. He shows the audience what is happening in scenes which are actable. His handling of the scenes of magic in *Friar Bacon and Friar Bungay* is more dramatic than the similar effects in Marlowe's *Faustus,* which are merely spectacular or, at most, only theatrical. In Greene's play, the scene of the wooing of Margaret by Lacy is made visible from afar to Prince Edward by means of Bacon's magical glass. Just as Friar Bungay is about to marry the lovers, Bacon strikes him dumb. Thus the magical element conducts the plot at this moment, if not in the conjuring scene in which Bacon gets the better of Vandermast.

Both plays show a new tendency towards the introduction of romantic love into plots of English plays. The characters are historical, but the love element introduces complications into *James IV* which entirely overshadow the historical element. The situations common to the chronicle play are replaced by scenes of a very different character except in the fifth act. The romantic scenes and the scenes of necromancy in *Friar Bacon and Friar Bungay* arouse an interest quite different from that of the chronicle play. Woven together as they are, they produce suspense, surprise and *coups de théâtre* in an amount approached only by Kyd.

Even Kyd and Marlowe often make the impression of having chosen scenes which tell the story. The scenes in these two plays by Greene not only tell the story but also are effective in themselves. One would pay attention to them, were they played separately. Greene brings his principal characters face to face; and they converse instead of merely talking in asides in each other's presence. The soliloquy is used sparingly. His characters and scenes would act well. Actors would find greater possibility of subtle characterization in his dialogue than in the dialogue interspersed with explanatory lines directed to the audience.

The ability to make the action rise to a climax was also possessed by Greene. *The Spanish Tragedy* and Marlowe's plays reach climaxes, but they are slow in starting. The spectator is not exactly sure how he should feel in regard to individual characters or what he may expect of them. From the first lines of these two plays by Greene, interest is aroused; and, degree by degree, it deepens into suspense. There is a cumulative sense of the action rising to a climax. Nash rightly placed him above his contemporaries in "plotting of plays."

Greene, even more successfully than Kyd, draws the many threads of his plots together into a whole. The story is very complicated in the play, but there is an interrelationship between the different episodes. The two or three series of events do not merely take place during the same time. Friar Bacon's magic affects the fate of Margaret. It would be impossible to suppress any part of *James IV* without seriously impairing the remainder.

The plot of the latter play is derived from an Italian story by Giraldi Cinthio who also dramatized it in his *Arrenopia*. Greene opens his play when James IV has just married Dorothea. The King, however, immediately declares his love to the countess Ida. In order to marry Ida he lays plans to have Queen Dorothea murdered. She tries to escape disguised as a man, is wounded by the assassin, but is rescued by Sir Cuthbert Anderson, who takes her to his home. Lady Anderson falls in love with Dorothea, believing her to be a knight. James IV believes her dead and repents his crimes when he hears of Ida's marriage to an English gentleman. The King of England, Dorothea's father, hearing that she has been murdered, comes to avenge her death. The discovery that she is alive ends the play.

Giraldi Cinthio begins his play after his heroine Arrenopia (Dorothea) has been rescued. She is known as the knight Agnoristo, and Semne (Lady Anderson) is in love with the supposed gentleman. Her husband is jealous. Partenia (Ida) never appears. The principal characters do not meet on the stage until the final scene. Successive monologues or else scenes between primary and secondary characters fill five long acts. The identity of Agnoristo is inartistically concealed from the audience. Suspense is sacrificed to surprise. Everything is sacrificed to unnecessary talk about the question of marital honor.

Greene's play has no such thesis. English drama of this period does not deal with problems of human life. The interlude had done so in a monotonous manner. Shakespeare will finally lift the play on revenge into a study of human psychology in *Hamlet*. He will find human problems of ambition, jealousy, paternal weakness where his predecessors saw only a story.

When Shakespeare began to write for the English stage about 1590, he had as models many forms of drama. The audience, for which he was to write, was not predisposed to accept any rules of classicism. It was content to have a story unfolded in any manner that rouses the emotions peculiar to the theatre. The audience was educated dramatically, but it did not allow theories of art to stand in the way of complete emotional enjoyment of a play. There was no deep reverence for the "ancients." The Elizabethan stage was best suited of all stages for telling a story. It had enough machinery to present any scene at any moment but not so much as to delay the performance for an instant. All the traditions of the theatre and of playwriting tended in the direction of freedom. Shakespeare knew the classical rules, but he did not allow them to keep him from telling a story on the stage in a manner that would seem effective to an audience that came to see as well as to hear a play.

The medieval influence overshadows all others in Shakespeare's chronicle plays or histories. Dr. Johnson defined a history as "a series of actions with no other than chronological succession, independent on each other and without any tendency to regulate the conclusion. His [Shakespeare's] histories being neither tragedy nor comedy are not subject to any of their laws; nothing more is necessary to all the praise which they expect, than that the changes of action be so prepared as to be understood, that the incidents be various and affecting and the characters consistent, natural and distinct."

Interesting as these plays must have been to contemporary audiences because of the historical element and their pageantry, they are of little importance in the development of dramatic art. They show events in chronological succession. At times the events are held together by the presence of such characters as Richard III or Hotspur. But such a series of events hardly constitutes a plot. There are climaxes and peripeteias, but they consist of such incidents as a king being deposed or dying and another proclaimed as his successor. The struggle is a clash of civil war. No grave, human principal is involved. The plays often begin with the news of a revolt against the king. No dramatic principle can be discovered in regard to the reasons for the selection of scenes, except that they show the progress of the revolt and its outcome. There is little preparation and foreshadowing. The events are understandable to the spectator, but unless he knows the course of history little suspense is aroused. Typical scenes are the reception of ambassadors, the defiance of the emissaries, the sentencing of traitors to death, musings of the hero before a battle, the battles themselves, the victory or defeat; while the whole is more or less interlarded with comic scenes which have little or nothing to do with the main action. The scenes, taken as separate units, are often admirable in their different effects; but, taken as a whole, they lack a spiritual or psychological motivation without which drama becomes merely what these plays are: a representation of events in which the dramatist has turned "the accomplishment of many years into an hour glass."

Shakespeare's art was a combination of medieval and Italian elements. Writing for a medieval, elastic stage he was primarily interested in representing a story by portraying most of the events before the audience. The complex plot, which he used in the majority of his plays, is a heritage of Renaissance drama rather than of medieval art. There is no evidence that he was inspired primarily to write a play because of a desire to treat a certain theme, problem or character. His point of departure was a story that would form a background for effective scenes of comedy and lyric beauty, or a story which could be represented at least theatrically, if not dramatically. He sacrificed the study of character to the presentation of his story, if it were necessary. His plays differ from Renaissance tragedy and comedy, not so much in subject matter or in the devices and situations used in the plot, as in the fact that he presented on the stage most of the scenes which arise in connection with the initial cause. Renaissance drama suppressed many scenes and presented only the comic or tragic reactions on the part of the characters to the events.

An early example of the importance which Shakespeare attached to the plot is found in his adaptation of the *Menæchmi*. The Plautine play has a complex situation which arises from an intricate plot, but the plot is kept in the background. Only those scenes which arouse laughter were selected by Plautus for presentation.

After the manner of the Italian writers of comedy, Shakespeare complicated the situation by introducing a second pair of twins, the two Dromios. But his most original and striking development of the plot is the creation of the rôles of Ægeon, Luciana and the Abbess. Their presence produces a romantic atmosphere wholly lacking in the Plautine play. Had Shakespeare based his comedy on a narrative version of this story, he might well have used the inclusive framework which he employed in *The Winter's Tale,* and have had the point of attack far enough back to show how the twins were separated. Unless he was influenced by special considerations, Shakespeare selected a point of attack early in the narrative, in the manner of the medieval playwright. In this case his immediate source was probably an English translation of the *Menæchmi* which he may have read in manuscript form. He did not alter the point of attack of his source; but he discarded the formal prologue and substituted a dramatic incident which gives the audience all necessary details and arouses sympathy and suspense. Inspired, perhaps, by a similar situation in *The Supposes,* Shakespeare introduced Ægeon, the father of the twins, who has come to Ephesus and who falls under the law that unless he can pay a ransom of a thousand marks he shall die. The play opens with a scene in court in which this sentence is passed. This incident gives Ægeon the opportunity to plead in his own behalf by telling of the loss of his wife and one of the boys whom he has sought for years. In this semi-tragic fashion the exposition is given dramatically, and a serious interest is supplied which was not emphasized in the original play.

The character of Luciana, the sister of Adriana, furnishes a touch of romance as well as comedy, for Antipholus of Syracuse falls in love with her; and when the mistaken identity is cleared up, their marriage is foreshadowed. The discovery that the Abbess is the wife of Ægeon is a *coup de théâtre* which is entirely romantic. Thus not only is the plot complicated by the increased number of chances in which the mistaken identity can supply scenes of comedy, but also by romantic situations which arouse sentiment.

The disguise of Viola in *Twelfth Night* is a device used in Italian comedy. On the Italian stage such disguises give rise to indelicate situations and humor. Shakespeare emphasized the love story and produced romantic situations through such devices. By bringing the love story on the stage, he made the plot a prominent element instead of a mere source of humorous scenes.

With an audience that enjoyed complex plots, with a stage well fitted to hold them, it is natural to find Shakespeare dramatizing intricate situations from almost the beginning to the end of his career. His point of departure was plot, and therefore he constructed his play so that he could present the story with the greatest dramatic effect. Many playwrights before his time had told stories. Marlowe had portrayed character especially, and had produced powerful, heroic dialogue. Lyly had refined the lighter characters of the stage and had furnished models of graceful, witty dialogue. Shakespeare excelled all his predecessors and contemporaries in depicting character in action and in writing dramatic lines; but he excelled them especially in telling a story dramatically, or at least theatrically. He also tells the story clearly, and never approaches the pitfall of obscurity into which Spanish writers and Frenchmen under their influence often fell. Shakespeare would have agreed with Aristotle that the action is the most important element of a play, while character is secondary. Whatever obscurity in his plays has baffled critics for three centuries arises in connection with the characters. If his plays are analyzed on the basis of plot as a point of departure, they are found to be the work of a masterful playwright who made a logical and complete use of the flexibility of the stage for which he wrote.

If the plots of Shakespeare were of "trifling importance" to him as Furness and other critics hold, it is difficult to understand why the playwright wove four stories into the plot of *The Merchant of Venice*, introduced the parallel action of the house of Gloster into *King Lear*, devised enough incidents in the first act of *Titus Andronicus* to fill out a whole play, and made the plot of the *Two Gentlemen of Verona* more intricate than the story in the source. If Shakespeare's plays are compared with their sources, it is found that he clarified and vivified many motives; but, in the majority of cases, he introduced more complications than were in the original version or at least retained so many situations that few of his plays, such as *As You Like It*, can be said to contain a slim narrative. His simplification is clarification, but is by no means a reduction of complexity.

In dramatizing narratives, Shakespeare chose an early opening. In *The Merchant of Venice* nothing of importance has happened before the first scene. *Romeo and Juliet* and *Othello* open where the actual stories begin in the narrative. In reading Holinshed's *Chronicles* one feels that the story of Macbeth commences when the incident of his meeting the three witches is described, and that scene comes early in the play. In no case has the dramatist opened his play after an incident has happened which ought to have been represented. To ascribe this practice of the early point of attack to his disregard of the unities is to give a negative reason. He was primarily interested in constructing a play which would represent a story without having to report or describe previous events in the plot.

As a result of this method, his scenes of exposition are clear and gripping. The spectator does not have to listen to intricate explanations and burden his memory with many details. From what is seen and heard one grasps the situation and assumes the correct mood in which to follow the ensuing action.

In *Two Gentlemen of Verona* the opening scene is somewhat classical with its explanatory dialogue between Valentine and Proteus and the following conversation between Proteus and Speed, the servant. The first two scenes of *The Merchant of Venice* are also deliberate in their movement. We learn of Bassanio's request for money so that he may woo Portia; and then the lady herself is disclosed to us in a scene with her waiting-gentlewoman Nerissa. Classical in form as it is, this scene between a heroine and a friend is far from its sordid Italian prototypes in poetic beauty and charming piquancy. The third scene instantly grips the attention as the sinister Shylock and Antonio make the astounding bargain of the money loaned with a pound of flesh as security. When this scene is over, the exposition has gradually merged into action with preparation for future development and foreshadowing of disaster for someone.

In *Cymbeline,* two protatic characters give a short explanation of the loss of the King's children and of the marriage of Imogen to Posthumus against her father's wish. The banishment of Posthumus by the King is then represented and with this touching incident of the parting lovers the story begins to unfold.

The opening monologue of *Richard III* is due to the influence of Renaissance classical tragedy, in which the villainous hero explains his fell designs directly to the audience. The transformation of another method of exposition of classical tragedy is exemplified in the opening of *Hamlet*. Instead of having the Ghost appear and demand vengeance in an undramatic monologue explaining the past events, Shakespeare dramatizes the scene with the sure touch of an artist. *Hamlet* opens as the watch is being changed. Horatio asks if "this thing" has appeared again tonight. In a moment, "the thing" comes. It resembles the dead King. They try to speak to it; but it is silent; and it disappears. Thus Shakespeare creates the atmosphere of the supernatural and a mood of wonderment and suspense. In the second scene, Hamlet dominates the stage, shedding over all his brooding melancholy and a grief which seems natural and yet to cover something—some vague suspicion too awful to be spoken or even thought of in words. Finally in the fourth scene, comes the meeting on the battlements of Hamlet and the Ghost. The story of the murder is told step by step with nerve-racking deliberateness. The spectator lives and feels through Hamlet's tortured mind. Indeed, this is one of the rare scenes in drama in which a member of the audience, learning the truth with the hero, ceases to be a mere spectator and becomes almost a part of the hero's own personality. Had Shakespeare placed the point of attack so as to include a representation of the murder of Hamlet's father, the audience, already in possession of that fact, would only watch Hamlet make the discovery and would lose the deep fellow feeling which enthrals it.

When Shakespeare used a play as a source, as in the case of *The Comedy of Errors* and *King Lear,* he did not change the point of attack of the original. In all probability the original *Hamlet* opened with the appearance of a ghost. If Kyd was the author of the first version, it is reasonably sure that he had used the Senecan opening of a ghost, especially since he had practically dragged in a ghost to begin *The Spanish Tragedy*. Thus Shakespeare seems again to have left the point of attack unchanged when using a play as a source. The whole construction and much of the dramatic beauty of his *Hamlet* are due to this indirect influence of Senecan tragedy.

Although these opening scenes of *Hamlet* are the most impressive of all his expository scenes because of the poignant situation, Shakespeare is no less skilful in handling other initial situations. He generally discloses an incident which not only appeals to the eye and the ear, but also strikes the keynote of the whole play. He creates atmosphere immediately, and throws the audience into the correct mood.

Thus in *Macbeth* we do not know exactly the significance of the witches when the curtain rises; but they are gruesome, awful in appearance and in their strange speech broken by flashes of lightning and rumblings of thunder. Certainly no spectator has ever failed to come under the supernatural, tragic spell which pervades the whole drama. This is the short prelude. In the next scene we learn of the victory and that Macbeth is to be greeted with the title of thane of Cawdor. Then the witches appear again and they hail Macbeth as thane of Cawdor and as "king hereafter." With Macbeth, the spectator turns his thoughts to the future fraught with prophecy. In Holinshed's *Chronicles* the first scene of the witches does not appear; but Shakespeare, with unerring skill, prepares the mind for the full emotional effect of the third scene by having introduced the weird sisters at the beginning. We know they will come to the heath, "when the battle's lost and won," to greet Macbeth. The suspense and supernatural awe are undiminished by vague surprise. A comparison of these three scenes in the order in which they come with the lifeless narrative paragraph from which they sprang bears witness to Shakespeare's magic skill as a dramatist.

In quite another mood but no less effectively, Shakespeare shows us the background in *Romeo and Juliet*. The curtain rises on a public place in Verona. A duel caused by the enmity of the Capulets and Montagues will bring tragedy to the young lovers. Within a few moments the servants of the two houses are engaged in a picturesque street brawl which prepares for the duel between Romeo and Mercutio. One is enveloped by the atmosphere of the impetuosity of the Italian Renaissance when flashing swords are hotly and carelessly drawn at a word. Though the meeting of Romeo and Juliet—the mainspring of the plot—comes at the end of the act, the knowledge that Romeo is going to the ball at the house of his enemies is enough to hold the attention until we see the boy and girl fall under the spell of romantic love.

Even more swiftly, the opening scenes of *Othello* unfold the situation by a series of incidents which strike the keynote of the tragedy. It is night in a street in Venice. Iago, stung to action by the appointment of Cassio as Othello's lieutenant, begins his slanderous revenge by arousing Brabantio from his sleep and telling him of Othello's marriage to Desdemona. Then he slinks away, as Brabantio comes forth. It is a play dealing with slander, sly insinuations which have a baffling appearance of truth, and jealousy which wrecks the happiness of a strange marriage. This scene in which Brabantio is aroused from his bed and told of the marriage of his daughter in brutal words is in cruel harmony with the tragedy which is to unfold.

In *King Lear,* the first scene contains the initial cause of the catastrophe. When Lear divides his kingdom between his elder daughters who flatter him and breaks out in blind rage against the too sincere Cordelia and refuses to harken to the loyal Kent, the tragedy which arises and the characters involved in it are presented in swift, powerful strokes. The avalanche of misfortune begins to move slowly but inexorably as the scene is enacted. Whatever happens during the rest of this vast tragedy is traceable to this first scene of exposition.

In *Coriolanus* and *Julius Cæsar,* plays dealing with the fortunes of a city in which the volatile crowd was to be reckoned with, the first scenes present the mob in action. Shakespeare is not merely creating local color and atmosphere, but is presenting in a colorful manner an important element in the situation. Instead of being a picturesque background, the mob is a force almost beyond human control. In *The Tempest,* the plot could be followed easily without the opening scene of the storm at sea; but again, this scene is more than a picturesque incident. It grips the attention by its stirring action and arouses some suspense, and therefore makes the following scene of exposition far more interesting, because the spectator, like Miranda, has seen the brave vessel dashed to pieces and is desirous of knowing the why and wherefore. One listens with real interest to many expository details given later by Prospero which would have aroused merely curiosity had the first scene been omitted.

Thus the opening scenes of Shakespeare's finer dramas are beautiful examples of exposition combined with a stirring incident which appeals to the eye as well as to the ear. They are picturesque even on a stage which had neither lighting system nor painted scenery. They furnish the correct atmosphere, and put the audience into the correct frame of mind. They contain many of the motives of the plot and generally show principal characters in action. They sound the keynote of the whole drama and cause the spectator to look toward the future with suspense. Neither Kyd nor Marlowe ever approached Shakespeare in the dramatic effect of opening scenes.

In preparation and foreshadowing Shakespeare is also preeminent. The plays of his contemporaries progress in an unexpected manner. In Shakespeare's theatre one may be disappointed or even deceived as to the outcome; but one always knows what to hope and what to fear as the action develops. The disappointment and the deception are not felt on artistic grounds, but arise from hoping against hope that the impending tragedy may be averted. Not only are situations in the opening scenes fraught with possibilities of disaster, but there is constant foreshadowing of events which do or do not take place. Romeo fears, as he goes to the Capulet's ball:

> Some consequence yet hanging in the stars
> Shall bitterly begin his fearful date
> With this night's revel.

These lines are somewhat obvious foreshadowing; but in *King Lear* the first suggestions of Lear's possible madness are very subtle. The old King's sudden outburst of wrath and his lack of judgment betray an absence of self-control. In the second act when Goneril has turned against him, he prays that his anger may be noble, that he may not weep. Then his last words as he leaves betray his lurking fear: "O Fool! I shall go mad." Again in the third act he cries out:

> O Regan, Goneril!
> Your old kind father, whose frank heart gave all—
> O, that way madness lies; let me shun that;
> No more of that.

Brabantio says to Othello:

> Look to her, Moor, if thou hast eyes to see.
> She has deceived her father and may thee.

In these few words an event is foreshadowed which does not come to pass; but, as Desdemona's father is speaking, a real fear is aroused in Othello and in the mind of the spectator. The remark is tragically just, in spite of Desdemona's innocence; and it implants the first grain of suspicion in Othello's heart. The lines spoken by Iago throughout the play constantly inform us of his diabolical plans. It seems impossible that he will be successful. His purpose is too vile. Desdemona is too pure. Yet each machination of his brain arouses suspense for the future, foreshadows the tragedy and prepares logically for each situation.

In *Julius Cæsar,* the prophetic words of the soothsayer and a foreshadowing dream are taken from the source. In *Macbeth,* the prophecies of the weird sisters, also suggested by the source, serve as unobtrusive but effective guideposts for the spectator. Shakespeare was eminently successful in concealing these technical devices by introducing them into scenes of great interest. Yet that he was conscious of the art seems plain from his foreshadowing and preparation in *Cymbeline.* In the fourth act Imogen must mistake the body of Cloten for that of her husband, Posthumus, through recognizing her husband's clothes. As far back as the second act, Imogen taunts Cloten by saying:

> His meanest garment
> That ever hath but clipped his body, is dearer
> In my respect than all the hairs above thee,
> Were they all made such men.

The insult strikes home. The words: "His meanest garment" burn into his stupid brain and Cloten forms the plan of dressing in the garments of Posthumus and slaying him. Before the revenge is accomplished, Cloten is slain, his head is cut off; and he is found by Imogen who believes him to be her husband. Such careful preparation is the result of conscious artistry.

This skill in exposition, preparation and foreshadowing is found to be still more striking when the closing scenes of his finest plays are considered in relation to the first act. His dénouements are the inexorable, logical results of his first situation. His tragedies end unhappily, not because he had decided to write a tragedy, but because he found the germs of misfortune in the situation. Undisturbed by conceptions of so-called poetic justice, unafraid of producing an "excess of tragic pain," he felt that even relatively slight mistakes in judgment, such as Lear made, spelled disaster even for the innocent who came within reach of their influence. Thus he changed the happy outcome of the original play to a catastrophe and transformed the silly old Lear of the first version into the tragic symbol of a rash, doting parent whose better judgment has been dulled by age. In *Macbeth* he punishes the guilty pair. They pay the mental as well as the physical penalty for their crimes; but Romeo, Juliet, Hamlet, Desdemona, even Othello, meet fates which are out of proportion to their mistakes and their flaws of character when the standards of poetic justice are invoked. Yet only crass sentimentalists could dream that the outcome of the situations in which these people are found could be different. Shakespeare idealized but never sentimentalized life.

The dénouements of his comedies are no less logical in their way. When he employs a recognition scene or the discovery of a long-lost child, he does not introduce the event without due preparation after the manner of classical comedy. In *The Winter's Tale* he shows how Perdita was lost. In *The Comedy of Errors* he introduces Ægeon searching for his boy. *The Merchant of Venice* ends with the trial scene, for those critics who erroneously believe that Shakespeare's main purpose in writing the play was to depict the character of Shylock. But Shakespeare carefully prepares for the last act of the plot by letting us see the exchange of rings.

Logical though these dénouements are, they are never commonplace and are often unexpected in the means by which they are accomplished. Shakespeare often introduced a thrilling *coup de théâtre* which, although foreshadowed and prepared for, produces a surprising peripeteia at a moment of climax. Also, in working up to these moments of climax he has accented either the element of hope or fear in arousing suspense in correct relation to the coming peripeteia. If the change from grief to joy is to take place, he has seemingly cut off all avenues of escape for his hero. Thus in the trial scene in *The Merchant of Venice*, judgment has been passed against Antonio. He has bared his breast for the knife. The letter of the law must be observed. His death is imminent, when suddenly Portia solemnly warns the Jew:

> Shed thou no blood nor cut thou less nor more
> But just a pound of flesh . . . nay, if the scale do turn
> But in the estimation of a hair,
> Thou diest and all thy goods are confiscate.

The preceding dialogue has logically prepared for this literal interpretation which brings the astonishing change of fortune.

In *The Comedy of Errors* the executioner stands ready for Ægeon when he is suddenly recognized by the Abbess. In *The Winter's Tale*, Leontes believes that Hermione is dead. He is shown her statue, marvellously like her. At last, the statue seems to come to life. It is the living Hermione. Thus the recognition scene, which in classical comedy had been merely a quick means to put an end to the plot when humorous scenes were exhausted, was transformed by Shakespeare into a dramatic scene of suspense and climax. In reaching the climax of his tragedies, Shakespeare correctly sheds a ray of hope over the situation. There seems to be some means of escape for his hero. In *Romeo and Juliet* the plan to have Juliet take the sleeping potion is fraught with danger. Yet all possible precautions have been taken. Even when the messenger fails to find Romeo, we know that the young lover is hastening to the tomb; we know that Juliet will awake; we hope she will awake before Romeo has drunk the poison. Time is working for happiness. The Friar, who knows all, is not far away; and, at least, Juliet has escaped the marriage with Paris. Then in one of the most dramatic and pathetic scenes in all drama, the balance of time swings against the lovers. It is neither chance nor destiny. The situation and the plan were unalterably tragic.

The balance between surprise and suspense in the ending of *Macbeth* is deftly kept. In this play our admiration for the hero is not strong enough to make us desire his success. We fear that he may not be punished and it seems likely that he may escape. For how is Birnam wood to come to Dunsinane; and what has one to fear if he cannot be slain by a man born of woman? But Birnam wood comes; and "Macduff was from his mother's womb untimely ripped."

When the fortunes of Lear seem to be at their lowest ebb, as the storm rages and his mind has given away, a vague, dim ray of hope gleams out of the darkness. Gloster confides to Edmund that "the injuries the king now bears will be revenged home; there is part of a power already footed." In the last scene of the fourth act, Lear has found a haven of refuge in the French camp with Cordelia. In a touching scene he begins to regain his reason under the gentle ministrations of his daughter. But hope is blasted by the defeat of the French. Lear and Cordelia are captured, and veiled orders of Edmund foreshadow their execution; but, with the downfall of Edmund and his confession, gleams one more hope that it will not be too late to revoke the order to murder Cordelia. Then once more, with dramatic swiftness, hope is changed to grief—this time irrevocably—as Lear bears in the dead Cordelia and dies of broken heart and tortured soul. All this happens while the fortunes of Edmund, Edgar, Goneril and Regan rise and fall with thrilling *coups de théâtre*. The original play ended happily, and Shakespeare has been accused of allowing chance—once more in the guise of time—to bring about an ending which produces an excess of tragic pain; but to change the dénouement would be to deny that in life mistakes of good men and machinations of evil brains result in tragedy for innocent human beings. Shakespeare, in *King Lear*, was true to life and to art, for in his own words: "Some innocents scape not the thunderbolt."

The dénouement of *Hamlet* is no less dramatic in its sudden events. We know that Laertes' foil is poisoned. We know that the cup contains poison. Hamlet is doomed. But that the foils should be changed when the young prince has received a mortal wound; that the queen should drink the wine; that Laertes should be wounded a moment later by the envenomed sword and should cry: "The king, the king's to blame"; that Hamlet should turn upon the king; these turns of the wheel of fortune create intense excitement.

Still more surprising, yet logical, is the *coup de théâtre* in *Othello*. Desdemona lies dead. Othello is a prisoner. He has learned the truth and is about to be led away, crushed into inactivity. He begins to speak quietly: "Soft you; a word or two before you go." He explains in calm words how he was deceived, was wrought upon, perplexed in the extreme. He quietly begs them to say of him:

> that in Aleppo once,
> Where a malignant and a turban'd Turk
> Beat a Venetian and traduced the state,
> I took by the throat the circumcised dog,
> And smote him, thus.

He plunges the knife into his own heart.

From one point of view, chance and coincidence may be working to bring forth these dénouements; but these events advance the action logically, not irrationally. The plots are based upon hidden designs. The characters are playing desperate games. In the last analysis, a happy ending would be due to chance when the odds are laid so heavily against success. These dénouements may be painfully tragic, but they are painfully true.

Shakespeare's point of departure was plot, and his predilection for complicated plots, full of suspense and surprising *coups de théâtre*, are strong factors in his scheme of playwriting. Broadly speaking, most of his plays observe a unity of action. The many threads of the story are finally gathered together and are unknotted generally in one dénouement. At the same time, the

mechanical conditions of the Elizabethan stage and the form
of dramatic art which he inherited, made the separate scenes of
his plays units in themselves. In Greek drama and in the modern well made play of the nineteenth century, the play itself is
the unit. In French romantic drama each act is likely to be a
unit; but in Shakespearean plays the smaller unity of the single
scene has a strong influence on his technique. This method of
playwriting leads to various results both fortunate and unfor-
unate. It is well suited for representing a complicated story
dramatically. Shakespeare's usual practice is to select scenes
which show the incidents of the story. The oratorical rôle of
the messenger did not appeal to him. Yet he did not always represent deaths. Regan and Goneril, Lady Macbeth die off-stage.
The murder of Duncan is handled in the effective manner of
Greek tragedy, in which the deed of violence is performed almost
if not quite within hearing. The scene in which Hamlet in disordered dress visits Ophelia is not represented, perhaps because
it might have appeared comic. But it is not clear why Shakespeare did not show us Cordelia reading the letter about her
father. However, important events off-stage are rare in Shakespearean drama. He does not hesitate to show murder and torture. The blinding of Gloster on the stage is dangerously close
to the horrible; but a playwright under Senecan influence would
have made the description disgusting. In *Titus Andronicus,*
he equals in bloodiness and horror any thriller of the Grand
Guignol.

Like the medieval theatre, Shakespeare's stage presents scenes
representing almost every phase of human life; but, instead of
being mere transcripts of reality, his scenes almost always serve
a dramatic purpose. The various incidents are unfolded with
kaleidoscopic variety and rapidity. Like the cinema, his dramas
often divide a scene in order to present a piece of information
or an impression which would be held back in other forms of
dramatic art. This method meets with success in the opening
of *Macbeth,* where normally the two scenes of the witches would
be coalesced into one. In the third act of *King Lear,* however,

he breaks into the representation of Lear's madness and the storm by inserting two scenes which foreshadow the coming of the French King. This procedure diminishes the cumulative effect of the scene on the heath. Also, in *Romeo and Juliet*, the rapid changes from the cell of Friar Lawrence to other localities partially destroys the continuity to which modern audiences are accustomed.

Only too often the brevity of separate scenes is disturbing. One scarcely has time to get into the mood and situation and to grasp fully the inner significance of the action before something new is presented. Sustained power is generally shown in the opening and closing acts of his plays. Such scenes as the one between Hamlet and his mother, the balcony scene in *Romeo and Juliet*, the trial scene in *The Merchant of Venice*, and many scenes in *Othello* bear witness to Shakespeare's ability to build up climactic effects. But unfortunately, the scenes are often sketchy. In *King Lear* the intrigue of Edmund with Regan and Goneril is so briefly presented that it scarcely makes a dramatic impression, and it keeps Lear and Cordelia off the stage. If interest lags in certain fourth acts of Shakespeare's plays, it is partially due to the short scenes introduced at this point to tell portions of the complicated plot and to prepare the action for the great catastrophe. Thus in *Macbeth*, the murder of Macduff's son is suddenly and briefly staged. The introduction of such incidents aids in telling the story; but not until Macbeth and Lady Macbeth are on the stage again, do we feel that the dramatic action is really unfolding.

These scenes are more narrative than dramatic, and once a principal has been moulded into an intensely interesting character, his absence is regrettable. The plot of a play should be unfolded by showing the effect of events on the important characters rather than by representing the actions of secondary personages. Had the Elizabethan stage been less flexible, Shakespeare would have had to be more rigorous in his selection of scenes. He could not have included in his plays so many incidents which only help to tell the story; and, very likely, he would have kept his important personages before us more than he does. Marlowe had made depiction of character the basis of selection of scenes. He had shown the events in the life of his hero. Shakespeare was more concerned with representing a plot in which many people were involved.

Yet Shakespeare, in spite of this difference in method, was able to differentiate his people and make of them individuals instead of types. There is no evidence that Shakespeare ever took a character as a point of departure and then constructed a plot to reveal that character in action. He never sacrifices plot to the study of character; but he often sets aside his chief personages in order to represent incidents of secondary importance which a modern dramatist, primarily interested in representing a character, would narrate in some manner. Othello and Iago hold the centre of the stage constantly; but Macbeth, Hamlet, Romeo, Lear, Cordelia, Antony, Cleopatra, suffer a temporary eclipse at moments when a Molière or even a Marlowe would keep them before us. Julius Cæsar and Shylock disappear before the plays are ended because of the exigencies of the complicated plots; but had Shakespeare taken these characters as points of departure he would have brought these plays to a conclusion when their rôles are ended. *The Merchant of Venice* has been produced in this manner, and the effect of the play is very different from what Shakespeare actually intended. It becomes practically a tragic study of character and ought to be called *Shylock*. Likewise, *Julius Cæsar*, if closed after Antony's oration, would better fit its title, but would be a play with a much simpler plot.

No other dramatist has ever produced such a great variety of people so skilfully drawn. Shakespeare's characters, even those of lesser importance, have a clearly defined individuality. His ability to produce a striking portrait by a few telling strokes is shown by the fact that Cordelia speaks less than a hundred lines. Yet having created this true, faithful child and having fixed our interest on her, he allows her to appear in only four out of twenty-six scenes.

The fact that boys played the rôles of women on the Elizabethan stage has been alleged as the reason why there were relatively fewer women than men in Shakespeare's plays. The disguises of girls as boys, such as Viola, have been ascribed to the same reason. But if the narrative sources of his plays are examined, it is found that he used the women he found in them; and, if they were disguised, he employed the situation as it existed. Also, the reason that so many of his heroines are motherless lies in the fact that they are motherless in the narrative or play that he dramatized or rewrote. Shakespeare created characters by endowing them with life; but he invented relatively few rôles and very few plots.

Shakespeare's skill in portraiture and his outstanding ability to develop the action out of the psychological reactions of the characters to events, have led many critics to analyze his plays as if character were of primary importance. This practice is unjust to the playwright. The construction of *Antony and Cleopatra* is a striking example of his method carried to such an extreme that the result is unfortunate. Here he had two characters around whom history and legend have woven a dramatic romance, in which a great leader loses all by succumbing to the sensuous charms of a woman. The glamour of centuries surrounds the theme; but Shakespeare followed the narrative source in Plutarch too closely. He introduced scene upon scene of troublesome brevity, dealing with changes in political fortunes and battles. The impression made by the hero and heroine is often dulled, at moments when it should be clearest, by these breaks in the continuity of the psychological struggle. It is fairly easy to pick up the many threads of a plot presented in this episodic manner; but it is difficult to make the necessary synthesis of character which has been interrupted by plot scenes, and even by scenes which have so slight a bearing on the plot that they are dropped in modern productions.

The spectator of a Shakespearean drama receives many different impressions and emotions in a short space of time. The element of contrast is introduced as the scenes follow in quick succession. It is difficult, however, to prove that Shakespeare consciously employed this method for the sake of contrast. He inherited the system, and he could not avoid contrast, once he had accepted it. He also inherited the medieval custom of introducing scenes of comedy into serious plays "in order to enliven the play," as the old playwrights said. When later English critics came under the influence of classical theory which demands continuity of scenes and forbids humor in tragedy, they attempted to justify the practice of their idol by asserting that he broke the continuity for the sake of introducing contrast and introduced humor to furnish comic relief from the otherwise excessive tragic pain. Historically these theories are false. Nor can the theory of comic relief be justified on artistic grounds. No truly great work of dramatic art is so tragic that unless our risibilities are tickled, we cannot bear it. No Greek or French audience ever longed for a scene of comedy in *Œdipus Rex* or *Phèdre*. English speaking people are certainly not more sensitive than those highly emotional races; nor is Greek drama less tragic than Elizabethan. These so-called scenes of comic relief such as the Porter's scene in *Macbeth,* and the scene in which Ophelia in her madness sings indecent songs, the Grave-diggers' scene in *Hamlet,* do introduce a contrast; but the contrast is so grim that, instead of relieving the emotion, it intensifies the tragedy. These scenes are played in the modern theatre in a grotesque tone; and to Shakespeare, more than to anyone else, belongs the credit of introducing the grotesque in order to heighten the beautiful and deepen the tragic. Victor Hugo, who proclaimed this theory, rightly gave full credit to Shakespeare for suggesting it in practice.

The influence of Shakespeare on the development of dramatic art has been variously felt. In the eighteenth and early nineteenth centuries his dramas were imitated on the Continent; and they helped to break down the rigorous respect for classical form. In England and later in America, critics came to look upon his plays as the pillars of Hercules beyond which we have been swept by the relentless tide of time. Too often we fix our gaze upon them; and, oblivious to other landmarks, we have tried to struggle back to them—always in vain. We have kept our eyes upon the past, teaching the children of every generation that there is nothing in dramatic art beyond Shakespeare; that the newer forms of drama are theatrical. The backwardness of English drama until recent years was due, to a great extent, to the blind worship of a great genius who wrote for a medieval stage.

CHAPTER VIII

SENECA

INTERESTING as it might be to trace the early history of Roman tragedy when Livius Andronicus, Ennius and Pacuvius and others were adapting Greek tragedy for the Roman stage, the lack of sufficient data and the fact that none of these plays are entirely preserved make the task difficult. Nor is the reconstruction necessary for our purpose. The Roman taste for spectacle seems to have modified the Greek technique, for a time came when in the presentation of an *Orestes*, Helen's entrance was shown with great magnificence. In the Euripidean version this was supposed to have taken place at night in order to avoid the insults of the people, but the later adaptation had the entrance by day. But the tragedy which was destined to exert the paramount influence in the Renaissance is tragedy which may not have been composed for representation, but for reading, or at most recitation. At least, Senecan drama is constructed as if it were to be read. On the stage it would lose in effectiveness.

In the tragedies of Euripides there were the germs of decadence of dramatic art. The outbursts of pure oratory, the debates on subjects only remotely suggested by the situation, the maxims and sententious sayings foreshadow a form of drama in which the action is subordinate to the lines and merely forms a background for the author's political, philosophical, mythological, religious, and geographical ideas and information. Also there is generally a trend in all tragedy toward the horrible or disgusting; and even a great genius must constantly be on guard against pushing his tragic element so far that it becomes a bloody episode in the life of mere criminals. Thus, Euripides in the *Bacchantes* describes the murder of Pentheus in terms which are more hair-raising than tragic:

> One awful blended cry
> Rose—the king's screams while life was yet in him,
> And triumph—yells from them. One bore an arm,
> One a foot sandal-shod. His ribs were stripped
> In mangled shreds; with blood-bedrabbled hands
> Each to and fro was tossing Pentheus' flesh.

The oratorical and the horrible became the aim of serious drama in the hands of Seneca. From one point of view it is unjust to apply the usual standards of criticism to Senecan tragedy, because Seneca's aim was to produce a poem in dialogue form in which he could describe, with an amazing flood of words and brilliancy of diction, scenes and deeds which he thought were tragic, but which, at most, give one a creepy thrill. Everything is sacrificed to this aim. But Senecan tragedy was the most artistic form of drama in the opinion of the men of the Renaissance, and contemporary ideals of dramatic technique were based upon these tragedies. Whether Senecan drama was written to be played or not, it finally became the supreme influence for many years in plays written for the stage. Therefore, absurd as it may seem to do so, the usual standards of dramatic criticism must be applied to this form of tragedy.

The Senecan formula of dramatic art was simple. He took a Greek tragedy and discarded everything which did not lend itself to description, oratory, debate and horror. His inventive power and his selection of incidents to be discarded, to be represented or described were conditioned by these considerations.

As a general rule the point of attack and the dénouement are at the same place in Senecan tragedy that they are in his Greek source. If a change was made, it was in order to introduce a descriptive passage. Thus *Hercules Œtœus* opens with Hercules still in Eubœa, whereas Sophocles' *Women of Trachis* begins just before his return home. The Senecan play is extended beyond the Euripidean version and closes with a description of the burning of the body of Hercules, the return of Alcmena with his ashes, and the vision of the hero in heaven. By this means, Seneca was able to introduce in the first act a long description by Hercules of his labors, and a description of the scene at the funeral pyre, and the oratorical lamentation of Alcmena in the last act. The play was enlarged in order to introduce undramatic material.

The opening scene is generally a monologue which is followed by a dialogue. So much knowledge of the myth is presupposed, that the situation remains obscure unless one is acquainted with it beforehand. In the scenes of exposition, as well as throughout the play, the story is so hidden in an avalanche of words that it is difficult to follow. There is none of the pictorial element in the opening scenes that is found in so many Greek tragedies. In Sophocles' *Œdipus Rex,* the eye would be attracted by the people kneeling in supplication before the monarch. We behold the stricken people; but Seneca is more concerned with describing in minute detail how the people are stricken. He prefers to depict in words the horror of the pestilence and the abject terror of the smitten populace, than to foreshadow the action and to arouse suspense. In his *Medea,* he has the heroine pour forth her emotions in a monologue instead of allowing the audience to hear the cries of the distressed woman. He does not show us the children and arouse suspense by foreshadowing their death as does Euripides. He lets his principal characters wail, and complain, and threaten dire vengeance; but he never arouses sympathy for them in the opening scenes.

Revenge is not a lofty motive and it is the chief motive of the typical Senecan play. In order to emphasize this idea of vengeance at the outset, certain plays, such as *Thyestes* and *Agamemnon,* open with a ghost or a fury who recounts the crime which is to be avenged. This procedure recalls the ghost of Polydorus in *Hecuba* and the furies at the beginning of the *Eumenides.* In Seneca's *Agamemnon,* the ghost of Thyestes tells the wrongs he suffered at the hands of Agamemnon's father, Atreus, and announces that the moment for revenge has come. To compare this bombastic spectre with the dramatic appearance of the Watchman in the Æschylean *Agamemnon* only makes one marvel at the bad taste of the Renaissance in drama. This motive of revenge, which puts the whole drama on a low plane, and substitutes a kind of grisly horror for the pulsating suspense and tragedy of fate portrayed by Æschylus, was to become the mainspring of Renaissance drama. And the ghost or fury vowing vengeance was a common device for exposition when Roman brutality was echoed in Italy, France and England. The sole consolation in the face of this lowered tone of a great art is that under the purifying genius of a Shakespeare a *Hamlet* will be refined from this base metal.

The action in Senecan drama limps along in a jerky fashion whenever it emerges, from time to time, in the press of description and oratory. There is scarcely any of the artistic swinging backward and forward of the pendulum of suspense from hope to fear which is found in Greek tragedy. What is left of this artistic device in Seneca's *Œdipus Rex,* for instance, has survived as if by chance. Instead of the scene wrought with consummate skill by Sophocles in which Tiresias, forced to speak by Œdipus, says: "Thou art the man," Seneca deliberately suppresses entirely the idea that Tiresias knows the identity of the murderer of Laius. Why? In order to turn the stage into a slaughter-house by having animals sacrificed so that Tiresias may divine from their bloody entrails the identity of the guilty man. Normally such a scene would take place off the stage, so that it could be described; but since Tiresias is blind, Seneca is able to have his daughter describe the sacrifice performed on the stage, and thus he attains one of his aims: to depict nauseating details which are only artistic to a person afflicted with blood-madness. That is the sole reason for introducing this scene which reaches only an anti-climax, for Tiresias cannot find out anything from the "vitals plucked from living breasts." He must summon the ghost of the murdered Laius.

This event leads to that other favorite device of Seneca: the appearance of a ghost; but he does not represent this scene on the stage, because he cannot forego the joy of describing it. So he has Creon, who has been present at the rites of necromancy, report the result to Œdipus. Now Creon, who knows that the ghost has accused Œdipus, is entirely able to hold back this astounding fact, until he has described minutely where and how the spectre appeared, and his own emotions during the scene. After a long harangue, he finally comes to the point. By this laborious method Seneca reaches an incident about the middle of his play, which comes fairly early in the Sophoclean version.

The original play furnished two other events which appealed to Seneca: the self-inflicted blindness of Œdipus and the suicide of Jocasta. The former is horrible enough in Seneca's opinion to merit the most careful handling. So he describes how Œdipus, with hooked fingers, rent his eyeballs from their deepest roots and then explored the wound. The death of Jocasta, however, is by comparison, tame, being a mere suicide. So Seneca allows it to be enacted on the stage.

Seneca, however, invents a scene between the bloody-eyed Œdipus and Jocasta just before her death; and by so doing, he again reaches a climax of horror. Hardly any situation can be truly tragic in the highest sense of the word, unless it is treated with delicacy. With the delicate feeling that belongs to the great artist, Sophocles never shows us the mother and son together after both are conscious of their crime. The instant that Jocasta knows the truth, she disappears. Only a morbid spectator would wish to see her. The tragedy does not degenerate into the indecent horror portrayed in Seneca's fifth act.

In *Medea*, Seneca substitutes for the dramatic scenes of the Euripidean play a fourth act consisting of a long description of Medea's incantations and of a representation on the stage of her necromancy as she prepares the fatal, poisoned robe. Euripides has her kill her children behind the scenes; but this double murder is a too delectable climax of horror for Seneca to miss. He has Medea slay one child on the stage; and in order to squeeze the last drop of horror out of this scene, worthy of the Grand-Guignol, Seneca brings Jason to witness the murder of the last child, dispatched on the housetops whither Medea has gone to mount her winged chariot.

The dramatic system of this playwright consists in describing scenes that are especially bloody, or which offer possibilities of depicting details which would be lost in being enacted. If a murder can be made more shocking by being witnessed by other characters, it is portrayed in plain sight contrary to the Greek practice. Thus in *Thyestes,* the scene in which Atreus kills and cuts up the children of Thyestes is messengered; but the scene in which Thyestes dines from their limbs, is represented. In each case the maximum of horror and nausea is produced. Greek playwrights portrayed the emotions aroused by a deed and the results of these emotions. Seneca portrays a horrible deed. The Greeks produced tragedy. Seneca produced "thrillers."

A description, however, does not have to be disgusting in order to appeal to Seneca as material for drama. He interrupts the action of *Hercules Furens* at one of the most exciting moments to allow Theseus, who has little connection with the plot, to describe the geography of Hades.

Although Seneca introduces these descriptions, he does keep his principal characters on the stage most of the time; but they talk at each other, rather than to each other. They accuse and bewail and plead; but always in such an oratorical way, that they seem to be aloof from each other, like debaters who speak one after the other on different sides of a subject. The poet too often makes them his mouthpiece and deprives them of individuality. It is impossible to be in sympathy with any one of them. Pale pity is all we feel; and generally we are left with an uncomfortable shudder. The impulsive, active, forceful Œdipus of Sophocles becomes under Seneca's hand a weary figure, who prays he may not survive his unhappy subjects. Senecan characters do not develop. Medea, at most, merely wavers in her feelings.

Another manner of delaying the action and of substituting narrative and description for dramatic scenes, lies in his extensive use of the chorus, which is often entirely unconnected with the plot. The chorus is only a confidant; and generally its function is to appear between the acts and comment on different questions suggested by the situation. In *Hercules Furens,* however, the first chorus consists of the band of captured maidens, of whom Iole is one; but this chorus is supplanted by a chorus of Ætolian women. Euripides has an excellent scene in which Iole and the captured maidens arrive; and Deianira, struck by the beauty of Iole, feels drawn to her and questions her; but Iole remains silent. This is a scene of great suspense and of capital importance, for a few moments later Deianira finds out that Iole is her husband's mistress. Although Seneca introduces Iole in the first act, with characteristic and consistent bungling, he suppresses the scene which contains the initial cause of the action. In his play the discovery that Iole is the mistress of Hercules occurs between the acts and is reported by the nurse. Once more the working of his system is plain. He has opened the play with Hercules still in Eubœa, in order to give Hercules an opportunity to describe his labors. His first act must end with a chorus and he introduces the captive maidens, who are conveniently present in Eubœa. After they have fulfilled this function they are promptly discarded, although Iole is an important character. In every phase of Senecan technique—exposition, point of attack, foreshadowing, obligatory scenes, climax, dénouement, characterization—the dramatic element is subservient to description, oratory, debate, horror, and the motive of revenge.

The culmination of this system is exemplified by his *Thyestes,* which unfortunately with the pseudo-Senecan *Octavia,* became the model of tragic drama for the Renaissance. In the first act of *Thyestes,* a fury goads the ghost of Tantalus to plunge his house into dire disorders and to awaken in Atreus and Thyestes an evil lust for blood. Act II. Atreus, in dialogue with an attendant, plans to recall Thyestes, who seduced the wife of Atreus and who tried to gain the throne. Pretending reconciliation he will offer Thyestes a place on the throne. Act III. A seemingly friendly meeting takes place between the two brothers, at the end of which Atreus places the crown on Thyestes' head. Act IV. A messenger describes to the chorus how Atreus killed and cut up the sons of Thyestes. Act V. Thyestes is shown at a banquet. Atreus gives him the blood of the children to drink and their limbs to eat. Thyestes recognizes the severed heads of his children. He vows vengeance. Comment is unnecessary.

In the pseudo-Senecan *Octavia,* the first act is an elegy by Octavia and her nurse on the subject of her grievous position. She despises Nero, her husband, and he loves a woman who turns out later to be Poppæa. Act II. Seneca, a character in the play, tries in vain to persuade Nero not to divorce Octavia for Poppæa. This scene, in which a confidant pleads with a tyrant for justice and clemency was to be often reproduced in neo-classical tragedy. Act III. The ghost of Agrippina rises, and curses Nero, and prophesies his death. Octavia tries to soothe the grief of the chorus at her divorce. Act IV. Poppæa tells her nurse how she was terrified by a dream, in which Agrippina's ghost and the spectre of her former husband appeared to her. A messenger announces to the chorus that the Roman people, aroused by love for Octavia, are threatening to burn the palace. Act V. Nero threatens vengeance on the people and orders a prefect to carry out his orders to exile Octavia and kill her. He leaves the stage. Octavia is dragged in by guards. The chorus laments and she is taken to exile.

This play, perhaps written by Maternus, is the sole surviving example of Roman historical drama. If it is a fair sample of its kind, one only regrets that it was preserved as a model for the Renaissance. It offends almost every canon of dramatic art. The protagonists and antagonists never meet on the stage, although, in order to avoid each other, they have to use opposite exits and entrances. There is no obligatory scene. The play is a succession of elegiac scenes, ghost scenes, vengeance scenes, and messengering. It was the prototype of many a play in the Renaissance. As Roman tragedy of this period accepted and emphasized the undramatic elements in Greek tragedy, so Renaissance tragedy exalts the undramatic elements in Roman tragedy. Dramatic action, which little by little came upon the stage, is finally drowned in a flood of words. It is a depressing spectacle of degeneration.

CHAPTER IX

ITALIAN TRAGEDY OF THE RENAISSANCE

KNOWLEDGE of classical tragedy came in the early Renaissance through the ten so-called Senecan tragedies, of which *Hercules Œtœus* probably and *Octavia* certainly were not written by Seneca, but were later imitations of his dramaturgy. *Hercules Œtœus* and *Octavia* are even less fitted for representation on a stage than the indubitably genuine Senecan plays. *Octavia,* which has been dated, though not convincingly, as late as the fourth century, is the least dramatic of them all, but exerted a strong influence on tragedy of the later Renaissance.

Interest in Seneca was revived by Nicolas Treveth who wrote a commentary on his works in the late thirteenth or early fourteenth century. Treveth was an Englishman who studied at Oxford and Paris. His work was well known throughout Europe, and especially in Italy, where the revival of classical scholarship was carried on diligently. Medieval drama had attained popularity in France by the beginning of the fourteenth century; but native Italian drama was relatively unimportant, and the mystery play became really popular in Italy only after the revival of the Senecan form of drama. The development of humanistic drama began in Italy in the fourteenth century, while the stage in France and England was wholly occupied by the medieval plays.

After Treveth's commentary on Seneca was published, a circle of scholars in Padua began the study of Senecan verse, and Albertino Mussato was inspired to imitate his tragedies. He seems to have assumed, perhaps correctly, that Senecan tragedy was intended to be read, not acted. His first play, *Ecerinus* (1315), is an historical tragedy in Latin and in Senecan style.

In the first act, Adelheita tells her children, Ecerinus and

Albricus, that their father is Satan. Ecerinus invokes the aid of Satan; and a chorus deplore the evil days into which they have fallen because of the overweening ambition of those in power. Act II. A messenger recounts to the chorus the misfortunes of the country and the rise in power of the cruel Ecerinus. The chorus ask Christ whether he is so entirely given up to the delights of Olympus that he has forgotten the faithful. Act III. The two brothers talk of their deeds and projects. They encourage each other to act as worthy sons of Satan. Lucas, a monk, tries in vain to win them over to better sentiments. A messenger, who announces that Padua has been captured by the Pope, is sentenced to be punished by having his foot cut off. A second messenger brings the same news and is tortured. Ecerinus orders his followers to prepare to lay siege to Padua. The chorus recount how he caused thousands of prisoners to be slain. Act IV. Ecerinus decides to abandon the siege and make war in the East. He prophesies victory; but a messenger describes the whole war and his death. Act V. A messenger recounts the capture of Albricus, how his children were murdered before his eyes, his death, and how his limbs were thrown to dogs.

The narration by messengers, the horror, the sententious, declamatory style, the scene in which the good counsellor pleads in vain, the choral rôle, the cruel villains instead of sympathetic heroes as principal characters in the story, the action behind the scenes, are due to Senecan influence. The point of attack, forty-six years before the close of the play, is medieval; but the play has none of the epic proportions of the medieval drama.

Loschi's *Achilleis* (*ca.* 1387) is constructed on broader lines. In the first three acts, at least one important character carries on the action. The scene changes from Troy to the camp of the Greeks, as the rule of the unity of place had not yet been formulated. The fourth act, however, consists of a recital, by a messenger to a chorus of Greeks, of the death of Achilles. The fifth act shows Agamemnon in his tent lamenting the death of the hero and calling for vengeance. Calchas says that, under the leadership of Achilles, Troy can be captured. After a fairly good beginning, Loschi reached only a climax of undramatic narration and elegy. *Achilleis,* however, is one of the first plays in which the Senecan vengeance motivates the action. Hecuba wishes to avenge the death of Hector by slaying Achilles. No Senecan ghost actually appears; but Hecuba dreams of Priam appearing to her dead and bloody, and begging her to avenge him.

The ghost appears in Corraro's *Progne* (before 1429), which is founded upon Ovid's *Metamorphoses* (VI. 5). The narrative tells how Tereus was married to Progne, who after five years of married life begged her husband to visit her father's land and bring her sister Philumena for a visit. Tereus did so; but as he was returning home, he was overcome with lust and violated Philumena. The horrified maiden begged for death, but Tereus cut out her tongue and imprisoned her.

Judging from the construction of *Titus Andronicus,* which contains a somewhat similar situation, we may conjecture that Shakespeare would have included these events in his play, had he dramatized this story. But Corraro has learned his lesson from Seneca and his opening act takes place after all this has happened. In Senecan fashion, the shade of Diomedes comes from Hades and predicts in obscure words that new horrors will be committed. The point of attack is *in mediis rebus,* according to the doctrine of Horace and the practice of Seneca. The motive of vengeance appears when Progne discovers what has happened to Philumena. She takes revenge upon her husband by slaying their son and serving his limbs to Tereus, after the manner of Seneca's Thyestean feast.

In 1471 Poliziano produced his *Orfeo,* which is the first play in Italian on a subject borrowed from classical mythology. In its first form this *favola,* as it is called, follows the technique of the *rappresentazioni,* or medieval Italian drama. The "annunciation," or medieval prologue, is pronounced by Mercury instead of an angel as in the plays on sacred subjects. The play then opens with a pastoral scene, in which the shepherd

Aristeo tells Mopso how he has fallen in love with a charming nymph whom he lately beheld. Mopso bids him beware of love, but Aristeo sings a song to his inamorata. Tirsi, returning from a search for one of Mopso's herd, speaks of having seen a beautiful maiden. Aristeo, sure she must be his lady, sets out in search of her. He finds the nymph, Eurydice; but she flees from him. Orfeo sings some Latin verses in praise of the Cardinal of Mantua. A shepherd informs him of the death of Eurydice through the sting of a serpent. Orfeo, chanting a lament, arrives at the gate of Hades; and, quieting the Furies and Cerberus with his song, he enters and begs Pluto to give him back his wife. Pluto, at the request of Proserpina, grants Orfeo's plea on condition that he will not look at Eurydice until they have ascended to earth; but Orfeo is unable to keep his eyes from her, and she bids him farewell forever. As he tries to follow her, a Fury bars his way. He breaks into lamentation. A Bacchante, indignant at his words against love and women, calls upon the women to slay him. They evidently pursue him off the stage, for the Bacchante returns with Orfeo's head. The play ends with a hymn and a sacrifice to Bacchus.

Some years later Teobaldo divided this play into five acts, introduced a chorus of Dryads in the second act and a chorus of Mænads in the last act, added a few speeches, and dropped the anachronistic reference to the Cardinal of Mantua. He thereupon called the play a tragedy. In substance and technique the second version is very close to the original form, which Symonds correctly styles "pastoral melodrama with a tragic climax." It had a greater influence on later pastoral drama and opera because of its lyric songs, than on Renaissance tragedy. The scene demands a medieval, simultaneous setting, which is incompatible with the tragic form of drama as produced by the imitators of Seneca.

During the latter half of the fifteenth century, mystery plays, comedies of Terence and Plautus, Senecan tragedies, and imitations of Senecan tragedies in Latin began to be presented in Rome, under the direction of Cardinal Raffaele Riario, and his nephew, Cardinal Pietro Riario. Vitruvius' description of the ancient theatre was rediscovered; and Raffaele Riario had a stage constructed with a setting consisting of a row of pillars with curtains hanging between them. This scenery could represent the public square for comedies, and the vestibule or exterior of a palace for tragedies. The adoption of this single scene instead of a medieval system of simultaneous setting would tend to facilitate the introduction of the rule of the unity of place. Also, it furnished that vague but indispensable locality for Senecan tragedy known as "behind the scenes," where most of the action in Renaissance drama will take place.

The influence of the simultaneous setting and the loose construction of medieval mysteries was still strong enough when Verardi was composing his *Historia Baetica* and his *Fernandus Servatus,* to cause these plays to be a combination of medieval and Senecan technique. Although he observes the unity of time in the *Historia Baetica* (produced in Riario's palace in 1492), the scene changes from the palace of Boabdil to the camp of Ferdinand. He also suppresses the chorus; but there is much messengering, and deliberations take the place of action. Dramatic dialogue is smothered by long discourses and harangues drawn from Livy and Sallust. The usual dream is introduced. In his other play, the Senecan Furies assume the medieval rôle of a devil as they tempt the would-be assassin of Ferdinand. Isabella's prayer to St. James, the appearance of the saint, and miraculous healing of Ferdinand's wound are typically medieval.

Dovizio's *Augustinus* (played about 1493), is even more medieval with its thirty-three scenes and no division into acts, its changes of scene from Africa to Milan, the sermon, and the introduction of comic episodes.

About the same time that these plays were written, other tragedies were being constructed on lines more strictly Senecan, in which elegy and narration almost completely overshadow any dramatic development of action. The first three acts of Laudivio's *De Captivitate Ducis Jacobi* (written before 1471) consist of deliberations and narrations. The hero enters in the

fourth act in time to be killed, and in the fifth act the announcement of his death is made.

Antonio Cammelli's *Filostrato e Panfila* (produced at Ferrara
in 1499) is a tragedy in the vernacular in Senecan style, although founded upon the first novel of the fourth day of the
Decameron. The prologue, which gives the plot, is spoken by
the Ghost of Seneca. Having fulfilled two technical exigencies
of introducing a ghost and pointing to Seneca as the sponsor for
his artistic methods, Cammelli begins his play with a rhetorical
scene between Demetrio, King of Thebes, and his daughter
Panfila. She is a widow and her father has no intention of marrying her to anyone, although he vaguely foreshadows the action
by commending a certain Filostrato, a servant but a man of
character. Panfila, in a monologue, discloses her love for
Filostrato; and as her father will not give her in marriage, she
resolves to become the mistress of Filostrato. In the second act
Filostrato learns of Panfila's love for him and how to enter her
room through a subterranean passage. The meeting of the lovers
takes place between the acts, and in the third act Filostrato tells
a courtier of his happiness. Demetrio informs us in monologue
that he was a concealed witness of the meeting. Pandaro introduces the necessary foreshadowing dream. In the fourth act
Pandaro pleads for clemency toward the lovers, but Demetrio
seeks bloody revenge. Neither of the lovers repents and
Demetrio resolves to have Filostrato put to death. The last act
opens with a description of the execution. The executioner gives
Filostrato's heart to Demetrio, who has it sent to Panfila.
She takes poison and dies on the stage. The play closes with the
repentance on the part of the father, a scene which will become
canonical.

In 1502 Galeotto del Carretto wrote *Sofonisba,* which was not
played until 1546, but which may have been known by Trissino,
who composed in 1515 a tragedy in Greek style on the same subject and with the same title. Both plays are drawn from Livy's
account of the defeat of Syphax and the fate of his wife Sophonisba; but they are very dissimilar in construction. The earlier

play contains a chorus, but is cast in the mould of medieval drama. Even the chorus is practically personified stage directions and narrative, for it describes what is happening as the characters go from one place to another, over the seas and finally to symbolic lands. There are many changes of scene and a long lapse of time. The point of attack is clearly medieval, as the play opens when Massanissa joins the Romans. Many of the events, which are recounted in the exposition of Trissino's version, are represented. The result is that Sophonisba herself, as so oftens happens in medieval drama, plays but a small part in the play bearing her name. The Greek tragic playwrights finally learned to keep the principal character in the story an active and dramatic character in the play, whereas in New Comedy, in Senecan tragedy and in the later mystery plays the principals are often overshadowed, although for different reasons, since these forms of drama are widely divergent.

Until the beginning of the sixteenth century Greek tragedy was little known; but Sophocles' tragedies were published in 1502 and those of Euripides in 1503. During this century Aristotle was constituted the supreme judge in the theory of dramatic art. Constant and voluminous discussion of his principles of criticism stimulated interest in Greek drama. The Greek tragic playwrights displaced Seneca as a model for certain Italian tragedies. Trissino was the first Italian dramatist to show good taste by preferring Greek tragedy to the plays of Seneca, which, as he said, are mostly fragments of Greek plays joined together with little art. His *Sofonisba* (1515) is not only classical, but in certain respects, more Greek than Senecan.

The play opens with a long recital by Sophonisba to her confidante, Erminia, of the history of Carthage. She tells that she was once affianced to Massinissa, but was given in marriage by her father to Syphas. The usual classical dream foreshadows allegorically the action which is to follow. The chorus wonders whether she should be told that the enemy is at the city gates. A servant informs her of the defeat and capture of Syphax by Massinissa; and a messenger announces the capture of the city. The real dramatic action now begins, for Massinissa and Sophonisba meet in a scene not without dignity and power. Sophonisba begs her former lover not to allow her to be taken as a captive to Rome and asks him to give his promise to protect her. They withdraw; and after a choral passage, a messenger informs Lælius that Massinissa has married the queen in order to protect her. Massinissa now appears and the question is whether the Romans will allow him to prevent his bride from being led to Rome as a captive. Cato comes to calm the hot dispute and it is agreed that Scipio shall make the decision. Syphax appears before Cato, and accuses Sophonisba of having incited him to war. Scipio orders Massinissa to give up his bride. The chorus sees a servant carrying a cup to Sophonisba. A servant tells how Sophonisba has drained the cup of poison. Sophonisba appears; and, taking leave of her child and her sister, she dies decorously in a chair and is borne away in it. Massinissa enters. He has committed a terrible blunder, and was only waiting for darkness to save Sophonisba, who took the poison too soon!

Trissino compressed many events into one day; but he did so without any thought of the unity of time since that theory had not yet been formulated. The scene really changes from the palace to the camp of Scipio; but the unity of place was even a later theory than that of the unity of time. The limits of time and of place introduced by Trissino are much narrower than those employed by Galeotto del Carretto; but they are due to imitation of Greek tragedy and not to observance of rules. Practice preceded critical theory as usual. Trissino chose his point of attack in accordance with the custom of Greek playwrights. It is farther from the climax than it will be in later Italian tragedy. There are long speeches and characterless messengers report too much of the action; but Trissino found justification for narration in Euripidean tragedy. There is no division into acts and the chorus is handled more after the manner of Euripides than of Seneca. The greatest departure from Senecan technique lies in the fact that there is no horror or bloody revenge with accompanying Furies or ghosts. The tragedy is on a high plane; and

Sophonisba, although pale in comparison to Greek heroines, is more dignified and more sympathetic than Senecan women. Sympathy is a very important emotion in dramatic art, but is rarely aroused by Senecan heroes. Trissino did not aim to shock his audience, but to move them to sympathetic tears. This is the result of Greek influence. Protagonists of medieval drama were sympathetic characters. Their death aroused religious exaltation because it was a triumphal apotheosis. Protagonists of Greek tragedy were sympathetic characters. Their death or defeat aroused tragic exaltation. Protagonists of Senecan drama are revengeful villains. Their death arouses horror.

Greek tragedy continued to exert its strongest influence until about 1530; but it was unfortunate for dramatic art that, even during this period, the dramatists were so imbued with the worst features of Senecan tragedy that they caricatured their Greek models. Rucellai based the first three acts of *Rosmunda* (1524) on *Antigone,* while the last two acts are a dramatization of the story of Donna Lombarda, who was forced by her husband to drink from her father's skull. This gruesome act is motivated by introducing the idea from *Antigone* that Rosmunda had buried her father's body against the orders of her husband. The joining of two plots resulted in producing a large amount of action in a rather short play. The Greek influence is manifest in the following features of the play: the point of attack is just before the initial cause of the action; the action is developed up to the fourth act almost entirely by the principal characters in a series of obligatory scenes; finally, the chorus takes a rather active rôle in the plot. The narration of horrible details by a messenger in the fifth act is Senecan. The character of Rosmunda, although drawn without any of the depth and beauty of her prototype, is at least not the revolting type of heroine who will appear in later tragedy of the Renaissance. The playwrights attempted to follow Greek models; but their inability to avoid the production of the horrible instead of the tragic is illustrated by Martelli's *Tullia* (*ca.* 1527). In order to produce this play, which is a travesty of Sophocles' *Electra,* the author has falsified entirely the historical incident of Tullia driving over the dead body of her father. Not content with inventing the character of Tarquinia to play the rôle of Clytemnestra, Martelli quenches utterly any sympathy for his heroine Tullia, who corresponds to the tragic Electra, by making her a woman who has already committed murder for the sordid motive of gaining power. Her husband, Lucio, the Orestes of this play, is a fitting mate for this hardened sinner of a wife.

The play follows Sophocles' *Electra* in many scenes and the Euripidean version in others, but the play is none the less a travesty of its sources. When Lucio faces his wife in the recognition scene, he pretends, like Orestes, to be carrying his own ashes; but as he does so in an epic speech of 211 lines the pathos turns to bathos. Martelli had evidently read his Aristotle carefully and was trying to make the most of the recognition scene. The death scene is handled in Greek fashion by having it take place within hearing of the audience, instead of having it narrated after it has occurred. However, the dénouement of the play does not follow its model, because it was not possible for Martelli to leave the question of the fate of his hero and heroine unanswered as could Sophocles or Euripides. When the people are reported to be rising against Lucio, the spirit of Romulus appears as a *deus ex machina* and bids them allow Lucio to reign in peace. Such is the Machiavellian reward for this Machiavellian pair.

Senecan influence is shown in the long-winded report of a dream of Tarquinia which is dragged into the play. Also, Martelli cannot fail to introduce a ghost, so he has the spectre òf the murdered king cry for vengeance. The revengeful spirit generally appears at the beginning of such plays, but this time the ghost just manages to crowd into the play at the climax.

Thus in spite of a praiseworthy attempt to follow the technique of Greek tragedy, of which the sole happy result was to have the principal characters develop the plot, Italian tragedy turned back to the imitation of the worst features of Senecan tragedy. Utterly failing to note or understand the delicacy with which the

Greek playwrights treated the *harmatia* or tragic fault of the hero, they present the fault so that it becomes a disgusting crime. One can admire their heroes only for the perfection of their villainy. They arouse fear, but never even pity. In *Tullia*, lust for power is the motive actuating these degenerate descendants of Electra and Orestes, who were impelled by Necessity or Fate and with whom we sympathize even if they are matricides. In Speroni's *Canace* the brother and sister commit incest knowingly, whereas Œdipus and Jocasta are innocent at heart of their crime. But *Œdipus Rex* in the hands of Anguillara becomes a shocking burlesque. The Italians did not understand that tragedy is not found in severed heads or gory limbs, but springs from the death struggle of a great soul against human circumstances.

The Greek influence was fostered by Alessandro Pazzi who translated *Iphigenia in Tauris* (1524), *Cyclops* and *Œdipus Rex* (1527), published a Greek text and revised a Latin text of Aristotle's *Poetics* (1536-7). In 1524 he wrote *Didone in Cartagine*, a play without act divisions, in which the chorus and dialogue is handled in Greek style. The play opens, however, at a point very close to the dénouement. Æneas has decided to set sail and abandon Dido. After the manner of Seneca, the ghost of Sychæus, Dido's husband, speaks a prologue, and his death at the hands of Pygmalion is revenged during the play. This gives an opportunity to introduce on the stage the severed hands and head of the murderer. The exposition of severed limbs on the stage will become one of the usual scenes of Italian tragedy. While Greek tragedies, such as Euripides' *Bacchantes*, are the ultimate source of such procedures, yet the attempt to arouse tragic horror in this way always seems to be more in the style of Latin and Italian tragedy. It is perhaps due to a restraining Greek influence that the bloody details of the scene are not insisted upon by Pazzi as they will be by later Italian dramatists. The whole play, however, is a dramatization of a dénouement and is an early example of the narrowing of the dramatic framework. This story, dramatized later in the century by Giraldi Cinthio and Dolce in Italy, by Jodelle in France, and by Marlowe in England readily lends itself to an elegiac form of drama consisting of lamentation and narration of the death of Dido. The theme of betrayed love is not very dramatic, especially if only the betrayal is represented; and the popularity of this story may well have had its share in making elegy out of tragedy. To make a drama out of this story, the point of attack must be set back so as to include the awakening love between Dido and Æneas. This was Virgil's way and afterward the way of Marlowe working under dramatic ideals different from the Italian.

Giraldi Cinthio in his *Discourse on Comedy and Tragedy* (1543) proclaimed the superiority of Latin over Greek tragedy on the ground that Seneca excelled the Greek dramatists in prudence, gravity, decorum, majesty and sententious maxims. Also he pointed out that all Seneca's tragedies end unhappily; and that if he, himself, had written tragedies with a happy ending it was to satisfy the wishes of the audience, for he deemed it better to produce a less praiseworthy play in order to please those for whom the play is enacted. Thus the criteria applied to serious drama are absolutely undramatic.

What difference does it make if Cinthio and many others study the "obscure" Aristotle and pour forth the results of their lucubrations in great tomes? They only succeed in foisting upon Aristotle the excuse for their theories of the unity of place and time. That is the one tangible result of their adoration of Aristotle. They talk learnedly of tragedy, of pity and compassion, and of horror. They sometimes write well of suspense and exposition and climax; but it is Seneca whom they admire and much of their task consists in twisting Aristotelian theory to apply to their own practice founded upon Seneca. It is not their critical theory, but their dramatic practice which is important. All their study of the *Poetics* could not save them from preferring the prudent, grave, decorous, majestic, sententious Seneca to the greatest dramas that the world had known.

In 1541 Giraldi produced his *Orbecche*, which was founded on his own novella, and which was the first regular neo-classic tragedy in Italian to be presented on a stage. The play opens with a formal prologue undoubtedly borrowed from comedy. It is an intimate talk with the audience in a familiar tone interspersed with flattery in which Giraldi justifies his attempt to produce tragedy, hitherto not a popular form of art.

The first act is a kind of second prologue, in Senecan style, introducing the plot. Nemesis calls for the Furies to take vengeance on Orbecche and her father Sulmone. The shade of Selina then appears and wonders very correctly why Nemesis does not entrust the question of wreaking vengeance to her. The answer is that Giraldi did not wish to miss any opportunity to represent every gruesome figure possible. And why must she be revenged? Simply because Sulmone discovered years ago, through the agency of his daughter Orbecche, that his wife, Selina, was committing incest with their eldest son and thereupon murdered both of them! This is the sordid motive of the plot. This "injustice" is to be avenged by the death of Orbecche and Sulmone.

In the second act the exposition of the plot is given laboriously, accompanied by line after line of reflections on life in general. Orbecche explains to her nurse that she is secretly married to Oronte and has two children by him, but that her father has informed her that she must marry the King of the Parthians. The position of the point of attack has forced the narration of this obligatory scene between Sulmone and Orbecche—a scene which would have been an excellent means of giving exposition and which contains the real motivating incident of the plot. The motivation of vengeance is merely trumped up in imitation of Seneca. The nurse promises to summon Oronte, but she spouts a monologue of such length that he finally appears unasked. The sole result of his interview with his wife is a decision to have Malecche intercede for them with Sulmone.

In the third act comes the inevitable scene, imitated from *Octavia*, in which Malecche pleads with the tyrant for clemency. Sulmone pretends to be won over to good counsel, and an apparent reconciliation takes place between the couple and the father. This situation of two lovers—here they are married—whom an irate father wishes to separate by marrying one of them to someone else for the sake of a large dowry, is one belonging to New Comedy rather than to tragedy. In New Comedy the father would relent, because the life story of one of the pair would be told at this point, and it would be proved that the apparent slave was a long-lost child. Curiously enough, Oronte makes this speech in a monologue and informs the audience that he was a child of noble birth, set adrift in the sea, rescued by pirates, and, when he reached Susa, was made to perform servile tasks. All this information, which would bring about the dénouement of comedy, has nothing to do with the unfolding of the plot of this play. It is only explicable, together with the prologue and the situation itself, as being the result of the influence of comic technique. Comedy was very popular at this time; and it is probable that Giraldi Cinthio was unconsciously influenced by its construction. Also the scene between Orbecche and Oronte begins with each one conscious of the other's presence and speaking in asides. This is a practice often found in comedy, but asides are extremely rare in tragedy.

This play illustrates the theory that the situation of New Comedy is inherently tragic and would often end unhappily were it not for the fact that the situation does not really exist. In this case, however, Giraldi is working toward the unhappy ending. So Oronte's life story, given in a monologue, changes nothing. Sulmone's reconciliation is only pretense; and the play, from this point on, is modelled on Seneca's *Thyestes*. In the fourth act, a messenger narrates to the chorus how Sulmone cut off Oronte's hands, murdered the children before their father's eyes, and then killed Oronte. Every harrowing incident is described with care.

In the last act, the severed limbs are presented in covered dishes by Sulmone to his daughter, after she has had time to tell her dream. Naturally she is somewhat aroused at discovering the limbs; and drawing the knife from one of the bodies, she stabs Sulmone, who decorously retires behind the scenes to die. Here is another body to cut up; and Orbecche appears with her father's head in her hands. Pouring forth imprecations and grief, she commits suicide. And after all this, Giraldi apologizes for breaking the rules by having Orbecche kill herself on the stage.

The vengeance motive; the appearance of the Furies and spectres in the opening; the point of attack no longer *in mediis rebus* but "at the end of things"; the scenes with confidants; the pleading in vain for clemency; the narrated horrors; the substitution of metaphors and harangues for action; the speeches and monologues with no connection with the plot and of unconscionable length; the chorus standing around and spouting platitudes; the author's satisfaction at having pointed a moral and adorned a tale with sententious maxims; the replacement of tragedy by horror, action by narration, the undramatic by the dramatic: these features all bear witness to the fact that Italian tragedy has at last come into its own.

The success of this play established tragedy in high favor, and inspired Sperone Speroni to outdo Giraldi in a piece on a similar subject. His *Canace* (1542) improves upon *Orbecche* only from the point of view of absurdity in its construction and in making the situation more disgusting. Were it not for the general inartistic impression made by *Orbecche,* one might have some sympathy for the hero and heroine. They have committed no crime. Giraldi keeps the incest out of his play proper; Speroni goes him one better by making the conscious incest of a brother and sister the motivating incident of his plot. These degenerates are the hero and heroine of this drama which observes all necessary decorum by having the deaths narrated.

In order to introduce the motive of vengeance, Venus, who speaks the formal prologue, is supposed to be desirous of taking revenge upon Æolus for having raised the storm, at Juno's request, about the fleet of Æneas. Venus, therefore, has inspired Æolus' twin son and daughter with incestuous love. Speroni solves the question of opening the play with the appearance of

a spectre, by introducing the shade of the child of this unhappy union, who was murdered by Æolus at birth. The culmination of absurdity is reached by having the next scene take
place just before the birth of the infant. The plot revolves
about its birth and death. The play actually begins after the
dénouement. Nothing illustrates better the importance attached
to having a spectre begin a play. In the controversy which
arose over this tragedy, the introduction of the shade of the
child was not questioned from the point of view of common
sense, but whether the Sixth Book of the *Æneid* was sufficient
authority for it! The rest of this curious act shows Æolus
happy with his son and daughter. A good counsellor fears that
misfortune may come. In the second act, Canace reveals the
approaching birth in a monologue; and in the next scene her
nurse tries to persuade her not to commit suicide. In the
third act Deiopea, the wife of Æolus, recounts her foreshadowing dream to her maid. The nurse appears with a basket containing the new-born infant; and telling Deiopea that it contains flowers, she gives the basket to a servant to place on the
altar of Juno. The next act contains the well-known scene of
a messenger narrating to the chorus how Æolus discovered the
child under the flowers and killed it, and the usual vain counsel
of clemency offered to Æolus by his counsellor and by his wife.
This meeting of Æolus and his wife is the only scene carried
on by two important characters, and even Deiopea is not a
principal. Only in the fifth act does Macareo make his first
appearance and the minister tells him how, under the orders
from Æolus, he bore steel and poison to Canace, who committed suicide. Macareo leaves in dispair. Æolus repents and
tries to save Macareo from suicide; but it is too late. The
servant narrates how he killed himself.

The prologue by Venus, the incest inspired by her, the scene
in which the nurse begs Canace not to die, the repentance of
Æolus too late to save his son, recall Seneca's *Hippolytus,* but
the whole construction and tone of the play is such that one
hesitates to make even Senecan influence responsible for it. Let

the responsibility rest upon Speroni and upon Giraldi for having inspired him with his *Orbecche*.

In spite of the popularity of this new form of Italian tragedy exemplified in *Orbecche* and *Canace*, Lodovico Dolce kept alive the influence of Greek technique. His *Giocasta* from *The Phœnician Women*, his *Iphigenia*, *Medea* and *Hecuba*, reborn, as he says, from Euripides, bear witness to an admiration for the Greek form, at the same time that his *Thieste* shows his interest in Senecan tragedy. *Didone* (1547) is composed along the usual lines of Latin tragedy and has most of the faults of the narrow, undramatic form.

Marianna, one of the bright spots in the darkness of dramatic art at this period, is a combination of Greek and Latin construction. Perhaps the form of the second prologue is due to an influence of medieval technique. Pluto comes forth from the obscure cavern where he torments the damned souls in eternal fire and announces that he desires to enrich Hell with Herod. He orders Jealousy to enter Herod's heart and Jealousy sets forth on this mission. The expressions employed, the Satanic attributes of Pluto, the conception and tone of the scene plainly recall scenes in medieval drama in which Satan sends forth a devil to take possession of a wicked tyrant. It is not a case of personal revenge, which is generally the motive of Italian tragedy. Although the introduction of the abstract character may be due to the influence of Plautus, the opening of Senecan tragedy by a Fury or a ghost could hardly have developed into such a scene had it not been for the influence of medieval drama. But here of course, after Herod has murdered his wife and children and repented of his crimes, there is no Virgin to forgive the hardened sinner, and either resuscitate his victims or receive him into Heaven. The climax is the usual narration of the deaths in the fourth and fifth acts, but the point of attack is so placed that the action has time, not only to unfold, but actually to arouse suspense. Herod is jealous of his wife, Marianna, who clears herself of the false charge of planning to poison her husband, but who is immediately afterward accused of guilty love for Soemo. Like the heroines of medieval drama she is innocent and her presence on the stage is like a breath of fresh air after the incestuous adulterous women whose fate we have been beholding with a mixture of pity and disgust. She is a forerunner of Desdemona, just as Herod is of Othello, and the very fact that we can sympathize with her shows she is not typically Senecan. There is the usual counsellor who gives good advice in vain, but instead of delivering his appeal in one long act, his pleading becomes more intense as the plot unfolds. The principals, instead of carefully avoiding each other, carry on the action and no obligatory scene is missing in the first three acts. Marianna fights a losing battle, but she fights it before our eyes.

Euripides' *Phœnician Women* is not one of his best plays from a technical point of view, but was very popular because of its oratorical effects. Dolce's *Giocasta* follows mainly a Latin translation of the Euripidean version in the arrangement of its scenes; and hence it avoids many of the usual infelicities of the narrower form of Italian tragedy based upon Seneca's *Octavia*. The opening of the play, however, contains certain additional scenes evidently devised to make the exposition clear. These playwrights of the Renaissance had to be explicit in explaining the situation, because the stories on which the plots were founded were not so familiar to their audience as they were to the Greeks. Their problem in exposition was the problem of the writers of New Comedy. They had much to explain; and they were working up to a climax of narration of deaths which occupied the fourth and fifth acts. It is for that reason that their exposition was long-winded and left little opportunity for development of the situation, even had it been their aim to unfold the action by events enacted on the stage. But it was not the aim of these playwrights to work up to a great clash of contending forces in the latter part of their play. They employed the first three acts in explaining the situation and in causing the action to develop through one or two events, imminent when the play begins, to a point where at least one character suffered death. To them, the culmination of their artistic efforts lay in the narration, not only of the death itself, but of what was said by the principal characters at that time. Cleverness in exposition; foreshadowing, except through the usual dream; suspense through arousing alternate emotions of hope and fear; character drawing, except to make the hero as villainous as possible—all this was of little importance. And when in certain of these plays there is a faint trace of technical artistry along these lines, it is due to either chance or to the classical source of the play. Thus Dolce's *Giocasta* is better constructed than his *Didone,* because he followed Euripides in the former and the narrower Senecan form in the latter. It is doubtful that he knew that his *Giocasta* was a higher form of dramatic art. Gascoigne's translation of Dolce's *Giocasta* was to be an important medium in acquainting Englishmen with classical tragedy.

Aretino's *Orazia* (1546) is also noteworthy because it is not a revenge play working up to a climax of narration describing a murder. At the opening of the play, the three Horatii have been chosen to decide the fate of Rome by a duel with the three Curiatii. The surviving conqueror, Horatius, enraged at Celia, his sister, who is affianced to one of the Curiatii and who upbraids her brother, slays her. Then the dramatic question arises as to what shall be done with a savior of his country who has murdered his sister; and for two acts this question is discussed in a very dramatic manner. From the point of view of technique this play is the best Italian tragedy of the sixteenth century; but it had no influence on the ensuing development of dramatic art. It was not *Orazia,* but *Orbecche* and *Canace,* which became the models. The critics soon put their stamp of approval upon the Senecan form, or rather the Senecan form as it had degenerated. Such plays as *Orazia* and *Marianna* were lost from view in the obfuscation produced by Scaliger and others through their admiration of Seneca. The faults of Senecan drama and misinterpretation of Aristotle became the bases of criticism of dramatic technique.

These critics of the Renaissance held that dramatic art was primarily a subdivision of the art of poetry, not an art which merely employs dialogue, in poetry or prose, with other arts, in order to produce true dramatic effect. For Aristotle, the art of poetry was the art of imitation, as well as an art of writing in verse. He was fully aware of the synthetic quality of dramatic art; but for the men of the Renaissance, drama became a literary art, predominantly rhetorical. Aristotle had pointed out that tragedy resembles epic poetry in certain respects, especially that tragedy was closer in tone to the epic than to comedy. On the basis of such resemblance and from the practice of playwrights, the critics of the sixteenth century evolved the theory of the complete separation of tragedy and comedy. It was considered inartistic to introduce any humor into a serious play. The separation of tragedy and comedy was a theory which lasted in France well into the nineteenth century. Comedy was considered a lower form of art. In the Renaissance, men apologized for writing it. Even in the early nineteenth century, writers of French tragedy stood a better chance of election to the Academy than did comic playwrights. This classification of dramatic art is false in every respect. Drama is an art in itself and is not a subdivision of literature. There is no strict line of demarcation between tragedy and comedy.

"Tragedy," said Scaliger in his *Poetics* (1561), "employs kings whose affairs are those of the city, fortress, and the camp. . . . All things wear a troubled look; there is a pervading sense of doom, there are exiles and death. . . . The matters of tragedy are great and terrible, as commands of kings, slaughters, despair, suicides, exiles, bereavements, parricides, incests, conflagrations, battles, the putting out of eyes, weeping, bewailing, eulogies and dirges. . . . A tragedy is the imitation of the adversity of a distinguished man." On the surface this is true of Greek tragedy, and it is profoundly true of the Italian tragedy of the Renaissance; but it no more represents the soul of Greek tragedy than a contorted face with bloody eyes represents the soul of Œdipus. These are mere externalities of tragedy.

Lest anyone assume from these passages that Scaliger believed in the introduction of many events into a tragedy, it is well to consider his model scenario. In speaking of the story of Ceyx, he says:

If a tragedy is to be composed from this last story, it should not begin with the departure of Ceyx, for, as the whole time for stage representation is only six or eight hours, it is not true to life to have a storm arise, and the ship founder, in a part of the sea from which no land is visible. Let the first act be a passionate lamentation, the chorus to follow with execrations of sea life; the second act, a priest with votive offerings conversing with Alcyone and her nurse, altars, fire, pious sentiments, the chorus following with approbation of the vows; the third act, a messenger announcing the rising of a storm, together with rumors as to the ship, the chorus to follow with mention of shipwrecks, and much apostrophizing of Neptune; the fourth act, tumultuous, the report found to be true, the shipwrecks described by sailors and merchants, the chorus bewailing the event as though all were lost; the fifth act, Alcyone peering anxiously over the sea and sighting far off a corpse, followed by the resolution, when she was about to take her own life. This sample outline can be expanded by the introduction of other characters.

Such a play is not tragedy, but is narration and elegy. Its construction is typical of tragedy of the Renaissance. "The action of tragedy should be prolonged until there is some change of fortune," said Minturno. Scaliger considered tragedy to be "the imitation of the adversity of a distinguished man." These critics failed to recognize that highly developed Greek tragedy contains a clash of contending forces or wills, personified by the protagonist and the antagonist. The portrayal of such a clash tends to bring these principal characters on the stage and to place them face to face in obligatory scenes. The "imitation of adversity" and the mere "change of fortune" do not imply a clash of wills and do not necessarily imply the existence of a great struggle or of an important antagonist, as is shown by the fact that Scaliger's scenario fulfills the requirements of a "change of fortune" and "imitation of adversity." Thus tragedy, because of this conception, became narrative. The principals lamented and were talked about, more than they acted. The protagonist and antagonist bewailed their lot to confidants, instead of fighting out the question man to man.

Although Aristotle's definition of tragedy was repeatedly quoted to prove that drama was acted, not narrated, the critics failed to see that the important question for the playwright was not the difference between an epic poem and a tragedy, but the difference between representing an event on the stage or narrating events off the stage. The critics and playwrights knew Aristotle's statement that there should be nothing improbable among the actual incidents, but if it be unavoidable it should be outside the tragedy, like the improbability in *Œdipus Rex* of Sophocles. But the playwright used the first three acts for exposition and possibly one or two events in the action, in order to reach the narrated climax or dénouement in the fourth and fifth acts.

In order to explain the reasons for narrating instead of representing the tragic events of the climax upon the stage, the critics relied upon the following statement from Horace's *Ars Poetica*:

An action is either represented on the stage, or, being done elsewhere, is there related. The things which enter by the ear affect the mind more languidly, than such as are submitted to the faithful eyes and what a spectator presents to himself. You must not, however, bring upon the stage things fit only to be acted behind the scenes; and you must take away from view many actions, which elegant description may soon after deliver in the presence of the spectators. Let not Medea murder her sons before the people; nor the execrable Atreus openly dress human entrails; nor let Progne be metamorphosed into a bird, Cadmus into a serpent. Whatever you show me in this manner, not able to give credit to, I detest.

The theory as a whole is sound dramatic technique and one which any dramatist might well ponder over. Had the dramatists, or even the theorists, grasped the full significance of the statement, there would have been far more dramatic action and less narration and vain philosophizing in classical tragedy of the Renaissance; but several factors militated against the application of the theory. Seneca constructed his tragedies so that they would contain rhetorical descriptions. He appealed to the ear and not to the eye. If he places action on the stage, it is only because by so doing he can still present horror in full detail. His Medea does murder her sons before the people, and human and animal entrails are openly exposed in his plays. The Italians did not have murders represented on the stage; but throughout the history of all classical and neo-classical drama there are suicides and deaths from poison enacted. Although they did not literally dress human entrails on the stage, they constantly exposed severed limbs and heads to view. But the narration and the philosophizing of Seneca were looked upon by them with favor. The place of the point of attack made lengthy exposition necessary and precluded much appeal to the eye. They found that description of horrible incidents was actually more horrible than enacting them. Therefore they did not apply the principle of appealing to the eye by placing action on the stage. The second half of this passage from Horace was the important part to them, for it justified "elegant" description. No dramatist or critic of the Renaissance would have thought of saying to the messenger, as does Macbeth: "Thou comest to use thy tongue: thy story quickly." They believed that deaths should not take place on the stage because they would be shocking. Giraldi Cinthio lays down a universal rule that the characters in a play should do or say nothing on the stage which they would not probably do or say in their own home. But if something indecent must be put on the comic stage, it should be veiled, so that maidens may hear it without censure. The *jeune fille au théâtre* was already beginning to influence dramatic art. Thus, for several reasons, the selection of scenes to be represented was made, not on dramatic grounds, but on the basis of decorum and of rhetorical appeal.

Horace said of the point of attack that the poet does not "trace the rise of the Trojan war from Leda's eggs; he always hastens on to the event; and hurries away his reader into the midst of interesting circumstances (*in medias res*), no otherwise than if they were already known." This theory may be well for the epic poet who has plenty of time and opportunity to explain by narration any previous circumstance; but the dramatic poet deals with characters who act; and it is not always possible to explain circumstances without committing the inartistic blunder of stopping the development of the action. Also the phrase *in medias res* is indefinite and many a play of the Renaissance begins "at the end of things."

Aristotle states his theory of the point of attack as follows: "Now a whole is that which has a beginning, middle, and end. A beginning is that which is not itself necessarily after anything else and which has naturally something else after it; an end is that which is naturally after something itself, either as its necessary or usual consequence, and with nothing else after it; and a middle, that which is by nature after one thing and also has another after it. A well constructed plot, therefore, cannot either begin or end at any point one likes."

This passage, translated and commented upon as it was by these critics, exerted no discernible influence upon the dramatists; and the critics themselves failed to understand all that it implies. In order to understand the problem of construction as viewed by Aristotle, it must be borne in mind that a plot to him is a series of events in necessary or probable sequence and that there is a great difference between a thing happening *propter hoc* and *post hoc*. Not temporal sequence but causal sequence of events is dramatic. One of the great differences between the technique of medieval drama and Greek tragedy is that the former is constructed on the plan of temporal sequence and the latter according to causal sequence. In the story of Œdipus the exposure of the child Œdipus by no means brings in its wake the future events, either from the point of view of necessity or probability. Nor does the murder of Laius by Œdipus, or even the marriage of Jocasta and Œdipus presuppose the rest of the tragedy. But when Œdipus receives the reply from the oracle that the only way to put an end to the suffering of the people is to discover the murderer of Laius, the rest of the plot follows in necessary and probable sequence. This is the Aristotelian "beginning," the correct point of attack. It is practically the beginning of Sophocles' play, being preceded only by the necessary scene of exposition. Thus the Aristotelian "beginning" corresponds to the initial cause of the action.

These theorists say very little in regard to the art of exposition. Naturally the first act is the place indicated by them for the explanation of antecedent events and present circumstances. Giraldi Cinthio says that the first act contains the argument or exposition; in the second act the things in the argument begin to move toward the end; in the third act come obstacles and troubles; in the fourth act means are offered for remedying the troubles; and in the fifth act is given the desired end with the necessary solution to the argument. Commenting on the division of a play formulated by Latin grammarians into protasis, epitasis and catastrophe he says the protasis, or exposition, may extend into the second act. Castelvetro would admit the formal prologue in comedy to explain the plot, because in comedy the subject not being historical or mythological is therefore unknown; but since the subject of tragedy is known to the spectator a formal prologue should not be employed. He criticizes the prologues of Euripides as being lacking in verisimilitude. According to Scaliger the beginning of a comedy presents a confused state of affairs, whereas a tragedy opens more tranquilly than a comedy.

The value of foreshadowing is apparent to Castelvetro, who says that the future should be predicted obscurely, but that the past should be clearly explained. Minturno says the audience must be kept in suspense until the end. Scaliger says that the protasis is the part of the play in which the substance of the affair is set forth and narrated without telling the outcome, for it is more artful to keep the mind of the auditor in suspense. If the outcome is foretold, it is made cold.

Giraldi Cinthio pointed out that the events of less cruel plays should happen so that the spectators will be in suspense until the end, which, being happy, will leave them consoled. He held that this keeping the audience in suspense ought to be so carried out by the poet that the auditor will not be in darkness; but the action should proceed step by step, unfolding the story so that the spectator will see the end brought about, but will be in doubt as to how it will come out. This is an excellent statement of the theory of suspense and even implies the use of foreshadowing and finger-posts; but keeping or half disclosing a secret is only a part of what is meant by suspense. The scenes arousing alternate hope and fear; the stressing of fear in a play with a happy ending and *vice versa;* Euripides' use of the prologue to foreshadow and arouse suspense; the unfolding of a plot, as in *Œdipus Rex,* in such a way that everything finally turns out contrary to our hope and desire and yet without breaking the logical and necessary sequence of events—these methods of arousing suspense, employed so artistically by the Greek dramatists, were apparently unknown to the Renaissance critics and dramatists. Even the suspense found in the original Greek play is sometimes entirely destroyed by the Italian who rewrites it. Anguillara in his version of *Œdipus,* introduces at the beginning a scene between Tiresias and his daughter in which every detail of the situation is described. Thus he breaks down the whole artistic construction of the play and lessens suspense immeasurably. A clear distinction must be made between knowledge of the plot brought into the theatre by the spectator and knowledge imparted to the spectator by a character in the play. The dramatist should never take into consideration pre-knowledge of the plot. It is something beyond his control and it rarely militates against suspense or enjoyment of the play, because if the spectator is interested in the representation he does not call to mind his previous information. Indeed, he can close his mind to his pre-knowledge of any circumstance. But when a character gives information and discloses secrets which should be kept, the spectator cannot close his ears; and knowledge gained in this way is all-important. As Scaliger said: "Although you may learn everything from the argument in the short analysis of a play, yet the indication is so summary and brief that it rather arouses curiosity than satisfies it."

Aristotle made no mention of acts; but Horace laid down the rule in regard to tragedy that there should be five acts, no more, no less. The division into acts probably grew up as the Greek chorus became a less vital part of the play and its songs marked pauses in the action. By the middle of the third century B.C., comedy, as well as tragedy, seems to have been divided into five acts. The dramatists and theorists of the Renaissance accepted this division. Of all the so-called rules of drama it was the least valid, the least questioned, and the least violated. An audience may need a few minutes of mental and physical repose during a play; but that there should be four such periods, no more nor less, is a theory with no reasonable or artistic basis. The practice was observed wherever and whenever neo-classical drama was produced. Even romanticists such as Hugo clung to it with strange tenacity, and Ibsen did not avoid this meaningless convention in his first important play, *Lady Inger of Ostrat*.

In the nineteenth century, the act had become a definite entity, marked by a drop curtain denoting a lapse of time. Each act was likely to represent a different scene and contained a new development of the action. Then the number of acts became important. But the five-fold division had no more effect on the construction of drama in the Renaissance than a three-, four- or six-fold division would have had, because the play, not the act, was the unit. One thinks of Shakespeare's plays as composed of scenes, of Hugo's plays as composed of acts, of Sophocles' plays as composing a complete entity. So neo-classical plays, in spite of their five acts, have no clearly marked divisions. The stage is simply left vacant four times during the play, for an empty stage, as Donatus said, marked the end of an act. In order to avoid an empty stage during an act, the rule of the linking of scenes was evolved. At least one character of a preceding scene had to take part in the following scene. The rule was so logical, so hampering and so useless that it survived for centuries. Nothing is more tenacious than a convention hoary with age.

Aristotle believed that the function of tragedy was to arouse certain emotions and to purge the mind of them through a kind of homeopathic treatment. Thus he justified the existence of tragedy which Plato would banish from his ideal republic on the ground that tragedy arouses emotions, and emotions are dangerous. For Aristotle, the ethical aim of tragedy was to induce a catharsis of troublesome, painful emotions or passions. Aristotle logically preferred an unhappy ending for tragedy, because such a dénouement performed the function of tragedy and fulfilled its ethical aim better than an outcome in which the virtuous were rewarded and the wicked were punished. He assigned this double ending of poetic justice to a lower rank in the artistic scale.

In general, the theorists and dramatists preferred an unhappy ending, although the critics admitted the happy ending in theory and the playwrights employed it at times, though rarely. Senecan drama aroused horror, and many Renaissance tragedies were composed in the same spirit. Certain critics grossly mistranslated the Greek word φόβος as *orrore* or *terrore*. Whatever emotion Aristotle meant by this word, he certainly did not mean "horror" or "terror." The theorists paid lip service to Aristotle's theory of the function of tragedy; but the whole spirit of the art had changed.

In place of the Aristotelian conception of the ethical aim of tragedy, the idea grew up that the aim was to teach morals by giving examples of vice and virtue. Scaliger held that it was not enough for a play to strike the spectator with admiration or consternation, but it should teach, move and please. This was the justification of the sententious sayings which, according to Scaliger, were the very foundation and props of tragedy. It was the justification of the tirades on life, power, the age, etc., which

Giraldi Cinthio said should be long. In addition to being rhetorical, tragedy became directly didactic.

The critics, following Aristotle, warned against having the dénouement depend upon the god from a machine. They held correctly that the solution of the plot should be brought about by the logical development of the action. They failed to see that, since a Greek tragedy contains a problem, the ending, happy or unhappy, must be the answer to the problem. The answer must satisfy, not man-made law, which is often unjust; nor poetic justice, which does not exist; but a human sense of justice, which is inexorable.

The Aristotelian ideal hero was a "man not pre-eminently virtuous and just, whose misfortune, however, is brought upon him, not by vice and depravity, but by some error of judgment, of the number of those in the enjoyment of great reputation and prosperity." Only too often in Italian tragedy, vice and depravity are the outstanding features of the hero. The Latin grammarians had insisted upon nobility of rank, rather than of character. The critics of this period accepted this transformation of the hero in theory. The dramatists had already produced plenty of examples of heroes whose tragic fault was not an error of judgment, but a desire for bloody revenge. The Marlovian Tamburlaines and Edwards, the Shakespearean Richards were not to escape the phenomenon of the degradation of the ideal tragic hero which took place in Italy. Yet, Hamlet is the purified hero, who must avenge a father's death with blood.

The dramatists chose a point of attack close to the dénouement for several reasons. This was the usual opening of Greek and Senecan tragedy. Horace was an authority for plunging *in medias res*. They were attempting to represent a single change of fortune and were more than willing to narrate the causes which led to the reversal. The critics of the Renaissance found an explanation for this procedure in the statement made by Aristotle that the epic differs from tragedy "in its length— which is due to its action having no fixed limit of time, whereas tragedy endeavors to keep as far as possible within a single revolution of the sun, or something near that." It is doubtful that any Greek dramatist modified the construction of his play in order to conform to this practice, which arose from the influence of worship of the dead hero on Greek tragedy. Aristotle did not advise it because it would make the action of tragedy seem more real or life-like. He was not a realist. Nor did he state it as an absolute rule to be followed. In the Renaissance this simple statement of fact was not only transformed into what was called the rule of the unity of time, but also a second rule of the unity of place was deduced from it and from the common practice of the dramatists.

Giraldi Cinthio makes the first reference to the unity of time when he says that the action of tragedy should occupy the space of a day or a little more. Robortello discusses the question as to whether "a single revolution of the sun" means twelve or twenty-four hours; and he restricts the time to twelve hours, because people are supposed to sleep at night. Segni, however, lengthens the unity of time to twenty-four hours on the ground that tragic acts are likely to be committed at night. Maggi explains the unity of time by the fact that the drama is represented before our eyes and if we should see the actions of a whole month performed in about the time that it takes to perform the play, that is, two or three hours, the performance would be absolutely incredible. "For example," says Maggi, "if in a tragedy we should send a messenger to Egypt, and he would return in an hour, would not the spectator regard this as ridiculous?" As Dr. Spingarn has pointed out, if the action is limited to the time of representation, it follows that the place of the action must be limited to the place of representation, although such a limitation is a piece of realism wholly out of keeping with the true dramatic illusion. Scaliger insisted that "as the whole time for stage representation is only six or eight hours, it is not in accordance with the exact appearance of truth to have a storm arise and the ship founder in a part of the sea from which no land is visible." He also says that no character must be sent from Delphi to Athens or from Athens to Thebes in a moment of time.

Castelvetro finally formulated the rule of the unity of place so easily deduced from these ideas. For him the unity of time was the time that it would take to accomplish the action in real life. He held that in tragedy the area of the place in which the action is accomplished is restricted, not only to a city or town or country or a similar situation, but to that space which could be visible to one person. Since the restricted place is the stage, thus the restricted time is that during which the spectators can sit at ease in the theatre. This cannot be longer than twelve hours, because of the necessity of eating, drinking and sleeping. "Tragedy," he continues, "ought to have as subject an action which happened in a small place and in a short time. It is not possible to have it understood by the spectators that many nights and days have passed when it is plainly evident to them that only a few hours have passed."

Following this argument to its logical conclusion, one can argue that a scene in Athens cannot be represented on a stage in Rome, and an actor speaking in Italian cannot represent the Greek Œdipus. Thus the whole case of dramatic art is thereby thrown out of court. Such is the logical conclusion of the arguments in favor of the unity of place and of time based upon verisimilitude! Aristotle's theory that a convincing impossibility is preferable to an unconvincing possibility, might have served to demolish such unsound arguments; but his ideal of artistic truth became an ideal of verisimilitude which meant an inartistic transcript of reality. The result was a drama which was neither true nor real, and hardly realistic. The critics failed to realize that the representation of facts of real life does not necessarily produce artistic truth.

The originality of these critics consisted in their explanation of the practice and their reasons for approving it. Most classical tragedies of the Italian Renaissance, written before Castelvetro formulated the rules of the unities, conformed to them. Thus no change was wrought by this theory on contemporary drama;

but the whole theory of play construction underwent a great change by the insistence upon the three unities and upon the ideal expressed by the awkward word "verisimilitude," which is so indefinite and capable of so many interpretations as to be almost meaningless.

The theory of the unity of action was, of course, Aristotelian and the phrases "unity of time" and "unity of place" were derived from the idea of the "oneness" of the action. The idea has been variously interpreted. From one point of view, the medieval plays on the Creation, the Fall, the Redemption and the Judgment observe a broad unity of action, although Aristotle would have denied that they observed the rule. Interpreted in the light of Greek tragedies which Aristotle admired, it makes for simplicity and yet completeness of the action. It militates against the introduction of all incidents, either by representation or narration, which are not vitally necessary to the development of the action. It means, as Aristotle said, that "the story, as an imitation of an action, must represent one action, a complete whole, with its several incidents so closely connected that the transposal or withdrawal of any one of them will disjoin and dislocate the whole."

Strictly applied it removes all episodes constituting a sub-plot and precludes the joining of two problems not interdependent, as is done in *The Merchant of Venice*. Not until the close of the nineteenth century will the rule of the unity of action be discarded as non-essential.

The strict application of the rule is often salutary for dramatic art. It sounded the death knell of the long-winded confusion of medieval drama. If the simple is the beautiful, the unity of action, applied with a skilful touch, produces beauty. But in the Renaissance it was the unity of time and the unity of place which became of paramount importance in the theory of dramatic art. Thus Castelvetro deduces the unity of action from the unities of time and place. He says: "But Aristotle might have well seen that in tragedy and in comedy the plot contains a single action or two, which, because of mutual interdependence can be considered one, and rather of one person than of a people, not because the plot is not fitted to contain more actions, but because the space of time, at the most twelve hours, in which the action is represented and the restricted space in which the action is represented, do not permit a multitude of actions, or indeed action of a people, indeed, very often do not permit an entire action, if the action is somewhat long."

Thus the unity of action becomes entirely subordinate to the unities of time and place, which in turn become the touchstone of dramatic technique. The observance of these two rules made tragedy more artistic according to Castelvetro, because "it is more marvellous when a great mutation of a hero's fortune is made in a very limited time and a very limited place, than when it is made in a longer time and in varied and larger places." Aristotle's wise theory of the point of attack goes by the board. Horace's *in medias res* had to be interpreted to mean a point in the story not more than twelve hours from the time of the climax. No matter what dramatic incident takes place more than twelve hours before the close, it had to be narrated. No matter what dramatic event happens away from the one place represented on the stage, it had to be narrated. The point of attack, exposition, the selection of scenes, the unity of action were conditioned by so-called rules based upon entirely fallacious arguments of verisimilitude. Artistic drama was sacrificed to inartistic realism. The true dramatic illusion was jeopardized in order to preserve a false illusion of place and time. This is the contribution of the Italian critics of the Renaissance to the theory of dramatic art!

CHAPTER X

ITALIAN COMEDY OF THE RENAISSANCE.
THE PASTORAL

PETRARCH'S love of classical literature inspired him to write a comedy, now lost, entitled *Philologia*. Other comedies in Latin and modelled on plays of Plautus and Terence were composed for the reader. Among them were Vergerio's *Paulus* (*ca.* 1390) and Ugolini's *Philogenia* (before 1437). But such plays were without special influence except that they prepared for the vogue of comedy in Italian based on classical models and produced on the stage.

In 1427 Cusanus brought from Germany to Rome a manuscript of twelve comedies of Plautus, whose work had been little known throughout the Middle Ages. Scholars began to study these plays, to fill in gaps in the dialogue, and even to add whole scenes to replace the lost ending of *Aulularia*. Terence had been better known than Plautus up to this time; but now his influence was no longer paramount. Comedies of both dramatists were produced by Pomponius Lætus in Rome. *Amphitryo* and the *Menæchmi* became so popular that people knew them by heart. Plots depending on mistaken identity through similarity of appearance were frequently employed in Italian comedies inspired by these plays.

Up to the beginning of the sixteenth century, comedy had not been rigorously classical. Boiardo's *Timone,* Accolti's *Virginia* are medieval in technique and stage setting. Even *Philogenia,* written in Latin, keeps the action on the stage, while the hero himself woos the heroine. Recognitions, mistaken identity, long-lost children were rarely used as plot material. *Stephanium* by Harmonius Marsus, however, is based upon *Aulularia* and is a typical classical comedy. Zamberti's *Dolo-*

techne (1504) also ends with a recognition, which removes the obstacles from the path of the lovers. It contains two pairs of lovers after the manner of Terence, and the situation is very complicated. Nardi's *Amicizia* (1509-12) is founded upon Boccaccio's 97th novella, but is cast in the classical mould. It is the story of a man who gives his wife to a friend; and when the man is wrongly accused of murder, the friend tries to assume responsibility for the crime. A happy ending ensues when the real murderer confesses. The plot is reminiscent of a miracle play without the miracle. It is far removed from the classical type of plot; and the play shows how unfit the construction of Latin comedy is for a romantic plot which contains striking scenes but which the author does not put on the stage. The trial, for example, has to be messengered because of the street-scene. The medieval dramatists had placed all situations on the stage. As soon as Latin comedy became the model, the playwrights confined themselves to a narrow range of enacted scenes. Unless they employed Latin plots, their work was awkward. *Amicizia* might have become at least a "thriller" under the hand of an English playwright of the sixteenth century. But the Italians turned more and more to the close imitation of classical comedy.

Ariosto's *Cassaria* (1508) and *Suppositi* (1509), Bibbiena's *Calandria* (1508, acted in 1513-1514), Machiavelli's *Clizia* (1512-1520) are plays built almost entirely on the framework of Latin comedy, especially of Plautine comedy. In *Calandria* the mistaken identity of twins, imitated from the *Menæchmi*, is made more complicated by having the twins a brother and sister, who dress at times in clothes of the opposite sex. The scenes in *Calandria* in which the old husband is shown by the tricky servant how to die and is loaded into a coffin to be carried to his supposed inamorata are more in the spirit of the novella than of Latin comedy. The unfaithful husband and wife, neither of whom suffers punishment for their extra-matrimonium activities, are medieval rather than classical figures. The general cynical tone is that of the farce, although Plautine influence would by no means preclude cynicism. Except in these respects, these plays contain little which would have seemed strange to the Roman audience before whom Plautine comedy was originally played.

Machiavelli's *Mandragola* (1530), Ariosto's *Lena* (1529) and his *Negromante* (1530), contain elements which are more original. The trick of placing a principal character in a box or chest, which is merely a humorous episode in *Calandria,* now becomes an integral part of the plot in the *Lena* and the *Negromante.* This points once more to the influence of the novella as a partial substitute for Latin comedy.

Of greater importance, however, is the introduction of the Necromancer who is a real character and is the central figure who keeps the action developing through his particular personality. Interest was not centred in the rise and fall of the fortunes of the lovers or of the characters which played the most active rôles in the unfolding of the plot. In the *Negromante* there is a plot involving the fortunes of lovers, and the obstacles separating them suddenly fade away in the light of a recognition scene, but the central figure is the Necromancer, a scoundrel who prepares the way for Molière's *Tartufe.* The play does not finish with the convenient and timely recognition, but with the downfall of this villain, who is really the hero, as the name of the piece implies. In *Calandria* there is also a necromancer; but the great difference between Ruffo and Ariosto's Necromancer is that, while both are impostors, the former is relatively unimportant. The plot of *Calandria* could develop almost as well without him; but in Ariosto's comedy the machinations and the character of the astrologer and his final downfall form the plot of the whole play. Out of elements which were episodic in *Calandria,* Ariosto constructed the mainspring of a plot. He introduced into comedy a hero of the villain type, such as is found in Italian tragedy and was to appear later in Elizabethan tragedy. As a result, interest in the plot assumes greater importance. The hard and fast mould of Latin comedy is broken.

Machiavelli's *Mandragola* is a curious combination of medieval, Italian, and classical elements. The play deals with a young man who has become enamored of Lucrezia, the young wife of the old Nicia, on merely hearing of her beauty. A journey from Paris to Florence in search of this far-away princess results in his falling completely in love with this woman, who at the beginning of the play is a virtuous spouse. This is all which is supposed to have taken place before the point of attack. There are no concealed or forgotten identities or long-lost children. There is no complicated series of events, no painful preparation for the introduction of the long arm of chance in the last act to solve any trumped-up problem. As in the medieval farce, the point of attack is practically at the beginning of the story and the situation actually exists.

The scenes of exposition, however, are handled as in Latin comedy. The young lover explains his sudden passion to his servant. The question to be solved is also the invariable question of how to overcome the obstacles separating a young lover and the object of his desires; but the fact that the heroine is married and is virtuous introduces an element which is by no means classical. Even in *Calandria* the question of marital infidelity forms a part of the situation; but the ending of the story was the regular "moral" ending, brought about by a sudden recognition. In the *Mandragola* the element of marital infidelity so modifies the whole situation that scenes and situations unknown in Latin comedy are introduced. The old husband is tricked, as old simpletons are deceived in the plays of Plautus and Terence. The heroine is also somewhat tricked; but two of the most important scenes show how a monk is persuaded to undertake the task of overcoming the virtuous scruples of the modest wife, and then how the monk, together with the mother, persuade Lucrezia to submit to an unspeakable plan to deceive her husband. Of the cynical immorality of these situations the less said the better; but nevertheless these scenes strike a note never heard even in Plautus. They give an opportunity for dramatic progression; whereas, in Latin comedy, most of the time was occupied with devising and at-

tempting to carry out plans to unite the lovers until one succeeded, or until an unexpected dénouement cleared up the situation. In the *Mandragola* two plans are discussed. One is
decided upon. It succeeds; and the play ends with Lucrezia
deciding that, since her husband is such an old simpleton, she will
accept the young Callimaco as her lover.

For the first time in comedy here is a young heroine whose
character develops and undergoes a complete change, who is
something more than a lay figure. The virtuous, modest, faithful wife of the first act becomes a cynical mistress, complacently
standing between her accepted lover and duped husband, and
ordering that ten ducats be given to the monk who has procured her so much unexpected happiness. One may deplore
the morals of the principals in Machiavelli's play, but his people
have individual characters. The comic stage had ceased temporarily to be the domain of marionettes or, at most, types cut
from the same patterns.

However, the cessation was only temporary. The Italians
realized that comedy should present a wide range of characters; but the theorists, following their classical ancestors, discussed and described the various types, and the characters remained simply types, as they had been in Latin comedy. The
Italians were particularly disposed to create stock characters. In
their *commedia dell' arte* the same actor always played the same
rôle. Scenarios were written which showed what the stock character did in each play. The dialogue was improvised. The
rôle was stencilled. This procedure might easily have been
followed in many Italian comedies, so stereotyped had become
the plot and characters in these neo-classical plays.

The *Mandragola* is more a highly developed medieval farce
in situation, tone, and conclusion than a Latin comedy. More
of the action, perhaps every scene, would have been represented
on the stage in purely medieval comedy. The heroine in this
play, as in most Italian comedies of the Renaissance, appears
rarely. Undoubtedly the setting of the scene in the street kept
many scenes off the stage; but the utterly indecent situations

in these Italian comedies, like the disgustingly horrible situations in Italian tragedies, could scarcely have been represented. The medieval dramatists were evidently almost ignorant of the possibility of reporting important events; but just as the Italian writers of tragedy led up to a messenger's speech describing horrors in every detail, so these comic playwrights found it expedient to describe their unrepresentable scenes. There is not much more action on the stage in Italian comedy than in Latin comedy, although these authors were familiar with medieval drama which kept events before the audience.

Machiavelli broke away from the traditional technique of Latin comedy in certain respects. Aretino and Grazzini emulated him in attempting to disengage Italian comedy from its Latin prototype. Aretino introduced the element of satire and emulated Ariosto in centering the interest upon a principal character, who is dominated by one characteristic, such as hypocrisy (*Ipocrito*), misogamy (*Marescalco*) or theorizing (*Filosofo*). This kind of character was a natural development of stock characters, which had become somewhat abstract even in Latin comedy. The slave was tricky; the parasite, a glutton; the old man, stupid. They were types with a dominant characteristic. Plautus had also produced in Euclio a personification of avariciousness, in the braggart warrior a personification of boastfulness. Ariosto and Aretino added to this gallery of portraits. The Italians thus prepared the way for the English comedy of humors, and for the long line of French plays in the seventeenth and eighteenth centuries, in which the principal character is the personification of some abstract trait, such as hypocrisy, flattery, avariciousness, mendacity, truthfulness, etc.

Unfortunately Aretino does not relate the action to his principal character in a dramatic manner. His plots do not develop, whether they are founded on simple or complex situations. The plot of the *Marescalco* rests upon the fact that the Duke of Mantua has ordered the overseer of his stables, a woman-hater, to take a wife. This gives an opportunity for satire on marriage and for joking the misogamist. The play is brought to a conclusion by dressing up a page as a pretended fiancée and unveiling the "bride."

Talanta has a very complicated situation founded on the *Menæchmi* in which Aretino goes Plautus one better by introducing triplets, whom he dresses in clothes of the opposite sex, and one of whom is painted to resemble a Moor. There are the usual tangled love affairs resulting from such a trumped-up situation, and these affairs are brought to a happy termination by a recognition scene. There is a difference, however, between a complicated situation and an interesting plot developing from the entanglement, as is proved by the fact that in this play there is practically no action at all. The situation is static, with the result that the actual plot is as unimportant in *Talanta* as in Aretino's other plays. Scene follows upon scene without affecting the fortunes of a single one of the many heroes and heroines. The several love affairs are loosely connected by the fact that two of these young people—the supposed Moor and the supposed slave—are given to the courtezan, Talanta, by two of her lovers; but the whole complicated situation, like the simple situation of the *Marescalco,* is merely a background for humorous scenes and satire. Almost any other set of circumstances would have served Aretino as well for his purpose. Many scenes in this comedy could be introduced into any other of Aretino's comedies without disturbing the framework of either play, for Aretino's plots are all buried under an avalanche of dialogue. With the possible exception of his hypocrite, his personages are mouthpieces for a satirist who is too wordy to be really humorous on the stage. The greatest fault of these comedies is that they would gain little or nothing by being acted.

Ariosto's *Negromante* had shown the way to a form of comedy in which there is a plot revolving about the character of the principal personage. Aretino's principal characters do little to carry on whatever action there is. Like the situations, they are static. The types which Aretino's people represent are satirized; but there is no rise and fall in their fortunes, no peripeteia causing a change in their outlook in life. Hence there is no dramatic sympathy aroused and little interest is created. The difference between a humorous story or satire in dialogue form and a comedy, lies in the fact that, while the reader will be content to laugh at the witty or satirical ideas, no matter who says them, the spectator of the play wishes to take sides for or against the character who is making witty or satirical remarks. In order to take sides, the spectator must become interested in the fate of some character or in some moral issue which is decided during the play. A reversal must not be wrought at the end of a play by a recognition scene or by a sudden change of character. The development must come slowly, logically and in such a way that one is constantly conscious of it. At least, the spectator must realize that a change is always possible. Thus in Aretino's *Talanta,* there is a happy ending which brings a change of fortune; but the peripeteia is too sudden, too mechanical and is not the result of anything said or done during the play.

Aretino produced satire in dialogue. As a rule, this is all that a bitter satirist can do. To be a great dramatist one must love humanity even because of its faults and weaknesses. The true dramatist must be intensely interested in the fate of his characters, both good and bad. He must work out their salvation or damnation. He cannot take as contemptuous a view of vice or virtue as does the born satirist. Aretino's fault as a dramatist was that in breaking with Latin comedy, he broke away from dramatic art.

Grazzini, known as Il Lasca, shows by his frequent references to certain technical matters in his prologues that the discussion of the technique of comedy was in the air. These dramatists were not blind followers of Plautus and Terence, unconscious as to why they were doing certain things in their art. However, these references to technical procedure found in prologues must not be taken too seriously. The spirit of the prologue to comedy was generally one of mockery and of playful boasting of the excellencies of the playwright's manner of composing comedy. In the prologue to the *Strega,* Grazzini says that

Aristotle and Horace are out of date. His own age and customs are different and comedies must be written in a different manner. There are no more slaves or adopted children; ruffians do not sell girls, soldiers do not seize young children any more and bring them up as their own.

In the prologue to *Gelosia* he asserts that the situation is new, that as soon as the audience hears in a prologue that in a capture of a city children have been lost, the public would like to get away. Hence in neither of these plays will there be recognition scenes or will long-lost children be found, because the public is tired of such tricks. Also he promises that in the *Strega* there will be no long, tiresome monologues. In this respect, he keeps his word in regard to all his plays. Although the recognition scene is not employed as a dénouement for certain of his plays, the ending of the *Parentadi* is brought about by an anagnorisis. Many a century will pass before this procedure will be discarded by playwrights who build up a complicated situation and wish to have the complications smoothed out in a manner satisfactory both to people on the stage and in the audience. The device was too convenient either to be convincing to the spectators or to be discarded by the playwrights.

Grazzini, with all his boasts of disregarding the ancients, remained a neo-classicist in playwriting. He was a more faithful imitator of Plautus than was Machiavelli. He used all the devices of Latin comedy at one time or another. Just as the example of Aretino did not suffice to cause Italian playwrights to discard the type of plot of Latin comedy, so Grazzini's attempt at novelty, which was not very serious, did not change greatly the framework of Italian comedy.

In order to break the classical mould and to allow comedy of this type to develop into romantic comedy, the point of attack must be pushed back and the events leading up to the situation with which most Latin and Italian comedies begin must be represented on the stage. Then the recognition scene can play its part in the dénouement; but Grazzini could not have changed the spirit or technique of classical drama even had he removed every recognition scene ever devised.

Together with this regular comedy, flourished the *commedia dell' arte* or improvised comedy. During the sixteenth century, troupes of Italian actors were formed who travelled far and wide in Italy, Spain, Germany and France, giving performances of Italian drama and especially *commedia dell' arte*. This form of drama was an outgrowth of the humble improvisations given in the public square by charlatans, mountebanks and acrobats of different kinds. By 1550 it reached a high stage of development.

Each troupe contained certain stock actors who played rôles such as the lovers, the crotchety old men, the braggart captains, the doctor, the pedant, and most important of all, the Zanni, or acrobatic clowns. Each member of the troupe, as a rule, used the same name in every comedy—a practice which was to extend down through the eighteenth century in certain French plays. Best known to English speaking peoples are such rôles as Columbine, Pantaloon, Doctor Gratiano, Captain Spavento or Fracasse, Harlequin, Polichinelle, the tricky clowns, etc. A distinctive part of the costume of the burlesque characters was the mask. The young heroines, however, appeared unmasked.

The scenarios of their comedies were written out in great detail, but each character improvised the dialogue to suit the action. By the latter part of the sixteenth century, they were aided in this improvisation by printed collections of speeches suited to each rôle, such as F. Andreini's *Le Bravure del Capitano Spavento,* published in 1515. Isabella Andreini, a lady of great culture and a member of an academy, shows in her *Letters* a careful study of the language, tone and Petrarchistic conceits suited to the rôle of prima donna, which she filled so brilliantly in the famous troupe of comedians known as the Gelosi. This improvisation of clever dialogue was a result of long practice and careful study.

The wide repertory of these troupes included tragedy, pastoral, comedy, ballet and the farce. The improvised scenarios which have been preserved—the earliest one dating back only to 1568—show a strong influence of the literary drama. There is no great difference in technique between the two forms except that the *commedia dell' arte* does not hold to the rule of five acts. Yet these troupes were a great influence in spreading Italian drama throughout Spain and France. Also, the repertory helped to keep alive the short farce in which, not the plot, but a comic situation bordering on a comedy of contemporary manners furnishes the main interest of the play. This influence of the farce will become important with the advent of Molière in France.

Another influence which came from Italy to the later drama of other European countries was that of the pastoral play. This form of theatrical art is an outgrowth of the eclogue in a dialogue form, which came to be recited before a courtly audience. Poliziano had put shepherds in his *Orfeo* even in the latter part of the fifteenth century; and Niccolo da Corregio had produced in 1487 his *Cefalo,* in which there is a pastoral setting with shepherds and nymphs and choruses of satyrs and fauns. Neither one of these plays, in spite of the settings, can be really considered the ultimate source of a form of drama of which the first real example was not produced until three-quarters of a century later when Beccari in 1554 wrote his *Sagrifizio.*

Tasso's *Aminta* (1572), Guarini's *Pastor Fido* (1590) and Bonarelli's *Filli di Sciro* (1607) are plays that mark the apogee of Italian pastoral drama and contain elements of dramatic art in new combinations which differentiate somewhat the pastoral form from contemporary tragedy and comedy.

Aminta was inspired by Argenti's *Sfortunato* (1567). The model is not dramatic. It lacks action, and the scenes are elegiac and lyric discussions of love. Also *Aminta,* though charming as pastoral poetry, has little to commend it dramatically. In the early dramatic eclogue, recited in dialogue on the stage, different subjects were discussed by two interlocutors, one of which was a good counsellor, as in Senecan drama. The influence of this scene is manifest in *Aminta.* In the first act, Dafne tries to persuade Sylvia to turn her thoughts from the delights of the chase to the joys of love, but Sylvia is obdurate. Aminta, in love with Sylvia, tells his confidant, Tirsi, how his love was awakened and bewails the cruelty of the object of his desires. Act II. A satyr, also in love with Sylvia, announces in a monologue his intention of lying in wait for the maid. Dafne bids Tirsi send Aminta to a pool where Sylvia will bathe. Tirsi informs Aminta that Sylvia awaits him; but Aminta is skeptical and undecided. Act III. Tirsi tells the chorus how Sylvia was attacked by the satyr; but, although saved by the timely arrival of Aminta, she fled from her protector. Nerina describes to Aminta the supposed death of Sylvia, overcome by a wolf; and she places Sylvia's veil, which was dropped in her flight, in her lover's hands. Aminta is now convinced that suicide is the only remedy for his unhappiness. Act IV. Sylvia recounts to Dafne how she escaped by stratagem from the wolf. Dafne informs her that Aminta has probably taken his own life and Sylvia repents her cruelty. Ergasto tells her that Aminta threw himself from a precipice. Sylvia laments his death. In the single scene of the last act, Elpino tells the chorus that Aminta was saved from death, his fall being broken by branches, and that the lovers are united.

This simple action is carried on by means of recitals of events given by secondary characters or with one principal character on the stage at a time. The hero and heroine never meet before our eyes. Neither Italian comedy nor tragedy would influence the pastoral dramatist to have the principals meet, and in the dramatic eclogue the nymph rarely appeared. The play is merely a pastoral story told in dialogue. Its importance to dramatic art lies in the fact that it places in the theatre a simple, serious love story, which is neither gross nor horrible as in Italy tragedy, nor vulgar and immoral as in Italian comedy. The charm of the play arises from the treatment of this kind of love in smoothly flowing lyricism. It is opera without an orchestral accompaniment.

This form of drama, however, lost much of its charm and all

of its simplicity in the development it received under the hand of Guarini in his *Pastor Fido*. He wished to outdo his rival Tasso in every respect. *Aminta* is pure pastoral drama and owes comparatively little to either tragedy or comedy. *Pastor Fido* is proudly described by Guarini as a tragi-comedy-pastoral, and this title is correct. The play is a combination of elements drawn from these three kinds of drama, with a ballet in the game of blind man's buff and at times a musical accompaniment in addition.

The plot is extremely complicated. When the play opens, Amarilli is betrothed to Silvio since, by the marriage of children of divine birth as an oracle has foretold, Arcadia can be released from its yearly sacrifice of a young woman. This situation, the oracles, the sacrifice, the plague which has visited the land, the dream, are elements of tragedy. Silvio—drawn from Seneca's character Hippolytus—loves only the chase. Amarilli loves a certain Mirtillo of unknown parentage; and although he returns her love, she feels she must be faithful to Silvio. Corisca, a mature and sophisticated nymph from the city, loves Mirtillo. She, in turn, is loved by Coridone and by the usual satyr. Silvio is loved by Dorinda. Each one of these episodes needs a separate exposition. It is given either in a monologue or in a discussion between a lover and a confidant, which serves as a dialogue on love, its pain and joys. These several love affairs with their cross purposes are a development of similar situations in Italian comedy. A kind of merry-go-round of affections is thus produced, which becomes characteristic of pastoral drama and passes into French classical tragedy and comedy.

The love motives work at cross purposes until finally, in a scene worthy of farce comedy, Amarilli is sent by Corisca into a cave where she expects to find Silvio, faithless to her, enjoying the charms of Lisetta. Mirtillo follows her expecting to find proof of Amarilli's infidelity, for the scheming Corisca has planned to entice Coridone, her lover, to the cave and have him found with Silvio. But before this can happen, the satyr closes the mouth of the cave with a rock, thinking to trap Corisca. There is also the usual scene of the satyr discomfited by the nymph, in this case Corisca. This scene is on a plane of very low comedy, for Guarini does not hesitate to introduce the vulgarity of Italian comedy, although he asserts that he employs words of double meaning in order to preserve the decorum of tragedy.

The discovery of Mirtillo and Amarilli in the cave leads to scenes and situations imitated from tragedy. The lovers are condemned to death; and Montano, the high priest, is charged with the sacrifice of Mirtillo, who is his unknown son. Here is one of the Aristotelian situations of tragedy. But a dénouement of comedy is introduced; and it is discovered that Mirtillo is the long-lost child of Montano. Guarini, however, is not satisfied with ending his play thus; and even after this recognition, Montano still believes he must sacrifice Mirtillo. Turning back to tragedy, Guarini introduces Tirenio, a blind soothsayer—the Tiresias of classical tragedy—who easily explains that since Mirtillo is the son of Montano and was first called Silvio, he is just as suitable a match for Amarilli as is Silvio. In the meantime, Silvio has fallen in love with Dorinda in true pastoral manner, by wounding her when she is disguised as a wolf; and his heart melts when he fears he has killed her. Most of this dénouement, or rather these dénouements, are messengered in true tragic style.

This complicated combination of tragedy, comedy, pastoral, ballet, and opera, displaced the simpler *Aminta* as a model; and future writers of pastorals turned to *Pastor Fido* as their source of inspiration. Four expositions and three dénouements are necessary to unravel the network of this too complicated plot.

It can scarcely be said that dramatic art gained much by the production of a form which could draw from both tragedy and comedy for its technique. Perhaps the sole advantage was that in the pastoral the main love motive was neither horrible nor vulgar, although the minor love motive was often indecent, because of the realistic treatment of the sensual passion of the satyr.

In structure, the outstanding feature of pastorals under the influence of Guarini is this merry-go-round of the love motive, complicated in every conceivable way by changed names, disguises, and characters of unknown identity. Thus in *Mirtilla*, by Isabella Andreini, Tirso loves Ardelia who, like Narcissus, loves herself. In Bonarelli's *Filli di Sciro*, Filli, known as Clori, loves Tirso, known as Nino, who loves Celia. She, in turn, is loved by Aminta, who will be recognized as the brother of Filli, while Celia will be found to be the sister of Tirso. A further complication, which could only arise in the curious handling of the love motive in pastoral drama, is introduced by having Celia equally in love with Aminta and Nino. Thus the outstanding feature of the plot of the pastoral is the love motive complicated in as many ways as can be devised by the playwright. The source of this motive is found in the complicated situations and in the concealed identity of Italian comedy. The pastoral simply developed the situation.

The importance of the pastoral in the development of dramatic technique will be manifest at a later period, when the Italian pastoral has been imitated in France in the first part of the seventeenth century. During the years 1620-1630, when both classical tragedy and comedy almost disappeared from the French stage, the pastoral, retaining elements of both tragedy and comedy, actually opened the way for the future development of the very forms of drama it had temporarily displaced. Corneille and other authors of comedy were to learn from the pastoral how to put into comedy themes of love which can be enjoyed without a blush. Voltaire said that Racine's *Bérénice* was nothing but a pastoral. The statement is exaggerated truth. In England, the pastoral brought lyricism and charming love stories into the plays of Lyly, who in turn handed these elements on to Shakespeare.

CHAPTER XI

FRENCH COMEDY OF THE RENAISSANCE AND THE SEVENTEENTH CENTURY

THE names and the works of the Latin comic playwrights were well known to the literary men of the French Renaissance; but as was the case in other forms of art, the French come into contact with classical comedy through the Italians. Even Grévin, who admired Plautus particularly, does not show in his plays the direct influence of Latin comedy.

The Frenchman interested in the theatre may have had an opportunity as early as 1520 to see Italian plays given by a troupe of comedians coming from the Peninsula; but the repertory even of an Italian company of that early date could scarcely have been very classical. Whatever form of dramatic entertainment these comedians offered, their journey was without lasting effect. In 1543, however, Charles Estienne translated *Gl'Ingannati*, written in 1531 by the Intronati, members of the Sienese Academy. The popularity of Ariosto's *Suppositi*, which was to exert a strong influence on later French comedy, was apparent even at this time through the translation or close imitation of the play by Jacques Bourgeois in 1545 and by Mesmes in 1552. In 1548, a troupe of Italian players produced Bibbiena's *Calandria* before Henri II and his court at Lyon. Firenzuola's *Lucidi* and Alamanni's *Flora* were played in 1555 at the court of Henri III in Paris. Indeed, the latter play was written by Alamanni in Paris.

In 1548 the Brotherhood of the Passion occupied the theatre called the Hôtel de Bourgogne, having been forced to leave the Hôtel de Flandres where they had been playing. On the seventeenth of November, Parliament decreed that they could no longer give plays on sacred themes. This decree was a blow to medieval drama since it made a great part of the repertory of these actors illegal. Although the Brotherhood continued to produce this forbidden part of their repertory in defiance of the law throughout the latter half of the century and although they could still represent lawfully "profane mysteries" and farces, this law was favorable to the introduction of a new form of drama in France. The decree must have been the result of discussion of the question as to what kind of drama was fitted for public representation. Critics may talk incessantly without noticeable effect; but when a part of the public begins to discuss drama, dramatic art begins to change in one way or another. On the other hand, this law decreed that no other troupe could play in Paris or the suburbs except under the name and for the profit of the Brotherhood of the Passion. This clause almost nullified the effect of banning sacred plays, for it left a company of players with a medieval repertory in sole control of the only theatre in Paris. Throughout the rest of the century plays imitated from classical models were probably never offered to the Brotherhood; and certainly no such plays were accepted. Medieval drama held the public theatre. The neo-classical drama found an occasional representation at colleges or at court.

The French dramatists of the Renaissance were confronted with a serious problem. They could scoff, as they did, at the mysteries and farces; but they could not dislodge them from the stage on which drama of medieval technique was presented. To win the day quickly or at all, they would have had to take possession of the theatre. But they were content with the printed page. Indeed, their comedies were often printed posthumously by a pious friend; or were published apologetically by the author as works composed lightly and as having lain for a long time forgotten "in an old batch of papers." It is doubtful that these authors ever realized how to introduce this new form of drama, or that, in spite of their Philistine attitude, they strongly desired to drive the old plays off the stage. Whatever was the case, the influence of Italian drama was slow in making itself felt in the theatre, no matter how strong it was in books; and this influence was noticeably exerted only after it had been combined with the influence of medieval drama by real men of the theatre in the seventeenth century. At most, the men of the Renaissance slowly and painfully prepared a public which would be ready in the next century to listen to a higher type of play than that offered by the Brotherhood of the Passion.

Charles Estienne, in the preface to the *Comédie du Sacrifice* (1543), expressed the attitude of the classicists in regard to the relative merits of medieval and ancient comedy. French farce, he said, keeps only one act of New Comedy. Many comedies consist of ridiculous words and badinage without rhyme or reason, without any plot or conclusion. The reforms which he implied or advocated consisted in lengthening the plays to five acts; dividing them into scenes; having characters leave the stage whenever their presence is not necessary; the introduction of a plot with an ending; the use of prose for dialogue in imitation of the Italians.

The first original French comedy produced as a result of the classical movement was *Eugène* (1552) by Jodelle. In his prologue he stated his purpose and ideas. Comedy is looked down upon, he said. Many people prefer tragedy; but the author wishes to please the lower populace and re-introduce comedy, which for so long has not been seen upon a stage. Although the plot owes nothing to an old Menander and the style is his own, the author owes nothing to the rubbish of the morality plays. He is going to follow an old trail in order that the French may dare to follow it. He will, however, break the law of comedy and make his characters graver than they would have been had he followed Latin comedy step by step. The characters are above the most vulgar populace. They are such people as we see among us. (This is a revolt at the outset against the idea that comedy must present the dregs of society as it so often did in Italy.) The setting is not so rich as it might be and there is no music between the acts. He will not tell the plot in the prologue. The audience will understand everything as soon as it hears the first scene.

The priest, Eugène and Jean, his chaplain, give the details of the situation. Eugène is in love with Alix and has married her to the stupid Guillaume; Jean is promised a benefice if he keeps the husband in ignorance of the amour of his wife and if he prevents Alix from turning her attention to some other gallant. The situation is still more complicated, as Jean explains in an ensuing monologue. Captain Florimond, who is in love with Eugène's sister Hélène and who was worn out by the lady's pitiless virtue, had turned his attention with success to Alix before his departure for the war. It was then that Eugène married Alix to the convenient Guillaume. In the next scene Guillaume extols his wife's virtue and chastity, while Alix throws in humorous asides. We learn that a certain creditor is demanding payment and the act closes with the arrival of Jean.

Act II. Florimond, back from the war, seeks Alix; and, after an episodic monologue and dialogue with his servant Arnauld, he sends the latter in search of his mistress. Hélène has seen Florimond pass by; and, after a monologue in which she repeats what is already known, she informs her brother Eugène of the relations between Florimond and Alix. The abbé is furious.

Act III. Arnauld reports the whole situation to Florimond. He has found Jean dining with Guillaume and Alix. They threaten to punish all the culprits. Jean tells his version of the incident in a monologue and enlarges upon the details of the appearance of Arnauld in a scene with Eugène and his sister. Florimond meets Alix, reproaches her, and orders his furniture removed from her house.

Act IV. Although Guillaume was present in the last scene, his monologue proves he believes no evil of his wife. The creditor, having heard that Florimond intends to strip the house of the furniture, arrives on the scene threatening prison for Guillaume if he is not paid. He encounters Eugène and Hélène who plead for Guillaume in vain. Arnauld offers his services to Florimond to kill Eugène. The act closes as Eugène laments over the whole affair to Jean, and asks Jean to withdraw while he thinks of what to do.

Act V. During the entr'acte Eugène has decided, so he tells Jean, to persuade Hélène to accept Florimond's love and thus all will be well. As for the creditor, Eugène will give him a cure. Hélène accepts the proposal, as does the creditor. Guillaume is not only satisfied with the return of his furniture; but also, when Eugène tells him he loves his wife and wishes to enjoy her favors without fear, the old fool blandly replies that he is not jealous. Florimond rejoices in the conquest of Hélène and the play closes with all the characters entering to enjoy a supper.

To insist categorically that the increase in plot material is wholly due to Italian influence would be unsafe. The farce had become more and more complicated and the despised *farceurs* had grown fairly adept in motivation and in developing action logically. *Eugène* marks a step forward in these respects; but this evolution may well have received little impulse from classical theory, for *Eugène* is a farce in five acts, with more complication of plot than usual. The setting, however, is a street as in Italian comedy.

The situation, characters, tone, the lack of liaison of scenes which follow each other at the will of the author, the ending, the versification, are characteristic of the farce. There is no more unity of action or plot than would be expected from a playwright who was acquainted with the more developed farces and who dared to develop this form still further. The situation is medieval for the reason that Alix is married. Latin comedy would have taken up the story before Eugène had married her to Guillaume. Florimond would have been the long-lost relation of someone of importance, and would have married Alix; whereas Hélène would have been married to someone else. Classical comedy does not use adultery as a motive. Farce comedy does; and these characters are stock characters of the farce. Florimond has a touch of the braggart captain, but he is still the "gallant" of the farce. The amorous priest, the wife bold in her infidelity, the stupid and complacent husband, belong to medieval comedy. Hélène is not the maiden of classical comedy. Her virtue is temporary. She has no thought of marriage with Florimond, but she accepts him in the frank, jesting manner of the farce. The ending is cynically medieval. There is no concealed or mistaken identity or disguise to mitigate the crudeness of the situation or to offer a relatively moral solution. In the manner of medieval drama of all kinds, the principal characters in the story carry on the action in the play. Most of the story is included within the limits of the play, although the situation is complicated enough to necessitate a rather more detailed exposition than is usual in the farce.

The point of attack, although not late in the story, causes certain anterior scenes to be narrated. Yet this is due to the complex situation rather than to Italian influence. The scene in which Arnauld discovers Guillaume, Alix and Jean dining together would certainly have been played on the purely medieval stage. It is a hilariously comic scene potentially; but it is reported, not enacted, in this play in which Italian influence is strong enough to introduce the street setting. From now on for many years, just such scenes will be lost to the comic stage in France.

Yet this attempt to evolve true comedy from the indigenous farce went for almost naught. Jodelle's emulators went to Italian comedy for their inspiration and were content to copy or adapt what they found beyond the Alps, with the result that their plays never saw the real stage.

One of the actors of the production of *Eugène* was Grévin, who wrote the *Trésorière* given at the Collège de Beauvais in 1558. This play is modelled closely on *Eugène* so far as situation, characters and dénouement are concerned. The rôle of the servant, however, was increased in importance; and less of the action takes place on the stage than in Jodelle's play. The last act is almost entirely narrative in the manner of Italian comedy. Also in dramatizing an actual event, Grévin followed the example of Grazzini and Machiavelli.

In Grévin's next play, the *Ébahis* (1561), one has to search for elements of the farce. The stupid, complacent husband of the farce has now become an old libertine of classical comedy, who, believing that his wife has disappeared for ever, is in love with Madelon, daughter of his neighbor Gerard. The unexpected return of his wife and the recognition in true Latin style solve the problem instead of having a frankly immoral situation accepted by a stupid husband for a dénouement as in the farce. The action is slow in starting, for the rest of the act is taken up with a recital by the servant Anthoine of how the old man makes a fool of himself at home playing his amorous rôle. The whole recital would make excellent comedy, were it enacted as it would have been in a strictly medieval play; but action even of this kind was going off the stage under the influence of this new way of constructing comedy.

In the second act, it is learned that Madelon is loved by a young advocate whose affection she returns, and by Pantaloon, an Italian, whom she disdains. The plot then develops in the regular Italian way to an Italian climax and ending. Go-betweens and servants contrive to bring the advocate, disguised as the amorous Josse, to Madelon. Her father sees the lovers through the keyhole, believes that the advocate is Josse and contents himself with joking his future son-in-law. A servant gives a new impulse to the action by accusing Pantaloon of having been the favored lover. The latter is captured but proves his innocence. In the meantime, a "Gentleman" has procured, through Dame Claude, a meeting with Agnes, the wife of Josse and former mistress of Pantaloon. When she appears on the scene the recognition and dénouement ensue.

The meeting of the lovers by means of disguise with the various mistakes which follow is a situation which becomes canonical in French comedy. Following the example of the Italians, Grévin, with his scene in the street, prefers to narrate the episode in all its details, instead of having it enacted up to a certain point in the manner of a similar scene in the old farce of the *Hen-House*. There is a refinement of indecency which is more revolting than the crude vulgarity of the farce. The action is necessarily behind the scenes. Secondary characters, such as servants and go-betweens, hold the stage. The heroine appears rarely. The situation is more complicated than in the case of the farce, although there is not much more action in the play than in the highly developed farce and there are fewer events on the stage.

Jean de la Taille composed in 1562 a comedy entitled *Les Corrivaux* which was published in 1573. His interest in Italian comedy is proved by his free translation, amounting at times to an adaptation of Ariosto's *Negromante,* and by a statement in the prologue to his play in which he openly avows that he followed Plautus and Terence and the Italians. He was the first playwright in France to proclaim the imitation of Italian comedy as the basis of his art. He discarded the versification of the farce and used prose for his dialogue as the Italian authors had done. His cast of characters is larger than that of his predecessors and much longer than the list of personages in the farce. His play also contains many scenes and a complicated plot, after the manner of the comedies produced in the Peninsula, although it is not quite so complex as the plot of its source, Parabosco's *Viluppo* (1547). Italian influence is now complete.

There is a double plot with two heroes and two heroines. One of the heroines appears in the first act to give the exposition, while the other does not appear at all. The latter, Fleurdalys, is a girl sought by two rivals who are introduced simultaneously into her house by tricky servants. This scene, as usual, is messengered. The plot is complicated by means of concealed identity and long-lost children. One of the lovers turns out to be the brother of his inamorata. This love of a brother for a sister is a motive well known in Italian drama. In tragedy it is frankly incestuous, and it leads to the climax and dénouement. In comedy it titillates the somewhat degenerate emotions of the audience and leads to the dénouement.

The only really interesting scene on the stage is the exposition in which the girl Restitue confesses to the nurse that her lover has deserted her and has become enamored of Fleurdalys; but there is no originality even in this kind of expository scene common to Italian comedy and best known to us in Ariosto's *Suppositi*. It is soon found that this situation has but little to do with the ensuing action, which develops into the messengered scene already mentioned. The rest of the play, after this obligatory scene off the stage, consists of recognition scenes and betrothals brought about unexpectedly. The French comic playwrights have all the parts of the Italian comic machine at their disposal, but they cannot fit them together so that the wheels revolve without squeaking. The result is that *Les Corrivaux* and the plays which follow it are in many ways much poorer examples of comedy than *Eugène*, which possesses some of the vigor of the medieval farce.

Belleau's *Reconnue*, finished by an unknown author after the death of Belleau in 1577, shows only too well the increasing misconception of what is humorous on the stage in the minds of men who were not writing plays for production. Belleau had played in Jodelle's *Eugène*, but his comedy is more effective when read than played. Very little of the action is on the stage. Even the climax is behind the scenes. Frequent monologues, asides and digressions recall Senecan tragedy. The technique of contemporary tragedy was based on the art of oratory and of narration. These same forces which kept action behind the scenes in tragedy were at work in comedy. The very title, *The Woman Recognized*, shows the influence of classical comedy with its recognition scene; and a remote source of the play is found in *Casina* by Plautus. Unlike the farce, Belleau's comedy is based upon a long series of antecedent events and the point of attack is late in the story.

Classicists, like Grévin, begged "all lovers of good literature to aid in driving out the monstrous farce." They gave the usual excuse for their lack of success: that the theatrical audience was ignorant. The answer to this accusation is that not one of the classical comedies of this period can compare favorably with *Pathelin* and other highly developed farces in fitness for presentation on a stage. The comedies written after 1560 were scarcely ever produced. The authors lacked the opportunity to see their works and to learn by experience what is effective on the comic stage. Many of them felt that comedy was an inferior form of dramatic art. They apologized for writing it and for having it published. Naturally they failed to dislodge the farce from its stronghold. Even in the seventeenth century, when Corneille and Molière adapted classical comedy to the public stage, the farce influenced these masters of the art of playmaking, both directly and indirectly.

Had it been possible to influence the real theatre at this time through plays built on the model of classical comedy, had the audience been prepared slowly for this new style of drama, Larivey might have become a real dramatist for the Hôtel de Bourgogne. In 1579 he published six comedies adapted from the Italian, although he implied in his prologue that Latin comedy was his primary source. In 1611 he published three more plays of the same kind. He improved the Italian originals by systematic reduction in the number of characters. Thus in the *Veuve* he dropped five rôles from the original *Vedova* by Buonaparte. Unfortunately he was too prone to cause feminine rôles to disappear. French classical comedy was not to come into its own until an active part both in the story and on the stage was given to the heroine. Critics have alleged as a reason for this suppression the fact that feminine rôles were generally played by men; they forget that Larivey was writing these plays to be read and that this custom had no effect on feminine rôles in tragedy.

Larivey also reduced long speeches and long scenes and even suppressed certain episodes, thus simplifying the action somewhat, but at times causing gaps in the plot. He also adapted local allusions and customs to fit French ideas. Yet in spite of the characteristic French impulse towards simplification, the plays remain entirely Italian in technique; and they merely reproduce the usual classical plots, motives, scenes and characters. Larivey excelled his contemporaries in the art of comic dialogue. He had an instinct for comic effect and the incisive line. It is here that his originality lies. Unfortunately these plays were never given a public hearing. Larivey did not become a real dramatist.

This lack of opportunity to produce plays of this type is felt to be all the more regrettable when one reads *Les Contens,* the masterpiece of French classical comedy of the Renaissance. This play, published in 1584 after the death of its author, Tournèbe, has dramatic merit. The plot is distinctly Italian. Tournèbe was more than a translator and adapter. He had a sense of the dramatic.

The plot rests upon the well-known situation of two or three men in love with the same girl; but the opening scene is handled in a manner very different from that of most classical comedies. The exposition, instead of being presented in a conversation carried on between one of the lovers and his father or a servant, is effected by an explanatory dialogue between the heroine, Geneviève, and her mother. An added interest is thus gained in that the sympathetic character is brought on the stage and the persons most concerned with the action explain the situation.

We learn from this dialogue that of her three lovers, Geneviève favors Basile; while her mother and the father of Eustache have decided to marry her to Eustache. The third lover is a braggart captain. It is found that Basile has been able to gain an interview with Geneviève the night before by appearing disguised as Eustache, with other maskers. Shakespeare would have put this scene on the stage as he did in *Romeo and Juliet;* but the meeting takes place indoors; and since Tournèbe has used the usual street-scene, he cannot include the scene within his play. The point of attack, therefore, comes later in the play than it should; but, since there is no long chain of antecedent events in this story, the point of attack is relatively early and is placed almost correctly. This is the only scene which ought to be enacted and is not on the stage.

The complication of the plot and the ensuing action arise from the fact that Basile, disguised once more as Eustache, gains entrance to Geneviève's house again, and, when discovered by her mother, he is thought to be Eustache. Further complications are introduced when Eustache, informed wrongly that

Geneviève has a physical infirmity, turns elsewhere for the gratification of his passion, and when the woman he is entertaining is dressed in his clothes and takes Basile's place beside Geneviève. This totally Italian situation depending upon disguise and similarity of appearance leads to the usual *quiproquo* and mistakes of classical comedy. The dénouement, however, is not brought about by recognition. The whole situation really exists at the beginning of the play; and the ending is caused when Geneviève's mother accepts Basile as a son-in-law. This is the logical ending; and the logical ending of a comedy based on a situation which really exists is very rare.

The servants occupy a secondary place in the action. No opportunity for humor is lost thereby; and the structure of this play proves that it is perfectly possible to make the principal and sympathetic characters in the story carry on much of the action on the stage and to increase greatly the interest in the plot, without sacrificing any of the comic effects arising from the tricky servant of classical comedy.

Geneviève appears on the stage much more often than the usual heroine of classical comedy. She furnishes a part of the comic effect. She is more respectable than the usual contemporary heroine. Although she receives her lover before they are legally married, the love of these two young people is relatively honorable when compared with the love in the farce and Italian comedy. Tournèbe stages a sympathetic, decent love scene between the hero and heroine, which raises the tone of the play and the interest in the pair far above the plane of the usual comedy based upon an immoral situation. This is the first example of the scene of gallant love which forms one of the foundations of later comedy.

Where had Tournèbe learned this art? He had seen Jodelle's *Eugène* acted. He had seen, therefore, a good deal of action on the stage. He did not imitate Italian comedy slavishly. Somewhere he had learned that much of the classical technique in comedy was faulty. He must have learned this from seeing medieval drama acted.

The influence of the farce increased. In 1589, Perrin asserted in his prologue to his *Escholliers* that he had not gone to foreign sources because he preferred the Gallic farce. He was more indebted to foreign comedy than he wished to admit, for the ultimate source of his play is Ariosto's *Suppositi*. Yet the fact that he made this statement is evidence that it was no longer necessary to despise the farce in order to be considered a gentleman and a playwright. Perrin made good his boast by adopting the versification of the farce, its cynical tone, and a simpler plot than is usual in Italian comedy.

Godard's *Desguisez* published in 1594, is also derived from the *Suppositi;* but again the plot is simplified and the characters are reduced in number. The plot deals with a lover who disguises himself as a servant in order to be near the woman he loves and to offer her honorable marriage. He declares his love in a scene on the stage. The heroine at first refuses; but later her heart is won. The hero and heroine were beginning to play opposite each other in French comedy more and more. Also, this play was given at least one performance.

Bonet's comedy *La Tasse* (1595) shows more plainly the influence of the acted drama and especially of the farce on classical comedy. In this play we first see a doctor and his valet who are going to the silversmith's to get a cup. Their plans are overheard by two sharpers or rather soldiers of fortune. The valet brings the cup to the doctor's wife. One of the swindlers brings two partridges, and assures the woman that they are a present from her husband and that the doctor wants the cup. She gives it to him. The doctor arrives and, when he learns what has happened, beats his wife, who refuses to beg his pardon for her stupidity. She faints. The servant threatens to yell "bloody murder." The doctor sets forth to seek the cup and one of the robbers mocks him. In the third act, the robber explains to the wife that one of the doctor's friends has played the trick, that the doctor now knows the truth and wants the birds brought to him so that he and his friend can eat them together. The enraged wife gives them up. The two robbers are ready to eat their stolen feast, when a third crook steals it. Each accuses the other. The wife now decides to avenge herself by being unfaithful to her husband, and sends for a "Monsieur Laure." The valet perceives what is happening and informs the doctor, who beholds the vengeance through the keyhole in regulation Italian fashion. He calls witnesses; but the maid, again in Italian fashion, changes clothes with Laure and she is discovered by the doctor. With the cynicism of the farce, Laure and the other witness decide to share the woman's favors in the future. She proves her "innocence" to her husband. Laure goes to seek the cup. He finds the robbers, who pass the cup back and forth to each other as they are searched, in a scene either inspired by the farce or the *commedia dell' arte*, at least from a popular acted form of drama, for such scenes are only effective when acted. Finally, Laure gets possession of the cup; and one of the robbers is recognized as the brother of the doctor, the other as the brother of his wife. This recognition, however, does not alter the typical farcical dénouement of the play.

Although certain incidents and tricks are borrowed from the Italian form, the greater part of the play is built along the lines of the farce. There is no late point of attack. The action develops from the situation as it exists at the rise of the curtain. There is concealed identity and a recognition, but these motives have little to do with the plot. The action is on the stage. Indeed, the setting may well have been of the medieval type and have shown the interior as well as the exterior of the house.

The *Corrivaux* (1612), by Pierre Troterel, also seems to demand a simultaneous setting. The author places his characters on the stage at will. The liaison of scenes is imperfect and the jerkiness of the action is characteristic of the medieval drama. The playwright was little concerned with explanations as to how the characters happen to appear. He was content to have them keep the action before the eyes of the audience. As a result, the psychology—if we may apply such a term to the minds of these characters—is as jerky as the action, although neither psychology nor action is halting.

In this play, the influence of Italian comedy can be found once more in the usual disguise motive; but the play is a farce with all the characteristic crude realism, obscenity, and cynicism. The technique is that of the farce. The point of attack is at the beginning of the story. The action develops on the stage and leaves little except utter indecency behind the scenes. The dénouement is the regular ending of the farce brought about by cynical disregard of truth and decency. Although such an ending can be found in the Italian *Mandragola* and in the novella, French comedy of the Renaissance did not have to learn this method of solving a problem from Italy. It was the ending through recognition and discovery that the French playwright had to learn from the land of Plautus and Terence.

It is commonly held that the French playwrights of the Renaissance learned to handle complex plots by imitating Italian comedy. The facts which we have attempted to establish do not entirely support that view. As time went on, the writers of French comedy, always prone to simplify Italian comedy, reduced this complexity more and more, until the double plot, the disguises, the long chain of antecedent events, the mistaken identity, concealed relationships, the round robin of three or four characters in love, the recognition and discoveries, all the mechanical devices for complicating plots, almost entirely disappeared or were used sparingly. These devices were to return in later French comedy; but Corneille, Rotrou and Molière did not learn these tricks from erudite imitators of the Italian comedy of Renaissance. Comedy was not in favor at the beginning of the French Renaissance, nor did it succeed in winning favor. *Les Contens,* alone, seems to have been held worthy of esteem. In fact, the authors of these plays treated them as step-children.

Not only were classical comedies denied representation on the popular stage up to 1600, but also Hardy, author of hundreds of other plays, probably wrote no comedies. The farce retained real vigor and finally forced its technique upon the erudite when they wrote humorous plays even based upon an Italian situation. Another reason for the failure of this transplanted comedy to impress its mould upon French acted drama was that humor found its outlet on the French stage not only in the farce, but in tragi-comedy and in the pastoral.

A comparison of *Les Contens, Les Escholliers, Les Desguisez,* and *Les Corrivaux* with Ariosto's *Suppositi* shows the difference between Italian classical comedy and French classical comedy that has been influenced by the farce. These French comedies use the motive of disguise; but, whereas in the *Suppositi* the disguise has taken place before the beginning of the play, in these comedies the point of attack is placed so as to include the disguise within the play. This is distinctively a medieval procedure, differing from the classical practice of placing the point of attack so close to the dénouement that many events and much of the situation have to be narrated. As a result of this procedure, much more of the action is on the stage and the plot develops more within the limits of the play. Also, the heroine and hero appear more frequently. Yet the plot was simplified by the French writers. Since the interest was sustained by having the action develop on the stage through the principal characters, it was not necessary to build up many complications brought about by antecedent events, to be talked about by secondary characters, as is generally the case in Italian comedy.

Mairet's *Galanteries du Duc d'Ossone* is the direct continuation of this method of building plays; and it carries the development one step farther in that the scene in which the lover gains admittance to his lady's room is on the stage in view of the audience, whereas in *Les Corrivaux* the audience saw only the disguised servant enter the house. In order to present this scene, Mairet, who was one of the advocates of the three unities, had to disregard the unities of place and of time. He wrote his play for a stage which permitted a system of simultaneous decoration. The street-scene of classical comedy was renounced. Medieval technique had triumphed enough to make it possible for the writer of comedy to put every scene on the stage. Of course, the single set was to return later in the French theatre; but by that time playwrights had learned how to avoid most of the infelicities caused by the unchanging set.

In the *Galanteries du Duc d'Ossone* at the rise of the curtain, Paulin, the aged husband of Emilie, has attempted to slay her lover, Camille. This is the sole important antecedent event. Paulin informs the Duke and asks for protection. The ensuing action arises from the fact that the Duke, although up to this time he has not been in love with Emilie, conceives the idea of sending Paulin away in order to have free access to his wife. The Duke enters the room of Emilie by means of a rope ladder. He finds her about to visit her wounded lover, Camille; and she begs the Duke, as a favor, to remain with the old woman who watches over her. The Duke gallantly consents and is rewarded by finding that the "old woman" is the young and attractive Flavie, who receives him with open arms. When Emilie returns, the play would seem to be over; but at the beginning of the fourth act, Camille solicits Flavie's love through his servant. Flavie accepts the proposal and grants a rendezvous. Emilie, however, grants a similar rendezvous to the Duke. In the darkness Flavie mistakes the Duke for Camille; but after a scene of recrimination and final reconciliation of the quartet of lovers, the husband of Emilie arrives. The Duke pretends that Camille is in command of a guard coming to arrest Paulin; and the duped husband flees, leaving the four lovers in possession of the field of battle.

On this situation, taken from an Italian novella, Mairet constructed a comedy by employing a technique by no means Italian. The servants do little until the fourth act. The principal characters are kept on the stage; and the action is in view of the audience, whenever it is within bounds of decency as interpreted by the free standards of the period. The Duke has borrowed a confidant from tragi-comedy who tries to dissuade his friend from carrying out his plan in a scene which is common in tragedy. The action arises from a simple situation and develops its complexity during the play. The two episodes in the action are not closely bound together; but there is plenty of action, and enough events take place on the stage to sustain the interest. The cynical ending is the regular ending of medieval French comedy. Finally, the people of this play are of high rank. Thus the materials are at hand for a comedy which will be interesting, if acted, and which will present characters of social rank higher than the usual people of either Renaissance or medieval comedy.

The problem now facing the comic playwright was how to make "honest people laugh." The indecency had to disappear. Corneille practically solved the problem in his *Mélite,* mainly through the influence of pastoral drama.

The influence of the pastoral on French dramatic technique was strongest during the years 1620-1630. During the latter half of the sixteenth century there were representations of pastorals at the courts, in the colleges and in the provinces. The real impulse towards the composition of pastoral plays came first with the translations of Tasso's *Aminta* (1584), Guarini's *Pastor Fido* (1595), Andreini's *Mirtilla* (1602), and Bracciolini's *Pentimento Amoroso* (1603).

By the beginning of the seventeenth century the French playwrights were acquainted with the technical elements found in the Italian pastoral, or as Guarini called his play, the tragi-comedy-pastoral. In the pastoral there is the complicated situation of crossed love motives, yet with very little action. The situation remains almost stationary until the dénouement solves the problems, generally by a recognition scene. The lyricism, the songs of unrequited love constituted the mainspring of the interest. As in tragedy, the monologue and the narrative abound; the confidant plays an important rôle; the plot is sometimes composed of parallel episodes, each of which could be played separately. It is thus that Montchrétien constructed his *Bergerie* with the result that the author himself forgot to complete one of the many love episodes. The interest arose, not from the situation as a whole, but from separate scenes consisting of lyric dialogues and monologues. The writer of pastorals did not yet attempt to introduce new situations and effects. He simply built up a complex framework by combining motives and situations which he inherited from the Italian pastoral. Montchrétien's play is a mosaic of traditional elements borrowed from Italian plays directly or indirectly. As Marsan says: "Nothing is lacking: chaste maidens, exalted lovers, passionate or cold shepherds, the confidants, the despairing father, the old woman expert in composing love philters, the satyr, the echo, the oracle, the interrupted sacrifice, the recognitions, bursts of anger, remorse, crimes, resurrections." All this we find, but no dramatic interest.

Out of these interests hurled together pell-mell to form a background for lyric effusions of tenderness, Hardy constructed plays with a dramatic action helping to arouse and sustain interest. Whether his situation is simple as in *Corine* and in *Alcée*, or complicated with a pastoral merry-go-round of love motives as in his *Alphée*, he was able to avoid the confusion and ineptitude of such plays as Montchrétien's *Bergerie*. The material is the same, but it is handled by a dramatist writing for an audience. His plots are simple, with the exception of the plot of *Alphée* in which he has introduced the merry-go-round of love; but even in this play the main episode is given enough importance so that the whole situation is made plain.

He begins usually in the middle of the action. Generally, principal characters open the play. The exposition is unobtrusive. From their conversation we learn incidentally what obstacles confront the lovers. The confidant is rarely employed. The principal characters carry on the action before our eyes. Scenes which are narrated in older pastorals, especially in *Aminta* and *Pastor Fido*, are put on the stage by Hardy. Thus the scene in which the satyr surprises the shepherdess at the bath, narrated in *Aminta*, is enacted in *Corine*. The rôle of the messenger, which is so important in earlier pastorals, does not exist in Hardy's extant plays of this class.

He shows the same care in leading up to his dénouements that he employs in his tragi-comedies. Thus in *Alcée*, the recognition of the son by his father which ends the play, is prepared by showing the father setting forth from his home in search of his child, and the arrival of the father in the land of the shepherds. The story is told clearly, and the correct scenes are chosen for representation. Emphasis is placed upon those in which the principal characters are concerned. There are enough events to give the play movement, and each act advances the plot.

These plays are a combination of heroic, marvellous, comic and melodramatic elements. The importance of Hardy's pastoral lies in the fact that it is a play founded upon a decent love story, in which the principal characters, not servants or confidants, carry on the action on the stage. It took the place which classical comedy might have occupied in the theatre during these years, because, in spite of its setting and its marvellous effects, the pastoral, as written by Hardy, is a comedy dealing with situations of everyday life.

Hardy opens his *Triomphe d'Amour* with a scene between three principal characters. Atys, a rich shepherd, and Cephée, a poor shepherd, dispute the question as to which one is loved by Clitie, daughter of Phædime. She does not wish to answer the question, but she promises to award her love to the one who can run the faster. As they withdraw to the starting point, she runs away, informing the audience that Cephée has known her inclination for him for a long time. When the race is run, the shepherds find their referee has flown. Clitie assures the shepherdess, Ægine, who loves Atys, that she will not accept the love of Atys. Phædime grants the hand of his daughter to Atys; but the maiden refuses to accept him as a husband.

Act II. A satyr laments his love for Clitie, and then overhears Clitie tell Mélice to ask Cephée to abduct her, in order to prevent her marriage to Atys. The satyr decides to upset this plan by abducting Clitie himself. Atys throws Cephée into amorous consternation by announcing his approaching marriage with Clitie; but Mélice reassures the lover by giving him Clitie's message. The satyr gets a second satyr to aid him in his plan of abducting Clitie.

Act III. Cephée and his friend, Pisandre, set out to abduct the willing Clitie. The satyrs arrive first. They are surprised by Cephée and Pisandre, who capture the first satyr; but the second satyr escapes, taking Clitie with him. Ægine declares her love for Atys, who repulses her. Cephée and Pisandre force the first satyr to show them where the second satyr has taken Clitie. He brings them to a cave, but they do not find her there. They beat the satyr and decide to have recourse to a sorceress in order to find out where Clitie is held prisoner.

Act IV. In a scene of incantation, the sorceress gives the answer that although the first satyr does not know where Clitie is, Diana will cause the place to be discovered. The scene then shifts to the cave where the second satyr is making violent love to Clitie, who wards him off with great difficulty. Led by a dog to this cave, the friends rescue the nymph.

Act V. As the unhappy Ægine is about to commit suicide, Philire suddenly appears and bids her go to the temple, where joy awaits her. Cephée demands Clitie as his bride in accordance with the law that a shepherd may marry a nymph whom he has saved from misfortune; but her avaricious father refuses to consent and invokes his paternal rights. The case is laid before the priest of Pan. The god himself appears and upholds the father. The lovers appeal to Cupid, who reverses the judgment. Ægine finds happiness with Atys, who now bestows his love on her.

Such plays are the source of the technique employed by Corneille in writing his first comedies. He says in his *Examen* of *Mélite* that his guide in playwriting was his common sense, together with the examples of the "late Hardy." It is doubtful that Hardy wrote any comedies in classical style. The Hôtel de Bourgogne evidently found the farce and the pastoral furnished satisfactory drama of a lighter vein. However that may be, Corneille's *Mélite* and his *Veuve* are not derived from the farce nor from classical comedy. Their construction can only be explained as a development of the technique of the lighter pastorals of Hardy, and not of such pastorals as Mairet's *Sylvie* and *Silvanire*, which are more in the style of tragi-comedy and which follow closely the construction of the *Pastor Fido*.

In *Mélite* (1629), we find Eraste and Tircis, two rivals for the love of the heroine, Mélite. Philandre is in love with Cloris, the sister of Tircis. The first act of exposition is handled as it would have been in a pastoral. The play opens with a scene between the two men; and then comes a series of love scenes in which the lady rebuffs or accepts her lover's advances as the plot requires. Eraste becomes jealous of Tircis, who he thinks is his rival. Although Tircis is an honorable friend, he falls in love with Mélite and she returns his affection. The jealous Eraste forges love letters purporting to be from Mélite, and he has them delivered to Philandre, who easily becomes enamored of Mélite, boasts to Tircis of his conquest, and shows him the false letters. Cloris accuses Mélite of winning Philandre from her, but Mélite protests her innocence. Mélite is informed that Tircis is dead and she faints. Eraste, when told that Tircis and also Mélite are dead, goes mad with remorse. Licis, however, assures Cloris that she announced the death of her brother to Mélite to see if she really loved him, for he still lives. Eraste, when told that both his friends are alive, asks forgiveness for his imposture. Cloris accepts him instead of Philandre; and Tircis and Mélite are united.

With the exception of the nurse, a minor character, there is nothing in this play which recalls the farce or classical comedy. Even the nurse could have been drawn from a pastoral. In construction, tone and effect it is a pastoral such as Hardy wrote, without the pastoral setting and the element of the marvellous. Although the play does not present certain scenes which appear in many pastorals, such as the magic incantation and the trial before a god, all the scenes which it does contain can be parallelled in pastoral comedy. The principal characters carry on the action. There are no tricky servants and no confidant. Unlike the plot of the farce and that of the *Galanteries du Duc d'Ossone,* this plot is founded on a decent love story; and the love element is not a mere background as it is so often in classical comedy. The rivals for the hand of the heroine; her hesitation to disclose her love; Cloris' rebuffal by Philandre; her sudden acceptance

of Eraste; the heroine's disclosure of her love at the news of
the death of her lover; the madness of Eraste when he hears
Mélite is dead; the lyric lamentations of the lovers; the tirades
expressing remorse—all these scenes are derived from the pastoral. Many lines are directly inspired by speeches in Mairet's
two pastorals, *Sylvie* and *Silvanire.*

In his *Examen,* Corneille explained the success of the play on
the ground of its novelty and the style of the dialogue, which
reproduced the conversation of honorable people. *Mélite* was
a novelty, and the dialogue is on a much higher plane than that
of the crude conversation of the characters in the farce and in
classical comedy of the Renaissance. Yet Corneille did not
produce a new kind of comedy without rules and models. He
had transferred the mechanism of the pastoral from Arcadia to
Paris by changing the costumes and the setting.

Corneille's second comedy, *La Veuve* (1633), follows the technique of the pastoral very closely. It presents the abduction of
the heroine in scenes similar to those in Hardy's *Triomphe
d'Amour.* Corneille does not depart from this system. *La Galerie
du Palais* (1634), *La Suivante* (1634), *La Place Royale* (1635)
are all founded upon a criss-cross of love motives. At the opening, two or three men and two or three women are bestowing
their affection upon each other. A sister tries to intercede for
a brother (*La Place Royale*); or a brother insists upon his sister
returning the affection of a friend (*La Veuve*). The lovers are
not settled in their affections; and the original situation is
quickly altered when one of the characters changes his mind on
a pretext so slight that the motive is plainly introduced to tangle
up the different strings by which the playwright moves his
characters around. The sudden jealousy or change of heart
does not result from the psychology of the characters. The ruse
and the resulting criss-cross are manufactured. If Corneille
wants a certain situation he, not his characters, causes it to
arise. The psychology of his comic characters reminds one of
Mélisée, in Scudery's *Amour Caché par l'Amour,* who explains

her attitude to her lover by saying: "Without reason, in loving him, I pretended to be cruel."

The tangled intrigues revolve, rather than evolve. When the fifth act is almost finished the threads are forcibly pulled apart; and, as in the pastoral, rather surprising marriages are foreshadowed. As Corneille admitted in his *Examen* of *La Place Royale*, his play ends with the marriage of episodic characters. His plot makes his characters. Thus Alidor, in this play, has to have a "wild mind" and find himself troubled by a love which attaches him too much to Angélique, in order that the wheels of the situation may revolve when he decides to give up his mistress to a friend. Then, as Corneille points out, "this love of repose does not hinder him in the fifth act from showing himself still in love with his mistress, in spite of the resolution he had made to get rid of her and the manner in which he betrayed her. Thus he seems to begin to love her truly only when he has given her reasons to hate him. The result is an unevenness of character which is very faulty."

Corneille realized that he sacrificed psychology to situation in these plays. He said in his dedicatory epistle to *La Suivante*: "Tricks and intrigues are the mainspring of comedy; the passions only enter accidentally." This describes his comedy; but Molière was to show that passions can be the mainspring of plot in comedy.

In composing these plays Corneille was not worrying about the unities, although his *Examens*, written about twenty-five years later, discuss them in the light of these classical rules. It happens that *La Suivante* observes the unity of time and that *La Galerie du Palais* does not. Thus his technique was not influenced by this rule. In the preface to the edition of *La Veuve* published in 1634, he said of the unity of place: "Sometimes I narrow it down to the size of the stage, sometimes I extend it to a whole town, as in this play. I enlarged it in *Clitandre* to places where one can go in twenty-four hours." Such a liberal interpretation of this rule made unnecessary any modification of the technique of these plays on account of the unity of place.

By the time he was writing his *Examens*, Corneille was distinctly troubled by the fact that his characters held in the street conversations which should have taken place indoors. He says:

Célidée and Hippolyte are two neighbors whose dwellings are only separated by a street, and their social status is not too high to allow the lovers to talk to them at their door. It is true that what they say would be better said in a chamber or in a drawing room, and it is only to show themselves that they leave the door, by which they should have been screened, and come to the middle of the stage to speak; but this is a theatrical licence which must be endured in order to find that rigorous unity of place which the great abiders by rules demand. It goes a little beyond reality and even decorum; but it is almost impossible to do otherwise; and the spectators are so accustomed to it that they find in it nothing shocking (*Examen de la Galerie du Palais*).

These ideas are afterthoughts. When he was writing these plays he interpreted the rules as he pleased. It was perfectly possible to stage interior scenes in the French theatre by withdrawing curtains, as in the *Galanteries du Duc d'Ossone*, or by using a simultaneous setting. Corneille was not hampered by rules or by lack of scenic appliances in constructing these plays. He simply transferred the out-door pastoral to the streets of Paris. Du Ryer, in his *Vendanges de Suresnes* (1635) employed the same method, but kept his scene in the suburbs. The shepherd Sylvain in Rotrou's *Diane* (1630) becomes a coachman in Paris in order to follow his beloved shepherdess to the city. No matter where the scene was laid, it had become possible to present a play with a light, charming love story, with a happy ending and without a recognition scene. The lovers became the principal characters on the stage; and the rôles of the tricky servant, the colorless confidant and the nurse were reduced to a minimum. Contemporary local customs and manners were substituted for those of an impossible Arcadia. Inevitably the French comedy of manners began to evolve.

The farce still furnished scenes of indelicate humor in such plays as Verronneau's *Impuissance* (1634). *Alizon* (1637) and the *Comédie de Chansons* (1640) are a series of farcical scenes held together in a very loose manner. They prepared the way for comedy of manners such as Desmarets' popular *Visionnaires* (1637). But when the plot was becoming simple in the hands of certain playwrights, the French discovered the rich mine of complex plots and astounding situations found beyond the Pyrenees. Unhampered by rules and with a system of stage setting consisting of back drops and of a few properties which allowed quick and innumerable changes, the Spaniards possessed a flexible theatre. Their ideal of honor, their duels, maskings, disguises, hair-breadth escapes, with the complexity of plot derived by Spanish dramatists from Italian comedy, produced a drama abounding in surprises. Endowed with a fertile romantic imagination, Lope de Vega alone used and re-used in his hundreds of plays probably every situation known to dramatic art. The Beaumarchais, the Scribes and the Sardous of later centuries will be the indirect heirs of this wealth of situation. The first writer to avail himself of the material was Metel d'Ouville who took his *Esprit Follet* (1641) from Calderon's *Dama Duende*.

The complex plot was not new in France. Italian comedy and the pastoral had furnished situations of great intricacy. Spanish comedy, however, had an advantage over the Italian comedy. Because medieval technique had survived to a greater extent in Spain, more of the action was on the stage. There were many incidents which led to extreme complications in the play itself. The action was easier for the audience to follow because it saw the complexities develop within the play itself. In Italian-Latin comedy many complications preceded the point of attack and were disclosed only at the dénouement. Many Spanish plays are extremely intricate and difficult to follow in book form; but much of this difficulty would vanish in a theatrical presentation. The reverse is partly true of many comedies of purely classical technique. Obscurity resulting from many incidents within a play is less inartistic than obscurity due to a few incidents beyond the ken of the audience in the theatre. Therefore the Spanish drama was a better model for French playwrights than was Italian comedy.

However, the inevitable difficulties arose in the attempt to adapt the freer Spanish form to a theatre which was beginning to observe the rules of the unities. On the French stage, scenes could change, since the unity of place was interpreted as meaning that the action takes place in one town. Corneille's *Illusion Comique* (1636) requires a multiple setting consisting of a palace in the centre of the stage; on one side, a cave in a mountain; and on the other side, a park. A modification of this system could be effected by setting a scene only in a particular act, as in Mairet's *Criséide et Arimant*, in which the "tomb and the altar appear only in the fifth act," according to the memorandum of Mahelot, the stage carpenter of the Hôtel de Bourgogne. In the *Galanteries du Duc d'Ossone* a procedure is found which is probably the beginning of a new method of changing the scene. In the second act the stage direction reads: "When he has entered, the drop which represents the façade of a house is drawn, and the interior of the small room appears." A second room is disclosed in the same scene, as is shown by the direction: "Here the second drop is drawn and Flavie appears on her bed." In the decade of the forties, scenes were changed between the acts when necessary, as in Corneille's *Menteur*, Scarron's *Jodelet, ou le Maître-Valet*, and Rotrou's *Laure Persecutée*. Yet French playwrights evidently preferred as few changes as possible, for Corneille reduced the number of sets in Alarcon's *Verdad Sospechosa* from six to two in his *Menteur*. He even expressed regret in 1660 that the change of setting drew attention to the change of scene.

The same conservative attitude toward the unity of time is illustrated by the fact that he reduced the three or four days through which the action extends in the Spanish original, to about thirty-six hours. Thus the rules were having their effect, although they were not so rigorously observed as they were later in the century. Even this relative freedom was not enough to insure the artistic construction of plays in which a developing action is one of the main sources of interest. The psychological analysis of a great emotional crisis, the development of a human soul in one or two dramatic situations may well be portrayed in a drama which observes the rules; but complex plots portraying many situations demand more time and space than French drama even of this period cared to allow. The more intricate the mechanism, the greater is the damage caused by the displacement or loss of even the smallest wheel. And Spanish plays were complicated machines, which lost certain parts in being transported to the French stage.

In writing the *Cid*, Corneille centred the interest upon a psychological problem. The incidents were subordinate to the developing action. His compression of the action and his excision of many of the events in the original play intensified the mental struggle of his principal characters and threw the problem into strong relief. In pure comedy and in romantic tragi-comedy, in which the greater part of the interest is centred upon a series of remarkable events causing intricate situations, the influence of the Spanish drama was less felicitous, because of the ever-increasing constraint of the rules. Thus Corneille in the *Menteur* and the *Suite du Menteur* (1643)—the latter derived from Lope's *Amar sin Saber a quién*—threw the mechanism somewhat out of gear by dropping certain scenes. If a play depends primarily upon events, these events ought to be enacted. If a plot is complicated, the spectators ought to see the complications develop. In Corneille's adaptations many of the important scenes are narrated. For example, in *Amar sin Saber a quién* the initial cause of the action is a duel in which one of the adversaries is slain. An innocent man arrives at this moment, is accused of murder and is imprisoned. Corneille begins his play after the hero is imprisoned.

Corneille also omitted, among other scenes, a very complicated situation in which the prevaricating hero seems to be making love to one girl by day and to the other by night. This scene takes place in the semi-darkness of a chapel. It would not have been credible in a public square. Because of French prejudice against laying a scene of comedy in such a locality, Corneille could not reproduce it, even had he wished to retain the plot in all its complexity. The rules of decorum forbade even the utterance of the word *église* on the French stage.

The dénouement of the French play is brought about by a change of affection on the part of the hero who transfers his love rather suddenly, but in a manner reminiscent of Corneille's young men, from one lady to another. The Spanish play is more convincing because the liar is forced to accept the woman he pretended to love. Thus he reaps the penalty of his weakness.

By such processes the Spanish drama was constantly robbed of much of its greatest asset: the swift, picturesque action. In the *Menteur*, the propensity of the hero to prevaricate, the mainspring of the whole plot, is not foreshadowed as it is in a scene in Alarcon's play. Thus not only the plot itself, but the characters often become less convincing when transported to France.

Such faults in these adaptations are manifest when they are compared with their sources. Yet in comparison with earlier French comedies, these plays mark a distinct advance. Obscure as they may be in certain points, they still retain some of the picturesque movement and the romantic gaiety of Spanish drama. "Honest men" can laugh and be thrilled by the duels and the clandestine meetings of lovers to whom a bit of romance is worth the risk of life and honor. The cynical indecency emanating from Italy and from the indigenous farce, as exemplified in the *Galanteries du Duc d'Ossone*, the artificial pastoral conception of love, as exemplified in Corneille's earlier comedies, are replaced by emotions much more dramatic and sympathetic. Spanish heroines, who run real danger with a brave smile as they meet their lovers, appeal to us more than do their Italian sisters, whose passions are tinged with cynical jesting, more than do the French heroines, who are often pouting shepherdesses from Arcadia.

In Scarron's plays, which are drawn from Spanish sources, this romantic and dramatic interest is so striking that there is little difference between his comedy and tragi-comedy. The conflict between love and honor is so real and the emotions of his characters are so human that the situations are theatrical, at least. One is actually interested in the outcome of the story. The action reaches a higher climax than in classical comedy, where generally a series of obstacles, which could occur in almost any order, is presented. The dénouement grows out of the plot instead of from a mere recognition. The conflict is a real problem. In a word, French comedy under Spanish influence is more than a series of comic scenes.

The *Menteur* had pointed the way which French writers were to follow for a few years; but Scarron's *Jodelet, ou le Maître-Valet* (1645) is of greater importance in the development of comedy because it not only kept the romance of Spanish plots, but also definitely introduced burlesque and the lowly farce into regular comedy. The principal character, Jodelet, is the ancestor of that long line of valets, Mascarille, Scapin, Crispin, etc., which will culminate in the brilliant Figaro. Jodelet himself comes of an old family which reaches back to the clever, though often cowardly slave of Latin comedy; but in this play he dominates all.

Don Juan goes to Madrid with his valet, Jodelet, to meet his intended bride, Isabelle, whom he has never seen. Jodelet confesses that, through a mistake, he has dispatched to Isabelle his own grotesque portrait, instead of his master's. On finding the house of his lady, Don Juan is no little disturbed when he beholds a gallant descend from the balcony. In order to observe the situation of affairs, he decides to change positions with his valet. Act II. Isabelle upbraids her maid for having allowed the unwelcome lover, Don Louis, to enter. Isabelle, judging Don Juan from Jodelet's portrait, is unwilling to marry him. Lucrèce, who turns out later to be Don Juan's sister, has been abandoned by Don Louis, who slew her brother. She begs aid from Don Fernand, Isabelle's father. The arrival of the long-nosed Jodelet as the future husband causes a disagreeable surprise. He is a grotesque figure, magnificently impossible as a lover and gentleman. Act III. Don Louis, in love with Isabelle, takes courage; but Isabelle, learning that he seduced Lucrèce, scorns him. Jodelet makes violent love to Isabelle, and beats Don Juan, who tries to interfere. Isabelle feels drawn to the supposed valet. Don Louis, meeting Lucrèce who is veiled, mistakes her for Isabelle and makes love to her. As she discloses her identity, Don Juan appears and challenges Don Louis to a duel on the spot. Don Fernand bursts into the room. Don Juan orders Don Louis to fight a duel with Jodelet who is supposed by Don Louis to be the master. Act IV. Jodelet, toothpick in hand, burlesques the *stances* of the *Cid* on honor, saying: "Be clean, my teeth, honor so commands." Informed of his approaching duel, he gives all his comic cowardice free play in a scene of burlesque humor, first with Don Fernand and then with his master Don Juan, who finally bids Jodelet summon Don Louis. Act V. Jodelet, after one lunge at Don Louis, puts out the light in the room so that Don Juan may do the real fighting. Don Fernand appears as they fight. Don Juan discloses his real identity, and Don Louis promises to marry Lucrèce while Don Juan is gladly accepted by Isabelle.

While other playwrights from 1645 to 1660 were reproducing plots of an intricacy bordering upon confusion, Scarron saw in Spanish comedy situations fitting for burlesque and buffoonery of the gayest sort. The duels, the clandestine meetings, the balcony scenes, the fine point of honor, the gallantry of words and deeds became sources of farce comedy without losing all of their melodramatic flavor. Were he alive today he would produce melodramas which satirize their own tricks, such as *The Seven Keys to Baldpate.* His originality consisted in not taking Spanish drama seriously. The result was a joyous mixture of melodrama and burlesque humor, with the latter element happily predominating, just at a time when romantic heroism on the French stage needed the corrective of laughter.

His *Don Japhet d'Arménie* (1652), drawn from Castillo Solórzano's *Marqués del Cigarral,* works up to scenes of Gargantuan humor in which the situations and dialogue are Rabelaisian, but undeniably funny. This retired court fool, while seeking his lady, finally climbs a balcony only to have the ladder removed. There he remains a prey to threats and stones from the crowd below, and deprived of his clothes; and the next morning he tries to explain his shivering condition on the pretext that he was going to bathe. The lines throughout the play are the crisp, incisive dialogue of the farce written by a master of burlesque and cynicism. Not since *Pathelin* had such comic brilliance sparkled on the French stage. Only Molière and Beaumarchais surpass Scarron in this respect.

Clever plotting is not sufficient to satisfy an audience for all time. After a period of a few years in which well-made plays have flourished, a reaction sets in against this type of drama. The Spanish *comedia* had been extremely valuable to French playwrights who have always been partial to drama of great technical artistry. French classical tragedy has been accused of a deficiency of action; but if the development of French drama is surveyed as a whole from Hardy down to the present time, it will be seen that, whether the unities are observed or not, French plays contain, as a rule, a well-balanced plot with enough *coups de théâtre* to satisfy an audience of almost any nationality. The fact that certain incidents were not usually enacted in classical tragedy must not cause one to believe that the French, after the jejune tragedies of the Renaissance, cared little for a developing dramatic action.

At this period, however, in spite of the two Corneilles with their intricate plays, the plot became less important. Scarron used it as a means to devise farcical situations. Cyrano de Bergerac, in his *Pédant Joué,* treated his story in a cavalier fashion. The farce reappeared with its octosyllabic verse in the short plays of Poisson. The comedy of character and the comedy of manners began to displace the comedy of plot. The transition was slow and gentle. The germs of these new comedies were present in the *Visionnaires,* in Corneille's comedies, and in such plays as *Alizon* in which contemporary life and manners are treated. Even Corneille's *Menteur*, produced under Spanish influence, foreshadowed a comedy in which a study of character would overbalance the interest in the development of the story. Scarron would not take melodramatic situations seriously even when tragi-comedy was popular. Jodelet and Don Japhet themselves, not the story of the plays in which they appear, focus our attention. Cyrano's pedant, Gillet de la Tessonnerie's character of the countryman in his *Campagnard*, not the plots of the plays, made them successful. The latter play is a series of episodes devised to portray a provincial who tries to succeed in urban society. Together with Tristan L'Hermite's *Parasite* these plays hark back both to Italian comedy and to the farce. The lovers are subsidiary to the parasite, the matamore or braggart captain, the false astrologer, the pedant, the irate parents. These characters can be found in Spanish plays, but they had already come from Italy before they arrived from Spain. In pure Spanish comedy, the lovers are important in the story and on the stage.

Quinault's *Amant Indiscret* (1654) is a comedy directly imitated either from Barbieri's *Inavvertito* or some other similar Italian play in which a stupid lover disarranges all the plans of the tricky servants to bring him and his mistress together. In all respects this piece is Italian not Spanish. Thus in the years when Molière was touring the provinces before his return to Paris in 1658, the comic form was once more in a fluid state awaiting a master hand to mould it into a master form.

Molière brought from his long tour in the provinces a few plays which bear the hall-marks of the *commedia dell' arte* and of the farce as modified by this form of Italian drama. His *Etourdi* is constructed along the same lines as Quinault's *Amant Indiscret*. A lover frustrates by his stupidity the ruses of his clever valet to win for him his lady love. The *Dépit Amoureux* is also a play in the Italian style, although the scenes of the lovers' quarrels and the burlesque of these episodes by the valet and the maid are probably from Lope de Vega's *Perro del Hortelano*. These two plays depend upon the plot for their interest, although the intrigue of the *Dépit Amoureux* has not the mechanical perfection of the *Étourdi*.

Had Molière been content to be merely a clever adapter of the ingenious plots found in superabundance in Spanish and Italian theatres, his importance in the development of drama would have been almost negligible. There were many playwrights of his time who could produce well-made plays. His indebtedness to his predecessors and contemporaries whether French, Italian or Spanish is so great, so constant, that one is often at a loss to decide from which of the many sources discovered by a host of modern investigators he drew certain scenes and plots. He, himself, would have been unable to point out the immediate source of his borrowings. He must not be thought of as a man with scissors and paste pot, clipping scenes from Spanish and Italian comedy and joining them in new combinations. Steeped in theatrical atmosphere and acquainted with all these plots, scenes and characters, he used them, not as a scholar arranges facts which he extracts from documents, but as a creative genius whose brain is a crucible for metal which may already have been moulded many times, but which comes forth from the new refining process purer and more beautifully formed. Molière borrowed, but he did not imitate, as did his predecessors, in the sense of taking a foreign play and adapting it to the French stage. One place where he found dramatic material, had been overlooked by his fellow playwrights. He delved into human character and society, and he drew from these unfailing sources of humor the highest forms of comedy: comedy of manners and comedy of character.

As an actor, he had learned what can be done on the stage. As a manager, he had learned to please an audience. As a playwright, he had learned all that a man in 1660 in France could know about dramatic technique. As a man, he learned to know human society. He was essentially and first of all a human being, whereas so many writers had been first of all playmakers. Corneille himself did not always penetrate deeply into the recesses of human psychology. The plot meant too much to him. Racine alone of Molière's contemporaries approached him in the delicate analysis of the human mind in dramatic form. These two dramatists were such masters of the art of constructing plays that they rarely allowed tricks of their trade to lead them into mere plotting for the sake of the plot.

The farce was the bridge over which Molière passed from comedy of plot to comedy of manners. Although disdained by the cultured, the farce was a too popular form of amusement to become extinct. It held its place in the theatre and in the street. During the years from 1619 to 1626, the celebrated Tabarin and his Italian wife played this kind of comedy on a temporary stage on the Pont Neuf, while such *farceurs* as Gros Guillaume caused the audiences in the Hôtel de Bourgogne to roar with Gargantuan laughter.

The farce underwent the influence of the *commedia dell' arte* in that it began to use stock characters, but with daubed and powdered faces instead of Italian masks. The medieval spirit is still manifest in the situations dealing with marital infidelity. In one of Tabarin's farces, which recalls the medieval *Naudet* and others, Tabarin and his wife begin with mutual recriminations. Tabarin overhears two old men bargain one after the other with his wife, who promises one of them a rendezvous at midnight, and the other a clandestine meeting two hours later. Tabarin accuses his wife of shocking infidelity, but she exculpates herself by asserting she is merely tricking the old fellows for their money. Tabarin then dresses in his wife's clothes, meets the gallants separately, gets the money, and beats them soundly.

The dialogue of these farces is in part only French, for Piphagne, the old man, speaks Italian and Captain Rodomont talks a jargon of Spanish. The fact that it is in prose instead of in the octosyllabic verse of the native farce shows the influence of *commedia dell' arte*. Farcical tricks, such as putting characters into sacks and beating them, were employed by Molière. There is no doubt that Molière saw just such farces and perhaps Tabarin himself. When Molière returned to Paris in 1658, Scaramouche and his troupe of *farceurs* were playing at the theatre of the Petit Bourbon. Molière shared the stage with them on alternate nights.

The farce often dealt with a situation borrowed from contemporary, real life. The plot was generally simple in comparison to the machine-made stories of more literary comedy. Thus this lowly form of theatrical entertainment, with all its tricks and burlesque, seems more realistic than the more highly developed drama of the period. It is a little play which represents contemporary manners. This simplicity of plot and the burlesque of customs had an influence on Molière even in his finest comedies, such as the *Précieuses Ridicules*, while many of his plays, such as the *Médecin malgré Lui* and *George Dandin*, are highly developed farces. In the latter play, an unfaithful wife and her lover, a man from the upper classes, successfully hoodwink the husband of humble birth and make him accept the situation in the true medieval style of the farce.

At the rise of the curtain on the *Précieuses Ridicules* (1659) we find two young men have been very coldly received by two young women who objected to their straightforward, manly proposal of marriage. These girls wish to be wooed in the long-winded, affected manner of the times, according to the codes laid down in the romantic novels. They are *précieuses* or high-brows who demand stilted phraseology and pedantry in conversation. The young men decide to play a farcical trick on them by sending their two valets to call costumed as marquis. Mascarille and Jodelet, characters of the comedy-of-masks, arrive dressed in the latest style. In scenes of gayest wit, they proceed to charm these young ladies with their foppish conversation, in which social customs are delightfully ridiculed. The young men return in the midst of a dance with which these so-called wits are regaling the feminine social climbers. They expose the trick, strip the valets of their borrowed finery and beat them in the usual manner of the slapstick farce. Then they leave, followed in a moment by their valets. The sensible old father beats the musicians who demand their pay; and then he informs the girls that this is what they have brought upon themselves by their nonsensical notions. The comedy is ended—ended as farces generally end, when the trick is played and someone is roundly thrashed in a boisterous scene. No marriage, no reconciliation is even hinted. It is the technique of the farce from quick beginning to sudden ending. But on this century-old framework Molière has delicately woven a short but incisive comedy of manners. The audience laughed and then went out of the theatre and thought, perhaps for the first time after having seen a comedy. The highest form of comedy causes laughter that makes an audience gasp before the laugh is ended and think of the foibles of human beings. Molière had produced such a comedy.

The *École des Maris* (1661) has the hall-marks of Italian comedy from the street-scene to the dénouement. It is primarily a comedy of plot, full of the gay situations and the clever tricks of the comedy-of-masks. Even the persons it portrays are stock characters. Yet the fundamental idea upon which the whole play is built is by no means merely farcical. Two brothers, Ariste and Sganarelle, have brought up two young girls whom they wish to marry. But the education of these wards has been very different. Ariste has allowed Léonor freedom and the pleasures of youth. Sganarelle has kept Isabelle under unnatural restraint. The result of these two systems is that Léonor loves Ariste and marries him, while Isabelle deceives her tyrannical guardian and marries a young man. The comedy is almost a problem play. Mere cleverness of plot no longer satisfied Molière.

"When you paint men (in comedy)," says Dorante in the *Critique de l'Ecole des Femmes,* "you must paint after nature; the portraits must be likenesses, and you have not succeeded if people do not recognize in them the men of the age." This is a part of Molière's confession of faith, and it reveals clearly the difference between him and other playwrights of the age. They were like painters who copy pictures. Molière took living models. This does not mean that, like Aristophanes, he produced comic portraits of certain individuals, except in one or two cases; but, like a skilled artist, he reproduced from his living models the characteristics of men and women of his age. His work quivered with the life of his time. It was not a copy of conventional types handed on from ancient comedy. Scarron, in writing his comedies in which Jodelet appears, had infused not a little life into this character, partially because he used Jodelet, the actor, as a model. Molière, like Scarron and like Shakespeare, incorporated certain physical characteristics of actors in the characters they were to play; but the psychological characteristics of his people are drawn from men and women, not from types of comic rôles or from actors.

Dorante also says that in comedy one must deal with the absurdities of men and show on the stage in a pleasing fashion the defects of all mankind. In the *École des Femmes* (1662), Molière handled his theme with this idea uppermost in his mind. The play deals with an old man, known as Arnolphe and as M. de la Souche, who has brought up Agnes in strict seclusion because he has the idea that ignorance and innocence are synonymous. He is about to marry his ward when the young Horace appears upon the scene. Horace falls in love with Agnes and meets her in secret. Not knowing that her cerberus, M. de la Souche, is Arnolphe, he makes a confidant of the old man and throws him constantly into spasms of fear and rage by telling him of his successful wooing of Agnes. A recognition of Agnes as a long-lost child brings the dénouement of this plot, which is patterned in its incidents after the Italian comedy-of-masks, with certain scenes drawn from the farce. The plot was taken from Scarron's translation of *El Prevenido Engañado*, a novel by Maria Zayas de Sotomayor.

In spite of these resemblances and borrowings, the *École des Femmes* marks a distinct advance in the technique of comedy. One of the objections raised against the play in the tempest of criticism which it aroused was that "in this comedy there is no action; the whole consists of narrations given by Horace and

Agnes" (*La Critique de l'École des Femmes,* sc. VII). If by "action" one means events such as the clandestine meetings of the lovers with which contemporary comedy filled many scenes, the charge is true. These traditional scenes are left out of sight. The lovers do not meet before our eyes until the middle of the last act. Dorante, Molière's spokesman, replies to this criticism: "There is a good deal of action on the stage; and according to the arrangement of the subject the narrations themselves are all action,—since they are innocently repeated to the person concerned, who by this means is thrown at every turn into a confusion which amuses the spectators,—and at every fresh piece of information he takes all the measures in his power to ward off the misfortunes he dreads."

What Corneille did for tragedy in the *Cid,* Molière did for comedy in the *École des Femmes.* They interpreted dramatic action to mean the psychological reactions produced by certain events, occurring in apparently inevitable sequence, on characters who are thereby stimulated to follow a certain line of conduct. Had Moliére arranged the subject according to the methods in vogue in comedy, he would have put the events on the stage and centred the interest in the plot, as he had often done in earlier plays.

Italian comedy of the Renaissance, following Latin comedy, had portrayed the tricks devised to unite the lovers, who rarely met on the stage. Corneille, under the influence of the pastoral, brought the love story on the stage. Spanish comedy gave French playwrights a more romantic conception of love. It showed the meetings, the jealousies, the danger of the lovers under the laws of honor. The scenes were theatrically effective because the more serious treatment of the love motive increased the suspense. In the *École des Femmes,* because of the "arrangement of the subject," such incidents are off the stage, as in early Italian comedy; but psychological action is introduced which more than compensates for the loss of physical action. True comedy arises from the effect of the events on the mind of Arnolphe, just as in the *Cid* true tragedy arises from the effect of the events on the minds of Rodrigue and Chimène. And both authors were subjected to attacks by their stupid enemies and were accused of writing poor plays which sinned against the rules!

With the *École des Femmes* and the *Précieuses Ridicules,* high comedy of character and comedy of manners come into existence in France. The setting for the *Précieuses Ridicules* is an interior, while in the later *Ecole des Femmes* the action takes place in the street in accordance with a tradition which can be traced back to Aristophanes' *Plutus.* In earlier plays of Scarron and of other writers, comedy had gone indoors, but generally into a bedroom, as in many a modern farce of French extraction. The scene was conditioned by the exigencies of the plot, which demanded that people be hidden or discovered in compromising situations. The true domestic interior—the common living rooms—was not shown until high comedy of manners and of character gained a foothold in such plays as *Tartufe,* the *Misanthrope* and the *Femmes Savantes.* The street-scene remained in plays which are distinctly of the Italian type, such as the *Fourberies de Scapin* and the *Comtesse d'Escarbagnas.* In the *Médecin malgré Lui* the scene changes from an exterior to an interior, as in the medieval farce. Exterior scenes, however, become less frequent after the success of Molière's comedies of manners; and in the eighteenth century they are very rare at the Comédie Française, because *Tartufe* and the *Misanthrope,* especially, were the models of comedy for many years to come.

Molière, like most successful dramatists, believed that the rule of rules was to please. He generally observed the unities, although he allowed himself the liberty of disregarding the unities of place and time in *Don Juan;* and the unity of action is not strictly retained in the *Fâcheux.* He refused to regard the unities as sacred, esoteric mysteries never to be disturbed. His usual observance of them did not cause him to omit important scenes. He was more likely to include the scene even in a somewhat unfitting setting. Thus in the *École des Femmes,* Arnolphe gives Agnes instructions as to the correct conduct of women and maxims for married life in a scene which would naturally take place indoors. Having chosen the setting of a street, Molière simply allows the dialogue to take place with the characters sitting on chairs in the open air.

His point of attack is relatively late. The situation which causes the action is already in existence when the play begins. Tartufe is installed in Orgon's family. The Misanthrope is in love with Célimène, the coquette. George Dandin already suspects his wife of infidelity. Yet in none of his plays can one point to a scene in the story before the point of attack and say with certainty that it should be included in the play.

He employs the usual means of exposition known in France at his time; but his sparkling wit and his directness enable him to avoid the dullness so often attendant upon expository scenes of classical drama. In the *Femmes Savantes* the whole situation and many details of character are imparted in scenes of high comedy, in which the learned Armande, the natural Henriette, and their silly spinster aunt, Bélise, discuss the question of which one is loved by Clitandre. We are thus given an enlightening first glimpse of this family, torn by the struggle between pretentious learning and common sense.

In *Tartufe,* however, Molière shows the greatest artistry in his daring form of exposition. Tartufe—his name, his actions, his health, his appearance, his ideas and finally the question of his sincerity or hypocrisy are discussed until keen suspense and desire to behold this creature are aroused. Not until the beginning of the third act does he enter. He is the central figure, and from his hypocrisy springs the whole plot. Until the dénouement, the play is an almost perfect piece of dramatic mechanism.

In this play, Molière maintained the correct balance between plot and characters. It is no mere gallery of portraits passed in review as in the *Fâcheux.* A whole family, consisting of persons of distinctly different temperaments, is shown in a struggle of life or death with a hypocrite. Tartufe has wormed his way into the good graces of the credulous father, Orgon. Not content with wishing to marry the daughter, he casts his slimy eyes upon the wife, Elmire. When he is exposed by Elmire, he defies Orgon, for he has not only gained possession of Orgon's property, but of certain compromising political papers. The situation is saved only by the intervention of the King's justice.

The situation is a gripping problem of life. Comedy has developed from a representation of the obstacles in the path of marionette lovers to a dramatic analysis of the psychology of a whole section of society. By reducing the importance of the plot, comedy has become almost serious drama. Yet the plot is by no means slight and overshadowed by the study of character, as is the case in the *Misanthrope*. The action in *Tartufe* leads through constant suspense to strong climaxes. Only Molière's unfailing wit and humor save the story from becoming so gripping as to be tragic.

He does not hesitate to draw humorous scenes from the inexhaustible source of the farce whenever his more serious plots begin to border too closely on sombre effects. Thus the scene in which Orgon tries to silence the garrulous maid, with its carefully worked out comic business, is a bit of farce comedy. In the *Misanthrope* the episode in which the breathless servant hunts through his pockets for an important letter and discovers that he has left it at home is nothing more than a trick of *commedia dell' arte*. Yet such incidents, though extraneous in a strict sense, are justifiable, because Molière, while treating serious themes, had to keep the general impression humorous. Such scenes are not inartistic comic relief. They are incidents introduced to keep the audience in the desired comic mood.

As a general rule, Molière was careful to prepare for and foreshadow the action in his plays. He keeps the audience in suspense not only in his comedies of plot, but also in his comedies of manners and of characters. He does not enlighten us so carefully as does the modern playwright in regard to the circumstances of the past and the heredity of his characters; but he never falls into the modern fault of making his plays a treatise of pseudo-biological or medical science. A careful analysis of his method in *Tartufe* shows that he has explained sufficiently the essential qualities of his characters. The credulity of Orgon and his attempted tyranny are explained and foreshadowed by the similar traits of character displayed by his mother in the first act. On the other hand, the audience hears of the valuable but compromising papers only at the end of the fourth act. In his finest comedies, one must look with meticulous care before characteristics or incidents are dicovered which are not motivated or which do not lead to dramatic action. Molière was far beyond his contemporaries in the study of the traits of human character which furnish material for drama.

If Molière is to be criticized at all, it is in his handling of the ending of many of his plays. A trivial comic plot can end about as the author pleases; but when a profound problem of human life is made the subject of a comedy, we have learned to demand a logical dénouement that evolves from the first hypothesis. The more serious the problem, the more difficult it is to keep the ending from being depressing.

There are two distinct types of dénouement in comedy. There is the ending brought about by a recognition or a discovery which generally shows that the supposed troubles of problem did not exist. Molière used this dénouement freely even in such plays as the *École des Femmes* and in *L'Avare*. In order to bring about a happy ending in *L'Avare,* four characters have to be shipwrecked, separated and have changed their names before the play begins. Also there is the cynical ending of the farce, which Molière employed in *George Dandin.* At the end of the play, the hero is in the same fix in which he was at the beginning, and he can think of nothing better to do than to jump head foremost into the water. Of course the problem of a peasant married to a coquette of noble birth was not viewed by Molière as it would have been by a Dumas or an Augier. Molière did not treat it seriously. He learned from the failure of his *Don Garcie* that his audience did not want him to write even tragicomedy; but he treated certain problems with such thought that we cannot dismiss them with a laugh as we do the situation in *George Dandin.* Perhaps we do Molière both honor and injustice by taking him more seriously than he would wish. When hypocrisy or avarice undermines a family, we want to know what is the logical outcome. We wish Molière had told us, instead of sweeping away the actual situation by the intervention of the King in *Tartufe* and by recognitions in *L'Avare*. In the *École des Maris* the ending is a logical result of the two systems of education employed by the brothers; but in the *École des Femmes*, Agnes escapes an odious marriage partially by a discovery. Molière, in the *Misanthrope*, did not hesitate to follow his problem of an upright, too outspoken man in love with a coquette to a logical end. The hero insists on telling the truth with unnecessary frankness. He was more of a comic figure to the Frenchman of his day than he is to us moderns because he departed too much from the usual ideal of a gentleman of that time. He was abnormal. His vice was a virtue carried to extreme. Yet the ending of the play is logical and it could not have impressed the contemporary audience as being the usual happy dénouement. The lovers are not united.

Why then does Molière seem to prefer a fortuitous dénouement to a logical ending in other plays, if the answer to the problem would naturally be tragic? Why, in *Tartufe*, does he prefer to pay a graceful compliment to the King and save the family from disaster by a fortunate discovery? He was undoubtedly influenced by the classical rule that comedy must end happily. He may have felt that he had answered his problem, and had shown that misanthropy, hypocrisy, avarice, social ambition, misalliance, tyranny over youth, intellectual pretentiousness are dangerous but are not fatal, as Othello's jealousy and Lear's mistakes in judgment are fatal to all who come in contact with them.

Also, his plays on such subjects may be considered as having as a point of departure a theme rather than a problem to be answered. *Tartufe* shows us hypocrisy but does not attempt to solve the problem of hypocrisy. Just as Galsworthy's *Loyalties* stops without trying to solve the problem of loyalty, so *Tartufe* comes to an end when the portrait of the hypocrite is complete and the hypocrisy has been presented in many of its forms. The dénouement of a play based upon an abstract theme is less important than the dénouement of a play dealing with a concrete problem.

George Dandin might have been called *Mésalliance* and Molière might have treated the problem of intermarriage of classes seriously. Had he done so, he would have created the *pièce à thèse;* and much incisive wit and gay laughter would have been lost to the world. But Molière treated serious themes of life with thoughtful humor. He left the implacable, pitiless logic of the dénouement to the dramatists of the nineteenth century.

CHAPTER XII

FRENCH TRAGEDY OF THE RENAISSANCE. HARDY

THROUGHOUT the Middle Ages the words "tragedy" and "comedy" had been applied to non-dramatic as well as dramatic literature. Any work in grandiose style, on an historical subject, dealing with characters of royal birth whose bloody downfall caused the misfortune of the state, could be entitled a tragedy, even though it was not written to be represented or in dialogue form. This conception of tragedy was derived from Donatus and Diomedes and was strengthened by ideas drawn from Horace, Vitruvius and Seneca, even after the discovery was made in Italy at the close of the fifteenth century that tragedies were intended for presentation on a stage. This medieval misconception was handed on to the humanists of the Renaissance by Badius in the preface to his edition of Terence (1504). He also pointed out on the authority of Donatus and of Horace that tragedy is divided into five acts and that the function of the chorus is to separate the acts. Characteristics of the art of tragedy were discussed in greater detail by Badius in his commentaries on the text of Seneca (1514). He held that the action of tragedy should develop from happiness to misfortune; deaths and scenes of violence should be narrated; the ending must be most turbulent. He described the rôle of the nurse as the chief confidante of the heroine. As the result of such practice and theories, the exposition given by a queen and her nurse was to rival in frequency the exposition given by a ghost or a supernatural character.

These were the outstanding elements in the art of tragedy in the first half of the sixteenth century in France. Even translations of Greek tragedy in Latin, such as *Hecuba* and *Iphigenia in Aulis* (Erasmus, 1506), and translations in French of *Electra*

(Lazare de Baïf, 1537), *Hecuba* (Bouchetel, 1545), *Iphigenia* (Sibilet, 1549), did not change or even add to this somewhat medieval conception. Nothing of the spirit and significance of Greek tragedy and indeed none of the deeper beauties of its technique was discovered by the humanists. The pathetic and atrocious elements of Greek tragedy, as exemplified by *Hecuba*, caused this tragedy to be often reprinted and translated. As the motive of mistaken identity had been furnished to comedy of the Renaissance by *Menæchmi*, so the misfortunes of this wife and mother, which call forth grandiose pathos and cries for vengeance and which exemplify the instability of human happiness, became a leading motive for the tragedy of the Renaissance.

The first original tragedies printed in France were written by the Italian Conti known among the humanists as Stoa. They are in Latin, and are entitled *Theoandrothanatos* (1508) and *Theocrisis* (1514). They are the Passion and Last Judgment of medieval drama reduced to five acts with a chorus. They are good examples of the humanistic Latin tragedy which spread from Italy through Europe at this time. Faulty as was this type of play, it introduced to France a form which was very different from the mystery and the morality. Stoa admitted that he did not introduce into his text the rhetorical descriptions which are the ornaments of tragedy; but, by this very admission, he indicated the road which dramatic art was to travel, where the action was to be lost from view in flowery by-paths and in a wilderness of sententious morality.

Barthelemy de Loches, perhaps a disciple of Stoa, continued this form of drama with his *Christus Xylonicus, tragœdia* (1529). This play, in four acts instead of the classical five, opens with a monologue of Christ which forms the first act. The third act deals with the Passion. The fourth represents Joseph of Arimathea and Nicodemus preparing for the entombment of Christ. The action passes in several localities, as in medieval drama.

These humanistic plays, medieval in subject, tragic from the

point of view of the outcome, show, at the same time, the influence of Latin comedy. Terence especially was admired as a
dramatist and moral philosopher. Comedy developed sooner
and more artistically in the Renaissance than did tragedy. It
could and perhaps did furnish the idea of both prologue and
epilogue, although medieval drama seems to have introduced the
prologue independently of classical comedy. The introduction
of sententious maxims was also the result of the practice of
Terence, although the later critics of the Renaissance will ascribe
this practice to the influence of Seneca alone. The five-act division of the action into exposition, unfolding of the action, introduction of obstacles, means of overcoming obstacles, dénouement,
was also introduced from comedy. Perhaps the rascals, Sanga,
Sannio, Dromo in *Christus Xylonicus* were borrowed from medieval drama; but their names recall classical comedy. One thing
is certain: pure classical tragedy was still contaminated by
medieval and comic elements.

At Bordeaux, in the college of Guyenne, Latin humanistic
tragedy reached its most artistic development. Buchanan translated *Medea* and *Alcestis;* he also wrote *Saint John The Baptist*
and *Jephtha,* and produced them all on the stage between 1539
and 1545. About 1546, Muretus' original play *Julius Cæsar,*
was played on the same stage.

As was the case in the development of Italian tragedy, the
Greek influence operated at a period before Seneca became the
accepted model; and, from our acquaintance with the later tragedies built upon the model of Latin tragedy, we may pronounce
it regrettable that the purer form of Greek art was not able
to hold its own against the view of the critics that Seneca was
the dramatist to be imitated.

Buchanan's two original plays have much of the Greek form.
The point of attack is far enough from the dénouement to allow
a development of the situation. It is true that much of the
dialogue of his *Saint John The Baptist* is oratorical debate after
the manner of Euripides; the scene of the dance of Salome and
the death of John are off the stage; but the recital of the death

is refreshingly restrained and dignified in comparison to what it would have been in an Italian tragedy of this period. There is no degenerate horror, no erotic detail, no display of the severed head in the manner of a Speroni, or indeed, of an Oscar Wilde. The medieval drama would have represented the dance and the execution; but the humanistic drama aims to discuss a situation and moralize upon it in an ornamental style. Therein lay the novelty. Dramatists had not yet learned to represent an event and to bring out all the finer shades of the situation. Another novelty in this neo-classical tragedy was the unhappy ending, the death of the hero, without even his ascent into Heaven, which had so mitigated the tragic element in the miracle and morality plays.

Buchanan's later play, *Jephtha,* follows much more closely the technique of Greek tragedy, especially *Iphigenia in Aulis* and *Hecuba.* The dramatist, for he has the right to that appellation, says in his autobiography that he wrote these plays to win over the youth of his time from the allegorical plays of the Middle Ages to the imitation of the ancients. Had he written them in French instead of Latin and had they been printed and circulated before instead of after Jodelle's *Cléopâtre,* they might have made French tragedy of the Renaissance an art more worthy of the name. His *Jephtha* is a play constructed along Greek lines, with a dramatic problem which develops in rapid action carried on by principal characters, with the exception of the usual messenger. It has none of the chaotic, loose construction of the medieval morality and none of the faults of Senecan tragedy.

After the manner of Euripides, a divine personage—in this case naturally an angel—announces the subject of the play in a prologue. It is the story of Jephtha's daughter taken from the short account in Judges, which Buchanan has not merely turned into action and dialogue by servilely following his source as did medieval playwrights, but which he has really dramatized in a manner not entirely unworthy of a Greek playwright. The exposition is given by Iphis, the daughter, and her mother. The classical dream is introduced for purposes of foreshadowing. A messenger announces the victory of Jephtha; and, in a scene of suspense delicately handled, Jephtha meets his daughter, and greets her with hesitancy and mysterious words foreboding tragedy. A priest, to whom he discloses his anguish, tries in vain to persuade him that the sacrifice of his daughter is not necessary. In a touching scene between the father and the daughter, with the mother present, the heroic Iphis learns what she must suffer. The messenger reports the fulfillment of the vow. The situation is even more poignant than the analogous episodes in *Iphigenia in Aulis,* which undoubtedly inspired Buchanan to dramatize this tragic story. The characters do not compare so favorably with their Greek prototypes; but *Jephtha* is a play the like of which we shall not find in France for many years to come.

The narrowing of the dramatic framework is exemplified in Muretus' Latin tragedy *Julius Cæsar,* written in emulation of Buchanan and played at Bordeaux about 1546. This short work of about 550 lines, of which 200 are assigned to the chorus, shows no influence of Greek tragedy and hence is much less artistic than *Jephtha.* The first act consists of a monologue delivered by Cæsar, in which he boasts of his power and security in spite of warnings from the seer and in spite of his enemies. In the second act, Brutus announces his intention of freeing the Roman citizens from the tyrant; and he gains the support of Cassius for the deed of violence. The third act still carries on the exposition, as Calpurnia tells her nurse of her fears and presentiments. In the fourth act, Calpurnia persuades Cæsar to remain at home; but, taunted by Brutus with being influenced by a woman's dream, he decides to go to the senate. Brutus acts as messenger of the news of Cæsar's death in the fifth act. Instead of ending the play at this moment, Muretus brings Calpurnia on the stage lamenting the death of her husband. Cæsar's ghost appears and announces his reception into Olympus in a manner that recalls the ending of many a medieval play. With this exception, the tragedy is purely classical according to the narrow view of the Renaissance. There is little action, five acts, a chorus, a dream, a nurse, a reported death, a discussion of tyrannicide in lofty declamation, and a royal hero. The influence of Seneca may not be direct; but the classical elements are too numerous to deny an indirect influence. Italy, by this time, was producing classical tragedy; and the relations between the two countries were so close that the educated Frenchman, especially, must have been acquainted with the new form of serious drama which was being produced beyond the Alps. In 1547, the architect Serlio published the fifth volume of his work on architecture and introduced to France the classical system of stage setting.

Muretus forms the connection between Paris and the provincial towns where humanistic tragedy was in favor. After leaving Bordeaux he went to Poitiers, where Faveau was writing tragedies in imitation of Seneca; and in 1551 he arrived in Paris. Jodelle, one of his friends, and Grévin, one of his pupils, must have become familiar with his work. Thus it is not surprising to find Jodelle producing in 1552-1553 the first classical tragedy in French on a subject allied to *Julius Cæsar,* namely *Cléopâtre Captive;* nor is it surprising that Grévin wrote a *Jules César* in French. Du Bellay, in his *Défense et Illustration de la Langue Française* (1549), had suggested to the classical scholars that they would know where to find models for tragedy and comedy if the rulers were willing to restore them to their ancient dignity. Henri II had shown himself thus inclined in 1548 by attending a representation of *Calandria* at Lyon. Ronsard's translation of *Plutus* had been played at the college of Coqueret in the same year. The way was open for classical tragedy. Jodelle may have known where to find the best models, but unfortunately he did not follow Greek tragedy as had Buchanan. His *Cléopâtre* is rather an imitation of the method of Muretus. He fell into the common mistake of neo-classicists who found their whole theory of art on imitation of the ancients but who are content to imitate the imitators of the ancients.

Cléopâtre is really an elegy in monologue and dialogue. The action—if we may call lamentation by this name—begins after the death of Marc Antony, whose ghost opens the play with a

monologue in Senecan fashion. Here is found the first reference
to the unity of time in France, for we are told that Cleopatra
will die before sunset. The point of attack is about as late in
the story as possible, and the whole play would scarcely furnish
material for a last act of a Shakespearean tragedy. Jodelle's aim
was not to produce a dramatic action which develops, but to
discourse upon the misfortunes of a queen.

The next scene introduces Cleopatra and her servants. She
has seen the vision of Antony's ghost, and the canonical dream
is thus preserved. In the second act, Octavian discusses with
two confidants what he shall do with Antony's betrayer. The
next act, it is true, contains a bit of action, but it is more comic
than tragic. Cleopatra, trying in vain to persuade Octavian not
to take her to Rome as a captive, flies into a rage and soundly
slaps Seleucus, who suggests that Octavian might possess her.
The fourth act shows her lamenting at the tomb of Antony;
and the usual messengering of her death occupies the short fifth
act. The chorus takes up more than half of the play.

This tenuous tragedy, performed before the court, was hailed
as a masterpiece of a new form of dramatic art. No greater
contrast can be found in two contemporaneous forms of drama
than that existing between the sprawling mysteries of epic length
where every event was enacted, and the narrow neo-classical
tragedy where action of any sort is scarcely visible.

Yet it was a tragedy, a play in which a sympathetic character
met death unrelieved by an ascent into Heaven. The audience
left the performance with a new sensation of tragic emotion.
However cold the play may seem to us, we must remember that
it furnished a new dramatic experience for the courtly audience
which was weary of medieval drama. This fact is enough to
explain the success of the tragedy of *Cléopâtre*.

One of the actors in Jodelle's double bill of tragedy and comedy
was Jean de La Péruse. Inspired by the success of the plays
which he had helped to produce, La Péruse almost immediately
set himself the task of writing a tragedy on which Sainte Marthe
put the finishing touches after the death of the author in 1554.

The play was published in 1555; and, while overpraised by the
scholarly coterie, the tragedy is an improvement on Jodelle's
work. This is due, in part, to the fact that La Péruse chose
the subject of Medea and did not hesitate to draw freely from
Seneca and, somewhat less, from Euripides. The play, generally
spoken of as a translation, is in reality an adaptation of Seneca's
tragedy. The scenes of the original are presented by La Péruse
in quite a different order; but nothing is gained by this re-
arrangement. The play has none of the delicately balanced
action of Euripides' tragedy, and La Péruse is much more
clumsy in handling the psychology than both Seneca and Euripides. Yet in comparison with Jodelle's play, *Médée* is actually
dramatic. The heroine plans and carries out her deed of violence. As in Seneca, the children are slain on the stage in direct
contravention of Horace's precept that Medea must not kill
the children before the eyes of the audience. While the point
of attack in *Cléopâtre* was at "the end of affairs," here the action
leaps *in medias res*. The exposition is carried by the queen and
her nurse in accordance with the ideas of Donatus. The rôle
of the messenger, however, in this and other French tragedies of
this period, is not nearly so important as it is in ancient tragedy
and in Italian plays. Seneca and the Italians worked up the
story to a narration of horror and emphasized thereby the terrible
deed of violence. The French emphasized the elegiac lamentation of the heroine because of the tragic situation. The death
is more of a dénouement than a climax in early French tragedy.
True dramatic action, the swinging of the pendulum of suspense
toward hope and fear alternately, are conspicuously absent in
both cases. On the other hand, Mellin de Saint Gelais in his
Sophonisbe (1556)—a free translation of Trissino's tragedy—
has the death of the queen narrated, although it occurred on the
stage in the original. The narration, however, is rather a pathetic
lamentation than an accumulation of horror. This change in
this play is evidence of the fact that Horace's dictum in regard
to deaths in tragedy was being more and more accepted as a
valid rule.

Whatever merit *Médée* possesses is due entirely to its sources. Just as Seneca's *Medea* is more dramatic than it otherwise would have been because it is founded on Euripides' play, so La Péruse's tragedy has more dramatic action than *Cléopâtre* because it is adapted from Seneca. The real ineptitude of the playwrights of this early period is entirely apparent when they attempt to dramatize a story without following some classical play.

Grévin is the first of the French writers of tragedy to show signs of dramatic ability. His *Jules César*, inspired by Muretus' play, is unmistakable evidence that he was unable to avoid Muretus' exposition by a monologue, but he prepares for a new scene in the last act in which Antony arouses the soldiers to vengeance. Of course, in comparison to Shakespeare's masterful handling of this situation, Grévin's scene pales into insignificance; but the existence of the scene shows that Grévin was alive to the possibility of making tragedy something more than an elegy. He also saw that the death of Cæsar is not merely a deed to be recounted and an event to cause Calpurnia to lament. Thus he places it in the fourth act of his play, whereas Muretus had used this material for his fifth act. Grévin's tragedy gains immeasurably in dramatic interest in comparison with Muretus' attempt. Grévin, rather than Jodelle, is the real founder of French classical tragedy, for he actually introduced a dramatic action.

Also his handling of the chorus, which, instead of being mere singers of moralizing commonplaces, is formed of Roman soldiers interested in the plot, gives evidence of dramatic instinct. He dared to introduce a novelty instead of following, in pious stupidity, worn-out customs of ancient drama which had lost their artistic significance. This is the first covert attack on the rôle of the chorus, which was thought to be so important but had become a lifeless literary excrescence, valueless in neoclassical tragedy for even pictorial effect.

Naturally, this new form of drama developed along two or three different lines. The playwrights were not yet in accord as to just what they wished to produce. Even the influence of medieval technique had not ceased to operate, especially in plays in which the plot is drawn from the Bible. In 1550, Théodore de Bèze had written the *Sacrifice d'Abraham* and had bestowed upon his play the appellation "tragedy." The piece is more medieval than classic. There is a good deal of action on the stage and the outcome is the happy ending of medieval drama. Desmasures' trilogy, *David Combattant, David Fugitif, David Triomphant* (1556) is also constructed on the framework of medieval drama although the author calls them, somewhat reluctantly, *tragédies saintes*. They only conform to the spirit of tragedy in the style of the dialogue, and in the fact that the action of each separate play observes the unity of time. The unity of place, however, gives way to a necessary multiple stage setting.

Two distinctly opposite tendencies are illustrated in Rouillet's *Philanire* (published in Latin in 1563, translated into French in 1577), and Filleul's *Lucrèce* (played in 1566). *Philanire* is founded on the same situation as Shakespeare's *Measure for Measure* and Cinthio's *Epitia*. In the first act, Philanire, having lamented, first in a monologue and then in the presence of her servants, the imprisonment of her husband, kneels before the provost, Sévère, and pleads for the release of her husband. Sévère agrees to show clemency provided Philanire will give herself to him. The second act opens with a wholly unclassical scene between Philanire and her children, one of whom is begging for a hobby-horse. The mother, overcome with pity for them, decides to plead with Sévère once more; and she finally gives in to his demands. In the third act, which occurs the next day, Philanire, bowed with shame, demands of Sévère that he fulfill his part of the terrible bargain. He does so by bringing on the stage her beheaded husband; and the lamentations of Philanire and the chorus are prolonged to a length, both boresome and disgusting. The story continues to develop, however, for in the next act the marriage of Philanire to Sévère is ordered by the governor and is consummated. In the fifth act the second husband is beheaded at the command of the governor, and Philanire comes on the stage to weep for her two husbands and to hint at suicide.

The plot, showing unmistakable evidence of Italian influence, is scarcely to be commended; but the action is well handled. The point of attack is correctly placed in order to allow the story to develop. The action is carried by principal characters on the stage in obligatory scenes. At the end of each act, the interest of the spectator is held in suspense as to what will happen. In spite of the grossness of the play with the tragic situation bordering on the burlesque, there is a distinct touch of pathos. The scene with the children, which motivates Philanire's surrender, is a relief in comparison to the motives of vengeance which dominate so often the characters of Renaissance tragedy. This broader framework, however, was not adopted by writers of tragedy. We shall find it only in tragi-comedies or serious plays with a happy ending.

The other tendency to narrow the scope of the action and to keep it either off the stage, or between the acts, appears plainly in Filleul's *Lucrèce*. In the first act, Tarquin tells of his love for Lucretia. Act II. She bewails her dishonor. Act III. Collatinus and Brutus arrive. Act IV. They desire to avenge the wrong. Act V. After Lucretia commits suicide off the stage, they take an oath to avenge her.

The taste for oratory and narrative, and the importance attributed to the rôle of the messenger are illustrated also in Guersens' *Panthée* (1571). In the fourth act, Panthée kills herself on the stage, contrary to the usual practice, but in the fifth act the deed is recounted first by the chorus and then by a messenger, who, so far as can be judged by the text, was not present in the preceding act when the suicide took place.

Had Scaliger's narrow conception of tragedy prevailed, such plays as Filleul's *Lucrèce* would have become the model; but, as is generally the case with dramatic critics, Scaliger's theories were out of date when they appeared in 1561. Through the critical and dramatic work of Jean de La Taille and of Garnier, a middle ground between purely oratorical tragedy and such plays as *Philanire* was reached.

Jean de La Taille published in 1572 his *Art de la Tragédie* which sums up the prevailing ideas of dramatic technique. The subject of tragedies, he says, deals with the pitiful downfall of lords, inconstancy of fortune, banishments, wars, plagues, famines, captivities and execrable cruelties of tyrants. A fitting subject would be a father who, unwittingly, ate his own sons; or one who finding no executioner to put an end to his own ills would resort to his own hands. He warns the playwright not to have anything done on the stage which cannot be done suitably and decorously. Hence violent deaths are inadmissible for everyone would see that such things are nothing but pretense. Thus he takes into consideration not only theoretical decorum, but also the difficulty of making such actions seem artistic. This betrays at least the correct attitude of mind for a playwright.

Owing to this theory and practice, tragedy of the Renaissance, as Professor Lanson points out, becomes a pathetic drama which draws emotion, not from the direct view of the tragic deed, but from the lamentations of its victims. The hero is the one who suffers, not the one who acts and struggles against adverse fortune. The playwright did not aim to show what caused the tragic situation or to represent the tragic deed. He forged no unbreakable chain of cause and effect leading to an inevitable dénouement. The situation and deeds were dramatic and tragic in so far as they furnished cause for lamentation.

For this reason, Jean de La Taille places the point of attack as close as possible to the end of the story. He says that one should not begin to relate the tragedy with the beginning of the story or the subject, but towards the middle or the end. This position of the point of attack, closer to the dénouement than even Horace would have it, forces the oratorical, narrative element to take full possession of the stage. Tragedy of the Renaissance corresponds in this respect to the early Greek tragedies.

A further result of this late beginning of the play is to preclude the calm or happy opening of tragedy, cited by the ancient critics and accepted by Renaissance critics as a rule of dramatic art. This is considered by La Taille as not always necessary. He does insist on the value of the peripeteia and holds that the spectators ought to see joy turned suddenly to grief and *vice versa;* but he does not realize, apparently, that his system of constructing tragedies makes such desirable developments in the plot practically impossible. By the time the play opens, as is the case in his own tragedies, the hero is so close to his doom that nothing but the gloomy part of the story remains.

He explains the chorus as an assemblage of men and women who, at the end of each act, discourse upon what has been said and explain what is supposed to happen behind the scenes. According to the accepted theory, there should be five acts, and an empty stage marks the ending of an act. Thus he establishes the rule of the linking of scenes found in Donatus, which requires that, except at the end of an act, a character remain upon the stage. This rule, however, was not strictly observed by the French dramatists until the seventeenth century.

The rule of the unity of time had been generally observed by French tragic playwrights from the time of Jodelle, and the lines of the play called attention of the spectators to the fact that the action took place in one day. The unity of place was implied by Scaliger in 1561. Castelvetro in Italy had given full expression to it in 1570; and now, in 1572, Jean de La Taille says succinctly of these two rules: "The story or play must be represented in one day, one time, and one place."

The ancient system of stage decoration, as reconstructed by Vitruvius and by Serlio in their treatises on architecture, was known to the French. The very indefiniteness of a scene of palaces in perspective served as a fitting background which did not call attention too plainly to the actual location of the action. Such a setting made it easy to observe the unity of place. Tragedy dealt with royal personages and only needed regal columns and arches as a background. It made little difference whether the scene was actually within or without the palace. Atmosphere was all that was necessary, and Serlio's scenery furnished the correct emotional surroundings without insisting too much on reality. The spectator was probably never troubled by the indefiniteness or confusion of places, which the modern critic can point out in certain plays of the period. He accepted an indefinite place because of the indefinite setting. We moderns have learned that a stage hung only with curtains is a fitting place for the representation of poetical drama in which the scene is simply "on the stage." Old prints show that such "scenery" was employed on the stage of the Renaissance.

Jean de La Taille's plays, *Saül, le Furieux* (written in 1563, published in 1572) and *La Famine ou les Gabéonites* (1573) correspond closely to his theories. In writing his *Saül, le Furieux* he made use of Seneca's *Mad Hercules* and from the third act of Seneca's *Trojan Women* he built up a part of the situation in *La Famine ou les Gabéonites*. The scene between the witch of Endor and Saul, in his first play, shows a dramatic instinct; and Saul is a more truly tragic hero than has been found in French tragedy up to this period. La Taille understood the theatre better than anyone of his time, but his time was against him. The art of tragedy was too young to bring forth a great playwright. Even though he showed flashes of dramatic ability, even though he understood the power of a well-constructed plot with an action swinging between hope and fear, he had too much tradition without experimentation behind him to be able to handle his chosen form of drama with success.

After Scaliger's activity as a theorist, after La Taille's theory and practice, the influence of Seneca naturally became dominant with Garnier. Whatever hesitation there had been between Greek or Latin tragedy as a model now disappears. The Italians had already chosen Seneca as their model. Greek tragedy became the source of only single scenes, as in Garnier's *Troade*. Even Aristotle was interpreted according to Horace, the practice of Seneca and of more modern playwrights. No one in the Renaissance had the slightest conception of the real meaning and deep significance of Aristotle's discussion of the technique of tragedy. Nothing remained of his theories except statements which were misconstrued or misunderstood.

Scévole de Sainte-Marthe says correctly of Garnier: "Since Seneca's manner of writing seemed to Garnier more exact and more regular, he tried to imitate this excellent author and succeeded perfectly." His first play, *Porcie* (1568), is made up of scenes without any real continuity drawn from several of Seneca's plays: *Thyestes, Hippolytus, Mad Hercules, Hercules at Œta, The Trojan Women.* The exposition is given by a Fury in imitation of Seneca's *Thyestes.* The play consists of monologues, political discussions leading up to the narration of three deaths, and the death of the nurse on the stage, which Garnier added, as he says, "to make the catastrophe bloody." Brutus, whose death leads to the death of Porcia, never appears on the stage. The nurse is evidently too minor a character to have oratory wasted upon her manner of demise, so she quietly stabs herself at the last line of the play.

In *Hippolyte* (1573), modelled upon Seneca's *Hippolytus* with ideas added from his *Agamemnon* and *Medea,* whatever faint gleams of drama are to be found can be explained as coming from Seneca, who in turn was indebted to Euripides' first version of the story. It is the thin infiltration of dramatic scenes such as the confession of Phædra of her love to Hippolytus, which saves these plays from being utterly ridiculous.

His *Cornélie* (1574), founded upon Seneca's *Octavia,* and his *Marc Antoine* (1578), which recalls the same play, both show a looseness of construction which results from attempting to use more material for the plot, but failing to combine the different episodes into a whole. *Cornélie* continues for four acts of oratory and lamentation before one can guess what all the talk is about. At the end of the fourth act, the action seems to be moving, with the speed and temperature of a glacier, towards the death of Cæsar; but, when the play is over, it is found that all the discursive exposition has been leading up to the climax of grief on the part of Cornelia, who has already wept for her husband, over the news of the death of her father. In comparison to Jodelle's *Cléopâtre*, there is too much opportunity for action in Garnier's *Marc Antoine*, since the playwright introduces three principals, Antony, Cleopatra and Octavian whose interests really clash. With great care, however, Garnier keeps on the very outskirts of this potentially dramatic situation, and so constructs the play that none of the chief characters ever meet each other alive.

One is struck by the repetition of two scenes in Garnier's plays. In one a conqueror, wishing to put an enemy to death, is opposed by a friend who pleads for a show of magnanimity. This type is illustrated in *Les Juives*, *Cornélie* and *Marc Antoine*. The other shows a confidant trying in vain to dissuade a person from committing suicide. These scenes are derived from Seneca and give opportunity for almost endless elegiac argument. Together with the description of deaths, they evidently form the obligatory scenes of Garnier's plays. If a ghost of a Fury, or some principal in a monologue gives the exposition and if these scenes are introduced, if the protagonists meet rarely or at all, we have a typical tragedy of this period. Garnier's principals are even less active than La Taille's heroes. When the play begins, they are so paralyzed by their misfortune that they can only weep, while secondary characters indulge in flowery oratory. Tears may have a value all their own in arousing sympathy in real life; but they have not the same power on the stage unless they are tears which cause events to unfold.

The process of adding material, which might have been used with dramatic effect by a more skilful hand, is carried so far in the *Troade* (1579) that the tendency towards an irregular form of drama, lacking a strict unity of action, is quite evident. Garnier points out in his argument preceding this play that the subject is taken in part from *Hecuba* and the *Trojan Women* of Euripides and from Seneca's *Trojan Women*. In the juxtaposition of episodes taken from different plays, Garnier parallels the practice of writers of comedy of the period. In this tragedy, Hecuba gives the exposition and tells in horrible detail of the death of Priam. Talthybius then announces the allotment of the women to their several conquerors. Cassandra prophesies the death of Agamemnon and is torn from her mother, who faints. Act II. Andromache, with Helen present, obeys the impulse of her dreams and hides the young Astyanax in a tomb. Ulysses enters, and in a scene following Seneca quite closely, the child is discovered and captured. Act III. Talthybius informs Hecuba that Achilles' ghost has announced that Polyxena must be put to death. The Greeks in council decide that the girl must die. Pyrrhus announces this decision to Hecuba, who begs for the life of her daughter, but Polyxena is led away. Act IV. A messenger relates the death of Astyanax to Hecuba and Andromache and spares no gruesome detail. Talthybius tells Hecuba of the death of Polyxena; and the chorus gives her another chance for lamentation by informing her of the discovery of the body of her son, Polydorus.

Any one of these episodes would have furnished enough material for a tragedy constructed after the formula of Scaliger, or according to the practice of Jodelle or Garnier himself in his earlier method. Not content, however, with this series of episodes, Garnier imagines that between the acts Hecuba has summoned Polymestor, the guardian and murderer of her son. He arrives at the beginning of the fifth act, and, when questioned by Hecuba, swears falsely that Polydorus is safe. She entices him into a tent and blinds him. When he comes forth, he confesses the murder of Polydorus. The play ends with a final outburst of grief from Hecuba.

Two things are evident from this analysis. When Greek drama is imitated there is much more action on the stage carried on by the chief characters, although the purpose of the playwright was only to imitate situations which led up to elegiac outbursts. Also, Garnier was trying to complicate the action, although he only succeeded in juxtaposing episodes in the story. Yet it is through just such experiments and clumsy attempts that playwrights learn finally to handle complicated situations successfully. While Garnier produced a play which is much more Senecan than Greek in its construction, the fact that he, the great admirer of the Latin philosopher, actually imitated certain scenes of Euripides in his attempt to improve French tragedy, is not to be overlooked. This is evidence that, however Senecan the theory of tragedy had become, a playwright had discovered that Greek tragedy was a source of dramatic effects not to be neglected. A hundred years later, Racine successfully brought French classical tragedy to its most artistic point of development by following with a sure step the path where Garnier had stumbled, but had shown the way.

Garnier's *Antigone* (1580) is constructed in the same manner as the *Troade*. It is a mosaic of Euripides' *Phœnician Women*, Seneca's version of the same play and Sophocles' *Antigone*. In order to give an appearance of unity of action to the different episodes, Garnier adds *La Piété* as a sub-title. Neither the unity of time nor place is preserved. Œdipus is weary of life and Antigone tries to console him. The scene changes to Thebes, and we find Jocasta deploring, in a dialogue with Antigone, the fratricidal war. Jocasta tries to bring her sons to reason, but in vain. The single long scene of the third act consists of the narrative of the brother's death, the suicide of Jocasta behind the scenes, and the attempt of Hæmon to console Antigone in the style of the poets of the Renaissance. The first scene of the fourth act is taken from Sophocles' *Antigone,* in which the two sisters discuss the question of burying Polynices. Creon forbids the burial. Antigone is brought before Creon and accused of having buried the body. Hæmon reports his quarrel with his father, and Antigone bids farewell to life. In the fifth act, one messenger reports the death of Hæmon and Antigone, and another messenger announces the death of Euridyce—making six deaths in all. The play ends with the usual lamentation on the part of Creon. Much of the play is in narrative form; but there is a wealth of plot material, even if it is clumsily handled. While one hesitates to compare Garnier to a Greek playwright, he reminds one of Euripides in these plays in which he juxtaposes episodes in order to bring out the pathos of the situations.

After his *Bradamante* (1582), a tragi-comedy in which he constructed a complicated plot, Garnier finally returns to a more regular form in *Les Juives* (1583). This play is built along well-known lines. A first act consists of a monologue, in which a prophet recounts the misfortunes of the Hebrews, and of a choral ode which enlarges upon the same idea. The action, as understood by the Renaissance playwrights, begins in the second act; and the second, third, and fourth acts consist of the usual scenes in which the principal and secondary characters plead in vain with a tyrant for clemency. The fifth act is a narrative of the blinding of Sédécie and the murder of his children and friends, together with the lamentation of Sédécie's mother, Amital, and the chorus. There is no real action but merely a kind of peripeteia, when the tyrant, after pretending to be merciful, carries out his vengeance. This form of peripeteia is distinctly Senecan. Yet the play is an improvement over Garnier's earlier tragedies. The situation is clear. The principals meet on the stage. Hence there is at least a unity of situation, lacking in *Porcie* and in *Cornélie*, although it is scarcely possible to speak of a unity of action in plays which do not aim to have the situation develop.

Les Juives and La Taille's *Saül, le Furieux* are the best examples of French tragedy of the Renaissance. With all their faults they fulfill the ideal of tragedy as it existed at that time. If the material they employ for five acts could have been used for the fourth and fifth acts alone, and had the principals been given an opportunity to act, instead of merely to suffer and lament, a difficult but yet artistic form of drama could have been produced. Unfortunately, for the next twenty years, tragedy made no advance in technique. The interest of a dramatic conflict and of a real plot was undiscovered. The hero remained the one who suffered. Any germ of a conflict, or any active hero that can be found, is to be explained as a faint echo from Greek tragedy, not as voluntarily and purposely introduced by the author for artistic reasons.

During the period from 1580 to 1600 the new form of tragedy

was acted before more popular audiences. It became less of a purely scholastic and courtly entertainment. Garnier's influence remained and the rhetorical narrative element prevailed in the long run. Yet the classical rules prescribing five acts, the unities of time and place, and the choruses are sometimes abandoned. The technique of the medieval drama did not die without a struggle and the popular audience was still too accustomed to the freer form of drama, in which there were events on the stage, to accept this narrative dialogue and monologue of Renaissance tragedy immediately. Thus in Beaubreuil's *Régulus*, even the battles are enacted, and the unity of time is not observed. Laudun, in his *Horace* (1596), stages the combat of the six champions, and Horace kills his sister in plain view of the audience. These defections from the camp of the classicists are to be explained by the influence of popular taste and of popular drama. Although instances of the deformation of classical procedure as exemplified in Garnier's *Les Juives* could be multiplied, the art of dramatic technique was at a standstill. The irregularities remained simply irregularities. These experiments did not bring forth any needed reforms in the construction of tragedy, such as the introduction of a real problem developing through dramatic action. At most, they kept the art of tragedy in a somewhat indefinite, fluid state; but no one was able to profit by this fluidity and mould a better form of drama.

Laudun set forth the ideals of irregular classical tragedy of this period in his *Art Poétique* (1597). Tragedy, he says, should contain five acts and the chorus should appear at the close of each act, with the exception of the fifth. It should not appear during the acts, as in Garnier's plays. The first act contains the lamentations; the second, the suspicions; the third, the councils; the fourth, the threats and preparations; the fifth, the executions and the shedding of blood. This formula is derived from Viperanis, and Laudun admits that the French do not follow it exactly.

The materials for tragedy are commands for kings, battles, murders, exiles, violation of women, betrayals, tears, cries, etc.

The characters are kings and princes; only if the plot requires it, is a man of low estate introduced. Laudun interprets Horace's rule that only three actors should speak at once, as having been formulated for the sake of the dignity of tragedy; but he insists that as many characters should appear as are necessary. Thus there might be a council of six or seven.

Ghosts, he holds, should appear only before the play begins, evidently as a prologue. Allegorical or divine characters should appear only in the prologue to tell what is going to happen, in order that the spectators may be attentive, or to explain the moral purpose of the play.

Laudun realized that tragedy was lacking in action, or at least, in events. Therefore, he was unwilling to accept the unities of time and place because their observance would deprive tragedy of so much material that it would lack charm. He considered that the rule of placing horrible events behind the scenes was due to the fact that many actions, such as dismembering a man, are impossible on the stage. He points out that half the tragedy is played behind the scenes, because that is where executions take place. It was natural, therefore, for him to have more action on the stage in his own plays.

Thus the theorists were keeping pace with the dramatists in the production of a somewhat irregular classical drama with a tendency toward more action. At the same time, the imitation of the narrower, so-called regular form, with entire emphasis on narration and sententious dialogue, was still being produced by such writers as Montchrétien, who follows in the footsteps of Garnier. His plays differ from those of his predecessor only in the fact that they are even more bare of events. Unity of action is very narrow. He never combines episodes, but treats one situation, after the manner of Garnier in *Les Juives*. However, it was at this time, the beginning of the seventeenth century, that Hardy began to write the tragedies played at the regular theatre in Paris, the Hôtel de Bourgogne.

Although many of these scholarly and literary tragedies had been represented in colleges, at the court, and later by professional actors, their authors were not professional playwrights. These plays, although composed with a view to production, were not written under normal theatrical conditions, in which a playwright is paid to produce something which must be enjoyed by a regular theatrical audience in order to be a success. In the first two or three years of the seventeenth century, Alexandre Hardy became the dramatist whose reputation and reward depended upon his ability to interest the normal audience of the Hôtel de Bourgogne. Unlike his learned predecessors in the art of writing tragedy, he could not be content with the applause and verbal and written commendation of intellectual friends. His plays had to get over the footlights to an audience which had paid an admission fee. The frequenters of this theatre were accustomed to the medieval system of dramatic technique and all that it implies in regard to the play and its mounting. On the other hand, Hardy had classical leanings, and was in sympathy with the new movements in dramatic art. Behind him were the rhetorical tragedies of Garnier, and also the more or less irregular plays. Before him was a medieval theatre where events, not rhetorical tirades, held the stage. By profession a playwright, he was the first Frenchman to realize that, while playwriting had been raised to a literary art, drama is an art which cannot be successful if the literary element is not subordinate, when necessary, to plot and action.

His tragedies can scarcely be called reactions against Garnier's technique, and against the irregular plays of which Laudun describes the construction, or even against medieval drama. To the best of his ability, he drew from these forms of drama whatever he found in them effective on the stage before his audience. He was not a man bound by a theoretical system. He retained the five acts, the Alexandrine line, the messengers, the ghosts in the first act. He portrayed suffering, vengeance and horror, expressed in lofty language. However, he finally banished the chorus as unreal and undramatic. He did not observe the unities of time and place unless he could do so without omitting any scene which he believed to be dramatic. He realized that his audience, accustomed to the portrayal of events in medieval plays, desired to have incidents, which Horace would relegate behind the scenes, enacted before their eyes. He did not fail to place such episodes on the stage. As a result, the rôle of the messenger and the rhetorical element, though still existing, lost materially in importance. The lines ceased to be merely a means of describing events and emotions. They became the means of developing the action. What is said in his plays is directly connected with what is being done. Action and dialogue go hand in hand to the end.

His point of attack is far enough back in the story so that his characters go through different emotions and so that the events calling forth these emotions happen within the play itself. There are hopes and fears, not merely two hours of impending, inescapable doom. Therefore, he was able to open his plays with a peaceful scene, and to represent the progression of emotions which had been lacking in earlier tragedies in France. In order to accomplish this advance towards a real plot, Hardy did not observe the unities of time and place when it was necessary to disregard them for the sake of his situation. He placed his scenes where he wished, because he was able to use the multiple system of stage decoration still in vogue in the theatre at Paris. The sets of five or six scenes represented places definitely, though summarily. Yet the definiteness of the separate scenes lent a clearness to his action in comparison to the vagueness shed over regular classical tragedy by the indefinite setting introduced by Serlio. The spectators of Hardy's plays knew where the event was taking place. Hence events are much more important in his plays than they are in Garnier's. In comparison to the plays of Corneille and Racine, it cannot be said that Hardy introduced a plot which develops logically to the end; but he did select the dramatic moments in his story and put them on the stage. He left out few obligatory scenes although in his *Ariadne,* lapsing into the usual practice of the earlier French dramatists, he fails to have Ariadne and Phædra meet on the stage. Liberty in regard to the unity of place and time are not enough to enable a dramatist to produce a dramatic action which develops through its different phases to an end, nor will many events in a play constitute a plot. To produce dramatic action, events and characters must mutually react upon each other. The event must result in a certain clearly defined psychological reaction, or else the mental state of the personages must cause the event. One or both of these phenomena must be taking place throughout a play. Renaissance tragedy in Italy portrayed the ghastly horrors resulting in an event. In France, tragedy had portrayed the tears and sorrow resulting from an event. Such is the aim of Jodelle's *Cléopâtre* and his *Didon*. Hardy, however, shows us Æneas making his decision to leave Dido. He realized that there are generally two characters concerned in the events of drama. Instead of making these characters avoid each other, he put them face to face. He failed, however, to make them develop psychologically in relation to what is happening around them. The gamut of their emotions is very limited. No fine shades of feeling suddenly cause an action to develop surprisingly yet logically. His people are at the end too much what they were at the beginning. He has no Old Horace who rises to unheard-of heights of austere patriotism; no Othello, vulnerable in his love at the beginning, who sinks to tragic depths of jealousy at the end; no Phædra, whose passion grows with the situation until it brings the downfall of all who are within reach of its uncontrollable fire. Able to represent dramatic moments, able to tell a story on the stage, Hardy could not construct a dramatic action on the stage and sustain it to the end. Garnier portrayed the emotional result of an event. Hardy portrayed the event and its emotional result. Tragedy of the highest form portrays the whole psychology of the hero as it develops from, or causes, each event.

Thus the influence of the unities of time and place on the development of a plot is not very important. The construction of his *Marianne* and *Didon*, in which the unity of time is observed, is not fundamentally different from that of *Coriolan* in which the events are spread over one year. The fact that the scene in *Didon* changes from Carthage to the country ruled by Iarbas, does not alter the fact that the events in the play deal with a single crisis in the life of the hero and heroine. Except in *Timoclée* and *Méléagre*, Hardy observed the strict rule of the unity of action. He observed them better than did many of his predecessors whose plays open a few hours before the dénouement and retain only a single scene of the action. To Hardy belongs the credit for having learned how to observe a strict unity of action dealing with one crisis while not observing unity of time and place. Victor Hugo could not do so much in many of his plays, notably *Hernani*, although he aimed at this very ideal. Hardy could not handle characters as Shakespeare could. He would not have constructed plots containing several crises as did Shakespeare. French playwrights were not forced to accept a strict unity of action because they accepted the unities of time and place. They accepted the unities of time and place because their observance was fairly easy under the strict rule of unity of action which French dramatists never seriously questioned. The French mind thinks keenly and deeply rather than broadly. The acceptance of the unity of action being inevitable, most of the other conventions of classical tragedy followed in its wake.

The suppression of the chorus, especially when these tragedies were represented, gave more opportunity for the development of the situation. Writing for a public accustomed to see events on the stage, Hardy was able to vary the kind of scenes in his tragedies, and avoid the monotony of earlier tragedies in which the range of scenes was restricted to the prophecy of a ghost, pleas for clemency, narrations of deaths, battles, and lamentations. Hardy understood the power of the appeal to the eye. Thus in his *Didon*, Æneas boards his boat and the boat sails away. Then Dido enters and finds that the vessel no longer lies at anchor. In *Scédase*, the two maidens are seized by their ravishers, and murdered; their bodies are cast into a well, and later, are discovered. He does not hesitate to show his characters in agony. Alcméon undergoes the torture of the poisoned necklace. Deaths occur frequently on the stage, no matter how violent. At the same time, unwilling to give up entirely the narration of such incidents, in *Coriolan* and in *Alcméon* the death is messengered after having been enacted. The importance attached to such narratives in classical tragedy is evident.

The element of spectacle, an inheritance of medieval drama, was not cast aside as unworthy of dramatic art. In the *Ravissement de Proserpine*, the earth opens and amid the spouting flames Pluto seizes the object of his desires. The *Gigantomachie* depends upon a series of spectacular pictures for its interest. Probably the properties and scenery formerly used for the spectacular setting of Hell in the mysteries represented the flaming forges of Ætna. Such scenes are clear evidence of Hardy's willingness to capture the eye as well as the ear. He employed theatrical effects and placed movement, if not pure dramatic action on his stage. Plays built in this manner are theatrically effective, if not dramatic.

With all these appeals to the eye, with all the variety of his settings, Hardy was still unable to arouse suspense as we understand it today. He arouses curiosity. His heroes are interesting because they call forth sympathy, not merely pity. They are much more active physically and mentally than are the tearful automatons of the sixteenth century. The rehabilitation of the hero from the bloody villain of Italian tragedy into the man or woman worthy of respect had taken place; and Hardy was responsible for this welcome development. Yet his whole system of dramaturgy was not capable of arousing poignant suspense as to what will happen and how it will happen. One is simply curious as to when the impending doom will fall. Hardy lacked the ability to combine the interplay of psychological reaction and events so as to arouse alternate hope and fear for a person who has won our sympathy. In spite of his power in selecting scenes and arranging them in an order which tells the story effectively, his characters do not grow and develop with fine gradation. Questions of life and death are discussed;

but decisions are arrived at too suddenly. There is no cumulative effect of hope and fear to constitute suspense. Without cumulation there is merely curiosity. Jean de La Taille had recognized vaguely the value of suspense and had said in his *Art de la Tragédie* that the spectators must be held "open mouthed"; but how to extract the full value of suspense was as yet an unknown art. As Professor Petit de Julleville says: "The theatre of the Middle Ages was ignorant of the art of surprises, of unexpected dénouements, of interest long in suspense and cleverly sustained. It disdained the means of arousing emotion which the modern theatre has abused." Classical tragedy of the Renaissance also disdained such peripeteias, although Greek tragedy employed them with great art. Thus to have introduced the element of curiosity, as Hardy does, marks an advance toward a goal reached by Corneille.

Even after *Bradamante,* tragi-comedy was cultivated but little. Having been overshadowed by regular classical tragedy, it now seems to have had its place usurped by irregular tragedy, which was more and more representing events and bursting the narrow framework set up by the earlier dramatists. This movement was carried on by Hardy until the form of tragi-comedy was reached. Had no plays of this type been written in the preceding century, tragi-comedy would have developed out of Hardy's conception of what a tragedy must be to interest his audience.

The importance of this development lies in the fact that the plot becomes the vital element in Hardy's tragi-comedies. Exercising more liberty than in his tragedies, he produced a series of striking events which moved towards one goal. He drew his ideas from romances and novels; but he joined the different adventures of his characters, if not in an inevitable chain of cause and effect, at least in a manner which is effective on a stage. He failed once more to represent the entire cumulative effect of passions and emotions. Yet he showed the cumulative effect of events. As Professor Rigal says: "In our tragic playwrights of the seventeenth century the action follows a straight line which is met from time to time by cross roads;—in Garnier it is transported, from time to time, to different roads without any word to inform us of the reason for these displacements;—in Hardy, finally, as frequently in Shakespeare, the action, like too large an army, divides into several corps and travels by several roads to a point where they reunite, where the corps are mingled, and where the march is finished."

Of course, Hardy is more classical than Shakespeare. He places his point of attack later in the story, after a part of the action has begun. Thus in *Frégonde*, he begins his play long after the lover of the virtuous wife has fallen a prey to her charms. He does not travel along by-paths of comedy, as does Shakespeare. But he fails where Shakespeare succeeded, not so much in character drawing as in not being able to handle events and characters in that strict interrelation which we demand of strict drama in which there is a plot. In *Frégonde* the interest lies in the psychology of the characters: a virtuous wife and an honorable husband, a lover who becomes honorable when he has saved the husband from bankruptcy. But Hardy insisted too much on events and not enough on the psychological reaction of the events on his characters.

The play begins with the Marquis de Cotron begging Frégonde's nurse to help him gain an interview with Frégonde. The nurse finally consents. The act closes with a short scene between the Marquis and a confidant, Count de Célane. The Count guesses from Cotron's face that the unknown object of his love has softened her heart. The situation would have been more dramatic had Don Yvan been introduced instead of a confidant.

Act II. The meeting between Frégonde and the Marquis, prepared for in the preceding act, takes place. Unfortunately, Hardy does not extract the full effect from the situation. Frégonde complains that she is besieged by the Marquis, but must keep her husband in ignorance of the fact that his friend is in love with her. The nurse begs her to allow the Marquis to speak to her. Frégonde realizes that the nurse has attempted to arrange the meeting and withdraws, after upbraiding both the nurse and the Marquis. One wishes she had allowed the Marquis to speak instead of showing her firmness in such a chaste manner; but Hardy prefers to impress his audience with the virtue of his heroine and thereby misses a scene which might have been most interesting psychologically. The next scene, however, is highly dramatic. Don Yvan informs his wife he is on the verge of bankruptcy. Only one friend remains to help him—the Marquis. Frégonde, without disclosing the situation, begs her husband, in vain, not to accept his aid.

The third act opens with a scene between the Marquis and his confidant. The Marquis rejoices because, now that he has aided Don Yvan by an act of friendship, he is cured of his passion for Frégonde. The next scene shows Frégonde and her husband. They have gone to the country. She still regrets that her husband has accepted aid from the Marquis. He can see no reason for her objections to such a friend. She grows pale with fear when a page announces the arrival of some hunters, one of whom must be the Marquis. Having worked up to dramatic obligatory scenes of the meeting, Hardy suddenly shifts the scene to Calabria and introduces an army of Turks whose leader exhorts them to attack the Christians. This is a curious moment to introduce a scene of preparation for later events. The monologue of the nurse then informs us of the first interview between Frégonde and the Marquis and that their rôles are now reversed. The Marquis is calm and respectful, but her love shines through her modesty. Their meeting on the stage, in which they both display their new feelings, is short in comparison with what the scene would be in a modern play; and the nurse should not have narrated what one is about to behold. Yet it is an obligatory scene depending on the psychology of the principal characters, rather than on events. It would have been more dramatic had the Marquis not suffered a change of heart; or if we had not been informed of his new attitude, and could see his character develop. But in drama of this period, the characters develop suddenly, and the psychological action often develops between the acts as physical action did in Renaissance tragedy. The struggle of souls has yet to be dramatized. Hardy can only vaguely point the way to attain this goal.

At the end of the third act, the Marquis departs. In the next act, the King offers the Marquis the governorship of Calabria. The Marquis requests that the office be given to his friend. Don Yvan accepts. A messenger announces that the province has been attacked by the Turks. A scene in which Frégonde talks with her nurse emphasizes her love for the Marquis; and, on learning that she must accompany her husband to Calabria, she expresses her regret at leaving Naples.

In the fifth act, Hardy successfully avoids the difficulty of working out his situation psychologically. Indeed, since the middle of the third act he has been preparing his dénouement with a care almost wholly lacking in the plays of his predecessors. His skill in foreshadowing and preparation is striking, although one regrets that he ends the play by events, rather than by solving the problem he has raised. The shade of Don Yvan, killed by the Turks, appears to Frégonde and bids her marry the Marquis, whose love for her, we learn from the scene between him and his confidant, still lives. The King grants his request to marry her.

In spite of its faults, this play reveals the importance of tragicomedy in the future development of dramatic technique in France. Without destroying the unity of action, it represents a variety of scenes on the stage, each one of which serves a purpose beyond merely harrowing the feelings of the audience. The action is skilfully foreshadowed. Hardy keeps his audience looking forward and awaiting events, instead of looking backward and listening to lamentations. His characters develop, not always as we think they should and their development is sudden; but they are not paralyzed by their misfortunes. Many of these plays set up a problem. It is in the logical solution of the problem that his art breaks down.

CHAPTER XIII

FRENCH TRAGEDY OF THE SEVENTEENTH AND EIGHTEENTH CENTURIES

DURING the last years of Hardy's activities as a dramatist, from about 1625 on, in front of the stage a change took place that was to be of great significance in the development of drama. The audience began to contain ladies and gentlemen instead of only the middle and lower classes who had frequented the Hôtel de Bourgogne and taken delight in the horse-play of the farce and the melodramatic *coups de théâtre* of tragi-comedy. The dramatist who wrote plays for production in the theatre became a man of distinction and his name appeared upon the playbills posted outside the door. The theatre became an important adjunct to dramatic art for the educated classes, who had been contented with the printed page or with occasional productions at court to bring them in contact with the art. The pastoral, with its trappings of chivalric and courtly love, helped to create an atmosphere which ladies, at least if masked, could breathe without apparent blushes. They wished to see enacted the pastoral love stories which they had been reading in romances for so many years. Scholars, poets, statesmen—including Richelieu—men who were to form the French Academy, become playwrights, critics, and spectators in a commercial theatre. Since these cultured spectators did not drive out the average citizen who brings to the playhouse a heart and mind unclouded by refinement, an ideal theatrical audience was formed. Drama must be a popular art in every sense of the word, if it is to exist in its highest form. Each class of society must give up what appertains to it alone and must become fused into a collection of men and women who are willing to have deep emotions aroused. Over-refinement and under-refinement must compromise. People who shrink from human emotion, as both the high-brow and the low-brow may do, are out of place in a great national theatre. The former may be compared to the scholarly critics, who, as Gombauld said, "understand best the rules of the theatre and frequent it the least."

Hardy ceased writing plays about 1628. The years from that date until 1636 or 1637, when the *Cid* was produced, mark a period of production of many different kinds of plays. Not until almost exactly two centuries have rolled by, will dramatists in France find the stage so open to whatever form of drama they wish to write. The farce, comedy, pastoral, tragi-comedy, tragi-comedy-pastoral, classical tragedy—all were produced either at the Hôtel de Bourgogne or at the new Théâtre du Marais, where a new troupe of actors, which had come to Paris in 1629, was installed in 1635. Whether a play was regular or irregular in its observance of classical rules, whether it was a combination of a prologue, a comedy and a tragedy such as Corneille's *Illusion Comique*, whether it was a mixture of pastoral, tragi-comedy and tragedy, such as Théophile's *Pyrame et Thisbé*, or a tragi-comedy with farcical scenes, such as Du Ryer's *Argénis et Poliarque*, the play was produced, if the actors believed it would interest the audience. Because of the system of simultaneous setting, together with the practice of withdrawing a kind of drop curtain to reveal a new scene, the dramatist was as free as he is today in his choice of scenes to be enacted. The plot could be simple to the point of almost complete disappearance, as in *Les Visionnaires*; or, under the combined influence of tragi-comedy and the new influence of Spanish comedy, it could be extremely complex and contain remarkable events, romanesque adventures, scenes of magic, women disguised as men and *vice versa*, mistaken identities and all that goes to make up what we call melodrama. It was a question as to what direction the evolution of dramatic art was to take. The dramatists themselves, Corneille especially, were regular and irregular by turns. Mairet re-imported the three unities from Italy and not only applied the unity of time strictly and the unity of place slightly less so in his *Silvanire* (1629), but also defended these principles in the preface to that play. Yet he disregarded the unities of time and place in his *Galanteries du Duc d'Ossone* (1632), and observed them both carefully in his *Sophonisbe* (1634).

Scudéry, who was to criticize the *Cid* for its neglect to observe the unity of time with verisimilitude, did not himself follow the same rule in his *Didon*. He placed the point of attack at a time previous to Dido's surrender to her love for Æneas. His third act is the place in the story where Hardy began his version. Thus even in 1636, tragedies on a classical subject might have a larger framework than at the beginning of the century or during the Renaissance.

The actors and authors connected with the older troupe of the Hôtel de Bourgogne, where plays not observing the unities had been given for thirty years after the discussion of the question abated, were less disposed to accept classical conventions. They did not wish to have their repertory disturbed. Those who wrote for the new troupe of Mondory at the Marais were inclined to give them more serious consideration.

It was natural that the rule of the unities should be received unfavorably by the French theatre-goers of the sixteenth century. The men who were observing the principles were not dramatists of great skill. Their conception of a play was undramatic. By this time, however, after Hardy had shown skill in handling events, after the pastoral by treating love stories in an actable way, had prepared the way for the great lovers of tragedy, after dramatists had learned that principal characters in a play must meet in obligatory scenes, instead of telling their few emotions to confidants or in soliloquy, it was possible for dramatists to meet these fundamental requirements of drama and check the movement towards irregularity by observing the unities of time and place. Even in the years of freedom the French dramatists never produced a *Life* or a *History* or a *Chronicle* as did the English dramatists. Clearness, simplicity, regularity were too ingrained in the French genius, after the Renaissance, to allow the medieval tendency towards formlessness to persist in drama. Thus the complexity of the plot, which had grown up in tragi-comedy and in the pastoral, and which was fostered by the new influence of Spanish drama, was met by the desire for the simplicity and regularity manifested in the classical rules, especially those of the unities.

In 1628, when the irregular tragi-comedy was still supreme, Ogier in a preface to Schelandre's *Tyr et Sidon,* protested against the unities of time both for technical reasons and on the ground of verisimilitude. He pointed out that a variety of events is necessary to make the representation agreeable, but that the unity of time causes too many events to occur in a short space of time. He felt that this offended the judicious spectator and made the play seem mechanical, in that the characters seem held in readiness to appear like gods from a machine. For this reason he objected to the recognition scenes in which the personages arrive as if by magic. Also, this manner of construction makes certain events, which should be separated by a lapse of time, follow each other closely. The compression of events into twenty-four hours caused too much narration by messengers stationed at every corner of the stage to tell what has happened on preceding days and to explain the motives of the actions which take place on the stage. In almost every act these "gentlemen" entertain the audience with a long account of troublesome intrigues, a practice which strains the listener's patience. "Indeed," he continues, putting his finger on the fault of French classical tragedy of the Renaissance, "it is very boring to have the same person always occupying the stage and it is more fitting for a good inn than for an excellent tragedy to see messengers arriving constantly." He gave the sound advice that in drama "tiresome discourses which recount the misfortunes of others must be avoided and the persons themselves must be put in action, while long narrations should be left to the historians."

There is much common sense in these views, and the criticism applies to the majority of French classical tragedies. The exposition is very likely to be tiresome and difficult to follow. There is too much narration throughout the plays. If attention is called by the dramatist to the lapse of time, events follow each other with mechanical swiftness and there are too many which happen within twenty-four hours, or else there are too few to keep the interest aroused and to allow characters to develop under the bludgeonings of fate.

Such arguments in favor of the unities as are based on respect for the ancients are—and were—of little weight in determining this question. The opinions for and against the acceptance of the rules were based primarily on the idea of *vraisemblance,* which in these discussions came to mean "likeness to reality." The spectator was supposed to behold things as if they were actually happening at the moment, and of which the principal aim is "the pleasure of the imagination." If the spectator, Mairet said, beholds events spreading over ten or twelve years, his "imagination will be diverted from the pleasure of the spectacle which he considers as in the present; and the imagination will have to work to understand how the same actor who, not long ago, was talking at Rome in the last scene of the first act, in the first scene of the second act is found in the city of Athens, or if you wish, in great Cairo; it is impossible for the imagination not to grow cold, not to be surprised by a sudden change of scene and be extremely disgusted, if it must always run after its object from province to province and, almost in a second, cross mountains and traverse the seas with it."

One does not feel that it is impossible for the scene to have changed, but it is true that one must accustom oneself to the new surroundings, and frequent changes of scene tend to break the continuity of the impression of the whole play. No doubt that is what Mairet and others felt when they saw, for example, Du Ryer's *Clitophon* (*ca.* 1628) with its many events and its complex stage setting calling for "a very superb temple . . . a prison in the form of a round tower . . . a beautiful garden . . . a high mountain, on the mountain a tomb, a pillar, a pillory, a rustic altar and a rock where one can climb in view of the audience . . . beside the rock a cave, a sea, half of a ship . . . under the rock, a prison for two people." Du Ryer, however.

devised such spectacular effects purposely. He believed that the public wished to have its eyes charmed by the diversity and change of the scenes. (Preface to *Lysandre et Caliste*.)

Chapelain based his arguments for the observance of the unities on the idea, which he called fundamental, "that imitations in all poems should be so perfect that no difference may appear between the thing imitated and that which imitates. . . ." Verisimilitude is necessary "for the sole purpose of removing from the spectators all occasions to reflect on what they are seeing and to doubt its reality."

The modern system of stage decoration, which sets scenes one after the other, is less likely to break down the impression of reality than the simultaneous system which placed on the stage, at the same time, localities which were known to be far separated geographically. It is easy to imagine a scene in Rome and then to imagine a scene in Athens following it; but, once the question of verisimilitude is raised, it is difficult for the spectator to admit that he can see Rome and Athens at one glance. It is difficult to accept such sudden changes of locality as Du Ryer allowed in *Argénis et Poliarque* in which the scene changes in the first act from Sicily to France and back to Sicily without a pause in the action. The question having been raised, there was nothing left for the defenders of this conception of verisimilitude but to admit that logically the scene should not change, and that the time of the action of the play should correspond exactly to the time of the representation. They did not hesitate to make this admission. But Chapelain expresses the opinion of his partizans by pointing out that less effort is required to imagine an action lasting twenty-four hours than lasting ten years. Also he says that "in the space of three hours as many things having happened as could reasonably happen in twenty-four, the mind easily believes, at least during the representation, that what has taken place has lasted about that length of time." One is much in sympathy with these arguments if he recalls that in the third act of Du Ryer's *Arétaphile* and in the fifth act of his *Argénis et Poliarque* events occur which require more than twenty-four hours. The dramatists were abusing their liberty; and the reaction against such a procedure was natural, although the arguments in favor of reform were at times illogical in their narrow logic and specious in their reliance upon a materialistic conception of realism.

However, had Chapelain ever attempted to write a play and keep the events portrayed within the limit of twenty-four hours without denuding the plot of action, he might have been less rigorous in his demands and less confident of the validity of his views. He might have recognized the justice of the view of a dramatist such as Gombauld, who said: "I know that the plot is one of the principal parts of a play; that is why I want to have as much of a plot as the fitness, the time, and nature of that action require." He might have seen that exact observance of the rules might make it impossible to treat certain fine plots, as Isnard said in a preface to Du Cros' *Fillis de Scire* (1631). But Chapelain refrained from playwriting—no doubt wisely.

Chapelain denied that the narrative passages spoken by messengers in drama are tiresome, and argued for the re-introduction of the chorus and of the musical accompaniment. However, having laid down verisimilitude as the foundation of his critical theory, he was forced to admit that the soliloquy, in which the actor gives information to the audience, is objectionable. He would always introduce someone, when such recitals are necessary, who would be interested in having them made to him. The soliloquy is only admissible if it is not a pure narration but an "interior discourse" such as comes to all men who are not absolutely stupid. Finally, he does not hesitate in his pitiless logic to advocate the banishment of dialogue in verse and rhyme on the ground that it is absurd. His conception of verisimilitude is so realistic, so inartistic, that it is strange he did not insist upon the real Cleopatra rising from her tomb to portray Cleopatra on the stage.

Whatever one may think of Chapelain's arguments, it was necessary to impose limits of some sort upon the dramatists who were confusing their plays by building them upon triple plots, were using and abusing the element of chance, and were fashioning plots by stringing together many events and by recounting many others in the exposition, as Du Ryer did in his *Cléomedon* (*ca.* 1634).

In this play we learn from the conversation of Queen Argire that twenty years ago she was seduced by King Policandre and had borne a son, Céliante, to him. When he married another princess, she married the King of the Santons to whom she bore a second son. She substituted her first born and sent the second child away. Her husband died. She sought to marry Policandre; and, when he rejected her suit, she sent Céliante to war against his own father, Policandre.

When this exposition has been given in the scene in Argire's tent, the scene changes to Policandre's court. The King is sore beset and is awaiting the arrival of Cléomedon, a freed slave who once saved him from a lion. A captured confidant of Argire is about to disclose to the King the fact that Céliante is the King's son, but the retainer dies before Cléomedon arrives. During the entr'acte the King wins a victory and captures Céliante. Both young men fall in love with the princess, but she loves only Cléomedon. Célanire and Bélise, her sister, fall in love with Céliante, and thus make the love imbroglio complete. Policandre has promised Célanire to Cléomedon; but he decides for reasons of state to marry her to Céliante and to give Bélise to Cléomedon. The latter opposes this solution and Cléomedon goes mad and seeks to kill Céliante. It is reported that Queen Argire has died while coming to attend the marriage of Céliante; but she appears opportunely to disclose the fact that Céliante is Policandre's son. This precludes a marriage between Céliante and his half-sister. It is discovered by a birth mark that Cléomedon is the son of Argire and the King of the Santons. He thus can marry Célanire. Bélise, found to be a step-daughter of Policandre, marries Céliante, while Policandre marries Argire.

Such a series of events, arising from causes manufactured by the dramatist or the novelist and brought to an end by equally forced means, does not produce the highest form of drama. The unity of action is destroyed by the shift in the interest from Argire and Policandre to their sons and daughters. It is true that the observance of the unity of time and place will not restore the unity of action to such a play; and yet, if the events in the play proper are limited to those which happen in one day and in one place, there is more likelihood that the dramatist will observe the unity of action, although he runs the risk of making his plot thin. Also he must give more thought to the psychology of his characters, if the events become less important.

About the same time that Du Ryer produced this play, Mairet, under the advice of Chapelain, wrote his *Sophonisbe* (1634) and followed the unities. Perhaps the fact that Trissino had written an early, regular Italian tragedy on this subject influenced him in his choice of theme. He produced a play which, in spite of certain lines, is worthy of respect. The story is difficult to put on the stage and to retain at the same time the sympathy of the audience for the heroine, because she is placed in the situation of marrying Massinissa just before or just after the death of Syphax, her first husband. Trissino had failed to portray the psychological tragedy in the situation. Monchrétien, in his *Cartarginoise*, had also been unable to portray anything but the physical tragedy. Mairet succeeds much better in making us conscious of a mental struggle caused by the events. As his preface tells us, he has Syphax die in battle so that Sophonisba will not have two living husbands, and he has Massinissa commit suicide. In Trissino's version, Massinissa makes a cold and unheroic impression by merely regretting that he sent the poison so soon to Sophonisba and did not wait until nightfall and rescue her. Also, in the Italian play, Sophonisba is not really in love with Massinissa, but marries him in order to avoid being led in captivity through the streets of Rome. Mairet, however, had learned from the pastoral the dramatic value of a real love interest which he introduced into his tragedy.

In the first act Syphax bitterly upbraids his wife Sophonisba for having written a letter to Massinissa, who is besieging the city. She tries to explain that her attempt to communicate with her former lover was due to a wish to gain a friend and protector among her enemies. Syphax is not convinced by this explanation. He tells his general, Philon, of his wife's perfidy and goes forth to fight a battle which he knows will end in his death. Sophonisba learns from her confidante that the man carrying her letter did not willingly betray her, but was captured and searched. She loves Massinissa; but her heart is torn, because she has deceived a husband who worships her. Mairet was not able to sustain this inner struggle as Corneille will later, when Pauline in *Polyeucte* finds herself in a similar situation; but he pointed the way to psychological tragedy.

Sophonisba is on the stage during the whole of the second act and we experience the events through the emotions which they call forth in her. The battle is about to be waged. In her cruel position she must long for the success of her enemies. Her brave subjects are defending her—the mortal enemy of their king, her husband. She learns that the battle is lost, her husband slain. She begs that one of her retainers slay her; but her confidante persuades her to try to win Massinissa.

In the third act, Massinissa appears. He orders that Sophonisba be captured and held carefully; otherwise the victory is only half won. The news is brought to Sophonisba that her lover is coming and the obligatory scene between the two, carefully prepared for, takes place immediately. It is a dramatic situation full of suspense and is well handled except for one or two unfortunate lines of comedy spoken by Sophonisba's confidante. Massinissa's heart is touched by the queen to whom he was formerly affianced and who now kneels before him begging that she may not be paraded in Rome as a captive. He lifts her up, and seals their troth with a kiss.

The first scene of the next act is pervaded by a foreboding calm before the storm. The two lovers have been married. They recall how years ago, when they were affianced, she was married to Syphax for reasons of state. In the midst of this tragic happiness, Massinissa is summoned by Scipio. This forebodes ill, but he swears to protect her. Scipio orders him to give up his wife. Massinissa pleads in vain. The marriage is declared null. He begs Lælius to plead for him.

In the fifth act, Lælius reports to Massinissa that his plea was vain. A messenger brings a letter from Sophonisba asking Massinissa to send the poison as he promised, if he could not bend the will of Scipio. He wishes to bear the cup himself, but Lælius informs him that he cannot see his wife. He goes to get the poison. Sophonisba recounts her tragic dream to her confidante. She receives the poison, drinks it and her attendants carry her away. Massinissa, informed of her death, begs to behold her body. "The room appears" and Massinissa pours forth his imprecations and despair. Scipio and Lælius withdraw. Massinissa stabs himself and dies on the body of his bride.

The observance of the unity of time has not caused any scene necessary to the plot to be left out. If the point of attack were removed farther from the climax, nothing would be gained from a dramatic point of view, since the events leading up to the situation are explained at the correct moment within the play. By considering the whole palace as the scene of the action—an allowable interpretation of the unity of place—Mairet has not been forced to omit any scene. Massinissa enters rather late in the play, but there is no reason for having him appear earlier. The plot happens to be one in which these rules can be observed without the loss of dramatic value. Only the hurried second marriage is dangerous to handle and Mairet was conscious of this pitfall. There are enough events to sustain the interest and to allow the characters, going through different phases of emotion, to be active in developing the situation. Yet there are not so many events that the author can rely upon them entirely. Mairet had to analyze the motives and thoughts of his people; and he had the time to do so which would have been lacking in a play built upon the melodramatic plan of presenting many incidents. Mairet succeeded, where Hardy failed, in producing a tragedy in which the action develops through an interplay of external events and internal feelings. The dramatic struggle has begun to enter the human mind instead of merely using the human body as a shuttlecock. Events in the plot have begun to follow each other psychologically, not merely temporally. Things have begun to happen because the hero and heroine think in a certain way, and not merely because they are shipwrecked or captured. Mairet's *Sophonisbe* is the most artistic French tragedy up to the time of its production, not, as Chapelain would have said, because it observes the unities, but because by observing the unities Mairet made the play a dramatic tragedy which unfolds partially in the human heart.

During these years an important influence of the Spanish drama had been gathering momentum. Hardy had taken the plots of some of his plays from French translations of Spanish romances and pastorals. His *Cornélie* and *La Force du Sang* revert to Cervantes' *Exemplary Novels* and his *Felismène* to Montemayor's *Diana;* but he owes nothing to Spanish drama. French tragi-comedy, however, as produced by him and his successors, with its complicated plot and melodramatic effects of suspense and surprise, its liberty in regard to place and time, prepared the way for the direct imitation of Spanish drama.

Beyond the Pyrenees, the classical rules of the unities had not been accepted by the playwrights. Lope de Vega had said in his *New Art of Writing Plays* that the public wanted to see everything from Genesis to the Last Judgment represented in two hours. Lope advises that the action should "take place in as little time as possible, except when the poet is writing history in which some years have to pass; these he can relegate to the space between the acts, wherein, if necessary, he can have a character go on some journey; a thing that generally offends whoever perceives it. But let not him who is offended go to see them." Wise advice to the critic; but unfortunately seldom followed because the critic's breath of life depends upon being offended. In complexity of plot the Spanish dramatist far surpassed the French. "The criterion of a fine plot," says Professor Martinenche, "seems to be for the Spanish to arouse surprise and to astonish by the wildest ingenuities." Love at cross purposes, abductions, disguises, duels, battles, sudden encounters, all that is melodramatic is poured indiscriminately, sometimes to the point of confusion, into the plots of their plays. Lope de Vega insisted upon the value of the unforeseen and even the ambiguous. He says of the play divided into three instead of five acts according to Spanish practice: "In the first act, set forth the case. In the second, weave together the events in such wise that until the middle of the third act one may hardly guess the outcome. Always trick expectancy; and hence it may come to pass that something quite far from what is promised may be left to the understanding. . . . To deceive the audience with the truth is a thing that has seemed well. . . . Equivoke and the uncertainty arising from ambiguity have always held a large place among the crowd, for it thinks that it alone understands what the other is saying." Also Lope pointed out that the male disguise of women is usually very pleasing. The Spanish employed more events in a single play than did their French contemporaries, with the exception of Du Ryer; and there are few, if any, dramatic situations which were not used by Lope de Vega. Thus, Spanish plays offered a rich mine for French dramatists who were seeking relatively complicated plots developing through melodramatic events and situations. Most of the lesser French playwrights who imitated the Spanish drama were content to borrow the plots and incidents. They did not even vaguely realize that in these complicated situations two powerful human emotions and ideals, love and honor, were personified and constantly clashing in a dramatic struggle.

The love portrayed in Italian tragedy was often horrible and gave rise to vengeance alone. In Italian comedy, love was voluptuous. In French tragedy of the sixteenth century, the love element caused tragic lamentation. In the farce, it was frankly indecent. Tragi-comedy portrayed romantic love such as would cause a hero to suffer and perform great deeds for his mistress. Love in pastoral comedy was gallant and made lyric poets out of the lovers; or in the case of the satyrs it was sexual passion. In French comedy, after 1629, love was gallant and capricious.

As for honor, after Tasso in his *Aminta* had described it as an *idolo d'errore, idol d'inganno,* the pastoral drama had portrayed this ideal as an obstacle in the path of love and pleasure.

In the Spanish drama, love is a deep, human emotion. It is active, powerful, sacrificing everything but honor. From such a conception of two ideals, which come constantly into conflict, springs a dramatic, emotional struggle which can take place between two human beings, or, better yet, in the heart of one person. "The subjects in which honor has a part," as Lope said, "stir everybody."

Rotrou, who founded several of his plays on the plots of Spanish dramas, was primarily led to these sources by his desire to put before the audience ingenious plots and theatrically effective situations. He is not afraid to represent incidents which purely classical dramatists would later narrate. In his *Iphigénie,* he puts the last scene on the stage and gives the following directions for the impending sacrifice: "Calchas has taken the knife, and, at the instant he is going to strike his victim, a clap of thunder is made; the Heavens open; Diana appears in a cloud; all the characters kneel." He saw the action and a stage picture, as few dramatists of his time did or would for many years to come. If not a great dramatist, he was a man of the theatre, which is more than can be said of many of his predecessors and contemporaries.

Writing for the troupe in the Hôtel de Bourgogne, he was not troubled by the question of the unities. He wanted to produce plays such as his *Laure Persecutée* (1638), which, from the rise to the fall of the curtain, would hold the attention of the audience by its rapid fire action, beginning in the very first line, when the count says to Prince Orantée: "My Lord, in the name of the King, I place Your Highness under arrest!" Swift in his exposition, which was more dramatic for being combined with an important event, Rotrou sweeps the action through many incidents typically Spanish. Thus his heroine is disguised as a page;

another woman impersonates the heroine, as in *Much Ado About Nothing*, while her lover sees his rival make love to her; the heroine appears disguised before the King who has ordered her to be put to death and causes the King to fall in love with her; daggers are drawn but not used. To all this are added scenes of "equivoke and uncertainty arising from ambiguity," brought about by criss-cross love affairs to be straightened out by the device of a long-lost child.

But Rotrou did not merely transport to the French stage the brilliant shell of Spanish comedy with its intricate convolutions, as did his contemporaries Beys and Pichou. He retained some of the spirit of love and honor and jealousy as they are portrayed in Spanish drama where they are emotions which rack the soul, instead of being merely convenient pegs upon which to hang a plot. The jealousy of the Prince Orantée in *Laure Persecutée* is drawn with subtle detail, as he longs and yet fears to see his mistress who, he thinks, has betrayed him. The lovers in *L'Heureuse Constance* are firm to the point of death in their mutual passion. In *Agésilan de Colchos* his heroine is in a dramatic situation which foreshadows the situation of Chimène in the *Cid*. She has been abandoned by her lover, Florisel, and her wounded sense of honor forced her to promise the hand of her daughter to the man who will slay Florisel, whom she still loves, whose death she demands while she longs for his life and love. Like Chimène, she faints when his supposed death is announced.

But Rotrou had not the power to sustain these dramatic situations. The jealousy of Orantée, well drawn as it is, does not become the mainspring of the plot as in *Othello*. Having sketched these human passions, Rotrou turns to the series of events for his main interest. His characters do not cause the successive situations to arrive because they are human beings animated by love, honor and jealousy. The problems of his earlier plays are still too external, founded too often on situations which do not actually exist, and recall the situations of both classical comedy and the novel.

The play was still to be written in which the dramatic struggle of the emotions and ideals of the character, faced by a tragic situation, caused events to unfold. The play was the *Cid;* and Corneille was the dramatist.

In 1632 Corneille had produced his *Clitandre.* He asserts in the preface that he wrote it to show that even if he had not observed the unity of time in *Mélite,* it was not because he was ignorant of the rule. In his *Examen* he says that, because *Mélite* had been criticized for its thin plot and familiar style, he undertook to write a play which observed the unity of time, was full of incidents, was in a more elevated style and was worthless, in order to justify his *Mélite.* He adds, and one easily agrees with him, "I succeeded perfectly."

The plot is so complicated that he admits that those who have only seen the play once are quite excusable if they do not understand it. To attempt to describe the situation and action in detail would be rather hopeless. Suffice it to say that the argument is a short story; and on the remarkable complex tangle of love motives recalling the pastoral he has built up a series of wild scenes. A woman is about to slay her sister when the sword is snatched from her hand by a man who needs it to defend himself. The same lady disguises herself as a man, and, when recognized by her would-be ravisher, puts out his eye with a hairpin. He is about to kill her, when a prince, whose horse has been killed under him by a thunderbolt, arrives. The lady trips her adversary and thus helps the prince to capture him. At the end of the play, when the usual marriages are being arranged, the lady begs her sister's pardon for having tried to kill her. The sister replies: "Sister, you mistake me for someone else if you believe I would remember that any more." So much for tragic problems at the beginning of his career!

Corneille points out in his preface that he has put the action on the stage instead of having messengers recount the marvellous incidents. "This novelty," he continues, "may please some; and anyone who wishes to weigh the advantage which action has over these long and tiresome recitals, will not find it strange that I preferred to divert the eyes rather than importune the ears." He admits, in his *Examen,* that the monologues are too long and too numerous in this play; but he also gives the reason for this defect of most of his work, including the *Cid.* The actors demanded them in order to show off their ability. About placing action on the stage and complexity of the story, Corneille had nothing to learn from Spanish drama. He was far removed from classical theories of the drama, although he was bothered by the existence of the rules of the unity of time and place. He could not dismiss them from his mind, as did Rotrou.

Mairet's production of *Sophonisbe* in 1634 gave dramatists such as Corneille, Scudéry, Rotrou and others food for thought. From 1634 to the time of the production of the *Cid* in 1637, about twelve mediocre tragedies were written. But here was a successful play which was a regular, classical tragedy. Naturally, Corneille was not to be outdone by a rival. In 1635 he produced his *Medée,* imitated from Seneca's and Euripides' versions. The chorus having disappeared from French tragedy, it was necessary to devise enough material to fill up the lacuna. Also, tragi-comedy had accustomed the audience to many events. Corneille, therefore, borrows certain effects from tragi-comedy with the result that the plot is more complicated and there are more incidents in the play than in Seneca's tragedy. Indeed, his *Medée* is a tragi-comedy without the happy ending.

He draws from Euripides' play the character of Ægeus and he actually represents the Athenian king as in love with Creusa, "to give," as he said, "the monarch more interest in the action." Ægeus tries to abduct her. She is saved by Jason, and Ægeus is thrown into prison. Medea visits him in prison and releases him by magic. He then offers to marry her. All this is pure tragi-comedy, as are also the pastoral scenes of incantation in the grotto and the incident of the magic wand, by which Medea makes the messenger suddenly stand motionless and tell her the effect of the poisoned robe.

Other melodramatic incidents, which depart from the original, are the deaths of Creon and Creusa on the stage, the avowed intention of Jason to slay the children himself, and his suicide at the end of the play when he finds that Medea has been able to kill the children first. "The spectacle of the deaths," said Corneille, "was necessary to fill up my fifth act. . . . But it has not the effect demanded by tragedy." He regretted the scene in the prison as being disagreeable; but there is no evidence that he regretted introducing the impulse on the part of Jason to slay the children, which is so "disagreeable" as to be laughable. Whatever change he makes in the psychology of his characters in this play is utterly undignified and inartistic.

When Corneille decided to use Castro's *Las Mocedades del Cid* as the source of his next play, he was in possession of a plot rich in dramatic situations and full of events. The rule of the unity of place, however, was now interpreted as meaning that the scenes represented must be confined to one town. The stage was set with scenes showing the palace of the King, the apartment of the Infanta, the house of Chimène, and a street or a public square. Corneille had decided that it was preferable to observe the unity of time, and to compress the events into twenty-four hours. He even calls attention in the lines to the length of the action, although he regretted it later for the perfectly valid reason that he thereby made the spectators conscious of the difficulty he experienced in compressing the action into one day. He did not learn until after he had written many plays that it is better for a dramatist who finds himself in a technical difficulty to avoid any attempt to explain or justify his procedure. Many inconsistencies and incongruities are unnoticed by an audience, provided the dramatist maintains a discreet silence.

With these interpretations of the unities as a starting point, it was necessary for Corneille to exercise great care in the selection of his point of attack, of the events to be enacted and of those to be included within the limits of his play, whether they were narrated or not. The original Spanish play is in two parts, each of which constitutes a separate play in three acts.

The scenes change to many different localities and the action extends over a period of many years. Even Corneille's somewhat liberal interpretation of the unities precluded the possibility of making the interest depend upon a series of romantic events. If he were not to repeat the mistake of his predecessors in the field of serious drama and merely represent the emotions arising from pathetic incidents, he had to centre the interest on the intensely dramatic situation offered by the Spanish original. He chose the latter course. Whether he did so with full consciousness of his artistry at the time or not, we do not know. The question is not important except for the fact that we are trying to discover the actual, conscious knowledge of dramatic technique possessed at the time; but we know that some years later he understood some of the reasons why his play is drama of the highest type. In the *Avertissement* of the edition of 1648 he says that the reason for the success of the *Cid* was that it fulfilled the two principal conditions as set forth by Aristotle. "The first is that the one who suffers and is persecuted is neither bad nor entirely virtuous, but a man more virtuous than bad, who by some human weakness which is not a crime falls into a misfortune which he does not deserve; the other, that the persecution and the danger do not come from an enemy, nor from one who is indifferent, but from a person who must love the one who suffers and must be loved by him." While others were splitting hairs over non-essential and even imaginary ideas of Aristotle, Corneille was the first dramatist to recognize the truth of these important ideas and to put them into practice. Like Shakespeare, Corneille placed the dramatic struggle of tragedy in the heart and soul of characters who arouse human sympathy.

The dramatic problem—the struggle between love and duty, or love and honor—exists in the Spanish original; but it is overshadowed by the series of events which seek to bring out the great deeds and chivalric heroism of the young knight. Corneille centres the interest from the first scene of his play on the emotions of the characters and the conflict of love and honor.

In the opening scene Chimène learns from her confidante that her father looks with entire favor upon her love for Rodrigue. The Count has just gone to the council where he expects to be made governor of the young prince. When the council is over, Rodrigue's father will formally request the hand of Chimène for his son. The Infanta confesses to Léonor that she loves Rodrigue; but, since a marriage to him is impossible because of the difference in rank, she will hasten the marriage of Chimène to Rodrigue, so as to quiet her own passion for the young knight. The Count and Don Diègue come from the council. Don Diègue has been made governor. The quarrel ensues. The Count slaps Don Diègue who draws his sword, which the Count strikes from his hand, and then departs with an insult on his lips. Don Diègue is thus stripped of all honor and is actually made unworthy of the post to which he has been appointed. He is as completely disgraced as a forger or a murderer would be in modern times. When his son arrives, Don Diègue tells him of the disgrace, which falls upon Rodrigue as well. Fully conscious of Rodrigue's love for Chimène, Don Diègue bids his son slay her father or die. In a monologue, Rodrigue weighs the heart-breaking situation, but only one course is open to him. He must wipe out the stain.

Act II. Don Arias pleads with the Count to make an honorable apology as the King has ordered. The Count refuses to consent to this humiliation. Rodrigue challenges him to a duel. They leave to fight to the death. The Infanta promises Chimène, who fears that a duel will be fought, to make Rodrigue a prisoner so that he may not see her father. She summons a page, who announces that the Count and Rodrigue have already met. The Infanta confesses to her confidante that should Rodrigue triumph, she could perhaps marry him, enobled by his exploits. The King hears that the Count has refused to offer an apology. He also announces that the Moors are about to attack the city. At this moment a courtier brings the news that Rodrigue has slain the Count. Chimène enters and demands vengeance. Don Diègue offers his life to pay for the crime his son has committed.

Act III. Rodrigue comes to Chimène's house; and her confidante hides him as Chimène enters accompanied by Don Sanche, who is also in love with her. He offers to be her avenger. She replies that she will accept his offer if it becomes necessary. Left alone with Elvire, she pours forth her grief. She is in honor bound to avenge her father's death, though she still loves Rodrigue.

ELVIRE

If you love Rodrigue, he cannot offend you.

CHIMÈNE

'Tis true.

ELVIRE

Then, after all, what will you do?

CHIMÈNE

I will avenge my father, and my woe.
I'll follow him, destroy him, then I'll die.
(RODRIGUE enters.)

RODRIGUE

Nay, madam, you shall find an easier way.
My life is in your hands; your honor's sure.

Few obligatory scenes are built upon more dramatic situations. The opponents are face to face; the problem is real; no *deus ex machina* can solve it. The conflict is in their souls. Corneille does not fail to rise to the situation and press the last drop of tragedy out of the problem. If he fails at all, it is, as he admits, in making his characters indulge in over-refinements of subtle argument at such a moment. Yet there is withal a touching pathos and dramatic power in their words unknown to French tragedy before the *Cid*. Tortured by their love, by their presence together, each is trying to do as honorable men and women should in accordance with the inexorable code of honor.

RODRIGUE

In thy dead father's name, for our love's sake,
In vengeance or in pity slay me here!
Thy wretched lover keener pain will know
To live and feel thy hate than meet thy blow.

CHIMÈNE

Leave me, I hate thee not.

RODRIGUE

'Tis my desert.

CHIMÈNE

I cannot.

RODRIGUE

When my deed is full known
And men can say that still thy passion burns,
Dost thou not fear the cruel stinging words
Of censure and of malice?   Silence them;
Save thine own fame by sending me to death.

. . . . .

CHIMÈNE

Depart.

RODRIGUE

What wilt thou do?

CHIMÈNE

The fires of wrath burn with the flames of love.
My father's death commands my utmost zeal;
'Tis duty drives me with its cruel goad,
And my dear wish is nothing to achieve.

RODRIGUE

O miracle of love!

CHIMÈNE

O weight of woe!

RODRIGUE

We pay our filial debt with suffering.

CHIMÈNE

Rodrigue, who would have thought!

RODRIGUE

Or could have dreamed,

CHIMÈNE

That joy so near so soon our grasp would miss.

RODRIGUE

Or storms so swift, already close to port,
Should shatter the dear bark of all our hope.

CHIMÈNE
   O mortal griefs!
RODRIGUE
   Regrets that count for naught!

The act closes with Don Diègue sending Rodrigue forth to
fight the Moors. One wonders what Shakespeare would have
written had Juliet been in honor bound to avenge the death of
Paris; but one does not attempt to answer the question.

Act IV. Elvire announces to Chimène the great victory won
by Rodrigue. She is torn by her admiration for him and her
duty to her father's memory. The Infanta tries to convince her
that now her duty wears a different face. She can no longer seek
vengeance upon the defender of the realm. The King confers
the title of "Cid" upon Rodrigue, who then describes his victory
in too great detail for modern ears. He withdraws as Chimène
comes once more to claim vengeance. When she is told by the
King, in order to test her feelings, that she has been avenged,
she betrays her love by fainting; but she insists that she has
fainted from joy. . The King refuses to be deceived, and she
asserts that she fainted from disappointment because his death
was supposedly glorious and not on a scaffold. She finally offers
to wed the man who will conquer Rodrigue in single combat.
Don Sanche offers to become her champion. She accepts him
and the King decrees she shall marry the one who is victorious.

Act V. Rodrigue comes to Chimène to bid her farewell forever. He does not intend to defend himself. Chimène replies
that he must defend himself for the sake of his honor; and at
last she confesses her love for him and bids him win the combat
of which she is the prize. With a wild cry of joy, he goes forth
to fight.

An episodic scene then occurs in which the Infanta, after hoping
that she may now love this hero, again decides not to betray
the love of Chimène and Rodrigue.

Chimène still fights her battle between love and filial piety,
when Don Sanche enters and lays his sword at her feet. Believ-

ing that Don Sanche has slain her lover she breaks down and confesses to him and to the King that she loved Rodrigue always. But Rodrigue appears. He had disarmed Don Sanche and told him to lay his sword before Chimène; but she can no longer pursue him for the sake of vengeance. Yet can she obey the King and marry him? The King suggests that she wait until time has dried her tears, and that Rodrigue go forth and win new glory by his valor.

It is true that the plot is to some extent a blind-alley theme. Since the action takes place within twenty-four hours, the idea of even discussing a marriage between the lovers is somewhat distasteful. In the Spanish original three years have passed. But does the modern theatre-goer stop to think any more than did the vast majority of the audience which saw the *Cid* when it was new? Jealous critics raised the cry that the *Cid* offended the rules of decorum. The naïve Chapelain suggested that it would have been more in accordance with the rules of decorum if the Count recovered from his wounds, or if Chimène were found to be not his daughter. In other words, he would have tragedy changed to melodrama for the sake of decorum. But everyone loved and admired Chimène and Rodrigue. Therein lay Corneille's success.

The two obligatory scenes, the interviews between the lovers, were also criticized on the same grounds; but Corneille, in his *Examen,* shows exactly why they were successful. He says: "Almost everyone wanted these interviews to be held; and I noticed in the first performances that when this unfortunate lover came to her, there arose a kind of quivering in the audience which showed a wonderful eagerness and redoubling of attention in regard to what they had to say to each other in such a pitiable situation."

The play is not technically faultless. The rôle of the Infanta is episodic and was finally deleted from the acting version. The description of the battle is too long, although it is connected with the action and is, as effectiveness demands, delivered by the hero and not by a mere messenger. The confidants play too large a part. It would have been more interesting to have the Count give his consent to Chimène's marriage to Rodrigue than to have her hear it from Elvire. The lovers should meet before our eyes before tragedy enters their love. Chimène need not witness the duel, as in the Spanish version, but she should know more definitely that it is taking place, and we should see her receiving the news of her father's death and witness her emotions torn by grief and love before they are torn by love and duty.

In respect to the number and variety of the incidents of the plot and the three perils which the hero undergoes, the play resembles the usual tragi-comedy. Only from 1648 on was the *Cid* called a tragedy. The love element harks back through Corneille's comedies to the pastoral. The lyric lamentation in monologue and in dialogue and certain narrations, such as that of the battle, recall French tragedy of the Renaissance.

Yet the great advance in serious drama has been accomplished by making the tragedy and the conflict psychological. The underlying motives are in Castro's play; and of all the important scenes in the *Cid,* the second interview of the lovers is the only one which has no prototype in the original Spanish play. But it was Corneille who centred the interest on the psychological problem by making the events of secondary importance. From one point of view this change in tone was an easy one to make. The observance of the non-essential rule of the unity of time had great influence on the dramatist in making this change; but the result was none the less a masterpiece.

A few jealous critics raised a tempest by trying to prove, vainly of course, that the *Cid* was not a good play, and the famous literary feud, the "quarrel of the *Cid,*" arose. This dispute was of importance to the development of drama in the fact that it caused the principles of playwriting to be widely discussed, and showed that after all the pedantic critic is only a pedantic critic—without influence. We are not concerned with the petty motives and results of the controversy.

In *Horace, Cinna* and *Polyeucte,* Corneille continued to centre the interest on the development of characters endowed with an indomitable will which overcomes all obstacles. His tragic situations are complicated, as in his comedies, by two men being in love with the same woman; but every event in the play has the sole purpose of showing how the hero becomes master of his fate and wills the dénouement even more than in the *Cid*. The passive, suffering hero or heroine, such as Cleopatra, Dido, Sophonisba, has given way to the strong-willed, active hero, such as Horace, who slays his sister, and Polyeucte, who becomes a Christian and suffers martyrdom with an obstinacy that is superhuman—and almost inhuman. One misses, more and more after the *Cid*, the human moment of hesitation in these personifications of will power. The delicate shades of psychology are lacking. Thus, transition scenes, when a principal character talks with a confidant, are often cold, because the principal character is one-sided in his greatness. But Corneille was a master dramatist in the obligatory scenes; and he rarely omits one. He even makes the recital of events off-stage an integral part of the action. Instead of being pathetic or nerve-racking recitations, serving as an undramatic dénouement, the announcement of the event causes some character to act and not merely to commit suicide, like Dido or Cleopatra in earlier tragedy. The narration of the death of Pompée in the tragedy of that name, takes place in the second act. It is actually the initial cause of the rest of the action.

The events in his plots follow in causal sequence, once the situation and characters are devised, because his hero wills that *this* shall happen since *that* has happened. The events are subordinated to his characters. Thus in the story of the three Horatii, one of the brothers kills his sister. Corneille knows that this will overstep the bounds of decorum, but he does not hesitate to portray the action practically on the stage, and the actress brought it even actually on the stage. This is, to him, an historic fact. His task is to show how the interplay of events and the psychology of his characters made this event unavoidable. Such is the method of a great dramatist. If Corneille divested his characters of human emotions, the fact remains that he swept aside the undramatic drama of the Renaissance and produced a form of drama which, down to the present day has never been successfully displaced, even though many critics have been loud in their condemnation of the well-made play.

Corneille was skilful in plotting. He searched history for dramatic situations which he developed into evenly balanced plots. In *Rodogune* a mother promises to place on the throne that one of her sons who will slay Rodogune. With geometrical precision Rodogune promises to marry the son who will slay his mother. In *Horace* the same balance of opposing forces and emotions is maintained. The feelings of his characters swing in the balance; their fates are inextricably intertwined. At times, as in *Héraclius,* he stretches the complexity so far beyond the breaking point that, as he admits, a spectator would have to see the play twice to understand it. Simplicity of plot in French tragedy was Racine's innovation. Corneille was too much under the influence of Spanish drama to use simple plots.

Like all successful playwrights and much to the disgust of most literary critics of all times, Corneille believed that the aim of drama was to please the audience. In order to please the spectator one must represent the "truth." The "truth" can be represented only by observing verisimilitude. "The truth being the aim," as Lanson says of Corneille's technique, "verisimilitude will be the law: all the rules are reduced to the aim of making the plays as verisimilar as possible."

Most dramatists and critics of Corneille's time would have subscribed in substance to this abstract theory, although they would have emphasized, as did D'Aubignac, the moral aim of drama. Yet Corneille's conception of what is true and what is verisimilar is much more psychological than the material conception that Chapelain, La Mesnardière and D'Aubignac had of these terms. Their chief concern was that drama should be life-like and so real that the spectator could not tell the difference between the imitation and the thing imitated. Thus La Mesnardière asserts in his *Poétique* (1640) that each play should contain only one peripeteia, because it is improbable that a change from joy to sorrow or *vice versa* would happen twice in one day. D'Aubignac in his *Pratique du Théâtre* (1657) measures exactly the size of the place of action by the "space in which the average eye can see a man walking without recognizing him." This is simply crass realism.

By the same kind of reasoning D'Aubignac would have reduced the unity of time from twenty-four to twelve hours. He argued that since the action should be a unity, if it is extended for twenty-four hours the characters would have to eat and sleep and do many things extraneous to the story; and that all men can do is to act during a day of twelve hours. A boss of a labor union could not argue more eloquently for an eight-hour day!

Corneille, himself, is not always above such meticulous interpretations of verisimilitude. For instance, he would extend the unity of time from twenty-four to thirty hours, as if six hours more made any real difference. He would keep the place of the action indefinite, so that the spectator would not notice any change of scene. But he is mostly concerned with making the psychology of his characters verisimilar or true. He criticizes the "two perils" which Horace undergoes, not because it is improbable that two crises could happen in twenty-four hours, but because the play is finished when the hero emerges from his first peril unless "the escape from this peril necessarily engages him in another." Corneille usually bases his arguments on artistic truth and not on realistic fact, as did his contemporaries. He says that "the dramatic poem is an imitation, or better yet, a portrait of the action of men and it is beyond a doubt that the more portraits resemble the original the more excellent they are." He concludes that the unity of time is founded on reason. Yet his common sense and his ability as a playwright led him to assume the position that we must observe it as much as possible, even up to forcing events a little to make them fit; but if this is not possible it can be neglected without scruple, and he "would not lose a good subject because of not being able to reduce it to the rule." The playwright with a true dramatic instinct always breaks any "rule" for the sake of a good play and the great dramatist is the one who can break any rule successfully.

The point of attack in drama of this period is partially governed by the rule of the unity of time. The first scene is supposed to be not more than twenty-four hours before the dénouement. Both Corneille and D'Aubignac insist that the action should begin the day that the catastrophe takes place. D'Aubignac would have the play "begin as close to the catastrophe as possible in order to employ less time for the business of the stage and to have more liberty to extend the passions and other discourses which may please." "The dramatist," he asserts, "must remember to take up the action at its last point and, so to speak, at its last moment. . . ." He does admit that some things which happened before the beginning must be supposed as happening that day; but the poet should assemble all the incidents in one day without events seeming feigned or forced. That such a procedure may reduce the material of the plot or the number of incidents does not trouble the worthy abbé.

He warns against complex plots as being undesirable, because they do not leave room for discourses, while he asserts that the "play which has almost no incidents but is sustained by excellent discourses will never fail to succceed." The greatest fault that the stage can incur, in his opinion, is to be silent. Whatever is done, someone must always be speaking. Silence has no place in the theatre except in the entr'acts. Such are the views of the seventeenth-century critic concerning what Voltaire will justly call "the great art of silence" on the stage. The art of acting was in its infancy. The inadequate lighting system did not make it possible for the actor to portray fine shades of emotions by facial expression. Dramatic grouping of characters was yet to be discovered. The scenery was a sketchy representation. On the other hand, eloquence and long discourses were considered as ornaments of conversation in real life. Conversation was oratorical in the salons where men and women discoursed upon psychological questions. In these circumstances, tragedy was naturally full of oratorical effects. The characters belonged to the highest class of society and they conducted themselves as they would conduct themselves in a salon or at court. They observed good form in their actions and in their words. Just as a gallows and executioners and gravediggers would be out of place in a salon and hence "shocking," so they were out of place on the tragic stage. They were "unworthy of the majesty of the Poem," said La Mesnardière. They could only be talked about in a polite manner and it was the business of the poet to merit praise by producing the same effect through discourses that would be produced by real spectacles.

Action on the stage, whether physical or psychological, was not important to D'Aubignac; but Corneille, while subscribing abstractly to this theory of the point of attack, actually pushed back the opening of his plays by forcing more events into one day than the critics would allow. He was too much interested in his art of plotting to do otherwise. In this way he was able, as a rule, to make his point of attack precede the initial cause of his action, although he could not show all the incidents leading up to the one which sets the plot in motion. In the *Cid* and in *Horace,* the opening scenes are peaceful or reassuring. We see the action begin. In *Polyeucte* the arrival of Pauline's former lover is the initial cause; but perhaps a modern playwright would have shown more gradually how Polyeucte was led to become a Christian since his conversion is an important link in the chain of events.

Because a relatively late point of attack forces the dramatist to begin the action quickly, the scenes of exposition in a classical drama are interesting, provided the action of a well-constructed plot ensues. Corneille always built up a dramatic situation immediately; and, if he is to be criticized for his plots, it is on the ground of complexity, with a few exceptions such as in the case of *Cinna.* He loses no time in gaining the attention of his auditors. He said that one must be sparing of "narrations of things which happened before the action began, because they are not expected and burden the mind of the auditor, who is obliged to charge his memory with what has been done ten or twelve years before to understand what he is going to see." Of course he could not always avoid such narrations. In *Polyeucte*, Pauline has to explain to a confidante her love for Sévère and her marriage to Polyeucte.

Corneille generally entrusts the exposition to the principal characters who, in conversation with confidants in the usual manner of neo-classical drama, give the essential facts. He uses an entirely protatic character, such as Pollux in *Medée*, very rarely, for he held that such characters should play some other part than that of mere listeners. His scenes of exposition, however, are usually narrative, although he will not allow a narrative monologue unless the character speaks under great emotion. He rarely introduces an incident, such as the council in *Pompée*, in order to give the exposition in connection with action.

The exposition of neo-classical tragedy was directed to the auditor, not to the spectator. The appeal was to the ear, not to the eye. There are no examples of expository scenes, such as are found in *Œdipus Rex* or the *Eumenides*, in which a spectacular event arouses the interest, in spite of the fact that D'Aubignac, relying on the authority of Vossius and the practice of the Greeks, advocated a striking opening.

Dreams and oracles were still the principal means of foreshadowing both in practice and theory, but the art of preparation was well understood. The first act, according to Corneille, not only should instruct the spectator in regard to all that has happened before the beginning of the play, but also in regard to all that he must know in order to understand what he is going to see. Each act should leave an expectation of something to happen in what follows. No character, with the exception of minor confidants and servants, should enter in the following acts who have not been made known and prepared for in the first act. D'Aubignac is very explicit on this point. It is not necessary, he says, to anticipate events and rob them of the element of surprise by preparing for them. "The preparation of an incident is not doing or saying things which will disclose it, but which can reasonably cause it without disclosing it." He gives full credit to Aristotle and Scaliger for having originated the theory of the art of preparation; but in all justice to the abbé it must be said that he states it more clearly than his precursors in the field of dramatic criticism.

The theory of the necessary sequence of events, originated by Aristotle and which Corneille put into practice with success, is clearly stated by La Mesnardière, who says: "The poet should take care when he is arranging a plot that all his events are so mutually dependent that the ones follow the others as by necessity. Let there be nothing in the action which may not seem to have occurred except in so far as it must occur after what has happened, so that all things may be so well enchained that one results from the other by a correct sequence." Thus, by 1640, in France the important law of the well-made play was fully recognized and was being put into practice. This marks the beginning of a new era in dramatic art, for it practically establishes the French conception of the unity of action. Corneille defines the unity of action as the "unity of peril." He criticizes *Horace* because the hero does not fall into the second peril as a direct result of issuing from the first. In other words, the unity of action ceases to exist when the necessary sequence of cause and effect is broken. Unity of action, according to this view, cannot mean the life of a hero or the fortunes of a city, such as Rome during the time of the Cæsars. Shakespeare's *Julius Cæsar* does not observe the unity of action, because it was not Shakespeare's purpose to show a necessary sequence of cause and effect in the plot. Unity of action has nothing to do, abstractly, with the unity of time or place. It is useless to compare what is called the larger English view and the narrow French view of the unity of action. The Elizabethan dramatists were not striving for this unity of action, as were the French.

Even in plays with a double plot the interdependence of the situations was insisted upon. D'Aubignac says, "the episode should be so incorporated with the principal subject that they cannot be separated without destroying the whole work." The episode must not be equal in importance to the main story, "but must be subordinated and depend on it in such a way that the events of the principal story are the cause of the emotions of the episode, and the catastrophe of the first must produce naturally that of the second."

In every way the continuity of the action was to be preserved. The stage could be left vacant only between the acts, and the scenes had to be so linked that an interlocutor of a preceding scene appeared on the following. Elaborate directions for linking scenes are supplied by Corneille and D'Aubignac. The principal characters had to be on the stage as much as possible, and, by going through the different emotions, not allow the spectator to believe that the action has ceased. On the other hand, entrances and exits were supposed to be carefully motivated; and in tragedy the same character did not appear more than once or at most twice in the same act, in order to avoid an appearance of indecorous hurry. In comedy, a character could appear several times in the same act.

The theory that the reward of the virtuous and the punishment of the guilty was the fitting ending of the plot was held by La Mesnardière and Corneille. Aristotle's theory of the purgation of the passions had given way to the theory that the theatre teaches morality by showing the deserved fate of the good and the wicked. But there is no evidence that Corneille ever modified the ending of the plot in order to conform to poetic justice. He accepted the ending of the story as he found it in history or fiction. The theory of poetic justice is incompatible with the spirit of classical tragedy in which the hero generally suffers misfortune out of proportion to his faults. According to Aristotle, the unhappy ending was best. Italian tragedy of the Renaissance aimed to portray a horrible ending. French classical tragedies as a rule end unhappily, and an unhappy ending does not mean that virtue has been rewarded and vice has been punished. Not until the more sentimental theatre of the eighteenth century has been influenced by English drama does the idea of poetic justice begin to influence the French playwright in ending his plays. In the seventeenth century the theory of poetic justice inherited from medieval drama was convenient evidence that drama had a moral value; but the maxims and sententious sayings, which were considered the very props of tragedy in the Renaissance, were now beginning to lose favor. Corneille advised that the playwright be sparing in his use of them and that they be put in concrete, particular language rather than in abstract, general terms.

Corneille, however, advocated lessening the horror of certain dénouements especially to maintain the sympathy of the audience for his hero. In *Rodogune,* the son does not force the mother to drink poison as history reports the episode. Had Corneille written an *Electra* he admits he would have had Orestes slay his mother by mistake when he was killing Ægisthus. Voltaire actually accepted this dénouement for his play *Oreste.* Corneille did not look with favor upon the suggestion of D'Aubignac that Camille run upon the sword of Horace instead of having the brother slay the sister. Yet the desire to lessen the horror of the dénouement and to make the hero as sympathetic as possible is evident.

Scenes of violent death and scenes which would be incredible or shocking, if represented, were still kept off the stage. Deaths by poison were allowed to take place in view of the audience, as in *Rodogune.* Corneille held that the rule of not shedding blood upon the stage was not inviolable. However, the tradition of narrating the deed of violence remained; but the length of these narrations decreased. No longer were they the emotional climax of the play spun out at great length by minute description of disgusting details and by abstract moralizing. Corneille realized that such narrations must be given by a sympathetic character in the presence of those who are most deeply affected, not by messengers to the audience. Because no sympathetic character was available to announce the death of Polyeucte, he reduced the narration to a simple announcement. In *Horace,* the news of the battle becomes a very important and dramatic incident of the action. While the narration of the deed of violence was reduced in length, it became an integral part of the action. In *Rodogune,* two lines inform the audience of the death of Seleucus which occurs between the acts; but the death causes the development of the plot in the fifth act. The question as to whether such incidents are on or off the stage is far less important than the question as to whether they are an integral part of the plot and are the causes of emotions which lead to further action. Corneille had solved the latter problem, and left the former to future generations.

French tragedy has been severely criticized for placing such actions behind the scenes; but when one considers all the circumstances which led the playwrights to adhere to this traditional handling of such scenes, the practice is at least explicable. Narrative passages were still considered an ornament. Tragedy was still poetry. The art of acting was in its infancy. Stage pictures were practically unknown. The playing space, encroached upon by spectators on the stage, was small. It is very difficult, even in a modern theatre, to keep a death scene from being comic. It would have been doubly difficult in such circumstances. The rule of decorum would have been quickly set aside had such scenes produced a dramatic effect on the stage of the period.

After the *Cid,* Corneille had written *Horace, Cinna,* and *Polyeucte.* The plots of these tragedies are dramatic but are not overloaded with complex action. Before composing his next tragedy, *Rodogune* (1644), Corneille had produced two comedies, *Le Menteur* and *La Suite du Menteur,* both drawn from Spanish plays with involved plots and remarkable situations. It is not strange, therefore, to find him working up to a very powerful situation in the fifth act of *Rodogune,* even though he had to sacrifice sympathy for his heroine by so doing.

Cleopatra has twin sons, Antiochus and Seleucus, both of whom are in love with the Princess Rodogune. Cleopatra has murdered her husband and she promises her sons that she will declare the one who slays Rodogune the eldest and heir to the throne. Rodogune then counters with the dramatic but inhuman proposition that she will marry the son who kills his mother. At the opening of the fifth act, Cleopatra has caused the death of Seleucus and plans to poison Antiochus and Rodogune with the marriage chalice. Antiochus is about to drink when he learns of the death of his brother by "a hand that was dear" to them. Was it the hand of his bride or his mother? Cleopatra accuses Rodogune of the foul deed. Antiochus is about to drink when Rodogune bids him beware the chalice prepared by the queen. Cleopatra seizes the cup in desperation and drinks. The poison works and she is led away to die.

Here is one of the few stage pictures in French classical tragedy and more action than usual on the stage. The power of the scene is undeniable. In its way it is the most striking fifth act of the century; but it helped to make Corneille exaggerate the importance of incidents and complex situations. From this time on, involved, theatrical plots became the aim of playwrights until the reaction set in with the advent of Racine.

Also the influence of Spanish drama, of classical comedy and of tragi-comedy tended to make tragic plots of extreme complexity. Corneille's *Héraclius* (1647) is a glaring example of this type of play. The situation is so intricate as to be utterly incomprehensible to the spectator; and even the reader, who can take his own time to study the intricacies of the plot, must be furnished with many explanatory details before he can comprehend what is happening. These details are so numerous that even the half of them cannot be quoted here, but an idea of their complexity may be gained from the following statement occurring in the text at the end of the second scene: "In these two scenes, Héraclius passes for Martian, and Martian passes for Léonce. Héraclius knows his own identity but Martian does not know his own identity." The spectator is entirely misled. Incident is piled upon incident to such an extent that, as Corneille admitted, the situation can be understood only by reflection after the play is finished.

Between the complexity of *Héraclius* and the simplicity of *Cinna*, there were tragedies of all degrees. D'Aubignac advocated simple plots for tragedy, although he did not know how to arrive at this ideal without reducing drama to narration. Racine solved the problem by placing the tragic conflict in the mind of one character. Instead of having two or more characters of equal importance arrayed on opposite sides of a question, he tends to subordinate everything to a mental struggle of one person. The Corneillian hero rarely hesitates, almost never weakens in his intention. He overcomes obstacle after obstacle. So far as will power and strength of character are concerned, he is one-sided. He develops in strength alone. In order to show this development, Corneille had to introduce many events and complications into his plots. Only when he produced a *Cinna*, whose purpose and intentions are not fixed from the beginning, was he able to reduce the number of incidents in his story.

Racine's characters show human weakness as well as strength when placed in tragic circumstances. Thus one event employed by Racine offers a double opportunity for action. His hero vacillates between the two courses open to him. He attempts to follow the right course and then finds that he cannot. The peripeteia furnished by the incident brings in its wake a psychological peripeteia on which the dramatic interest is centred. Racinian characters have some of Hamlet's indecision which causes suspense and enables the playwright to show both sides of the situation. The conflict of passions against will power is ever present and is equally balanced. The pendulum swings back and forth. In Corneille's tragedies the pendulum swings generally in one direction. His characters do not vacillate in a human, and at the same time, dramatic manner. Corneille complicates the situation and the plot. The psychology of his characters is not complex. Racine complicates the psychology of his characters. His plots are not complex, with the exception of the plot of *Bajazet* (1667), which is built on Corneillian lines.

For this reason, Racine's plays from *Andromaque* on are psychological studies in dramatic form in which events are important only as they influence the characters. His *Bérénice* is the most striking example of the simplicity of plot and situation employed by him. Throughout the whole play the question as to whether Tite will marry Bérénice or send her away is discussed. The dramatic struggle goes on in the hearts of the two lovers as they waver between the sacrifice of their love and the sacrifice of the interest of the state. The vacillation produces the suspense.

Racine chose naturally the late point of attack. The dramatic situation is already in existence when the curtains are drawn apart on his first act. His expositions are easily understood and are very dramatic. Corneille had to explain a complex situation and inform the audience as best he could how this situation arose. Racine only has to have his principal characters explain how they fell into their tragic state of mind. They must confess that they are faced by a psychological problem. The very act of confession is dramatic because it bares their inmost souls. His hero must make a decision; and whichever course is followed, tragedy is likely to result. Andromaque must either betray her love and respect for her dead husband by marrying Pyrrhus or else allow her child to be put to death. Phèdre must choose between succumbing to her passion for Hippolyte and remaining an unhappy, though faithful woman. She must choose between the banishment of the innocent Hippolyte and seeing him the husband of another woman. The drama lies in the struggle first to decide what ought to be done, then in trying to do it.

French classical tragedy attained the highest degree of dramatic artistry and beauty in Racine's *Phèdre,* in which he applied his system of playwriting with greatest success.

Act I. Hippolyte tells Théramène that he loves Aricie, but that his father, Thésée, does not wish him to marry her because she belongs to an ill-starred family. Thésée has long been absent, no one knows where. His wife, Phèdre, who has been persecuting Hippolyte, her step-son, is ill with some unknown mortal malady. Hippolyte resolves to seek his father.

In a scene of unsurpassed dramatic power, Phèdre confesses to her nurse, Œnone, the cause of her illness. Restless, she has risen from her darkened couch and sought the sunlight. Robed in all her gorgeous, queenly attire, she walks with faltering steps. Even the jewels and veils weigh upon her too heavily. For the last time she has come to look upon the sun. She longs for death but refuses to explain why. Œnone exhorts her to live and not to give up the royal power to Hippolyte. She trembles when that name is spoken. Only when Œnone upbraids her for her silence, does she confess. Instead of hating her step-son, she loves him. All her persecution, her banishment of him, was a vain attempt to smother her passion. Every line of this exposition is intensely dramatic and tragic.

News comes that her husband is dead. The crafty nurse recognizes what this means. Aricie is now an aspirant to the throne at Athens. No blame attaches to Phèdre's passion now. She must win Hippolyte; and they together will oppose Aricie's aspirations. Phèdre consents.

Act II. Aricie is told by her confidante that Hippolyte wishes to see her. He has never told her of his love; but Ismène assures her that Hippolyte's coldness is feigned, and she is happy in the thought that he may love her. When he appears, he bids her go to Athens and reign. Then, unable to control himself longer, he confesses that he loves her. Before she can admit her love for him, Phèdre sends word that she wishes to speak with Hippolyte. Aricie and Ismène withdraw.

Phèdre is brought face to face with Hippolyte—the object of her passion. She upbraids herself for her cruelty toward him. She mourns for her dead husband, but gradually her words become tinged with double meaning. Her grief for Thésée becomes a veiled avowal of love for his son. Outraged, Hippolyte cries out: "Have you forgotten that Thésée is my father and your husband!" She replies: "Why should you fancy I have lost remembrance, and am regardless of mine honor?" Hippolyte asks her pardon for misconstruing words of innocence. He starts to go. She suddenly throws herself on her knees and pours out her passion unrestrainedly. She bids him slay her. As he remains motionless, stunned by this horror, she draws his sword and seeks to slay herself. The nurse stays her hand and leads her away, still clinging to the sword.

Théramène enters with the news that the son of Phèdre has been elected King of Athens. "A faint rumor meanwhile whispers that Thésée is not dead."

Act III. Phèdre, bitterly unhappy, is brooding over the disgrace of her confession, when Œnone brings the news that her husband is still alive. Her position is unbearable. She knows that in some way Thésée will hear of her love for his son—a love once again incestuous. Death is her only means of escape from disgrace. But the nurse rouses her to a plan of action, saying:

> Venture to accuse him first,
> As guilty of the charge which he may bring
> This day against you. Who can say 'tis false?
> All tells against him: in your hands his sword
> Happily left behind, your present trouble,
> Your past distress, your warnings to his father,
> His exile which your earnest prayers obtained.

Phèdre revolts for a moment, then humanly accedes to this plan. Thésée and Hippolyte appear. Phèdre evades the embrace of her husband as unfit to meet his caresses, and leaves. He turns to Hippolyte for an explanation of Phèdre's strange welcome; but his son replies that Phèdre alone can solve the mystery, that he asks only to disappear for ever. Thésée finally demands to know who has betrayed him, why he was not avenged. Hippolyte is silent. Thésée goes to Phèdre to demand the truth.

Act IV. When the curtain discloses the scene, Œnone has finished her lying accusation against Hippolyte, and holds forth his sword as evidence of the truth of her words. Thésée believes her and faces Hippolyte with the story which cannot be refuted, unless Hippolyte accuses Phèdre, which he will not stoop to do. In vain he tries to defend himself, tries to show the impossibility of it all because of his love for Aricie. Thésée brands his words as lies, accusing him of adultery and incest, and orders him away from his wrath. When Hippolyte has gone, the guilty Phèdre enters and intercedes for the innocent boy. Thésée tells her he will pray to Neptune to destroy his son, who seeks to defend himself by confessing that he loves Aricie. These words strike Phèdre like a thunderbolt. Ready to save Hippolyte by confessing the frightful truth, now she is dumb. To save him for another woman is beyond her power. Left alone with her nurse, she pours out upon her the agony of her soul, and, with rising anger, curses Œnone for being the cause of her undoing.

Act V. Hippolyte has told Aricie of the accusation. She asks him if he is going to keep silent. He answers that to tell more would disgrace his father. They plan to flee together. Hippolyte departs as Thésée enters. He accuses his son to Aricie. She warns him and is close to disclosing the truth. She rouses a shadow of doubt in the mind of Thésée. When she has gone he demands that Œnone come, so that he may question her alone. He learns immediately that Œnone has committed suicide, that Phèdre is on the verge of madness, but has thrice started to write a message to him. The doubt of his son's guilt increases. He cries out that Hippolyte must return and defend himself. Théramène messengers the death of Hippolyte, dashed from his chariot on the rocks, when a monster of the deep frightened the horses. Phèdre enters and confesses the truth to the grief-stricken father. She has taken poison and she dies.

By making Phèdre instead of Hippolyte the central figure of the tragedy, Racine was able to produce not only a study of passion and jealousy, but also to make the situation much more tragic and dramatic. The added circumstance of Hippolyte's love for Aricie is necessary to bring out the complete conception of the character of Phèdre. This motive is not a mere sub-plot. It gives the reason for Phèdre's silence when she knows Hippolyte is going to his doom. A passionate woman would have saved him even at the price of confessing her guilt, but a jealous woman would act as she does. Were this circumstance suppressed the whole psychological development of the character would ring false and the play would become only a thriller.

As the tragedy is constructed, Phèdre dominates all other characters. Externally the nurse may seem to guide her; but in reality Œnone gives voice to one side of Phèdre's complex nature. Phèdre struggles not against destiny, but against something just as unconquerable—herself. She speaks of destiny, but human beings who sin unwillingly against moral laws explain their acts as due to destiny. Phèdre, above all, is human. The tragedy lies in the fact that she is fully conscious of her sins and is almost, but not quite strong enough to conquer her sinful emotions. There, also, lies the drama. The struggle is within her soul. External events arouse and keep the struggle at fever heat. Every event acts upon her emotions. Every emotion, every thought she has involves the other characters in her downfall. In that the heroine is fully conscious of the horror of the situation, Phèdre is more dramatic than Œdipus Rex, in which Œdipus is blind to the circumstances. Œdipus Rex is a remarkable example of dramatic technique, but only when the situation is plain to the principal character can there be a study of psychology. The dramatic action must at least take place because of the hero's blind acts, as in Œdipus Rex; but better still, it should unfold because of the conscious reactions to each situation of the dominating character as in Phèdre.

Racine depends very little on concealed or mistaken identity to bolster up his plots. His situations are real in the sense that the spectator is not deceived in regard to what is happening. He states his problem and rarely dodges the issue, although in Iphigénie he introduces Eriphyle, an unknown sister of Iphigénie, who is sacrificed in her stead, in order to avoid introducing Diana as a supernatural means of ending the story. Whenever chance does enter his story, it never becomes obtrusive, because the events are so overshadowed by the emotions they arouse. Since events are unimportant in this respect, Racine easily observes the unity of place and time. So long as we behold a dramatic struggle in the mind of a person, we merely wish to know first, what has caused the struggle. This forms the exposition of Racine's plays. Secondly, we wish to know what keeps up the struggle. It is not so necessary to behold the physical action when psychological action in the mind of one person is of paramount importance. The one person, however, must be on the stage as much as possible, for we must get his reactions to any event of the past, or incident off the stage, instantly and at first hand.

Racine, therefore, fails rarely to include the really obligatory scenes within the scope of the vision of the spectator. Yet it will always be a matter of regret that he began the fourth act of *Phèdre* after the accusation of Hippolyte made by Œnone to Thésée. One misses the dramatic moment when Thésée first hears the story of the supposed guilt of his son. One would like to know how Œnone began, how she led up to the accusation, how she was able to make her lie plausible. Yet, to Racine's glory, let it be said that he did not allow decorum or any other classical rule to keep him from bringing all characters face to face in this tragedy in scenes which require a master hand not to become shocking and merely horrible. Some day the story of Phædra may be dramatized again, so that use can be made of the richness of the art of the modern theatre with its colors and form and lights. Yet Racine's *Phèdre* will remain a work of highest art so long as jealousy and uncontrollable passion exist in human nature.

Racine's masterful handling of classic tragedy proves that certain subjects gain dramatic power by being treated according to the laws of classical technique. The Frenchman of the classical centuries made the mistake of believing that all dramatic stories were improved by being poured into the narrow classical mould. The Spanish drama, French comedy, and the contemporary novels furnished the dramatists with a complete assortment of theatrical situations and *coups de théâtre*. Plots of the most amazing complexity were more familiar to the Frenchman of the seventeenth century than to the average theatre-goer of today. Much of the stuff that melodrama was made of is in the French classical tragedies. Disguises, long-lost children, letters lost and found, all were on the stage. Instead of lacking incidents and complications, French tragedy was too full of them. Only master technicians like Racine, and sometimes Corneille, could compress their material within the limits of the form, without making the play either difficult to follow or wordy because of lengthy explanations. The usual love of complexity and *coups de théâtre* was the undoing of the dramatists. They tried to pour too much into a mould that is unsuited to complex plots and many events.

The dramatists of the latter part of the seventeenth century and early eighteenth century realized that tragedy was losing its power. They believed that the decline was due to simplicity of plot and lack of events. La Grange-Chancel set about producing tragedies on melodramatic lines; and Crébillon added the element of horror to his situations. These melodramatic elements were not a new development. They existed in Hardy's plays, in novels, in Spanish plays, and were employed by such writers as Thomas Corneille, and even by his illustrious brother in *Rodogune*.

The melodramatic and the horrible were employed by Crébillon as the main interest in the play, while the psychological element practically disappeared. Society in France was so ultra-refined that plain, unvarnished tragedies of blood, crime, and incest would have been shocking. Therefore, Crébillon used mistaken and concealed identity in order to build his plots in such a way that the rules of good taste were observed. His plots, as a result, are complicated. Much must be told in the exposition, and narrative expositions are difficult to follow. Much must also be concealed from the audience. The spectator does not know enough of the why and the wherefore to be able to grasp the situations as a whole. One does not know what situations actually exist and what only apparently exist.

Thus in *Rhadamiste et Zénobie* the heroine is loved by her

husband, her brother-in-law, and her father-in-law. She believes that her husband is dead. She loves her brother-in-law. She knows her own identity, but he does not know who she is. Numerous other complications make the psychological study of character impossible. No one knows what a woman thinks or does in such circumstances. Crébillon's plays are not good tragedies because there are so many curious events in them that the intellectual element is obscured. They are not good melodramas because there are not enough curious events on the stage to hold the spectator breathless. The late point of attack cuts off half the plot. Melodrama must be seen, not heard about in speeches of messengers.

The first important plea for a modification of the rules of tragedy was made by Houdar de la Motte in prefaces to his plays. He was in favor of liberty, especially in regard to the unities of time and place, in order to introduce more action on the stage. He realized that these rules made exposition difficult and deprived the spectator of the emotional pleasure of witnessing many striking scenes which in classical tragedy take place before the late point of attack, or between the acts, or behind the scenes. He took the sound position that scenes which can be dramatic should not be sacrificed to the unities.

He saw no reason why spoken tragedy should not appeal to the eye as musical tragedy did at the Opéra, where remarkable scenic effects were in strong contrast to the vestibule of a palace, that eternal setting of classical drama. He called attention to the effectiveness of the nuptial ceremony in the fifth act of *Rodogune* with the large number of people on the stage and with the poisoned cup passed from hand to hand. In all French tragedy he could cite only one other such scene; and that one is in *Athalie*. This insistence upon stage pictures as a legitimate part of dramatic art is very striking at this relatively early date. Only in operas were scenery and groupings of characters employed for dramatic effect. The presence of the spectators on the stage in the Théâtre Français narrowed the playing space to an area about twelve feet square. The proximity of the spectators rendered the art of acting difficult. The actors had to be constantly on their guard lest some action, such as falling on the knees, would become laughable. There was nothing left for them but a recital of lines. Everything seemed to conspire to make tragedy a conversation under a chandelier in five acts.

La Motte also suggested that long speeches be cut down and monologues used sparingly. He did not attempt to drive out verse; but he held the sensible view that since there undoubtedly were men who could construct a good play and who were not poets, therefore tragedies in prose should be acceptable. He was in favor of complex plots as oppposed to the simple plot, because they held the attention more easily by their variety of incident.

In spite of his advocacy of all these liberties he was most conservative in his practice. In theory he was a century in advance of his age. Many of his ideas were repeated by Hugo in his *Préface de Cromwell*. Hugo, however, made use of these liberties in writing his plays. The only real advance in playwriting made by La Motte was his elimination of the confidant. His cast of *Inès de Castro* is delightfully free from this walking eartrumpet, which, when it speaks, voices platitudes. As La Motte says, scenes in which confidants appear are almost always disguised monologues. Racine had made his confidants much more important in the plot than they generally were in contemporary tragedy; but La Motte's attack upon this undramatic rôle and the practical application of the doctrine in his *Inès de Castro* are landmarks in the evolution of French tragedy.

The use of the confidant was one of the greatest handicaps under which these playwrights had voluntarily placed themselves. The confidant took over certain functions of the chorus when the choral rôle had lost its picturesque and dramatic functions. This character was a great convenience; but it was such a convenience that its rôle was abused. The scenes of narrative exposition, of elegy, of undramatic emotions were constantly staged between a principal and a confidant. The Greek chorus was always picturesque and often was employed to produce dramatic stage pictures. The opening of Sophocles' *Œdipus Rex* with the citizens of Thebes kneeling in supplication to the god-like hero forms a picture which is essentially dramatic. Such scenes were impossible when a single confidant had assumed the choral rôle.

Voltaire opened his *Œdipe* with a secondary character and a confidant; but he introduced spectacle in the second scene of the act, in which "the door of the temple opens and the high priest appears in the midst of the people." Racine himself had re-intro-duced a chorus on the stage in *Esther* and had employed the de-vice of opening doors to disclose a new scene in *Athalie*. Thus Voltaire was not entirely an innovator; but this imitation of Racine in these particulars foreshadows his future activity in introducing more spectacle on the French stage.

Voltaire's stay in England (1726-1729) brought him in con-tact with a theatre and a drama which had undergone a consider-able classical influence, but were still highly romantic in com-parison with theatrical art in France. Although he opposed the views of La Motte, on his return from England he was firmly convinced that more action and spectacle should be introduced into classical tragedies.

In his *Discours sur la Tragédie* he admits that French tragedy is conversation rather than the representation of an event. The excessive delicacy of the French forces playwrights to narrate events which they would like to expose to the eyes. The presence of spectators on the stage makes almost every action impracti-cable and causes the scenery rarely to be fitting to the play. The ghost of a Pompey or a Brutus could not appear surrounded by spectators ready to scoff at the unusual. The body of Marcus could not be brought before Cato, his father, as it is in the effec-tive scene in Addison's *Cato*. The parterre would howl. Ladies would turn their eyes away. A large number of characters is impossible on the French stage. Thus the effective scene of the conspiracy in Otway's *Venice Preserved* had to be dropped by La Fosse in his French adaptation, entitled *Manlius*.

The scene of Antony's oration in *Julius Cæsar* had delighted

Voltaire and he pointed out that the Greeks had hazarded just as daring actions. He did not wish to have the stage become a scene of carnage; but he did not see why certain situations, which seemed disgusting and horrible to the French, could not furnish a pleasure as yet unexperienced if handled artistically. He felt that the laws of decorum were not so important as the law of the three unities. To break the unity of action is to admit the inability to fill up a play with a single deed. To disregard the unities of place and time is to harm verisimilitude. But a horrible spectacle does not shock verisimilitude. In order to stage it, a great genius would have to put true grandeur by his verses into an action which would otherwise be disgusting.

So long as verisimilitude and the poetical, literary element were preserved, Voltaire was ready to experiment with new spectacular effects. He was ready to appeal to the eye as did the English, to pay more attention to the action; but he never swerved from the idea that "it is much more difficult to write well than to put on the stage assassinations, torture wheels, gallows, witches, and ghosts."

The stage direction appearing at the beginning of his play *Brutus* (1730) shows his first attempts to introduce scenery and spectacle: "The stage represents a part of the house of the consuls on the Tarpeian rock. The temple of the Capitol is seen in the background. The senators are assembled between the temple and the house, before the altar of Mars. Brutus and Valerius Publicola, consuls, are presiding over the assembly: the senators are ranged in a semicircle. Lictors with their fasces stand behind the senators." During the play the scene changes, or is supposed to change, to the interior of the house of Brutus and an apartment in the house of the consuls. In the fourth act the scenery at the rear opens, and Brutus is disclosed in a melodramatic manner. While Voltaire does not actually break the law of the unity of place, which he interpreted to mean a whole city, yet real changes or even supposed changes of place were as unusual as the spectacular picture with which the play opens.

The Senecan ghost calling for vengeance had long ago been discarded in France. This same ghost had entered English drama in the Renaissance, and had appeared dramatically in *Hamlet*. Voltaire had been greatly stirred by this scene when he saw it acted in London, and determined to employ the ghost on the French stage. In *Ériphyle* (1732) the ghost of Amphiaraus appears in the fourth act and bids his son Alcméon avenge his death at the hands of Ériphyle, his wife, and mother of Alcméon. In this manner Ériphyle is prevented from marrying Alcméon, who turns out to be her son. Voltaire was surprised that this very decorous and classical ghost, which appears in broad daylight merely for the sake of appearing, did not have the dramatic effect of the ghost in *Hamlet*. He did not realize that it is one thing to see a ghost on the stage and quite another to have the appearance of a ghost set in motion a psychological conflict in the soul of a man. Voltaire never understood why the technique of Shakespeare was dramatic. He only realized that there were effective scenes in Shakespeare. As a result, under Voltaire's hand these scenes and situations become, at best, strong *coups de théâtre*.

His *Mort de César* (played publicly in 1743) gave Voltaire an opportunity to imitate the scene of Antony's oration over the dead body of Cæsar which was disclosed to view. The audience was not greatly impressed by this pale and distant imitation, which retains only the external trappings of the dramatic original. When the sound of a cannon announced in *Adélaïde du Guesclin* (1734) that Nemours had been put to death, and when Nemours appeared with his arm in a sling, the audience was entirely recalcitrant. Perhaps the parterre also chuckled because Nemours was not really dead after all. Not until 1765, when the play was revived, was a French audience willing to have climaxes brought about by sounds. A few months afterwards the three knocks at the door were to cause the climax of the *Philosophe sans le Savoir*.

Gresset, under the influence of English drama, produced his *Edouard III* (1740) in which a murder takes place in plain view of the audience. Voltaire had not dared to stage a murder even in his *Mort de César*. Two years after, however, in *Mahomet*, Voltaire has the scenery open and disclose an altar. Séide "goes behind the altar where Zopire is" and strikes him down; a moment after Zopire appears, leaning on the altar, having risen from behind the altar where he has received the blow. Zopire dies as the act ends. Voltaire thus stages a murder according to the rules of decorum; but at least he is putting on the stage everything he dares at the time when theatrical audiences are vociferous in their condemnation of novelties which could be made ridiculous. Death scenes always border dangerously upon the comic even when played with the greatest art and care. According to Voltaire the French audience did not want "new pleasures." He had to introduce new effects with great caution.

Sémiramis (1748) with its carefully devised and spectacular setting and stage pictures, its four changes of scene, and the appearance of a ghost, resembles in many ways a melodramatic opera. Concealed identity and recognitions form the basis of its plot. Voltaire employed such situations with more artistry than did Crébillon, but he none the less accepted them as material to furnish *coups de théâtre*. Even in his *Mort de César* he attempted to make the situation more poignant by having Brutus discovered to be the child of Cæsar. Whether or not this heightens the tragedy, it produced a totally different play since the murder of Cæsar is made a problem of parricide. In *Mérope* a mother is about to murder an unrecognized son. In *Sémiramis* the queen, with the help of Assur, has murdered her husband Ninus. She falls in love with a brave young warrior, Arsace, who turns out to be Ninias, her son. The shade of Ninus orders Ninias to avenge his death. The son, thinking to kill Assur, slays his mother in the darkness of the tomb. The play is magnificent, spectacular melodrama, filled with complications and *coups de théâtre* in every scene. It speaks to the eye and to the ear and to the emotions, but not to the soul.

Although Louis XV gave a large amount of money for the mounting of the play, the spectators on the stage interfered with the effectiveness of the production at the first performance.

They were removed for the succeeding performances; but the problem of seats on the stage still remained, as this reform was only temporary. When Voltaire's *Oreste* was produced in Paris it was necessary to leave out the cries of Clytemnestra, which had made a great effect when the play was given at Versailles on a stage which, though small, was free of spectators. Voltaire was therefore untiring in his efforts to clear the stage for scenery and action; and finally in 1759, through the generous subvention of 10,000 livres given by the Comte de Lauraguais, the comedians agreed to remove the seats. At last the stage was cleared for action and spectacle.

CHAPTER XIV

TEARFUL COMEDY. DOMESTIC DRAMA

THE immediate successors of Molière had a rich heritage; and, as is generally the case with heirs, they were content to enjoy their blessings without attempting to develop their fortune along new lines. In one respect, however, the evolution of the technique of comedy is patent. The playwrights show a marked tendency to satirize contemporary manners. Dancourt even introduced actual events into his plays. De Visé treated subjects based upon local incidents and characters. The farce comedies produced at the Théâtre Italien and later at the Théâtre de la Foire were up-to-date in their realism. As many of Molière's successors begin their careers as playwrights in these minor theatres, it is not surprising to find them producing plays for the Comédie Française which contain realistic satire of contemporary conditions.

This cynical realism brought forth comedies of contemporary manners, in which the satire is more concrete and less universal. It also had a direct influence on the ending of comedy. The plot is worked out to what seems a logical conclusion, instead of ending with a manufactured dénouement. In Dancourt's *Chevalier à la Mode,* the gay, deceiving Chevalier is unmasked finally by his own mistakes, after having lied himself out of many embarrassing situations.

Le Sage produced in *Turcaret* a notable example of dramaturgic skill in that generation. The play deals with the machinations of an unscrupulous and amorous farmer general, duped by a frivolous baroness, who, in turn, is the plaything of a chevalier who extracts from her the money she cajoles from Turcaret. In the end two servants triumph in this cynical game of love and high finance. The dénouement is not only dramatically effective and bitterly logical, but also realistic in view of the prevailing social conditions.

The reaction in the form of sentiment or sensibility against this cynical tone was bound to come and it appeared sporadically even before the Regency. La Bruyère had wondered why people laugh freely but are ashamed to weep in the theatre. This was in 1688. By 1733 La Chaussée began to produce *comédie larmoyante* (tearful comedy) in which humorous scenes are episodic. However seriously we moderns may interpret certain scenes in Molière's plays, he never devised a situation or wrote a line that was a bid for tears. In praising the *Misanthrope* in his *Art Poétique*, Boileau reaffirmed the rule of the separation of tragedy and comedy, which he styled "the enemy of sighs and tears." But sighs entered comedy bringing tears in their wake.

An early example of the introduction of sentimental scenes into comedy is found in Baron's *Andrienne* (1703), an adaptation of Terence's *Andria*. For the first three acts the *Andrienne* is practically a translation in verse of the original. *Andria* is distinctly a comedy; but like so many Latin plays, its story is founded on a romantic situation of a clandestine love match between a young man and a long-lost child. As usual with Terence, the romance and sentiment inherent in the plot are carefully kept off the stage together with the heroine. The scenes selected for representation are humorous. Baron, however, brings the heroine on the stage in the fourth act. She is recognized by Criton in a scene which is not comic. Then she laments her state of injured innocence to Dave and finally kneels before Chrémès, her unknown father, begging him to recognize the validity of her marriage contract with Pamphile. Chrémès is strangely agitated by the *voix du sang*, which will talk so loudly in sentimental comedy of later years. These scenes of sentiment and tears are more restrained than in later comedy; but their introduction by Baron shows the tendency to represent the romance and sensibility inherent in the plots of Latin comedy.

Destouches, even in his early plays, showed a tendency to

moralize and to react against the cynicism of contemporary comedy. In England, from 1696 when Cibber's *Love's Last Shift* had introduced sentimental comedy to an audience which wept "honest tears," there was a marked trend toward the drama of sensibility. From 1717 to 1723 Destouches lived in England and was one of the first Frenchmen to find something to admire in English plays. In 1736 he adapted Addison's *Drummer* for the French stage under the title *Le Tambour Nocturne;* and he praised English drama in the preface. How much or how consciously he was influenced by the trend of sensibility in England is hard to tell; but his sojourn in London would tend to strengthen the tendency toward moralizing which he had already shown. His *Philosophe Marié* (1727), founded upon his own secret marriage, is a serious comedy. In the *Envieux* he has one of the characters speak of this play as one which causes "serious emotions" and which breathes "honor, modesty and virtue," and which contains "serious characters."

The real transition between comedy and *comédie larmoyante* is found in Destouches' *Glorieux* produced just a year before La Chaussée's *Fausse Antipathie* (1733). The plot is partly based upon a romantic situation of a father who has lost his fortune and who has two children who have not seen him for years. His son is proud and pompous. The daughter does not know who were her parents and has been brought up in a convent as a child not of gentle birth. At the opening of the play, she is half servant, half companion to the daughter of a newly rich bourgeois, who shows her too marked attentions, which she virtuously rejects. She is loved by the son of the household; and in spite of her supposedly humble condition, he offers her honorable marriage in scenes which are distinctly of the sentimental type. Her brother, unknown to her, is in love with, or at least willing to marry the daughter of the rich bourgeois.

The humor of the play is furnished by the overweening pride of the young Tufière, by the bourgeois, and also by the inevitable valet. The humor outweighs the sentiment. Yet there are several scenes of emotion such as the recognition between the father and daughter; and the scenes in which the father breaks his son's pride and brings about his repentance are by no means entirely comic. To transform such plays into tearful comedy it is only necessary to emphasize more strongly the romantic, sentimental elements of the plot and make the humorous scenes episodic.

This is precisely what was done by La Chaussée. One of the episodes in Regnard's *Démocrite* (1700) concerns Strabo whose wife drove him away by her shrewish manners. After many years they meet and fall in love with each other, until they discover their real relationship, when they promptly despise each other. Finally, they are reconciled, deciding after all that they may as well live together. Where Regnard saw cynical humor, La Chaussée saw material for sentimental comedy. In the *Fausse Antipathie*, Léonor and Damon fall in love with each other. Damon is willing to divorce his wife, whom he has not seen since the day of his marriage when he fled after a duel. Léonor, the virtuous wife, is not willing to divorce her husband, who, she learns, is alive after having been believed to be dead. Yet she loves Damon deeply. At the end of three acts, they find that they are the couple married years ago and separated by the unfortunate duel.

The play was successful. A new kind of drama was recognized. The usual literary battle ensued as to whether this new form was legitimate or not. Comedy had begun to arouse tender emotions instead of laughter by presenting a new series of scenes. Terence was cited by the defenders of this new kind of drama as authority for the procedure of arousing sentiment by the representation of incidents in the lives of ordinary people. However, if La Chaussée is to be compared with any classical playwright, it is not Terence but Euripides whom he resembles in his choice of scenes to be placed on the stage. The situation in the *Fausse Antipathie* is exactly the situation in Euripides' *Helen*, when Helen and Menelaus meet and do not recognize each other. Madame Argant persecutes Marianne not knowing she is her own daughter (*L'École des Mères*). She believes that Marianne is the mistress of her husband. In a similar way, Creusa in *Ion* is ready to slay her own child because she believes that he is the illegitimate child of her husband. Euripides, Terence and La Chaussée founded their plots on the same kind of romantic situations of disguises and concealed relationships. Euripides chose the scenes which arouse tragic emotions, bordering upon sentimentality. La Chaussée selected the same scenes, but aroused only sentimental emotions. Terence disregarded such scenes and represented the situations which arouse laughter. Only super-sentimentalists of the eighteenth century, whose sensibility could be excited by the sight of a dead donkey, could really malign Terence by asserting that his plays are the justification of tearful comedy.

The disappearance of the element of comedy and of the comic rôles of the valet and the soubrette is more or less complete in La Chaussée's plays, until in *Mélanide* there is no humorous line or rôle. In all his dramas the comic is episodic. He presents problems of family life and marriage. He differs from modern writers of serious drama in the fact that he is prone to surround his problems with the romantic atmosphere of concealed relationships of people who have changed their names. Thus the problem is generally non-existent, if the truth be known.

In *Mélanide,* for instance, the heroine has come to live with Dorisée. Mélanide's nephew, Darviane, has fallen in love with Rosalie, Dorisée's daughter, who is also wooed by the rich Marquis d'Orvigny. Mélanide agrees to send her nephew away. His lack of fortune makes his marriage impossible. Mélanide was separated years before from her lover, the Count d'Ormancé, by whom she had a child. She sees Orvigny (off-stage) and recognizes her former lover, Ormancé. The Count is informed by Théodon of Mélanide's presence; but he refuses to give up Rosalie. Mélanide at last allows her supposed nephew to guess that he is her illegitimate child. She bids him respect the Count. In a dramatic scene the young man forces the Count to admit that he is his father. Father and son then are rivals; but when

Ormancé finally sees Mélanide, his love for her is revived and Rosalie's hand is bestowed upon their son.

Much of the technique of these plays depends upon the unveiling of the past, not merely for exposition and dénouement, but for the purpose of developing the action. The plot unfolds swiftly. The spectator is kept in suspense, theatric though it may be, by the air of mystery surrounding certain characters. Each disclosure is interesting and brings in its wake a development of the plot. The scenes are carried on by the chief characters. The rôles of servants are materially reduced. Thus the first scene of *Mélanide*, in which the two mothers are discussing the marriage of their children, is more dramatic than it would have been had the situation been explained in the usual manner by secondary characters.

La Chaussée believed that plays should be a series of emotional crises of sentiment. But they are not studies of real problems of marriage and family life. Their plots are too complicated and the situations are too strange. The mistakes in identity are often trumped up. The characters are not sufficiently motivated. Mothers dislike their children merely for reasons of plot. La Chaussée sometimes has to hurry a character off the stage in order that he may not discover the actual state of affairs before the fifth act. Thus his plays consist of correcting external mistakes and delusions under which his characters are laboring, instead of solving psychological problems which confront most people in married life.

Supposedly his characters are normal individuals of the upper classes. They are respectable and very virtuous. The ingenue of unbelievable innocence and virtue is a child of La Chaussée. His men and women are persons such as most theatre-goers imagine themselves to be; but they are in curious situations in which normal people almost never find themselves.

His plays were successful because they presented scenes which aroused sentiment and caused tears that were not hot or bitter, and because the characters seemed to be more like ordinary citizens than did the heroes and heroines of tragedy. Tearful comedy also differed from contemporary tragedy in its dénouement which was happy, and in its general tone, which was sentimental, not tragic. But the plots, the scenes represented on the stage, and the construction of tearful comedy resemble the technique of the contemporary tragedy. La Chaussée was an eighteenth-century Euripides.

Gresset's plays maintained the serious tone. His *Méchant*, inspired by Congreve's *Double Dealer*, is a rather sombre comedy, while his *Sidnei* is a study of a romantic hero meditating suicide, perhaps inspired by *Hamlet*. The French were becoming fairly well acquainted with English drama, through reviews and excerpts from plays in journals and the free translation of English plays by La Place, Patu, Bocage and others.

La Place presented the English arguments against the unities in the preface to his *Théâtre Anglais* (1745). He advocated more action, more attention to scenic details and less narration in the French theatre. He suggested that the same liberties allowed in opera be permitted in classical tragedy. Had his ideas been followed, romantic tragedy would have resulted; but bourgeois tragedy and the *drame* were the products of English influence at this time. It was not Shakespeare or Dryden, but Lillo and Moore who furnished the models for French bourgeois drama.

On the third day of April, 1792, a play entitled *The Lamentable and True Tragedy of M. Arden of Feversham in Kent* was entered on the Stationers' register and was published anonymously, probably after having been acted seven years before. It was a domestic tragedy founded upon an incident recounted by Holinshed in his *Chronicles of England, Scotland and Ireland*. As a work of dramatic art, the play has little to commend it. The author follows the source very carefully, almost slavishly. From a less dramatic passage in the same *Chronicles*, Shakespeare constructed his *Macbeth*; but the author of *Arden of Feversham* did not aim to do more than to produce "a naked tragedy," as he calls it in the epilogue. In stark realism the play stands apart from the majority of contemporary tragedies which presented heroes of high rank and not ordinary citizens.

Several plays of this type have been preserved, such as *A York-shire Tragedy* (1608), *A Warning for Fair Women* (1599), and Heywood's *A Woman Killed with Kindness*. Others have been lost. The number of plays based on contemporary incident seems to have been small; but *Arden of Feversham* was an important step in the development of modern dramatic art because of its realistic and serious treatment of a situation involving bourgeois life and characters.

Alice Arden is in love with a certain Mosbie and plots to slay her husband as the play opens. After repeated attempts in which she and ruffians hired by her and Mosbie are unsuccessful, Arden is finally murdered by them in his own home while playing cards. The guilty lovers and their servants are apprehended and punished. Far too much of the play is given over to the attempts on Arden's life. Too many scenes merely tell a story where a modern dramatist would make a study of the motives of the crime. This is all the more regrettable because the character of Alice is drawn with some skill. The scenes between her and Arden and those between her and Mosbie are portrayed with dramatic effect. She is no lay figure nor bloody villainess, but a woman swept along by a passion against which she revolts. She is conscious of her sin and her conscience works dramatically. Her lover, Mosbie, also shows sparks of life; but Arden himself arouses little sympathy or interest. The framework of a modern realistic play was at hand, but the playwright was more intent on telling the whole story as he found it in Holinshed, than in analyzing a situation which will become the basis of countless modern problem plays.

The tendency in comedy to treat domestic problems seriously, the tendency in tragedy to get away from heroic, romantic situations, the moralizing and sentimental trend of both forms of drama combined to produce *The London Merchant* by Lillo. The reaction from the brilliant but cynical comedy of the Restoration was inevitable. Lillo felt that the time had come to enlarge "the province of the graver kind of poetry" which had dealt with the misfortunes of princes. He suggested that "plays

founded on moral tales in private life may be of admirable use
. . . by stifling vice in its first principles." He was undoubtedly
familiar with *Arden of Feversham* in 1731 for he adapted it
for the more modern stage in 1736.

Both plays are "naked tragedies" and "tales of private woe."
They are both founded upon fact, and stand apart from contemporary plays as being distinct innovations. *The London
Merchant* probably would not have been written in 1731 had it
not been preceded by a generation of sentimental comedy. But
the tragic ending of *The London Merchant* with the death of
George Barnwell, the sympathetic hero, differentiates the play
sharply even from comedy which caused a few honest tears to
fall in the middle of the play. The hero, a "London 'Prentice
ruin'd" is far below the social scale of the protagonists of South-
ern's *Fatal Marriage*, Rowe's *Fair Penitent* or Otway's *Orphan*
about whom there is a romantic glamour wholly lacking so far as
Barnwell is concerned. The historian can trace influences which
produced this play, yet *The London Merchant* impressed the
theatre-goers of 1731 as a novelty and as an innovation. It makes
the same impression today on the reader who has been studying
the English plays of the period. Not only is the atmosphere of
the play realistic, but the plot has the simplicity of modern realistic drama in comparison with the plots of contemporary tragedy
which generally combined a situation of criss-cross love affairs
with a political question.

The first scene is laid in a room in the house of Thorowgood,
an upright and highly respected London merchant. The dialogue
between him and his clerk, Truman, serves to bring out the
solidity, honor and power for good in the position of a merchant.
This is followed by a scene between the merchant and his daughter, Maria, showing the kindness of Thorowgood as a father and
the complete understanding between him and his daughter. The
next scene takes us to the boudoir of the courtezan, Millwood.
She tells her maid, Lucy, of the acquaintance she has made of
a certain George Barnwell. On the pretext of having an affair

of importance to discuss with him, she has tricked him into calling upon her.

Like the opening of modern realistic plays, these scenes are not introduced to give the exposition of the plot, but to create atmosphere and to depict the *milieux* in which the action is to unfold.

The innocent Barnwell arrives and succumbs to the wiles of the courtezan, who schemes to have him furnish money by robbing his employer, Thorowgood. The second act opens with a monologue by Barnwell, who informs us that, to the crime of guilty love, he has added the crime of theft. His tortured conscience is revealed when his brother clerk, Truman, tries to find out the cause of his evident unhappiness. But confession would betray Millwood whom he loves, not knowing her real character. Yet the kindness of his employer brings him to the point of avowal; but Thorowgood silences him with the words: "This remorse makes thee dearer to me than if thou hadst never offended; whatever is your fault, of this I'm certain: 'twas harder for you to offend than me to pardon." Millwood and Lucy are then received coldly by Barnwell, but she finally wins him back by playing upon his pity. She trumps up the false story that she has been ruined financially by her guardian and is homeless. Barnwell once more steals gold from his employer and gives it to her.

At the beginning of the third act, Thorowgood is asking an accounting from his clerks. Truman is ready. Barnwell has disappeared. Truman goes to seek him; but he returns with a letter from Barnwell confessing the embezzlement. He reads this note to Maria, who immediately plans to restore the missing sum, so that Barnwell's crime may remain undiscovered. It is now more or less plain that Maria loves Barnwell. The scene then changes to Millwood's house. Lucy describes at length the interview between Millwood and Barnwell and even quotes dialogue from this scene, which should have been acted on the stage. It is an obligatory scene and is given in direct discourse and in detail in the ballad on which the play is founded. Why an English dramatist of the period would merely report the scene is a mystery. However, Lucy tells Blunt how Barnwell arrived and threw himself on Millwood's mercy, how she rebuffed him as a stranger until he showed her a bag of gold, and how she persuaded him to rob and murder his uncle. Partially through fear, Lucy decides to prevent the deed, if possible. The next scene reveals the uncle's country seat. Barnwell is hesitating, but his passion for Millwood conquers. He dons a mask. His uncle appears. Barnwell cannot bring himself to shoot. He drops the pistol. His uncle suddenly perceives this masked figure. Fearing discovery, Barnwell runs him through with his sword. As the uncle dies, he asks a blessing upon his nephew and pardon for the murderer. These dying words bring instant and lasting repentance to Barnwell.

When the fourth act opens, Maria has made up the shortage in the accounts. Lucy has arrived and has told Thorowgood what she knows of Barnwell. The merchant finds difficulty in believing her story because Barnwell's account balances. However, he prepares to visit Millwood and face her with the accusation. Before he arrives, Barnwell comes in with hands still bloody, dazed but repentant. Millwood is furious because he has dared to come empty handed. She sends for an officer to arrest him as a confessed murderer. When Thorowgood confronts Millwood, she dissembles very cleverly. She admits Barnwell visited her house; but she asserts that he came to see her maid Lucy. She leaves the room to get proof of her story. Lucy and the officer enter. Millwood returns with a pistol but is overpowered. With very effective speeches she denounces society as the cause of her moral downfall. She comes very close to justifying, or at least to explaining herself. One is reminded of the fallen women on the modern stage. If such speeches are trite today, they were new in 1731. Lillo was intent upon his thesis, as well as upon the story.

Indeed, the fifth act, which passes in the prison just before the execution of Barnwell and Millwood, presents no great climax such as always occurs at the end of previous tragedies. The scenes present the results of Barnwell's previous course of action as they affect him and those about him. His resignation is dignified and pathetic without being mawkish. The scene in which Maria confesses her love for him is remarkably simple and effective, if some allowance is made for the sentimental age. Even in the depiction of Millwood, the dramatist has established an artistic balance. Had he followed the usual treatment of such characters, he would have made her repent, or he might have kept her the personification of evil and lust. But Millwood neither rants sentimentally nor glories in her crimes. She is stunned, overcome by her fate. Mercy is beyond her hope— almost beyond her wish. "She goes to death encompassed with horror, loathing life, and yet afraid to die; no tongue can tell her anguish and despair." Among contemporary paragons of virtue and of injured innocence, and among lustful tragic queens Millwood stands out as a real character. She has left a long line of descendants on the modern stage, beginning as far back as Marwood in Lessing's *Miss Sara Sampson* down to Shaw's Mrs. Warren.

The language of the play is overwrought in many passages; the moral is pointed too plainly; asides and monologues impair the subtlety of many scenes. Yet the play has a modern flavor. The prose in the dialogue, in spite of its overadornment, strikes a very different note from that of heroic verse. The point of departure is a theme, a problem of life, not a story. In tone and construction, *The London Merchant* resembles many social dramas produced after the reaction against the well-made play of the last century had set in and frequent changes of scene, avoided by the French and by English dramatists under the influence of Ibsen, were once more allowed. *The London Merchant* does not remind one of plays produced before 1731, but of dramas of Lessing, Diderot and Sedaine.

Moore's *Gamester* (1753) was unimportant in the development of contemporary English drama, but had an influence on French drama. It is a tragedy in prose dealing with the downfall of

Beverly through gambling and through the villainous machinations of his false friend, Stukely.

What Lillo and Moore had done in England, Diderot wished
to do in France, for he considered *The London Merchant* a
"sublime thing." Moore's *Gamester* may well have been in his
mind when he lauded the dramatic effect of a "passion which
leads a man to his ruin, from his ruin to despair, from despair
to a violent death." He made a free translation of the play in
1760 which was not played. In 1762 Bruté de Loirelle made
another translation, and Saurin produced successfully in 1768
an adaptation of *The Gamester* entitled *Beverlei*. The frequent
adaptations of these two English plays and Diderot's enthusiasm
are evidence that they are important forces in the development
of the *drame* in France, which has been defined by Professor
Gaiffe as "a spectacle intended for a bourgeois or popular audience and presenting a moral and affecting picture of its own surroundings." The appellation *drame* had been applied to *Mélanide*
in discussions of the play, but Beaumarchais' *Eugénie* was the
first piece officially entitled *drame* by the author.

Bourgeois or domestic drama had been produced by Landois
in his *Sylvie* (1741), a one-act tragedy in prose, which was a
failure. The preface, a prologue in dialogue form, anticipated
Diderot's theories to some extent in regard to stage setting and
acting; and Diderot recognized his indebtedness to Landois,
especially in regard to the use of stage pictures.

Landois admitted that to write a domestic tragedy in one act
in prose was to court failure; but he insisted that criticism of
such a procedure was due to unjustifiable prejudice. He ridiculed the regal heroes of tragedy, the sententious and heroic
lines, the flowery figures of speech, the dreams and the messenger.
He held that tragedy departs so much from reality that if one
saw the French king and his court acting and talking as do tragic
heroes, one would think them crazy or indulging in a masquer-
ade. He instructed the actors not to go beyond a natural manner of acting. His characters were not to advance to the footlights to spout moral commonplaces and heroic rodomontades.

Without wishing to keep great heroes off the stage, he imagined that one could present persons who would be of greater interest, because their life was more closely related to that of the audience. Such are the theories, briefly stated by Landois, which were to be discussed at length some years later by Diderot in his *Entretiens sur le Fils Naturel*.

Landois' play deals with a man who is convinced of his wife's infidelity. The curtain rises on a scene in a bare room. The husband, Des Francs, has summoned his wife, Sylvie, to appear before him. He believes that she is feigning a stupor. In the meantime a friend, Des Ronais, appears. Des Francs tells him that he has surprised his wife with a certain Galouin, whom he wounded, but who escaped. Des Ronais insists upon Sylvie's innocence. He himself was dining the night before with Galouin and Sylvie. When he has left, Sylvie appears in a half stupor. Her husband accuses her in a scene that has a good deal of suspense and dramatic power. He takes her stupefied innocence for clever feigning. He offers her the choice between death by poison or by a hunting knife. She protests her love for him. At last, overcome by his emotions, he attempts to commit suicide. Des Ronais arrives in time to stop him. He has seen the dying Galouin, who confessed that he bribed Sylvie's maid to drug her. Sylvie is innocent. But the French audience was not ready for bourgeois tragedy, in one act, in prose. The play failed and was forgotten by everyone except Diderot. Yet the dramatic theories which it exemplified lived on and *Sylvie* is one of the stones in the foundations of modern drama.

Diderot was a realist a century before the word was used as a critical term. In 1748 he said in the *Bijoux Indiscrets:* "The perfection of a spectacle consists in the imitation of an action, so exact, that the spectator, deceived without interruption, imagines that he is present at the action itself." Classical tragedy, he felt, had passed its highest point of perfection. The plot was so complicated that only through a miracle could so many events happen in so short a time. It was unnatural because of the stilted manners of the actors, the oddness of their costumes, the extravagance of their gestures, the emphasis of the strange, cadenced, rimed dialogue. Also, tragedy was unnatural because the author made mouthpieces of his characters, and because the actors stood in semi-circles, always faced the audience, and almost never sat down.

Diderot became the advocate of realistic domestic tragedy and of the *genre serieux*—plays which are neither tragic or comic. "Do you not realize," he says, "the effect produced by a real scene, true costumes, dialogue fitting to the action, simple plots, dangers which must have made you tremble for your relations, your friends, yourself? A reversal of fortune, fear of ignominy, the results of poverty, a passion which leads a man to his ruin, from his ruin to despair, from despair to a violent death are not unusual events; and do you believe that they would not affect you as much as the fabulous death of a tyrant or the sacrifice of a child on the altars of the gods of Athens or of Rome?"

Believing in realism and that the function of art was to reveal the chain of cause and effect in nature, Diderot wished to retain the unities. Mercier, alone, of the theorists of the latter half of the eighteenth century, attacked the unities. It is not classical, nor realistic, but romantic drama which finds the unities an obstacle in presenting dramatic action. The observance of the unity of place was not to preclude a reform in stage setting and the possibility of changing scenes. Diderot objected to the presence of spectators on the stage which allowed only a back drop for scenery. It was also "unreal" to him to have conspirators against a prince meet in the very room in the palace where the prince had just been consulting them on a most important affair. The setting, therefore, should change every time that the scene changes, and every change should mark a new act. The play would be easier to follow, more varied and more interesting. Since the scenery was highly developed at the opera, he saw no reason why it should not be introduced on the dramatic stage. "In order to change the whole conception of drama," he says, "I would only ask for a very large stage where one would show, when the subject of a play demanded it, a large square with the adjacent edifices, such as the peristyle of a palace, the entrance of a temple, different places distributed so that the spectator would see the whole action and so that there would be a place behind the scenes for the actors."

Just such a setting had been specially constructed for Voltaire's *Sémiramis* under the influence of stage decoration for opera. This scheme is practically the simultaneous setting of the medieval theatre; and in describing the possible action of a domestic tragedy, Diderot imagined a setting consisting of two rooms separated by a space. He would have on the stage, in direct defiance of tragic decorum, a bed, a mother and father asleep, a crucifix, the dead body of a son, scenes alternately in dialogue and in pantomime.

In order to bring dramatists closer to the truth in their plots and dialogue, and actors closer to natural action and declamation, he insisted that the setting should be exact. If the scene is in the salon of Clairville, as in his *Fils Naturel*, the salon of Clairville must be transported on the stage as it exists in real life. (Antoine and Belasco who bought interior furnishings of real rooms and placed them on the stage were not such innovators as has been believed.) The utmost simplicity, however, should reign unless the play demands expressly the contrary, so that there may be no distraction to the eye. (Only in the last four years have modern producers rediscovered this valid theory set forth by Diderot.)

A room on the stage had a fourth wall in Diderot's imagination; but it was placed behind the audience in the parterre. He did not make the naïve blunder of our modern realists who imagine a transparent fourth wall built in the proscenium. He wanted a fireplace in the side wall, instead of in the rear centre; but he would not have put it in the footlights, nor would he have placed chairs with their backs to the audience in the extreme foreground, as do modern realists. He was enough of a realist to know that we do not see the back of furniture which stands against a wall.

Diderot's theory of the fourth wall was a legitimate conception. It meant that the spectator was *in* the room, not *outside* of it, and endowed with X-ray eyes. Hence, the movements, attitudes, facial expression of the actor assumed an importance in his scheme that they never had possessed in tragedy or comedy. Actors of his generation moved in a stagy manner, with exaggerated gestures. The art of facial expression was in its infancy. The actors rarely sat down, but stood in a semi-circle and faced the audience. Stage pictures were only spectacles. They did not have a psychological value. They did not help to tell the story. Their emotional value was negligible.

Under Diderot's theory that the invisible spectator is present in the room, the actor was to betray the state of his soul by acting. "He speaks, or is silent, he walks or stops, is seated or standing, appears in front of me or on one side. . . . What difference does it make that he turns his back on me [the spectator], that he looks at me, or that, in profile, he is in a chair, his legs crossed, and his head in his hands?" His aim was to substitute real people for the usual mannequins, walking with measured steps, acting according to wooden rules, but which got out of the picture and sought applause by addressing the parterre.

Such ideas, together with his work as an art critic, naturally led Diderot to discover and insist upon the value of the stage picture, which he defined as "an arrangement of persons on the stage so natural and so true that, rendered faithfully by a painter, would please me on canvas." Theatrical art was to learn to execute "other pictures than those which had been seen for a century." In painting, artists were telling pathetic and senti-mental stories on their canvases. So actors were to be grouped, not only to be pleasing to the eye, but also to produce the correct emotional atmosphere. Indeed, the new domestic tragedies of the time seem to have actually reproduced contemporary paintings on the stage. The stage pictures became an integral part of the play. They helped to tell the story.

The pictures led to pantomime. Diderot knew many rôles and he used to close his ears and see if the acting misled him. Few players, he found, could undergo successfully this test of their ability. With his customary enthusiasm, he exclaimed of the sleep-walking scene in *Macbeth*: "There are some sublime gestures which all the resources of oratory can never express. . . . I know of nothing in discourse more pathetic than the silence of that woman and the motion of her hands. What a picture of re-morse!" After Clairon's performance in *Tancrède* (1760), he wrote to Voltaire: "Ah, my dear master, if you could see Clairon passing across the stage half fainting in the arms of the execu-tioners who surround her, her knees bending under her, her eyes closed, her arms falling stiff by her side as though she were dead; if you heard the cry she utters when she perceives Tan-crède, you should be more convinced than ever that silence and pantomime sometimes have a pathos to which all the resources of oratory can never attain."

Thus a new source of artistic emotion was introduced on the French stage. "The great art of silence," as Voltaire called it, was fully appreciated for the first time. For Diderot, effective panto-mime was more artistic than poetical dialogue; but Voltaire maintained that a monologue written by a Racine is finer than any theatrical action that can be devised. Diderot advocated that scenes of pantomime alternate with scenes of dialogue. Manuscripts of plays began to be filled with state directions. The supremacy of the literary element in drama was challenged. The playwright no longer had to be a poet or even a man of literary ability.

The difference between the points of view of Voltaire and Diderot can be illustrated by an episode in Racine's *Britannicus*. At the beginning of the second act, Nero describes how Junie was abducted and brought to the palace at his command. A helpless woman, surrounded by brutal soldiers, she subdued the brutal emperor by her timid innocence; and, with her eyes glis-tening with tears, in the light of the flickering torches she passed unharmed from his presence. The narrative in harmonious Alexandrine lines is effective dramatic poetry; but just such scenes as this lend themselves to dramatic action. After the middle of the eighteenth century, a playwright would be likely to turn Racine's poetry into prose stage directions. Instead of being described at the opening of the second act, the scene would be acted at the end of the first act, possibly without one word being spoken. Instead of writing descriptive narrative lines, the playwright would rely for his effects on the suspense aroused by the pantomime and by the dramatic series of stage pictures inherent in the scene. Only those who prefer to read plays will insist that the modern audience is to be criticized because it wishes to see such events instead of hearing them described, even in poetry written by Racine.

It is true that when the dénouement of Racine's *Iphigénie* was put into action in 1769, it failed to please the audience. This experiment, however, shows plainly the trend of dramatic art at that time towards action and away from poetical narration, although the wrong scene was evidently selected for representation in this experiment.

Dialogue, according to Diderot, was to be in prose. It was to be a transcript of speech in real life. Under strong emotion, the sentences were to be broken into phrases. "The violence of a thought cutting off respiration and bringing confusion to the mind, a man passes from one idea to another; he begins a multitude of discourse, he does not finish any." . . . The long tirades of tragedy were frowned upon as stopping the action, and when the action is suspended the stage is empty. He states a theory which La Chaussée had put into practice almost a generation before. Under the influence of his intense emotion Durval in the *Préjugé à la Mode* speaks in broken phrases in the manner described by Diderot.

Since Diderot believed in the chain of cause and effect in nature, much of his technical theory was founded upon this idea. "Dramatic art," he said, "prepares for events only to link them; and it links them in its productions only because they are linked in nature." His point of attack, however, was not chosen in relation to this theory. Holding to the unity of time, he was not free to begin the play more than twenty-four hours before the close.

Stage pictures, pantomime, pathetic and dramatic scenes, such as the opening of Sophocles' *Philoctetes* which he cites as a model, were considered the best means of exposition. He was in favor of letting the spectator into the secret of the whole situation and even of the dénouement. The interest would lie in the psychology of the characters in a given situation. Concealed relationships bringing about *coups de théâtre* were to be shunned. The spectator would be more interested if the relationship were known to him. His tears would flow sooner and not only at the moment when the characters themselves discovered their true identity. "Ignorance and perplexity excite the curiosity of the spectator and sustain it; but it is the things known and always expected which trouble him and agitate him." These ideas are an attack upon the plots of tragedy complicated in order to produce *coups de théâtre*. For complication, he would substitute simplicity; for *coups de théâtre*, stage pictures.

With his customary agility in suddenly appearing in the vanguard of an advance which bade fair to be successful, Voltaire produced his *Ecossaise* in 1760. The scene represents simultaneously the common room and a private room in an English café, although on the stage in Paris only one room was set to serve for both. A curtain was dropped momentarily to represent the change of scene from one room to another. The location of the scene was a novel bit of realism. Few of the audience remembered that the scene of one of J. B. Rousseau's comedies had been laid in a café.

The play deals with a young Scotch girl, Lindane, who has lost both family and fortune. She is in love with Lord Murray, the son of the man who is responsible for her misfortunes. Through the machinations of Lady Alton, also enamored of Murray, she believes he has deserted her. The virtuous and modest Lindane refuses financial aid offered by the bluff and eccentric merchant, Freeport; but he goes bail for her when she is denounced by Lady Alton and arrested as a spy. Monrose, about whom hangs a mystery calculated to arouse suspense, learns from a newspaper that he is condemned to death for political reasons. The good-hearted landlord warns him that already the police are searching for him. He discovers Lindane to be his child and prepares to slay Murray, scion of the house which has ruined him. Murray enters. Swords are drawn, but Murray casts his at the feet of Monrose and holds out to him the pardon he has procured.

Such is the stuff that the *drame* and the later *mélodrame* are made of. There is the virtuous persecuted heroine, a long-lost child, in love with the noble son of a man who has persecuted her family; the scheming villainess, Lady Alton, who is seconded by the unscrupulous Frelon; the kindly landlord with his napkin, which was then a questionable realistic touch; the gruff but kind merchant who offers aid, while drinking chocolate and reading a newspaper. This "scene of the chocolate" was especially applauded for its realism. There is Monrose saved at the end by the necessary papers, when swords have been drawn for a duel. Each act ends with a climax—a "big curtain." In the first act, habitués of the inn gather for dinner and keep up a continuous chatter on politics and what not, in order to produce realistic atmosphere, as it would be called today.

Diderot's *Père de Famille* achieved success in 1761 and later in 1769. It is always on the verge of being dramatic and never becomes so. Diderot was too much of a moralist and a conversationalist to be a good dramatist. In this play and in his *Fils Naturel,* which he wrote to illustrate his theories of stagecraft, he succeeded in following his own precepts, except that his plots are more involved than the simple plot he advocated. The stage pictures, the pantomime, the emotional dialogue, the transcript of real life are all in his plays. Single scenes are effective, such as the opening of the *Père de Famille* showing the family anxiously awaiting the return of the son and the explanation of his absence. The worried father interrogating the servant, the daughter playing backgammon with the uncle, their trivial conversation concerning the game, the candles burning out in the dawn, this whole picture is very different from the eternal exposition of valet and soubrette, or hero and valet in comedy. But taken as a whole, these plays are not dramatic. The characters are overwrought; they talk too much; they weep too much; they act too much. The play is engulfed in a flood of emotionalism in praise of virtue. The success of the *Père de Famille* was due to the realistic treatment of scenes of family life which made the contemporary audience weep. La Chaussée's comedies were also being given frequent revivals during these years. Sentimentality was overflowing in the theatre.

The *drame* needed a dramatist. It found one in Sedaine. His *Philosophe sans le Savoir* (1765) is not only the finest example of the eighteenth-century *drame,* but may well be called the first modern drama, so similar is it to plays of the nineteenth and early twentieth centuries.

The curtain rises on a large business office in the home of Vanderk, a banker. Antoine, Vanderk's trusted clerk, finds his daughter, Victorine, weeping. When pressed for the cause of her tears, she confesses that she has heard talk of a duel to follow a quarrel in a café and fears that Vanderk, Jr., may be going to fight. It is the day before the wedding of Vanderk's daughter Sophie. Dressed in her bridal robes, Sophie interviews her father, pretending she is a client, to see if he recognizes her. He pretends not to know his daughter in a scene which is so restrained that it serves to bring out the charming atmosphere of the happy household without overstepping the bounds of sentiment.

Vanderk, Jr., enters. He is slightly distraught. Sophie presents him with a watch. The act closes with the following dialogue:

VICTORINE (to VANDERK, JR.)
  You have worried me a great deal. A quarrel in a café!
VANDERK, JR.
  Does my father know that?
VICTORINE
  Is it true?
VANDERK, JR.
  No, no, Victorine! (*Exit into the salon.*)

VICTORINE
Oh, how worried I am!

This restraint in dialogue, the suspense and foreshadowing brought out with such simplicity, the combination of happiness and tragedy hanging over a peaceful household are new and modern elements in dramatic art in 1765.

In the second act, Vanderk assures his son that the profession of a banker is honorable and of great value to the world. Young Vanderk is disturbed by the contemporary prejudice which makes only the nobility respectable. Vanderk discloses the fact that he is of noble birth. Sedaine then introduces Vanderk's sister, a fussy old lady who is obsessed by prejudice against all professions except those of law and the sword. Towards the close of the act comes a remarkable scene between Victorine and Vanderk, Jr., in which they talk of his watch, but in such a manner as to foreshadow the possibility of his death. He gives her the watch to keep until the morning.

VANDERK, JR.
And will you give it back to me?
VICTORINE
Surely.
VANDERK, JR.
To me alone?
VICTORINE
Why, to whom else?
VANDERK, JR.
To me alone.
VICTORINE
Why yes, surely.
VANDERK, JR.
Goodnight, Victorine . . . Good-bye . . . Goodnight . . . To me alone. To me alone.

It is a procedure of modern realists, especially of Ibsen and his followers, to express impending tragedy by indirect methods, to allow the audience to get by implication the dramatic emotions which are behind such common incidents of real life. The tragic atmosphere is heightened by being in contrast with the apparent triviality of the incident, while the very triviality of the incident makes the tragedy seem more real. The spectator enjoys making the necessary deductions from the simple words of the dialogue which become fraught with dramatic emotion.

The third act opens at dawn. Vanderk, Jr., is trying to leave the house without arousing anyone. The doors are locked. He arouses Antoine to obtain the keys, but his father has them. Vanderk, Sr., enters, and a strong obligatory scene ensues in which his son explains that he overheard a young officer brand business men as knaves and that he challenged the officer in a moment of impulsive anger. They are to fight with pistols. The father realizes that the duel must take place in spite of the fact that it is a barbarous custom and the result of a worn-out code of honor. He gives his son the necessary letters to enable him to escape to England if he still lives; and he sends him forth.

The sole incident in the fourth act consists in Vanderk, Sr., sending Antoine to the scene of the duel with instructions to help his son to escape if he lives, and if he is dead—to return and knock upon the door three times. The whole act is surcharged with suspense and impending tragedy. Preparations for the wedding continue, but the son is absent. Why? Victorine is tortured with apprehension. The old aunt fusses about nonessentials. Antoine almost loses control of his emotions. Madame Vanderk is happy; and yet—why is her son absent? The father is outwardly calm, controlled, but shows that his heart is breaking.

In the last act, a M. Desparville presents a letter of credit to Vanderk who pays it instantly without discount. Desparville is in trouble. His son is fighting a duel! Vanderk guesses the truth. As the business transaction is concluded, there is a knock at the door, then a second and a third. Vanderk betrays his agony only by one phrase: "Ah, sir! All fathers are not unhappy." The musicians arrive for the wedding. Antoine brings the word that both young men fell. Victorine breaks down. Vanderk starts to go to his dead son when the boy suddenly appears with his adversary, young Desparville. Vanderk, Jr., fired in the air when young Desparville had missed him narrowly. Both leaped from their horses, and an apology and reconciliation ensued. The knowledge of the whole affair is withheld from the rest of the household and the curtain descends quietly.

The *Philosophe sans le Savoir* is an excellent example of the results obtained from Diderot's theories when they are applied to drama by a man who is first of all a dramatist. Where Diderot failed in practice, Sedaine succeeded. Not since Racine, had any French dramatist been able to build a play full of dramatic suspense on such a simple situation, although simplicity of plot was constantly insisted upon by French playwrights and critics in theory. Marivaux alone employed uninvolved plots, but he did not aim to create suspense. He relied upon the brilliance of his dialogue and minute psychological analysis of character to hold his audience. Sedaine, however, creates suspense and maintains it to the end.

The power of the whole play is the result of simplicity and restraint. Sedaine's technique is the antithesis of the technique of contemporary tragedy. His dialogue is apparently only a skeleton. There is not a line of what would have been called "poetry" then or "literature" today. But each line implies a hundredfold more than it says. The virtue of his characters is brought out by what they do, not by long tirades, telling how virtuous they are. Their deep emotion is betrayed as much by what they do not say as by what they do express in words. After La Chaussée's and Diderot's outbursts, this is a great relief.

The climax of the play is ushered in by sounds, not by tirades of messengers or even of a principal character. Drama has proved that it is not necessarily a literary art.

Perhaps in one respect alone, the *Philosophe sans le Savoir* differs from a drama of the latter half of the nineteenth century.

Victorine is the transformed soubrette of comedy, just as Antoine is the tricky valet metamorphosed into the faithful confidential clerk. Victorine is in love with Vanderk, Jr. Much of the tragedy of the situation is brought out through her emotions; but she does not marry the son of her employer in the eighteenth century. Not until almost a century has passed is she finally married to this man of rank by George Sand in her sequel to this drama entitled *Le Mariage de Victorine* (1861).

Unfortunately for the future history of this new form of drama, the conservative actors at the Comédie Française did little to encourage Sedaine in spite of the success of this play. These *drâmes* required a new art of acting, and the comedians were so rooted in the tradition of their robust heroic declamation that they did not feel at home in these rôles which demanded simplicity and naturalness. Sedaine began once more to write plays for the Opéra-Comique, where he had attained his first success. The lesser theatres of Paris, where tradition was weaker but where the audience was less educated, became the sponsors of the *drame*.

The effect on the *drame* of being closely associated with comic operas and with pantomimes given with elaborate scenery and orchestral accompaniment was to cause it to become more melodramatic. Indeed, the term melodrama in the modern sense came into use during this period. In 1775 Rousseau applied the descriptive term *mélodrame* to his *Pygmalion* which is a monologue accompanied by music. The practice of sustaining certain passages of dialogue with music soon grew up in the lesser theatres on the Boulevard du Temple managed by Nicolet and by Audinot. These two impresarios produced spectacular plays and historical pantomimes with musical accompaniment, and the word "melodrama" began to assume its modern meaning of a play full of hair-raising adventures and unexpected *coups de théâtre*.

After such a play as the *Philosophe san le Savoir* this tendency toward the melodramatic is all the more regrettable. Beaumarchais' *Eugénie* was one of the few plays which carried on the ideals of the *drame* successfully, but Beaumarchais turned back to classical comedy in his two masterpieces the *Barbier de Séville* and the *Mariage de Figaro*. Just at the time when the valet and soubrette and all the other parts of the formula of classical comedy seemed on the wane, Beaumarchais, using the old tricks, produced marvelous examples of technical skill. He weaves the intricate action of the *Mariage de Figaro* through situation after situation, reaching climax after climax of the gayest farce comedy. And all through the play, Figaro delivers rapier thrusts to the Old Régime. The initial cause of the action is the fact that Almaviva wishes to exercise a medieval right at the marriage of Figaro to Suzanne. From this situation, explained in the first act with sparkling wit, arises a long series of complications and mistaken identities. The plot is a maze of intrigues; but the action is always clear, because the audience sees the whole machinery revolving smoothly. Beaumarchais produced a masterpiece because he combined wit, clever characters and skilful plotting in a play which contains a vital theme: the conflict between traditional authority and the rights of the Third Estate. There is no finer example in all dramatic art of a comedy founded upon an important theme, and containing, at the same time, a complicated plot which does not obscure the basic idea.

While the Comédie Française was holding strongly to classical tradition and to the rules of good taste, there was an increasing desire on the part of the French audiences to experience new thrills. Even in tragedy, Voltaire had catered to this taste, although circumspectly. The adaptations of *The London Merchant* and *The Gamester* were also very much softened. Mercier did not allow his Jenneval (Barnwell) to murder his uncle and thus turned the grim English play into a rather sentimental story of regeneration. The courtezan, Millwood, was also much reformed by Mercier. Saurin, in his *Beverlei* (*The Gamester*), transferred much of the interest of the spectator from Stukely, the villain, to his hero. The arch villain was still too strong for French taste, as were such characters as Millwood. Both Sedaine and Collé were inspired to draw plays from Dodsley's *Miller of*

Mansfield, which had been translated by Patu; but Sedaine in *Le Roi et le Fermier* and Collé in the *Partie de Chasse de Henri IV* kept the heroine pure, although in the original version she had been seduced by Lord Lurewell. A false marriage was almost the only fault allowed the virtuous heroines of the French *drame*. The themes involving adultery were left for the writers of the nineteenth century.

Secondary characters and changes of scene, especially within an act, were materially reduced in number by French playwrights in their adaptations of English plays. Scenes of comedy, risqué dialogue and lyric passages were carefully deleted. Yet in comparison with plays constructed in accordance with strict classical rules, the *drame* was much freer. Although the scene did not change with such frequency as on the English stage, under the influence of the Opéra-Comique and the Opéra and the pantomimes, the scenic element became important and changes of scene took place from act to act, provided the localities represented were not far distant from each other. Instead of the public square or the drawing-room of comedy, and the vestibule of a palace of tragedy, the *drame* showed the spectators forest scenes, interiors of peasant huts, the interior of a prison, etc.

Mercier and Marmontel both insisted upon the emotional effect of scenery. The trivial, sordid details so dear to the realists of the nineteenth century were emphasized in the settings for the *drame*. The scene, the stage picture and the pantomime of the first scene of Mercier's *Indigent* are described with great care. The stage represents a miserable room without a fireplace. The furniture is dilapidated. The broken windows are patched with paper. A lamp is burning low. Through a door is seen a young woman lying on a small bed. A man is weaving. He gets up to see if this woman, his sister, is sleeping. The noise of a lively party and music of an orchestra are heard. The man blows upon his cold fingers. One might believe that this is a modern play dealing with the lower depths of society in the style of the modern realists. Other scenes represent the apartments of a rich young man, a stair and a hallway in the same building. A scene in a notary's office, carefully set in all its confusion, is no unworthy predecessor of similar interiors described by Balzac with a wealth of commonplace details.

Such scenes are very different from the drawing-room of La Chaussée or even of Diderot. Some of the people who come and go in these surroundings are poverty-stricken; but the cynicism of the Regency had long ago given way to sentimentality; and these characters are too sentimentally virtuous to be realistic. They resemble closely the people of tearful comedy. They are in the usual ignorance of their real relationships. The problem is only superficial. The heroine in this case turns out to be the sister of her would-be seducer.

Thus the *drame* introduced realism in details of scenery, costume, dialogue and acting; but the plots and characters remained romantic in these realistic surroundings. Yet the *drame* was too realistic for the conservative actors of the Comédie Française. They did not wish to modify their routine methods. Such playwrights as Sedaine and Mercier were forced into the lesser theatre in Paris and into the provincial playhouses. The *drame* tended to become melodramatic, because it had to make its appeal to less intellectual audiences that wanted thrills and even shudders, provided they came wrapped in a romantic haze of triumphant virtue.

Sharing the stage with spectacular pantomimes and with melodramas, the scenery became more romantic, more thrilling and even grisly. Scenes of every description were represented with careful attention to details. Even lighting effects began to be developed, not merely to differentiate night from day in a realistic manner, but in order to give an added beauty. Favart in the *Moissonneurs* directed that "in the first act, the sky grows bright gradually, the morning mist disappears, the sun rises, etc." This is an early example of the light-scenario which plays such an important part in the modern theatre.

The *drame*, as conceived by Diderot and as written by Sedaine and Beaumarchais, was too realistic for the actors of

the Comédie Française; but it was not romantic enough for
the theatres on the Boulevards. Thus it was more or less absorbed by the melodrama; and the new combination, instead of
leading directly to such realistic plays as those of the younger
Dumas and of Augier, paved the way for the romantic dramas
of the elder Dumas and of Hugo.

CHAPTER XV

GERMAN DRAMA OF THE EIGHTEENTH CENTURY

THE Thirty Years' War left Germany in a deplorable condition. There was no intellectual centre, no flourishing capital where art and wealth could combine to produce drama. Theatrical activities were in the hands of nomadic troupes of actors. Repertory companies of English, French, Dutch and Italians toured the country, sometimes settling down more or less permanently at the court of some principality which had been created by the Peace of Westphalia. German troupes were also formed in imitation of these foreign companies and took over their plays in translation.

The repertory of these wandering comedians included many forms of drama: Italian *commedia dell' arte* and opera; pseudo-Shakespearean dramas, such as the *Bestrafte Brudermord;* biblical mysteries; farces; adaptations of Spanish and Italian dramas; French tragedy and comedy; and Dutch plays. Because of the custom of having the actors improvise much of the dialogue, the original authors would have recognized their offspring with difficulty.

The principal rôle on the German stage was that of the clown known as Hanswurst, Pickelherring or Harlequin. He appeared in farces and comedies as the important character and was even introduced into the serious plays as a humorous commentator on the plot and characters. In such a theatre it is not surprising to find coarse humor in place of comedy, blood-curdling horror in place of tragedy, bombast in place of dramatic dialogue. To bring forth a national drama, Germany had to build up a national spirit and an intellectual centre. Dramatic art had to have leaders who, by precept and example, would bring some order out of the theatrical chaos.

The nationalization of Germany became possible after the Peace of Westphalia. Leipzig became the artistic and intellectual centre in the first quarter of the eighteenth century. In 1724, Gottsched, a young Prussian, came there in order to escape the recruiting officers of the famous stalwart guards and to try to realize his ambitions to become chief-of-staff of the German intellectuals. He possessed the tenacity and the ability for organization of a Prussian drill sergeant. He made up his mind that German drama—indeed all literature—should be reformed according to the rules of French classicism, particularly as laid down by Boileau in his *Art Poétique*.

This decision and his efforts to carry out his plan were to bring down upon his head the wrath and contempt of many of his own generation. He was reviled as a worshipper of false gods. He lacked creative ability. His artistic sense was underdeveloped. Yet the German theatre needed drastic reform. Purification was necessary in every sense of the word. There were three forms of dramatic art which he might have chosen as a model for German drama: the Greek, the English, or the French. In selecting French drama he believed that he was including whatever the Greeks had to teach the moderns. The neo-classical form, more than English drama, offered the correctives of simplicity, of unity and of good taste which had to be applied to German dramatic art. The ideals of classicism may be narrow; but they are very valuable in drama, as in all art, in checking artistic Bolshevism. Had Gottsched set up the Shakespearean drama as the ideal, he would have misunderstood the content and have stamped his approval on a form which would not have offered correctives necessary for German drama at that time. In order to attain true liberty, without anarchy, it was well for the German stage to be ruled for a time by the absolutism of French classicism.

Gottsched suggested to Hoffmann, the manager of a troupe of actors, that he present translations of French tragedies; but Hoffmann felt that the German public would not support serious plays without the rôle of the clown. When Neuber and his talented wife took over the management of this company, they sought the advice of Gottsched on their arrival in Leipzig in 1727. He saw in them actors of high ideals. They had already tried the experiment of playing regular tragedies and comedies. They saw in him the avowed reformer of the German stage, who could guide them in their career. Thus a co-partnership between the practical and theoretical sides of dramatic art was formed.

A new repertory had to be created, and there were practically no German playwrights. Gottsched decided to have French drama translated and produced until the Germans could learn to write their own plays. Not a spark of originality was shown by Gottsched in his confession of faith—*Versuch einer Kritischen Dichtkunst* (1730)—in which he merely reiterated the ideas of Horace and Boileau. The adaptations and translations of French plays made by him or under his direction are mere hack-work. He built his *Sterbende Cato* (1731) out of fragments of Deschamps' *Caton d'Utique* and Addison's *Cato*. Yet in spite of its defects it achieved success and held the stage for many years. The repertory was published as the *Deutsche Schaubühne* (1740) in six volumes. The first three volumes contain translations of well-known French tragedies and comedies. The last three are devoted to plays by German authors such as Grimm, J. E. Schlegel and Frau Gottsched.

In selecting the French drama as the model, Gottsched did not intend to remain satisfied with the production of French plays. He was extremely patriotic and wanted to show the rest of the world that Germans, once having been given correct models, could produce plays as fine as those of any nationality. In his *Kritische Dichtkunst* (1730) he said that Germans would have to be contented with translations of French plays until they could develop their own dramatists. In the preface of the first volume of the *Deutsche Schaubühne* he insisted that Germany did not lack men capable of defending the national honor against the claims of the French. He was by no means a totally blind admirer of French drama. He encouraged the study and translation of Holberg's plays in which the bourgeois German could find more of his domestic environment represented than in French drama.

He fought, together with the Neubers, the difficult battle of driving the clown off the stage. Karoline Neuber wrote a one-act play which dramatized the banishment of Hanswurst from the stage. The clown frequently returned, for the German public delighted in his coarse jokes; but Gottsched's reform was finally effective, though after he had been discredited as a leader. In charging him with lacking originality, it must be remembered that when he attempted to reform the costume of actors, his idea of having actors dress in costumes of the period of the play was so novel that it met stony opposition. When the Neubers had broken off relations with their erstwhile guide, they lampooned his idea of exact costume by playing the third act of his *Sterbende Cato* with burlesque Roman costumes. The audience roared with joy. Real genius would have been wasted on a public that was not willing to accept simple reforms based on obvious common sense.

Deserted by the Neubers and attacked by Breitinger and Bodmer for attempting to impose rules of French classicism on German literature, Gottsched began to lose his power. Younger men, such as J. E. Schlegel, began to found their theories of dramatic art on Greek ideals and to admire Shakespeare's *Julius Cæsar* which was translated in 1741. Holberg's plays outstripped Molière's comedies in popularity. Under the influence of this Danish playwright, Borkenstein wrote *Der Bookesbeutel* (1742) which gave evidence that other plays beside the French were worthy of study and imitation. Thus the Gottschedian domination was severely shaken before Lessing arrived in Leipzig in 1746.

Lessing was closely affiliated for two years with the Neubers, who produced his comedy *Der Junge Gelehrte*. He became an intense student of dramatic art on the stage, and learned from observation and practice the possibilities and limitations of living drama. With Weisse he translated, among other plays, Regnard's *Joueur,* Voltaire's *Mariamne,* Marivaux's *Annibal* and, for some unknown reason, Thompson's dreary *Sophonisba*. He also planned and wrote fragments of many dramas as experiments in the art of playwriting.

His complete plays and scenarios of this period of apprenticeship show him to be strongly under French influence, especially that of Molière whom he always admired even when he attacked French classicism. He observed the unities and employed the conventional characters of French comedy, even giving them French names. Though it does not seem that he had read Shakespeare as yet, he was acquainted with Restoration drama. His scenario *Der Leichtgläubige* is founded on Wycherly's *Country Wife;* and Congreve's *Double Dealer* forms the basis of his sketch *Der Gute Mann*. However, he simplified the plots, as a French playwright would have done, by deleting characters and events which are not closely related to the main action. His conception of the unity of action was at least as severe as that of Voltaire, whom he admired and met in Berlin in 1751. If they talked on drama together they must have been in full agreement, although some years afterward Lessing attacked Voltaire's theories vigorously.

By 1750 he had reached the conclusion that Shakespeare, Dryden, Wycherly, Vanbrugh, Cibber and Congreve, who were known only by name in Germany, deserved admiration as well as the French poets; and he believed that if the German followed his own nature in dramatic art, the German stage would resemble the English more than the French. He did not include in this list George Lillo who was soon to exert a strong influence on Lessing, himself, through his *London Merchant*. Moore's *Gamester*, which was to be popular in Germany, had not yet been written.

In 1754 Lessing began to publish the *Theatralische Bibliothek*, and in the first number he included discussions of sentimental comedy by Chassiron and by Gellert. In commenting on this form of drama, Lessing took the ground that true comedy may contain both humorous and emotional scenes. He accepted the plays of Destouches, which were both comic and sentimental, but he rejected the purely tearful comedy of La Chaussée. Voltaire had expressed similar views in his preface to *Nanine* (1749). Later when Lessing had become acquainted with the theories of Diderot and had seen La Chaussée's *Mélanide*, Gresset's *Sidnei* and Mme. de Graffigny's *Cénie*, he changed his views and accepted purely sentimental comedy as a form of drama which gave legitimate pleasure.

Lessing was not in advance of his times in his theory. In practice, however, he was soon to outstrip the French dramatists, for in 1752 he was engaged in writing his *Miss Sara Sampson* (1755) under the influence of the English novel and drama. This play is a domestic tragedy, a kind of drama then known to the French only in the translation of Lillo's *London Merchant*, which was also translated into German, and played at Leipzig in 1754. Moore's *Gamester* was translated by Bode in the same year. Richardson's *Clarissa Harlowe* and *Grandison* were the sources for the idea, though not the actual plot of Lessing's play; but, unlike Lillo in *The London Merchant*, he did not dramatize a narrative story. He constructed his plot and selected his scenes with entire freedom. True to his theory of the similarity of taste in drama between the English and Germans, he not only treated a story laid in England involving English characters, but also employed a form of drama somewhat freer than the French.

The first scene represents a public room in an English inn. Sir Sampson and his faithful servant, Waitwell, have found that Sara Sampson, who has eloped, is there with her lover, Mellefont. Her old father is ready to forgive her. The scene changes to Mellefont's room. Mellefont upbraids himself for seducing Sara and carrying her away. His servant, Norton, mentions a certain Marwood, among other wicked women, on whom Mellefont has wasted his patrimony. Sara enters and pleads with Mellefont not to delay their marriage. For nine weeks he has been putting it off. In relating an allegorical dream, she foreshadows the course of the action. Mellefont seems to love her deeply, but he must delay their nuptials longer because of an inheritance which he would lose if he married her then. A letter arrives from Marwood. She is in the same town and demands an interview.

The second act takes place in Marwood's room at another inn. She is disclosed at her toilet, with her maid, Hannah. Mellefont is received warmly by her, but he repulses her. She seeks to win him back, trying all her weapons in vain. At last she brings in their daughter, Arabella. They kneel before him. He is shaken to whatever depths his being contains. He leaves, and Marwood believes she has won her game; but Mellefont returns, having "recovered his senses." He refuses to leave Sara. Marwood, Medea-like, threatens to slay their child. She draws a dagger and tries to stab Mellefont, who wrests the dagger from her. Marwood demands that she be allowed to visit Sara as a "Lady Solmes." Mellefont consents for no valid psychological reason. The dramatist has intervened to arrange a meeting which is an obligatory scene but is weakly motivated.

The third act opens in a room in the first inn. Sir William gives Waitwell a letter for Sara, which will assure her of his forgiveness. He chooses this method ostensibly to save Sara from embarrassment, but really so that the dramatist can stage a scene, which proves ineffective dramatically. Sara, seeing the letter, first jumps to the conclusion that her father is dead, and then says she cannot read a letter of forgiveness. A meeting of the father and daughter would have been much more dramatic than the interview between Sara and the old servant, which is full of sentimental shilly-shallying and curious psychology. The meeting of "Lady Solmes" and Sara, however, is well handled. The situation is charged with suspense. Marwood conducts herself as a lady. When she finds out that the fact that she has put Sir William on the track of his daughter has resulted in a reconciliation she withdraws, alleging faintness.

In the opening scene of the fourth act, Sara is radiant with happiness; but when she has left the stage, Mellefont doubts that he really wishes to marry her. He does not understand himself. Marwood arrives once more. She demands to see Sara.

Mellefont once more consents weakly. Marwood gets rid of Mellefont by a trick. The two women face each other in a scene that was to appear in many a modern drama. "Lady Solmes" pleads for Marwood; she discloses her past; she describes how Mellefont won her love; she tells of the child and begs Sara to be generous. Sara is deeply stirred, but revolts at the idea of giving up her lover. At last she throws herself on her knees before "Lady Solmes" begging her not to place her in the same class with Marwood. "Lady Solmes" discloses her identity. Sara, in terror, recognizes the woman with the dagger of whom she dreamed. She rushes wildly from the room. Marwood's monologue vaguely foreshadows her atrocious design to poison Sara.

In the fifth act Sara has recovered from her terror; but strange pains are seizing her. Mellefont returns. A letter is brought to him. It is from Marwood who is escaping to the coast. She has poisoned the medicine which Betty gave Sara. Sir William enters and Sara dies in his arms. Mellefont commits suicide with Marwood's dagger.

That the play scored a success on the German stage until it was overshadowed by *Emilia Galotti* (1771) is no cause for surprise. *Miss Sara Sampson,* although not flawless, is unquestionably the most powerful domestic drama of the century. Sedaine's *Philosophe sans le Savoir*—not yet written—was to be more artistic in its technique; but its climax depends on a mistake. Lessing's situation exists. It has none of the mistaken identities and the long arms of chance found in La Chaussée's manufactured plots. Marwood's disguise is perfectly legitimate, since it is not employed for purposes of dénouement. Lessing faced his tragic situation boldly and carried it through to an ending that is logical in its pathos. If the motivation of some of Mellefont's acts is weak, we must remember that he himself is an unstable weakling, given to lawless acts. It is far better to have the action unfold with such motivation, than to have the plot depend upon the mistakes and chance meetings which many plays had inherited from Roman comedy. There is too much didacticism, too much weeping, too much sentimentality for the modern stage; but in comparison with Diderot's tearful dummies or Lillo's preaching personages, Lessing's characters are very human in an age when the stage was dominated by didactic ideals and sentimentality. Even Lessing, artist though he was, decided for or against certain forms of drama partially on their power to teach morals and reform mankind. The opposition of the clergy in all countries to the theatre was responsible in a large measure for such false standards of dramatic criticism.

Many influences were operative in the construction of *Miss Sara Sampson*. Lillo had produced domestic tragedy and Lessing was inspired to emulate him in the unhappy outcome instead of producing merely a sentimental comedy. The mother of Lessing's Marwood was Lillo's Millwood. Sara, Mellefont and Sir William recall Richardson's characters of the same types. The virtuous heroine abducted or eloping with a Lovelace, her death, the sentimental tone can be ascribed to the vogue of *Clarissa Harlowe;* but the dominating factor in the actual situation is Seneca's *Medea*. Lessing studied Seneca carefully. As in *Medea*, a man is deserting a woman who is the mother of his child. She threatens to murder the child; and her language is manifestly Senecan in its disgusting details describing how she will cut up the child. She slays the bride with poison and escapes in triumph. Rightly, Marwood calls herself a "new Medea." If she is somewhat baffling in her brutality and in the sympathy she arouses at times, it is because we cannot understand a Medea in modern surroundings even though she be debased from a queen to a courtezan. Even Medea, as conceived by Euripides, was a strange barbarian to the Greeks.

No Frenchman would have written a play in 1755 dealing with the situation of *Miss Sara Sampson,* given it a tragic ending, and placed on the stage a heroine who had willingly given herself to her lover. The French would have demanded that Sara should have been tricked by a false marriage. They would not have accepted Marwood at all. They would not have allowed a change of scene within an act, and would have been loathe to permit the change from act to act. Yet the construction of the play is French rather than English because of its compactness. Lessing believed that the unities of time and place were not sacred rules, that they could be sacrificed, if necessary, as in Plautus' *Captives*. He changed the scene several times in *Miss Sara Sampson*, but not so often as did English dramatists in their plays. He observed the unity of time. He introduced no scenes merely for the sake of representing incidents of the story. He did not show Mellefont being led through the town by Marwood's accomplices, nor Marwood poisoning Sara, nor Marwood's escape. An English playwright would not only have represented such events but also might have placed the point of attack so as to include the decision of Sara to elope, in order to show more of the story in action. Lessing's point of attack is strictly classical. It is correctly placed just at the moment before the dramatic action begins. The initial cause is Marwood's plan to face Mellefont once more. As a result, the play shows more of the psychological reaction of events, the theme is more emphasized, characters are more carefully analyzed, than in English domestic drama. The play is compact and well made in comparison with *The Gamester* or *The London Merchant*. It is true that the English prototypes contain only one action as does the German play; but they are exceptions to the rule. English drama generally combined two actions or at least had more episodes than Continental drama.

The scenes of the German play are sustained discussions of the theme. They rise to climaxes gradually. The second scene between Sara and Marwood is especially fine in its change from tense calmness to the tragic outburst from Sara when she recognizes Marwood. It unveils the past with profound emotional effect. Lessing learned this dramatic method of telling a story from classical drama; but he also pointed the way to many scenes of this kind in modern dramas of Hebbel and Ibsen. Classical, but not so felicitous, is his use of the allegorical, foreshadowing dream. The device was threadbare even in his time. Diderot was soon to say: "The devil take this race of dreamers."

The servants which Lessing gave to each principal character stepped out of French comedy and assumed the rôles of confidants. Betty is the only one which is at all vital to the plot. Waitwell and Norton are mere sentimental moralizers. Had Lessing followed English drama entirely in constructing *Miss Sara Sampson,* he would probably have avoided none of the flaws in his play; and it might have lost much of its effectiveness as close-knit drama.

Lessing had given Germany a well-written domestic tragedy, a play dealing with family life without melodramatic scenes in a prison. By 1758 he was engaged in writing *Emilia Galotti* which was planned to be in three acts instead of the classical five. He intended to take advantage of all the liberty of the English stage. The next year found him attacking Gottsched once more for having introduced French tragedy as the model for German dramatists. His attacks on French drama were almost always confined to classical tragedy. He admired Molière and Destouches. He considered Diderot on a plane with Aristotle; and he acknowledged, even to the point of exaggeration, the debt he owed to this mediocre playwright but excellent critic, whose plays he translated into German. However, he proclaimed in 1759 the superiority of English tragedy over the French. "In our tragedies we wish to see and think more than the timid French tragedy gives us occasion to see or think. . . . The great, the terrible, the melancholy . . . affect us more deeply than the good, the tender, the loving. . . . Too great simplicity tires us more than too great complexity." He believed that Shakespeare was greater than Corneille; that Corneille was closer to the ancients in technique, but Shakespeare was nearer them in what is essentially tragic. Shakespeare was to become the model of the Germans. Lessing proclaimed his power; but he did not imitate the Shakespearean form in his own plays, even with the "modest alterations" which he admitted were necessary.

His *Minna von Barnhelm* is the most truly German comedy in spirit produced up to 1767. He reproduced in it the life and customs of his country. He created German characters and put them in a situation arising from the Seven Years' War, instead of taking them from the English or French stage. Franciska is no Lisette. The valet, Just, is not a Frontin. Werner, the landlord, is drawn from life. Minna and Tellheim are distinct personalities possessing more than the one trait of character shown by most people in classical comedy.

Yet the construction of the play is French. It observes the unities carefully. Unlike the action in contemporary English comedy, the plot of *Minna von Barnhelm* is uninvolved. Although Lessing had criticized the simplicity of French tragedy, he did not like the complex plots of English comedy "which distract and tire our attention." There is no trace of any English influence except that the episode of the rings recalls *The Merchant of Venice*. If Lessing prolonged the situations arising from the exchange of rings, he was simply juggling too deftly after the manner of French dramatists. Goethe justly admired the masterful process of the exposition of plot. Without detracting from Lessing's originality or skill, it may be said that Molière in his *Tartufe* had shown him the way. Also, Goethe pointed out the greatest defect in this otherwise well-built play. The secondary characters are too much in evidence in the third act. After Minna and Tellheim have met, the spectator wants to see them fight their charming battle of love and honor.

Lessing's dramaturgic skill is no less striking in his *Emilia Galotti* which is based on the story of the Roman maiden Virginia, slain by her father in order to preserve her honor. He modernized the setting by placing the characters in an Italian court of the eighteenth century; and many of the spectators must have thought in terms of contemporary German courts when they saw the play. The plot, unlike that of heroic tragedy, does not involve any political question; but since the characters are of high rank, it can scarcely be called a domestic tragedy. A romantic atmosphere pervades certain scenes, such as that in which Angelo, the bandit, plans the abduction of Emilia. The attack on her carriage and the murder of her lover, Appiani, although off the stage, are also devices belonging to the romantic playwrights.

Lessing observed the unity of time; but the scene changes from the Prince's palace to Galotti's house. No vitally important scene is kept off the stage; but an English dramatist would have shown the meeting of the Prince and Emilia in the church and also would probably have shown their first introduction to each other. Once more Lessing's training in the French school of dramatic art seems to have kept him from employing all the liberty and freedom of English drama. However, the features of French drama objectionable to Lessing are conspicuously absent. There are no confidants, declamatory tirades, nor messengers. The foreshadowing dream is reduced to a few lines. Odoardo stabs his daughter and her death occurs on the stage. The plot unfolds through events and not through the explanation of the reaction of the characters to the events, as it does in French tragedy.

The incidents which Lessing devised to advance the action and to develop the characters were effective and novel in the eighteenth century. The Prince shows his impulsive love for Emilia Galotti by granting a request to a woman because she, too, is named Emilia. Later, he is ready to sign a death warrant without looking at it, so absorbed is he in his new passion. Much of the exposition is given by having a painter bring to the Prince a portrait of Orsina, his mistress, and one of Emilia. To develop character and action by introducing incidents not closely connected with the plot is a method of modern playwrights but was a striking novelty in the eighteenth century. To make each act a unit ending with a distinct climax, as Lessing does, was also an important factor in the dramatic technique of the eighteenth century. The Frenchman, Sedaine, was the only dramatist up to this time who seems to have realized the value of this procedure. The English still made the scene the unit. For the French, the whole play was the unit; but Lessing and Sedaine understood the value of a climax just before an entr'acte curtain.

There are many touches of theatrical skill throughout the play.

Indeed, Lessing borders upon the melodramatic in the development of his action. Odoardo stabs his daughter in order to bring about a tragic ending. Emilia is in the Prince's palace. The Prince is a sensualist, but he does not offer her violence. Her father is fully informed of everything. The Prince insists that he must send his daughter to the house of the chancellor pending an investigation of the death of her fiancé. In order to justify the slaying of Emilia, Lessing has her beg for death because of the astounding confession that she makes: Grimaldi's house is one of revelry; she has felt its influence; she has a passionate nature and might not control herself! With no preparation, Lessing destroys the Emilia of the first four acts. If anyone should be killed by the outraged father, it is the Prince, not the innocent daughter; but he escapes with Marinelli, the real villain. It is neither Shakespearean nor Aristotelian. It is melodramatic. That the Lessing who insisted so strongly in the *Hamburgische Dramaturgie* on Aristotle's theory of logical probability, should so falsify character and situation for the sake of theatrical effect is very significant. Romantic tragedy and melodrama are in the air.

In Germany, as in France, Shakespeare was becoming a name to conjure with in the latter half of the eighteenth century when the attack on classical tragedy began. The age delighted in paradoxes and Shakespeare exemplified a dramatist who aroused tragic emotions without observing the "rules" of tragedy. He was the "voice of nature," yet he had not imitated the ancients in order to follow nature. Pope had come to the conclusion that the Aristotelian rules could not be the measuring rod for Shakespeare's plays. Shakespeare did not speak of nature but through her. Dryden said that Shakespeare "needed not the spectacles of books to read nature; he looked inwards and found her there." The German playwrights were soon going to be content to seek for nature in Shakespeare instead of looking either inwards or outwards.

Young, in his *Conjectures on Original Criticism* (1759), became the champion of Shakespeare. He was not the son of the ancients but their brother; "their equal and that in spite of all his faults." He was master of two books: the book of nature and of man. He was original, not an imitator. Young's treatise was translated into German twice, immediately after its publication. Kame's *Elements of Criticism* also were translated (1763-66) and the German scholars found in them the following ideas: Shakespeare is superior to all other writers in delineating passion and sentiments; his dialogue is the language of nature; his plays are defective in the mechanical part and are full of irregularities; but he excels all the ancients and moderns in knowledge of human nature; in drawing character, he is masterful.

These English estimates of Shakespeare were eagerly read and echoed in Germany. Wieland published a translation of his plays which, though inexact and defective in many places, offered an opportunity to become acquainted with the work of this natural genius, this voice of nature which sang untrammelled by rules. Lessing placed him on a plane with Sophocles, far above Corneille and Voltaire. Corneille's plays resembled the Greek drama in mechanics, Shakespeare's resembled them in spirit. Gerstenberg praised them as "pictures of moral nature." In spite of his defects, Shakespeare was a great artist. Such was the general verdict.

But that was not all. Gerstenberg and others pointed out that Shakespeare was great because he had imitated nature and had not followed the ancients. Lessing was willing to couple Shakespeare with Sophocles, but he was too profound an admirer of Aristotle and the Greek dramatists to admit that all rules, especially the actual rules of Aristotle, could be disregarded. For him Aristotle was as irrefutable as Euclid. Gerstenberg insisted that Aristotle wrote for his own time; that the moderns have more liberty; that Shakespeare is not to be judged by rules made two thousand years ago under different theatrical conditions. Warning against such revolutionary ideas, Lessing said that "tragedy cannot depart one step from the guidance of Aristotle without departing just so far from perfection." Lessing reached this point of view by having swept aside the pseudo-

Aristotelian rules and the involved lubrications of scholars. He studied Aristotle's *Poetics* as a manual of playwriting. He tested dramatic art on the stage in the light of Aristotle's ideas. He understood Greek dramatic craftsmanship better than anyone up to his time and far better than most modern Aristotelian scholars, because he was a man of the theatre and they are theorizers at a desk. Anyone who studies the *Poetics* from Lessing's point of view and who discards pseudo-Aristotelianism of all ages, will be likely to reach his conclusion as to the value of the *Poetics* for the dramatist.

Lessing's statement of the case of German drama may be summarized as follows: The French stage is supposed to be entirely fashioned according to the rules of Aristotle, and critics have tried to convince Germans that it has reached its high degree of perfection through the observance of these rules. Thus the Germans have imitated the French. Germans have been happily awakened from their slumber by certain English plays; they have finally discovered that tragedy is capable of quite a different effect than Corneille and Racine were able to make it produce. Blinded by this sudden gleam of truth, Germans have bounded back to the edge of another abyss. The English lack plainly certain known rules contained in French drama. Germans have concluded that the aim of tragedy is reached without these rules, indeed that it is less well attained by following the rules. Even that opinion might be accepted, but to confound all rules of dramatic art with these rules of French tragedy and to renounce them all, to consider prescribing what shall and what shall not be done as mere pedantry, to forget what has been learned and to insist that every playwright discover dramatic art for himself —that Lessing will not countenance.

Yet, in a measure, that is just what was done. The idea that Shakespeare was a great playwright in spite of not observing rules was transformed to the theory that he attained the aim of tragedy by not observing rules. Shakespeare was "original." He was "the voice of nature." No longer "the brother of the ancients," he became their opponent. Even the mechanics of his plays, which Gerstenberg had admitted were weak, now began to be praised. Herder insisted that Shakespeare, far from incapable of inventing a plot, conceived stories of which the view alone gave one vertigo. His plays were like successive waves of the sea, vast pictures of life. A new form of drama must be created such as Shakespeare had invented. Lenz had taken up the battle against classicism and Aristotle. He formulated the new rule that dramatic unity consisted not in the unity of action, but in the unity of the hero, thus reversing absolutely the theory of Aristotle in the light of what he considered Shakespeare's practice.

Shakespeare employed plot not character, as a point of departure. Aristotle considered plot more important than character, and Shakespeare was more Aristotelian in this respect than most critics admit. But he made his characters such outstanding personalities, he differentiated all classes and individuals so clearly that his admirers have generally believed that in order to imitate Shakespeare one only has to put many different kinds of people on the stage and have them go through many events. Character has become more important in modern drama than it was in Greek drama. Even Lessing exalts the importance of character far more than do his masters, Aristotle and Diderot. Yet few modern dramatists make the delineation of character the primary purpose of their art any more than did Shakespeare.

Did Lessing ever regret having criticized Gottsched for not having offered Shakespeare instead of Corneille as a model for German playwrights? Lessing certainly never followed the Elizabethan conception of dramatic art. His *Emilia Galotti* and even *Nathan der Weise* are far more French than English in technique.

Lessing justly upbraided the critics who asserted that genius is stifled by rules. Nothing can stifle genius. Mediocre talent, by following accepted canons of drama, can produce plays worthy of some consideration. But mediocre talent, which disregards all guidance, depends on its own inspiration, and invokes the name of Shakespeare, brings forth five acts of nonsense such as Gerstenberg's *Ugolino* (1768). The dramatist thought that he was imitating the originality and the voice of nature in Shakespeare. Original it was, but the voice of nature was merely the wild hysteria of Ugolino and his sons dying of starvation for five acts in a melodramatic tower.

Enthusiasm for Shakespeare, because he disregarded the unities and produced great pictures of life and whole galleries of portraits, enveloped the young Goethe. He wrote *Goetz von Berlichingen* (1773) without consideration for the special conditions and limitations of the physical theatre. When Shakespeare wrote, he thought of the spectator. When Goethe wrote *Goetz,* he thought of the reader. Goethe assumed a freedom which Shakespeare, though writing for a flexible stage, never allowed himself. *Goetz* contains fifty-four changes of scene in comparison to thirty-eight in *Antony and Cleopatra* and eighteen in *Julius Cæsar.* There are forty-one speaking characters in *Goetz* as against thirty-one in *Julius Cæsar.* Goethe did not realize that the scene could change easily in the Elizabethan playhouse, because there was practically no scenery to change; whereas in the German theatre scenery had to change with every shift of the scene of the action. Not only was this procedure difficult mechanically, but also psychologically. Each time that different scenery is disclosed to the eye, it communicates new impressions to the mind. Less attention is paid to the actors for some minutes with the disclosure of each different set. In the Shakespearean playhouse this distraction was reduced to a minimum. Notwithstanding the difference between the German and Elizabethan systems of stage decoration, some of the scenes in *Goetz* contain only five or six lines. Goethe said that Shakespeare's plays were "curiosity boxes" and the "technique of the curiosity box" actually became the ideal of such men as Klinger.

Lessing was shocked. Even Herder, who was directly responsible for Goethe's admiration for Shakespeare, admitted that Goethe had been spoiled by Shakespeare. The young playwright had surpassed his master in producing a kaleidoscopic series of scenes and characters; but, like his contemporaries, with the exception of Lessing, he failed to realize that Shakespeare was a master in the art of plotting, and therefore was careful in handling, foreshadowing, preparation, suspense, surprise, climax and dénouement. Whether these elements of dramatic art are fundamental or are so important as depiction of character or as literary quality, does not enter into the question. The important point is that Goethe paid little or no attention to these very things which Shakespeare watched with care in constructing his plays. Goethe had condemned unity of action together with the unities of time and place. He had insisted that Shakespeare's plots were not plots in the usual meaning of the word; but that his plays were the free expression of the ego. Shakespeare held the mirror up to nature; the romanticists held the mirror up themselves. Shakespeare is bafflingly impersonal as his would-be biographers soon learn. Goethe knew what he was doing; but he had a curious idea of what Shakespeare had done, although his view is still held by many admirers of Shakespeare who ascribe his greatness as a dramatist to a disregard of dramatic art. The grossest misinterpretation of Shakespeare's art was that which led these young playwrights, including Goethe and Schiller, to believe that in writing closet drama they were imitating the Elizabethan dramatist. Of all dramatists, Shakespeare was the last who would have wasted his time composing unplayable plays. Indeed, he spent much of his time merely rewriting plays in order to make them more playable.

Goetz von Berlichingen became popular in book form and was produced on the stage. As a result of its success a premium was placed on loose construction in drama. Not only were the rules of French drama discarded, but also playwrights imitated the sketchiness of the Shakespearean form without regard for the logical development of his plots. This looseness of construction is especially apparent in the first dramas of Klinger. His *Otto* contains four plots and requires fifty-two changes of scenery. *Das Leidende Weib* requires thirty. Such exaggerated "technique of the curiosity box" could not last. When Klinger composed *Die Zwillinge,* which he wrote for production on the stage, he allowed the scene to change only once within the act. The other changes occur at the beginning of the acts and only three settings are necessary.

Klinger was correct in his belief that the Germans preferred the "life, action and events" of Shakespeare to the "resounding declamation" of French tragedy; but he failed to see that the life, action and events of Shakespeare were carefully arranged in relation to a dénouement. He believed erroneously that Shakespeare's secondary episodes and parallel actions were independent of the plot instead of being carefully interwoven. Thus Klinger's plays often contain events and characters which are totally unrelated.

In imitation of Shakespeare he combined tragic and comic scenes and characters; and he had his melodramatic events accompanied by supposedly sympathetic manifestations of nature, such as storms and gruesome nights. This practice was piously carried on by later melodramatic dramatists in Germany and France.

He was so intent upon having his characters express their emotions that he failed to make clear the causes. Irritating obscurity pervades scene after scene in all his plays. Only by careful analysis and by piecing together details can one discover who the characters are and why they are acting as they do. In *Das Leidende Weib* he does not explain why the woman confesses her infidelity to her husband, nor does he show her so doing. One merely realizes rather vaguely that she must have made this confession on which the action depends.

In 1776 Klinger produced *Sturm und Drang* (*Storm and Stress*) from which the period in German literature derived its name. His first title for this work, *Wirrwarr* (*Imbroglio* or *Jumble*) is more fitting, for the plot is submerged in a succession of scenes in which characters indulge in curious explosions of passion. The voices of untrammelled nature are speaking; but nature is more restrained, more "regular" than these neurotic gentlemen of the Storm and Stress supposed. In Klinger's plays, the passionate outbursts border often upon the abnormal. The

Freudians would find his characters a precious collection of personalities to psychoanalyze. The modern dramatist who deals with pathological cases is not so original as he flatters himself to be. Klinger was the Strindberg of the eighteenth century. If one of his plays were produced anonymously with cubistic scenery at special matinées, long-haired men and short-haired women would believe that they had discovered an ultra-modern genius. Fortunately, theatre-goers are pretty normal individuals, and soon tire of abnormality when the apparent novelty has worn off. Unbridled romanticism must either calm down or it will be replaced entirely by common sense. German romantic drama calmed down even in the heydey of the Storm and Stress. The physical stage and the human audience are good balance wheels for dramatic art. Whether there are rules or not, there are certain limits which drama has never successfully overstepped.

In his *Anmerkung übers Theater* (1774), Lenz attacked not only the French theorists, but also Aristotle. All rules must be abolished. Characters must take the place of unity of action, because events are caused by character. German tragedy must be a series of events, which follow each other like thunderbolts, dominated by a principal character. Unity of action is preserved if it concerns one person.

In putting these theories into practice he wrote plays such as *Die Soldaten* (1776) in which secondary actions and unrelated events conceal the principal plot. The triviality and crudeness of many of the episodes produces a curious realism of which not a Diderot, but a Zola would approve.

Heinrich Wagner was no less realistic but was more regular in the construction of some of his plots. His *Kindermörderin* (1776), as he first wrote it, might have been produced at the Théâtre Antoine in Paris at the end of the next century. It is a domestic tragedy of a girl who is betrayed and then murders her starving baby. In spite of an unexplained and inexplicable villain who forges a fatal letter for no reason, the play is powerful in its stark realism exhibited in such scenes as the one in which the girl croons a lullaby to her dead child. This situation, so easily made shocking, is actually dramatic. Still more daring is the scene in a low inn of the first act. Wagner's *Die Reue nach der That* (1775) is also striking in its simplicity in an age when jumbled plots were the vogue. This play is a domestic tragedy which furnished ideas for *Kabale und Liebe*, and it was a connecting link between Lessing and Schiller.

Wagner's technique shows the influence of Mercier whose essay on dramatic art, *Du Théâtre* (1773), he translated in 1776. Mercier was more revolutionary than his compatriots in regard to the unities of time and place and the number of acts. He advocated the removal of all barriers between dramatic forms. Yet no Frenchman of that time would have dreamed of disregarding the unity of action. Wagner constructed a simple, direct action, although he did not write primarily for the stage. He differs from the French in that his realism is not only a transcript of life but includes scenes and details which would have shocked the French. Indeed, when his *Kindermörderin* was produced in Germany, the whole first act had to be dropped; and the tragic ending was unfortunately transformed into a weak, sentimental outcome.

When the playwrights, including Schiller and Goethe, faced the question of presenting their plays on the stage before an audience, the voice of nature singing of the new freedom without regard to rules did not seem quite so enthralling. No matter how sincere an author may be in assuring the public that his play was not written for the stage, no matter how strongly he may believe that his muse cannot have its wings clipped by the shears of a stage director or be caged in a theatre, one has yet to discover the writer of closet drama who objected to his work being played. Generally after he has scored a success he finds that he can express his ideas on the stage before spectators.

Schiller and Wagner altered the dénouements of their plays "written for the reader." Klinger ceased to construct dramas needing over fifty changes of scenery, when a prize was offered in 1775 by the Ackermann players for a drama to be produced. Goethe wrote *Egmont*. Schroeder adapted Lenz's *Hofmeister* for the stage and produced it. Lenz, who had written scornfully of the unity of place, began to apologize for Shakespeare's frequent changes of scene. He wrote plays more fitted for production than his earlier work; and he remarked that Shakespeare's practice did not justify young poets in imitating him in his peculiarities and that they should not try to make us believe that Shakespeare's beauties lie simply in his irregularity. This statement from Lenz is significant, and a little amusing, in view of his earlier caustic remarks about regularity. In the glare of the footlights and in the sound of applause, certain ideals of freedom do not seem quite so indispensable to dramatic art. The theatre and the audience were calming down considerably the Storm and Stress of these passionate young lovers of liberty in art.

In spite of the admiration of Shakespeare and the hostility towards French tragedy, the French *drame* was exerting a healthful influence in the direction of regularity. Lessing had produced in *Miss Sara Sampson* a play which anticipated the *drame* in many ways. Diderot's and Mercier's plays and theories had met with success in Germany. The interest in family life inherent in Germans was favorable to the cultivation of a drama dealing with domestic problems. Lessing said correctly in 1781 that Diderot had exerted more influence on German drama than on French. Yet this influence consisted in furnishing the theory and examples of a form of dramatic art which Lessing had first created independently of Diderot. The French *drame* did not bring forth, but strongly reinforced and supported the development of German domestic drama. Otto von Gemmingen's *Der Deutsche Hausvater* was inspired by Diderot's *Père de Famille*. Schiller's *Kabale und Liebe* is indebted to von Gemmingen; but Lessing had given the German playwrights a finer example of that form of drama than Diderot ever produced.

The strong interest in this kind of drama kept Germans in contact with well-made plays because Lessing, Diderot, Mercier, Saurin, etc., produced domestic dramas which were carefully constructed. Their admiration for Shakespeare did not lead them to the conclusion that all rules should be abolished, that drama should be a "jumble" or a "curiosity box." Diderot relegated plot to a position of secondary importance; but no French playwright ever broke entirely with the Aristotelian ideal of the inevitable development of an action with a beginning, a middle and an end. A French Klinger is unthinkable even in periods of revolt against rules. Although Klinger was dealing with domestic themes in what he naïvely believed was a Shakespearean manner, the majority of playwrights, including Schiller in his *Kabale und Liebe,* were naturally under the influence of the well-made play when they built their plots dealing with domestic problems. Schiller, himself, admired Diderot greatly. In this play, the dramatist employed the form which Lessing had introduced first in *Miss Sara Sampson* and later in *Emilia Galotti. Kabale und Liebe* is more complex and has more characters than the usual domestic tragedy, for Schiller learned simplicity with difficulty; but he added nothing new to dramatic art in this drama, although it is the best constructed play of his youthful period.

Only *Fiesko* of his early plays was originally written to be played. He said of *Die Räuber:* "This play is to be regarded as a dramatic narrative, in which, for the purpose of tracing out the innermost workings of the soul, advantage has been taken of the dramatic method, without otherwise conforming to the stringent rules of theatrical composition, or seeking the dubious advantage of stage adaptation." Unmindful of Lessing's sound exposition of the true Aristotelian theory, he classed Aristotle with Batteux as having prescribed narrow limits for drama. Completely under the spell of what was then thought to be Shakespearean dramatic art, and especially inspired by *King Lear,* Schiller wrote a play which totally disregards that strict economy necessary for dramatic art. Had his play never been produced or had he not as a rule produced dramas of many episodes and motives, his choice of the form of large proportions would be without significance. But Schiller's work is important in this respect in the history of German drama and in the development of French drama. Like Schiller, even partially because of Schiller's example, the same prolixity and vastness enters the work of the elder Dumas and Hugo. The latter's *Cromwell* is of even greater length than *Die Räuber*.

Plays containing many characters and episodes and written by poets such as Goethe and Schiller, who have deep insight into the human soul and its problems, are baffling problems both to director and dramatic critic. They have undeniable power. Because they are works of thoughtful men, they contain a central idea. This central idea is easily interpreted as constituting unity of action. It is constantly said of such plays that "they represent real life"; "they depict a world catastrophe"; "they are man struggling with destiny." By careful critical study extending over years upon years the relationship of every episode to the dramatist's main idea can be discovered. The play is found to resemble a vast mural painting, with intricate but unified design. But just as the physical eye can behold only fragmentary beauties of a mural painting on more than one wall, so it seems that the mind's eye cannot understand the whole inner unity of a drama of many different episodes in the theatre. The play may be a "world in itself"; but the world in itself is too great to be set before us on the stage. Many critics conclude that, because dramatic art has psychological and physical limitations, dramatic narrative transcends drama. It would be just as enlightening and just as true to hold that the epic transcends the sonnet.

It would be going too far to say that Schiller was not at home on the stage; yet this embarrassment at the narrow limits of classical tragedy or even of any form of drama is manifest in all his plays except *Kabale und Liebe, Maria Stuart* and *Die Braut von Messina*. There are two distinct groups of scenes in *Die Räuber* portraying events which happen to the brothers. These two actions join in the latter part of the play. About four and a half acts are devoted to preparation. *Wilhelm Tell* has three actions. *Don Carlos* is a maze of intrigue. Schiller found a prologue necessary in addition to the five acts full of events for the presentation of *Die Jungfrau von Orleans*. To treat the subject of Wallenstein, Schiller was content with no less than three plays—two of them in five acts. The plot of *Fiesko* has more ramifications than that of *Othello*. These dramas resemble powerful but ponderous German sentences with many modifying phrases and parentheses, each of which has a bearing on the main idea but whose very presence is distracting. Just as powerful an impression and a clearer one could have been made, if a simpler and less prolix form had been employed.

In order to give the background of the subject of Wallenstein, the dramatist takes a whole play to represent the army and its life. He presents it completely and minutely. The influence of the army is a part of the action, but it is not so important as to require such careful presentation. This overemphasis distorts the action of the following ten acts. The Roman citizens are the background of *Julius Cæsar;* but Shakespeare did not need a whole play to paint that background vividly and completely enough for the spectator to experience the sensations aroused by the mob and to understand its effect on the situation. Schiller learned from Shakespeare the dramatic value of the crowd and of mass actions. Unfortunately he did not acquire, at the same time, the feeling for balance and for dramatic economy. He overemphasized, and did not illumine with quick strokes which vivify because they come like flashes of light.

However, in spite of this prolixity, Schiller's use of mass effects was a notable development of dramatic art. Greek drama with its chorus, Shakespearean drama with its mobs, had not only presented an interesting spectacle but also a psychological element in human life. When dramatic art came under the sway of French classicism, mass effects disappeared. Through his admiration for *Julius Cæsar*, Schiller revived this element of drama which is effective but very difficult to handle. His plays glow with colorful pictures as his many characters or his crowds come and go in ever-varying combinations. They are like a kaleidoscope. How rich and varied they must have seemed to the audience in comparison with the severe French dramas or even those of Lessing! And these scenes do not merely furnish local color picturesquely. Schiller's ensemble scenes have a dramatic significance. One cannot say so much for all of Hugo's and Dumas' scenes which they staged under his inspiration. Such moments in their plays often resemble Schiller's scenes outwardly but not inwardly. The French were too content with producing merely local color. That a scene is historically correct, or even atmospherically correct is not sufficient reason for its existence. An ensemble scene is only justified completely if it is a vital part of the interpretation of the central idea of the drama.

This quality of dramatic significance which Schiller put into his mass effects makes them artistic; but his too frequent and prolonged use of them sometimes obscures the central theme. Schiller appeals so strongly to the eye, he calls upon the spectator to witness so many characters in different combinations that the inner meaning of his play becomes vague at times, although the reader of his dramas can follow the development of the ideas with comparative ease. In this respect Schiller is not at home in the theatre. The ability of an audience of the highest mentality to understand certain plays is limited as well as enlarged by the fact that the impressions come through the eye and ear simultaneously. The phrase "too vast for the stage" often means "too vast for the audience," even though the audience be composed of the keenest critics who use the first expression to justify their admiration for some play in book form.

The development of distinct characters is also one of Schiller's contributions to dramatic art. Since Shakespeare, no playwright had succeeded so well as Schiller in making most of his personages distinct entities. Molière's and Racine's creations are more abstract and general types. Schiller was able to differentiate even the minor characters and to endow with personality rôles that he does not trouble to name.

His principal characters such as Wallenstein, Johanna, Maria Stuart, Posa and Fiesko are dynamic personalities. Whatever they do or think, whether they show will power or a lack of will power, they are interesting individuals to watch. For many dramatists, characters only have an existence in the play itself. Their past is disregarded. Hamlet would be clearer to us had Shakespeare told us what kind of a child and boy he was. Schiller has supplied us with important information in several instances. The prologue of *Die Jungfrau von Orleans* serves to show us what Johanna was in her village. The use of this device illustrates once more Schiller's insistence upon background or environment, as it would be called today. It also shows how he sacrificed dramatic economy. In *Maria Stuart*, however, he is eminently successful in showing the heroine's past and giving a complete analysis of her whole character as affected by her past without using the device of the prologue. In *Don Carlos* he calls up events which took place before the first act in order to illumine his characters. This procedure is similar to the Greek practice of unveiling the past to cause a development in the plot; but the Greek dramatists did not disclose the past in relation to character.

Interesting as Schiller's characters are, they are not always consistent. The action does not always follow logically from their state of mind. Only in *Wallenstein's Tod* and *Maria Stuart* is one impressed by the inevitability of the action as a result of the interplay of character and event. Goethe in a conversation with Eckermann summed up Schiller's defects as a dramatist as follows: "He seized boldly on a great subject and turned it this way and that. But he saw his object, as it were, only on the outside; a quiet development from its interior was not within his province. His talent was more desultory. Thus he was never decided—could never have done. He often changed a part just before a rehearsal. And as he went boldly to work, he did not take sufficient pains about motivating his plays."

This criticism applies to Schiller's early dramas; and perhaps Goethe is partially responsible for these faults, because his *Goetz*, which Schiller admired, is lacking in motivation. Schiller's *Don Carlos* is marred by the number of changes made in the play and by the different conceptions of the action which the dramatist had from time to time while writing it. Schiller seems never to have been sure whether Posa or Don Carlos is the hero. Both characters lose in effectiveness, because interest and sympathy are divided. Two or three Schillers seem to have collaborated in producing the tragedy. Each seems to have added something germane to the subject, but not absolutely necessary to the action.

The lack of preparation is most unfortunate in *Die Jungfrau von Orleans.* Johanna has been presented to us as a woman so inspired by her divine mission that earthly love, love of woman for man, is unthinkable for her, although she is urged to marry. The idea has been hammered home throughout a whole scene. She is fighting a certain Lionel, is victorious and is about to slay him, when suddenly she loves him. That she loves and that she loves him—in whom neither she nor the spectator has had any interest—are almost incredible facts suddenly brought before our eyes. Yet the rest of the action develops from this *coup de théâtre,* so surprising, so unmotivated as to be false to her character. That Johanna, winsome though sexless, was loved by any man is not strange; but that she should love needs careful motivation and explanation. Timme gave Schiller the sound advice to study *Goetz* less and Lessing more. Had he followed this suggestion he would have introduced fewer surprises into his actions. His plots would have been less artificial and his characters would not have acted so often on flimsy pretexts or on no pretext at all.

He had a strong tendency towards the melodramatic; and he introduced thrilling incidents which excite but do not convince the spectator. He introduced such scenes when his theme should be receiving all his attention. In *Fiesko*, when the whole question of the destiny of Genoa and of liberty is at stake, he stages a scene, laboriously prepared in enigmatic lines which arouse only curiosity, in which Fiesko shows his true feeling of contempt for the coquette Julia while his wife is concealed behind the tapestry. At the end of the play Fiesko's wife dons the scarlet cloak of Gianetto. Fiesko, catching sight of the cloaked figure, believes it is his enemy and stabs his own wife. The whole act is a series of similar theatrical incidents, which take place without reason or even preparation, in spite of Schiller's statement in the preface that drama does not allow the interposition either of chance or of a particular providence.

Such lapses into melodramatic and theatrical effects are all the more regrettable because of Schiller's ability to characterize and because he always tried to give his plays a profound meaning. His ultimate aim was not a stirring drama. Like many playwrights of the century, he used drama to teach directly certain ideals, such as liberty, and to inveigh against social and political tyranny. A dramatist who has something to prove must employ sparingly theatrical tricks, which may be used with impunity by a Scribe whose ultimate aim is to fascinate for three hours.

Schiller was not content to hold the mirror up to nature, to allow the audience to see human life in its manifold problems, both grave and gay. He could not always refrain from taking possession of a character and speaking through it. Louisa is too sophisticated, didactic and sententious in the latter part of *Kabale und Liebe,* especially in her interview with Lady Milford. If drama must teach, it must do so unobtrusively, by guiding the spectator in making deductions from the story that is unfolded on the stage. Whether the play be tragic or comic, if one comes out of the theatre with deeper insight into human nature and with the conviction that the moral law prevails, the dramatist has fulfilled his function completely. We do not go to the theatre to listen to the Ten Commandments in versions less forcible than the original.

This enumeration of Schiller's faults must not blind us to his power as a dramatist. His ability to create character, to endow whole groups of people with dramatic life, to present so much of humanity and of human nature to an audience during a few hours marks him as a man of genius. His talent was desultory but it was flexible. Though embarrassed by the stage, he showed that the theatre could contain vaster themes than it had held since Shakespeare's time. When Schiller became more at home in the playhouse, he turned more and more to Greek drama. *Œdipus Rex* became his model. He wrote to Goethe (October 2nd, 1797) that he was seeking tragic material of the kind of *Œdipus Rex* which is a "tragic analysis" of past events. Everything has happened and only needs to be unfolded. Also, as he pointed out, the past is more terrible because it is unalterable and the fear that something has happened affects our feelings very differently from the fear that it might happen. He was the first of the moderns to realize the dramatic effectiveness of unveiling the past. So he wrote *Die Braut von Messina* (1802) in imitation of Sophocles. Together with Goethe's *Iphigenie,* it brought back a form of dramatic art which had been discredited because pseudo-classical tragedy had lost most of the essential elements of true classicism.

It was a long journey from *Die Räuber,* a dramatic narrative, to *Die Braut von Messina;* but Schiller accomplished it. When dramatic art in England and in France had fallen upon evil days of triviality and of academic sterility, Schiller was bearing the torch from which other men were to receive guidance and to kindle their own fires of inspiration. The young romanticists in France took from him many a theatrical scene; but they also learned from him how to depict life in glowing colors. His great contribution to dramatic art is the mass effect, the presentation of a little world on the modern stage. His art was not flawless in this respect and he sacrificed much to these effects; but the stage was richer and glowed with life and color because he wrote of many men.

CHAPTER XVI

FRENCH MELODRAMA. FRENCH ROMANTIC DRAMA

THE last decade of the eighteenth century brought a political and economic revolution, but dramatic art remained
practically unchanged in France. Plays with republican sentiments were popular and the sentimental *drame* had a revival.
Fenouillot de Falbaire's *Honnête Criminel* scored a success in
1790; and in the same year Arnaud's *Comte de Comminges*, a
sombre *drame* written in 1764, was finally produced. There was
nothing new until Lemercier's *Pinto* (1799) in which are traces
of the influence of *Macbeth* in the scene of the murder and the
scene in which Égisthe tries to soothe the remorse of Clytemnes-
tre. Like Voltaire, Lemercier felt that French tragedy needed
new inspiration, but he was far from becoming a romanticist.

His *Pinto* is an historical comedy in which the grave is mingled with the gay, although the rule of separation of tragedy
and comedy was enforced as strictly as possible by critics and
the Academicians. Lemercier presented characters of high rank
in situations of farce comedy. He observed the unity of time
rather loosely, and the scene changed from act to act. The
plot deals with a conspiracy to place the Duc de Bragance on the
throne of Portugal. Plots and characters of this kind had formed
the material of countless tedious tragedies; but Lemercier makes
Pinto, a kind of Figaro, the principal plotter. By weaving in
love episodes of a light nature, by using disguises, *quiproquo*,
rope ladders, closets from which unexpected people come, he
turned the play into a comedy which resembles Beaumarchais'
Mariage de Figaro in some of its tricks of legerdemain. The
apparatus was being prepared for the greatest of all dramatic
tricksters—Eugène Scribe. Indeed, the romanticists, who thirty
years later were to take themselves so seriously, did not disdain

such situations as a background for their poetical melodramas.

In the Boulevard theatres the melodrama was continuing to develop. Monvel in his *Victimes Cloitrées* (1791) produced a fourth act which offered inspiration scenically and theatrically for future thrillers. Dorval, the hero, has been thrown into a dungeon by the traitorous Père Laurent. On the other side of the double subterranean vault languishes his fiancée, Eugénie, who has been abducted by the "traitor." Both compartments are exposed to view.

Dorval discovers in a tomb of a former prisoner a letter written in blood which shows him how to procure tools left by the unfortunate victim. He makes his escape and rescues the heroine. The persecuted virtuous woman and the villain or "traitor," as he was called, are two stock characters of melodrama.

The *Château du Diable* (1792) by Loaisel Tréogate also offers a melodramatic story embellished with spectres and other strange inhabitants of a mysterious castle where iron cages and warning inscriptions suddenly appear. The hero, of course, is passing through terrifying dangers for the sake of the lovely Adélaïde. All these tests, however, have been merely devised by the heroine's uncle to prove the virtue and bravery of the hero!

In the *Forêt Périlleuse* (1797) Loaisel Tréogate sends Colisan through a series of real adventures in his quest for his lady. Here are the brigands, Schiller's brigands, who were growing in popularity on the melodramatic stage. They capture the heroine and imprison her in a cave. Colisan discovers her, is caught, condemned to death and executed—or rather would have been, had not Morgan, pretending to be a bandit, saved him just before the curtain!

In the same year, the great master of melodrama, Pixerécourt, made his début as author of a one-act comedy, the *Petits Auvergnats*, which contains in miniature much of his technique. Here is a virtuous wife who has been abducted from her husband by the traitor Rosambel. The husband believes she has deserted him; but she returns after two years spent in a dungeon, and her innocence is proved by a letter. The comic rôle, which was to become very important in melodrama, was also introduced in this play.

A few months later, *Victor ou l'Enfant de la Forêt* was produced. Pixerécourt had written it as an opera, with scenes of spoken dialogue; but another lyric drama of the same name was accepted at the Théâtre Favart. So he gave his version to the Ambigu Comique where it was produced successfully without lyric passages but with a musical accompaniment in certain scenes. *Victor* opened a long series of successful melodramas written by Pixerécourt, Caigniez and others for the delight of the bourgeois audiences in the opening years of the nineteenth century, while senescent classical tragedy was boring the intellectuals and before romantic drama furnished its compromise form for both classes. Roger, the bandit in Pixerécourt's *Victor*, owes his existence to Schiller's Karl von Moor in *Die Räuber*. Hernani will also be an outlaw. Pixerécourt, as well as Dumas and Hugo, read Shakespeare, Scott, Goethe, Schiller and Kotzebue; but Pixerécourt was a writer of plays for the people who care naught whence comes their amusement. He borrowed scenes and situations from these foreign writers without throwing down the gauntlet to any literary coterie and without enrolling himself under the banner of Shakespeare, as will Dumas and Hugo. Yet he blazed the trail for the romanticists.

These melodramas follow a basic formula. A virtuous woman undergoes dire sufferings at the hands of a traitor; but strict poetic justice is meted out. The virtuous characters are rewarded and the traitors are either punished or die repenting their sins. A comic character is usually numbered among the virtuous and often plays an important rôle in the dénouement. This character is an old soldier, a servant of some sort, or may be a rather good-natured coward on the side of the traitor.

In order to furnish the requisite number of exciting situations leading to suspense and *coups de théâtre*, the events leading up to the initial cause are numerous and strange. Abductions, disguises, supposed deaths, unknown identities, all the old tricks of classical comedy are brought into play. In order to arouse suspense these events are explained to the audience earlier than in classical comedy, in which the explanation serves as a dénouement. The point of attack is late in the story; and the melodramas observe the unities, as a rule, although the scene changes from act to act. Although unhampered by classical traditions, these playwrights did not imitate the story-telling methods of either English or German dramatists.

The late point of attack and the necessity of explaining many events made the expositions inartistic. A monologue or a long recital in dialogue were the frank methods employed. However, since confidants were not introduced, these expositions escaped much of the solemn tedium of the corresponding scenes of contemporary tragedy. They are as direct as possible, and are often enlivened by comedy. The novel scenery also lends an interest to the exposition. In Caigniez' *Forêt d'Hermanstad*, a ghostly, ruined gothic hall stimulates attention; and in Pixeré-court's *Tékéli*, the hero is discovered in a tree while a storm rages through the forest. The aim of the melodrama is to produce thrills as often and as early as possible.

The plot unfolds rapidly. The plays consist of three acts; and the act itself is treated as a separate unit, ending with a climax and a striking line. The change of scene from act to act emphasizes this unity. Most of the events are on the stage, only those being reported which cannot happen in the particular place which is represented by the scenery. No problem or theme or character is portrayed with rigorous logic. The point of departure is a plot filled with strange events and thrills to which everything is sacrificed, except the virtue and life of the heroine. Innocence, as well as murder, will out in melodrama.

Even in Pixerécourt's *Femme à Deux Maris*, Elisa, the wife of the two men, is a paragon of virtue. She was forced to marry the villain. She bore him a son, but she believes the father to be dead. She has made a happy second marriage. The first husband, Fritz, returns to blackmail her. Count Edo·1ard, the second husband, saves Fritz from death when he is recognized as an old deserter from the army. He is planning to send Fritz away with money. Edouard also is going to leave his wife until death decides which man shall be her husband. Fritz orders Walter, one of his henchmen, to kill the "second man" who crosses the garden at a certain hour that night. The faithful Bataille, the comic character, overhears the plan. At the appointed hour, Bataille crosses the garden first. Then comes Fritz, now the "second man." Walter slays him. "Papers" in his portfolio prove the innocence of Elisa.

An added attraction for the audience in these plays is a spectacle in form of a fête with a dance, or a review and parade of soldiers. The divertissement, however, grows out of the situation. There are also sieges of châteaux, battles and duels to hold the audience breathless over the fate of the hero and heroine. The scenery is very elaborate and the directions for it are given in detail. Forests, gardens, inn-yards, gothic halls, palaces, courtyards, peasants' huts, landscapes with bridges and waterfalls, decks of ships, caverns and mines were constructed with care. The back drop was painted like a large picture; but in many plays the rocks, walls, stairways and bridges had to be practical. The stage carpenters of the Opéra, Matis and Desroches, did not consider it beneath their dignity to build complicated sets for the melodrama, which made the "vestibule of a palace" of classical tragedy appear as monotonous and flat as the tragedy itself. The audience of a melodrama had plenty to see, as well as to hear. Spectacle, which had been a novelty except at the Opéra and the Opéra-Comique, had now become a regular part of the plays in the lesser theatres.

Classical tragedy was both senescent and obsolescent. It was being kept alive artificially. The Napoleonic era witnessed a revival of Greek and Roman ideals in art. Napoleon himself posed as a Roman clad in a toga and wearing a Roman crown of leaves. Classical tragedy was considered the glorious inheritance of the past. It was almost the official form of drama in the opinion of Napoleon and of the Academy. A writer of tragedy outranked a comic playwright in the hierarchy of the intellectuals. The art of the greatest actors, among whom was Talma, was employed to vivify these inferior imitations of great tragedies of a bygone age. Costumes were specially designed and fresh settings were painted for new productions. Talma carried on the reform in costume begun by Lekain. He was a friend of David, the classical painter, who helped to inspire him with a taste for exact local color. In 1789, Talma appeared in the play *Brutus* wearing a Roman toga. He also toned down the emphasis of tragic declamation. If anyone could have saved tragedy, it was Talma. But all the learned doctors, skilled nurses and loving friends could not save the venerable and eminently respectable patient.

Reform, not revolution, was the desire of Lemercier who had written in 1796, apropos of *Pinto,* that he had striven "to strip a great action of all poetic ornament which might disguise it; to present persons speaking and acting as one does in real life, and to reject the sometimes false prestige of tragedy and felicitous verses." The dialogue in his plays is often terse and direct; but he did not give up the tirades so beloved by the declamatory actors.

In his *Christophe Colomb* (1809), he went so far as to break the unities of time and of place. The first act is in front of the house of Columbus. The second act passes at the court of Isabella, while the third reveals the very unclassical scene of the cabin of the ship of Columbus just before land is sighted. When the play was produced at the Odéon, the audience indulged in more than a preliminary skirmish to the battle of *Hernani.* Several heads were cracked over the question of the unities in spite of the fact that the author had apologized in advance in a *Note de l'Auteur* for infringing for once the sacred classical rules in which he professed absolute faith. He denied any intention "of opening up new roads." He only wished to try all those that art could offer. At the second performance of his so-called Shakespearean comedy, a spectator was killed in the pit. The classical audience evidently objected only to bloodshed and scenes of violence on the stage. Horace had failed to lay down rules in his *Ars Poetica* protecting the audience. Just who these gentlemen were who fought so valiantly that night against classicism, history does not record. They were not yet an organized band calling themselves romanticists; but they rioted partially under the Shakespearean banner.

Lemercier himself was not a romanticist and never became one. His lectures on dramatic art given in 1810-1811 at the Athénée prove his orthodoxy in regard to classicism in theory, even if he sinned at times in practice. The classical Academy accepted him into their holy-of-holies, though not without reproof for his lapses from the true classical faith.

The war, which was to last until the battle of *Hernani* in 1830, was started. Lessing had bitterly attacked French classical drama in his *Hamburgische Dramaturgie* with little effect so far as the French were concerned. In 1808, Schlegel launched his criticism of the drama of the Old Régime. He found a devoted pupil and follower in the brilliant though prolix Mme. de Staël, who admitted her inability to keep silent on any interesting subject. In her book *De l'Allemagne* (1813), she echoed certain ideas of Schlegel and added suggestions of her own in regard to a new form of drama for the French. She brought the word "romantic" into prominence as the appellation of a new theory of art. She complained, as had Schlegel, that any innovation in tragedy was met with the cry of "melodrama." The unities of time and place hamper the dramatist. The pomp of Alexandrine verse and the rules of good taste banish many legitimate emotions from the theatre. The less regular foreign plays produce stronger emotions. "In some French tragedies there are as violent situations as in English or German tragedies; but these situations are not presented with all their force and sometimes by affectation the effect is softened, or rather effaced." The vulgar, in nature, often mingles with the sublime and sometimes increases its effect; but the French audience cannot be convinced that a comic scene is employed to bring out a tragic situation. The finest French tragedies no longer interest the people. Is it not necessary to find out why the melodramas are so popular? French literature is menaced by sterility. Foreign plays may well be studied, not necessarily in view of adopting their technique, but to stimulate new ideas.

Benjamin Constant praised German drama, while upholding the severity of French technique, in his preface to an adaptation of Schiller's *Wallenstein* published in 1809. He forced the German trilogy into a single play in five acts in order to observe the unities. He omitted many scenes and characters with some regret. Although he admired the scene of the conspirators, he could not reproduce it because "the language of these assassins is as vulgar as their condition and sentiments." He pointed out that characters in French tragedy are only types, while Richard III is an individual because all his characteristics are included in Shakespeare's delineation of the man. The limitations of French tragedy are clearly explained; but, Constant, like Voltaire of old, feared that if the French playwrights were allowed liberty, nothing would be seen on the stage except "scaffolds, combats, fêtes, spectres and changes of scenery."

In 1820, Lebrun felt that he was the awaited innovator when he produced a pale imitation of Schiller's *Maria Stuart*. He hoped, not without fear, that people would be grateful to him for "having brought about the alliance of two Muses who seemed to have been irreconcilable enemies and for having finally introduced on the French stage, without wounding the severity of our taste and our rules, forms and colors which our dramatic literature lacked," and which he believed "to be indispensable to modern tragedy." He was attempting the impossible, for French tragedy could not be reformed or enlarged without offending the rules. He suppressed the local color, and all familiar human touches of the original play. He simplified the plot and either toned down or left out many dramatic scenes. Whatever was strikingly novel or romantic was sacrificed to the rules; and the result was merely another classical tragedy.

Another attack on the unities came from beyond the frontiers of France from Manzoni, a disciple of Goethe and a student of Schlegel, in a *Lettre à M. Chauvet* and in the preface to his romantic play, the *Conte di Carmagnola* (1820). This historical drama was translated into French and published in the *Chefs d'Œuvre des Théâtres Étrangers* (1822). This collection in several volumes offered translations of German, English, Danish, Spanish, Dutch, Polish, Portugese, Russian and Swedish dramas translated by Andrieux, Constant, Guizot, Nodier, Rémusat, Villemain and others. The education of the French theatre-goer in regard to foreign dramatic art was progressing. Trognon, the translator of the *Conte di Carmagnola*, remarked: "This tragedy is composed in the system that we have agreed, somewhat unfittingly, to call *romantic*." The adjective employed by Mme. de Staël was being used. Trognon defined romantic drama as one which, aiming to represent human life with all its principal accidents, to revive history in its entirety, oversteps the arbitrary limits of classical tragedy. He carefully refrained from passing judgment on either form of drama.

Stendhal, however, had the courage of his convictions. He had seen Shakespeare's plays performed in London. He boldly proclaimed that romanticism is the art of presenting to different peoples the works of literature which, in the present state of their customs and beliefs are susceptible of giving them the greatest possible pleasure; that classicism presents to them the literature which gave the greatest pleasure to their great-grandfathers. Here was not a foreigner, but a Frenchman declaring war upon classical tragedy and attacking the unities. The arguments set forth in his *Racine et Shakespeare* (1822) were not new, but they are brilliantly and fearlessly expressed. He pointed out the enemies: The old classical rhetoricians, the Academicians, the classical playwrights who were making money, the newspapers that gave an erroneous impression of romanticism. He struck at the great idol: Racine no longer pleases. Shakespeare does. Frenchmen must imitate Shakespeare.

Even Lemercier took courage and produced in 1823 his *Richard III et Jeanne Shore, drame historique imité de Shakespeare et de Rowe.* Actually the play is founded almost entirely on Rowe's *Jane Shore.* The mention of Shakespeare is pure advertisement, for only a few unimportant details of Lemercier's portraiture of Richard are drawn from *Richard III.* However, the fact that Shakespeare's name comes first on the title page, where it hardly belongs at all, shows the increasing prestige of the Bard of Avon in France in spite of the occurrence of the year before when, on the thirty-first of July, 1822, a troupe of English actors playing *Othello* at the Porte-Saint-Martin had been driven off the stage with cries of: "Down with Shakespeare! He is an aide of Wellington!" But it was one thing to play *Othello* in English and quite another to adapt one of Shakespeare's plays in order to make it "bearable to the noble and delicate taste of the French public," and to have Talma in the cast.

Lemercier did not allow the scenery to change during the act. "Such an irregularity wounds our perfected art." He preferred to allow Jeanne Shore to wander about the Tower of London, where she does not belong, than to change the scene to her home. However, the second act shows her apartment, at night, illuminated by lamps. "Everything in gothic style," in this scene; and "everything in the style of architecture with ornaments of the fifteenth century" in the set of the third act representing the council hall of the palace. The fifth act takes place in a public square. The gothic style, local color and change of scenery smack of melodrama and foreshadow the romantic settings of 1830.

Finding that the change of scenery from act to act and the nonobservance of the unity of place had not brought down upon his head the wrath of the gods, Lemercier ventured to state in his preface, in italics, that Aristotle had not absolutely prescribed the unity of place. Here spoke the playwright, not the professor of the *Cours Analytique de Littérature* who had proclaimed the unities inviolable.

The play was called historic drama; but "tragic dignity" was invoked by the author to explain his "corrections" of the English play. Thus he could not have Shore disguised as an old servant, nor could the lackey repulse Jeanne on Alicia's doorstep, nor could Alicia pour vindictive imprecations upon Jeanne. Lemercier had to tone down the sins of Jeanne after the usual classical custom. The duel between Shore and Hastings had to be omitted. It was a trick of the "lower theatre," *i.e.*, melodrama; while in his opinion the substitution of the "papers" by Alicia was a bit of thimble-rigging unworthy of a comic opera. He suppressed the very things in 1823 which Dumas and Hugo were to introduce on the French stage in 1830.

Yet he allowed his heroine to die of hunger miserably—in the street. He invented a beggar, who is too sentimental, but is certainly not a classical figure. Finally, he said in his preface: "The local color, which the accusation of this magic spreads over this terrible picture of the physical and moral deformities of Gloster, makes the epoch live in the eyes of the spectator." In Talma's representation of the deformed Gloster, was there a touch of the "grotesque"—that other watchword of Hugo? If there was, Boileau must have begun to turn in his grave; and Lemercier would turn in his, if he were classed among the hated romanticists.

"The public wanted something new but was on guard against the new," said Lebrun in regard to the failure of his *Cid d'Andalousie* (1825). This play was too close an imitation of the *Estrella de Sevilla* (wrongly attributed to Lope de Vega) to suit the classicists and not revolutionary enough to arouse the interest of the romanticists.

Stendhal had said that Scott's novels were romantic tragedy mingled with long descriptions. The reading public devoured his stories with avidity. It was brought into contact with stirring historical scenes and local color in book form. In 1827 the lesser dramatists began to use *Kenilworth*, *Quentin Durward* and other novels as sources of their plays. Hugo began to write his *Cromwell*, which was not to be played. Dumas was studying Schiller's plays, which had been translated in 1821. Neither of these young men had found himself as a dramatist. A *coup de théâtre* was needed to arouse the future leaders of the dramatic revolution. It came in the shape of performances of Shakespeare by English actors at the Odéon.

On September 11, 1827, Kemble and Miss Smithson were enthusiastically received in *Hamlet*. *Romeo and Juliet* also succeeded in spite of cuts in the text and the mediocrity of the actors in the secondary rôles. *Othello* aroused criticism. The scene of the murder, as usually played at that time, in which Desdemona was stabbed three or four times as well as smothered, was too brutal. It was denounced by critics as a "hideous and disgusting butchery." According to the *Pandore* neither the men nor the women in the audience could bear the spectacle. The "brutal" scenes of Shakespeare affected the French audience as the ultra-realistic plays of the Grand Guignol affect us today. They produced a new, but unpleasant thrill.

Hugo, Gautier, Dumas, Berlioz were among the young men in the audiences. They did not understand English but followed the plays by studying Guizot's translation (1821). To young Dumas, Shakespeare was a revelation which threw him into a delirium of enthusiasm and inspired him to write plays. He hailed Shakespeare as "the man who created most, after God." Berlioz got wrought up to such a pitch of excitement that he married Miss Smithson with whom he played a stormy romantic drama in real life. Not so much could be expected of the sixteen-year-old Gautier, but he soon began to dream of the scarlet waistcoat and pea-green trousers with which he was to grace in romantic fashion the première of *Hernani,* and incidentally to insult the sombre classicists.

Hugo soon published the *Préface de Cromwell* in which he placed Shakespeare and the Bible on the same plane. This document is the Declaration of Independence of the new literature of freedom which Dumas styled "this literary America." Hugo's ideas on dramatic art were not new. Even his theory that the grotesque must be combined with the beautiful in the drama had been suggested by previous critics. His originality consisted in the eloquence with which he argued. His ideas are expressed in his usual trumpet-like fashion which makes his prose resemble a brass band playing *fortissimo* and often a little sharp. One cannot choose but hear. But brass bands never won a war.

The English actors did more to prepare for the victory of romantic tragedy than was accomplished by such propaganda. Their success continued. With few exceptions the journalistic critics were won over to praise. Smithson scored a veritable triumph. Kean, Kemble and Macready were lauded to the skies. French playwrights and actors were advised by the critics to study English dramatic art. In spite of reforms attempted first by Lekain and later by Talma, the actors still grouped themselves in a semi-circle and declaimed the Alexandrine verse. English acting had a wider range and was more realistic. The French actors began to study the interpretation of madness and of death scenes; and thus they prepared unconsciously to act such scenes in the new drama that was to come.

Macready's production of Knowles' *Virginius* in April, 1828, was of special importance. The same subject had been dramatized in classical form by Campistron and by Laharpe. Here was an excellent opportunity to compare the classical and romantic systems. The *Globe* (April 16th) pointed out the superiority of romantic drama for historical subjects. "Only by adopting the Shakespearean system could one trace in all its beauty the character of Virginius." Thus actors, playwrights and public were given an opportunity to study a different form of dramatic art on the stage, whereas previously they had only read about it or had studied it from the printed page of translations.

"The time was propitious," said Dumas in speaking of this period. Talma, the great interpreter of classic rôles, had died in 1826. If one did not know what one wanted, one at least knew what one wanted no longer: classical tragedy. Dumas burned his tragedy *Les Gracques*. He thought that he burned a translation of Schiller's *Fiesko*. He wanted to make his début with an original work, and Ancelot's adaptation, *Fiesque*, had scored a success in 1824 when the sound of a cannon announcing the hour had echoed from afar the cannon in Voltaire's *Adélaïde du Guesclin* and prepared for the three cannon shots in *Hernani*,

so jarring to the sensitive classical ears. Inspired by a small
bas-relief of Christine causing the assassination of Monaldeschi,
he wrote *Christine,* a dramatic trilogy in five acts, in verse, with
a prologue and epilogue thrown in for good measure. The prologue, the first and second acts are at Stockholm. The third,
fourth and fifth acts are at Fontainbleau; and the epilogue is
at Rome. So much for the unities of time and place! Accepted
at the Comédie, intrigues back-stage delayed its presentation.
Henri III et Sa Cour was written in three months and presented
on the eleventh of February, 1829. "From the third act to the end
it was no longer a success, it was an increasing delirium," said
Dumas of the first night. Gœthe's *Faust,* Schiller's *Don Carlos*
and *Fiesko,* Scott's *Astrologer, Abbot* and *Quentin Durward* furnished the dramatist with many details.

The first act opens in the study of the astrologer, Ruggieri,
in Paris. It is Sunday night, July 20, 1578. (Historical details and local color have come into their own.) Catherine de
Medici comes to consult her magician. She is losing power over
her son, Henri III. Guise is forming the League and aspires
to the throne. Young Saint Mégrin is too much in the King's
favor. These men must destroy each other. Saint Mégrin loves
the Duchess of Guise with silent, hopeless passion. Ruggieri
must bring them together. Saint Mégrin is coming to have
Ruggieri cast his horoscope. Catherine has drugged the Duchess
and brought her, asleep, to an adjoining alcove which opens with
a spring. Thus fortified with information and plans, Ruggieri
bids Saint Mégrin gaze into a magic mirror. The spurious
Mephistopheles opens the alcove and shows him the reflection
of his sleeping "Marguerite." A moment later, by pressing another spring, Ruggieri causes the couch, on which the Duchess
lies, to roll into the room. The Duchess wakens, but the love
scene is rudely interrupted by the sound of her husband's voice.
Ruggieri spirits her away through a secret door; but the Duchess,
like Leonora in Schiller's *Fiesko,* has left on the divan her
Shakespearean handkerchief—a real *mouchoir* this time. The
Duke has seen Saint Mégrin. He finds the handkerchief and

calls to one of his henchmen: "Find me the men who assassinated Dugast."

Act II. A great hall in the Louvre. The young men are amusing themselves and producing local color by fencing and playing with pea shooters, while they indulge in the latest gossip. Saint Mégrin challenges Guise to a duel by shooting a bonbon at him —in the presence of the King. (O tragic dignity, where art thou fled!) The Duke accepts; but mutters, aside: "You challenge me too late. Your fate is sealed." Dumas feared the dangerous scene of the pea shooter, but it "passed without opposition."

Act III. The oratory of the Duchess. The faithful Arthur reads aloud to the Duchess Ronsard's latest poem. Guise enters and dismisses the boy. He bids the Duchess write a letter at his dictation. The note tells someone how to enter the apartment of the Duchess. She refuses to write. The Duke forces her by seizing her arm with his mailed fist. The address is to Saint Mégrin. Arthur is summoned. The Duke conceals himself. Arthur is to be instructed to deliver the letter. "A single sign, a single word and the child is dead." The Duchess gives the instructions. The Duke locks the door, which is to open only to Saint Mégrin.

Arthur delivers the note to Saint Mégrin in the fourth act. It is night. Ruggieri warns Saint Mégrin that a cloud will soon obscure his star. But the King gives him a talisman to wear during his duel on the morrow. A melodramatic storm breaks as Saint Mégrin goes to the fatal rendezvous.

Act V. The Duchess awaits her lover in torture, praying that he may not come. He arrives. She tells him of the trap. But these moments "have been the sweetest of his life." She loves him. "Society has no more bonds, the world has no more prejudices," cries the young hero in true romantic frenzy. Noise without. He calmly draws his sword. The Duchess cries for help out of the window. A rope ladder is thrown in. The little page has discovered the plot. The Duke hammers at the door. Time is needed to fasten the ladder. The Duchess passes her arm through the iron ring of the door as a bar. Saint Mégrin puts his·sword between his teeth and descends the ladder. The Duke breaks in the door. From the street comes the sound of clashing swords. The Duke rushes to the window.

SAINT PAUL (*below*)
  Here he is.
DUKE OF GUISE
  Dead?
SAINT PAUL
  No, covered with wounds, but breathing still.
DUCHESS
  He breathes!   He can be saved!   Duke, in the name of Heaven. . .
SAINT PAUL
  He must have some talisman against steel and fire. . . .
DUKE OF GUISE (*throwing the handkerchief of the* DUCHESS *out of the window*)
  Well, strangle him with this handkerchief. Death will be sweeter to him; it bears the arms of the Duchess of Guise.

And the curtain of the Comédie Française—the temple of classicism—begins to descend on high-class melodrama at advanced prices.

Except for the five acts and the fact that the unities happen to be preserved, this play contains almost everything, including picturesque oaths, which would shock the classicists. Whole scenes are given over to local color, as a result of a careful study of Scott. Humor is introduced. Familiar talk about contemporary events replaces the poetic tirade. The dialogue is direct, without metaphorical circumlocution of classical tragedy or of Schiller, and without the lyricism of later romantic drama. Dumas was too much a dramatist to hold up the action in order to sing operatic arias as did Hugo. The dialogue is dramatic prose. The classicists were spared the desecration of the Alexandrine verse. Perhaps that fact delayed the battle until Hugo offended them with overflow lines and displaced cæsural pauses at the Comédie, a year later.

In the last analysis, *Henri III* is melodrama with an unhappy ending. It is not Shakespearean in construction. The play is well made. Had Dumas not seen Shakespeare's plays on the stage, he might not have become a dramatist. Had he not read Schiller and Scott, he would not have introduced certain scenes. He did not choose a theme as a point of departure as did Schiller; but, as in melodrama and in Shakespearean drama, the point of departure is a thrilling plot. Had he not seen melodrama, he could not have written *Henri III* in the form in which it is constructed.

On the thirtieth of May, 1829, Delavigne produced his *Marino Faliero* at the Porte Saint-Martin instead of at the Comédie Française. This play was an attempt at compromise. He refused to state to which of the two systems of literature this play belonged. It was inspired by Byron's closet drama of the same title; but, since it was written for the stage, the differences between the two plays are marked. Delavigne's aim was to produce a freer drama in harmonious verse and to consider as a sacred trust "the beautiful and flexible language" handed down by the great masters. So much for Dumas' staccato prose, with the further implication that if prose melodrama could succeed at the Comédie, literary tragedy could succeed at the Porte Saint-Martin provided the play has some of the new tricks! Thus the heroine reads Dante; and a picture by Giotto of Paolo and Francesca recalls her own situation. The Doge plots while playing chess. The villain, disguised in a domino, shadows the heroine at a masked ball. The Doge wrapped in a cloak discloses himself to conspirators assembled in a public square at midnight. A gondola arrives from which two men step forth and fight a duel to the death. The plot rests upon a political conspiracy and a marital problem. The heroine is not guiltless and the dénouement is tragic; but the plot and the setting and much of the action remind one of Pixérécourt's heroes and conspiring villains in dominos, involved in a political problem and a concealed marriage, while fêtes, gondolas, and masks furnish local color.

Marino Faliero scored a success as a play, but not as a compromise form of drama. The war had gone too far to be settled by a peace without victory. The classicists looked upon Delavigne as a deserter to the Boulevard theatre. The romanticists found his vocabulary too classical for their taste. Like most premature peacemakers he got slapped on both cheeks.

Of quite a different temper was Alfred de Vigny who threw off with an effort his contemplative mood of philosophical poet in order to battle against the old order. He chose as a weapon Shakespeare's *Othello*, which he translated freely, but sympathetically into Alexandrine verse. He omitted certain unimportant scenes and shortened many others. He dropped the clown; and Bianca, the courtezan, did not appear on the stage, although he added her rôle in later editions. He suppressed vulgar lines, on the ground that the genius of great poets does not reside in indecent words. The version played by the English actors contained similar cuts. But he retained the *mouchoir* with a mischievous smile. In order to preserve faithfully the effect of emotional dialogue combined with hurried action, he used overflow verse.

The play was produced on the twenty-fourth of October, 1829, at the Comédie. The cast was excellent, and the settings designed by Cicéri received high praise from both parties. As to the play itself, opinion was naturally divided. It was a pretty strong dose for the conservatives to swallow. They choked and sputtered with rage in their journals; but Shakespeare, "the great Shakespeare," as the actor said who announced the author, had won his place in the sun on the stage founded by Louis XIV— *le roi soleil!*

"A simple question has to be answered," wrote Vigny a few days later. "Will the French stage be open or not to a modern tragedy producing;—in its conception a broad picture of life, instead of the cramped picture of the catastrophe of a plot;— in its composition, characters, not rôles, peaceful scenes without dramatic action, mingled with comic and tragic scenes;—in its

execution, a style familiar, comic, tragic and sometimes epic?"
(*Lettre à Lord * * *.*)

This question, which he silently addressed to the first-night
audience, was answered affirmatively. Vigny speaks of the old
system "which had just died out." Certainly in 1829 its flame
was burning low in spite of the desperate puffs of the classicists.
Soumet's *Fête de Néron,* produced December 18, was one of the
last flickers. Poppæa died on the stage, revealing a large bloody
wound; and a disgusted critic of the *Quotidienne* remarked:
"Horror for horror, Othello's pillow is better!"

The only ammunition left the conservatives were hisses and
fisticuffs which they saved for *Hernani,* produced on the twenty-
fifth of February, 1830. For several weeks the approaching storm
had loomed on the horizon. The air is charged with electricity
as the negative and positive poles assemble at the Comédie.
There is mutual jeering and recrimination. Then the curtain
rises.

The scene represents the apartment of Doña Sol in the ducal
palace of her old uncle. It is night. A lamp burns on the table.
Doña Josefa, the duenna, is alone. She draws the crimson curtains. A knock is heard at a little secret door. She listens. A
second knock.

DOÑA JOSEFA
Serait-ce déjà lui? C'est bien à l'escalier
Dérobé.

(The audience is in an uproar. The first line contains an overflow highly offensive to delicate classical ears. The battle is
on.) She opens the door. A man enters. His face is muffled
in his cloak, in melodramatic fashion. He drops his cloak. It
is not Hernani, but Don Carlos, the King. He inquires if this
is the place where Doña Sol, affianced to the old Duke, her
uncle, meets her young lover, Hernani. It is. The duenna can
choose between a purse for hiding the King in a closet, or a dagger. She takes the purse. (More uproar in the audience. A
king hiding in a closet! A king who puns and jokes and uses

commonplace words, in verses with a strange cæsuras and overflow! It is too much!) Doña Sol enters and a moment later,
Hernani, the bandit, her lover, sweeps in out of the storm.
(And all this is in the Comédie Française not in the Porte Saint-
Martin: the virtuous heroine, her bandit lover, her comic servant,
her uncle preparing an unwelcome marriage, a "villain," who
had slain the lover's father, and upon whom the hero seeks to
be avenged, listening in a closet.)

Doña Sol and Hernani intone their love duet. Hernani vows
vengeance on the King who condemned his father to the scaffold.
Doña Sol swears to follow Hernani to his mountains and become
an outlaw's mate. The closet opens and the cloaked figure steps
forth. The unknown man jokes and jeers at Hernani and
calmly declares his love for Doña Sol. Swords are drawn and
crossed. Don Ruy Gomez, Doña Sol's uncle, enters suddenly
with servants bearing lights. As he is to marry his niece he
feels that three men with her "are by two too many." He calls
for his "dagger of Toledo, axe and dirk," when the unknown
figure reveals his face. It is the King. He asserts that he has
come to discuss his succession to the Imperial crown; and he
proceeds to do so at Hugoesque length. As he leaves, he hears
Hernani and Doña Sol agree to meet at midnight on the morrow.
Don Ruy Gomez asks the King who is this lord. The King
replies: "One of my followers." All exit except Hernani, who
delivers a fiery invective playing upon—not to say punning upon
—the word "follower," as the curtain falls amid wild cheers
and booing.

The second act discloses the square before the ducal palace.
Night. Here and there a few windows are illuminated. The
King and four of his nobles, wrapped in long cloaks, hats pulled
down, arrive. The King watches for a light in the window before which there is a Juliet balcony. It gleams forth. His
Majesty orders his nobles to withdraw, and then he gives the
signal agreed upon by Doña Sol and Hernani. She descends
from the balcony only to find herself held by the King. He
promises that she shall be his queen—his empress. Faithful to

her outlaw she snatches the dagger from the King's girdle. "Another step and I kill you—and myself." Hernani arrives like a thunderbolt. The duel begun last night can be finished. But no. Now they know each other. The King will not fight an outlaw, though the outlaw murder him. Hernani "plays a moment with the hilt of his sword, turns sharply towards the King and—snaps the blade on the pavement." "We shall have fitter meetings—. Go!" He throws his cloak about the King's shoulders so that his bandits in ambuscade will not recognize and slay His Majesty. Doña Sol offers the sound advice to fly immediately, but Hugo is not going to miss the chance for a dramatic-lyric scene. Hernani finds that it is too late. (This Byronic Romeo is a bit of a Hamlet in his indecision.) They stay "to speak of love in stillness of the night when nature rests," until the tocsin sounds. Instead of seeking refuge with the woman whose life and honor he has endangered, he gallantly kisses her, but rather ungallantly leaves her fainting on the stone bench as he dashes off to protect his followers. However, this is romantic drama, not a book of etiquette.

The curtain of the third act rises upon the gallery of family portraits of the Duke. Doña Sol is to become his bride within the hour. A pilgrim appears asking asylum. Doña Sol enters in bridal attire. Pages bear in a silver casket of jewels. The pilgrim tears off his robe. He is Hernani. He bids the lackeys seize him. His head is worth a thousand crowns. The Duke, in honor bound to protect his guest, goes forth to close the palace gates. Hernani waxes sarcastic at the sight of the bridal jewels until Doña Sol causes his wrath to melt by showing him a dagger at the bottom of the casket. At the end of their love duet, the Duke finds them clasped in each other's arms. Addressing the portraits of his honorable ancestors, the Duke asks for guidance. Trumpets announce the arrival of the King. The Duke goes to his own portrait, presses a spring and it opens, revealing a hiding place. Hernani conceals himself in it as the King enters. When His Majesty demands that Hernani be surrendered, the Duke once more points to his ancestors; and,

having rehearsed their honor, he points to his own portrait.
Will he open it? No. He will not be a traitor. The furious
King departs, taking Doña Sol with him as a hostage. Hernani
comes forth. The Duke is ready to fight. Hernani offers him his
life, until he learns that Doña Sol has been abducted by the
King who loves her. He asks to be allowed to live until he
saves her. He offers the Duke his horn.

HERNANI

    Listen! take you this horn, and whatsoe'er
    May happen—what the place or what the hour—
    Whenever to thy mind it seems the time
    Has come for me to die, blow on this horn.
    And take no other care; all will be done.

DON RUY GOMEZ (*offering his hand*)

    Your hand.

    (*They clasp hands.   To the portraits*)

    And all of you are witnesses.

The vaults of the tomb of Charlemagne, mysterious arches,
steps and columns are the sombre shadowy setting of the fourth
act. Unities of time and place have been broken to bits. Unity
of action has been stretched almost to the breaking point. For
the classicists, it has snapped. Don Carlos and his noblemen
await the conclave, which is to elect the emperor. A cannon will
boom thrice if Don Carlos is chosen. Left alone, he meditates
at length in the famous monologue on several subjects, including clemency. (Meditative monologues in the style either of
Figaro or Hamlet were considered essential to romantic drama.)
He enters the tomb. The cloaked conspirators, among whom
are the Duke and Hernani, file in softly in the light of a single
torch. Hernani is chosen by lot to slay Don Carlos. A cannon
booms—again—thrice. The tomb opens, Carlos appears. Every
light is suddenly quenched. He strikes the bronze door with
his key, soldiers seize the conspirators. Doña Sol is brought
in. The Emperor pardons Hernani and bestows Doña Sol on
him as his bride.

Act V. The nuptials. A moonlit terrace of the palace of Aragon. Music. Masks and dominos. Another setting of the melodrama. Young lords laughing and chatting. Hernani and Doña Sol have been married. Happiness and plenty of local color; but a sinister figure—a black domino—crosses the terrace. Flame seems to shine in his eyes. At last the guests retire. Doña Sol and Hernani are left alone in the quiet beauty of the perfumed night. In lyric poetry such as was never heard on the French stage, they pour forth their ecstasy in one of the most beautiful love duets ever spoken. The silence is too deep. Doña Sol longs to "hear a voice of night . . . a bird that in the meadow sings . . . a nightingale in moss or shadow lost, or flute afar." The sound of a horn is heard. Her prayer is answered, but—it is the sound of Hernani's hunting horn—his death note sounded by Ruy Gomez, who appears shrouded in his black domino. The lovers beg for mercy, but Hernani is in honor bound. Doña Sol snatches the poison from her husband and drinks half of it. She gives him back the vial. He drains it; and the modern Romeo and Juliet die in each other's arms. The curtain falls as romantic drama wins the day. It is melodrama lifted to a high plane by a poet under the influence of Shakespeare, by a playwright under the influence of two centuries of French dramatic craftsmanship.

The lyricism was due, in part, to Shakespeare's direct influence and also to the fact that the author was a lyric poet in a lyric age. The juxtaposition of the grotesque and the beautiful had been exemplified in Shakespearean drama. The theory had been formulated briefly by Walpole, Schlegel, Mme de Staël and others, and had been developed at length by Hugo. The balcony scene of *Romeo and Juliet* inspired Hugo. A part of the death scene is modelled on Garrick's adaptation of *Romeo and Juliet* which was the version played by the English troupe, and witnessed by Hugo. In this scene Juliet awakens before Romeo dies; and they indulge in a tragic lyric duet before they die, as do Hernani and Doña Sol.

Yet French romantic drama is not Shakespearean. These

young playwrights justified their theories and practice by calling upon the authority of the great Elizabethan dramatist whenever it was possible. They considered themselves his devoted disciples. They conjured by his name; but they wrote well-made plays. His influence was less immediate than they believed; it was actually less operative than Schiller's. The melodrama was the medium with which they worked and from which they derived much of their technique.

The melodrama was in three acts, but the romanticists usually retained the five-act form. Where Pixerécourt was short of breath, Hugo was long-winded. The romantic playwright rarely permitted a change of scene within the act. This was another Shakespearean liberty which smacked too much of anarchy for the Frenchman. Unlike Shakespeare, unlike the classicists, but like the writers of melodrama and like Schiller, the romanticists made each act a unit ending with a climax and a striking final line. The scene is the unit in Shakespeare. The whole play is the unit in classic drama. Neither of these forms has a clearly marked act division where the curtain must fall. Alfred de Musset alone was under the direct inspiration of Shakespeare; but after the failure of his *Nuit Vénitienne* in 1830, he did not write his plays with a view to stage presentation. Although his charming lyric dramas were finally produced, the Shakespearean looseness of their construction kept them from influencing the development of French dramatic art until after romantic drama had run its course.

The scenery of romantic tragedy reproduces the settings of the melodramas with the same care for detail. The scenery is an integral part of the play and not a mere background. Shakespeare's plays and classical tragedy can be produced intelligently without any decoration; but to remove the sets from the stage would make melodrama and romantic drama unintelligible. Thus in Hugo's *Le Roi s'Amuse*, the place de la Grève and the interior of two rooms must be visible in order to follow the action of the fourth act. The settings aim to bring out the local color of the place and period; and Hugo made the setting an integral part of his dramatic art. He introduced effects of mass, light and shade, and color for psychological and emotional purposes. His gothic windows suffused with light foreshadow Maeterlinckian settings. Crowds, monks, soldiers, maskers are employed for pictorial-dramatic effects. He transformed the divertissement of the melodrama into a carnival ballet in the opening of *Lucrèce Borgia*. In the final act of *Hernani* he dramatizes light, color, sound, silence and lyric poetry. He calls upon our sensations as well as upon our intellect. Synthetic dramatic art is not far away. Richard Wagner was soon to revive the Aristotelian synthesis by adding the element of expressionistic music in perfect harmony with the dramatic situation.

The point of departure in romantic drama is a plot which can be divided into five acts, each one furnishing at least one great *coup de théâtre*. Nothing is too melodramatic in any sense of the word for these romantic playwrights. The plot may be highly complex, as in *Hernani* or *Henri III*, or much simpler, as in *Ruy Blas* or *Marion Delorme*. It must have thrills arising from remarkable situations. Thus the whole machinery of disguises and concealed identities, as used in melodrama, is brought into play. Forbid the use of masks and cloaks, and both forms of drama cease to exist.

The plots leap forward by means of overheard conversations and actions beheld by concealed personages. The characters arrive on the scene "pat, like the catastrophe of the old comedy." If they came a few seconds earlier or later, the whole course of the action would be altered. If a greater thrill can be produced, they come down the chimney, as does Don César in *Ruy Blas* or through a window, as does Didier in *Marion Delorme*. If, as in the latter play, one character must not recognize another, for the sake of the plot a lamp is overturned. The lame reason is given, aside, that a rival is looking at the heroine with bold eyes. In such circumstances the study of a theme or a character is difficult. The psychological element is often unheard amid the whirring of the machinery, no matter how smoothly the wheels revolve. Analysis of character cannot be made effectively in monologues and tirades. Character unfolds in action; and the action of romantic tragedy is a series of thrills. Hugo's people are not always marionettes; but they become so at any moment for the sake of the plot. The range of characters is greater than in melodrama. The melodramatic formula of the virtuous woman persecuted by the "traitor" is not monotonously maintained. The humor is not confined to a single comic character. Yet, like the hero of the melodrama, Didier, Gennaro and Ruy Blas are children of mysterious parentage. Gennaro, ignorant that he is the son of the evil Lucretia, is first cousin to Pixerécourt's Victor who does not know that his father is the notorious bandit. Parental love for innocent offspring controls the actions of both "villains." In *Le Roi s'Amuse,* the pander Triboulet is the father of the heroine, Blanche; and he is punished by bringing destruction unwittingly upon his own child, the only creature in the world whom he loves and respects. The rôle of the evil-doer, which appears in so many romantic tragedies, is handled much less crudely than in melodrama. The heroine is not always a paragon of virtue. Blanche actually loves the King and deceives her father in *Le Roi s'Amuse.* Marion Delorme is a courtezan who enlists our sympathy. By endowing their principals with both vices and virtues, the romanticists began to differentiate characters and create individuals, not mere rôles cut out by pattern. Not since Figaro, had any characters appeared on the French stage with such distinct personalities as Triboulet, Marion Delorme, Ruy Blas. Had they been in less strange circumstances and gone through fewer astounding adventures, they would have been more human.

The classical dramatists often made their personages vague abstractions. The romanticists insisted upon the "characteristic." They exaggerated the characteristic to such an extent that it borders constantly on caricature. Their personages are individuals; but they are very strange individuals in strange circumstances. We know them; but we do not know anyone like them.

The construction of romantic tragedy differs from that of melodrama in two respects. The point of attack is earlier in the newer form of drama. Thus the narrative exposition of the melodrama is generally replaced by exposition in action in romantic tragedy. This is a distinct gain, for nothing is more inartistic in the theatre than mere narrative before suspense has been aroused. Had the romantic playwrights followed Shakespeare's practice, they would have chosen a still earlier point of attack.

The greatest difference between the two forms appears in the last act. The melodrama ended happily. Romanticists could not be so bourgeois as to believe in the reward for virtue. No means of escape from death was allowed in their scheme of art for hero or heroine. The final impression left by romantic drama is tragic; but it is not well to inquire as to the inexorable logic of the dénouement either of melodrama or of romantic drama. A tragic last act is only apparently inevitable when the determining element in the action is chance.

The influence of the melodrama is clearly seen in Hugo's *Lucrèce Borgia,* which even retains the three-act division and the prose dialogue. The play opens at Venice before an illuminated palace. Maskers dance a ballet, after which the exposition is given, not in action, but, as in the melodrama, by narrative dialogue telling of the criminal Lucretia and of her mysterious child. Among the young men who listen is the Spaniard, Gubetta, a traitor who turns out to be the semi-comic, lesser villain of melodrama. Young Gennaro falls asleep on a bench. Lucretia finds him. He is her son. She kisses him and thus arouses the jealousy of the Duke d'Este, her second husband, who enters masked and unperceived, and exits vowing vengeance. Gennaro wakens. He is attracted to this unknown woman whom he neither knows as his mother nor as the hated Borgia. Gennaro's friends enter. They tear the mask from her face. Gennaro is horror-stricken to find she is Lucretia Borgia.

Act II. The young men have arrived at Ferrara on an embassy. They are before the Borgia palace. Lucretia vows venge-

ance upon Gennaro's friends for having caused him to manifest hate for her—his unknown mother. She plans a poisoned
banquet for them. Gennaro is not to be harmed; but the Duke
d'Este has Gennaro seized and brought before him and Lucretia.
He confesses that he erased the B from the word Borgia on
the palace. Lucretia, who has demanded the death of the unknown culprit, is horror-stricken. Her husband forces her to
pour out poison for Gennaro, whom he has pretended to pardon.
Gennaro drinks it; but Lucretia gives him an antidote, and
bids him fly from Ferrara.

Act III. The banquet hall of a palace. Gennaro has delayed his departure—for reasons of plot—and has partaken of
the poisoned wine with his young friends. Gubetta, pretending
to have drunk of the wine, begins a drinking song. Monks are
heard chanting. The lights go down. The chant comes nearer.
Large curtains open, disclosing an altar. Six monks enter.
Lucretia appears. The curtains close. She announces that the
banqueters are poisoned. The curtains disclose five coffins ready
for them. Gennaro asks for the sixth. Lucretia had thought
him, her son, safe on the road to Venice. She stabs Gubetta
for not having saved him. Gennaro still has the antidote; but
there is not enough of it for his friends. He refuses to take
it, and he seizes a knife from the table. She pleads, but
in vain. He stabs her as his friends die. She cries: "I am your
mother!" With a scream of despair he falls dead. Lucretia
crawls to his body and dies as the monks take up their chant.

Nothing more hair-raising than this play by Hugo and *La
Tour de Nesle* by Dumas had ever been produced on the Boulevards by Pixerécourt. It is not strange that the French intellectuals soon began to tire of such effects and to demand a
new drama of "good sense." The reaction commenced when the
actress Rachel, a volcano covered with snow, successfully revived many of the great classic rôles in 1838. Even Hugo's
finest drama, *Ruy Blas*, of the same year could not stem the tide
that was setting in against romanticism on the stage. In 1843
the *Burgraves* failed dismally. Hugo's first play, *Cromwell*,

was too vast for the stage. His *Burgraves* is an epic poem in dialogue under which the delicate framework of drama cracked. Involved and lumbering in its plot, it can scarcely be followed by the spectator. The characters are, as Sainte Beuve remarked, "gigantic marionettes." They stalk about the stage gorgeously but heavily in their concealed identities and disguises. They boom forth long speeches full of confusing details of uninteresting history. No one is the person he seems to be, and only the spectator who enjoys a Chinese puzzle really cares who the characters are or is interested in what they are doing. In the *Burgraves*, Hugo is at his worst; and the greater the genius, the worse he is when he exaggerates his virtues into vices. Hugo was done as a dramatist; and romantic drama ended in 1843 with the failure of the *Burgraves*. Like its heroes, it had lived a short and riotous life. It was "born too late in a world too old."

A month after this Waterloo of romantic drama, the Restoration of classical tragedy took place with Ponsard's *Lucrèce*. In its period of exile this drama of the Old Régime had learned some liberalism. The unities of time and place are not observed in *Lucrèce;* but interminable narrative passages, including an allegorical dream, were piously ground out by the author in a style imitated from Corneille and Racine. "Good sense," which results in mediocrity, could help to discredit the excesses of romantic drama, but it could not revive classical tragedy for long. The age was becoming realistic. The word had not yet been used in regard to art, but Balzac was writing his *Comédie Humaine*. The preface in which he explains his method appeared in 1842. Contemporary manners, not ancient or medieval history, were being portrayed in the novel. It was only a matter of time before the drama, as usual, would follow in the footsteps of narrative fiction and study problems of everyday life, in everyday surroundings.

CHAPTER XVII

FRENCH REALISTIC DRAMA. THE PROBLEM PLAY

THE *Mariage de Figaro* had combined a discussion of a social problem with an intricate plot handled with great dexterity. During the Revolution the theatre had been given over to propaganda. The characters were mere masks. The plots were often inartistically sacrificed for the sake of satire in comedy, and in order to voice republican sentiments in serious plays. Drama, like all other arts, was at low ebb. But, while the war over tragedy was being waged, comedy began a peaceful development which was to culminate in the work of Scribe and, through him, to exert a powerful influence on all European drama of the nineteenth century.

Picard, an actor-dramatist, was chiefly responsible for the reestablishment of true comedy on the stage. His *Médiocre et Rampant* (1797) was an artistic success in comparison to the plays of the *sans culottes* of the revolutionary period, although it was no novelty in comparison to the comedies of the Old Régime. In his *Entrée dans le Monde* (1799), Picard consciously sacrificed plot to a discussion of manners. He pointed out in his preface that he introduced episodic scenes and a large number of characters in order to show a part of the society of Paris in 1799, that he hurried events in an improbable manner, and that the dénouement does not spring either from the action or the characters. In 1801 he produced a study of the provincial manners entitled *La Petite Ville*. His point of departure was the theme of the unattractiveness of society in small towns. Realizing that there was no unified plot in the play, Picard called it an episodic comedy. He even deleted one of the acts without seriously harming what plot there was;

but the element of plot, though insignificant in these two plays, was to become increasingly important in his work.

His *Duhautcours* (1801) was a step towards realistic comedy. Inspired by *Turcaret* and by Noland de Fatouville's *Banqueroutier,* Picard presents in this play a study of the world of high finance, which was to become the subject of countless plays in the new century. This comedy becomes a serious drama in the fourth act when Durville and his advisor, Duhautcours, try to effect a bankruptcy which will enrich them. They are finally foiled and exposed by Franval in a realistic scene which foreshadows many such episodes in modern drama in which, during a brilliant soirée, guests, creditors and lawyers assemble in the home of a captain of industry. The plot does not overshadow the study of high finance in 1801; but the question as to whether the would-be bankrupt can succeed in his nefarious plans is important enough to satisfy anyone who insists that every play must have a story. A secondary love story between the nephew of Durville and a young girl whose father is being ruined by the financier is loosely connected with the main action. Picard was still inclined to be episodic instead of neatly dovetailing the component parts of his action as Beaumarchais had done and as he himself was to do in a few years.

He said that his *Marionettes* (1806) was a play based on character and hence the plot was subordinate to the characters. However, his aim was to show that people are governed by events, not by will power or personal traits. In a word, we are all marionettes and when circumstance pulls the strings we dance accordingly. He developed this view of life still further in his *Ricochets* (1807). He says of the plot: "My little groom obeys his mistress. The son of the minister obeys his, the mistress obeys her own caprice; and the caprice, by which he is dominated, dominates and decides by a series of ricochets, the fate of all the personages. Finally, in destroying all hopes by the loss of a little dog, in causing them to be reborn, in realizing them, in bringing about marriages and getting positions by the gift of a canary bird, I prove that small causes often produced great results." That such a chain of cause and effect acts upon people that are marionettes was Picard's view of life. Scribe's method of constructing plays was to be based on this theory.

When Pascal remarked that if Cleopatra's nose had been shorter, the history of the world would have been different, he implied that small causes bring forth great effects; but the statement also embodies the idea that chance plays an important rôle in the drama of life. Fate and Chance are as far apart as the two poles and quite as similar in effect. The concepts expressed in these two words are diametrically opposed to each other, and yet, are so constantly interchanged, that they seem to the average man to be interchangeable. Is it Fate or Chance which rules the destiny of an Œdipus or a Romeo? The individual may answer the question according to the state of his digestion; but anyone who believes that small causes produce great results, that kingdoms are lost for want of a horseshoe nail, that the upsetting of a glass of water may bring political upheavals, will allow the element of chance free play in his philosophy of life.

Many of Scribe's contemporaries believed that the destruction of class distinction by the Revolution had made the comedy of manners impossible. Scribe went much further and insisted that the stage never had been and never could be the mirror of society. Perhaps he was wearied of the solemn reiteration of the opposite view by the Academicians. It was his fate to mirror the larger part of contemporary society better than they did and better than the nervous romanticists who believed so ecstatically in missions and purposes of art. Holding these conceptions of life and of drama and becoming the master-builder of the well-made play, Scribe's influence on dramatic art in the nineteenth century was universally condemned by serious critics and dramatists. The critics were content to censure him. The dramatists criticized him consciously and imitated him unconsciously.

"You go to the theatre, not for instruction or correction, but for relaxation and amusement. Now what amuses you most is not truth, but fiction. To represent what is before your eyes every day is not the way to please you; but what does not come to you in your usual life, the extraordinary, the romantic, that is what charms you, that is what one is eager to offer you. . . . The theatre is then very rarely the expression of society; . . . it is very often the inverse expression."

Thus spoke Scribe to the Academicians in 1836. Not since Molière had a dramatist had the temerity to insist that the principal aim of the theatre is amusement. He began his career by writing *comédies-vaudevilles*. The *vaudeville* aims solely to entertain. It is a play in one to three acts in which songs are introduced. The plot is often based upon some curious, actual incident, and the *quiproquo* is constantly employed. A descendant of the farce, the vaudeville was often satirical. As Molière developed the farce into high comedy in the seventeenth century, so Scribe started with the *vaudeville*, and with the aid of the example of Picard, he gradually transformed the *vaudeville* into a comedy which actually deals with manners and society, but in which the plot is carefully stressed. Scribe's ability to build intricate situations and to extract from them the maximum amounts of surprise and suspense, has caused him to be considered usually as a playwright who sacrifices all to dramaturgic dexterity. The charge is true; but in spite of this sacrifice, some of his plays contain social problems.

His formula for constructing plays is simple. The variations of his method are many. As a rule, his point of departure is a plot. If he begins with a social problem, such as marriage, and money, or with the idea of showing how great results arise from small causes, or with a character, the plot assumes finally such importance that the problem, character or theme is overshadowed.

His point of attack is fairly close to his dénouement. Though his plots contain many incidents, he feels no need of the large framework of romantic drama. His *Bertrand et Raton* (1833), produced in the heyday of romanticism, is a compact historical comedy. When the curtain rises on any of his full length comedies, there is often much to be explained. Scribe is deliberate in his first act. He would be boring in some of his openings were it not for his wit. If a social problem is involved in the plot, he states it lucidly and discusses it clearly. If events of the past are to influence the present, he explains them and their effect on his characters. He does not avoid long speeches, asides or monologues, and does not mystify the spectator by keeping secrets.

By the end of the first act or in the first part of the second, all the important circumstances are clear. Then the fireworks begin. Letters miscarry. The *quiproquo* occurs at any moment. He weaves together the many threads of his plot and dexterously unties them at the end. It is the incidents which develop, not his characters.

An outstanding example of his dramatic juggling is his *Bataille de Dames* (1851). Henri de Flavigneul has been condemned to death for conspiracy and is hiding, disguised as a servant, in the home of the Countess d'Autreval. She is secretly in love with him. Her niece, Léonie, does not know who this valet is, but finds herself uncomfortably attracted by him. The juggling of the question: Will he be discovered? then begins. Henri is constantly on the point of revealing his identity by his gentlemanly manners and conduct. He confesses his identity to Léonie because she felt insulted at his attitude toward her after he rescued her from a bolting horse. Henri is in love with Léonie, but he is in a very awkward position. The Countess loves him, and is saving him from death.

Montrichard is searching for Henri in order to capture him. Henri meets him, and pretends to aid him in his search. Léonie, questioned by Montrichard, practically betrays Henri through agitated answers. The Countess saves Henri by having an admirer of hers, De Grignan, dress as a servant and pose as Henri. Montrichard actually gives Henri a pass and a horse to carry a message. Henri escapes but learns that De Grignan has been taken. He returns. Montrichard discovers he has captured the wrong man. He returns. Henri conceals himself behind the broad skirts of the two ladies. Montrichard announces that Henri has been pardoned. Henri reveals himself. Montrichard immediately arrests him. His statement was a trick. He has won. The Countess is in consternation for a moment. Then she announces that Montrichard is joking; that his statement was true. Montrichard laughingly admits it. Henri is free. The Countess, however, is defeated. She must renounce Henri for the sake of Léonie; but she is partially consoled by accepting De Grignan.

Artificial as the plot is, it is deftly handled and enlivened by sparkling wit. The suspense, surprises and sudden appearances are mechanical; but the machinery runs so smoothly, so quietly, that one is not disturbed by it. Scribe sweeps gracefully to a climax while his contemporaries labored heavily to reach it. His theatrical effects may be meretricious, but they are never dull. Hugo piled up heavy complications and romantic drama cracked under them. Scribe wove complications into a piece of lace work—light and diaphanous.

The plausibility of the development of his situations has been a thorn in the flesh of his hostile critics. He was careful in his preparation. In *Adrienne Lecouvreur* his heroine dies through breathing a subtle poison. This event is not foreshadowed but is fully prepared in the first act. Scribe's characters always enter at the psychological moment; but their entrances are never improbable. Letters bring the dénouements of the *Mariage d'Argent* and of *Camaraderie;* but the spectator does not feel that the situation of the characters as the curtain falls is illogical. In *Bertrand et Raton* many suprising events take place, but he shows that those who actively conspire against a government, especially the bourgeois, are not the people who reap the benefits of a revolution. Much can be said for this idea. It is a sensible view; and common sense—meaning the point of view of the average man—dominates Scribe's plays. His popularity with the majority of theatre-goers and his unpopularity with the feverish romanticists were due partially to his common sense. The accusation that he was not a profound thinker is true; but he cannot be accused justly of being illogical. He had a sane outlook on life. He avoided sentimentality. He sacrificed the romantic to the reasonable. Even his theory of the small cause leading to great results has a certain plausible logic in it as he presents it in his developing actions.

His play *Une Chaine* is based upon the situation of a young musician who has succeeded in obtaining recognition through the efforts of a young married woman. They are lovers. He feels deep gratitude towards her; but when he falls in love with his cousin and wishes to marry her, his mistress becomes a chain. This idea is stated clearly three or four times during the play; but there is no study of the problem. The action develops through a series of events that is full of surprise, suspense, and Scribian tricks. The situation becomes complex to a high degree, but always remains clear. The play is more than well made; it is beautifully made. The interest lies in the plot, not in the problem. Yet the ending is logical and sensible although it is brought about by a trick. But the time was soon to come when Augier and the younger Dumas were to place much more emphasis on the problem and somewhat less on the plot. The well-made play, however, was to continue its vogue for many years. Scribe invented nothing. French playwrights for two centuries had shown great skill in construction. But Scribe used all the tricks of the trade all the time. Others used some of them some of the time. He excelled everyone in dramaturgic dexterity, and he taught the dramatists of the nineteenth century their art of playmaking. His greatest virtue was his greatest fault: he was too skilful. But as Sarcey says, "One must know Scribe. One must study, but not imitate him."

Augier and the younger Dumas owed much to Scribe; but, unlike him, they held that drama reflects contemporary society. Augier was content to treat problems impassively. Dumas sought to give the answer to the problem. He was militant, argumentative, presenting one side of the question with logic that seems, for the moment, irrefutable. Augier presented both sides of the problem with delicate balance. He concluded on the side of common sense like Scribe, like Molière; but the conclusion is unobtrusive. The final curtain of a play by the younger Dumas reminds one of the Q.E.D. of a geometrical problem. One has experienced a demonstration. The point has been hammered home.

The elder Dumas was the most romantic of all romantic playwrights. He was still producing great historical spectacles when the realistic problem play was evolving in the middle of the century. His *Antony* (1831) is an extravagant example of romanticism; yet it foreshadows the problem play as it was to be produced by his son. Vigny's *Chatterton* (1835) contains a romantic poet as a hero, but it is a conscious attempt to introduce that form of drama in which plot is relegated to the background and the idea or thought is the important element in the synthesis.

The curtain of *Antony* rises on the salon of Adèle d'Hervey. She receives a letter from Antony, who was in love with her before her marriage, but who has dropped out of her life for three years. He wishes to see her; but Adèle, the mother of a three-year-old child, fears to see him lest her former love for him revive. She arranges to go out in her carriage, leaving her sister Clara to interview Antony and dismiss him. Out of a window, Clara sees the horses take fright and a young man leap forward and save Adèle. It is Antony. He is badly injured. Adèle enters and is given a portfolio found on Antony. It contains her picture, her only letter to him—and a dagger. Antony is carried in. Adèle, feeling her love for him once more, says he may remain only if his life is in danger. He tears off the bandages and cries: "Now I can stay—can't I?"

The explanation of the situation is given in the second act. Antony is still at Adèle's home. The veils are withdrawn from the past. Antony left Adèle three years before, because a marriage was proposed between her and Colonel d'Hervey. Antony is a foundling without family, rank or occupation. He had asked for a space of two weeks in order to solve the secret of his birth. He was unsuccessful. Because of the prejudice of society against such men as he, Antony could not be the rival of Colonel d'Hervey. Adèle comes more and more under the spell of the pale, young romanticist as he talks of his life and love. Adèle confesses her love for him; but she has decided to seek the protection of her husband stationed in Strasbourg. Antony leaves her, knowing nothing of her decision which is to be communicated to him in a cold letter.

The third act is at an inn two leagues from Strasbourg. Antony arrives. He engages the two vacant rooms. He makes it impossible for any traveller to obtain fresh horses; but he tells the hostess he may give up the extra room if a guest arrives. He sends his servant to Strasbourg to watch Colonel d'Hervey. At the slightest sign of the Colonel's departure for Paris at any time, the servant is to inform Antony. In a passionate monologue, punctuated by driving his dagger into the table, he informs us that he has passed Adèle on the way. He is going to demand an explanation of her departure. He exits. Adèle arrives. The hostess gives her the extra room, since she cannot continue her journey. She hears a noise in the next room. She is beside herself with fear. Antony appears on the balcony, breaks the window and enters. Adèle screams. Antony takes her in his arms and, putting a handkerchief over her mouth, draws her into the other room as the curtain falls.

The fourth act passes some time later at a ball given by the Vicomtesse de Lacy. Adèle has ventured into society with Antony. Under the cloak of a discussion of literature, a Madame de Camps cites their case only too plainly. Left alone with Antony, Adèle is crushed by the impending scandal. Antony takes her in his arms, but the Vicomtesse enters too suddenly. Adèle rushes from the room. Antony's servant informs him that Colonel d'Hervey is nearing Paris.

The fifth act reveals a room in D'Hervey's house. Adèle has reached home. Antony arrives with the crushing news of her husband's arrival. They must fly. A pounding is heard at the door. The Colonel is outside. Nothing remains but death. Antony stabs Adèle. The door is broken down.

ANTONY (*throwing the dagger at the* COLONEL'S *feet*)
Yes. Dead. She resisted me and I killed her.

To the modern realist such a series of *coups de théâtre* so neatly dovetailed seems too melodramatic to represent life. The characters are too exceptional. Their psychological reactions seem as superannuated as the medicine practised by the doctor who bleeds Antony for an injury which has already caused a loss of blood. The passions displayed by Antony made him seem false to certain contemporaries. The element of chance in the action seems overworked, with the timely and untimely appearances of the personages and the remarkable succession of events of the past and present.

But Dumas was entirely conscious of what he was trying to do in constructing this *"drame d'exception,"* as he called it. The dialogue contains a running comment on his ideas. In the fourth act, Eugène, a dramatist, is asked why he does not write a play on a subject of modern society instead of the Middle Ages. "That is what I repeat to him every minute," says the Vicomtesse. "Do something of real life. Are we not much more interested in people of our own times, dressed like us, speaking the same language?" Beaumarchais and Diderot had asked the same question, years before, in regard to classical tragedy. It was pertinent to the new romantic historical drama. A baron replies for Eugène: "It is easier to take subjects from chronicles than from the imagination. One finds in them plays almost entirely written." Eugène—probably speaking for Dumas—says that comedy of manners is very difficult because the Revolution levelled all differences of rank. He continues:

The drama of passion remains, and here another difficulty presents itself. History gives us facts, they belong to us by right of inheritance, they are incontestable, they belong to the poet. He revives the men of bygone times, clothes them in their costumes, agitates them with their passions which increase or diminish to the degree to which he desires to carry the dramatic. But if we tried, in the midst of our modern society, in our short-tailed, awkward coats, to lay bare the heart of man, one would not recognize it. The resemblance between the hero and the audience would be too great, the analogy too close. The spectator who follows, in the actor, the development of the passion will want to stop it where it would have stopped in his own heart. If it surpasses his own power of feeling or expressing, he will not understand it any longer, he will say: "That is false; I do not feel thus; when the woman I love deceives me, I suffer without doubt . . . yes . . . for a time . . . but I don't stab her and die, and the proof is, here I am." Then the cries of exaggeration and melodrama, covering the applause of these few men, who, more happily or unhappily organized than the others, feel that passions are the same from the fifteenth to the nineteenth century.

This passage contains the indictment by the realists before they pronounced it upon romantic drama. Indeed, it is a common indictment of all drama. It implies the eternal question: Just how melodramatic can an art be which seems to represent real life actually before us? The point of melodramatic saturation depends entirely upon the views of contemporary society.

Dumas felt that in *Antony* he was writing something much more realistic than the romantic historical drama. Though some contemporaries called the hero false, he is the incarnation on the stage, not only of the romantic lovers in novels and poems of the time, but of the romanticists as they imagined themselves to be, as they were, in so far as was possible in an everyday world of reality. The success of the play would otherwise have been impossible.

Antony, the foundling of mysterious parentage, has descended from a long line of children, beginning with Euripides' Ion, who are lost for theatrical purposes in both tragedy and comedy. But Dumas' treatment of this idea of the foundling was both new and dramatic. The fact that Antony is an orphan of unknown parents is the determining factor in his character and raises the problem of the attitude of society towards foundlings. The play, therefore, not only foreshadows realistic drama because it deals with contemporary characters, but also because it raises a social problem. This question is the basis of the plot and is directly discussed in the second act in a manner resembling that of the later problem play. The unfaithful wife had appeared on the German stage in Kotzebue's *Menschenhass und Reue* in 1789; and his play had been given in French adaptations in 1792, 1799 and 1823. The grown-up, illegitimate child had been a source of sentimental emotion in European bourgeois drama from the time of Diderot's *Fils Naturel*. In *Antony*, however, the unfaithful wife and the illegitimate child are tragic characters. Their lives give rise to problems, rather than to sentimentality. The fallen woman on the stage can no longer always escape punishment by repentance and by living a life of charity and virtue. Thus *Antony* rightly belongs to the nineteenth century, while *Menschenhass und Reue* is clearly a product of the sentimental optimism of the eighteenth century.

Having struck this modern note in *Antony*, Dumas turned once more to romantic melodrama. It was easier for his active brain to construct plots than to study carefully problems of his society. But Alfred de Vigny, the most profound thinker of all the French romanticists, was deeply impressed by this drama. He insisted that it contained a dominating thought, that it was a moral satire against the atheism, materialism and egoism of the age. He denied that the play was too "talky." While the stage was ringing with the sonorous lyricism of Hugo and the spectators were being dazzled by theatrical surprises, Vigny revolted against the complicated mechanism of romantic drama. He said in his preface to *Chatterton* that the time had come for the "Drama of Thought." He proposed to show "the spiritual man stifled by a materialistic society." He chose the simplest possible plot: "the story of a man who has written a letter in the morning and who awaits the reply until evening; it comes and it kills him." Had there been a simpler plot, he would have chosen it, because in this play "the moral action is every-thing." The action is in the heart of Chatterton, the symbolic figure of the Poet; in the hearts of Kitty Bell and the Quaker.

In *Chatterton,* Vigny consciously produced a problem play before the expression itself was used as a term of dramatic criticism. Many dramatists before him had written eloquent prefaces to show how their plays taught morality by stripping vice of its mask and rewarding virtue. Social problems had been mirrored more or less consciously. But no dramatist had so clearly stated his problem, and deliberately reduced the plot to a bare skeleton in order to spend all the time on the "moral action." If dramatists had employed this method consciously, they had kept silent in regard to it. Diderot had advocated simplicity of plot and a study of family life, of profession and positions, such as *The Father,* instead of characters and characteristics such as *The Flatterer.* Sedaine, under the influence of Diderot, depicted a family in a charming manner and even introduced the problem of the duel in *Le Philosophe sans le Savoir.* But the bourgeois drama was not primarily a problem play as is *Chatterton* in which every character and every scene arise from the point of departure of "the spiritual man stifled by a materialistic society."

It is probable that Vigny was influenced by Sedaine rather than by Racine in re-introducing a simple plot into French drama. He admired Sedaine's *Philosophe sans le Savoir.* It was a beautiful work to him; and the result of careful study of human nature and art. The rarity of such plays was evidence of their extreme difficulty. He prophesied that this form of drama would gain in power as it treated graver and greater problems. The characters were "happy creations which time cannot wither." The simplicity of the dialogue, the gracious nobility of the scenes following each other with such ease and naturalness appealed to him. These words of high praise were written in 1841; but *Le Philosophe sans le Savoir* was constantly played and Vigny's knowledge and delight in this drama are certainly of earlier date.

The material action of *Chatterton* observes the unities strictly. It takes place in the house of John Bell, a gross materialist, in which Chatterton, the poet, has rented a room. He is starving. His brain refuses to work. He has pledged his body as security for a loan. He has written the Lord Mayor asking for a position. He has fallen in love with Bell's wife, Kitty; and she loves him, although both have locked their secret in their hearts. The Lord Mayor offers the poet a position as his valet. Chatterton drinks opium and dies. Kitty Bell's death follows symbolically and actually from his kiss.

The moral action is the clash of spirituality and materialism. The spiritual world is represented by Chatterton, Kitty Bell, her children, and the Quaker. John Bell is the successful industrialist, surrounded by young lords who live riotously and see in Kitty only a woman to seduce. The Lord Mayor is the personification of a thankless national government which sees in a poet only a worthless citizen.

Those who looked for a plot in the play saw only a justification of suicide; but fortunately the majority of the spectators caught the deeper meaning. The stupid keepers of their brother's morals are always with us in the theatre; but this time their vapid cry of immorality was soon drowned in applause. The *drame serieux* had returned to the French stage in the form of a problem play even while Hugo and Dumas were thundering forth their gorgeous melodramas and Eugène Scribe was playing his clever parlor tricks.

Throughout the period of romanticism, Scribe had preserved the compact classical form of drama. Augier was even more classical. The point of attack in his plays is almost as close to the dénouement as it is in the comedies of Molière or Regnard. The scene changes from one salon to another, but it does not wander from place to place as in romantic drama. The element of time is unimportant. One does not ask how many hours or days have elapsed between the acts. The epic and lyric elements of Hugo have disappeared. The striking settings, local color and the melodrama are things of the past so far as Augier is concerned.

His plots are complex but they are never imbroglios giving rise to surprising events. Mistaken identity and the *quiproquo* have no place in problem plays. When Augier employs a *coup de théâtre* or any technical device, it is not for the purpose of dazzling the spectator with his brilliant dexterity, but in order to show a new development of his plot. He holds a middle ground between Scribe and the later realists who would banish all the devices of the well-made play.

His situations are skilfully articulated. Just as he discusses both sides of the question, so he balances delicately both his characters and their fortunes. This equilibrium is beautifully exemplified in his *Gendre de M. Poirier,* which he wrote in collaboration with Landeau. In this comedy the clash between the ideals of the newly enriched bourgeois and the old nobility is depicted. Poirier, the rich bourgeois, has married his daughter, Antoinette, to Gaston, a young marquis riddled with debts. On both sides it is a marriage of convenience. Poirier wishes to become a peer of France. Gaston desires to live a life of idleness and luxury. They represent the extremists of their respective classes. Montmeyran personifies the more moderate wing of the nobility. He has accepted the fate of his class and become a soldier. Verdelet, Poirier's friend and Antoinette's godfather, is a bourgeois willing to remain a simple, solid citizen. Between the two parties stands Antoinette. Gaston, utterly egoistic, is not unconscious of the fact that she is attractive and charming; but he considers her merely the source of his income. He is carrying on an intrigue with a Madame de Montjay, more through force of habit than because he loves her. To have a mistress is a part of his scheme of life. The duel which he is to fight on her account is also a part of the code of his world. In spite of his faults, which are presented as those of his class, Gaston is a likeable character. Poirier also has grave faults, but the right is often enough on his side to make the audience sympathize with him at times.

The first three acts of the play deal with questions arising from the intermingling of the two classes. The attitudes of the nobleman and of the bourgeois in regard to honor, money, marriage, ambition, and usefulness to society are brilliantly set forth. The virtues and vices of each class are depicted with incisive wit. Neither side is entirely condemned or exonerated. Finally, the concrete question as to whether Gaston and Antoinette can continue to live together boils out of the social ferment. Gaston has learned to love her because she has shown true nobility of character, but will he give up his ideal of honor in order to prove his love for her, by refusing to fight the duel? Thus even the sentimental interest is the result of the clash of social ideas. Scribe sacrificed the study of a problem to the development of his plot; but it is the problem not the development of the story, which dominates the construction of this play from start to finish.

Social questions had formed the basis of many a play in past ages, but in the middle of the nineteenth century the problem play came into its own. So long as the rule of the separation of tragedy and comedy was observed, the canonical happy ending of comedy was often a false note, destroying the harmony of the developing action. Now, for practically the first time in France, the dramatist could observe social conditions and treat them on the stage with freedom from tradition or rules. The question as to whether comic scenes can be mingled with tragic situations is far less important than the question as to whether a dramatist is allowed to take a situation involving customs of contemporary society and develop it to its logical outcome, happy or bitter as the end may be. When dramatic art threw off the incubus of the rule of the separation of comedy and tragedy it scored a veritable triumph.

Looking back over the centuries of dramatic art one is impressed by the dearth of plays which deal with problems of men and women in their everyday life. Without detracting one iota from the tragedies and comedies of the Greeks, the Elizabethans, the French and the Germans, one feels that the human, personal touch is too often lacking, that a whole section of joys and sorrows of men and women has been left unrepresented. The dramatists depicted vice and virtue, true ideals and perverted ideals. But where was the picture of the normal man and woman laughing and weeping by turns in the comedy of life which ends with tragic tears? English, German and French domestic tragedy had attempted to supply such pictures of life; but they were often pictures and nothing more. The problem play, as the expression implies, deals with certain conditions in society which cause trouble. It seeks to analyze the opposition between social custom and the law, or between custom and justice. The dramatist does not consider the problem as merely ridiculous. He sees that there is right and wrong on both sides, although he concludes for or against one side of the question. This method is very different from the dramatic presentation of such vices as avarice, hypocrisy, affectation, etc., as ridiculous foibles of man. Molière could employ any means to end his play *Tartufe* after he had shown the effects of hypocrisy. The dénouement was unimportant, provided vice had been held up to ridicule. The portrait of the hypocrite was complete. In the problem play, each step must be logical. The dénouement becomes highly important for it contains the answer to the whole question. Thus the younger Dumas founded his whole scheme of dramaturgy on the basis of the problem. Social questions had been discussed in drama before his time; but he finally made the problem the point of departure.

His first drama, *La Dame aux Camélias* (1852), is a play which tells a story. He did not write it in order to discuss the question of a courtezan regenerated through love. His formula of playmaking had not yet been devised. *Diane de Lys* (1853) likewise depends more upon its dramatic plot than upon the presentation of a problem of marital infidelity for its interest. However, the situations upon which these plays are based contain moral questions which only need to be discussed at length to turn the dramas into *pièces à thèse*. The problem of marital infidelity is inherent in the plot of *Antony;* but the rôle of the husband exists for purposes of plot and dénouement alone. What he thinks, what are his rights, are questions of vital importance in a *pièce à thèse;* but they are not raised by the elder Dumas. In the final analysis, *Antony* is the portrayal of enthralling passion of the decade of the thirties, done in romantic style. In *Diane de Lys* the rôle of the husband is important. His situation, his rights are carefully set forth. The plot is still of greater interest than the discussion of the question of infidelity; but there is a marked development in the importance of the problem between *Antony* and *Diane de Lys.*

La Dame aux Camélias and *Diane de Lys* opened a long series of realistic plays which remains unbroken to the present day. The erring woman and her relation to society had been presented in the theatre sporadically; but from 1852 on she holds the centre of the stage. After three-quarters of a century of such plays and at a time when motion pictures rehabilitate the courtezan continuously every day from noon until midnight, it is difficult to imagine the younger Dumas' first play as being considered a rather shocking novelty when it was first produced. Its realism seems a bit sentimental. The pistol shot which brings down the curtain of *Diane de Lys* has become as banal as the arrival of the long-lost father or son with a fortune.

Scribe's *Dix Ans dans la Vie d'une Femme* (1832) was a realistic study of a woman who became a courtezan; but it was an isolated example without influence. These dramas of the younger Dumas ushered in a new development of dramatic art. When he wrote the *Demi-Monde,* the playwright turned still more to the study of a social problem. The plot is complicated; but on leaving the theatre one is not thinking merely of the fact that Suzanne, a member of the *demi-monde,* has not been able to rise out of it by marrying Raymond. Much less is one concerned with the marriage of Olivier to Marcelle by which she will escape from her surroundings. It is the whole social problem of the *demi-monde,* which is uppermost in one's thoughts. The spectator feels that a case has been tried and settled before him.

Hugo had used the five acts to present a complicated story embellished with long speeches resembling operatic arias. Scribe had taken advantage of the full length play to dazzle the spectators with kaleidoscopic developments of his plot. Dumas belongs to the Scribian school in that he usually devised a plot full of surprising turns; but he left plenty of time to argue his point and to paint his portraits fully. Especially impressive in this respect is the *Demi-Monde*. He presents several different types of people belonging to this society. Each one is clearly differentiated from the other. Little by little we learn of their past, their present, their ambitions, their habits, their incomes, and their previous relations with each other. He even succeeds in making a striking personality of Madame de Lornan who plays a part in the action, but who never appears on the stage. Likewise, a Monsieur de Latour does not enter but is sketched into the picture as a type of the men who frequent this society.

The concrete question which forms the plot is: Can Suzanne, a woman with a past, rise out of the *demi-monde* by marrying Raymond? This causes the gradual disclosure, not only of her past, but that of all the other characters. The technique of developing the action by withdrawing veils from the past was employed by Dumas with great effectiveness. As each discovery takes place the action moves forward and the resultant phase of the moral problem is discussed.

While the audience is supposed to draw inferences from the development of the plot and especially from the dénouement in regard to the problem and its answer, much of the discussion is direct. It is a debate or argument, thinly disguised, in which each character presents his case. The whole drama is plainly a conflict of opposing forces, and the action works up to the point in which the opposing wills clash in an obligatory scene. One character is pre-eminent in leading the discussion and in presenting the author's views. In the *Demi-Monde*, Olivier de Jalin fills the rôle of the *raisonneur*, as it was called. This rôle has been compared to that of the chorus or the confidant in classical tragedy; but at least these characters are not mere moralizers. They are active and effective. They fight for a moral principle. They give their views; but they dominate the action to such an extent, that they resemble dangerously an exhibitor of marionettes as he moves the strings. Only Dumas' skill saves him from too apparently manipulating everything through the person of his *raisonneur*. While the rôle of the confidant persists in many modern dramas as a friend of the family or a kindly old uncle, the *raisonneur* is more than a mouthpiece for aphorisms. He may represent the crux of the whole action for the intellectuals in the audience, although he may not be the hero of the concrete story to the sentimentally inclined. Thouvenin, the *raisonneur* in *Denise,* harangues André for four and one-half minutes in order to prove to him that he should marry Marthe who is the mother of an illegitimate child. So far as the problem is concerned, this lecture, as Dumas called it, is the culmination of the drama.

Dumas believed that the *Demi-Monde* was more a portrayal of manners than a problem play; but in writing the *Fils Naturel* (1858) he reached the goal of the *pièce à thèse*. He said in the preface (1868): "For the first time, it is true, I was trying to develop a social thesis and to render, through the theatre, more than the depiction of manners, of characters, of ridiculous foibles and of passions. I hoped that the spectator would carry away from this spectacle something to think about a little." As Vigny's wish had been to introduce a theatre of "thought," so the younger Dumas dreamed of a "useful" and "legislative" theatre. "Through comedy, through tragedy, through drama, through buffoonery, in the form which fits us best, let us inaugurate the *useful* theatre, at the risk of hearing cry out the apostles of *art for art's sake*—four words absolutely empty of meaning."

The theatre was not the end but the means. Eleven years after writing this preface he admitted, in his preface to *L'Etrangère,* that people would not look to the theatre for the solution of great problems; but he was none the less sincere in his belief that the theatre should attempt to solve problems.

Sarcey held that the theatre never had reformed anyone and never will. He saw no reason, therefore, for treating Dumas' favorite theme: adultery. Sarcey was correct in his first contention. The theatre can only reform people indirectly, by showing life; but there is no reason why adultery or any other phase of society should not be represented on the stage, provided the portrayal is true. Innocence and ignorance were once practically synonymous terms when applied to women—especially young women. Even Dumas advocated veiling the dialogue so that certain passages could be understood only by men. The *jeune fille* had an influence on dramatic art far greater than that of the "tired business man." Happily both these innocents belong to the past.

Dumas considered drama as an art by itself and not as a mere branch of literature. When he said that drama ought always to be written as if it were only to be read, he meant that a play, in order to live, must contain ideas. He pointed out that the reader often does not find the emotion in the printed play which he did in the representation, because a word, a look, a gesture, a silence, a purely atmospheric combination had held him under its charm. The language of great writers would only teach the dramatist words and a number of these would have to be excluded because they lack "relief, vigor, almost the triviality necessary to put in action the true man on this false ground" (the stage). "The language of the theatre does not have to be grammatically correct. It must be clear, full of color, incisive." He cited the line by Racine: *"Je t'aimais inconstant: qu'aurai-je fait fidèle!"*—as an example of bad grammar but as an excellent line on the stage. The style of Scribe would be acceptable to Dumas if it contained a thought.

Such ideas are a bold challenge to the literary critic. They had been expressed, in part, by Diderot a century before. In the nineteenth century dialogue grew less and less stylistic, but Dumas' lines are by no means devoid of embellishment. In comparison with dialogue in our contemporary drama, his speeches are often rhetorical. In scenes of action he is clear and concise. The illuminating phrase came to him naturally. Not since Sedaine and Beaumarchais had a playwright expressed his ideas so brilliantly, so tersely when brevity is demanded in the particular scene. His greatest fault was the constant use of aphorisms. It is easier for an author to be brilliant than to be life-like in dialogue. His use of the aside and the monologue is regrettable because he could be subtle, and subtlety is extinguished by the aside and the monologue used to explain facts obvious to the modern audience.

Dumas fought valiantly to set drama free to tell the truth about life. Whether he succeeded or not in always telling the truth is not now a vital question. He set up an ideal of sincerity in drama. He was never false to his conscience. He insisted upon the necessity of being a master in the art. He said in the preface to *Un Père Prodigue*: "A man without any value as a thinker, as a moralist, as a philosopher, as a writer, can be a man of the first order as a dramatic author. To be a master in this art, one must be clever in the business." He admired Scribe's ability as a technician, though he deplored his lack of depth and sincerity. If it were possible, he would think like Æschylus and write like Scribe. "The dramatic author who would know *man* like Balzac and the *theatre* like Scribe would be the greatest dramatic author that ever existed." He learned from Scribe to know the theatre. Indeed, at the close of his career, Dumas' plays were criticized for being too well made. Yet he never sacrificed what he felt was the logical demonstration of his thesis to a striking theatrical effect, although he devised *coups de théâtre* in order to prove his point. "The real in the foundation, the possible in the fact, the ingenious in the means, that is what can be demanded of us." But he never swerved from the belief that "the most indispensable quality is logic, which includes good sense and clearness."

"The truth (of a play)," he held, "can be absolute or relative according to the importance of the subject and the place that it occupies; the logic must be implacable between the starting point and the place of arrival, which it must never lose from view in the development of the idea or the fact." There must be "the mathematical, inexorable and fatal progression which multiplies scene by scene, event by event, act by act up to the dénouement which ought to be the total and the proof."

Thus the dénouement of a play assumed great importance. The desire of an audience for a happy ending, and the rule that comedy must end happily and tragedy unhappily went by the board. The whole construction of the play depended upon the ending. In the preface to *La Princesse Georges* Dumas said: "You can make mistakes in the details of execution; you have no right to be mistaken in the logic and in the linking of the sentiments and facts, still less in their conclusion. One ought never to modify a dénouement. One ought always to begin a play with the dénouement, that is, not begin the work until one has the scene, the movement and the word of the end." One cannot help wondering how much Molière would have changed the endings of his plays had he constructed them after this method.

Naturally a great deal of controversy arose over the dénouements of Dumas' plays. Were they logical? Were they moral? Were they practical solutions of the problems raised? He was accused of representing special cases and deducing general conclusions.

He did create situations which were extraordinary. He complicated his plots so much that the later naturalists dismissed them as improbable. It is very improbable that an illegitimate child could be brought up in affluence by its mother who had been poor; that the child as a young man should wish to marry his father's niece; that he would save France; that his father's brother would offer him a title; that his father would wish to recognize him in order to gain the title, etc. But that all happens in the *Fils Naturel*. Such a plot is not the result of observation of life, but is devised to present a thesis. His demonstration of his hypothesis may be perfectly logical, but the hypothesis is so far-fetched that he has not represented the usual, but an unusual problem of the illegitimate child. Dumas was quite correct in pointing out in his preface the advance he made in treating this subject. "It was agreed formerly, in the theatre, that an illegitimate child should groan, for five acts, at not having been recognized, and that at the end, after all kinds of trials, each more pathetic than the others, he would see his father repent and they would throw themselves in each other's arms crying: 'My father! My son!' to the applause of an audience in tears." This particular brand of sentimentality Dumas made ridiculous.

Scribe was a master technician who merely wished to amuse an audience. Dumas was a master technician who felt he had something to prove and wished to make an audience think. He finally constructed plays in which the plot was of secondary importance. In the *Question d'Argent* (1857), he was so intent upon presenting the various phases of the influence of money on contemporary society that the plot almost disappeared. The first and second acts are discussions of the thesis: money means success. By the end of the third act, Eliza, the daughter of an honorable but poverty-stricken nobleman, is going to marry Giraud, a man of the people, who has amassed a fortune by methods which are within the law but are questionable from the strict moral point of view. The audience knows that such a marriage spells tragedy; and Eliza finally repudiates her engagement. The interest of the play does not lie primarily in the story, but in the discussion of the whole money question and in the idea that one should win a fortune by esteem, not win esteem through a fortune.

As a rule, Dumas was careful to build up a gripping plot which unfolds with surprise and suspense. He insisted upon the "ingenious in the means." The ingeniousness appears somewhat overdone, now that the reaction against the *coup de théâtre* has put us on guard against the too cleverly devised scene. But if he forced events or characters it was in order to demonstrate his thesis. In *L'Ami des Femmes* he frankly used the legerdemain of Scribe throughout the play. De Ryons pulls the strings. He foretells what will happen. It seems as if what he prophesies is impossible. Then, presto, it comes to pass, but the thesis is proved. At the close of all his plays there is a surprising peripeteia. The unexpected happens. The last scenes form an exciting climax in which all the strings of the plot are gathered together and suddenly untied in an ingenious manner.

In *La Princesse Georges*, the husband of the heroine is apparently going to meet his certain death; but the bullet strikes another lover of Sylvanie. Césarine, in *La Femme de Claude*, seems on the verge of successfully betraying her husband and making good her escape. She has seduced his young assistant. The plans of the invention are in her grasp. Her confederate is just outside the window, and she is about to throw them to him when the sound of her husband's voice makes her stop involuntarily. Then the bullet strikes her. The climax of the *Demi-Monde* is produced when Olivier makes Suzanne—and the audience—believe he has killed Raymond. By this trick, he unmasks Suzanne, who declares her love for Olivier when she believes that Raymond is dead. Even in the *Question d'Argent*, the least exciting of his plays, Giraud's unexpected return, when everyone considers him an absconder, constitutes a surprising *coup de théâtre*.

Generally the last few minutes of Dumas' plays contain the psychological and dramatic climax. The curtain descends almost instantly after the line and event which bring the solution of the problem. The tension is not relaxed gradually with explanations or prophecies of the future, as in Shakespearean and Greek tragedy. The tension snaps. The knot is cut with one stroke. The spectator is left gasping with theatrical excitement. Dumas insisted that the dénouement should be unforeseen, but logical. This procedure was commonly followed by the realists. When Freytag was expounding his theory of the rise and fall of the dramatic action, the playwrights had ceased to represent the fall.

The objection was made, especially in regard to the pistol shot as a climax and dénouement, that social problems in real life were not solved by bullets. Alphonse Royer said in 1878:

"This simple procedure which charges the arms manufacturer with the decision of questions that logic cannot solve has been the *pons asinorum* of the realistic school which has used and abused it as long as the public was willing to lend itself to this trickery against which it protests to-day." From the point of view that realism is a transcript of real life, the objection is sound. Dumas' attempt to answer such objections is found in the preface to *L'Étrangère*.

"When we attack a law on the stage, we can only do it by means of the theatre and most often without even mentioning the law. The public must draw the conclusions and say: 'Indeed, that is a case in which the law is wrong!' Our means are a certain combination of events drawn from the possible, laughter and tears, passion and interest, with an unforeseen dénouement, personal initiative, the intervention of a *deus ex machina*, mandatory of a Providence which does not always manifest itself so aptly in real life, and which, playing the rôle which the law should have undertaken, employs in the face of unsolvable situations, the great argument of the old theatre, the argument without reply—death."

To such arguments the naturalists replied: "That is not life, hence not truth." Dumas retorted: "That is logic, hence it is truth." He insisted that there is a vast difference between truth in life and truth in the theatre. Zola denied the existence of any such difference. The reason for this distinction, according to Dumas, was that audiences were governed by mob psychology, were enormous masses and had to be attracted and held by gross means. Truth had to make concessions; and he relied upon Goethe's prologue to *Faust* to show that "the public has been and always will be a child, both ignorant and wishing to learn nothing, curious and convinced that there are many things very natural, very true, of which the theatre should never speak, impressionable and heedless, sensitive and teasing . . . deaf to reasoning and always open to an emotion."

Such arguments voiced by a sincere man who had spent his life trying to reason even in his theatrical manner are depressing, far more depressing than if they came from Goethe, who was more of a poet-philosopher than a dramatist. This theory of the audience was widely accepted. But though an audience has some characteristics of a mob and though there are audiences of varying degrees of intelligence, people are enough the same in a theatre as outside of it to make it unnecessary to misrepresent life on the stage. A dramatist must write for an audience. He does not have to write down to an audience. He can tell the truth in the theatre, if he knows how to tell the truth in the theatre. Sooner or later popular success will be his. Where is the dramatist of ability who was faithful to the truth who failed to be recognized by the crowd as a great artist? At least, he has left no trace of his plays in written form.

When a subject fitted for dramatic representation and demonstration had occurred to Dumas, he studied it in all its ramifications. He knew the life history of all his characters. Thus in the preface to *Monsieur Alphonse* he gave a full biographical account of his principals up to the opening of the play. Such complete details cannot be presented in the play itself. The limit of time precludes that possibility. Yet such careful analysis of character and of the problem has its effect upon the drama. One may or may not agree with the author's conception of the development of the action; but one realizes that Dumas knew why his people are what they are and do what they do.

But they are what they are because of the problem; and they do what they do in order to prove his thesis. His characters impress one as his creations, not as people observed in life. In that period of naturalism when novel writers were striving to be impartial observers, Dumas sacrificed whatever power of objective observation he possessed to his thesis. His characters tend to become generalizations and in *La Femme de Claude,* allegorical abstractions. He admitted that he spoke through them. As Zola said, his characters are "colorless, stiff as arguments, which disappear from the mind as soon as the book is closed or the curtain falls. . . . All that he touches instead of becoming animate grows heavy and turns towards dissertation. . . . Balzac wants to paint and M. Dumas wants to prove." He was like a lawyer in court. He convinced his auditors by his arguments. But just as a lawyer may win a case by a clever array of facts which are not the real truth, so a dramatist writing a problem play is in danger of convincing an audience in a theatre only to have them question his conclusion on calmer consideration.

REALISTIC DRAMA

CHAPTER XVIII

NATURALISTIC DRAMA

IN 1859 Sarcey saw a revival of Balzac's *Marâtre* originally
produced in 1848. He hailed the play as a first attempt at
a new kind of drama. "It is not a masterpiece; far from it; it
is much better than that: it is a revolution. Hats off, please.
Realism is taking possession of the theatre." Zola in later years
gave Balzac full credit for the realistic elements in the play and
for defying contemporary conventions of playmaking in *Mercadet*
(1851).

La Marâtre is a clumsy, yet powerful piece of work. The plot
is somewhat romantic with its stolen letters, deaths by poison,
and the appearance of Pauline after she seems to have died.
The dialogue is inept, labored and full of asides which explain
badly the real sentiments and purposes of the characters.

The play presents a woman who has married an old Napoleonic general in order to inherit his money and then to marry
her lover, Ferdinand, who is the son of one of the betrayers of
Napoleon. Ferdinand falls in love with Pauline, the step-
daughter of his former mistress. The two women fight for Ferdinand with drugs, poison, stolen letters and threats of blackmail.
Pauline, the daughter, finally commits suicide by swallowing
arsenic known to be in her step-mother's possession. Gertrude
is accused of murder; but Pauline, apparently dead, rouses herself long enough to exonerate her. The old general is on the
point of insanity when the curtain falls. This overwrought situation belongs rather to romantic drama with a setting and costumes of the Renaissance; but the setting of the play was modern, there was no sympathetic character, no *raisonneur;* and
Balzac drew his people objectively, and with powerful crude-

ness. Hence the play seemed realistic in the middle years of the nineteenth century.

Balzac's plays were not a revolution but only a revolt. His attempts to make the theatre present real life were cut short by his death. His name, however, was invoked by the later naturalists and his plays were cited as early examples of the new form of drama. This was good advertising for their cause, for Balzac was a name to conjure by. Yet one only has to compare *La Marâtre* with Turgeniev's *A Month in the Country* (1855), founded on a similar situation, to realize what exaggerated theatrical people Balzac created. Gertrude is a melodramatic villainess. The others are monomaniacs and therefore as abstract as characters in classical comedy. *La Marâtre* is dated. *A Month in the Country* is still modern.

The old rules were dead. No one discussed the unities, the number of acts, the separation of tragedy or comedy. But a new set had taken their place: the rules of the well-made play with its obligatory scene, the rules of the problem play. Zola tells how as a young man he learned that complicated code of convention which critics called "the theatre": how characters should enter and exit; the symmetrical division of scenes; the necessity of sympathetic and moral rôles; the art of juggling truth by a gesture or a tirade. It seemed that when one wanted to write a play one had to forget life and manœuvre characters according to particular tactics of which one learned the rules.

"We must clear the ground," he wrote in his preface to *Thérèse Raquin* (1873). "The well-known recipes for tying and untying a plot have served their time; now we must have a simple, broad picture of men and things, a drama such as Molière might have written. Outside of certain scenic necessities, what is called to-day the science of the theatre is only a heap of clever tricks, a kind of narrow tradition which cramps the stage, a code of language agreed upon and situations worked out in advance which any original mind will strongly refuse to employ."

He revolted against the whole procedure. In the theatre, he said, characters must enter, talk and exit. "That is all; the author remains after that the absolute master of his work." "What is the use of a thesis," he asks, "when life is sufficient?" Why should the playwright descend to play the rôle of a lawyer? "Problem plays argue instead of living." Authors can make them mean what they wish. They are a plea, not the truth. They are as fragile as a house of cards.

He insisted that playwrights should observe life and transport it to the stage instead of building clever but improbable plots and introducing striking *coups de théâtre*. Without advocating a revival of classical drama, he pointed to the simplicity of the plot and the absence of tricks in the plays of Corneille and of Molière. "I believe that one should go back to tragedy, not, Just Heaven, to borrow any more its rhetoric, its system of confidants, of declamation and interminable recitals; but to return to the simplicity of action and to the sole psychological and physiological study of characters. The tragic form thus understood is excellent: an event unfolding in its reality and arousing in its characters passions and sentiments of which the exact analysis would be the sole interest of the play!"

Theatrical situations must no longer dominate and reduce characters to manikins. The simpler the peripeteia the stronger it is. The dénouement especially should not depend upon a string to be pulled. Zola admired the ending of Augier's *Lionnes Pauvres* because Pommeau, having learned of his wife's infidelity, left the stage quietly but tragically to go forth a broken-hearted old man. The ingenious, surprising dénouement of the usual play by Dumas or Sardou seemed false to him. He accused Sardou of replacing peripeteias of passions by peripeteias of bits of paper.

Zola objected strenuously to sleight-of-hand tricks by which authors softened their situations or got out of difficulties because they did away with true passions and profound analysis of life at the same time. After seeing a well-made play one often wonders what would usually happen in real life in circumstances which have developed so miraculously on the stage. Zola was not tilting at windmills. Sleight-of-hand was a part of the playwright's equipment. The theatre was not supposed to have the liberty of the novel. Certain pictures had to be softened. Zola held that if such was the case it was better not to try to put them on the stage than to misrepresent them.

In dramatizing his novel *Thérèse Raquin,* Zola tried to make the play a study of human life. The action did not consist of a manufactured plot, but was to be found in the inner struggle of the characters. There was to be no logic of facts, but a logic of sensations and sentiments. He said in the preface: "The dénouement was the mathematical result of the proposed problem. I followed the novel step by step; I laid the play in the same room, dark and damp, in order not to lose relief or the sense of impending doom; I chose supernumerary fools, who were unnecessary from the point of view of strict technique in order to place side by side with the fearful agony of my protagonists the drab life of every day; I tried constantly to make my setting in perfect accord with the occupations of my characters, in order that they might not play but *live*. I counted, I confess, and with good reason, on the intrinsic power of the drama to make up in the minds of the audience for the absence of intrigue and the usual details."

French drama had been depicting the *"monde"* and the *"demi-monde."* Here was a representation of the life of the lower middle-class shopkeepers. It was a tragedy much more brutal than any except those that the German dramatists had produced during the eighteenth century when bourgeois tragedy enjoyed its fleeting vogue on the European stage.

The first act develops the environment of the drab protagonists. Thérèse has married her sickly cousin Camille. They live with his mother. About the only distraction in the household is a game of dominoes once a week with some equally uninteresting neighbors. However, life has suddenly become tense for Thérèse. She has become the mistress of Laurent, a boyhood friend of Camille. They dream of being free to marry. A year later, the second act shows Thérèse a widow. She and Laurent purposely upset a boat in which Camille and they were rowing. The husband was drowned. Laurent has taken his place in the household. The third act takes place on the wedding night of Laurent and Thérèse. The awful memory of their deed haunts them. In their hysterical outburst, the mother learns the truth. She is paralyzed in limbs and tongue by the shock. In the last act, the mutual revulsion of the guilty pair for each other develops. The old woman sits motionless and mute. She gains temporary use of a hand and begins to trace words accusing them. But her hand stops. Thérèse and Laurent now loathe each other to the point of each wishing to murder the other. Finally Mother Raquin speaks. She will not denounce them. Her vengeance will be to watch their mutual loathing. They commit suicide.

The plot is not complicated, but it is certainly astounding. Zola complained that the play would not have failed had he dished up the story with romantic trappings. However that may be, the situation is too remarkable. Zola invoked Molière as a model. What would Molière have thought of a picture of life which resembles Shakespeare's *Titus Andronicus!* No amount of bourgeois *milieu* can save such a plot from being melodrama of the sixteenth century.

Zola did succeed, however, in producing a cast of characters in which there is no *raisonneur* or sympathetic rôle. His protagonists have no glamour of morality or of sentimental, magnificent villainy about them. There is no character who adorns the dialogue with aphorisms or discusses any problem. The public, accustomed to the glittering characters of Dumas and Sardou and to the unusual sympathetic young lovers, was shocked by what Zola called these "lower middle-class shopkeepers that presume to participate in a drama in their own house, with their oil-cloth table cover." The great distinction between bourgeois tragedy of the eighteenth century and that of the nineteenth century lies in the fact that the earlier form was thickly coated with sentimentality and the special brand of virtue of the time. The naturalists did not seek to stimulate the tear ducts of "honest people." Though the bourgeois *milieu* was similar, the two forms of drama were vastly different in effect.

Naturalism was to enter the theatre unobtrusively but more effectively in plays of entirely opposite tone, such as Erckmann-Chatrian's *Ami Fritz* (1876). This play presents a rustic picture of Alsace in simple idyllic form. The plot is devoid of complications and *coups de théâtre*. It contains no problem, no thesis. Fritz is a generous easy-going but well-to-do squire. He seems to be a confirmed bachelor, happy with his friends, who enjoy with him plentiful dinners washed down with deep potations. David Sichel, an old rabbi, believes that Fritz should marry. With a wife and children, life will have a deeper significance for him. During the bounteous meal in the first act, little Suzel arrives. She is the pretty little daughter of one of Fritz's farmers. He falls in love with the child without knowing exactly what has happened.

In order to escape from the kindly designs of Rabbi Sichel he goes to his farm which is cared for by Suzel's father. The second act represents the famous cherry tree from which Suzel tosses down cherries to Fritz who is succumbing more and more to this mysterious feeling. There is a well near by. Here the old rabbi comes. He wishes to find out whether Suzel's heart has answered Fritz's unconscious love. Sichel asks for a drink. Suzel fills the jug; and, in response to his question as to whether she knows the story of Rebecca at the well, she repeats the text of the Bible.

In the third act, Fritz has returned home, having run away in fear from this ever-growing love. The act is almost without incident. Of course Suzel and Sichel come; and finally Fritz can bear it no longer. He fears he may hurt the feelings of his old housekeeper, who has watched over his comfort since he was a child, if he marries. He confides in her, and she draws a rosy picture of married life. When Suzel enters, he tells her simply and directly of his love for her and she slips into his arms.

Accustomed as we are to consider naturalism as a drab and

brutal representation of the seamy side of life, it is difficult to
discover at first glance any relationship between this rustic idyl
and the kind of drama that Zola wanted to see on the stage.
L'Ami Fritz, however, became a small storm centre. Many declared it to be boresome and gross. They objected to the constant references to food and drink, sauerkraut and beer. They
criticized sharply the lack of action. They were not interested
in the picture of Alsatian life. But in this controversy, Sarcey
and Zola, often bitter opponents in their theories of dramatic
art, found themselves in accord. To them it was a true representation of life. The realistic scenery, especially the cherry tree
and the well, with real water, the detailed representation of the
dining-room, contributed greatly to the ultimate success of the
play. The settings became famous. Sarcey deplored realism
in scenery for the sake of realism; but in this case he insisted
that the scenery was an integral part of the action. Zola was
ecstatic over the faithful representation of the *milieu*, the observation of life and the simplicity of the action. They differed,
however, on one important point. Zola cited the play as a modest
example of what drama should aim to be. Sarcey warned against
trying to imitate it. For him *L'Ami Fritz* was a happy exception
—but an exception, nevertheless, because of its simple plot.

The naturalists, under the spell of Balzac and Flaubert, insisted upon exactness in stage setting to the most minute detail.
The physical stage was the environment without which their
characters would remain largely incomprehensible. "An exact
decoration," said Zola, "a salon, for instance, with its furniture,
its jardinières, its ornaments establishes instantly the situation,
the society where one is, tells the habits of the characters." He
believed that the naturalistic evolution had begun in the theatre
necessarily on the material side, by exact reproduction of environ-
ments. The machinists had done their part; but the playwrights were still groping. "Sardou," he said, "wanted real cups
of the Directoire period in *Les Merveilleuses;* Erckmann-Chatrian demanded in *L'Ami Fritz* a spring which gave real water,
Gondinet in *Le Club* demanded all the real accessories of a club.

One can smile, shrug his shoulders, say that this does not make the works better. But, behind all these whims of careful authors, there is, more or less confusedly, the great thought of a methodical and analytical art marching along with science" (*Le Naturalisme au Théâtre*).

In their desire to transfer real life to the stage the naturalists changed the manner of mounting plays. They revived unconsciously the theories of Diderot. Everything heard and seen on the stage must be an exact reproduction of what would be heard and seen if the action were actually taking place. In Diderot's discussion of scenery the existence of the "fourth wall" is not mentioned, but is implied. So far as can be deduced from his arguments, Diderot would have placed this imaginary wall behind the last person in the theatre. The spectator was invisible, but was within the room. The naturalists, however, placed the fourth wall in the proscenium arch. Chairs were placed with their backs against the footlights. Even fireplaces were represented by andirons or grates with a ruddy light streaming from them. Actors constantly stood and sat with their backs to the audience. Their diction was purposely slovenly, because real people do not enunciate carefully.

The result was most unfortunate. The theatre tended to become a peep-show in which one saw imperfectly and understood less. Instead of feeling the effect of reality, one was baffled. One was conscious of actors who delivered their lines badly or too rapidly. The whole picture was wrong, indeed was unlifelike because no human being is endowed with X-ray vision enabling him to see through a wall. Thus reality was utterly disregarded by these realists. The spectator was a rank outsider who was placed so he could see and hear only with great difficulty. Seats on the side were often better than seats directly in front of the stage.

Still another attempt to produce reality was made by setting the walls of a room on the bias and with unexpected angles. This was successful if the room was supposed to be a part of an attic or in some rambling house. But usually rooms are square or oblong. One does not think of them as if he were seated in one corner looking at another. Thus this method of setting interiors always produces the impression that the room has a queer shape, whether or not that is the effect desired. So these settings produced an impression of cubism in which dramas of ordinary commonplace life were strangely incongruous.

The properties and furnishing were as exact as possible. If the scene was a butcher's shop, as in the *Bouchers*, real quarters of beef proved to the audience that they were in a meat market. Who could deny it? When Antoine produced *Old Heidelberg* he bought the interior of a students' room in Heidelberg and transferred it to the stage. The stage was so overloaded and such a restless impression was made that one had to make an effort to forget the reality of the scene in order to grasp the truth of the play. Real trees were actually set up on stages. In the optics of the theatre they were pitifully inadequate to represent themselves. Drama cannot compete with nature by employing nature's own methods. In such procedures, the naturalists were like naïve little girls who pretend to be grandmother by dressing in grandmother's hat and shawl.

Since the *milieu* was a determining factor of character in the naturalistic theory of art, it had to be carefully represented. There is no valid objection to a photographic reproduction of environment on the stage, provided it expresses the inner spirit of the play as well as the outward form of the place. Scenery had been a decorative adjunct to the physical action. The naturalists were correct in their theory that it should be a part of the spiritual action; but their methods and results were not successful.

Throughout the nineteenth century, persons on the stage talked more and more like ordinary people; but it was still necessary to differentiate the many types of human beings. The differentiation in language had lagged behind the differentiation in costume and make-up. On the stage people of all classes had used substantially the same vocabulary. Under the impulse of naturalism the incongruity of conventionalized dialogue disappeared. Free speech came with the Free Theatre. Greater variety of effect and contrast was introduced. Manner of speech is an externality; but a person in real life and on the stage reveals much of his character as soon as he speaks. When kept within artistic limits, naturalistic dialogue—meaning language befitting the character and situation—is an asset to drama. It is one of the means by which these playwrights were able to present studies of each individual. Drama had ceased to represent the abstract types of classicism. The romanticists had created strange individuals. Under the influence of the problem of the play, many of Dumas' characters became abstractions. The naturalists aimed to differentiate ordinary citizens.

Aphorisms were frowned upon. Brilliancy gave way to the commonplace. Hugo had democratized the noble vocabulary and style of classical drama. The naturalists believed that the dialogue of drama was still too rhetorical and prudish. When Zola employed a few words of slang in his *Bouton de Rose,* the audience was scandalized. The playwrights were undaunted. As they depicted the seamy side of life, so they used defiantly the crude or obscene vocabulary of the *milieu,* each vying with the other to see how far he could go.

Any kind of language, didactic, poetical, brilliant or crude is inartistic, if it causes the spectator to think of the author or the actor instead of the character. Dumas intrudes in his didacticism; Hugo in his poetry; Wilde and Shaw in their brilliancy. In naturalistic drama, when vulgar expressions are used, the spectator is very likely to get merely the impression that the actor has spoken an indecent line. Whether one approves or not, the spell of the drama has been broken for the moment.

The use of crude language and the depiction of sordid scenes were not the exception but the rule in naturalistic drama. But the idea of fitting the dialogue to the characters and the *milieu* was legitimate. The naturalists left nothing to the imagination in setting, costumes and dialogue. On the other hand, they constantly called upon the imagination to fill in the gaps between their pictures. They plastered on the *milieu* and scarcely sketched the connection between the events of the action. Preparation was studiously neglected. Their formula was to observe a part of life and to present the results of their observations in a series of scenes. Too often, they represented only externalities of life.

Another phase of the controversy concerned the artistic value of the *pièce bien faite* (well-made play). The expression, when used approvingly, denotes a play in which the action develops through an inevitable sequence of cause and effect, in which every scene is so placed and so treated that to change it in the slightest degree would harm the total effect. Furthermore, the expression describes—and still with approval—a plot which unfolds with suspense and surprise and rises to several crises, as in *Œdipus Rex*. Aristotle's *Poetics* is the first and in many ways the best discussion of the well-made play.

When Scribe was turning out his clever plots, full of suspense, surprise and crises, the phrase was naturally applied to his plays; but, when critics began to point out that Scribe employed mere tricks to arouse theatrical excitement, the expression *"pièce bien faite"* became a doubtful compliment. Sarcey says that about 1850 Scribe began to lose his reputation and by 1859 the public no longer wanted his *pièces bien faites*. Sarcey felt in 1878 that Zola was tilting at windmills in attacking the well-made play. He denied that the plays of Labiche, Meilhac and Halévy, and Augier had the slightest relation to the well-made plays of Scribe. Sarcey's statement is too sweeping. These authors were not abusing theatrical tricks as had Scribe; but Sardou and Dumas were devising very complicated plots with the scenes neatly dovetailed. Their dénouements were clever— too clever for the naturalists in theory. Dumas was presenting theses with many *coups de théâtre*. The naturalists demanded real life with few, if any, *coups de théâtre*. On one point the critics and public were in agreement: the expression "well-made play" connoted disapproval by 1878. The idea is relative. In comparison with Scribe's plays, Dumas' *Question. d'Argent* is not well made; but in comparison with Becque's *Corbeaux* it is.

Compared with Gorky's *Lower Depths*, Becque's drama is beautifully made.

A play should be a *lambeau d'existence* (fragment of existence) according to Zola. It was Jean Jullien who coined the famous phrase, *une tranche de vie* (a slice of life), which was the ideal of the naturalists and which now is used in a deprecatory sense to describe plays which pretend to be real life because of their brutality.

In his campaign against the complicated plot, Zola pointed out many examples of plays which owed their success to observation of life, analysis of character and depiction of *milieu*. He considered Labiche superior to Sardou because his plots were not needlessly complicated. In praising Meilhac and Halévy's *Mari de la Débutante* he said: "Once again, it is proved that the subject does not matter, that plot can be lacking, that the characters do not even need to have any connection with the action; it is enough if the pictures offered to the public are living and make it laugh or cry." This bold statement, expressing the attitude of the naturalists, implicitly denies in general all the accepted ideals of dramatic art. The pictures can be held together by a very thin thread. An obligatory scene is not necessary. Peripeteias may or may not take place. The dénouement does not matter. The interest is no longer in an ingenious mechanism, but in a series of true pictures.

Allowance may be made for a certain amount of exaggeration in these statements enunciated in the heat of battle. Zola's own plays are by no means lacking in plot, peripeteia or obligatory scenes. He insisted upon a logical dénouement in his *Thérèse Raquin*. Nevertheless these principles were later put into effect to a remarkable degree; and, even when Zola enunciated them, he could at least point to plays which succeeded although they were lacking in most of the elements of the old dramatic code.

Gondinet's *Club* illustrates the growth of the naturalistic method. The plot is unimportant. It rests on the traditional situation of marital infidelity, treated in a serio-comic manner, but the interest lies in the keen and witty representation of a men's club. In the second act we are shown an evening at the club, the different types of habitués, and all that goes on. Only men are present; and yet the plot develops in their conversation, which is delightful satire on club life. The third and fourth acts present a charity bazar, no less cleverly. Such pictures were hailed enthusiastically by the naturalists. A revival of Barrière's *Faux Bonshommes*, first produced in 1856, gave Zola an opportunity to point out that this play, with almost no plot, had outlived Scribe's clever concoctions, because of its incisive and somewhat acrid pictures of bourgeois life. Sarcey said, in 1889 after the foundation of the Théâtre Libre, that this play proved that the "pessimists of the Théâtre Libre invented nothing."

Such dramas, however, were naturalistic by chance, not because the authors were striving to produce dramas in which a series of life-like pictures would be substituted for clever intrigue. These plays succeeded in spite of the lack of plotting. The popularity of Sardou's plays, constructed along Scribian lines, is evidence that the public enjoyed, as it always does, an intricate story unfolded with theatrical tricks. The dominating influence throughout the whole European theatre was the technique of Scribe and of Sardou, his most brilliant disciple. Their plays were produced constantly in all theatrical centres and even penetrated America. The well-made play, whether combined with the problem of Dumas' type or not, was in popular favor. Zola and the Goncourts could not stem the tide.

Henri Becque tried for years to get *Les Corbeaux* produced. Here was a drama written consciously in the naturalistic method. Finally, in 1882, it was accepted by the Comédie Française. That the stronghold of tradition should even open its doors to naturalism is significant of the fact that the movement had progressed. Perrin, the director, was fully aware of the dangers of producing the play. He wanted changes made. Becque refused to alter his work. Once more the air of the old playhouse was charged with electricity as the curtain rose on this drama which aimed to destroy the conventions of the well-made play.

The first act presents the characters and the environment. It is a series of pictures of bourgeois life, such as Diderot had advocated over a century before. Monsieur and Madame Vigneron are a bourgeois couple who have risen to a position of relative wealth through a factory which is their source of income. Vigneron is associated in the business with Teissier, who is not liked by the family. Their notary, Bourdon, has a rather shady reputation. The youngest of the four daughters is engaged to Georges de Saint·Genis, who is so splendidly null that he plays a mute rôle. His scheming mother controls his actions. Gaston, son of the Vignerons, is portrayed as a naturalistic study in heredity. He is spoiled by his father and has inherited his weaker qualities. The daughter Judith has some musical talent which is overpraised by her teacher, Merckens. Marie is calm, sensible and practical. These characters are brought together by the well-worn device of a dinner party which the naturalistic playwrights did not hesitate to employ. When all are assembled, a doctor enters. Vigneron, who has been slightly indisposed, has suffered a stroke of apoplexy and is dead.

This act is a prologue, so far as the plot is concerned. Scarcely the slightest hint is given as to what may develop. There is preparation but no foreshadowing. Naturalistic drama relegates plot to a secondary rôle, and often gives up the whole of the first act to just such analyses of the situation, the environment and the characters. The analytical method of the novelists, introduced by Balzac, was now influencing the dramatists.

The second act opens a month after the death of Vigneron. Madame Vigneron and her daughters are in the throes of financial affairs of which they understand little. Bourdon, Teissier and Lefort, the architect, are advising them—badly. Vigneron had a large income, a potential fortune; but his affairs are in such a state that only fifty thousand francs will remain as capital, if the "Vultures" are able to carry out their plans. The question is: Must the factory be sold? Teissier has a legal right to dispose of it after the death of his partner. The women are utterly bewildered. The curtain falls as Judith reads aloud letter after letter demanding immediate settlement of their debts.

The bewilderment of the women is intensified in the third act. They do not know whom to trust or where to turn. They suspect Bourdon and Teissier, but do not dare nor know how to break with them. Marie shows a little understanding of the situation. Teissier, sixty years of age, is attracted by her. He offers her a way out of the difficulty. He will take her into his house and support her. Later, he may marry her. She refuses hotly this none too honorable offer. In the meantime, Madame de Saint-Genis has discovered the painful situation of their finances. She breaks off the engagement of her son to Blanche. The young girl loses her reason. She had given herself to the weakling.

In the fourth act the financial affairs have been settled. The Vignerons have moved into a miserable apartment. They are living on their small capital. When Judith asks Merckens, her flattering music master of the first act, if she cannot support the family by her talent, he laughs at her and leaves. Teissier now makes a formal offer of marriage to Marie through Bourdon. The question is discussed in a dull, bitter, business-like manner. It is their way out. Teissier cannot live forever. Marie accepts his offer. "I am shameful, shameful in doing it. I would be guilty in not doing it," she says. The scene is remarkable in its heavy, quiet tragedy. The last episode presents a so-called creditor trying to collect a bill that has already been paid. Teissier foils him and remarks only too truthfully to Marie: "You have been surrounded by rascals since your father's death."

There are only two scenes in the play which are clearly "du théâtre" (of the theatre). One is the unexpected death of Vigneron. The other is the dramatic interview between Blanche and Madame de Saint-Genis. Becque unfortunately introduces this meeting with a monologue in which Madame de Saint-Genis informs the audience what she is going to do. This procedure is more than unnecessary. It is inartistic and robs the scene of legitimate suspense. Becque abuses the monologue throughout his plays. He may have done so consciously in order to show his contempt for the well-made play. On the other hand, Scribe and his followers never balked at the use of this device. The mono-

logue and the aside came under the ban only about the year
1900.

The rest of the scenes are analytical. The situation develops
very slowly. The play represents the slow crumbling rather than
the dramatic crash of the household. The old order of dramatic
art, said the critics, gave the effect of life through movement.
The new drama presented movement through life. Becque strove
to construct an objective analysis of what happened to a family
after the death of the breadwinner. No *raisonneur* guides the
plot or the opinion of the audience. The objective attitude
produced pessimism in drama as it had in the novel. The characters, including Marie, arouse only pity. We feel for them,
almost never with them. The sympathetic hero—the *bête noire*
of the naturalists—is conspicuously absent.

The dénouement is neither sentimental nor grandly tragic. It
is unobtrusively inevitable, pessimistic and cynical. It lacks,
purposely, theatrical excitement. In comparison with the tense
last moments of plays by Dumas or Sardou, *Les Corbeaux* contains no climax. Yet the scene between Marie, Teissier and the
false creditor sums up the whole theme. It is far more difficult
to devise such endings, than to fire a pistol shot and kill either
hero or villain. The final impression on the audience of 1882
was very different from that made by the usual play of the
period. Only the ending of Augier's *Lionnes Pauvres* could approach this dénouement in its dull hopelessness.

The play did not achieve popular success; but Becque did not
lack admirers. His play became the model for the naturalists,
who proclaimed its value almost too noisily. *Les Corbeaux,* however, is much more a well-made play than his *Michel Pauper*
which had failed utterly in 1870. This drama is a series of pictures which follow each other in temporal sequence. First one
character and then another dominates the scene. The composition resembles that of the naturalistic novel, and was therefore
too loose for the taste of the period.

The art of playwriting had become too much of a cut-and-dried
"business." The dramatist pulled too many strings to keep his

action moving. Those who are fully acquainted with the well-made play are so conscious of its mechanism that scenes and dialogue become too obvious. One can often foretell the whole development of the action. Seeing such a play is like watching a magician perform tricks of which the mechanics are known beforehand. Drama was in danger of becoming as banal as the ending of a motion picture. Thus the naturalists revolted against invention and composition, because they were products of the imagination, which, they held, was the primordial cause of the falsity of the drama. For imagination the dramatists strove to substitute observation of life. Their plays were to be "slices of life." The phrase has become as much a term of mild contempt as the expression "well-made play"; but this movement exerted a salutary influence on dramatic art. However, a grave danger for the dramatist lurks in the presentation of slices of life on the stage. The dramatist who presents a series of pictures after the manner of the realistic novel and who deliberately presents them in a "beautiful disorder" is liable to obscure his meaning. Preparation, said older playwrights, is necessary for the sake of clarity. Without clarity there is no theatre. Preparation, replied the naturalist, is too mechanical. The dovetailing of scenes is unreal. Both contentions are correct; but the naturalistic dramatist sometimes forgot that in the novel there were long passages of analysis and explanation which welded the slices of life into a unified whole, and which take the place of preparation on the stage. Slices of life in the theatre often give the effect of being merely juxtaposed. The spectator is called upon to supply the transition which the novelist gives the reader.

This is not an utterly impossible demand to make of the audience. In the last forty years, the spectator has learned to receive impressions and to unify them; but the dramatist who aims to use this method must weigh every scene, every line. He must guide the spectator more skilfully, if he elects to guide him delicately and unobviously. It is more difficult to write a non-well-made play than a well-made play. Shakespeares and Mussets are rarer than Scribes. Their "beautiful disorder," their impressionism and even obscurity were cited as arguments in favor of the naturalistic method.

The progress of the non-well-made play can be illustrated by the fate of Daudet's *L'Arlésienne*. When first produced in 1872 it was a failure. Daudet was informed that he had not the gift of playwriting. The plot was considered too tenuous and the situation remained static. The play is a dramatization of a short story which is masterful in its vivid brevity. The bare situation presents a young peasant who is madly in love with a girl of Arles. His family consents to their marriage. A horse-jockey arrives; and, in order to prevent the marriage, he informs the family that he is the girl's lover. The young peasant throws himself from a lofty window.

Daudet expanded the sketch into a play in three acts and five scenes accompanied by Bizet's music. He added a young peasant girl, Vivette, in love with Frédéri, the hero. Also he introduced a backward younger brother, known as The Innocent, and other secondary rôles. A striking element in the construction of the short story is that the girl from Arles is, so to speak, behind the scenes. Still more surprising is the fact that she never appears in the play, to which she gives the title. We do not even know her name.

There is very little of what was then considered dramatic in the play. The marriage is broken off when the jockey produces love letters from the girl. Frédéri is finally affianced to Vivette; but when he overhears the jockey tell how he is going to carry off the girl, his mad passion for her returns. Then comes the suicide. There is little preparation and only a few lines of foreshadowing. Mention is made of the superstition that a dull child brings happiness and protection, and thus doom is foreboded when The Innocent begins "to awaken."

That such simplicity of plot and lack of development caused the play to fail in 1872 is not surprising. But in 1885, the revival of *L'Arlésienne* was a complete success. The press critics, according to Sarcey, insisted that now anything could be put on the stage with success, an idyl, a short story without a trace of dramatic form. As for himself, he found the play a "mortal bore," which happened to please the public mostly because of Bizet's music. The present writer saw the play in 1906 and he agreed heartily with Sarcey. A play without movement in which the heroine did not appear seemed undramatic. Many years have passed and now he is not so sure of the meaning of the word dramatic. As for the non-appearance of the heroine, that may be due to great art or to lack of art on the part of Daudet. Sarcey held it was the latter. But just such departures from usual procedure have become a part of the new dramatic technique in the Little Theatre in its search for sensations.

Because of the failure of his plays, Zola could be only the theoretical leader of naturalism in the theatre. A practical leader was needed. He appeared in the person of André Antoine—an employé of the Gas Company, who had a passion for the theatre. Imbued with Zola's theories, he came to the conclusion that the modern stage was false in every respect. He formed a band of young enthusiasts who shared his views; and, in 1887, he produced two bills in a cramped hall with benches for seats. The first bill, given in March, was saved from complete failure by the success of *Jacques Damour,* a play in one act by Hennique from Zola's novel; but Méténier's *En Famille* and Bergerat's *Nuit Bergamasque,* produced in May, established artistically the Théâtre Libre, as Antoine called his group. The undertaking was financially unstable and only seven or eight bills were given a year; but naturalism had found a theatre. Soon the established playhouses, including the Comédie and the Odéon, had to reckon with Antoine's Théâtre Libre, where many of the living French playwrights found a stage for their early plays and where the realistic drama of other nations was first produced in France. The name Théâtre Libre had to be given up by Antoine for business reasons, but the movement of the Free Theatre continued as he founded the Théâtre Antoine. Indeed, the name became a synonym of naturalism in the drama.

Tolstoi's *Power of Darkness* was written in 1886, but the censorship forbade its production on the Russian stage. The play was destined to be one of the important influences in the revolution of dramatic art, for Antoine produced it in 1888 with success in Paris and later took it to Brussels where it was also acclaimed. Inspired by Antoine's example, the society of the Freie Bühne gave the play in Berlin. The influence of the Russians undermined the belief that drama must conform to certain traditions. Dramatic art differs from the art of writing fiction; but it does not follow, as was believed, that certain themes and situations can only be given artistic treatment on the printed page. Everything in life can be presented on the stage. The Free Theatre, it is true, inclined too much towards winning a place for naturalism. Other directors, such as Lugné-Poë in Paris and Stanislavsky in Moscow had to open the theatre to symbolic drama and to static drama. Yet the Théâtre Libre in Paris was largely instrumental in making the old cry *"Ce n'est pas du théâtre"* ridiculous. Catulle Mendez wrote to Antoine in 1887: *"Ce qui n'est pas du théâtre, vous le jouez sur votre théâtre."*

When Antoine announced the production of *The Power of Darkness,* the Parisian newspapers asked some of the older dramatists their opinion of the undertaking. Dumas replied that the play was too sombre and contained no sympathetic character. Sardou felt that the play could only be read, although it was "cruelly true and very beautiful." For Augier it was a novel in dialogue form and too long for the French stage. These supposed faults turned out to be virtues for the audience, which was weary of sympathetic characters, and wanted sober, cruel truth represented without the romance of patent-leather shoes and costumes of the drawing-rooms of Dumas.

Tolstoi found it difficult to turn his creative effort from the novel to the drama. Dialogue in his fiction is of secondary importance. He introduced monologues with a feeling of guilt. Nevertheless he succeeded in producing a play which was far more "of the theatre" than Gorky's later *Lower Depths.* However, in 1888, *The Power of Darkness* seemed to hostile critics undramatic in many scenes and excessively melodramatic in others.

It is a study of peasant life and naturalistic in the sense that repulsive and gruesome details abound in the dialogue and situations. At the same time, *The Power of Darkness* is Tolstoi's protest against the ignorance, evil and the darkness in which peasants were forced to dwell in Russia. He shows how crime follows upon crime, for, as Akim warns his son: "If but one claw is caught the whole bird is lost."

The story is short. Nikita, a young peasant, has become the lover of Anisya, wife of his employer. He refuses to marry a girl he has seduced, and helps Anisya give her husband slow poison furnished by his mother. Married to Anisya, he makes love to his half-witted step-daughter and becomes the father of her child. In order to marry off Akulina, he kills the child a few minutes after its birth, at the instigation of his wife and his mother. When Akulina is being married, he confesses all his crimes.

Tolstoi wrote the scene of the murder and burial of the child in two different forms. Antoine produced it in the ghastly version in which the action practically passes before our eyes. Nikita is concealed in the cellar, but the dialogue between him and the women describes the gruesome act as it takes place. No doubt Antoine wished to give his public the strongest possible dose of naturalism; but just such scenes form an indictment of the naturalistic method carried to excess. The play is now produced by Pitoëff with the variant scene, in which the action comes to us through the ears of a frightened child who cannot sleep but hears vague, though significant sounds; and then Nikita appears, horror-stricken at his deed. Thus presented, the scene is dramatic and tragic, whereas the first version is so gruesome that it arouses disgust.

Thalasso, the sympathetic historian of the Théâtre Libre said in 1909 that when Antoine produced his second bill on May 30, 1887, "contemporary dramatic art was born." But contemporary drama has gone beyond naturalism, and other European countries had a share in the creation of the transcript of life on the stage. By 1890, France no longer held the undisputed leadership in dramatic art. Norwegian, Swedish, Danish, Russian, German and Belgian dramas began to be produced by Antoine and others who formed Little Theatre groups. Thus one of the important effects of the war waged by the Théâtre Libre was to live up to its name and to set the theatre free. Developments in dramatic art became less national and more European. Naturalism was to become as conventionalized in many respects as the older forms of drama; but in the struggle to introduce it on the stage, all conventions were declared invalid. A period of experimentation ensued. Not only in France but all through Europe, the repertory theatre had to compete with the laboratory theatre. Complacency, which arises from pride in tradition, was severely jarred by bands of iconoclasts who set up stages in purlieus of great capitals and produced all kinds of dramas which were not "in accord with the rules." They were often failures, but somehow were interesting. Thus the naturalistic movement in drama not only fought the conventions of the well-made play but also was a manifestation, if not the cause, of the broadening and the development of dramatic art along many lines.

The season of 1892-1893 was the *quatre-vingt-treize* of the Free Theatre. At that time drama finally freed itself from the old conventions and limitations which are not inherent in the art itself. Many different forms of drama found a hearing on the European stage. Shaw's first play, *Widowers' Houses,* was produced in London. Pinero's *Second Mrs. Tanqueray* gave the Londoners an example of Ibsen's methods applied to a problem in British surroundings. Ibsen's *Master Builder,* a combination of realism and symbolism, was performed for the first time on any stage in Berlin and later in London. Björnson's *Beyond Human Power* reached the Parisian stage. Maeterlinck's symbolistic *Pelléas and Mélisande* had its world première in Paris. Oscar Wilde's *Salome* was prohibited after the first performance in Paris but was published in French. Sudermann produced his masterpiece *Magda* (*Heimat*). Schnitzler wrote *Anatol.* Hauptmann's naturalistic and plotless *Weavers* was played first in Berlin and then in Paris. In his *Assumption of Hannele* he left the naturalistic world for a land of poetry and dreams. *Hannele* borders on expressionism. The season was rich in performance and in promise.

The Weavers delivered a strong blow against the old ideals of plot and individual characters. The play presents a series of facts and pictures of conditions of the weavers of Germany about 1840. Their misery and their revolt are depicted. Whether they triumphed over their employers or ameliorated their condition we do not know. The play has no dénouement. It simply stops. The acts might well be the dramatization of five special articles written for a newspaper during a period of social unrest. The play contains no more plot than does a newspaper story. Certain events are represented. Each act presents a different *milieu*. New characters are introduced in each act. There is no single hero, no careful analysis of any character, no love story of any kind. The weavers, both those endowed with individual rôles and the collective mob, are the protagonists. In this respect they resemble the chorus in early Greek tragedy.

The old test of the relation of plot and character cannot be applied to this play. Although drama was to become more completely static in Gorky's *Lower Depths*, this play was revolutionary in 1893 in its disregard of the importance of action as the indispensable element of dramatic art. When Sarcey reviewed *The Weavers* he admitted that even unity of action was no longer necessary. Unity of impression was sufficient. Thus the last of the pseudo-Aristotelian unities remains as a valid law only in academic circles. In 1894 Brunetière formulated his "law of the drama"; but even this law, which dominated academic criticism for years, has had to give way before the steady advance of a theatre which refuses to be bound by conventions.

CHAPTER XIX

GERMAN FATE–TRAGEDY. HEBBEL. IBSEN

TRAGEDY has been defined as the spectacle of a man struggling against the unconquerable. If the unconquerable is also the invisible and intangible and works mysteriously, the spectacle seems to be more thrilling whether it be a Greek presentation of the operation of the curse on the house of Atreus, the coming of Death in Maeterlinck's *Intruse*, the influence of social environment in Hebbel's *Maria Magdalena*, or of heredity in Ibsen's *Ghosts*. Even today many critics in their overwrought enthusiasm consider all tragedies which they admire as representations of the working of Fate, Destiny or Nemesis—spelled with a capital. The words have became as meaningless as the recurrent description of a tragic hero as a "man face to face with the Universe," which sounds so overwhelmingly tragic and is so trite. The common denominator of all these expressions is an invisible, intangible, invincible force opposing an individual. It would be well if the critics would declare a moratorium on the word "fate," and call this force by its right name whether it be an oracular curse of the gods or the action of the thyroid gland.

A curious manifestation of the action of fate in drama is found in the German *Schicksalstragödie* (fate-tragedy), which flourished in the first part of the nineteenth century. Schiller's study of Greek tragedy led him to the introduction of the idea of Nemesis into his own plays. The action of his *Braut von Messina* is based upon the fulfillment of an oracle in a surprising manner. The play foreshadows the fate-tragedies in which a curse becomes operative. Occultism, spiritualism and superstition also contributed to the success of this form of drama of which the first example and the model for many years was Werner's *Vierundzwanzigste Februar*.

The idea of the play was suggested to Werner by Goethe who produced this one-act tragedy in Weimar on the 24th of February, 1810, before an audience that was both thrilled and horrified. The plot of the play is reminiscent of Lillo's *Fatal Curiosity* in which a long-lost son returns to his poverty-stricken parents, conceals his identity in order to make their joy complete the next day, and is murdered by his father for his wealth. In Lillo's play there is but a faint idea of the operation of fate. Werner employs almost every device of the supernatural and fatalistic in constructing this thriller which anticipated the clap-trap of the Grand Guignol by a century.

The curtain discloses the interior of an isolated Alpine inn. The clock strikes eleven at night. The tempest is howling. Trude, the innkeeper's wife, indulges in a monologue as she spins. Her husband does not return. They have naught to eat. No fire. The curse is fulfilled. An owl knocks on the window. Another knock. This time it is Kuruth, her husband. He bears an order—written that day, the 24th of February, 1804—to pay his creditor or to be arrested for debt on the morrow at eight o'clock. Nothing is left for him but suicide. The fatal 24th of February, 'twas then in 1776 that his father died and pronounced the curse. Another knock. A stranger enters who immediately explains to the audience in a convenient aside that he is the long-lost son, Kurt. (Playmaking was easy in those days.) The stranger gives them food and drink. He also seems to know an uncanny amount about them and the curse. Kuruth finally tells the whole story. His father was hot-headed, and one day, the fatal 24th of February, abused his son's wife. Kuruth hurled at him a knife with which he had been sharpening a scythe. It missed, but his father cried out: "May you be murderer of a murderer, as you have murdered me"; and promptly died of apoplexy. Two children were born to them—a boy and a girl. The boy bore the mark of Cain—a blood-red scythe. When the boy was seven, he saw his mother kill a chicken on the 24th of February. In a spirit of imitative play he took the knife and killed his sister. His father cursed him. The child was sent away to an uncle to protect him from his father. Misfortune after misfortune arrived—always on the 24th of February. Kurt is deeply touched. He would like to relieve their misery. (Of course there is no real reason why he should not, for he knows that the curse on him has been withdrawn by his father; but if he disclosed his identity the whole play would be spoiled.) So Kurt tells his story. He also tells them that their son was a victim of the French Revolution and died in his arms. He is rich. He is going to bring happiness to his parents who live near. The constables will arrive at eight. Well, let them awaken him at seven. He enters the small bedroom. As he hangs up his clothes, he pulls out the nail. Putting it back, he causes the fatal knife to fall at Trude's feet on the other side of the partition. Kuruth finally decides to kill the stranger and rob him. He was a suspicious character anyway, and admitted being a murderer. He plunges the knife home. The victim hands them his passport. He is Kurt, their son. The curse has operated. "Another 24th of February. Most unhappy day. God's mercy is eternal. Amen."

When Goethe was reproached for having permitted such a play on the stage at Weimar, he replied: "You are right, but one doesn't always drink wine, sometimes one drinks brandy." Had he known that this play was to call forth a legion of melodramatic imitations he would have thought that he had been drinking wood alcohol, for German fate-tragedy is denatured Greek tragedy in a very raw form. Nemesis becomes the superstition of old wives' tales.

When Aristotle insisted that drama should represent the inevitable development of an action, he referred to the inevitable psychological development. Nemesis or fate or destiny which makes an otherwise reasonable character act like a moron is a travesty worthy of farce-comedy at best. The idea of fate controlling the destiny of man in a surprising fashion would have persisted in drama without these German plays; but their existence is significant of the tenacity of the idea which they helped to emphasize. The influence of heredity and environment as portrayed by Hebbel, Ibsen and their successors is a variation of this dramatic idea in a rational age of scientific and philosophical determinism.

Bourgeois drama was more successful in Germany than in France. The treatment of the themes of the illegitimate child, intermarriage of classes, maidens betrayed by men of noble birth was naturally more sentimental than tragic in an age of sensibility. Structurally these plays hold a middle ground between the close-knit French *drame* and the more loosely constructed English plays. Their importance lies in the fact that they treated the themes which were to become the tragic problems in drama of the nineteenth century. As there were no traditional rules of decorum in the German theatre, scenes of realism were mingled with scenes of sentimentality. The dialogue was much coarser than that permitted on the French stage until the close of the century. Thus, when Madame Molé adapted Kotzbue's *Menschenhass und Reue* she suppressed most of the purely homely Germanic local color, dropped several commonplace scenes, and re-arranged the play so that there would be no change of scene within the acts.

It frequently happens that the second-rate playwright attains international reputation, especially if he combines theatrical effectiveness with sentimentality. Such was the case of Kotzebue. He won success not only in Germany but in England, Russia and even France. All kinds of plays flowed from his facile pen in great numbers. His *Menschenhass und Reue* (1789) is one of the first modern dramas in which the heroine is an unfaithful wife, a character destined to dominate the serious theatre of the nineteenth century. However, she is much more sentimental than tragic. Much of the play consists of scenes presenting her as a wholly repentant woman spending her life in performing good deeds. Her husband is depicted as a charitable misanthrope but his hatred of mankind is only skin-deep.

Before the play opens, Eulalia has left her husband, Meinau, because he did not gratify her desire to live a life of luxury. Her lover never appears and his character is only sketched. He was a mere trifler. None of the usual phases of the question of infidelity such as were to be treated in the nineteenth century are discussed. The situation is given a romantic, sentimental coloring. Eulalia has been given charge of an estate. For four months an unknown man has been renting a small lodge near the château. Neither one has seen the other, since their meeting is to be the climax of the play in the last act. When the recognition takes place by chance each vies with the other in generosity. Eulalia offers her husband a divorce; he offers her a fortune. Both are refused. They are about to separate forever when their children appear as gods from the machine, and their mutual love conquers. The curtain falls on the usual sentimental tableau of the re-united family which was so dear to artists and dramatists of this period. This solution of the problem of the unfaithful wife aroused criticism and it is a far cry from such a dénouement to the usual unhappy fate of such heroines in the next century.

This play was produced in Paris in 1792. A second version was made by Madame Molé and produced with success first in 1799 and later in 1823, with Talma and Mlle. Mars in the cast. Gérard de Nerval adapted it for the stage in 1855, and it was revived once more in 1862. Several literary translations were also published. Thus the unfaithful wife first reached the French stage by way of Germany.

Even in Germany, however, the bourgeois drama was finally discredited. Hebbel assigned the cause of this reaction to the fact that the plays dealt with externalities rather than with the inner elements of character. The love affairs of a bourgeois maiden with a nobleman, lack of money, class distinction, were pathetic but not tragic situations. If external circumstances were different, the problem would not exist. Partially anticipating Brunetière's law of the drama, Hebbel pointed out in 1843 that tragedy arises from the operation of the will, "the obstinate extension of the ego," especially from the struggle between the individual will and the world-will, or a will inherent in the universe. In his theory character was far more important than the dramatic fable. (*Mein Wort über das Drama.*) He advocated the presentation of situations brought about by inner experience rather than external circumstances such as class distinction. (Preface to *Maria Magdalena*.)

In his *Maria Magdalena* (1844) he presents a tragedy of the middle classes arising from the bourgeois psychology of Anton rather than from any externality, such as the betrayal of his daughter by a man of rank. Her betrayer is of her own class. *Maria Magdalena* is a picture of bourgeois society, practically an indictment of the middle classes. Sentimentality has given way to realism.

It is a Sunday morning in the home of Anton, the master-joiner. His wife is putting on her wedding-dress to go to church in order to give thanks for her recovery from a dangerous illness. Karl, the son, is depicted as a wayward boy, demanding money, revolting at the narrowness of the home. His father's stern-ness and intolerance have totally estranged the youth. Leonhard is in love with the daughter Klara. In a scene between them, we find that he has forced her to give herself to him. He was jealous of her childhood friend who has lately returned as a Secretary. Leonhard has gained the position of cashier by get-ting the other candidate drunk before the examination. Klara is disgusted at being chained to such a man. Leonhard learns that Klara has no dowry. Her stern but just father has given it to help his old benefactor. When Karl is arrested for rob-bery, Leonhard breaks his troth with Klara. The news of her son's disgrace kills the mother.

In the second act, old Anton is shown a prey to the fear of what people will say of him—the father of a thief. His words burn into Klara's soul. He would cut his throat if she were not innocent. Karl is freed from prison. He was wrongly accused. Now, Klara alone bears the burden. Her friend, the Secretary, declares his love for her. She confesses the truth to him.

The third act takes us to Leonhard's room. Klara asks him to marry her, now that her brother's innocence is proved. He refuses brutally. When she has gone, the Secretary comes and takes Leonhard away to fight a duel. The scene changes to Anton's house. Karl has returned. "If you had done it, he'd have killed himself," Karl says to Klara. She goes forth. The Secretary comes. He is wounded but has killed Leonhard. Klara is avenged. The Secretary makes Anton promise not to turn her out if she . . . but she has thrown herself down the well. "You sent her on the road to death," cries the Secretary to Anton, "and I, I'm to blame that she didn't turn back. When you suspected her misfortune, you thought of the tongues that would hiss at it, but not of the worthlessness of the snakes that own them. You said things that drove her to despair. And I, instead of folding her in my arms, when she opened her heart to me in nameless terror, thought of the knave that might mock at me." The curtain falls on Anton's line, expressive of the completeness of the tragedy: "I don't understand the world any more."

Maria Magdalena is the tragedy of Anton rather than of Klara who is a victim of the bourgeois virtues of Anton which he magnified into vices. His rectitude, piety, thrift, pride and sense of morality have made him the inhuman instrument of destruction of his family. The play is a dramatization of Hebbel's statement made in his diary: "There is no worse tyrant than the common man in his own family circle." But more than that, it is an analysis of a segment of society and the turmoil resulting from its social ideals and prejudices. Hebbel's substitution of inner conflict for the conflict of externalities produced social tragedy. The theme is treated with such objectivity and is so free from sentimentality that the final impression is realistic. Indeed, the play was not fully appreciated until after realism had won its place in the theatre towards the close of the century.

But Hebbel did not continue to treat themes of middle-class society. Nor was Ludwig's *Erbförster* (1850) nor Freytag's *Die Valentine* (1847) and *Graf Waldemar* (1848) powerful enough to foster the development of bourgeois tragedy. Ludwig's play deals with middle-class people, but the plot turns into a melodramatic situation in which a father shoots his daughter by mistake. He is led to act by his uncompromising, stubborn nature. The play is more a portrayal of character than a representation of a social problem. So much of the interest depends upon chance and circumstantial evidence of murders, that it represents a special case.

The old themes of class distinction and the difference in class ideals continued to form the basis of dramatic conflict until Ibsen began to carry on the work begun by Hebbel in *Maria Magdalena* and dramatized the struggle between the individual and social laws. Hebbel treated the problem of the woman who is considered to be the man's chattel in *Gyges und sein Ring* and in *Herodes und Mariamne* before Ibsen founded *A Doll's House* on this situation. In *Judith,* Hebbel speaks of ill-assorted marriages as productive of ghosts. But the setting of these dramas is not in the far distant past and the treatment of the problems is more mystical than realistic.

These two playwrights held many ideas in common; but the idea that Hebbel introduced the unveiling of the past or analytic method of playwriting and that Ibsen derived his practice from Hebbel is a partial misconception. English playwrights had not employed this method in bourgeois drama. They employed an early point of attack and presented most of the events on the stage. The French dramatists, especially Diderot, naturally observed the unity of time and placed the point of attack late in the story. Schiller had realized that the analytic method was effective, not because it preserved a realistic unity of time, but because it made possible the presentation of a composite action in a brief space of time. He had employed this method both for purposes of plot and analysis of character. Although the Germans were never so strict as the French in regard to changes of scene and lapse of time, they usually employed a late point of attack in bourgeois drama. The analytic method and the unveiling of the past were a natural result and were introduced long before Hebbel's time as a consequence of the imitation of the structure of the French *drame* of the eighteenth century. Although Hebbel did not introduce the analytic method, he showed how effective it may be as a means of analyzing character and showing the cumulative effect of apparently minor elements of the past upon a tragic crisis of the present.

Hebbel prepared the way for Ibsen and the development of the social drama of the latter half of the century; but he was not responsible for the ensuing evolution of dramatic art, because he did not continue to produce plays of the type of *Maria Magdalena*. For this reason a Norwegian was hailed by the German naturalists and founders of the Freie Bühne as the innovator in dramatic art at the close of the nineteenth century, after German drama had reached the low level of mediocrity in the seventies and early eighties. In 1889 the Freie Bühne was founded in Berlin on the model of Antoine's Théâtre Libre of Paris. Ibsen's *Ghosts* was given as its first offering. It was then that Hebbel, Ludwig and Anzengruber began to be fully appreciated as dramatists who had long carried the torch of realistic drama. When Ibsen was hailed by the Germans as the regenerator of dramatic art, he said: "They had long had their Hebbel."

Until 1850 there was no Norwegian drama. In 1851 young Ibsen was appointed director of the newly established theatre in Bergen. He held this post for six years. When he died in 1906, his dramas had been acclaimed in all European theatres and his art of playwriting had become the model for students of dramatic technique and for many dramatists of the late nineteenth century. Ibsen was the outstanding figure of his age in dramatic art. Otto Brahm said: "The gates to the most modern German drama were opened when *Ghosts* appeared on the stage" (of the Freie Bühne). The remark applies equally well to all stages upon which that play and his other dramas were produced. The Free Theatre—the theatre in which audiences are supposed to be over twenty-five years of age mentally—is the legacy of Ibsen wherever it exists. The drama of ideas came into its own as he produced, at intervals of two years, his series of plays beginning with *A Doll's House* (1879) and ending with *When We Dead Awaken* (1899).

His first method of playmaking was derived from German and French romantic dramatists and from Scribe. Under his direction in Bergen, one hundred and forty-five plays were produced. Of these, seventy-five were by French authors and twenty-one were by Scribe himself. He learned the tricks of the well-made play. He employed them and then cast them aside.

His first play of importance, *Lady Inger of Ostrat* (1855), is a romantic tragedy in the regulation five acts. It contains all the elements common to that type of drama which had flourished in Germany and France. Lady Inger, thinking to raise her long-lost son to kingship, orders the murder of a rival claimant who is discovered by a token, in the shape of a ring, to be her son. Her daughter falls in love with the betrayer of an elder sister. Confusion of names, unknown strangers, ghosts, papers, poison cups, vaults, love at first sight, sudden entrances through windows, fatal mistakes of identity, ambuscades make the plot too complex to be clear. The characters are subservient to the situation. Ibsen showed a knowledge of all the devices of dramatic art of the previous generation; but he did not yet employ them with the deftness of Scribe.

The influence of Scribian technique on Ibsen during his years of apprenticeship has been clearly demonstrated by Mr. William Archer who says of *The Feast at Solhoug:* "It may indeed be called Scribe's *Bataille de Dames* writ tragic. . . . All the ingenious dovetailing of incidents and working-up of misunderstandings, Ibsen unquestionably learned from the French. The French language, indeed, is the only one which has a word—*quiproquo*—to indicate the class of misunderstanding which from *Lady Inger* down to *The League of Youth*, Ibsen employed without scruple."

The League of Youth (1869) is a tissue of misunderstandings and *quiproquo* which eclipses the theme of the play. It is an outstanding example of what havoc to truth can be wrought by these methods of building plays, and shows how a comedy can be turned into that most unfortunate kind of drama: a farce with pretensions of ideas. Ibsen had now acquired much of the deftness of Scribe; but in order to be the real Ibsen whom we know, he had to discard the art of plotting he had learned.

Pillars of Society (1877) is a better piece of dramatic art because the theme is not obscured by obvious tricks. It was received enthusiastically in Germany. Ibsen began to enjoy an international reputation; but had his activities as a playwright ceased with this play, he would have gone down to posterity as an excellent imitator of the French school of dramatic art as practiced by Augier and Dumas. In November, 1878, he jotted down "Notes for the Modern Tragedy." The phrase is significant, for these notes were to expand into *A Doll's House;* and this drama is the transition from the old to a new form of tragedy.

There are two kinds of spiritual law, two kinds of conscience, one in man, and another, altogether different, in woman. They do not understand each other; but in practical life the woman is judged by man's law, as though she were not a woman but a man.

The wife in the play ends by having no idea of what is right or wrong; natural feeling on the one hand, belief in authority on the other have altogether bewildered her.

A woman cannot be herself in the society of the present day, which is exclusively a masculine society, with laws framed by men and with a judicial system that judges feminine conduct from a masculine point of view.

She has committed forgery, and she is proud of it; for she did it out of love for her husband to save his life. But this husband with his commonplace principles of honor is on the side of the law and regards the question with masculine eyes.

It was thus that the impulse came to Ibsen to write *A Doll's House.* His point of departure was a problem, called in those days "The Woman Question." The French dramatists had produced the problem play and the drama of ideas; but they wrote like lawyers who have something to prove. The *pièce à thèse* is literally and actually a play with a thesis. For that reason it often departs from true life in order to carry its point. The *raisonneur* is an advocate. Ibsen took sides. He thought too deeply, too passionately to assume a calm, judicial position. Yet he presented this problem in a way that shocked the sentimental optimists who want a happy ending to all human questions on the stage, and grieved the sentimental pessimists who think that unsolvable problems can be solved by a pistol shot. He was a naturalist in the best sense of the word, for he presented life without trying to solve one of its greatest enigmas.

The curtain rises on the living room of Nora and Helmer. There is nothing new in the setting. It is merely realistic representation. Ibsen never came under the influence of the new stagecraft because his life work was completed before that movement revolutionized dramatic art.

Into this room comes Nora. It is Christmas time. A joyous atmosphere pervades this house. Without wasting a word, Ibsen quickly shows us that Nora does not have masculine ideas of money. She is relieved of some financial burden. She wants to be extravagant. She is capable of deception. Helmer treats her as a charming doll—as had her father—and as a sweet little song bird. This opening scene gives impressions unobtrusively. Up to this point it is exposition in the new style. But with the entrance of Mrs. Linden, the old form of exposition is employed. She is a friend whom Nora has not seen for years, to whom Nora tells a part of her story. Nora's husband was ill. A journey to Italy was necessary to save his life. She procured the money in a mysterious manner. She has been paying the debt ever since that time. Her husband knows nothing about it. Was the money furnished by an admirer of hers, possibly Dr. Rank? Probably not. Her husband has been appointed to a high position in a bank. The debt is almost paid.

Nora, left alone with her children, is wildly romping with them about the Christmas tree when Krogstad enters. Rank has described him as a moral incurable. His past is dishonorable. He is trying to rise but Helmer has decided to dismiss him from the bank. Krogstad asks Nora to intercede for him. He loaned her the money years ago. She forged her father's name to the note. He threatens exposure. Nora cannot understand that she committed a crime—that the law is against her. She did it to save her husband's life!

With this scene the exposition and the unveiling of events of the past come temporarily to an end. Curiosity has become suspense. The situation is fraught with dramatic tenseness; and the plot seems to be of paramount importance, when Helmer refuses to retain Krogstad in his employ in spite of Nora's intercession. The psychological element, however, enters the drama at this moment. Helmer shocks and bewilders Nora by telling her that a lying mother corrupts her children. In speaking of Krogstad, Helmer says: ". . . In such an atmosphere of lies home life is poisoned and contaminated in every fibre. Every breath the children draw contains some germ of evil." The act ends with Nora crying out "Corrupt my children!— Poison my home! It's not true! It can never be true!"

The tragedy of the modern woman begins to overshadow the dramatic plot. The question as to whether Nora's forgery will be discovered pales in comparison with the question of the status of woman in relation to masculine ideals. Nora begins to think. The spectator does likewise. However, the interest in the plot does not disappear. Ibsen had not yet given up any of the traditional methods of arousing suspense and excitement. The entrances and exits of his characters are carefully timed. Indeed, the time element is as important as in any one of Scribe's plays. The plot even hinges upon letters, the moment of their arrival and of the disclosure of their contents.

The second act opens as Nora anxiously searches the letter box for Krogstad's incriminating message. Sardou, in *Pattes de Mouche* (*A Scrap of Paper*), was no more dexterous than Ibsen. Nora is preparing a costume for a fancy dress ball at which she is to dance a tarantella. She makes a second attempt to persuade her husband to let Krogstad keep his place in the bank; but Helmer is obdurate and sends the letter of dismissal. Nora is about to appeal to Dr. Rank for money to make the last payment on the debt; but this last avenue of escape is closed to her when she discovers that Rank loves her. Krogstad arrives. He has received his dismissal. He will keep the forged note as a weapon. Helmer will be in his power. As he leaves, he drops his letter of accusation in the box. Mrs. Linden offers a ray of hope as she goes to try to persuade Krogstad to take the letter back unread. Helmer is going to open the box when Nora stops him by dancing the wild tarantella. Whether the scene be called theatrical or dramatic, it is the last time that Ibsen employed such methods of the older form of drama calculated to arouse intense emotional excitement.

The curtain of the third act rises upon Mrs. Linden and Krogstad. They loved each other in the past. She had married someone else for protection. Now she offers to return to him. In his happiness he is ready to recall his letter; but she insists that he leave it. Helmer and Nora must come to a complete understanding. As Krogstad exits, Ibsen's last villain leaves his stage. Mrs. Linden is the goddess from the machine for the plot, for Krogstad is to write another letter promising not to blackmail Helmer.

Dr. Rank then takes leave of Nora. He is going to die of an inherited disease. Ibsen could not allow the audience to conjecture that perhaps Nora would seek protection from a lover. Helmer opens the letter of denunciation. With masculine egoism he fails Nora in the crisis. He thinks of nothing but himself and his position. Then comes the second letter. The plot is solved. The whole problem is solved for Helmer. He is saved. Therefore he will protect Nora—now that she needs no protection from him. "Only open your heart to me, and I will be both will and conscience to you," is his fatuous comment on the solution. The stage is set for a happy ending. There is some evidence that Ibsen first intended to have a scene of reconciliation. But the husband and wife sit down on opposite sides of the table and the real tragedy begins. A new form of tragedy evolves from this scene in which Nora explains her position, her ideals, her whole feminine psychology in plain, direct language. The eight years of her married life have been spent with a stranger in a doll's house. They cannot live together until the miracle comes to pass that communion between them shall be a marriage. She leaves quietly. From below is heard the reverberation of a heavy door closing.

The last scene makes the play a masterpiece of nineteenth-century drama. It caused a storm of protest. For its production, Ibsen preferred to tack on a happy ending than to leave the salving of wounded feelings to some bungling play-doctor. The American cinema version also performs the miracle before our eyes lest we should leave the motion picture house pondering over a problem. But the lesson has been learned from *A Doll's House* that dramatic art does not consist in scenes like that of the tarantella but rather in searching the souls of men and women for the motives of their acts. The expression "obligatory scene" took on a new meaning when Helmer and Nora faced each other in the last act. It was no longer the keystone of a well-built plot, but the scene which presents the basic idea of the whole play. This scene is the dramatization of Ibsen's "Notes for the Modern Tragedy."

A Doll's House, therefore, marked the parting of the ways between the old and new drama of the nineteenth century. Ibsen had shown himself master of French craftsmanship. Up to the last scene, *A Doll's House* is a well-made play. Each entrance and exit is perfectly timed, and produces a more or less striking turn of affairs. Letters and rings of the door bell arouse suspense. Strong contrasts of joy and despair, hope and fear are employed in the manner of Victor Hugo and other romanticists. The play can hold the interest of the unthinking spectator through its plot alone. But *A Doll's House* is more than a perfect machine. It is a living organism.

As if conscious of reaching the limits of the domain of the old drama, Ibsen said of his next play, *Ghosts:* "It may well be that the play is in several respects rather daring. But it seemed to me that the time had come for moving some boundary posts." "My object," the dramatist also said, "was to make the reader feel that he was going through a piece of real experience." No matter how fascinating the development of such plots as that of *A Doll's House* may be, the spectator knows that such a succession of events, such striking contrasts, do not produce the effect of a real experience.

Ghosts is a close-knit drama. The action takes place in one room and in a few hours; but the dramatic development is an analysis of the past much more than in *A Doll's House*. "To marry for external reasons, even if they be religious or moral, brings Nemesis on the progeny." *Ghosts* is the dramatization of this statement of Ibsen; and of the *via crucis* of the wife and mother involved in such a marriage.

Ghosts recalls *Œdipus Rex* in the fact that Ibsen has chosen as a point of attack the moment when the past must be disclosed and when the modern Nemesis—heredity—is about to descend upon its victim. Yet there are fewer *coups de théâtre* and less suspense in *Ghosts* than in *Œdipus Rex*. The unveiling of the past in the Greek tragedy is an unveiling of events. In the modern tragedy, the unveiling of the past reveals the psychology of human beings, especially of Helen Alving. It reveals the results of a marriage for external, social reasons.

Helen had married Captain Alving because her mother and her two aunts proved to her clearly that it would be downright madness to refuse such an offer. He turned out to be an utterly dissolute man. She went to Pastor Manders and said: "Take me." But he sent her back to her husband, to her path of duty, as he believed. A child, Oswald, was born to them. Alving also had a daughter, Regina, by one of the maids in the house. A few years later, he died. When the play opens,

Oswald, now a young artist, has returned home from Paris. Mrs. Alving has built an orphanage with her husband's money —her purchase price. Pastor Manders has arrived to dedicate it.

The first act is entirely retrospective. Not until the last minute is there an important incident in the present. Mrs. Alving tells Manders that from the day after tomorrow she will act in every way as though he who is dead had never lived in this house. "There shall be no one here but my boy and his mother."

> (*From the dining-room comes the noise of a chair overturned, and at the same moment is heard*)
>
> REGINA (*sharply, but in a whisper*)
>
> Oswald! take care! are you mad? Let me go!
>
> MRS. ALVING (*starts in terror*)
>
> Ah—!
>
> (*She starts wildly towards the half-open door.* OSWALD *is heard laughing and humming. A bottle is uncorked*)
>
> MANDERS (*agitated*)
>
> What can be the matter? What is it, Mrs. Alving?
>
> MRS. ALVING (*hoarsely*)
>
> Ghosts! The couple from the conservatory—risen again!
>
> MANDERS
>
> Is it possible! Regina—? Is she—?
>
> MRS. ALVING
>
> Yes. Come. Not a word—!
>
> (*She seizes* PASTOR MANDERS *by the arm, and walks unsteadily towards the dining-room*)

The scene is strikingly dramatic. Ibsen did not give up entirely such moments of tenseness; but he employed them sparingly in his plays after *A Doll's House*. The scene is typical of his method. With strict economy of dialogue he advances the situation; but he also reveals the past at the same time. Indeed, the chief value of the scene lies in the fact that it paints a vivid picture of Alving's relations with Regina's mother, of all the tragedy of years gone by and points to the tragedy of heredity that is to come to pass in a few short hours.

The second act is almost entirely retrospective. Oswald tells his pitiful, horrible story. He is the physical victim of his father's excesses. Regina alone can bring him happiness. The act closes with the burning of the orphanage.

The last act portrays the physical disintegration of Oswald. His mother does not oppose the union of Regina and Oswald; but after she has revealed their true relationship, Regina leaves. Oswald forces his mother to promise to take away the life she gave him when his impending mental breakdown occurs. The curtain falls upon Oswald demanding the sun. His heredity has overtaken him. His mother holds the morphia tablets in her hand and is staring at him in speechless horror.

"The fault lies in that all mankind has failed," said Ibsen of this play in his preliminary notes. No more depressing tragedy has ever been written. The remedy for the situation in *A Doll's House* was a "miracle," but even this tenuous hope was removed in *Ghosts*. The Russians, with their will to hope and their belief in a better future no matter how remote, are optimists in comparison with this stern Norwegian. This relentless picture of modern life, as he saw it, showed dramatists that the theatre was not merely a place in which to behold exciting heroics, sentimental propaganda, or melodramatic events.

Ibsen never ceased to exercise a certain amount of dramaturgic dexterity which he learned from the French school of dramatic art. He resembled the younger Dumas more than he would have wished to admit, for he had no admiration for the virtual creator of the problem play. In *The League of Youth*, the situation and effects are meretricious. In *Pillars of Society*, the dénouement is so carefully articulated that one is conscious of the technical devices which lead up to it. The first two acts of *A Doll's House* are so full of antitheses, contrasts, unexpected but pat arrivals of personages that one still feels the skill of the dramatist in keeping up suspense. Too much of the plot depends upon the hour that events take place and on the time that letters are sent, received and read. Until the last scene, the plot is a very interesting element of the whole play, just because it is so beautifully manipulated. But never again did Ibsen allow his dramaturgic dexterity to overshadow for an instant his characters and his presentation of human problems. The only possible exception would be *Hedda Gabler*. Yet the character of Hedda is so dominating that one cannot follow the ingenious development of the plot except in relation to this perverse fascinating woman who, in striving for power over a human being and in seeking for beauty at all costs, destroys Lövborg and herself.

Events which are placed in the unchangeable past seem to be inevitable. Their revelation generally brings a peripeteia. When a dramatist is hammering home ideas, it is well for him not to have to spend time showing the physical causes of his problem or to have to consider the temporal sequence of incidents. He is not hampered by the question of showing when or where all these events came to pass. He can select a locality where they can be revealed at the time when he wishes to bring them to light.

Therefore, Ibsen observed a relatively strict unity of place and of time. In many of his plays the scene does not change at all, and the action is completed within twenty-four hours. In *John Gabriel Borkman* the actual time of representation is longer than the ideal duration of the action. At the end of the first act we hear, from the room above, the strains of the *Danse Macabre*. When the curtain rises on the second act, the last bars are being played.

Although Ibsen helped to introduce the static drama, his whole scheme of playwriting kept his dramas in a close-knit form and shed an atmosphere of realism over them. These were piously imitated by his followers as essential elements of dramatic art. Nothing in the actual structure of his later dramas led to the disintegration of the well-made play. In structure and in spirit his earlier *Peer Gynt* with its veiled expressionism is closer to the drama of the present day than is any one of his later plays,

even including the obscurely symbolic *When We Dead Awaken.*
The late point of attack, however, sometimes causes bewilderment on the part of the spectator. *Rosmersholm* is so introspective that many scenes are not fully understood the first time
that the play is seen. Ibsen makes every line and every action
of his characters significant. No dramatist has ever equalled
him in dramatic economy.

Although he employed symbolism more and more in his later
years, he was not seeking to veil his meaning after the manner
of many modern playwrights. Yet the first scene of *Rosmersholm* is baffling. Rebecca West and Madame Helseth are
watching Rosmer out of the window. Will he cross the bridge
over the mill-race—"a place where a thing like that happened."
No. He goes around it. "They cling to their dead here at
Rosmersholm." If they didn't, there would be no White Horse.
But the rector, "he goes straight over the foot bridge, he does.
And yet she was his sister, his own flesh and blood." When
one sees the play a second time and knows that Rebecca West
drove Beata, Rosmer's wife, to commit suicide by leaping from
this bridge, the scene contains a deep significance instead of an
elusive mystery. Indeed, the whole drama, on second sight,
produces a different effect, because the mysterious becomes clear
and significant. Yet one would not wish to alter this masterpiece of dramatic narration. As Mr. Archer said: "In unskilful
hands this method might doubtless become very tedious; but
when, as in *Rosmersholm,* every phase of the retrospect has a
definite reaction upon the drama—the psychological process—
actually passing on the stage, the effect attained is surely one of
peculiar richness and depth. The drama of the past and the
drama of the present are interwoven in such a complex yet clear
and stately harmony as Ibsen himself has not often rivalled."

Though his plays are retrospective and tend towards the static
form, they never give the effect of stagnating action. His opening scenes are quiet. Sometimes, as in *A Doll's House,* they are
peaceful for the purpose of contrast to the coming storm. Unobtrusively he gains our interest because he builds from the

very outset. In the art of preparation and foreshadowing he belongs to the older school of dramatists. He points to the course of the action and uses recurrent lines, such as the words of Hedda: "And then at ten o'clock—Eilert Lövborg will be here—with vine leaves in his hair." For if at ten o'clock Lövborg does not come like an inspired Dionysus, tragedy will ensue. The third act opens at dawn the next day. The two women have waited for him in vain. One sometimes regrets that modern drama frowns upon significant lines of preparation, especially after listening to the skilful exposition and foreshadowing in *Hedda Gabler,* where every speech is a vivid revelation of character or situation and leads one into the dramatic future, fraught with suspense.

Hedda Gabler, through cowardice, gave up Eilert Lövborg and married Tesman, who has nothing but a Ph.D. degree. Lövborg, under the inspiration of Thea Elvsted, wrote an epoch-making book which would have brought him fame. Tesman, in the meantime, has been at work on what is known as a "scholarly article," dealing with the domestic industries of Brabant during the Middle Ages. When Hedda meets Lövborg again her old desire to mould a human destiny returns. She is jealous of Thea, whose flaxen hair she always wanted to pull, for the fragile Thea possessed the courage which the dashing daughter of General Gabler lacked, although she amuses herself with her father's pistols. Hedda sends Lövborg to a drinking party. In the interval, marked by an entr'acte, he loses his precious manuscript and later visits a notorious Mademoiselle Diana and becomes involved with the police.

Tesman has found the manuscript, and brings it to Hedda. When Lövborg appears and speaks of it as his child and Thea's, Hedda gives him one of the pistols and tells him to use it now —and beautifully. He takes it; and, when he is gone, Hedda burns the manuscript. Lövborg has committed suicide, shooting himself not in the breast but in the bowels, as Hedda's admirer, Judge Brack, informs her with cruel pleasure. Furthermore, Brack has recognized the pistol. Scandal will ensue if he speaks;

but if Madame Hedda is tractable, all will be well. Thea and
Tesman have set to work to reconstruct the book from the
notes. The former situation has recurred in a tragi-comic variation.

Hedda crosses to the table where Tesman and Thea are working; and, suppressing an involuntary smile, she imitates Tesman's
intonation. "Well? Are you getting on, George? Eh?" This
vapid "Eh" sums up his character. Hedda passes her hands
through Thea's hair which always irritated her.

HEDDA
Doesn't it seem strange to you, Thea? Here are you sitting
with Tesman—just as you used to sit with Eilert Lövborg?
MRS. ELVSTED
Ah, if I could only inspire your husband in the same way!
HEDDA
Oh, that will come too—in time.
TESMAN
Yes, do you know, Hedda—I really think I begin to feel some-
thing of the sort. But won't you go and sit with Brack again?
HEDDA
Is there nothing I can do to help you two?
TESMAN
Nothing, nothing in the world. I trust to you to keep Hedda
company, my dear Brack.
BRACK
With the very greatest pleasure.

Each line of this dialogue has a double significance. Beneath
the superficial meaning, lies the revelation of the tragic situation.

Ibsen now produces one of his contrasts. Hedda goes into
another room and draws the curtains. Suddenly she is heard
playing a wild dance on the piano. Tesman protests at dance
music in moments of grief. She promises to be quiet. Tesman
suggests that in the future Thea and he will work at his Aunt
Julia's house. Brack will entertain Hedda. They will get on
capitally together.

HEDDA (*speaking loud and clear*)

Yes, don't you flatter yourself we will, Judge Brack? Now that you are the one cock in the basket—

(*A shot is heard within.* TESMAN, MRS. ELVSTED *and* BRACK *leap to their feet*)

TESMAN

Oh, now she is playing with those pistols again.

But this time, it is more than playing. She has shot herself with the one that remained when she sent Lövborg forth with the other. She used it "beautifully," for Tesman shrieks: "Shot herself. Shot herself in the temple"; and he adds his usual vapid comment, grotesquely tragic at that moment: "Fancy that!" Then comes Brack's recurrent phrase: "Good God!— people don't do such things."

Whether such ingenious and skilful handling of tense moments is to disappear entirely from drama of the future only time can tell. The reaction against the well-made play has made us suspect that such technique is meretricious; but we must remember that there is a difference between the theatric employed to excite and the dramatic which convinces. Surely this dé- nouement is dramatic.

Closing scenes of high tension with a surprising though logical peripeteia are typical of most of Ibsen's plays. Even his last drama, *When We Dead Awaken,* rises to a final dramatic climax. Maia's triumphant song of freedom is heard far down in the valley. Then "suddenly a sound like thunder is heard from high up on the snow-field, which glides and whirls downwards with headlong speed. Professor Rubek and Irene can be dimly discerned as they are whirled along with the masses of snow and buried in them."

The dénouements of *Little Eyolf* and of *John Gabriel Bork-man* are exceptions to his general practice and are examples of the quieter drama of the twentieth century such as Chekhov produced. Mr. Archer believed that the last scenes of these dramas resemble the choral odes and the mournful antiphones of Greek tragedy. Yet there is more than lamentation and lyricism in these scenes evoking the past. Rita and Allmers are doing more than "looking back over their shattered lives and playing chorus to their own tragedy." They are saving what is left from the wreckage and are going to build anew. Ella and Borkman are coming to a realization of things that were enigmas in the past. The peace which descends upon the people in these plays is not the peace of resignation to the inexorable will of the gods as in Greek drama. It is not the peace of defeat after a half-hearted battle, when nothing remains but the will to hope for a better future, centuries distant, as in Russian tragedies. It is the peace which comes from finally understanding the bewildering past. Ibsen's characters act until the end. Unlike the Russian and Greek heroes, they never cease thinking only to suffer patiently. There is psychological, dramatic progression until the curtain falls. I cannot, therefore, agree with Mr. Archer that in Ibsen "the poet definitely triumphs over the mere playwright," in these dénouements. Ibsen's scenes are never static in the sense that they merely induce an elegiac mood. The story of events may come to an end but the story of the souls of his characters continues to the last line. The spectator must do more than experience moods. He must think with Ibsen's men and women, if he would get the full effect of the drama. Audiences had first worshiped in the theatre. When the religious element disappeared, they had been content to laugh or weep. Now they began to think. They wanted to listen to clear, detailed arguments and to use their reason. In the ultra-modern theatre, with its symbolism, expressionism and new stagecraft, the audience experiences sensations and receives impressions.

Yet Ibsen was among the first to sow the seeds of the deintellectualization of dramatic art. Even before Verlaine was proclaiming that art is "beautiful eyes behind a veil," that the elusive nuance is preferable to the clear color, Ibsen began to draw a veil over his precise meaning by the use of symbolism. There is not a line in *A Doll's House* which is not clear. In

Ghosts there are one or two figures of speech which border on the symbolistic. After the orphanage has been destroyed by fire, Oswald says: "Everything will burn. All that recalls father's memory is doomed. Here am I, too, burning down." Hedda's classic line: "And then—at ten o'clock—Eilert Lövborg will be here with vine leaves in his hair," contains that balance of clarity and obscurity which stimulates the imagination. It is given strong emphasis by its position as the last line of the second act, and by the frequent recurrence of the idea. The sensitive auditor develops the image and the idea that are evoked beyond what the words state into what they may imply. He collaborates with the playwright in the process of creation. Subtle suggestion takes the place of clear statement.

This method is not a new one for Ibsen at this period of his career. His earlier plays abound in symbolistic figures of speech. *Peer Gynt* especially, contains a hidden meaning which is more or less vaguely grasped rather than clearly understood. When Ibsen first turned to realism in his dramas, when the problem became of paramount importance in his scheme of playwriting, he sought for the clarity, logic and precision which naturally accompany a deterministic philosophy. His impressionistic imagery gave way temporarily to exact pictures of life. His settings went indoors—into the four walls of ordinary houses. His dialogue, without being commonplace, became more concrete. It was concise and incisive conversation such as people ought to carry on in the given circumstances but never do, because real life is not art.

Then little by little, the rich imagination of the poet began to reassert itself and go hand in hand with the ideas of the realistic dramatist. Figures of speech half reveal a realm of phantasy which one seeks to penetrate as an initiate. Characters appear such as the Rat-Wife in *Little Eyolf*, Hilda and Solness in *The Master Builder*, which can be regarded either as symbols or real people. He uses symbolistic titles such as, *The Wild Duck* and *The Lady from the Sea*. It is not necessary to interpret any of his plays symbolically except *When We Dead*

Awaken. There is a concrete explanation for all his characters and scenes. The Rat-Wife may be Death, may be Almer's companion in the mountains, or may be simply a woman who rids houses of rats and mice. The element of the supernatural can be explained away in terms of the natural.

Ibsen seems to have constructed his plays in several strata. On the exterior is the plot. *A Doll's House* furnishes theatrical enjoyment in the unfolding of its story, charged with suspense, as completely as any melodramatic thriller. Even in his more static dramas, such as *Ghosts, Little Eyolf, Rosmersholm, John Gabriel Borkman,* there is enough story in the past and present to arouse interest in the fate of the characters. But beneath the theatrical enjoyment, lies our personal concern over Nora, Mrs. Alving, Rita and Almers, Rebecca and Rosmer, Borkman and the sisters who love him. We can look upon them as people like ourselves in special circumstances. *A Doll's House* can be interpreted as the study of a woman. Or it can be studied as a dramatic presentation of "The Woman Question." Finally, in his later plays, there is the sub-stratum of symbolism, which stimulates the imagination by subtle suggestion. Ibsen invites one to penetrate esoteric mysteries, but he never forces one, except, perchance, in *When We Dead Awaken.*

Even *The Wild Duck*, which is highly symbolistic, can be followed as a concrete series of events proving that it is dangerous to destroy illusion and to substitute the devastating truth for the life-giving lie. Ibsen did not, and perchance could not, clearly explain exactly what he meant in certain passages. Weary of being interpreted he said at times: "Well, some commentator or other will come along and tell me what I really meant by that."

It is not the business of the critic to interpret and explain this symbolism. Analysis is fatal to phantasy. There is a secret compact between each individual and the artist. The dramatist unlocks the gates and points the way. The spectator wanders where his imagination leads him in this realm of limitless fancy. If he goes astray, he and the artist should not indulge in mutual recriminations, for the artist has purposely dulled the power of reason in order to give free play to the imagination. Once the dramatist has set the spectator free, the critical annotator must not impair this freedom by trying to superimpose his own interpretation, unless he would set himself above the creative artist and destroy the mutual compact between the artist and each individual. We share our methods of reasoning with minds of countless others. One's imagination is peculiarly his own. What one thinks, others may think. What one imagines, no one else can imagine.

Ibsen wrote *A Doll's House* and *Ghosts* in order to convince every spectator of certain truths as he saw them. We may or may not agree with him, but we know what he meant. When he wrote *When We Dead Awaken* he invited collaboration with each of us singly. We cannot prove that we know what he meant; but each of us is at liberty to build up his own interpretation, which is essential to him and absolutely non-essential to everyone else. Whether some of the obscurity in this play be due to Ibsen's failing powers or not, *When We Dead Awaken* is the natural outcome of the trend towards the deintellectualization of dramatic art which began when symbolism commenced to replace clarity and precision in drama.

Ibsen was fully conscious that he was introducing recondite meanings into his plays. He said of *The Wild Duck:* "In some ways this new play occupies a position by itself among my dramatic works; in its method it differs in several respects from my former ones. . . . I hope that my critics will discover the points alluded to,—they will at any rate, find several things to squabble about and several things to interpret. I also think that *The Wild Duck* may very probably entice some of our young dramatists into new paths; and this I consider a result to be desired." His prophecy and desire came true. The critics are still squabbling about the inner meaning of *The Wild Duck*. Younger dramatists, such as Maeterlinck, embraced the symbolistic method. And from Maeterlinck's symbolism sprang Strindberg's expressionism.

Beginning as a romantic dramatist Ibsen passed through the Scribian school, became a relentless realist and ended as a symbolist. His career exemplifies the development of drama of the nineteenth century in Europe, whether he be imitating others, or striking out on new lines. He has been anathematized and worshiped. He cannot be dismissed. The English censor may keep *Ghosts* off the stage but that play of Ibsen's, like all his others, is constantly played in other versions by other men. Dramatists of widely divergent ideals owe much to Ibsen directly or indirectly. The realist or the symbolist, the impressionist or the expressionist, the deft dramaturge or static dramatist can look to him for justification of their art. Brieux, Shaw, Maeterlinck, Werfel, Craig, Antoine, Reinhardt, Stanislavsky, D'Annunzio, Benavente—and the list is scarcely begun—would differ as to what is dramatic art; but they could, and no doubt would drive home their arguments by illustrations drawn from the art of Henrik Ibsen.

CHAPTER XX

RUSSIAN DRAMA

BEFORE "realism" or "naturalism" became critical terms in other European countries, Gogol had founded the "Natural School" of Russian literature by writing his novel *Dead Souls* (1842). During the nineteenth century, Russian realism developed first in the novel and then in drama to such a high degree of artistry that it became a strong factor in European literature. In the dramatic field the movement culminated in the Moscow Art Theatre.

The theatre in Russia in the seventeenth and eighteenth centuries had been under the domination of foreign ideas. Most of the comedies were founded on Molière. Romanticism and classicism clashed in the theatre, with the victory going finally to the romanticists. Shakespeare replaced Racine and Voltaire as the model for playwrights. Scott's novels furnished much material for plots. The strict censorship of the stage had hindered the development of originality. Nothing of international significance was produced.

By the beginning of the nineteenth century the Russian middle classes had begun to attend the theatre; and the bourgeois dramas of Kotzebue, who lived in Russia, were translated and produced with success. As a result, a school of imitators, called "Kotzebuists," arose to supply the demand for plays in which the virtuous side of family life was portrayed. These dramas cannot be correctly designated as realistic in the later meaning of the word. They contain too much sentimentality. There are too many mysterious persons who are apparently of the peasant class but turn out to be noblemen in disguise. Yet dramas portraying family life are always potentially realistic. In comparison with classical drama or with Pushkin's romantic

Boris Godunov, the bourgeois play seems to be a transcript of life.

Griboyedov's *Intelligence Comes to Grief* (1831) was the result of a careful study of Moscow society in the early twenties. Although he was constantly hampered by the strict censorship, the author succeeded in attacking the weak points in Russian society. The dramatic action is sacrificed to long discourses and dialogues, as is often the case in later realistic plays.

Gogol's *Revizor* (*Inspector-General*) (1836) is both a masterpiece of technique and of realism. It is the dramatization of a situation suggested to Gogol by Pushkin. The latter had once been mistaken by the dignitaries of a town for an Inspector-General. Gogol expanded the incidents into a comedy of keen satire combined with farcical situations. Except for the five-act form and the opening of the second act by a monologue delivered by a servant, there are no stereotyped elements in its construction. The plot is uninvolved and contains no real love episode. There is no hero nor heroine. The absence of a sympathetic hero, which was one of the criticisms directed at the play, is characteristic of the drama at the end of the century. This was one of the rôles to which Zola and his school strenuously objected.

The characters are drawn from real life with careful observation. Gogol's notes on the characters and costumes are evidence of his naturalistic methods as a creative artist. He brings on the stage a whole Russian village and yet differentiates clearly all the numerous characters. His people are not mere types, but individuals, each possessing some personal, distinctive traits. To paint such a large gallery of portraits in the short time allowed a playwright to produce his effects shows a marvellous understanding of dramatic economy.

The dénouement of the comedy is especially noteworthy. The municipal dignitaries have mistaken a worthless young rascal, Khlestakov, as the Inspector-General. They are all grafters. One of them, at least, "steals more than his rank warrants." All are quaking with guilty fear. Khlestakov has made the most of his gorgeous opportunity by borrowing money right and left and becoming engaged to the Governor's gullible daughter. When he has made his escape, his real identity is discovered by a letter which he has written to one of his friends. The postmaster has been instructed by the Governor to "open a little" all letters to see that they contained no incriminating accusations against him. Mutual recriminations are being exchanged by the duped gentlemen when a gendarme announces that the real Inspector-General has arrived! The curtain falls on a carefully devised pantomime and stage picture portraying the tragi-comic consternation of all.

Aside from the dramatic effectiveness of this sudden peripeteia, the dénouement is strikingly realistic in its merciless humor. Here is no virtue rewarded. There is none to reward. The play leaves neither the impression of peacefulness of comedy nor of the loftiness of tragedy. The particular situation has been brought to a close. The ending is logical, pitilessly inexorable. But the imagination is so stirred by the news of the arrival of the Inspector-General, that the people in the play do not seem merely to be on the stage and to cease to exist when the curtain falls. Their life must continue. To make such vivid impressions of reality as opposed to theatricality is the aim of the naturalistic playwrights. Seldom has the aim been attained so completely as in this case. That Gogol was consciously striving for this effect of action continuing after the fall of the curtain is shown by the fact that the first act ends in the same general manner. The Governor's wife and daughter are at the window talking to someone outside, and the wife "keeps on shouting and they both stand at the window until the curtain has fallen."

Unfortunately the *Inspector-General* remained an isolated masterpiece of realistic comedy on the Russian stage. It would not have been produced had not the Czar himself protected it from the censors. Gogol had many imitators; but they either lacked his skill or encountered the censorship to such an extent that Russian dramatists produced nothing of importance for many years.

The repertory of the Moscow theatre consisted mainly of Gogol's plays, Griboyedov's satirical drama in a rather mutilated version, adaptations of French melodramas and vaudevilles, an occasional Shakespearean play, and the works of a few native Russians. As if in compensation for the dearth of first-class dramatists, the art of the actor developed to a high degree at Moscow. The declamatory style and the traditional manners and poses of the French were discarded. The actors sought to create each rôle as a distinct entity, instead of playing it as if it belonged to a certain class of characters which were to be interpreted according to traditional conventions. Routine acting gave way to creative acting. Simplicity and naturalness took the place of over-refinement of histrionic art. The dramatist and actor strove to collaborate in the creation of every character. The Russian critic believed that the dramatist should rely on the actor to a great extent. Thus by the middle of the century the Russians were consciously working on the theory that drama, in its highest form, is a unified synthesis of all the arts it employs, not a mere concatenation of playwright, actor and scene painter, each struggling to make his share in the production prominent even to the detriment of the whole. With such theories evolving, the time was not far off when the director would be called upon to harmonize all the many elements of each production.

The development of a realistic school of acting is not surprising. Russian writers were primarily observers of life. They cared less for artistic form than did their Western neighbors. Their aim was to give a physical and spiritual picture of society rather than to tell a story for the story's sake. M. J. Olgin says of the literature of this period: "We notice a preponderance of matter over form, of content over construction. As a rule, Russian writers do not construct their works carefully. They are hardly concerned over a plot. They are not very fastidious as to the choice of expressions. What is their real interest and what gives their work a peculiar value is the palpitation of actual life, the soaring of the spirit, the sincerity of a human soul speaking directly and freely. Literary productions called by their authors a story or a novel are quite often neither the one nor the other. They are just a morsel of real life, an illuminating episode, a study in human character, or a string of such episodes and studies loosely connected."

Both classical and romantic forms of drama were transplanted. There was nothing distinctly Russian in either kind. No national traditions held the stage nor hindered its development. When the natural school of novelists had developed, the theatre was open to the realists without any battle. When Ostrovski began to produce his realistic dramas, he did not have to enter into competition with any tradition or even memory of a national dramatic art. Turgeniev had already prepared the way for the transfer to the drama of the methods of the realistic novelist.

His play *A Month in the Country* (1855) is a psychological study of a group of people who find themselves in a situation so similar in some respects to that of Balzac's *Marâtre* that direct influence is not improbable. Natalia Petrovna is the wife of a rich land-owner, Arkadi Islaev. She is in love with Rakitin; but, as she says to Rakitin: "You and I have a moral right to look not only into Arkadi's face, but into the face of the whole world." She finds herself strongly drawn to her son's tutor, Bieliaev, who has but lately arrived. Viera Aleksandrovna, a young girl of seventeen, and a foundling, brought up by Islaev, also falls in love with Bieliaev.

The play unfolds quietly as a psychological study of people who find themselves thus entangled. Each one tries to understand himself and tries to act the rôle of an honorable person. There are no climaxes or scenes of theatrical tensity. The solution of the problem comes when Rakitin and Bieliaev go away forever. In comparison with the whirring machinery of *La Marâtre* and its overdrawn characters, Turgeniev's play is almost static. Throughout the whole work there is no trace of the usual devices of the well-made play. The technique of the Russian playwrights of the early twentieth century will scarcely differ from that employed by Turgeniev. *A Month in the Country* is a drama presenting a human problem in a manner that would still be called a novel in dialogue by those who believe that drama means action, although the sole requirement of drama is that it be acted.

Ostrovski began his career as a playwright in 1846. His first plays, which were really only dramatic sketches, failed to get a hearing. The censor forbade the production of his first full length play, *It's a Family Affair—We'll Settle It Ourselves,* until 1861, although it was published in the *Muscovite* in 1850. In 1853, however, his comedy, *Keep Out of a Stranger's Sleigh,* was performed in Moscow, and from that time until his death in 1886 he was a dominant factor in the Russian drama and in the theatre, being the first Russian writer to devote his entire life to dramatic art as a profession. The important year in his career was 1859 when a volume of his plays was published and his masterpiece, *The Storm,* was produced with great success. It was during 1859 and 1860 that the critic Dobrolyubov analyzed the dramatic technique of Ostrovski in articles called *The Realm of Darkness* and *A Ray of Light in the Realm of Darkness.* The latter referred to *The Storm.* The Russians realized that they possessed the beginnings of a national school of dramatic art which was to develop brilliantly and become of great international significance.

Ostrovski was an observer. He reproduced scenes of life with photographic exactness, especially those in the life of the Moscow merchants. His talent did not turn to dramas of intrigue. The well-made plot appeared on the Russian stage only in adaptations of foreign plays. The original situation in which his characters are found develops slowly; and, while the drama is not static, it does not unfold with surprising events nor in a manner that removes it to any degree from the way in which it would probably develop in real life. His scenes are rarely theatrically tense. *Coups de théâtre* are conspicuously absent. He does not employ finger-posts and foreshadowing in order to create suspense, but only to make his action proceed logically and to guide the spectator in his emotions and understanding. He does not rise to great climaxes, nor does he make his people debate problems of life with forensic passion.

His dénouements are usually quiet. Sometimes they are even purposely incomplete in order to give an effect of actuality. Thus at the end of *A Protégée of the Mistress*, Nadya will be forced to marry a worthless drunkard or else she will end her life in a pond. We do not know which event finally takes place. According to the usual theory of playwrights, to leave an audience in uncertainty as to the fate of a heroine is inartistic; but Ostrovski was not concerned with such details, although they would form the dramatic dénouement of most plays of this type. He aimed to present in this drama a series of episodes illustrating a phase of Russian life on an estate. Having fully depicted the tragedy of the situation, it makes little difference what happens to the heroine.

Both plot and even character are of secondary importance in "dramas of life" as Dobrolyubov called these plays. His characters exist objectively for the spectator. He does not force us to take sides for or against them. Some are morally better than others. Some are more evil than others. Ostrovski does not present the sympathetic hero or the arch villain. In not creating sympathetic characters he was following in the footsteps of Gogol. Even his antagonists do not arouse admiration as do the villains of romantic drama. They are only the products of their sordid surroundings. Glumov in *Enough Stupidity in Every Wise Man* describes himself as a kind of Iago. He says to his mother: "I am intelligent, crafty, envious: just like you. . . . How do people attain their ends? Not always through achievements, but oftener than not through a glib tongue. We like to talk here in Moscow. Is there any reason why I should not reach success in this spacious gossip shop? No! I'll gain the good will of the bigwigs, and I'll become their protégé, you'll see! It's silly to annoy them. We should flatter them to their heart's content. There's the whole secret of success!"

Ostrovski does not proceed to show Glumov as a magnificently sinister Iago destroying innocent happiness of good men and women. He unfolds a picture of the satiric Glumov trying to get a wife and a fortune by flattering and tricking people who are perhaps no better than himself and are surely less intelligent. Glumov has diagnosed the malady of his social group correctly. He would have succeeded, had he not been stupid enough to lose his diary in which he wrote what he actually thought of his associates! When he is exposed, he retaliates by exposing their shallowness, their dependence upon him.

Interest does not centre in the story which is told unobtrusively, nor in the character of Glumov, but in the depiction of the shallow, sordid society in which he moves. No problem is discussed. No moral is taught. The characters are not mouthpieces for the author. Ostrovski has been sharply criticized for not drawing moral conclusions; but he was content to present life as he saw it, while, in France, Dumas was reasoning and preaching through his characters. Realism that preaches directly is very unreal. No one character is analyzed by Ostrovski for dramatic purposes. But many characters are presented. Each one has his idiosyncrasies; and Ostrovski was not afraid to spend time in allowing them to show these minor characteristics. He was criticized for not observing dramatic economy; but he knew that realism thrives on the representation of minor and commonplace details. His characters lend themselves to careful study and realistic interpretation by actors. They are not subtle, as Iago is subtle; but they need delicate interpretation by the actor in order to bring out their minor peculiarities. Indeed, the Russian actors have brought out in these rôles certain characteristics which Ostrovski merely sketched. His realism is impressionistic, springs from within his characters and does not depend upon crude or brutal externalities, as the realism in Western Europe often does.

Dobrolyubov said of Ostrovski's *Storm:* "The need for justice, for respect for personal rights, this is the cry . . . that rises up to the ear of every attentive reader. Well, can we deny the wide application of this need in Russia? Can we fail to see that such a dramatic background corresponds to the true condition of Russian society? Take history, think of our life, look about you, everywhere you will find justification of our words. . . . Our history up to the most recent times has not fostered among us the development of a respect for equity, has not created any solid guaranties for personal rights, and has left a wide field to arbitrary tyranny and caprice." *The Storm* is the dramatization of these ideas, which form the basis of the whole work rather than merely serving as the dramatic background. The plot is the background. Into the situation, Ostrovski has woven many characters, all carefully differentiated; and one of them, Katerina, is minutely analyzed. As the plot is subservient to the characters, so plot and characters exist solely to present the theme as stated by Dobrolyubov.

The story of the drama is almost trite when separated from the other elements of the play. Katerina and her husband are bullied by his mother. In the absence of her husband she gives herself to Boris, "a young man of good education"—and nothing more. When the husband returns, Katerina, in a state of nervous excitement during a storm, confesses her sin. Boris is sent away. Her life is so miserable that she throws herself into the Volga.

Boris and Katerina have only two scenes alone together during the play: one at the end of the third act and their scene of parting in the fifth act. Boris appears momentarily in the fourth act; but, while his presence is dramatic, no words are spoken between them. This situation involving unlawful love and marital infidelity would have given rise to a very different series of scenes in the hands of a contemporary French, German or English dramatist. Either a problem play or a semi-romantic tragedy would have evolved. Ostrovski does not emphasize either plot or the discussion of the problem of marriage. Therefore he has plenty of time to analyze his characters and to present his theme through their actions, personalities and conversations, especially as the actual story of the play does not begin to unfold until towards the close of the third act.

Taking complete advantage of the analytical method, Ostrovski created a group of characters who typify the tyranny, superstition, idealism, sensitiveness, the spirit of revolt and the fatalistic passivity which existed in Russian life in that period. Certain minor personages have little if anything to do with the evolution of the plot, but are indispensable to the picture of the society represented. Feklusha, a female pilgrim, represents the religious superstition and ignorance. Kuligin is described as "a man of artisan class, a self-taught watchmaker, engaged in trying to discover the secret of perpetual motion." He is the idealist, the dreamer who clashes with the brutal bully, Dikoy, a merchant. The importance of this episode is attested by the fact that Ostrovski reserves the scene until the fourth act. From the point of view of the plot, the scene is unnecessary and even questionable at that moment; but, since the play is founded on a theme, the scene is obligatory and is staged at the correct moment.

The analysis of the character of Katerina, the heroine, is remarkably complete. She is highly imaginative and supersensitive. Even as a child she was happy but highstrung, and given to religious ecstasy in which prayer and bursts of tears mingled. She has unfulfilled, vague desires, is subject to daydreams, visions, and has had sensations of flying like a bird. Now, because of her mother-in-law's unreasoning tyranny, her married life is complex. She feels caged. She is sorry for her husband, she wants him to protect her against herself; she wants to be loyal to him but her feelings for him go no farther. She is obsessed by the idea of death; but fears life more than death. She has a half-waking, recurrent dream of being held in a man's arms. She tries not to admit that this man is Boris, but represses constantly, fearing sin. Her maternal instinct has been thwarted. Children, she feels, would have been her safeguard. In spite of her passivity and nervous fear, she revolts. To the Russians she is the spirit of revolt. When her husband is away temporarily, she gives herself to Boris—the young man of good education. Having revolted, she is unable to face the consequences. It is difficult to find such a minute keen analysis of a woman in any play produced before 1860. Katerina does not exist primarily as a study of a dramatic character. She is entirely subservient to the theme; but diminution of the element of plot made such analysis of character possible in drama as well as in the novel in which the element of time is not a vital question.

There are few scenes in the play which are dramatic in the sense of the word as it was used in the nineteenth century. The scene of confession, however, in the fourth act is handled in a very tense manner. A series of insignificant events and circumstances so wring Katerina's nerves that they snap. It is a case of conscience and a desire to lighten her soul by unburdening it with a confession; but it is also the result of a loss of self-control when she catches sight of Boris, when the old half-witted woman addresses her with words that seem to be a curse, when the storm breaks and the people are frightened, when she chances to look upon the half-effaced mural painting of the tortures of Hell.

The scene of farewell between Boris and Katerina is a restrained moment of pathos and hopelessness expressed with artistic simplicity. The play would have been more tragic had Ostrovski let the curtain fall upon her at this moment instead of having her put an end to her troubles by suicide. Perhaps the dramatist felt that he could not use the quieter climax which he had employed in the *Protégée of the Mistress*, because *The Storm* was more than a mere piece of actualism and he had to round out the theme.

Thus while other European theatres were perfecting the well-made play, Ostrovski was disregarding, when necessary, every canon of its constitution. He was anticipating the reaction against this form of drama. The Russian cares little for the ideal of art for art's sake. He cares even less for the ideal of drama for the sake of clever technique. Ostrovski's influence was not felt during his lifetime outside of Russia; but, whenever the effect of Chekhov, Gorky and the Moscow Art Theatre on the drama of the present is measured, it must be remembered that Ostrovski's technique is the foundation of Russian dramatic art.

Such plays lend themselves to indeed demand careful production. No plot and no single character is strong enough to insure success. Where so much depends upon atmosphere which is created by the portrayal of small significant facts, the whole production must be the result of unified acting, awkwardly called "ensemble." The Russians were among the first to realize the importance of ensemble playing. In 1868 A. K. Tolstoi discussed the question in an article entitled *Project for the Production of the Tragedy Tsar Fedor Ivanovich.* He described the spirit of the play and analyzed the architecture of the scenery, the coloring, the costumes and the characters as parts of a unified whole. Much of this unification was to be produced by ensemble acting or the careful relation of each rôle to every other rôle in the play with its proper emphasis. Thus the responsibility of every actor, whether star or supernumerary, was greatly increased. The example of the Meiningen players strengthened the convictions of such Russians as Korch, who was one of the chief producers of Ostrovski during the last two decades of the nineteenth century. It was with Korch that Chekhov began his career as a playwright; and Chekhov became closely identified with the Moscow Art Theatre, founded about ten years later in 1898. Finally, the Moscow Art Theatre has opened up to Europe Russian dramatic art, not only by the presentation of its own plays, but by stimulating interest in all forms of Russian drama.

The revolt against artificiality was led by Stanislavsky and Nemirovitch-Danchenko who founded the Moscow Art Theatre. At first it resulted in their attempts to reform the methods of production rather than to introduce a new form of playwriting. The Russian plays of the first order were not machine-made. The Russian theatre only had to present the dramas of Ostrovski, Turgeniev or Tolstoi in a manner befitting their spirit and structure in order to make a great stride in the direction of naturalism. But what kind of naturalism or realism did Stanislavsky and his colleagues set up as their ideal and in how far were they suc-

cessful in attaining it? Their adverse critics assert that they
sought and attained only the realism of external fact.

The Moscow Art Theatre accepted the convention of the
fourth wall in the proscenium arch and all that it implies. In its
production of *The Storm* light was cast upon the stage in a
manner to represent sunlight coming through windows in the
imaginary fourth wall. Such a procedure is pure hokum and
provocative of no artistic reaction. On the contrary, the sound
of crickets in another play met with undeserved condemnation.
The chirping was not introduced because crickets are heard in
the country but in order to produce the sensation of loneliness
of the country. The Moscow Art Theatre certainly held to the
theory of realism and representation of life shorn of traditional
theatricality; but Stanislavsky has stated his attitude towards
the naturalism of external fact and has explained why the Moscow Art Theatre was sometimes misunderstood. "Like all revo-
lutionists," he says, "we broke with the old and exaggerated the
new. All that was new was good simply because it was new.
Those who think that we sought for naturalism on the stage are
mistaken. We never leaned toward such a principle. Always,
then as well as now, we sought for inner truth, for the truth of
feeling and experience; but as spiritual technique was only in
its embryo stage among actors of our company, we, because of
necessity and helplessness, and against our desires, fell now and
then into an outward and coarse naturalism." (*My Life in Art.*)

The realism of the Moscow Art Theatre during the first few
years of its existence aimed to use external facts to reveal the
inner truth. This ideal is very different from the realism which
puts real trees on the stage in order to make the audience believe they are in a forest. The scenery was not symbolic nor at
all stylized. It aimed to represent the locality as it would appear in real life. The actors acted as if they were real people.
They sought to avoid the traditional theatricality which made
the actor a poser and a declaimer; and they were unconscious
of the new theatricality of the twentieth century which frankly
admits that an actor is an actor. They sought to reproduce the

halftones of life. They were finally to seek the overtones of symbolism.

This organization found in Chekhov a playwright who was attuned to its theory of production. He had already become skilled as a story writer, in revealing the half-hidden phases of human life and emotion. He was untrammelled by any set of rules or traditions of playmaking. He distrusted his ability to become a dramatist. Indeed, many a critic denies him that appellation because his plays cannot be reduced to any of the old formulas of structure.

His ideals as a dramatist have been summed up by Nemirovitch-Danchenko as follows:

To free the stage from routine and literary stereotypes.

To give back to the stage a living psychology and simple speech.

To examine life not only through rising heights and falling abysses, but through the everyday life surrounding us.

To seek theatricality of dramatic production not in exceptional staging, which has given over the theatre for many years to a special kind of masters and has turned away from it the contemporary literary talents, but in the hidden inner psychologic life.

The art of Chekhov is the art of artistic freedom and artistic truth.

It is often said that only the superb acting of this Russian company can save his plays from failure. That is true; but it does not follow that Chekhov is not a dramatist. It proves that only these players have learned how to interpret his moods. His dramas on the printed page are far more lifeless than those of Scribe. When they are portrayed in the Moscow Art Theatre they live—not brilliantly nor even clearly—but like a vivid dream.

One sometimes awakens from a dream with a feeling of longing or fear or sadness or despair. One tries to remember the subject, perhaps the plot of the dream and its characters. More or less vaguely the experience is recalled. It does not become clear, no matter how vivid the dream has been or how poignant the emotion may be. Yet for hours the mystic experience envelops one and partially obscures reality.

Thus it is when we have seen a Chekhovian play. The mystic emotion is very real, but it is difficult to analyze clearly in words the plot and the characters. To attempt to do so is as fatuous as trying to interpret a Russian symphony in the manner of well-meaning gentlemen who write program notes. In our own lives, there is the external reality, the plate-glass front, that one presents to the other plate-glass fronts. Behind the show window is the real human being—a complex tissue of thoughts, dreams, moods, sensations, emotions, which he himself is incapable of analyzing. There lie the ideas, motives, manifestations of the will, velleities which arise from hidden or half-hidden sources.

Thus in Chekhov's plays there is the external reality in the scenery and in the actors. Then, in the words he gives his characters to speak, in the pauses of the dialogue, in the words left unspoken, he reveals, as no one would dare or even could reveal in real life, the inner lives of his people. All these things of which human beings are half conscious and which make us what we really are, appear as in a glass, darkly.

His dialogue is not flamboyantly brilliant or obtrusively incisive. He advised the playwright to avoid "choice diction." The language should be simple and forceful. He employs Maeterlinckian silences and pauses in the dialogue with great effect. When he is purposely not entirely clear, he is never irritatingly obscure, because one does not feel that he is concealing philosophical thought in riddles as Strindberg does in *To Damascus*. In such passages, Chekhov is revealing the vague thoughts and sensations of his people.

In general, his plays resemble those of Ostrovski and Turgeniev in structure. His art is unobtrusive. His tone is subdued. The scene in *Uncle Vanya* in which Voynitsky attempts to shoot Serebryakov is anomalous. The poignant moments of his later plays are restrained. He intensifies his situations gradually without striving to produce amazement or astonishment. Although his early *Ivanov* was written in climactic form, his later plays, such as *The Cherry Orchard*, do not build up to great climaxes.

His characters are neither heroic nor trivial. "Modern playwrights," said Chekhov, "begin their plays with angels, scoundrels and clowns exclusively. Well, go seek these elements in all Russia! Yes, you may find them, but not in such extreme types as the playwrights need. Unwillingly, you begin forging them out of the mind and the imagination. You perspire and give the matter up. I wanted to be original. I did not portray a single villain, not a single angel (though I could not refrain when it came to the clown), did not accuse anyone or exculpate." The will to act of Chekhov's characters is weak; but their suffering therefrom is very human. Their will to hope is strong; and their resultant faith is almost divine.

His point of departure is a theme. He seeks to present a phase of human suffering arising from the will to hope, to dream, but not to act or accomplish. At the end of his plays, all is lost except that someone like Nina in *The Sea Gull* has learned "to bear one's cross and have faith"; or like Sonya in *Uncle Vanya* has learned to say: "We must go on living! We shall go on living, Uncle Vanya. We shall live through a long chain of days and weary evenings; we shall patiently bear the trials which fate sends us. . . . I have faith, I have faith."

He said of playwrights in 1889: "The subject ought to be new but there need be no fable." In other words, plot complication is unnecessary. He differs in that respect from Ibsen, his favorite author. The Norwegian dramatist always constructed a clear plot. His plays open at a climactic moment in the story. The scenario of *A Doll's House* shows how Ibsen built his plays about events. Nora and Hedda go through a remarkable series of circumstances. No character of Chekhov's could dream of such astounding things happening to one person in a whole lifetime. Chekhov's scenario for the *Demon of the Woods* consists of a minute study of the characters and notes as to what they did in the past. It abounds in small, significant facts of their lives. That is the reason why his characters often seem to be indulging in monologues even in ensemble scenes. They are revealing their personalities by recounting incidents of their lives. They constantly "remember" petty actions and give bits of their personal views. When Ibsen unveils the past, he develops the present action and reveals character. When Chekhov withdraws veils, he reveals character and creates the spiritual environment of his people. His plots, therefore, are often static for almost a whole act. *The Cherry Orchard* is particularly devoid of progressive action. The initial situation simply becomes more intense. The orchard is sold and its destruction begins as the play ends. This is symbolic—and turned out to be prophetic —of the disintegration of Old Russia. The plot is entirely without suspense. Yet the play is interesting on the stage because it reveals delicately and minutely the forces at work in this disintegration.

Chekhov's plays open at a moment when he can portray the circumstances which will lead his characters to their Garden of Gethsemane. The shadows have begun to fall, but the darkness is long in coming. Chekhov's people struggle but little. We see them suffer a long time. Sometimes years pass and the situation changes only in intensity; and the change is gradual. Chekhov is so deliberate, so quiet in his development of the situation that he is said to have dramatized moods rather than plots.

Treplev says in *The Sea Gull*, expressing, no doubt, Chekhov's own views: "I come more and more to the conviction that it is not a question of old and new forms, but that what matters is that a man should write without thinking at all, write because it springs freely from his soul." We cannot imagine Chekhov working with any formula.

He has no thesis or problem to demonstrate. Hence, he does not stage obligatory scenes in which protagonist and antagonist directly debate the question as do Helmar and Nora in *A Doll's House*. He has nothing to prove except that Russians of a certain class act in a certain way in a certain situation. Thus his theme may be abstract, as in *The Three Sisters*, which is a study of wistful longing for something never attained. Chekhov said that exhaustion, feeling of guilt, boredom and loneliness are distinctly Russian characteristics, that "disappointment, apathy, nervous limpness and exhaustion are consequences of extreme excitability and such excitability is extremely characteristic of our young people." His plays portray these forces operating in society. His scenes show his characters in these moods rather than causing things to happen. His people do not understand themselves as Cyrano, for instance, understands himself. They never finally learn the why and the wherefore as does Nora. His plays are portrayals of states of mind of characters and the particular state of mind of the dominant characters becomes the theme of the play. The scenes of the plot, which any other contemporary European dramatist would have chosen for representation, are often omitted by Chekhov; or they are presented with such quietness and reserve that they are branded as undramatic by those who believe that only plays with a noisy climax are dramatic.

The Sea Gull deals with the fate of a young woman, Nina, who is deeply loved by Treplev. He is trying to become a sincere playwright. She is fascinated by Trigorin, an author who has already arrived, a man of shallow personality, the lover of Treplev's mother. Not until the second act does one know what to look for when Trigorin says significantly: "A subject for a short story: a young girl, such as you, has lived all her life beside a lake; she loves the lake like a sea-gull and is as free and happy as a sea-gull. But a man comes by chance, sees her, and having nothing better to do, destroys her, like that sea-gull here." Nina is to be the sea gull that Trigorin destroys. Two acts have been devoted to giving impressions of character and circumstances.

Between the second and third acts, Treplev tries to commit suicide. He wishes to challenge Trigorin to a duel. These facts, which the average dramatist would represent, are merely told in a most casual, unobtrusive manner. At the end of the third act, Nina is going to Moscow to try to become an actress. She promises to meet Trigorin there. The fourth act begins two years later and all the tragic events in that interval are communicated in the following quiet dialogue:

DORN

... How is she [Nina] getting on?

TREPLEV

I expect she is quite well.

DORN

I was told that she was leading a rather peculiar life. How was that?

TREPLEV

That's a long story, doctor.

DORN

Well, tell it us shortly (*a pause*).

TREPLEV

She ran away from home and had an affair with Trigorin. You know that?

DORN

I know.

TREPLEV

She had a child. The child died. Trigorin got tired of her and went back to his old ties, as might have been expected. Though, indeed, he had never abandoned them, but in his weak-willed way contrived to keep them both going. As far as I can make out from what I have heard, Nina's private life was a complete failure.

DORN

And the stage?

TREPLEV

I fancy that was worse still. She made her début at some holiday place near Moscow, then went to the provinces. All that time I did not lose sight of her, and wherever she went I followed her. . . .

This story would have served as the material for two acts of the usual play of the early twentieth century; but Chekhov was carrying on the disintegration of the play made up of violent and highly colored climaxes. When he does come to the tragic moment, he usually combines it with some bit of everyday life. In the final scene of *The Sea Gull,* the whole family is gathered for tea and cards. Shamraev shows Trigorin the stuffed sea gull, symbolic of Nina. "I don't remember," says Trigorin. The sound of a shot is heard. (Konstantin Treplev has killed himself because of Nina whom Trigorin doesn't remember.) Dorn leaves the room a moment. On his return he quiets Konstantin's mother with a word. Then comes the following speech:

DORN (*turning over the leaves of the magazine, to* TRIGORIN)
There was an article in this two months ago—a letter from America—and I wanted to ask you, among other things (*puts his arm around* TRIGORIN'S *waist and leads him to the footlights*) as I am very much interested in the question. (*In a lower tone, dropping his voice.*) Get Irina Nikolayevna away somehow. The fact is, Konstantin Gavrilitch has shot himself. . . .

The curtain falls on this tragic situation, outwardly so calm. The scene is a combination of external realism, symbolism, the commonplace and the tragic that is difficult to equal. With amazing delicacy of touch and with few strokes he paints his final picture in which the whole drama is summed up and brought to an end. The closing minutes of *Uncle Vanya, The Three Sisters* and *The Cherry Orchard* are no less poignant and significant in their combined symbolism and realism so artistically restrained.

The entire collapse of the principles and formulas of playwriting, old as Aristotle, can finally be observed in Gorky's *Lower Depths* produced by the Moscow Art Theatre in 1902. The title of the play is curiously significant. It seems to signify the *ne plus ultra* of naturalism and of formlessness in structure.

In a squalid doss house about twenty characters of the underworld are gathered. There is no plot whatsoever. Certain events happen. A woman dies of tuberculosis. The landlord of this foul basement is killed in a fight. His wife accuses Vaska, her paramour, of the murder because he is forsaking her for her younger sister. Vaska in turn throws the guilt upon the wife. They are being arraigned in court when the play ends with the suicide of the actor. The outcome of the trial is never disclosed. The events do not even constitute a connected story, much less a plot. They are not introduced for the purpose of depicting the characters, for the characters do not change because of them. The personalities would have been just as clearly revealed if none of these things had happened. They serve the purpose of giving the spectator the sensation of "the lower depths," for the main effect of the play is that one has experienced that phase of society. The character of Luka, the philosophical pilgrim, serves the same purpose. He comes into this den. He shows us that these people are not beasts but human beings with longing hopes that go unfulfilled. "We are all human beings," he says; but had he never come into their lives neither they nor we would have known how human they really are. Whether his philosophy of life—that things exist only if we believe in them—is true or false, whether Gorky was cynical or idealistic in his depiction of the influence of this philosophy is of little importance. The effect of the whole play is not sordid or vile; but one is left with the distinct sensation of having penetrated the physical and emotional lives of people such as one merely sees in slums and reads of in reports from minor police courts. One feels *The Lower Depths*.

"It is not drama," cried many critics in protest; and they proved to their own satisfaction that the play broke with all formulas and laws of dramatic art. Yet the play has impressed thousands of spectators as a true picture of that phase of life. Here is no sickening sentimentality, no criminal little Eva ascending the heavenly ladder of the social scale, no heroics, no inquiry into causes, no placing of blame on society, none of the usual elements which make "crook plays" outrageous falsifications of life, no matter how dramatic they may be.

The Lower Depths is static because the lower depths are static. People who fall into them do not rise from them physically or mentally. Regeneration is a miracle. Gorky was not trying to dramatize an improbable possibility. Life is sometimes dramatic. Generally it is undramatic. Is the theatre to be closed to a presentation of life as it usually is? Is a dramatist to relinquish to the novelist the presentation of static situations and people who are not consciously manifesting their will? Is it true, as Brunetière said, that such people as Gil Blas cannot be portrayed as central characters in a play? There is nothing in dramatic art which forces it to relinquish to the novelist any portion of human life and truth. The fact that it may have done so is no proof that it must continue to do so. Drama is a representation of life by actors. There is no law, no limitation, save the limitations of the human beings who produce the representation.

CHAPTER XXI

SYNTHETIC DRAMATIC ART. THE NEW STAGECRAFT

THE Greeks realized that drama is a synthesis of all the arts. Aristotle defined the synthesis when he said that "every tragedy must have six parts which determine its quality —namely plot, character, diction, thought, spectacle and song." Plot was to him the soul of a tragedy. Character was of secondary importance. Spectacle was the least important element, "because spectacular effects depend more on the art of the stage machinist than on that of the poet."

After the Renaissance, the Aristotelian theory and the practice of the dramatists tended to bring forth the well-made play. The Greeks had been such consummate artists in this respect and Aristotle had analyzed and exalted this form of drama to such an extent that the spectacular and musical elements were entirely overshadowed. Dramatic criticism dealt mainly with plot and character. Indeed, character became the crux of dramatic art. Plot assumed a position of secondary importance. A play was considered a masterpiece only if it contained deep analysis of character. During the nineteenth century the playwright dominated the stage. With the dawn of the twentieth century the director became the vital factor in the theatre.

The court players of the Duke of Meiningen were a factor in the development of synthetic drama. Their patron had seen Kean's gorgeous production of Shakespeare in London and was deeply impressed by the processional scenes and the mob scenes. Bodenstedt had also attended these performances in 1859, and he became director of the Meininger in 1865. The strong financial position of this troupe enabled it to mount plays with great care and beauty. They developed what is known as ensemble playing. This expression applies primarily to the handling of crowds and mass effects of human beings on the stage. No matter how great was the reputation of any actor, he could be called upon to play a rôle generally assigned to untrained, awkward supernumeraries. Shakespeare's and Schiller's dramas offered the finest opportunities for ensemble scenes; but in later years when the troupe was touring Europe (1874-1890), under the direction of Chronegk, they produced modern plays by Ibsen, Björnson, Echegaray, etc. The Russians were especially impressed by this communistic spirit in drama, and the Russian theatre of the present day owes much to the ideals of the Meininger. Antoine saw them in Belgium in 1888 and realized that their grouping in ensemble scenes produced an extraordinary illusion of truth. He praised their light effects, costumes and scenery with some reservation.

Mass effects of human beings in the theatre may be handled in general in two ways. The Greek chorus is a unit. It speaks and dances in unison even though it may be divided into semi-choruses. The Shakespearean mob is a collection of individuals who speak and act as separate units. They are actual people in the drama whereas the Greek chorus may become practically impalpable, invisible spectators and interpreters of the drama for the actual audience. Both methods may be combined as in the modern production of *Carmencita and the Soldier* by the Moscow Art Theatre Musical Studio. The figurants on the stage proper are individuals in the drama. Those who are on the steps and archways above the stage are invisible to the persons in the play but reflect by poses and songs the thoughts and emotions of the characters below. Their function is not only to explain but also to guide the emotions of the spectators as did the Greek chorus. In any case, the crowd, if properly handled in relation to the basic idea of the play, becomes not merely a transference of reality to the stage but an integral part of the work of art. By dissolving pictures and by articulate sounds it helps to create the inner meaning of the play and becomes expressionistic.

The Meininger showed by example the value of ensemble playing, and, because they extended the spirit of ensemble to light effects and costume, they helped to re-create the ideals of synthesis and expressionism in dramatic art. They made it possible to produce such plays as Hauptmann's *Weavers* with great effectiveness. They showed that drama does not merely consist of a single character played by a "star" in the centre of the stage in front of blazing footlights; but that drama can be the gorgeous, emotional presentation of masses of men and can reflect large pictures of human life within the four walls of a building. The effects of which Schiller dreamed have now been realized.

The first modern artist to foresee the development which dramatic art was to undergo was Richard Wagner. He restated the theory of synthesis. "The highest conjoint work of art," he wrote in 1849, "is the Drama: it can only be at hand in all its possible fulness, when in it each separate branch of art is at hand in its utmost fulness. The true is only conceivable as proceeding from a common urgence of every art towards the most direct appeal to a common public. In this Drama, each separate art can only bare its utmost secret to their common public through a mutual parleying with other arts; for the purpose of each separate branch of art can only be fully attained by the reciprocal agreement and co-operation of all the branches in their common message." (*Das Kunstwerk der Zukunft.*)

This is the Greek conception of dramatic art, but one which had ceased to exist, partially because of the influence of Aristotle's insistence upon plot and character. This conception has become the basis of modern drama which calls upon all the arts in order to make a complete artistic effect.

Wagner was chiefly concerned with the revival of the musical element in drama, for he correctly held that opera of his day was scarcely drama. The music did not express the dramatic idea. The music of one opera was just as fitting or really unfitting for any other. An aria from *Rigoletto* could be transferred to *Traviata* or to *Mignon* without violating any artistic principle. Wagner made music the essential expression of each particular scene in his operas. He was also interested in the spectacular element furnished by the fine arts and the groupings of the actors. Scenery had been employed only for the purpose of creating illusion. It was a representation of the place of the action, whether gorgeous or drab. Wagner foresaw a more effective use of the plastic arts. They could create not only beauty but truth. He showed how each art can be employed in connection with the others to bring out the essential meaning of the drama. He said: "Thus the illusion of plastic art will turn to truth in drama: the plastic artist will reach out hands to the dancer, to the mime, will lose himself in them and thus become both mime and dancer. So far as lies within his power, he will have to impart the inner man, his feeling and his willing to the eye."

That is Wagner's prophecy of stylization through synthesis. The plastic arts were for the first time put upon a plane with the work of the dramatist. Wagner also made a prophetic statement in regard to lighting, before the discovery of the electric light. In speaking of the scene-painter, he said: "The illusion which his brush and finest blend of colors could only hint at, could only distantly approach, he will here bring to its consummation by artistic practice of every known device, by use of all the art of lighting."

Wagner would scarcely have been content to make the playwright and the musical composer subservient to the director; but he advocated allowing the director to control all other elements of synthesis. Thus both in theory and practice, Wagner was bringing forth a modern conception of drama which insists upon stylization and an harmonious synthesis of all the arts in which each art creates through its own medium artistic truth and beauty. Mere illusion is the work of a machinist. Truth and beauty are the work of an artist whether he employs musical instruments, colored lights, painted canvas, or the spoken word and movement to attain his end.

In the modern synthesis, special attention has been paid to

the use of the plastic arts which include in the theatre, color, light and shade as produced by lighting and the grouping and posing of human beings. Indeed the term "plastic arts" takes on a deep significance when applied to dramatic art. The theatre presents a living picture. As Appia said: "The *mise-en-scène* is a picture composed in time." Drama is the only living art. It possesses all the advantages and disadvantages of life. The fine arts are not plastic in the sense that drama is. A painting, a piece of sculpture or of architecture is frozen, unchangeable once it is completed. It exists until forces of nature or of man destroy it. Drama exists only while it is being produced by human agency. Though we may apply the term "static" to plots of certain plays, the play itself is never static. Something in it changes, develops every instant. It quivers with life until the final curtain. Then it exists only in memory, like a human being that has lived and died.

The problem of setting a play has many ramifications. The production can be actual or ideal. Many people, endowed with a certain kind of imaginative power, read a drama and imagine the action as taking place in the same manner that it would happen in real life. That we may call the ideal production. It is entirely divorced from the theatre. Macbeth is really on the blasted heath. Clytemnestra is in front of a Greek palace. Cyrano is in the old Hôtel de Bourgogne. Lear is buffeted by a real storm. Everything is as it was; but everything is imaginary.

The actual production is on a stage, in theatrical conditions. It may be wholly imagined by the reader of a play or it may be the real representation. The theatre is primarily concerned only with the actual production real or imagined; but the theatre must reckon with the realm of phantasy in which the ideal production is made. The theatre is all pretense. Other arts are only partially pretense, with the exception of music which need not pretend to be anything which it is not. A painting does not pretend to be the actual object represented. Michelangelo's statue of David does not pretend to be David; but the actor pretends to be Macbeth. The question is: How

far can the setting pretend to be the actual place in which Macbeth is? Of one thing we are sure: the actual place is somewhere else. Thus the setting, whether realistic, symbolic, expressionistic, archeological or the back wall of the playhouse,
is pretense. In the last analysis the theatre must reckon with
illusion. But what kind of illusion? Illusion of reality or illusion of phantasy or illusion of inner truth?

Looking back over the development of stage decoration one
is impressed by the fact that the setting has been in harmony
with the form of drama for which it was devised; but when
plays originally produced with certain fitting scenery are later
played before scenery conforming to new ideals, the results
are unsatisfactory. The architectural background of the Greek
theatre was a dignified setting for Greek drama. It expressed
the spirit of the play. The plastic evolutions of the chorus
must have been effective against the stately wall pierced with
massive doors leading to a mysterious realm of phantasy. The
medieval drama, produced within a church, was in the correct
symbolic environment. When played on the parvis in front of
a cathedral, the gothic structure was in complete harmony with
the play. The Elizabethan stage was well suited to the technique employed by Shakespeare; but, while it formed an unobtrusive background, it did not express the inner spirit of his
plays. The multiple system of stage decoration employed in
French theatres was an inheritance from medieval drama in which
symbolism had given way to realism. The system actually
broke down when stricter methods of realism were employed.
The painted back drop with its inartistic perspective originated
in Italy and in the seventeenth century was employed both in
England and in France. Designed to give the illusion of reality, it destroyed the illusion as soon as an actor appeared on
the stage. In the eighteenth century, the scenery for opera
was aiming to produce amazing and gorgeous spectacles. The
spectacular element began to creep into the setting of drama
without music. De Loutherbourg, in England, produced back
drops of pictorial effectiveness, but they were really gigantic

oil paintings. The romantic drama in France sought for settings full of atmosphere and local color.

About 1852 Kean began to mount Shakespeare's plays in England with historical exactness. In Germany, about 1840, Tieck and Immermann designed a modified Elizabethan setting for Shakespearean productions. These two methods are diametrically opposed. Kean's aim was to reproduce exactly the setting of the place of action. Tieck insisted upon playing Shakespeare in conditions resembling those in which his plays were originally produced. Neither one is satisfactory. Shakespeare's plays were not composed for scenery of historical realism. They belong to the realm of phantasy in that respect. A production of his dramas in exact or modified Elizabethan surroundings makes an archeological impression upon an audience. Nothing is farther removed from art than archeology. With the age of realism in drama, came scenery still more realistic. Interiors of rooms were made exact replicas of the rooms in which the action was supposed to take place. Antoine, Belasco and Stanislavsky tried to have all properties the actual objects which would have been employed in real life. For his production of *Old Heidelberg,* Antoine transported to the Paris stage the furnishings of a student's room in Heidelberg. Trees made of cork in such a manner as to deceive a woodpecker were placed upon the stage. Even real saplings were given the impossible task of representing themselves artistically. Lighting, which had served as illumination, now was employed to create realistic illusion, to copy nature. The revolving stage, the wagon stage, the elevator stage, the sliding stage were invented. The plaster dome, the canvas cyclorama were set up. The realist had done his worst. The machinist had done his best. The drama awaited a creative artist.

The German critic, A. W. Schlegel, had pointed out the errors of stage decoration at the beginning of the nineteenth century. "The errors which may be avoided are want of simplicity and of great reposeful masses; the overloading of the scene with superfluous and distracting objects, either because the painter is desirous of showing off his strength in perspective or because he does not know how otherwise to fill up the space; an architecture full of mannerism, often altogether unconnected, nay, even at variance with possibility, colored in a motley manner which resembles no species of stone in the world." In 1880 Feuerbach, not a man of the theatre but a painter, sounded clearly the note of the future ideal of stagecraft when he said: "Unobtrusive suggestion is what is needed, not bewildering effects." For once in the history of dramatic art, theory was preceding practice.

The next important contribution to the theory of the new stagecraft was made by Appia in *Die Musik und die Inscenierung* (1899). He developed Wagner's theories of the synthetic theatre in relation to scenery, lighting and the actor. The lighting harmonizes the setting and actor.

Appia found a two-dimensional stage decorated with two-dimensional paintings serving as back drops. In this area a three-dimensional living actor moved about in front of a dead setting. The whole inharmonious combination was illuminated by a lighting system that was crude and often cast meaningless and disturbing shadows. He insisted that false perspective must go; that the stage must make use of the dimension of height; that no matter where the actor walked the setting must retain its true proportion; that everything on the stage must be in three dimensions.

The painted back drop gave way to simple mass effects which were bathed in light and shadow, in harmony with the developing action of the play. Thus in speaking of the forest scene in Wagner's *Siegfried*, he says: "We must no longer try to create the illusion of a forest; but instead the illusion of a man in the atmosphere of a forest. When the forest trees, stirred by the breeze, attract the attention of Siegfried, we, the spectators, should see Siegfried bathed in the moving lights and shadows, and not the movement of rags of canvas agitated by stage tricks. The scenic illusion lies in the living presence of the actor."

The light that plays upon the scenes is dynamic. It is an integral part of the drama. In the last act of *Tristan und Isolde* the light, no less than the music, must accompany the action. Appia tells exactly what the light should be and where shadows must fall. As the curtain rises Tristan lies in the shadow. He is dying. The sunlight, becoming more and more golden, filters through the branches of a great tree and strikes the ground near his feet. Then slowly, it begins to flow over his body, until, when Isolde comes to him, it sheds its radiance over both of them. As the Liebestod is sung, the golden light has passed beyond the dead Tristan. "The light fades little by little, until the scene is enveloped in a darkening twilight. The curtain falls on a calm, peaceful picture, of uniform tone, where the eye distinguishes only the last reflection of the sunset playing softly over the white form of Isolde." Stage setting was transformed by Appia from a means of illusion into a means of expression.

In his epoch-making book entitled *The Art of the Theatre* (1905), Gordon Craig delivered a body blow against the academic, bookish theories of drama. Eleven years before, Brunetière had promulgated his "law of the drama," and by 1905 it had become the basis of dramatic criticism. But Craig was interested in the living drama in the theatre, not merely in the play. "The art of the theatre is neither acting nor the play, nor the dance; but it consists of all the elements of which these things are composed: action which is the very spirit of acting; words which are the body of the play; line and color, which are the very heart of the scene; rhythm, which is the very essence of dance." Such is Craig's description of the Greek synthesis; but, unlike Aristotle, Craig expressly denied that one element was more important than the other. The literary and academic world greeted this theory of dramatic art as heresy which smelled of grease-paint, and turned up its offended nose as high as its brow. To realize that Aristotle placed plot above character was disconcerting; but at least the Greek critic had placed spectacle last. Now to find that the play itself was held as no more important than spectacle, that was too fantastic. Besides, Craig could have his art of the theatre. Cultured gentlemen and scholars, cultured and uncultured, were content with their dramatic literature—whatever that may be.

In order to produce this new art—new because it must be a synthesis—Craig dreams of a master mind capable of creating and directing every element. In the meantime, the theatre has had to be content with one man who can synthesize and harmonize the different arts. Although he may not actually write or act the play, or design the scenery and costumes, the director has assumed almost supreme authority in the creation of dramatic art. The scenic artist, the actor, even the dramatist must bow to his will, for, as Craig has said, "it is impossible for a work of art ever to be produced where more than one brain is permitted to direct." It is even more impossible when several brains work independently. The dramatist can tell what effect he wants to make, but he is rarely able to produce that effect when called upon to direct a production of his play. Dramatic art still awaits its "poet" or creator; and it will never attain perfection until such a creative genius appears. But some day the super-Wagner will be born.

Craig's influence on dramatic art has been most potent in regard to spectacle. After Appia and Craig, we can surely employ the word spectacle in a new sense meaning that part of a drama which produces legitimate and artistic effect upon the human mind through the eye. Color, form, light and shadow, *all* in movement, are found to have deep significance. Craig taught us to give up the vain search for perspective of depth and to substitute perspective of height towering to infinity. He made the pictorial back drop ridiculous. He showed us that it is possible to paint with light in color and in intensity befitting the moving action of the play. His light "travels." It is dynamic. It "caresses or cuts."

He fights realism valiantly and has won so many supporters that the old minotaur is gasping, if not dead. In choosing colors for a scene he would not look first at nature but in the play of the poet. Even that is not enough. "I let my scenes grow out of not merely the play, but from broad sweeps of thought which the play has conjured up in me, or even other plays by the same author have conjured up." Hamlet seems to him to be a lonely man in a dark place. Hence the setting must suggest this inner meaning of the play. In this conception of Hamlet, Craig may be right or wrong; but his method is artistically sound.

In every possible way he seeks to express the inner spirit of the drama unobtrusively. He stimulates the imagination through the senses, while the realist killed the imagination by the presentation of the actual thing or a deceiving replica. "By means of suggestion," Craig holds, "you may bring on the stage a sense of all things—the rain, the sun, the wind, the snow, the hail, the intense heat—but you will never bring them there by attempting to wrestle and close with Nature in order so that you may seize some of her treasure and lay it before the eyes of the multitude. By means of suggestion in movement you may translate all passions and the thoughts of vast numbers of people, or by means of the same you can assist your actor to convey the thought and the emotions of the particular character he impersonates. Actuality, accuracy of detail, is useless upon the stage."

Appia and Craig are the prophets of the new art of drama. Lest anyone object that the art is not new, let us immediately admit that it is as old as Greek tragedy. But through the influence of the tragedies and of Aristotle's commentaries, we erected the theory of the unity of action into the supreme law. It was broadened and narrowed by turns; but no one dared to leave it out of consideration. Now a new unity or rather the old unity of the Greek drama is set up as the ideal. By a synthesis of all the arts the spiritual meaning of the drama is brought out. To this process the term "style" or "stylization" may be applied. We have re-discovered that drama is not words; that, with all its limitations, it is limitless in its infinite variety. When the creative dramatic artist finds that one of the component arts is failing to produce the desired effect, he brings into play another art to supplement or to substitute for the one which, because of its very nature, is found wanting at that particular moment. The supreme test of a drama is based upon the question as to whether all the arts employed have been used in a manner to evoke completely the inner meaning of the drama.

The theatre of the twentieth century is constantly being torn down and rebuilt. It is seething with experiments, with new syntheses. The proscenium arch, footlights, cloth cycloramas, plaster domes, constructivist scenery, architectural scenery, the mingling of actors and audience, improvisation like the *commedia dell' arte*, stages painted with oils, stages painted with light, stages painted with colored cloth, sets on different levels, steps, and more steps, ladders, machines for effects, machines for setting, silhouettes, bas-reliefs, two dimensions, three dimensions, all this and more goes and comes in countless variations. Plays of all ages are produced in as many different "styles" as there are directors. *Phèdre* and *Macbeth* are given cubistic scenery.

In Craig's production of *Hamlet* at the Moscow Art Theatre certain scenes were staged in a monodramatic manner so that the audience saw the place and the characters as Hamlet saw them in his tortured mind. Stanislavsky has described in *My Life in Art* one of the scenes as follows: "The King and the Queen sat on a high throne in golden and brocaded costumes, among the golden walls of the throne room, and from their shoulders there spread downwards a cloak of golden porphyry, widening until it occupied the entire width of the stage and fell into the trap. In this tremendous cloak there were cut holes through which appeared a great number of courtiers' heads, looking upward at the throne. . . . Add to this scene, so remarkable for its imagination and mystic impressionism, the impudent, threatening, piercing fanfares of brass instruments with unbelievable dissonances, which proclaimed to the whole world the criminal greatness and hypocrisy of the King who rose to the throne." In Elmer Rice's *Adding Machine* the walls of Mr. Zero's house are covered with numbers. One of the acts in Molnar's *Liliom* represents heaven in the shape of a minor police court as it might appear to a criminal. Even Ibsen's plays have been produced with stylized settings. The objective naturalists show the effect of environment on character. The subjective expressionists show the effect of character on environment.

Back of the movement known as the New Stagecraft lies the old yet new spirit of the Greek synthetic art of drama. "The theatre is ceasing to be intellectual," cry the timid reactionaries. "The theatre is beginning to live again now that you word-worshippers are being put into your proper places," these men of the New Theatre retort. "We cannot understand this new drama," complain the intellectuals. "Don't try to understand it! Experience it," is the answer. The theatre is a place in which to listen. The theatre is a place in which to see. Yes, it has been each one and both of these places. The New Theatre is the place to feel, to experience all life in all arts. The New Theatre is the most complex of all the arts. We must be patient while it experiments, forgiving whenever it fails, keeping our eyes on its possibilities, rather than on its performance.

CHAPTER XXII

SYMBOLISM. EXPRESSIONISM

THE naturalists sought to substitute reproductions of every-day life for the dagger strokes and pistol shots of conventional tragedy. In removing heroics from drama they introduced the commonplace; but they still depicted life in its moments of struggle and violence. Maeterlinck considered drama dominated by anachronism because it depicted the life of violence. "Indeed, when I go to a theatre," he complained, "I feel as though I were spending a few hours with my ancestors, who conceived life as something that was primitive, arid and brutal . . . I am shown a deceived husband killing his wife, a woman poisoning her lover, a son avenging his father, a father slaughtering his children, children putting their father to death, murdered kings, ravished virgins, imprisoned citizens —in a word, all the sublimity of tradition, but alas, how superficial and material. Blood, surface tears and death . . . I was yearning for one of the strange moments of a higher life that flit unperceived through my dreariest hours; whereas, almost invariably, all that I beheld was but a man who would tell me, at wearisome length, why he was jealous, why he poisoned, or why he killed."

Maeterlinck, like the naturalists, found the true tragic element in the life of every day; but instead of finding it in material and psychological struggles as did they, he saw it in moments of tranquillity and silence. "I have grown to believe," he said, "that an old man seated in his armchair, waiting patiently, with his lamp beside him; giving unconscious ear to all the eternal laws that reign about his house, interpreting, without comprehending, the silence of doors and windows and the quivering voice of light, submitting with bent head to the presence of his soul and his destiny—an old man, who conceives not that all the powers of this world, like so many heedful servants, are mingling and keeping vigil in his room, who suspects not that the very sun itself is supporting in space the table against which he leans, or that every star in heaven and every fibre of his soul are directly concerned in the movement of an eyelid that closes, or a thought that springs to birth—I have grown to believe that he, motionless as he is, does yet live in reality a deeper, more human, and more universal life than the lover who strangles his mistress, the captain who conquers in battle, or the husband who avenges his honor."

Such is Maeterlinck's theory of the static theatre as set forth in *The Tragical in Daily Life*. He saw examples of it in Greek tragedies in which not only the material action, but the psychological action were diminished in a "truly marvelous fashion, with the result that the interest centres solely and entirely in the individual face to face with the universe." The physical action in *Philoctetes* is simple and ordinary. The chief interest of the tragedy for Maeterlinck lies neither in it nor in "the struggle we witness between cunning and loyalty, between love of country, rancor and headstrong pride." The beauty and greatness, therefore, are not in plot or psychology, but in the words. There are two kinds of dialogue. There are "the words which accompany and explain the action"; and there is another dialogue that seems superfluous at first, but "examine it carefully and it will be borne home to you that this is the only one that the soul can listen to profoundly, for here alone is it the soul that is being addressed. . . . One may even affirm that a poem draws nearer to beauty and loftier truth in the measure that it eliminates words that merely explain the action and substitutes for them others that reveal not the so-called 'soul-state' but I know not what intangible and unceasing striving of the soul towards its own beauty and truth."

Maeterlinck found in Ibsen's *Master Builder* a drama in which this dialogue of the second degree attains the deepest tragedy. "Hilda and Solness are, I believe, the first characters in drama who feel, for an instant, that they are living in an atmosphere of the soul; and the discovery of this essential life that exists in them, beyond the life of every day, comes fraught with terror." For Maeterlinck, at least, there is a new kind of dramatic suspense which lies deeper than the suspense of the material action or the suspense of the psychological action. Maeterlinck has called it the "anguish of the unintelligible" which he finds in Ibsen's *Ghosts* and in Tolstoi's *Power of Darkness*.

"Their conversation," he says of Hilda and Solness, "resembles nothing that we have ever heard, inasmuch as the poet has endeavored to blend in one expression both the inner and outer dialogue. A new, indescribable power dominates this somnambulistic drama. All that is said therein at once hides and reveals the sources of an unknown life. And if we are bewildered at times, let us not forget that our soul often appears to our feeble eyes to be but the maddest of forces, and that there are in man many regions more fertile, more profound and more interesting than those of his reason and intelligence."

Thus Maeterlinck advocated the deintellectualization of dramatic art, the static drama and the dramatization of the "meditation that comes to us in the tranquil moments of life," when the veil is partially lifted from the mystery of the universe.

"In a symbol," said Carlyle, "there is concealment and yet revelation: hence, therefore by silence and speech acting together comes a double significance." "The great art of silence," as Voltaire called it, had been employed for dramatic purposes by Æschylus. With Maeterlinck it assumed the function ascribed to it by Carlyle. Silence is not merely a means of intensifying dramatic suspense but is "the angel of the supreme truth, the messenger that brings to the heart tidings of the unknown." Even the dialogue of the second degree must be combined with silence, "for the soul tests its weight in silence and the words we let fall have no meaning apart from the silence that wraps them round."

In the *Philosophe sans le Savoir* we have called attention to the effectiveness of the dialogue about the watch which, without

any symbolism, is really about the possible death of young Vanderk. Akin to such methods, without being a direct outgrowth,
is the use of symbolism as employed by Ibsen. With Maeterlinck, comes not only symbolism with its double significance,
but also the significance of the words left unspoken. His tragic
old man is supposed to interpret "without comprehending the
silence of doors and windows and the quivering voice of light."

This may seem impossible and to be the rhetoric of a mystic.
Yet attempts to put his theories into practice have not been
failures. Indeed, the motionless life becomes visible in certain
static scenes. When Pelléas and Mélisande, in the music drama,
are watching the ship sail out to sea, the dialogue continues with
orchestral accompaniment; but the final effect of the scene is
one of silence, of the communion of the souls of these somnambulistic lovers. Maeterlinck, with the aid of Debussy's music,
approaches what he calls the "new theatre, a theatre of peace,
and of beauty without tears."

Corresponding to his dialogue of the first and second degree
is what may be called his action of the first and second degree.
The visible action on the stage evokes the invisible action behind the scenes in such plays as *The Intruder* (*L'Intruse*) and
The Death of Tintagiles (*La Mort de Tintagiles*). The visible
and invisible action are simultaneous, as was sometimes the case
in Greek tragedy, notably in the death scene in *Agamemnon*,
and in the opening of the *Eumenides*. As one infers a mystic
meaning from the spoken dialogue, so one infers the mystic
action from the visible action. Sarcey used the phrase "The
Maeterlinckian Beyond" with some contempt; but it is an apt
description of his invisible place which is just beyond the visible
scene of the action. Much of Maeterlinck's action occurs in
"The Beyond." That is the reason that doors and windows are
so important in his settings and in his symbolism. Doors separate the physical from the psychical, life from death. Doors
that will not close, doors that will not open, doors that guard
treasures, ghosts, plagues, women who will not be free, all have
symbolic and dramatic significance.

One of his most effective scenes is that in which Golaud holds little Yniold up to the window of the room in which are Pelléas and Mélisande. We do not actually see the young lovers, but like Golaud, we see them in the simple, broken words of the child. They are motionless—looking at the light—standing upright against the wall—they never close their eyes. . . . Then, the child will tell no more—will look no more. If eyes are the windows of the soul of man, windows are the eyes of the soul of Maeterlinck's drama.

The Intruder is Maeterlinck's most successful attempt to carry out his theories of dramatic art as they existed at this period of his career. He dramatized the coming of Death and exemplified his tragic old man who, though almost totally blind, sees more than those whose eyes are undimmed. He alone penetrates partially the mystery and feels the terror of the moment. He interprets the silences without comprehending.

The setting is a gloomy room in an old château. "At the back, stained glass windows in which green is the dominant color and a glass door opening upon a terrace. A big Dutch clock in a corner. A lighted lamp."

The Grandfather seats himself under the lamp. His daughter has been ill for weeks since she gave birth to a baby that has never made a sound. "She is out of danger," says the Father; but the Grandfather believes she is not doing well. A nun, the Father's sister, is coming to visit the sick woman. The stars are out. It is moonlight. The nightingales are singing. Now they are hushed. Someone must have entered the garden. The silent, frightened swans have swum to the other bank. The dogs do not bark. "There is a stillness of death." Cold comes into the room. The glass door is open. They cannot shut it. All at once the sound of the sharpening of a scythe is heard outside. The gardener is mowing in the garden; but to the sensitive ears of the Grandfather it seems as if he were mowing in the house. The lamp is burning dimly. A noise, as if someone coming into the house. It must be the nun. A knock on the secret door. It is the maid-servant. She did not make the noise. The Grandfather feels a presence in the room. No. There is no one here but the family. The lamp burns out. Silence. "One could hear an angel's step." Silence. Silence. "I am afraid, too, my children." Then a ray of moonlight penetrates through a corner of the stained glass, and spreads strange gleams here and there in the room. Midnight strikes; and at the last stroke it seems to some that a sound is heard, very vaguely, as of someone rising in all haste. Who rose? No one. A wail of fright is heard from the child's room. "Listen! the child! He has never cried before." Heavy, headlong steps are heard in the wife's room.—Then a deathly stillness.—The Sister of Charity, clad in black, appears on the threshold. She makes the sign of the cross to announce the death of the wife. All but the Grandfather silently enter the room. He gropes excitedly about the table in darkness. "They have left me all alone."

Here is a play without plot, without depiction of character. Maeterlinck's people are marionettes, as he frankly admitted. It makes little difference who speaks the lines. The sounds, especially the knocking, the ensuing silence, the light, the doors and windows, the repetitions, "the perilous simplicity of speech and act," as he called it, are all characteristic of Maeterlinck's dramaturgy. He described *The Master Builder* as a somnambulistic drama. The dialogue of his *Princesse Maleine* gives "the characters the appearance of somnambulists who are a little deaf and are being continually awakened from a painful dream." Tyltyl and Mytyl in *The Blue Bird* (*L'Oiseau Bleu*) are dreaming somnambulists trying to penetrate the mysteries of life and death. This dream-like atmosphere pervades all his plays. His settings of forests, sombre Gothic halls and towers with doors and windows behind which lurks the mysterious, are designed to enhance this effect and to harmonize with the mood of the scene. Light plays an important rôle in his plays and is actually personified in *The Blue Bird*. He was one of the first playwrights after Wagner to recognize the dynamic quality of light and colors which change and dissolve in accompaniment to the spiritual action.

His stage directions describe the effect he wishes to obtain and the dialogue notes the change in the light scenario. He runs the whole scale from darkness to light that is "unbearable." His personification of Light in *The Blue Bird* says: "I have not a voice like Water; I have only my brightness, which Man does not understand. . . . But I watch over him to the end of his days. . . . Never forget that I am speaking to you in every spreading moonbeam, in every twinkling star, in every dawn that rises, in every lamp that is lit, in every good and bright thought in your soul." The rôle of light in the modern theatre is no less important than in Maeterlinck's philosophy. Appia and Craig personify light and speak of its function in drama in similar terms.

Sound, silence, light and color, together with the veiled implications of the spoken words, are the most important elements of his symbolism and his dramatic effects. They are the means he employs to evoke the invisible, the intangible, the subconscious and the unintelligible. As a result, his symbolistic dramas lend themselves to productions in expressionistic style.

Maeterlinck has become convinced that purely static drama is impossible. "Whatever the temptation," he says, in his essay on *The Modern Drama,* "he (the dramatist) dare not sink into inactivity, become a mere philosopher or observer. Do what one will, discover what marvels one may, the sovereign law of the stage, its essential demand will always be *action.* . . . And there are no words so profound, so noble and admirable, but they will soon weary us if they leave the situation unchanged, if they lead to no action, bring about no decisive conflict, or hasten no definite solution." Yet Maeterlinck himself has been largely responsible for what he calls the "paralysis of external action" in modern drama.

He is not a man of the theatre, and like Charles Lamb, he believes that dramas presented by human agency lose some of their beauty. He feels so conscious of the actor that he forgets the character. He prefers plays in his imagination to those on the stage. Yet he has had a profound influence on the modern stage not merely in his use of symbolism but in showing the power of expressionism in dramatic art. Whatever we may think of his mysticism and of his philosophy, he has made us hear certain overtones which heretofore were inaudible in drama of violent situations and were lost in the hammering on rather obvious social problems. The production of *The Blue Bird* in expressionistic style by the Moscow Art Theatre in 1910 is an important date in modern drama. Debussy's musical version of *Pelléas and Mélisande* is an early example of synthetic art in which the separate arts are finely balanced. *The Intruder* and *The Death of Tintagiles* have shown us that drama can be something other than a violent struggle of human passions and discussions of social laws and customs.

When Sarcey saw the first production of *Pelléas and Mélisande*, which was made in Paris by Lugne-Poë in 1893, he wrote a witty review of the play; but his views illustrate the change which was taking place in dramatic art. Belonging to the older generation which admired the problem play, with its geometrical demonstration, he complained of the obscurity of the symbolistic drama. Commenting on the line: "She was born without reason . . . to die; and she dies without reason," Sarcey wrote: "That is precisely what I complain about. For only the knowledge of the reason for things entertains me in the theatre." But this form of drama makes a conscious break with reason and our reasoning powers. We are supposed to experience the play. Sarcey quotes a friend, probably imaginary, as saying: "The theatre, in the new school, is a sombre wall behind which something mysterious is happening. You perceive at intervals, through an opening, a shadow which glides by murmuring enigmatic words; you guess the rest." Though written in a spirit of mockery these words define exactly the aim and the source of artistic pleasure of Maeterlinck's dramas.

Strindberg began as a romanticist, became a naturalist, passed from naturalism to symbolism under the influence of Maeterlinck and finally introduced expressionism into dramatic art. His naturalistic period in drama began with his play *The Father* (1887), which was produced by Antoine in 1888 and which gave Strindberg an international reputation as dramatist. His preface to *Miss Julia* was a reply to the hostile criticism evoked by *The Father* and it set forth much of his naturalistic theory of dramatic art, especially in regard to the Little or Intimate Theatre.

He advocated physical changes such as the abolition of footlights, less make-up for actors, a small stage in a small auditorium. He dared not dream of beholding the actor's back throughout an important scene, but he hoped that crucial scenes might not be played in the centre of the proscenium. "To make a real room of the stage, with the fourth wall missing, and a part of the furniture placed back towards the audience, would probably produce a disturbing effect at present." But the rear wall of the scene in *Miss Julia* was placed diagonally across the stage. "Having only a single setting, one may demand to have it real." He objected to pots and pans painted on the scenery. He tried to abolish the division into acts because he feared that "our decreasing capacity for illusion might be unfavorably affected by intermissions during which the spectator would have time to reflect and to get away from the suggestive influence of the author-hypnotist." He filled in the pauses of the action by the dance, pantomime, and monologue. He sought to prove that the monologue is a justifiable procedure provided it is employed at moments when a person in real life would talk to himself.

All these suggestions, including that of the fourth wall, were adopted by the realistic theatre; but in 1909 Strindberg said of this search for actuality: "I cannot but regard all that pottering with stage properties as useless." In a brief discussion of "stylization" in his *Dramaturgy*, Strindberg has described how he came under the influence of Maeterlinck. He read in 1890 a criticism of Maeterlinck's plays. It seemed to him satire or nonsense. When he read the plays themselves, Maeterlinck was a closed book to him because he was so deeply sunk in materialism. "But I felt," he continues, "a certain unrest and a sadness that I could not grasp the beauty and depth that I sensed and for which I yearned as a damned soul yearns for the company of the Blessed. Only after I had passed through the Inferno years (1896-99) did I find Maeterlinck again, and then he seemed like a new land and a new era."

Strindberg felt that Maeterlinck's characters live on another plane; that Maeterlinck is in communication with a higher world; and that in this wonderful world of the poet everything has different dimensions, different light, different tone. Strindberg disliked Ibsen, but he found in Maeterlinck that "transcendental soul" and the "essential life" that exists beyond the life of every day which Maeterlinck found in *The Master Builder.*

Such is the life in a world stripped of reality that Strindberg depicts in his trilogy *To Damascus.* Even his early *Lucky Pehr* (1883) is an allegorical play of an unreal world in which objects such as a funeral pall and a broom are endowed with life. Certain human characters are abstractions. Pehr himself is Youth, who goes forth into the world and returns home to find happiness in unselfish love. The world depicted in *Lucky Pehr* is the world of the medieval allegory. It is doubtful that Strindberg would have produced even symbolic drama had he not undergone the influence of Maeterlinck; yet he was less a stranger in Maeterlinck's dream world of *The Blue Bird* because he had depicted an allegorical world in *Lucky Pehr.*

Even his naturalistic conception of character was a preparation for his depiction of character in *To Damascus.* In the preface to *Miss Julia* he stated his theory as follows:

In the course of the ages the word character has assumed many meanings. Originally it signified probably the ground-note in the complex mass of self, and as such it was confused with temperament. Afterward it became the middle-class term for an automaton, so that an individual whose nature had come to a stand-still, or who had adapted himself to a certain part in life—who had ceased to grow, in a word—was named a character. . . . This middle-class notion about the immobility of the soul was transplanted to the stage, where the middle-class element has always held sway. There a character became synonymous with a gentleman fixed and finished once for all—one who invariably appeared drunk, jolly, sad. . . . This manner of regarding human beings as homogeneous is preserved even by the great Molière. Harpagon is nothing but miserly, although Harpagon might as well have been at once miserly and a financial genius, a fine father, and a public spirited citizen. . . . I do not believe, therefore, in simple characters on the stage. And the summary judgments of the author upon men—this one stupid, and that one brutal, this one jealous and that one stingy—should be challenged by the naturalists, who know the fertility of the soul complex, and who realize that "vice" has a reverse very much resembling virtue. . . .

My souls (or characters) are conglomerates, made up of past and present stages of civilization, scraps of humanity, torn-off pieces of sundry clothing turned into rags—all patched together as is the human soul itself.

The character of Julia is a conglomerate. The action of the play arises from her complex psychology which is the result of her heredity, her environment, events in her past life, the present circumstances and the influence of others, such as her fiancé and her parents, who do not appear in the play. The action, as Strindberg said, cannot be traced back to a single motive but it springs from a whole series of more or less deep-lying motives. The primary emphasis, however, is placed upon the theme of social ascendancy and decline of classes. The deeplying motives and the complex psychology of Julia are given as causes of the action. But the action passes in a world as real as the devices of the naturalistic theatre can make it. Therefore, whatever lies in the past or outside of the one room must be narrated in dialogue. Julia is the embodiment of a conglomerate soul. We see her act as she does because of certain influences; but she is a naturalistic individual in a naturalistic world. For these reasons the deep-lying motives and the elements which compose her complex soul are in the background. Strindberg brought them into the foreground when he left his naturalistic world for his expressionistic world.

In his trilogy *To Damascus,* Strindberg entered the Maeterlinckian dream world where reality cannot enchain the dreamer's thought and imagination. He analyzed his own conglomerate soul. He is the character called The Unknown. This character sub-divides. The Unknown meets himself in different phases of his own entity. He beholds himself as he was in certain periods of his life. Cæsar, the madman, and The Beggar are parts of his own personality. The Woman is a concept, or rather several concepts which appear to him at different times. Strindberg described his new method of playwriting in a prefatory note to *The Dream Play* (1902) as follows:

As he did in his previous dream play [*To Damascus*], so in this one the author has tried to imitate the disconnected but seemingly logical form of the dream. Anything may happen; everything is possible and probable. Time and space do not exist. On an insignificant background of reality, imagination designs and embroiders novel patterns, free fancies, absurdities and improvisations.

The characters split, double, multiply, vanish, solidify, blur, clarify. But one consciousness reigns above them all—that of the dreamer; and before it there are no secrets, no incongruities, no scruples, no laws.

Maeterlinck's dream world is inhabited by people who are personifications and symbols. His characters are mysterious because they live in a world beyond reality. But they have few attributes. They are not conglomerate souls.

Strindberg's dream world is the world of Strindberg's soul. His characters are concepts of all the elements and influences which form the human soul. His people are never fixed. They are changing organisms. Strindberg was abnormally subjective and introspective. He indulged in self-inflicted torture through constant mental vivisection. He personified emotions in his plays. External events with "an insignificant background of reality" lose their externality and become completely identified with psychological reactions of the characters. In the motion picture *The Cabinet of Dr. Caligari* we see the action and the setting through the eyes and brain of a madman. So in Strindberg's *To Damascus*, the drama comes to us through the character called The Unknown, who appears in every scene and is off the stage for only a few minutes during the whole trilogy. We behold this strange world through his eyes. The result is what has been called "monodrama."

The medieval mystery plays and the allegorical plays aimed to interpret the spiritual life through realistic methods. Strindberg tried to interpret real life through spiritual methods. The aim of medieval drama was to save souls for the after life. Strindberg attempted to save souls for this life by analyzing the deep-lying motives of our acts and by revealing the hidden recesses of the subconscious.

Strindberg's theatre has been called anarchistic. It knows no rules, save that there must be impersonation. It knows no limits, for it is as vast and as flexible as the mind of the dreamer. Under his influence the last fetters of the old dramatic traditions have been struck off, for the realistic concepts of time and space do not exist in his dream world.

In such plays as *To Damascus, The Dream Play* and *The Spook Sonata* there is inartistic obscurity and too much pseudo-profundity. Yet they reveal the processes and the infinite variations of the mind of a conscious dreamer. They half illumine hidden recesses of human nature by methods which had never been so fully and frankly employed in the theatre. Strindberg did not employ these methods with complete success. Expressionism is still in its experimental period in the theatre. But all expressionistic dramatists who strip the external film of the world of reality from their conceptions of life in order to present their interpretation of the human soul are either conscious or unconscious disciples of Strindberg, the inspired madman.

The serious drama of the nineteenth century presented man

in his relation to social laws and customs. It depicted the struggle of the sexes in relation to society. A large part of the drama of the twentieth century seeks to depict man's struggle with himself. Instead of trying to solve the riddle of the universe, drama is attempting to solve the riddle of personality. The struggle of man against the gods, fate, destiny, heredity or environment has been replaced by the struggle of man to understand himself. In *To Damascus* the man is mentally unbalanced at times and he sees himself as the madman. Modern psychology has taught us that we are not hopelessly unbalanced if we have divided personalities. We no longer believe that a man who shows one side of his nature to the world or who masks his real personality is a hypocrite.

The modern dramatic hero does not eternally proclaim to the world: "I have a great will. See what I do in this situation!" He asks: "Why do I do this? What am I?" At the end of *Maria Magdalena*, Anton says: "I don't understand the world any more." He means that all his ideas of social law and custom have become incomprehensible. That is his tragedy in the nineteenth century. When the last curtain comes down on Pirandello's *Six Characters in Search of an Author, Henry IVth*, or *Right You Are, If You Think You Are*, his people are saying: "What are we? Do we exist? When do we exist?" That is their tragedy in the twentieth century.

The modern dramatist seeks to analyze the human mind. He employs any method that seems suitable to his particular task. In Pellerin's *Têtes de Rechanges* the principal character starts out to dine. By the time he arrives, he has become six separate persons. The title of Alice Gerstenberg's *Overtones* is typical of this form of drama. The play presents an interview between two women, each of whom is represented by her primitive self, Hetty and Maggie, and her cultured self, Harriet and Margaret. "The primitive and cultured selves never come into actual physical contact but try to sustain the impression of mental conflict. Harriet never sees Hetty, never talks to her, but rather thinks aloud looking into space. Hetty, however, looks at Harriet, talks intently and shadows her continually. The same is true of Margaret and Maggie." The cultured selves are the subtle overtones of the primitive selves who wear chiffon veils. Both Margaret and Harriet are married; but Harriet loves Margaret's husband whom she refused to marry because he was too poor. During the interview the veiled, primitive selves reveal the thoughts behind the words of the cultured selves.

The title of Evreinov's *Theatre of the Soul,* a monodrama in one act, is typical of another phase of this form of drama. The scene of the action is the human breast where the soul is supposed to reside. The setting is a pulsating heart. In the prologue to the play The Professor says: "The human soul is not indivisible, but on the contrary, is composed of several selves, the natures of which are different. Thus if M represents I myself (*He writes on the board*), $M = M_1 \; M_2 \; M_3 \; \ldots \; M_n$." He explains that M_1 is the rational self or the Reason; M_2 is the emotional self or Feeling; M_3 is the physical self or the Eternal.

The Rational Entity and the Emotional Entity are in conflict over a Dancer. The Emotional Entity's concept of the Dancer appears. She is seductive and "she sings and dances to the rhythm of the heart which beats joyously." The Rational Entity summons its concept of the Dancer. She is old and hideous and the Emotional Entity pushes her away. The Rational Entity's Concept of the Wife appears. She is nursing a child and croons a lullaby. The Emotional Entity pushes her away. She is the "eternal housemaid." The Emotional Entity's Concept of the Wife is an ordinary slovenly bourgeoise. Finally the Emotional Entity kills the Rational Entity and throws himself at the feet of the seductive Concept of the Dancer. She laughs at him. He has no money. He commits suicide. The Subliminal Entity awakens. A railroad Porter says it is time to change cars and the Subliminal Entity goes forth.

Another example of the personification and analysis of abstract elements in the life of man is found in Toller's *Man and the Masses* (*Masse-Mensch*). When Hauptmann dramatized the condition of the weavers in Germany he made a collective crowd the protagonist in his play. He employed naturalistic methods. His crowd does and says nothing which a crowd could not do or say in real life. He depicted the psychology of a mob as it is manifested externally. Toller employed expressionistic methods. He depicted the inner psychology of the Masses as it is manifested externally in the symbolic figure of the Nameless One who is described as The Spirit of the Masses. As the program of the American production tells us, the theme of the play is "the inevitable tragic nature of the conflict between man, the individual, and the needs of the masses. The protagonist is a woman profoundly convinced that no cause can be really won if it is won at the price of war and bloodshed." The Woman is a radical but has strong humanitarian instincts. She is the only character in the play who has a name, Sonia Irene L., and even her name seems to be symbolic of the Russian communist movement. The Man, her husband, is the State.

Three of the nine scenes "take place in the woman's mind, projecting through a dream medium her horror of capitalistic control, of proletarian warfare, and her pity for its victims." In a *Letter to a Creative Producer* which appears as a preface, Toller explains his method as follows:

"There are critics who complain that, although the 'dream scenes' are sufficiently dream-like, you gave the 'realistic scenes' a visionary air, and that thus you blur the boundary between dream and reality. I wish emphatically to declare that you have altogether realized my intention. These 'realistic' pictures are no typical naturalistic scenes. With the exception of Sonia, the types are not individualized. What can be realistic in my drama *Man and the Masses?* Only the spiritual, intellectual qualities."

By such methods and with the aid of expressionistic settings which banish all ideas of concrete realism, Toller analyzes and dramatizes the spiritual intellectual qualities of his theme. The play reveals many psychological elements in the conflict between man and the masses which remain hidden perforce in Hauptmann's naturalistic *Weavers*. Yet a danger lurks in blurring the boundary between dream and reality. The play does not aim to give the spectator merely the sensation of a revolution. It has a definite intellectual theme. The program of the American production gave a detailed synopsis of each scene and an explanation of the symbolism without which perhaps not one spectator in a thousand would have grasped the true significance of many of the lines. The modern dramatist who uses such methods in order to reveal truths must differentiate between obscurity which explains and obscurity which needs explanation.

Instead of employing separate actors to personify aspects of a personality, Eugene O'Neill has employed masks which the character dons or removes as his personality changes or as he wishes to present his internal or external self to other characters in his drama *The Great God Brown*. In his *Lazarus Laughed* the crowds and the choruses are masked according to a very elaborate scheme in order to show their ages and characteristics. The masks vary from scene to scene and over three hundred are required. In the first scene all the figurants except Lazarus are masked in accordance with the following scheme:

There are seven periods of life shown: Boyhood (or Girlhood), Youth, Young Manhood (or Womanhood), Manhood (or Womanhood), Middle Age, Maturity and Old Age; and each of these periods is represented by seven masks of general types of character as follows: The Simple, Ignorant; the Happy, Eager; the Self-Tortured, Introspective; the Proud, Self-Reliant; the Servile, Hypocritical; the Revengeful, Cruel; the Sorrowful, Resigned. . . . Each type has a distinct predominant color for its costumes which varies in kind according to its period. The masks of the Chorus of Old Men are double the size of the others.

Lazarus Laughed is a massive piece of synthetic drama in which all the arts are called upon and must be employed lavishly to carry the idea: "Death is dead! Fear no more! There is only life! There is only laughter!" Such is the message that

Lazarus brings back from the grave and tries to teach men—but "men forget."

The Great God Brown is a drama which minutely analyzes personalities and at the same time attempts to carry, as an overtone, a mystical background of conflicting tides in the soul of Man. O'Neill's explanation of his methods and aims is an important document in the history of modern drama. It shows the possibilities and the limitations as yet inherent in such forms of art. When speculation was rife as to the meaning of this interesting but complicated play, O'Neill wrote as follows:

I realize that when a playwright takes to explaining he thereby automatically places himself "in the dock." But where an open avowal by the play itself of the abstract theme underlying it is made impossible by the very nature of that hidden theme, then perhaps it is justifiable for the author to confess the mystical pattern which manifests itself as an overtone in *The Great God Brown*, dimly behind and beyond the words and actions of the characters.

I had hoped the names chosen for my people would give a strong hint of this. (An old scheme, admitted—Shakespeare and multitudes since.) Dion Anthony—Dionysus and St. Anthony—the creative pagan acceptance of life, fighting eternal war with the masochistic, life-denying spirit of Christianity as represented by St. Anthony—the whole struggle resulting in this modern day in mutual exhaustion—creative joy in life for life's sake frustrated, rendered abortive, distorted by morality from Pan into Satan, into a Mephistopheles mocking himself in order to feel alive; Christianity, once heroic in martyrs for its intense faith now pleading weakly for intense belief in anything, even Godhead itself. (In the play it is Cybele, the Pagan Earth Mother, who makes the assertion with authority: "Our Father, Who Art!" to the dying Brown, as it is she who tries to inspire Dion Anthony with her certainty in life for its own sake.)

Margaret is my image of the modern direct descendant of the Marguerite of *Faust*—the eternal girl-woman with a virtuous simplicity of instinct, properly oblivious to everything but the means to her end of maintaining the race.

Cybel is an incarnation of Cybele, the Earth Mother doomed to segregation as a pariah in a world of unnatural laws but patronized by her segregators who are thus the first victims of their laws.

Brown is the visionless demi-god of our new materialistic myth— a Success—building his life of exterior things, inwardly empty and resourceless, an uncreative creature of superficial preordained social grooves, a by-product forced aside into slack waters by the deep main current of life-desire.

Dion's mask of Pan which he puts on as a boy is not only a defense against the world for the supersensitive painter-poet underneath it but also an integral part of his character as the artist. The world is not only blind to the man beneath but it also sneers at and condemns the Pan-mask it sees. After that Dion's inner self retrogresses along the line of Christian resignation until it partakes of the nature of the Saint while at the same time the outer Pan is slowly transformed by his struggle with reality into Mephistopheles. It is as Mephistopheles he falls stricken at Brown's feet after having condemned Brown to destruction by willing him his mask, but, this mask falling off as he dies, it is the Saint who kisses Brown's feet in abject contrition and pleads as a little boy to a big brother to tell him a prayer.

Brown has always envied the creative life force in Dion—what he himself lacks. When he steals the mask of Mephistopheles he thinks he is gaining the power to live creatively while in reality he is only stealing that creative power made self-destructive by complete frustration. This devil of mocking doubt makes short work of him. It enters him, rending him apart, torturing him and transfiguring him until he is even forced to wear a mask of his Success, William A. Brown, before the world, as well as Dion's mask towards wife and children. Thus Billy Brown becomes not himself to anyone. And thus he partakes of Dion's anguish—more poignantly, for Dion had the Mother, Cybele—and in the end out of his anguish his soul is born, a tortured Christian soul such as the dying Dion's, begging for belief, and at the last finding it on the lips of Cybele.

And now for an explanation regarding this explanation. It was far from my idea in writing *Brown* that his background pattern of conflicting tides in the soul of Man should ever overshadow and thus throw out of proportion the living drama of the recognizable human beings, Dion, Brown, Margaret and Cybele. I meant it always to be mystically within and behind them, giving them a significance beyond themselves, forcing itself through them to expression in mysterious words, symbols, actions they do not themselves comprehend. And that is as clearly as I wish an audience to comprehend it. It is Mystery—the mystery any one man or woman can feel but not understand as the meaning of any event—or accident—in any life on earth. And it is this mystery I want to realize in the theatre. The solution, if there ever be any, will probably have to be produced in a test tube and turn out to be discouragingly undramatic.

Having seen the play and having read O'Neill's explanation one understands; but is it going to be necessary to have annotated programs for modern drama? *The Great God Brown* is too overburdened with meaning to be clear either to spectator or reader without elucidation. We have a right to demand that a work of art be self-contained. Dramatic art is the richest of all the arts. A dramatist ought not to be forced to rely upon printed explanations or synopses of scenes in order to communicate completely his ideas to an intelligent audience. The use of masks in *The Great God Brown* was enlightening and baffling by turns. The blurring of symbolism and reality was often troublesome. When a man is dead can you steal his mask which represents his personality? Certainly, because he may be only symbolistically dead. But if Dion Anthony is symbolistically dead why does Brown fear the police? Are they symbols? No. The spectator is willing to play any game, to pretend anything the dramatist requests in order to penetrate the mystery of life and the enigma of personality. But *The Great God Brown* befogs the brain and then asks the brain to function. *Lazarus Laughed* is a finer work of art in that the theme is clear and simple; and the symbolism and masks and crowds are employed to help us experience and sense the message of Lazarus to the world. There is no blurring of the spiritual with the real because there is no touch of realism in the whole drama.

If *The Great God Brown* is irritatingly obscure, *Strange Interlude* is the clearest and the most minute analysis of the enigma of human personality in all drama. The title means "life," for Nina says: "Strange interlude! Yes, our lives are merely strange dark interludes in the electrical display of God the Father." O'Neill has not tried to solve the mystery of life or to paint a whole world. He has taken four people when life really begins for them and he shows how they lived for years and years externally and in their own secret selves; what they said; what they did; what they hoped. Other dramas have done as much; but no drama except *Strange Interlude* has ever told us clearly what people thought as they spoke and hoped and acted.

We had learned long ago to read hidden motives behind spoken words. We had tuned our ears to the Chekhovian silence and to the Maeterlinckian dialogue of the second degree. In *Strange Interlude* each character speaks his inmost thoughts in a monologue or an aside. However, the terms monologue and aside are somewhat misleading. When a character is speaking his thoughts all actors on the stage are motionless and the awkward effect of the old aside is entirely absent. The audience easily accepts the convention that the other characters do not hear; and it seems as if we were divining with absolute accuracy the thoughts of the character. These monologues cast an artistic spell because they contain the illuminating truth. The dialogue makes the desired impression of external illusion. The thoughts are the inner reality of each character. They come in quick, short phrases like plashes of light that reveal the raw, pulsating personality behind the false shell which protects it from mortal view.

It is said that O'Neill has used the method of a novelist. The play is long. It takes four hours playing time to present the nine acts of this drama. The monologues have been compared to the comments of a novelist and to narrative passages. But *Strange Interlude* is a play in every sense of the word. One is never conscious of the writer's comments or of narration. The thoughts of the characters are theirs alone. The characters are before our eyes in flesh and blood. We see their lives unfold before us. We hear them speak. We do not guess, we know what they think and how they feel. The effect is one that the novel can never produce. The spectator has a sensation of omniscience, as if for the first time he were penetrating the inner personality of living human beings.

Nothing whatsoever is left to our imagination. What little symbolism there is, such as Gordon's departure in an airplane, is perfectly obvious. The play is not subtle in the sense that we must indulge in creative thinking, as we must in symbolistic or expressionistic drama. We see into the inmost hearts of the characters; but we do not live in them as we live in Hamlet. We are absolutely objective spectators. The naturalists, such as Henri Becque, have shown us the externalities of life. The spectator at a performance of *Les Corbeaux* knows exactly as much of the characters and their actions as if he had been permitted to be an invisible spectator of these episodes in real life. But he knows nothing more. Nor does he feel that there is anything beyond these externalities. In symbolic dramas such as Heiberg's *Tragedy of Love*, D'Annunzio's *Gioconda*, or Ibsen's *Master Builder*, we are conscious of a deeper meaning half-hidden behind the external manifestation of the life on the stage. We can speculate on the hidden meaning, if we wish. The dramas of Maeterlinck are played in a Beyond, which lies behind doors, windows, curtains, walls and which we must penetrate if we are to grasp or even vaguely feel the significance of the play. In expressionistic drama, such as Toller's *Man and the Masses*, O'Neill's *Lazarus Laughed*, we are in a spiritual world of abstract ideas personified by human beings, light, form, color and sound. In *Strange Interlude* externalities of life are depicted exactly in all necessary detail. But since the innermost thoughts of the people are also presented exactly in all necessary detail and since nothing is left to the creative imagination of the spectator, perhaps we may call *Strange Interlude* a super-naturalistic drama.

Will *Strange Interlude* create a new form of drama that will compete in length and in method with the novel? Or is the play merely an example of the new spirit in dramatic art which permits a dramatist to use whatever form and whatever method that will best interpret life? Only time can tell. We do not know what our grandchildren will see in the theatre when the plays of the first generation of the twentieth century have become old-fashioned and are dated. They will smile, with kindly indulgence, at plays we admire. They will declare their faith in new forms of art. But it is hoped that they will be grateful to this age which set the drama free.

BIBLIOGRAPHY

I

A SELECTIVE BIBLIOGRAPHY OF IMPORTANT PLAYS TREATED
IN THE TEXT WITH SPECIAL REFERENCE TO COLLECTIONS
AND ANTHOLOGIES AND TO TRANSLATIONS IN ENGLISH

CHAPTERS I-IV AND VIII

ÆSCHYLUS, *Tragedies*, translated by H. W. Smyth, Loeb Library;
by J. S. Blackie, Everyman's Library.

ARISTOPHANES, *Comedies*, text with translation by B. B. Rogers,
each play in a separate vol.; by W. J. Hickie, Bohn Library.

EURIPIDES, *Tragedies*, translated by A. S. Way, Loeb Library; by
various authors, Everyman's Library.

MENANDER, *Comedies*, translated by F. G. Allinson, Loeb Library.

PLAUTUS, *Comedies*, translated by H. T. Riley, Bohn Library; by
Paul Nixon, Loeb Library.

SENECA, *Tragedies*, translated by F. J. Miller, Loeb Library.

SOPHOCLES, *Tragedies*, translated by F. Storr, Loeb Library; by
George Young, Everyman's Library.

TERENCE, *Comedies*, translated by H. T. Riley, Bohn Library; by
John Sargeaunt, Loeb Library.

CHAPTERS VI-VII, IX-X

Ancien théâtre françois, ed. by M. Viollet-le-Duc, 1854-57 (10
vols.) (Contains farces, moralities, tragedies, and comedies.)

Antichrist and Adam, translated by S. F. Barrow and W. H.
Hulme, *Western Reserve University Bulletin*, 1925.

BÈZE, THÉODORE DE, *A Tragedie of Abraham's Sacrifice*, translation
by M. W. Wallace (University of Toronto Studies, 1906).

Dodsley's Old English Plays, ed. by W. C. Hazlitt, 1874-76
(15 vols.).

Drames liturgiques, ed. by C. E. H. de Coussemaker, 1860. (Text with translation in French.)

English Miracle Plays, Moralities and Interludes, ed. by A. W. Pollard, 1923.

GASCOIGNE, GEORGE, *Supposes* and *Jocasta*, ed. by J. W. Cunliffe, 1906.

Love in a French Kitchen, a medieval farce, translated by C. C. Clements and J. M. Saunders (*Poet-Lore*, 1917).

Le théâtre français au XVIe et au XVIIe siècle, ed. by E. Fournier.

Le théâtre français avant la Renaissance, ed. by E. Fournier, 1872.

Minor Elizabethan Drama, Vol. I, "Pre-Shakespearean Tragedies," Vol. II, "Pre-Shakespearean Comedies," ed. by A. Thorndyke, Everyman's Library.

Miracles de Notre-Dame, ed. by G. Paris and U. Robert, 1876-93 (8 vols.) (Société des anciens textes français.)

Representative English Comedies, ed. by C. M. Gayley, 1903.

Specimens of the Pre-Shakespearean Drama, ed. by J. M. Manley, 1897 (2 vols.). (Contains examples of all forms of English drama of the Middle Ages and the Renaissance.)

Teatro italiano antico, ed. by G. D. Poggiali, 1808 (10 vols.).

The Farce of Master Pierre Patelin, translated by R. Holbrook, 1905.

Théâtre français au moyen-âge, ed. by L. J. N. D. Monmerqué and F. X. Michel, 1842. (Specimens of medieval drama with translation in modern French.)

Tudor Facsimile Texts, ed. by J. S. Farmer (1907)f.

CHAPTERS XI-XIV AND XXII

AUGIER, E., and SANDEAU, JULES, *The Son-in-law of M. Poirier* (*Le gendre de M. Poirier*) in *Chief European Dramatists*.

BALZAC, H. DE, *Dramas*, ed. by J. W. McSpadden, 1901.

BECQUE, H., *The Vultures, The Woman of Paris, The Merry-Go-Round*, translated by F. Tilden, 1913, Modern Drama Series.

Chief Contemporary Dramatists, ed. by T. H. Dickinson, 1915 (2d series, 1921).

Chief European Dramatists, ed. by Brander Matthews, 1916.

CORNEILLE, P., *Œuvres complètes,* ed. by Marty-Laveaux, 1862-68 (12 vols.).

———— *The Cid,* translation in *Chief European Dramatists,* ed. by Brander Matthews, 1916.

DUMAS, ALEXANDRE, the younger, *The Foreigner (L'Etrangère),* New York, F. Rullman, 1881.

———— *The Money-Question (La question d'argent)* in *Poet-Lore,* 1915.

———— *The Outer Edge of Society (Le demi-monde)* in *Chief European Dramatists.*

GOETHE, J. W. VON, *Dramatic Works,* Bohn Library.

HAUPTMANN, G., *Dramatic Works,* ed. by L. Lewisohn, 1912-17 (7 vols.).

HEBBEL, C. F., *Three Plays (Gyges and His Ring, Herod and Mariamne, Maria Magdalena),* Everyman's Library.

HUGO, V., *The Dramatic Works,* 1900 (3 vols.).

———— *Hernani,* in *Chief European Dramatists.*

IBSEN, HENRIK, *Collected Works,* ed. by W. Archer, 1911 (12 vols.).

LESSING, G. E., *Dramatic Works,* Bohn Library, 1878 (2 vols.).

LILLO, GEORGE, *The London Merchant and Fatal Curiosity,* ed. by A. W. Ward, 1906.

LUDWIG, O., *The Hereditary Forester (Der Erbförster),* in *The German Classics,* 1914.

MAETERLINCK, M., *Plays,* translation by R. Hovey, 1913-19 (7 vols.).

MOLIÈRE, J. B. P., *Œuvres complètes,* ed. by E. Despois, 1873-1900 (13 vols.).

———— *The Dramatic Works,* translation by Van Laun, H., 1875 (6 vols.). Also an excellent translation of several plays by C. H. Page, 1908 (2 vols.).

PIRANDELLO, LUIGI, *Three Plays,* translated by E. Storer and A. Livingston, 1923.

RACINE, JEAN, *Œuvres complètes,* ed. by P. Mesnard, 1865-73.

———— *Phedra,* in *Chief European Dramatists.*

Representative Continental Dramas, Revolutionary and Transitional, ed. by M. J. Moses, 1924.

SCHILLER, J. C. F. VON, *Works,* ed. by N. H. Dole, 1902, Vols. III and IV.

SCRIBE, E., *The Ladies' Battle* (*Bataille de Dames*), French's acting edition of plays, Vol. CVIII.

SEDAINE, M. J., *Le philosophe sans le savoir,* ed. by T. E. Oliver, 1914.

STRINDBERG, A., *Plays,* translated by E. Björkman, 1912-16, 4 series.
———— *Lucky Pehr,* translated by V. S. Howard, 1912.

VOLTAIRE, F. M. A., *Works* (St. Hubert Guild), 1901-03 (22 vols.). Selected plays, including *Nanine* and *The Scotch Woman* (*L'Ecossaise*), in Vols. VIII-X.

WERNER, F. L. Z., *The Twenty-Fourth of February* (*Der Vierundzwanzigste Februar*), in *The Drama,* 1903.

CHAPTER XX

CHEKHOV, A., *Plays,* translated by M. Fell, 1916 (2 vols.).
———— *The Cherry Orchard,* in *Chief Contemporary Dramatists.*

EVREINOV, N. M., *The Theatre of the Soul,* translated by M. Potapenko and C. St. John, 1915.

GOGOL, M. V., *The Inspector-General,* translated by T. Seltzer, 1916.

GORKY, M., *The Lower Depths,* in *Chief Contemporary Dramatists,* 2d series, 1921.

GRIBOYEDOV, A. S., *The Misfortune of Being Clever,* translated by S. W. Pring, 1914.

OSTROVSKY, A., *Plays,* translated by G. R. Noyes, 1917.
———— *The Storm,* translated by C. Garnett, 1899.

TOLSTOI, L. N., *Plays,* translated by Louise and Aylmer Maude, 1914.

TURGENIEV, I. S., *Plays,* translated by M. S. Mandel, 1924.

II

A SELECTIVE BIBLIOGRAPHY OF WORKS ON DRAMATIC ART

GENERAL WORKS ON DRAMA AND DRAMATIC TECHNIQUE
AND THE THEATRE

ARCHER, WILLIAM, *Playmaking, a Manual of Craftsmanship,* 1912.
BAKER, G. P., *Dramatic Technique,* 1919.

BELLINGER, M. F., *A Short History of the Drama*, 1927.

BULTHAUPT, H., *Dramaturgie des Schauspiels*, 1908 (4 vols.).

CLARK, BARRETT, *European Theories of the Drama*. An anthology from Aristotle to the present day.

CREIZENACH, W. M. A., *Geschichte des neueren Dramas*, 2d ed., 1911-23.

DINGER, H., *Dramaturgie als Wissenschaft*, 1904-05 (2 vols.).

FREYTAG, GUSTAV, *Die Technik des Dramas*, 1863, translated as *The Technique of the Drama*, by E. J. MacEwan, 1895.

HAMILTON, CLAYTON, *The Theory of the Theatre*, 1910.

KLEIN, J. L., *Geschichte des Dramas*, 1865-76 (13 vols.).

MANTZIUS, K., *A History of Theatrical Art*, translated by Louise von Cossel, 1903-09.

MATTHEWS, BRANDER, *Development of Drama*, 1903.

——— *The Principles of Playmaking*, 1919.

NICOLL, A., *The Development of the Theatre*, 1927.

——— *An Introduction to Dramatic Theory*, 1903.

PROLSS, R., *Geschichte des neueren Dramas*, 1880-83 (3 vols.).

ROYER, ALPHONSE, *Histoire universelle du théâtre*, 1878, Vols. V and VI.

SCHLEGEL, A. W., *Vorlesungen über dramatische Kunst und Literatur*, 1809-11, translated by J. Black as *Lectures on Dramatic Art and Literature*, Bohn Library.

CHAPTERS I-V

ALLEN, J. T., *Stage Antiquities of the Greeks and Romans and their Influence*, 1927.

BYWATER, I., *Aristotle on the Art of Poetry* (Text, translation, and notes), 1909.

BETHE, E., *Prologomena zur Geschichte des Theaters im Altertum*, 1896.

CORNFORD, F. M., *The Origin of Attic Comedy*, 1914.

CAPPS, E., *Greek Comedy*, in Columbia University Lectures on Greek Literature, 1912.

DENIS, J., *La comédie grecque*, 1886.

COUAT, A., *Aristophane et l'ancienne comédie attique*, 1892.

DECHARME, P., *Euripides and the Spirit of His Dramas*, translated by James Loeb, 1905.

FLICKINGER, R. C., *The Greek Theatre and its Drama*, 2d ed., 1926.

GOODELL, T. D., *Athenian Tragedy*, 1920.

HAIGH, A. E., *The Attic Theatre*, 3d ed., 1907.

—— *The Tragic Drama of the Greeks*, 1907.

HARBERTON, J. S. P., *The Lately Discovered Fragments of Menander, Text and Translation*, 1909.

JEBB, R. C., see Introduction to his separate editions of the plays of Sophocles.

LEO, F., *Plautinische Forschungen*, 1895.

LEGRAND, P. E., *The New Greek Comedy*, translated by James Loeb, 1917.

LUCAS, F. C., *Tragedy in Relation to Aristotle's Poetics*, 1927.

MICHAUT, G., *Histoire de la comédie romaine*, 1920.

MAZON, PAUL, *Essai sur la composition des comédies d'Aristophane*, 1911.

NAVARRE, O., *Les origines et la structure technique de la comédie ancienne*, in *Revue des études anciennes*, 1911.

NORWOOD, G., *The Art of Terence*, 1923.

—— *Greek Tragedy*, 1920.

PATIN, H. J. G., *Etudes sur les tragiques grecs*, 1841 (4 vols.).

RIDGEWAY, W., *The Dramas and Dramatic Dances of non-European Races in Special Reference to the Origin of Greek Tragedy*, 1910.

SHEPPARD, J. T., *Greek Tragedy*, 1920.

VAUGHN, C. E., *Types of Tragic Drama*, 1908.

WILAMOWITZ-MOELLENDORFF, TYCHO, *Die dramatische Technik des Sophokles*, 1917.

WEIL, H., *Etudes sur le drame antique*, 2d ed., 1908.

ZIELINSKI, TH., *Die Gliederung der altattischen Komodie*, 1885.

CHAPTER VI

D'ANCONA, A., *Origini del teatro italiano*, 1891 (2 vols.).

BAPST, G., *Essai sur l'histoire du théâtre*, 1893.

COHEN, G., *Histoire de la mise-en-scène dans le théâtre religieux français du moyen-âge*, 1906.

CHAMBERS, E., *The Medieval Stage*, 1903.

DU MÉRIL, E., *Histoire de la comédie*, 1864.

GAYLEY, C. M., *Plays of Our Forefathers*, 1909.

LINTILHAC, E. F., *Histoire générale du théâtre en France*, 1904, Vols. I and II.

MAGNIN, C., *Les origines du théâtre moderne*, 1838.

PETIT DE JULLEVILLE, L., *Les mystères*, 1880 (2 vols.).

——— *La comédie et les mœurs en France au moyen-âge*, 1886.

REICH, H., *Der Mimus*, 1903 (2 vols.).

ROY, E., *Etudes sur le théâtre français du XIVe et XVe siècles*, 1901.

SEPET, M., *Les origines catholiques du théâtre moderne*, 1901.

CHAPTERS I-V AND VIII

ALBRIGHT, V. E., *The Shakespearian Stage*, 1909.

ASCHAM, R., *The Scholemaster*, ed. by Arber, 1870.

BAKER, G. P., *The Development of Shakespeare as a Dramatist*, 1907.

BOAS, F. S., *Shakespeare and his Predecessors in the English Drama*, 1896.

BROOKE, C. F. T., *The Tudor Drama*, 1911.

CREIZENACH, W. M. A., *English Drama in the Age of Shakespeare*, 1916.

CUNLIFFE, J. W., *The Influence of Italian on Early Elizabethan Drama*, in *Modern Philology*, 1907, Vol. IV.

——— *The Influence of Seneca on Elizabethan Tragedy*, 1893.

FANSLER, H. E., *The Evolution of Technic in Elizabethan Tragedy*, 1914.

GAYLEY, C. M., *An Historical View of the Beginnings of English Comedy*, in his *Representative English Comedies*, 1903.

GREG, W. W., *Pastoral Poetry and Pastoral Drama*, 1906.

HERFORD, C. H., *Studies in the Literary Relations of England and Germany in the Sixteenth Century*, 1886.

LEE, S., *The French Renaissance in England*, 1910.

LOUNSBURY, T. R., *Shakespeare as a Dramatic Artist*, 1901.

LUCAS, F. L., *Seneca and Elizabethan Tragedy*, 1922.

MACKENZIE, W. R., *The English Moralities*, 1914.

MATTHEWS, BRANDER, *Shakespeare as a Playwright*, 1913.

POLLARD, A. W., *English Miracle Plays, Moralities and Interludes*, 5th ed., 1909.

REED, A. W., *The Beginning of the English Secular and Romantic Drama*, 1922.

SCHELLING, F. E., *Elizabethan Drama*, 1908 (2 vols.).

SIDNEY, PHILIP, *An Apology for Poetrie*, ed. by Arber, 1595.

SKELTON, JOHN, *Magnyfycence*, ed. by R. L. Ramsay, 1908.

SYMONDS, J. A., *Shakespeare's Predecessors in the English Drama*, 1884.

The Cambridge History of English Literature, ed. by A. W. Ward and M. A. Waller, 1910, Vols. V and VI.

VERITY, A. W., *Marlowe's Influence on Shakespeare*, 1886.

YOUNG, K., *The Influence of the French Farce upon the Plays of Heywood*, in *Modern Philology*, 1904-05, Vol. II.

CHAPTERS VIII-X

APOLLINAIRE, G., *Le théâtre italien*, 1910.

BIANCALE, A., *La tragedia italiana del 500*, 1901.

CASTELVETRO, L., *Poetica d'Aristotle*, 1576.

CHARLTON, H. B., *Castelvetro's Theory of Poetry*, 1913.

DANIELLO, B., *La Poetica*, 1536.

GIRALDI, CINTHIO, *Discorso sulle comedie e sulle tragedie*, written in 1543, published 1554 (Daelli's *Biblioteca Rara*, 1864, Vols. LII-LIII).

HORACE, *The Art of Poetry*, translated by C. Sharp.

KARSTEN, H. T., Ed., *De commenti Donatiani ad Terenti fabulas*, 1912 (2 vols.).

MINTURNO, A. S., *L'arte poetica*, 1564.

NERI, F., *La tragedia italiana del cinquecento*, 1904.

PADELFORD, F. M., *Select Translations from Scaliger's Poetics*, 1905.

ROBORTELLI, F., *In Librum Aristotelis de Arte Poetica Explicationes*, 1548.

SCALIGER, J. C., *Poetices libri septem*, 1561.

SMITH, WINIFRED, *The Commedia dell'Arte*, 1912.

SPERONI, SPERONE, *Opere*, 1740 (5 vols.).

SPINGARN, J. E., *A History of Literary Criticism in the Renaissance*, 1908.

SYMONDS, J. A., *The Renaissance in Italy*, 1900.

TRISSINO, G. B., *Tutte le opere*, 1729 (2 vols.).

CHAPTERS XI-XIV

ARNAUD, C., *Etude sur la vie et les œuvres de l'abbé d'Aubignac et les théories dramatiques au XVIIe siècle*, 1887.

BERNBAUM, ERNEST, *The Drama of Sensibility*, 1915.

CHASSANG, M. A. A., *Des essais dramatiques imités de l'antiquité au XIVe et XVe siècles*, 1852.

M.M.D.C. (DE CHASSIRON), *Réflexions sur le comique-larmoyante*, 1749.

CORNEILLE, PIERRE, *Œuvres complètes*, ed. by Marty-Laveaux.

DIDEROT, DENIS, *Œuvres complètes*, ed. by Assézat, 1875-77.

FAGUET, E., *La tragédie en France au XVIe siècle*, 1883.

FOURNEL, V., *Le théâtre au XVIIe siècle*, 1892.

GAIFFE, F., *Etude sur le drame en France au XVIIIe siècle*, 1910.

HÉDELIN, F. (Abbé d'Aubignac), *Pratique du théâtre*, 1657.

HUSZAR, G., *Corneille et le théâtre espagnol*, 1903.

JOURDAIN, E. F., *Dramatic Theory and Practice in France*, 1690-1808, 1921.

LA MESNARDIÈRE, *Art poétique*, 1640.

LA MOTTE, ANTOINE HOUDAR DE, *Premier discours sur la tragédie*, and his three "Discours sur la tragédie," prefixed to his plays.

LANCASTER, H. C., *The French Tragi-comedy*, 1907.

LANSON, G., *Nivelle de la Chaussée et la comédie larmoyante*, 2d ed., 1903.

———— *L'idée de la tragédie avant Jodelle*, in *Revue d'histoire littéraire de la France*, 1904.

———— *Esquisse d'une histoire de la tragédie française*, 1920.

———— *Corneille*, 1898.

———— *Les origines de la tragédie classique en France*, in *Revue d'histoire littéraire de la France*, 1903.

LARROUMET, G., *La comédie de Molière*, 1887.

LA TAILLE, JEAN DE, *Art de la tragédie*, 1572.

LINTILHAC, E. F., *Histoire générale du théâtre en France*, 1904-10, Vols. IV and V.

LION, H. G. M., *Les tragédies et les théories dramatiques de Voltaire*, 1895.

LOPE DE VEGA, *Arte nuevo de hacer comedias*, translated by W. T. Brewster in *Papers on Play-making* (Dramatic Museum of Columbia University), 1914.

LOUNSBURY, T. R., *Shakespeare and Voltaire*, 1902.

MAIRET, JEAN DE, Preface to his *Silvanire*, ed. by Otto, 1890.

MARSAN, J., *La pastorale dramatique en France*, 1905.

MARTINENCHE, E., *Molière et le théâtre espagnol*, 1906.

—— *La comédie espagnol en France*, 1900.

MATTHEWS, BRANDER, *Molière*, 1910.

MOLAND, L., *Molière et la comédie italienne*, 1867.

MOLIÈRE, J. P. B., *Œuvres complètes*, ed. by Despois et Mesnard, 1873-1900.

OGIER, F., Preface to Schélandre's *Tyr et Sidon*, 1628, in *Ancien théâtre françois*, 1856, Vol. VIII.

RACINE, JEAN, *Œuvres complètes*, ed. by Mesnard, 1865-73.

RIGAL, E., *Molière*, 1908.

—— *Alexandre Hardy et le théâtre français*, 1889.

SEARLES, COLBERT, *Les sentiments de l'Academie française sur la tragedie-comédie du Cid*, 1916.

SEGALL, J. B., *Corneille and the Spanish Drama*, 1902.

TOLDO, P., *La comédie française de la Renaissance*, in *Revue d'histoire littéraire de la France*, 1897-1900.

VAUQUELIN DE LA FRESNAYE, *L'art poétique*, ed. by Pellissier, 1885.

VOLTAIRE, *Œuvres complètes*, ed. by Moland, 1877-85.

CHAPTER XV

BELOUIN, G., *De Gottsched à Lessing*, 1909.

BLANCHET, F. A., *Du théâtre de Schiller*, 1855.

BRENNING, EMIL, *Lessing als Dramatiker und Lessing's Nathan der Weise*, 1878.

ELOESSER, A., *Das bürgerliche Drama*, 1898.

GOTSCHLICH, EMIL, *Lessing's aristotelische Studien und der Einfluss derselben auf seine Werke*, 1876.

GOTTSCHED, J. C., *Versuch einer kritischen Dichtkunst*, 1730.

GRUCKER, E., *Histoire des doctrines litteraires et esthétiques en Allemagne*, 1883.

KONTZ, A., *Les drames et la jeunesse de Schiller*, 1899.

KUHNEMANN, E., *Schiller*, translated by Katherine Royce, 1912 (2 vols.).

LESSING, G. E., *Hamburgische Dramaturgie*, 1769, translated by E. C. Beasley and Helen Zimmern as *Hamburg Dramaturgy*, Bohn Library.

PETERSON, J., *Schiller und die Bühne*, 1904.

PETSCH, R., *Deutsche Dramaturgie von Lessing bis Hebbel*, 1912.

POENSGEN, MAX, *Geschichte der Theorie der Tragödie von Gottsched bis Lessing*, 1899.

CHAPTER XVI

BORGERHOFF, J. L., *Le théâtre anglais à Paris sous la restauration*.

GINISTY, P., *Le mélodrame*, 1911.

GLACHANT, P. et V., *Essai sur le théâtre de Victor Hugo*.

HUGO, VICTOR, *Préface de Cromwell*, 1827.

LATREILLE, C., *La fin du théâtre romantique et François Ponsard*, 1899.

LE ROY, A., *L'aube du théâtre romantique*, 1904.

MARSAN, J., *Le mélodrame et G. de Pixerécourt*, in *Revue d'histoire littéraire de la France*, Vol. VII.

NEBOUT, P., *Le drame romantique*, 1899.

MANZONI, *Lettres sur l'unité de temps et de lieu, traduites par Fauriel*, 1823.

PARIGOT, H., *Le drame d'Alexandre Dumas*, 1898.

PITOU, A., *Les origines du mélodrame*, in *Revue d'histoire littéraire de la France*, 1911, Vol. XVIII.

SAKELLARIDES, E., *Alfred de Vigny, auteur dramatique*, 1902.

SOURIAU, M., *De la convention dans la tragédie classique et dans le drame romantique*, 1885.

STENDHAL (Pierre Beyle), *Racine et Shakespeare*, 1823.

ALLARD, L., *La comédie de mœurs en France au dix-neuvième siècle*, 1923.

BENOIST-HANAPPIER, L., *Le drame naturaliste en Allemagne*, 1905.

BRAHM, OTTO, *Kritische Schriften über Drama und Theater*, 1913.

BRUNETIÈRE, F., *La loi du théâtre*, translated by P. M. Hayden as *The Law of the Theatre* in *Papers on Play-making* (Dramatic Museum of Columbia University), 1914.

CHANDLER, F. W., *Aspects of Modern Drama*, 1914.

—— *The Contemporary Drama of France*, 1920.

CLARK, BARRETT, *A Story of the Modern Drama*, 1925.

DAWSON, E., *Henri Becque*, 1923.

DOUMIC, R., *De Scribe à Ibsen*, 1896.

DUKES, ASHLEY, *Modern Dramatists*, 1911.

GAILLARD, H., *Emile Augier et la comédie sociale*, 1910.

GOT, A., *Henri Becque*, 1920.

HENDERSON, A., *The Changing Drama*, 1919.

—— *European Dramatists*, 1914.

JAMESON, S., *The Modern Drama in Europe*, 1920.

JULLIEN, JEAN, *Le théâtre vivant*, 1892-96.

LEWISOHN, L., *The Modern Drama*, 1915.

LINTILHAC, E., *Histoire générale du théâtre en France*, 1910, Vol. V.

MORRILLOT, PAUL, *Emile Augier*, 1901.

PARIGOT, H., *Emile Augier*, 1890.

—— *Le théâtre d'hier*, 1893.

SARCEY, F., *Quarante ans de théâtre*, 1900-1902 (8 vols.).

SÉCHÉ, A., et BERTAUT, J., *L'Evolution du théâtre contemporaire*, 1908.

SHAW, G. B., *Dramatic Opinion and Essays*, 1906 (2 vols.).

SMITH, H. A., *Main Currents of Modern French Drama*, 1925.

STOECKIUS, ALFRED, *Naturalism in the Recent German Drama*, 1903.

THALASSO, A., *Le Théâtre-libre*, 1909.

WAXMAN, S. M., *Antoine and the Théâtre-libre*.

WITKOWSKI, G., *The German Drama of the Nineteenth Century*.

ZOLA, E., *Nos auteurs dramatiques*, 1881.

—— *Le naturalisme au théâtre*, 1881.

CHAPTER XIX

ARCHER, W., see introductions to his translations of Ibsen's plays, 1907.

CAMPBELL, T. M., *Hebbel, Ibsen and the Analytic Exposition* (Contains translations of Hebbel's *My Views on Drama* and his Preface to *Maria Magdalena*), 1922.

HELLER, O., *Henrik Ibsen*, 1912.

LENEVEU, G., *Ibsen et Maeterlinck*, 1902.

LITZMANN, B., *Ibsens Dramen*, 1901.

MINOR, J., *Die Schicksalstragödie in ihren Hauptvertretern*, 1883.

MOSES, M. J., *Henrik Ibsen*, 1908.

STEIGER, E., *Das Werden des neueren Dramas*, 1903 (2 vols.).

WEIGAND, H. J., *The Modern Ibsen*, 1925.

CHAPTER XX

CARTER, H., *The New Theatre and Cinema of Soviet Russia*, 1925.

BAKSHY, A., *The Path of the Modern Russian Stage*, 1916.

GREGOR, J., and FULOP-MILLER, R., *Das Russische Theater*, 1927.

OLGIN, M. J., *A Guide to Russian Literature*, 1920.

SAYLER, O. M., *The Russian Theatre*, 1922.

——— *The Russian Theatre under the Revolution*, 1920.

STANISLAVSKY, C., *My Life in Art*, 1924.

WIENER, L., *The Contemporary Drama of Russia*, 1924.

CHAPTER XXI

CARTER, HUNTLEY, *The New Spirit in Drama and Art*, 1912.

CHENEY, SHELDON, *The New Movement in the Theatre*, 1914.

——— *Stage Decoration*, 1927.

CRAIG, E. GORDON, *On the Art of the Theatre*, 1911.

——— *Scene*, 1923.

——— *The Theatre-Advancing*, 1921.

——— *Towards a New Theatre*, 1913.

GRUBE, M., *Geschichte der Meininger*.

LOHMEYER, W., *Die Dramaturgie der Massen*, 1913.

MACGOWAN, K., *The Theatre To-Morrow*, 1921.

MACGOWAN, K., and JONES, R. E., *Continental Stagecraft*, 1922.

MODERWELL, H., *The Theatre of Today*, 1914.

NIESSEN, C., *Das Bühnenbild*, 1924 *ff.*

SAYLER, O. M., *Max Reinhardt and His Theatre*, 1923.

WAGNER, RICHARD, *Prose Works*, translated by W. A. Ellis, 1892 *ff.*

CHAPTER XXII

BAKSHY, A., *The Theatre Unbound*, 1924.

CARTER, H., *The New Spirit in the European Theatre*, 1925.

DICKINSON, T. H., *The Insurgent Theatre*, 1917.

DUKES, A., *The Youngest Drama*, 1924.

GOLDBERG, I., *The Drama of Transition*, 1922.

JOURDAIN, E., *The Drama in Europe*, 1924.

LEWISOHN, L., *The Drama and the Stage*, 1922.

MOSES, M. J., *Maurice Maeterlinck*, 1911.

QUINN, A. H., *A History of the American Drama*, 1927 (2 vols.).

PALMER, JOHN, *The Future of the Theatre*, 1913.

—————— *Studies in the Contemporary Theatre*.

ROSE, H., *Maeterlinck's Symbolism*, 1911.

SHEFFAUER, H. G., *The New Vision in the German Arts*, 1924.

STRINDBERG, A., *Dramaturgie*, translated in German by E. Schering, 1911.

SYMONDS, A., *The Symbolist Movement in Literature*, 1917.

TILGHER, A., *Studî sul teatro contemporaneo*, 1923.

VERNON, F., *The Twentieth Century Theatre*, 1924.

YOUNG, S., *The Flower in Drama*, 1923.

INDEX

WORLD DRAMA
46 plays in two volumes

selected by Barrett H. Clark

This anthology was designed not only for the serious student of world literature and the drama, but for everyone interested in the stage. It is an unusual collection, containing many great plays which are not ordinarily to be found in anthologies, and several which are not currently to be found in print in English in any edition. Virtually every great dramatic tradition is represented — Greek, Roman, Indian, Chinese, Japanese, Medieval, as well as such national traditions of Europe as Italian, Spanish, English, French, German, Danish, Russian, and Norwegian.

VOLUME I: Aeschylus: *Prometheus Bound;* Sophocles: *Antigone;* Euripides: *Alcestis;* Aristophanes: *The Clouds;* Plautus: *The Captives;* Terence: *Phormio;* Seneca: *Medea;* Kálidása: *Sakoontalá;* The Oriental plays: *The Chalk Circle, Abstraction, Nakamitsu,* and *Fair Lady at a Game of Poem-Cards;* The anonymous Medieval plays: *Adam, The Wise Virgins and the Foolish Virgins, The Second Shepherds Play, The Farce of the Worthy Master Pierre Patelin, Everyman,* and *St. George;* Sachs: *The Wandering Scholar from Paradise;* Marlowe: *The Tragical History of Dr. Faustus;* Johnson: *Every Man in his Humour;* Heywood: *A Woman Killed with Kindness;* Beaumont and Fletcher: *The Maid's Tragedy;* Farquhar: *The Beaux-Stratagem;* Goldsmith: *She Stoops to Conquer;* Sheridan: *School for Scandal.*

VOLUME II: Beolco: *Bilora;* Scala: *The Portrait;* Goldoni: *The Fan;* Alfieri: *Saul;* Cervantes: *The Cave of Salamanca;* Lope de Vega: *The King, the Greatest Alcalde;* Calderón: *The Constant Prince;* Corneille: *The Cid;* Racine: *Berenice;* Molière: *The Cit Turned Gentleman;* Beaumarchais: *The Barber of Seville;* Hugo: *Hernani;* Augier and Sandeau: *M. Poirer's Son-in-Law;* Dumas fils: *The Demi-Monde;* Lessing: *Miss Sara Sampson;* Goethe: *Egmont;* Schiller: *William Tell;* Holberg: *Jeppe of the Hill;* Ostrovsky: *The Thunderstorm;* Ibsen: *A Doll's House.*

Two volumes. Volume I: 26 plays; Volume II: 20 plays. Introduction. Reading lists. Total of 1362pp. 5⅜ x 8.

Vol. I, paperbound $2.25

Vol. II paperbound $2.25

THE DRAMA OF LUIGI PIRANDELLO
by Domenico Vittorini

Every play that Pirandello wrote between 1918 and 1935 is analyzed in this authorized study. Each play is placed in its background of Italian cultural history, and examined for its place in Pirandello's development and for its contribution to European dramaturgy.

Dr. Vittorini demonstrates that Pirandello's plays illustrate ideological problems, and shows how Pirandello, at various times, used different symbolic media for their solution. These techniques range from near naturalism to ironic grotesqueness, to social criticism, to character study, to the "intellectual speculation" so prominent in **Six Characters in Search of an Author**. In each case the reader is guided carefully through Pirandello's complex symbolism and original dramatic techniques by means of detailed synopses, which are so animated that they retain much of the atmosphere of the original work.

THE DRAMA OF LUIGI PIRANDELLO is especially important because of the few translations of Pirandello's work. It is also important in providing an approved interpretation of a notoriously difficult dramatist. Since it compresses Pirandello's entire range of thought into a single easily followed book, it will enable you to get a wider comprehension of the work of Nobel Laureate Pirandello than you could obtain from a single play or selection of plays.

"The introduction dealing with Pirandello's life and the detailed accounts of the plays . . . are the useful parts," TIMES [London]. "Clarifies Pirandello's position . . . offers an analysis of his philosophy," THEATRE ARTS MONTHLY. "I thank you cordially, dear Vittorini," PIRANDELLO.

Foreword by Pirandello. Biographical introduction. Bibliography of plays & English translations of plays, novels, poetry; critical studies. Portrait of Pirandello. xiii + 350pp. 5⅜ x 8.

T435 Paperbound $2.00

THE WORLD'S GREAT SPEECHES
edited by Lewis Copeland

255 speeches by 216 speakers are included in this monumental collection. Invaluable for speakers, debaters, etc., they will form a unique reference work for powerful and effective openings, speech transitions, organization, humorous snatches, provocative themes, and impressive endings. By following the speeches of the greatest speakers of all time you can learn the art of holding your audience and conveying impressions which will remain long after the occasion of the speech.

Speeches of every time and nearly every nation are represented in this truly cosmopolitan collection. From ancient Greece there is the Funeral Oration of Pericles, Socrates speech on his condemnation to death, two speeches of Demosthenes, etc.; speeches of Cicero, Julius Caesar, Catiline, and others represent ancient Rome; early Europe is covered by such illustrious names as St. Francis, Martin Luther, John Calvin, Frederick the Great, Mirabeau, Robespierre, Napoleon Bonaparte, Victor Hugo, Pope Leo XIII, Leon Trotsky, Marshal Foch, and many more; the profusion of important speakers from modern times can only be suggested by the following sample: George Bernard Shaw, Sun Yat-sen, Mahatma Gandhi, John L. Lewis, Herbert Hoover, Winston Churchill, Adolf Hitler, Benito Mussolini, Molotov, Joseph Stalin, Pope Pius XII, Franklin Delano Roosevelt, Fulton J. Sheen, Bernard Baruch, Harry S. Truman, Frank Lloyd Wright, William Faulkner, Dylan Thomas, Walter Reuther, and many more. In addition, there is a fine selection of historically important speeches from the earliest days of the United States and from other nations of the western hemisphere such as Brazil, Canada and Bolivia. While most of the material is unabridged, some has been skillfully condensed (retaining the author's words) so as to permit the inclusion of important works otherwise too long.

New Dover edition enlarged to include speeches to 1957. 255 speeches; 216 speakers. 3 indices: Topic, Author, Nation. xx + 745pp. 5⅜ x 8.

T468 Paperbound $2.49

MASTERS OF THE DRAMA
by John Gassner

This enormous half-million word volume is the only up-to-date history of world drama in English, the best introduction to world dramatic literature. It is unmatched in scope, ranging from the prehistoric religious festivals ancestral to the modern play, to the psychological and social drama of the 1950's in America. It describes in full detail the life and works of every major dramatist in history, from Aeschylus and Sophocles to Tennessee Williams and Arthur Miller.

This one-volume library of history and criticism is unmatched in its coverage of dramatic traditions not generally known to the American reader: the Japanese theatre, Chinese theatre, Classical Sanskrit plays, Italian Renaissance plays, and dozens of other areas. It is entirely adequate in its coverage of major dramatics, and unique in its coverage of minor plays and playwrights of interest—more than 800 authors, more than 2,000 plays!

Gassner's MASTERS OF THE DRAMA is not a bald summary of dates and plots. Brilliantly written, it demonstrates chains of developement in dramatic history, analyzes recurring dramatic needs of each epoch, and examines the cultural and social environment of each dramatist. You will find it an unsurpassed reference work; a most useful introduction to new fields of exploration in the drama; a necessary commentary to the modern stage; and, itself, a fascinating classic of modern literature.

PARTNAL CONTENTS: 1. Primitive drama. 2. Aeschylus. 3. Sophocles. 4. Euripides. 5. Aristophanes. 6. Menander, Platus, Terence. 7. Hebrew, Sanskrit drama, Kalidasa, etc. 8. Chinese, Tibetan, Japanese. 9. Medieval drama, religious and secular. 10. Italian Renaissance—Tasso, Bardi, Ariesto, Machiavelli, etc. 11. Lope de Vega, Calderon. 12. Marlowe. 13. Shakespeare. 14. Jonson, Beaumont & Fletcher, Webster. 15. Corneille, Racine. 16. Molière. 17. Goethe, Schiller, etc. 18. German, French romanticism, Hugo, etc. 19. Ibsen. 20. Björnson, Strindberg. 21. Zola, naturalism, Maeterlinck, etc. 22. Pirandello, etc. 23. Hauptmann. 24. Sudermann, Schnitzler, etc. 25. Chekhov, etc. 26. Gorky. 27. Synge, etc. 28. Shaw. 29. O'Neill. 30. Modern Americans 31. Post-war theatre in EUROPE. Appendix: Jewish, Polish theatre, etc.

3rd enlarged edition. Bibliography of 30 pages; index of 50 pages. xxi + 890pp. 5⅝ x 8¾   Clothbound $5.95

Catalog
of
DOVER BOOKS

BOOKS EXPLAINING SCIENCE

(Note: The books listed under this category are general introductions, surveys, reviews, and non-technical expositions of science for the interested layman or scientist who wishes to brush up. Dover also publishes the largest list of inexpensive reprints of books on inter-mediate and higher mathematics, mathematical physics, engineering, chemistry, astronomy, etc., for the professional mathematician or scientist. For our complete Science Catalog, write Dept. catrr., Dover Publications, Inc., 180 Varick Street, New York 14, N. Y.)

CONCERNING THE NATURE OF THINGS, Sir William Bragg. Royal Institute Christmas Lectures by Nobel Laureate. Excellent plain-language introduction to gases, molecules, crystal struc-ture, etc. explains "building blocks" of universe, basic properties of matter, with simplest, clearest examples, demonstrations. 32pp. of photos; 57 figures. 244pp. 5⅜ x 8.
T31 Paperbound **$1.35**

MATTER AND LIGHT, THE NEW PHYSICS, Louis de Broglie. Non-technical explanations by a Nobel Laureate of electro-magnetic theory, relativity, wave mechanics, quantum physics, philosophies of science, etc. Simple, yet accurate introduction to work of Planck, Bohr, Einstein, other modern physicists. Only 2 of 12 chapters require mathematics. 300pp. 5⅜ x 8.
T35 Paperbound **$1.60**

THE COMMON SENSE OF THE EXACT SCIENCES, W. K. Clifford. For 70 years, Clifford's work has been acclaimed as one of the clearest, yet most precise introductions to mathematical symbolism, measurement, surface boundaries, position, space, motion, mass and force, etc. Prefaces by Bertrand Russell and Karl Pearson. Introduction by James Newman. 130 figures. 249pp. 5⅜ x 8.
T61 Paperbound **$1.60**

THE NATURE OF LIGHT AND COLOUR IN THE OPEN AIR, M. Minnaert. What causes mirages? haloes? "multiple" suns and moons? Professor Minnaert explains these and hundreds of other fascinating natural optical phenomena in simple terms, tells how to observe them, suggests hundreds of experiments. 200 illus; 42 photos. xvi + 362pp.
T196 Paperbound **$1.95**

SPINNING TOPS AND GYROSCOPIC MOTION, John Perry. Classic elementary text on dynamics of rotation treats gyroscopes, tops, how quasi-rigidity is induced in paper disks, smoke rings, chains, etc, by rapid motion, precession, earth's motion, etc. Contains many easy-to-perform experiments. Appendix on practical uses of gyroscopes. 62 figures. 128pp.
T416 Paperbound **$1.00**

A CONCISE HISTORY OF MATHEMATICS, D. Struik. This lucid, easily followed history of mathematics from the Ancient Near East to modern times requires no mathematical back-ground itself, yet introduces both mathematicians and laymen to basic concepts and discoveries and the men who made them. Contains a collection of 31 portraits of eminent mathematicians. Bibliography. xix + 299pp. 5⅜ x 8.
T255 Paperbound **$1.75**

THE RESTLESS UNIVERSE, Max Born. A remarkably clear, thorough exposition of gases, electrons, ions, waves and particles, electronic structure of the atom, nuclear physics, written for the layman by a Nobel Laureate. "Much more thorough and deep than most attempts . . . easy and delightful," CHEMICAL AND ENGINEERING NEWS. Includes 7 animated sequences showing motion of molecules, alpha particles, etc. 11 full-page plates of photo-graphs. Total of nearly 600 illus. 315pp. 6⅛ x 9¼.
T412 Paperbound **$2.00**

WHAT IS SCIENCE?, N. Campbell. The role of experiment, the function of mathematics, the nature of scientific laws, the limitations of science, and many other provocative topics are explored without technicalities by an eminent scientist. "Still an excellent introduction to scientific philosophy," H. Margenau in PHYSICS TODAY. 192pp. 5⅜ x 8.
S43 Paperbound **$1.25**

FADS AND FALLACIES IN THE NAME OF SCIENCE, Martin Gardner. The standard account of the various cults, quack systems and delusions which have recently masqueraded as science: hollow earth theory, Atlantis, dianetics, Reich's orgone theory, flying saucers, Bridey Murphy, psionics, irridiagnosis, many other fascinating fallacies that deluded tens of thousands. "Should be read by everyone, scientist and non-scientist alike," R. T. Birge, Prof. Emeritus, Univ. of California; Former President, American Physical Society. Formerly titled, "In the Name of Science." Revised and enlarged edition. x + 365pp. 5⅜ x 8.
T394 Paperbound **$1.50**

THE STUDY OF THE HISTORY OF MATHEMATICS, THE STUDY OF THE HISTORY OF SCIENCE, G. Sarton. Two books bound as one. Both volumes are standard introductions to their fields by an eminent science historian. They discuss problems of historical research, teaching, pitfalls, other matters of interest to the historically oriented writer, teacher, or student. Both have extensive bibliographies. 10 illustrations. 188pp. 5⅜ x 8. T240 Paperbound **$1.25**

THE PRINCIPLES OF SCIENCE, W. S. Jevons. Unabridged reprinting of a milestone in the development of symbolic logic and other subjects concerning scientific methodology, probability, inferential validity, etc. Also describes Jevons' "logic machine," an early precursor of modern electronic calculators. Preface by E. Nagel. 839pp. 5⅜ x 8. S446 Paperbound **$2.98**

SCIENCE THEORY AND MAN, Erwin Schroedinger. Complete, unabridged reprinting of "Science and the Human Temperament" plus an additional essay "What is an Elementary Particle?" Nobel Laureate Schroedinger discusses many aspects of modern physics from novel points of view which provide unusual insights for both laymen and physicists. 192 pp. 5⅜ x 8.
T428 Paperbound **$1.35**

BRIDGES AND THEIR BUILDERS, D. B. Steinman & S. R. Watson. Information about ancient, medieval, modern bridges; how they were built; who built them; the structural principles employed; the materials they are built of; etc. Written by one of the world's leading authorities on bridge design and construction. New, revised, expanded edition. 23 photos; 26 line drawings, xvii + 401pp. 5⅜ x 8. T431 Paperbound **$1.95**

HISTORY OF MATHEMATICS, D. E. Smith. Most comprehensive non-technical history of math in English. In two volumes. Vol. I: A chronological examination of the growth of mathematics from primitive concepts up to 1900. Vol. II: The development of ideas in specific fields and areas, up through elementary calculus. The lives and works of over a thousand mathematicians are covered; thousands of specific historical problems and their solutions are clearly explained. Total of 510 illustrations, 1355pp. 5⅜ x 8. Set boxed in attractive container. T429, T430 Paperbound, the set **$5.00**

PHILOSOPHY AND THE PHYSICISTS, L. S. Stebbing. A philosopher examines the philosophical implications of modern science by posing a lively critical attack on the popular science expositions of Sir James Jeans and Arthur Eddington. xvi + 295pp. 5⅜ x 8.
T480 Paperbound **$1.65**

ON MATHEMATICS AND MATHEMATICIANS, R. E. Moritz. The first collection of quotations by and about mathematicians in English. 1140 anecdotes, aphorisms, definitions, speculations, etc. give both mathematicians and layman stimulating new insights into what mathematics is, and into the personalities of the great mathematicians from Archimedes to Euler, Gauss, Klein, Weierstrass. Invaluable to teachers, writers. Extensive cross index. 410pp. 5⅜ x 8.
T489 Paperbound **$1.95**

NATURAL SCIENCE, BIOLOGY, GEOLOGY, TRAVEL

A SHORT HISTORY OF ANATOMY AND PHYSIOLOGY FROM THE GREEKS TO HARVEY, C. Singer. A great medical historian's fascinating intermediate account of the slow advance of anatomical and physiological knowledge from pre-scientific times to Vesalius, Harvey. 139 unusually interesting illustrations. 221pp. 5⅜ x 8. T389 Paperbound **$1.75**

THE BEHAVIOUR AND SOCIAL LIFE OF HONEYBEES, Ronald Ribbands. The most comprehensive, lucid and authoritative book on bee habits, communication, duties, cell life, motivations, etc. "A MUST for every scientist, experimenter, and educator, and a happy and valuable selection for all interested in the honeybee," AMERICAN BEE JOURNAL. 690-item bibliography. 127 illus.; 11 photographic plates. 352pp. 5⅜ x 8⅜. S410 Clothbound **$4.50**

TRAVELS OF WILLIAM BARTRAM, edited by Mark Van Doren. One of the 18th century's most delightful books, and one of the few first-hand sources of information about American geography, natural history, and anthropology of American Indian tribes of the time. "The mind of a scientist with the soul of a poet," John Livingston Lowes. 13 original illustrations, maps. Introduction by Mark Van Doren. 448pp. 5⅜ x 8. T326 Paperbound **$2.00**

STUDIES ON THE STRUCTURE AND DEVELOPMENT OF VERTEBRATES, Edwin Goodrich. The definitive study of the skeleton, fins and limbs, head region, divisions of the body cavity, vascular, respiratory, excretory systems, etc., of vertebrates from fish to higher mammals, by the greatest comparative anatomist of recent times. "The standard textbook," JOURNAL OF ANATOMY. 754 illus. 69-page biographical study. 1186-item bibliography. 2 vols. Total of 906pp. 5⅜ x 8. Vol. I: S449 Paperbound **$2.50**
Vol. II: S450 Paperbound **$2.50**

DOVER BOOKS

THE BIRTH AND DEVELOPMENT OF THE GEOLOGICAL SCIENCES, F. D. Adams. The most complete and thorough history of the earth sciences in print. Covers over 300 geological thinkers and systems; treats fossils, theories of stone growth, paleontology, earthquakes, vulcanists vs. neptunists, odd theories, etc. 91 illustrations, including medieval, Renaissance wood cuts, etc. 632 footnotes and bibliographic notes. 511pp. 308pp. 5⅜ x 8.   T5 Paperbound **$2.00**

FROM MAGIC TO SCIENCE, Charles Singer. A close study of aspects of medical science from the Roman Empire through the Renaissance. The sections on early herbals, and "The Visions of Hildegarde of Bingen," are probably the best studies of these subjects available. 158 unusual classic and medieval illustrations. xxvii + 365pp. 5⅜ x 8.   T390 Paperbound **$2.00**

SAILING ALONE AROUND THE WORLD, Captain Joshua Slocum. Captain Slocum's personal account of his single-handed voyage around the world in a 34-foot boat he rebuilt himself. A classic of both seamanship and descriptive writing. "A nautical equivalent of Thoreau's account," Van Wyck Brooks. 67 illus. 308pp. 5⅜ x 8.   T326 Paperbound **$1.00**

TREES OF THE EASTERN AND CENTRAL UNITED STATES AND CANADA, W. M. Harlow. Standard middle-level guide designed to help you know the characteristics of Eastern trees and identify them at sight by means of an 8-page synoptic key. More than 600 drawings and photographs of twigs, leaves, fruit, other features. xiii + 288pp. 4⅝ x 6½.
T395 Paperbound **$1.35**

FRUIT KEY AND TWIG KEY ("Fruit Key to Northeastern Trees," "Twig Key to Deciduous Woody Plants of Eastern North America"), **W. M. Harlow.** Identify trees in fall, winter, spring. Easy-to-use, synoptic keys, with photographs of every twig and fruit identified. Covers 120 different fruits, 160 different twigs. Over 350 photos. Bibliographies. Glossaries. Total of 143pp. 5⅝ x 8⅜.   T511 Paperbound **$1.25**

INTRODUCTION TO THE STUDY OF EXPERIMENTAL MEDICINE, Claude Bernard. This classic records Bernard's far-reaching efforts to transform physiology into an exact science. It covers problems of vivisection, the limits of physiological experiment, hypotheses in medical experimentation, hundreds of others. Many of his own famous experiments on the liver, the pancreas, etc., are used as examples. Foreword by I. B. Cohen. xxv + 266pp. 5⅜ x 8.
T400 Paperbound **$1.50**

THE ORIGIN OF LIFE, A. I. Oparin. The first modern statement that life evolved from complex nitro-carbon compounds, carefully presented according to modern biochemical knowledge of primary colloids, organic molecules, etc. Begins with historical introduction to the problem of the origin of life. Bibliography. xxv + 270pp. 5⅜ x 8.   S213 Paperbound **$1.75**

A HISTORY OF ASTRONOMY FROM THALES TO KEPLER, J. L. E. Dreyer. The only work in English which provides a detailed picture of man's cosmological views from Egypt, Babylonia, Greece, and Alexandria to Copernicus, Tycho Brahe and Kepler. "Standard reference on Greek astronomy and the Copernican revolution," SKY AND TELESCOPE. Formerly called "A History of Planetary Systems From Thales to Kepler." Bibliography. 21 diagrams. xvii + 430pp. 5⅜ x 8.
S79 Paperbound **$1.98**

URANIUM PROSPECTING, H. L. Barnes. A professional geologist tells you what you need to know. Hundreds of facts about minerals, tests, detectors, sampling, assays, claiming, developing, government regulations, etc. Glossary of technical terms. Annotated bibliography. x + 117pp. 5⅜ x 8.   T309 Paperbound **$1.00**

DE RE METALLICA, Georgius Agricola. All 12 books of this 400 year old classic on metals and metal production, fully annotated, and containing all 289 of the 16th century woodcuts which made the original an artistic masterpiece. A superb gift for geologists, engineers, libraries, artists, historians. Translated by Herbert Hoover & L. H. Hoover. Bibliography, survey of ancient authors. 289 illustrations of the excavating, assaying, smelting, refining, and countless other metal production operations described in the text. 672pp. 6¾ x 10¾. Deluxe library edition.   S6 Clothbound **$10.00**

DE MAGNETE, William Gilbert. A landmark of science by the man who first used the word "electricity," distinguished between static electricity and magnetism, and founded a new science. P. F. Mottelay translation. 90 figures. lix + 368pp. 5⅜ x 8.   S470 Paperbound **$2.00**

THE AUTOBIOGRAPHY OF CHARLES DARWIN AND SELECTED LETTERS, Francis Darwin, ed. Fascinating documents on Darwin's early life, the voyage of the "Beagle," the discovery of evolution, Darwin's thought on mimicry, plant development, vivisection, evolution, many other subjects. Letters to Henslow, Lyell, Hooker, Wallace, Kingsley, etc. Appendix. 365pp. 5⅜ x 8.   T479 Paperbound **$1.65**

A WAY OF LIFE AND OTHER SELECTED WRITINGS OF SIR WILLIAM OSLER. 16 of the great physician, teacher and humanist's most inspiring writings on a practical philosophy of life, science and the humanities, and the history of medicine. 5 photographs. Introduction by G. L. Keynes, M.D., F.R.C.S. xx + 278pp. 5⅜ x 8.   T488 Paperbound **$1.50**

WORLD DRAMA, B. H. Clark. 46 plays from Ancient Greece, Rome, to India, China, Japan. Plays by Aeschylus, Sophocles, Euripides, Aristophanes, Plautus, Marlowe, Jonson, Farquhar, Goldsmith, Cervantes, Molière, Dumas, Goethe, Schiller, Ibsen, many others. One of the most comprehensive collections of important plays from all literature available in English. Over ⅓ of this material is unavailable in any other current edition. Reading lists. 2 volumes. Total of 1364pp. 5⅜ x 8.

Vol. I, T57 Paperbound **$2.00**
Vol. II, T59 Paperbound **$2.00**

MASTERS OF THE DRAMA, John Gassner. The most comprehensive history of the drama in print. Covers more than 800 dramatists and over 2000 plays from the Greeks to modern Western, Near Eastern, Oriental drama. Plot summaries, theatre history, etc. "Best of its kind in English," NEW REPUBLIC. 35 pages of bibliography. 77 photos and drawings. Deluxe edition. xxii + 890pp. 5⅜ x 8.
T100 Clothbound **$5.95**

THE DRAMA OF LUIGI PIRANDELLO, D. Vittorini. All 38 of Pirandello's plays (to 1935) summarized and analyzed in terms of symbolic techniques, plot structure, etc. The only authorized work. Foreword by Pirandello. Biography. Bibliography. xiii + 350pp. 5⅜ x 8.
T435 Paperbound **$1.98**

ARISTOTLE'S THEORY OF POETRY AND THE FINE ARTS, S. H. Butcher, ed. The celebrated "Butcher translation" faced page by page with the Greek text; Butcher's 300-page introduction to Greek poetic, dramatic thought. Modern Aristotelian criticism discussed by John Gassner. lxxvi + 421pp. 5⅜ x 8.

T42 Paperbound **$2.00**

EUGENE O'NEILL: THE MAN AND HIS PLAYS, B. H. Clark. The first published source-book on O'Neill's life and work. Analyzes each play from the early THE WEB up to THE ICEMAN COMETH. Supplies much information about environmental and dramatic influences. ix + 182pp. 5⅜ x 8.
T379 Paperbound **$1.25**

INTRODUCTION TO ENGLISH LITERATURE, B. Dobrée, ed. Most compendious literary aid in its price range. Extensive, categorized bibliography (with entries up to 1949) of more than 5,000 poets, dramatists, novelists, as well as historians, philosophers, economists, religious writers, travellers, and scientists of literary stature. Information about manuscripts, important biographical data. Critical, historical, background works not simply listed, but evaluated. Each volume also contains a long introduction to the period it covers.

Vol. I: **THE BEGINNINGS OF ENGLISH LITERATURE TO SKELTON, 1509,** W. L. Renwick. H. Orton. 450pp. 5⅛ x 7⅛.
T75 Clothbound **$3.50**

Vol. II: **THE ENGLISH RENAISSANCE, 1510-1688,** V. de Sola Pinto. 381pp. 5⅛ x 7⅛.
T76 Clothbound **$3.50**

Vol. III: **THE AUGUSTANS AND ROMANTICS, 1689-1830,** H. Dyson, J. Butt. 320pp. 5⅛ x·7⅛.
T77 Clothbound **$3.50**

Vol. IV: **THE VICTORIANS AND AFTER, 1830-1914,** E. Batho, B. Dobrée. 360pp. 5⅛ x 7⅛.
T78 Clothbound **$3.50**

EPIC AND ROMANCE, W. P. Ker. The standard survey of Medieval epic and romance by a foremost authority on Medieval literature. Covers historical background, plot, literary analysis, significance of Teutonic epics, Icelandic sagas, Beowulf, French chansons de geste, the Niebelungenlied, Arthurian romances, much more. 422pp. 5⅜ x 8.
T355 Paperbound **$1.95**

THE HEART OF EMERSON'S JOURNALS, Bliss Perry, ed. Emerson's most intimate thoughts, impressions, records of conversations with Channing, Hawthorne, Thoreau, etc., carefully chosen from the 10 volumes of The Journals. "The essays do not reveal the power of Emerson's mind . . .as do these hasty and informal writings," N. Y. TIMES. Preface by B. Perry. 370pp. 5⅜ x 8.
T447 Paperbound **$1.85**

A SOURCE BOOK IN THEATRICAL HISTORY, A. M. Nagler. (Formerly, "Sources of Theatrical History.") Over 300 selected passages by contemporary observers tell about styles of acting, direction, make-up, scene designing, etc., in the theatre's great periods from ancient Greece to the Théâtre Libre. "Indispensable complement to the study of drama," EDUCATIONAL THEATRE JOURNAL. Prof. Nagler, Yale Univ. School of Drama, also supplies notes, references. 85 illustrations. 611pp. 5⅜ x 8.
T515 Paperbound **$2.75**

THE ART OF THE STORY-TELLER, M. L. Shedlock. Regarded as the finest, most helpful book on telling stories to children, by a great story-teller. How to catch, hold, recapture attention; how to choose material; many other aspects. Also includes: a 99-page selection of Miss Shedlock's most successful stories; extensive bibliography of other stories. xxi + 320pp. 5⅜ x 8.
T245 Clothbound **$3.50**

THE DEVIL'S DICTIONARY, Ambrose Bierce. Over 1000 short, ironic definitions in alphabetical order, by America's greatest satirist in the classical tradition. "Some of the most gorgeous witticisms in the English language," H. L. Mencken. 144pp. 5⅜ x 8.   T487 Paperbound **$1.00**

MUSIC

A DICTIONARY OF HYMNOLOGY, John Julian. More than 30,000 entries on individual hymns, their authorship, textual variations, location of texts, dates and circumstances of composition, denominational and ritual usages, the biographies of more than 9,000 hymn writers, essays on important topics such as children's hymns and Christmas carols, and hundreds of thousands of other important facts about hymns which are virtually impossible to find anywhere else. Convenient alphabetical listing, and a 200-page double-columned index of first lines enable you to track down virtually any hymn ever written. Total of 1786pp. 6¼ x 9¼. 2 volumes. T133. The Set, Clothbound **$15.00**

STRUCTURAL HEARING, TONAL COHERENCE IN MUSIC, Felix Salzer. Extends the well-known Schenker approach to include modern music, music of the middle ages, and Renaissance music. Explores the phenomenon of tonal organization by discussing more than 500 compositions, and offers unusual new insights into the theory of composition and musical relationships. "The foundation on which all teaching in music theory has been based at this college," Leopold Mannes, President, The Mannes College of Music. Total of 658pp. 6½ x 9¼. 2 volumes. S418 The set, Clothbound **$8.00**

A GENERAL HISTORY OF MUSIC, Charles Burney. The complete history of music from the Greeks up to 1789 by the 18th century musical historian who personally knew the great Baroque composers. Covers sacred and secular, vocal and instrumental, operatic and symphonic music; treats theory, notation, forms, instruments; discusses composers, performers, important works. Invaluable as a source of information on the period for students, historians, musicians. "Surprisingly few of Burney's statements have been invalidated by modern research . . . still of great value," NEW YORK TIMES. Edited and corrected by Frank Mercer. 35 figures. 1915pp. 5½ x 8½. 2 volumes. T36 The set, Clothbound **$12.50**

JOHANN SEBASTIAN BACH, Phillip Spitta. Recognized as one of the greatest accomplishments of musical scholarship and far and away the definitive coverage of Bach's works. Hundreds of individual pieces are analyzed. Major works, such as the B Minor Mass and the St. Matthew Passion are examined in minute detail. Spitta also deals with the works of Buxtehude, Pachelbel, and others of the period. Can be read with profit even by those without a knowledge of the technicalities of musical composition. "Unchallenged as the last word on one of the supreme geniuses of music," John Barkham, SATURDAY REVIEW SYNDICATE. Total of 1819pp. 5⅜ x 8. 2 volumes. T252 The set, Clothbound **$10.00**

HISTORY

THE IDEA OF PROGRESS, J. B. Bury. Prof. Bury traces the evolution of a central concept of Western civilization in Greek, Roman, Medieval, and Renaissance thought to its flowering in the 17th and 18th centuries. Introduction by Charles Beard. xl + 357pp. 5⅜ x 8.
T39 Clothbound **$3.95**
T40 Paperbound **$1.95**

THE ANCIENT GREEK HISTORIANS, J. B. Bury. Greek historians such as Herodotus, Thucydides, Xenophon; Roman historians such as Tacitus, Caesar, Livy; scores of others fully analyzed in terms of sources, concepts, influences, etc., by a great scholar and historian. 291pp. 5⅜ x 8. T397 Paperbound **$1.50**

HISTORY OF THE LATER ROMAN EMPIRE, J. B. Bury. The standard work on the Byzantine Empire from 395 A.D. to the death of Justinian in 565 A.D., by the leading Byzantine scholar of our time. Covers political, social, cultural, theological, military history. Quotes contemporary documents extensively. "Most unlikely that it will ever be superseded," Glanville Downey, Dumbarton Oaks Research Library. Genealogical tables. 5 maps. Bibliography. 2 vols. Total of 965pp. 5⅜ x 8. T398, T399 Paperbound, the set **$4.00**

GARDNER'S PHOTOGRAPHIC SKETCH BOOK OF THE CIVIL WAR, Alexander Gardner. One of the rarest and most valuable Civil War photographic collections exactly reproduced for the first time since 1866. Scenes of Manassas, Bull Run, Harper's Ferry, Appomattox, Mechanicsville, Fredericksburg, Gettysburg, etc.; battle ruins, prisons, arsenals, a slave pen, fortifications; Lincoln on the field, officers, men, corpses. By one of the most famous pioneers in documentary photography. Original copies of the "Sketch Book" sold for $425 in 1952. Introduction by E. Bleiler. 100 full-page 7 x 10 photographs (original size). 244pp. 10¾ x 8½.
T476 Clothbound **$6.00**

THE WORLD'S GREAT SPEECHES, L. Copeland and L. Lamm, eds. 255 speeches from Pericles to Churchill, Dylan Thomas. Invaluable as a guide to speakers; fascinating as history past and present; a source of much difficult-to-find material. Includes an extensive section of informal and humorous speeches. 3 indices: Topic, Author, Nation. xx + 745pp. 5⅜ x 8.
T468 Paperbound **$2.49**

FOUNDERS OF THE MIDDLE AGES, E. K. Rand. The best non-technical discussion of the transformation of Latin paganism into medieval civilization. Tertullian, Gregory, Jerome, Boethius, Augustine, the Neoplatonists, other crucial figures, philosophies examined. Excellent for the intelligent non-specialist. "Extraordinarily accurate," Richard McKeon, THE NATION. ix + 365pp. 5⅜ x 8. T369 Paperbound **$1.85**

THE POLITICAL THOUGHT OF PLATO AND ARISTOTLE, Ernest Barker. The standard, comprehensive exposition of Greek political thought. Covers every aspect of the "Republic" and the "Politics" as well as minor writings, other philosophers, theorists of the period, and the later history of Greek political thought. Unabridged edition. 584pp. 5⅜ x 8.
T521 Paperbound **$1.85**

PHILOSOPHY

THE GIFT OF LANGUAGE, M. Schlauch. (Formerly, "The Gift of Tongues.") A sound, middle-level treatment of linguistic families, word histories, grammatical processes, semantics, language taboos, word-coining of Joyce, Cummings, Stein, etc. 232 bibliographical notes. 350pp. 5⅜ x 8.
T243 Paperbound **$1.85**

THE PHILOSOPHY OF HEGEL, W. T. Stace. The first work in English to give a complete and connected view of Hegel's entire system. Especially valuable to those who do not have time to study the highly complicated original texts, yet want an accurate presentation by a most reputable scholar of one of the most influential 19th century thinkers. Includes a 14 x 20 fold-out chart of Hegelian system. 536pp. 5⅜ x 8.
T254 Paperbound **$2.00**

ARISTOTLE, A. E. Taylor. A lucid, non-technical account of Aristotle written by a foremost Platonist. Covers life and works; thought on matter, form, causes, logic, God, physics, metaphysics, etc. Bibliography. New index compiled for this edition. 128pp. 5⅜ x 8.
T280 Paperbound **$1.00**

GUIDE TO PHILOSOPHY, C. E. M. Joad. This basic work describes the major philosophic problems and evaluates the answers propounded by great philosophers from the Greeks to Whitehead, Russell. "The finest introduction," BOSTON TRANSCRIPT. Bibliography, 592pp. 5⅜ x 8.
T297 Paperbound **$2.00**

LANGUAGE AND MYTH, E. Cassirer. Cassirer's brilliant demonstration that beneath both language and myth lies an unconscious "grammar" of experience whose categories and canons are not those of logical thought. Introduction and translation by Susanne Langer. Index. x + 103pp. 5⅜ x 8.
T51 Paperbound **$1.25**

SUBSTANCE AND FUNCTION, EINSTEIN'S THEORY OF RELATIVITY, E. Cassirer. This double volume contains the German philosopher's profound philosophical formulation of the differences between traditional logic and the new logic of science. Number, space, energy, relativity, many other topics are treated in detail. Authorized translation by W. C. and M. C. Swabey. xii + 465pp. 5⅜ x 8.
T50 Paperbound **$2.00**

THE PHILOSOPHICAL WORKS OF DESCARTES. The definitive English edition, in two volumes, of all major philosophical works and letters of René Descartes, father of modern philosophy of knowledge and science. Translated by E. S. Haldane and G. Ross. Introductory notes. Total of 842pp. 5⅜ x 8.
T71 Vol. 1, Paperbound **$2.00**
T72 Vol. 2, Paperbound **$2.00**

ESSAYS IN EXPERIMENTAL LOGIC, J. Dewey. Based upon Dewey's theory that knowledge implies a judgment which in turn implies an inquiry, these papers consider such topics as the thought of Bertrand Russell, pragmatism, the logic of values, antecedents of thought, data and meanings. 452pp. 5⅜ x 8.
T73 Paperbound **$1.95**

THE PHILOSOPHY OF HISTORY, G. W. F. Hegel. This classic of Western thought is Hegel's detailed formulation of the thesis that history is not chance but a rational process, the realization of the Spirit of Freedom. Translated and introduced by J. Sibree. Introduction by C. Hegel. Special introduction for this edition by Prof. Carl Friedrich, Harvard University. xxxix + 447pp. 5⅜ x 8.
T112 Paperbound **$1.85**

THE WILL TO BELIEVE and **HUMAN IMMORTALITY, W. James.** Two of James's most profound investigations of human belief in God and immortality, bound as one volume. Both are powerful expressions of James's views on chance vs. determinism, pluralism vs. monism, will and intellect, arguments for survival after death, etc. Two prefaces. 429pp. 5⅜ x 8.
T294 Clothbound **$3.75**
T291 Paperbound **$1.65**

INTRODUCTION TO SYMBOLIC LOGIC, S. Langer. A lucid, general introduction to modern logic, covering forms, classes, the use of symbols, the calculus of propositions, the Boole-Schroeder and the Russell-Whitehead systems, etc. "One of the clearest and simplest introductions," MATHEMATICS GAZETTE. Second, enlarged, revised edition. 368pp. 5⅜ x 8.
S164 Paperbound **$1.75**

MIND AND THE WORLD-ORDER, C. I. Lewis. Building upon the work of Peirce, James, and Dewey, Professor Lewis outlines a theory of knowledge in terms of "conceptual pragmatism," and demonstrates why the traditional understanding of the a priori must be abandoned. Appendices. xiv + 446pp. 5⅜ x 8.
T359 Paperbound **$1.95**

THE GUIDE FOR THE PERPLEXED, M. Maimonides One of the great philosophical works of all time, Maimonides' formulation of the meeting-ground between Old Testament and Aristotelian thought is essential to anyone interested in Jewish, Christian, and Moslem thought in the Middle Ages. 2nd revised edition of the Friedländer translation. Extensive introduction. lix + 414pp. 5⅜ x 8.
T351 Paperbound **$1.85**

DOVER BOOKS

THE PHILOSOPHICAL WRITINGS OF PEIRCE, J. Buchler, ed. (Formerly, "The Philosophy of Peirce.") This carefully integrated selection of Peirce's papers is considered the best coverage of the complete thought of one of the greatest philosophers of modern times. Covers Peirce's work on the theory of signs, pragmatism, epistemology, symbolic logic, the scientific method, chance, etc. xvi + 386pp. 5 ⅜ x 8.   T216 Clothbound **$5.00**
                                                                        T217 Paperbound **$1.95**

HISTORY OF ANCIENT PHILOSOPHY, W. Windelband. Considered the clearest survey of Greek and Roman philosophy. Examines Thales, Anaximander, Anaximenes, Heraclitus, the Eleatics, Empedocles, the Pythagoreans, the Sophists, Socrates, Democritus, Stoics, Epicureans, Sceptics, Neo-platonists, etc. 50 pages on Plato; 70 on Aristotle. 2nd German edition tr. by H. E. Cushman. xv + 393pp. 5⅜ x 8.   T357 Paperbound **$1.75**

INTRODUCTION TO SYMBOLIC LOGIC AND ITS APPLICATIONS, R. Carnap. A comprehensive, rigorous introduction to modern logic by perhaps its greatest living master. Includes demonstrations of applications in mathematics, physics, biology. "Of the rank of a masterpiece," Z. für Mathematik und ihre Grenzgebiete. Over 300 exercises. xvi + 241pp. 5⅜ x 8.   Clothbound **$4.00**
                                                                        S453 Paperbound **$1.85**

SCEPTICISM AND ANIMAL FAITH, G. Santayana. Santayana's unusually lucid exposition of the difference between the independent existence of objects and the essence our mind attributes to them, and of the necessity of scepticism as a form of belief and animal faith as a necessary condition of knowledge. Discusses belief, memory, intuition, symbols, etc. xii + 314pp. 5⅜ x 8.   T235 Clothbound **$3.50**
                                                                        T236 Paperbound **$1.50**

THE ANALYSIS OF MATTER, B. Russell. With his usual brilliance, Russell analyzes physics, causality, scientific inference, Weyl's theory, tensors, invariants, periodicity, etc. in order to discover the basic concepts of scientific thought about matter. "Most thorough treatment of the subject," THE NATION. Introduction. 8 figures. viii + 408pp. 5⅜ x 8.
                                                                        T231 Paperbound **$1.95**

THE SENSE OF BEAUTY, G. Santayana. This important philosophical study of why, when, and how beauty appears, and what conditions must be fulfilled, is in itself a revelation of the beauty of language. "It is doubtful if a better treatment of the subject has since appeared," PEABODY JOURNAL. ix + 275pp. 5⅜ x 8.   T238 Paperbound **$1.00**

THE CHIEF WORKS OF SPINOZA. In two volumes. Vol. I: The Theologico-Political Treatise and the Political Treatise. Vol. II: On the Improvement of Understanding, The Ethics, and Selected Letters. The permanent and enduring ideas in these works on God, the universe, religion, society, etc., have had tremendous impact on later philosophical works. Introduction. Total of 862pp. 5⅜ x 8.   T249 Vol. I, Paperbound **$1.50**
                                                                        T250 Vol. II, Paperbound **$1.50**

TRAGIC SENSE OF LIFE, M. de Unamuno. The acknowledged masterpiece of one of Spain's most influential thinkers. Between the despair at the inevitable death of man and all his works, and the desire for immortality, Unamuno finds a "saving incertitude." Called "a masterpiece," by the ENCYCLOPAEDIA BRITANNICA. xxx + 332pp. 5⅜ x 8.
                                                                        T257 Paperbound **$1.95**

EXPERIENCE AND NATURE, John Dewey. The enlarged, revised edition of the Paul Carus lectures (1925). One of Dewey's clearest presentations of the philosophy of empirical naturalism which reestablishes the continuity between "inner" experience and "outer" nature. These lectures are among the most significant ever delivered by an American philosopher. 457pp. 5⅜ x 8.   T471 Paperbound **$1.85**

PHILOSOPHY AND CIVILIZATION IN THE MIDDLE AGES, M. de Wulf. A semi-popular survey of medieval intellectual life, religion, philosophy, science, the arts, etc. that covers feudalism vs. Catholicism, rise of the universities, mendicant orders, and similar topics. Bibliography. viii + 320pp. 5⅜ x 8.   T284 Paperbound **$1.75**

AN INTRODUCTION TO SCHOLASTIC PHILOSOPHY, M. de Wulf. (Formerly, "Scholasticism Old and New.") Prof. de Wulf covers the central scholastic tradition from St. Anselm, Albertus Magnus, Thomas Aquinas, up to Suarez in the 17th century; and then treats the modern revival of. scholasticism, the Louvain position, relations with Kantianism and positivism, etc. xvi + 271pp. 5⅜ x 8.   T296 Clothbound **$3.50**
                                                                        T283 Paperbound **$1.75**

A HISTORY OF MODERN PHILOSOPHY, H. Höffding. An exceptionally clear and detailed coverage of Western philosophy from the Renaissance to the end of the 19th century. Both major and minor figures are examined in terms of theory of knowledge, logic, cosmology, psychology. Covers Pomponazzi, Bodin, Boehme, Telesius, Bruno, Copernicus, Descartes, Spinoza, Hobbes, Locke, Hume, Kant, Fichte, Schopenhauer, Mill, Spencer, Langer, scores of others. A standard reference work. 2 volumes. Total of 1159pp. 5⅜ x 8.   T117 Vol. 1, Paperbound **$2.00**
                                                                        T118 Vol. 2, Paperbound **$2.00**

LANGUAGE, TRUTH AND LOGIC, A. J. Ayer. The first full-length development of Logical Posivitism in English. Building on the work of Schlick, Russell, Carnap, and the Vienna school, Ayer presents the tenets of one of the most important systems of modern philosophical thought. 160pp. 5⅜ x 8.   T10 Paperbound **$1.25**

ORIENTALIA AND RELIGION

THE MYSTERIES OF MITHRA, F. Cumont. The great Belgian scholar's definitive study of the Persian mystery religion that almost vanquished Christianity in the ideological struggle for the Roman Empire. A masterpiece of scholarly detection that reconstructs secret doctrines, organization, rites. Mithraic art is discussed and analyzed. 70 illus. 239pp. 5⅜ x 8.
T323 Paperbound **$1.85**

CHRISTIAN AND ORIENTAL PHILOSOPHY OF ART. A. K. Coomaraswamy. The late art historian and orientalist discusses artistic symbolism, the role of traditional culture in enriching art, medieval art, folklore, philosophy of art, other similar topics. Bibliography. 148pp. 5⅜ x 8.
T378 Paperbound **$1.25**

TRANSFORMATION OF NATURE IN ART, A. K. Coomaraswamy. A basic work on Asiatic religious art. Includes discussions of religious art in Asia and Medieval Europe (exemplified by Meister Eckhart), the origin and use of images in Indian art, Indian Medieval aesthetic manuals, and other fascinating, little known topics. Glossaries of Sanskrit and Chinese terms. Bibliography. 41pp. of notes. 245pp. 5⅜ x 8.
T368 Paperbound **$1.75**

ORIENTAL RELIGIONS IN ROMAN PAGANISM, F. Cumont. This well-known study treats the ecstatic cults of Syria and Phrygia (Cybele, Attis, Adonis, their orgies and mutilatory rites); the mysteries of Egypt (Serapis, Isis, Osiris); Persian dualism; Mithraic cults; Hermes Trismegistus, Ishtar, Astarte, etc. and their influence on the religious thought of the Roman Empire. Introduction. 55pp. of notes; extensive bibliography. xxiv + 298pp. 5⅜ x 8.
T321 Paperbound **$1.75**

ANTHROPOLOGY, SOCIOLOGY, AND PSYCHOLOGY

PRIMITIVE MAN AS PHILOSOPHER, P. Radin. A standard anthropological work based on Radin's investigations of the Winnebago, Maori, Batak, Zuni, other primitive tribes. Describes primitive thought on the purpose of life, marital relations, death, personality, gods, etc. Extensive selections of õriginal primitive documents. Bibliography. xviii + 420pp. 5⅜ x 8.
T392 Paperbound **$2.00**

PRIMITIVE RELIGION, P. Radin. Radin's thoroughgoing treatment of supernatural beliefs, shamanism, initiations, religious expression, etc. in primitive societies. Arunta, Ashanti, Aztec, Bushman, Crow, Fijian, many other tribes examined. "Excellent," NATURE. New preface by the author. Bibliographic notes. x + 322pp. 5⅜ x 8.   T393 Paperbound **$1.85**

SEX IN PSYCHO-ANALYSIS, S. Ferenczi. (Formerly, "Contributions to Psycho-analysis.") 14 selected papers on impotence, transference, analysis and children, dreams, obscene words, homosexuality, paranoia, etc. by an associate of Freud. Also included: THE DEVELOPMENT OF PSYCHO-ANALYSIS, by Ferenczi and Otto Rank. Two books bound as one. Total of 406pp. 5⅜ x 8.
T324 Paperbound **$1.85**

THE PRINCIPLES OF PSYCHOLOGY, William James. The complete text of the famous "long course," one of the great books of Western thought. An almost incredible amount of information about psychological processes, the stream of consciousness, habit, time perception, memory, emotions, reason, consciousness of self, abnormal phenomena, and similar topics. Based on James's own discoveries integrated with the work of Descartes, Locke, Hume, Royce, Wundt, Berkeley, Lotse, Herbart, scores of others. "A classic of interpretation," PSYCHIATRIC QUARTERLY. 94 illus. 1408pp. 2 volumes. 5⅜ x 8.
T381 Vol. 1, Paperbound **$2.50**
T382 Vol. 2, Paperbound **$2.50**

THE POLISH PEASANT IN EUROPE AND AMERICA, W. I. Thomas, F. Znaniecki. Monumental sociological study of peasant primary groups (family and community) and the disruptions produced by a new industrial system and emigration to America, by two of the foremost sociologists of recent times. One of the most important works in sociological thought. Includes hundreds of pages of primary documentation; point by point analysis of causes of social decay, breakdown of morality, crime, drunkenness, prostitution, etc. 2nd revised edition. 2 volumes. Total of 2250pp. 6 x 9.   T478 2 volume set, Clothbound **$12.50**

FOLKWAYS, W. G. Sumner. The great Yale sociologist's detailed exposition of thousands of social, sexual, and religious customs in hundreds of cultures from ancient Greece to Modern Western societies. Preface by A. G. Keller. Introduction by William Lyon Phelps. 705pp. 5⅜ x 8.
S508 Paperbound **$2.49**

BEYOND PSYCHOLOGY, Otto Rank. The author, an early associate of Freud, uses psychoanalytic techniques of myth-analysis to explore ultimates of human existence. Treats love, immortality, the soul, sexual identity, kingship, sources of state power, many other topics which illuminate the irrational basis of human existence. 291pp. 5⅜ x 8.   T485 Paperbound **$1.75**

ILLUSIONS AND DELUSIONS OF THE SUPERNATURAL AND THE OCCULT, D. H. Rawcliffe. A rational, scientific examination of crystal gazing, automatic writing, table turning, stigmata, the Indian rope trick, dowsing, telepathy, clairvoyance, ghosts, ESP, PK, thousands of other supposedly occult phenomena. Originally titled "The Psychology of the Occult." 14 illustrations. 551pp. 5⅜ x 8.
T503 Paperbound **$2.00**

DOVER BOOKS

YOGA: A SCIENTIFIC EVALUATION, Kovoor T. Behanan. A scientific study of the physiological and psychological effects of Yoga discipline, written under the auspices of the Yale University Institute of Human Relations. Foreword by W. A. Miles, Yale Univ. 17 photographs. 290pp. 5⅜ x 8.   T505 Paperbound **$1.65**

HOAXES, C. D. MacDougall. Delightful, entertaining, yet scholarly exposition of how hoaxes start, why they succeed, documented with stories of hundreds of the most famous hoaxes. "A stupendous collection . . . and shrewd analysis, "NEW YORKER. New, revised edition. 54 photographs. 320pp. 5⅜ x 8.   T465 Paperbound **$1.75**

CREATIVE POWER: THE EDUCATION OF YOUTH IN THE CREATIVE ARTS, Hughes Mearns. Named by the National Education Association as one of the 20 foremost books on education in recent times. Tells how to help children express themselves in drama, poetry, music, art, develop latent creative power. Should be read by every parent, teacher. New, enlarged, revised edition. Introduction. 272pp. 5⅜ x 8.   T490 Paperbound **$1.50**

LANGUAGES

NEW RUSSIAN-ENGLISH, ENGLISH-RUSSIAN DICTIONARY, M. A. O'Brien. Over· 70,000 entries in new orthography! Idiomatic usages, colloquialisms. One of the few dictionaries that indicate accent changes in conjugation and declension. "One of the best," Prof. E. J. Simmons, Cornell. First names, geographical terms, bibliography, many other features. 738pp. 4½ x 6¼.   T208 Paperbound **$2.00**

MONEY CONVERTER AND TIPPING GUIDE FOR EUROPEAN TRAVEL, C. Vomacka. Invaluable, handy source of currency regulations, conversion tables, tipping rules, postal rates, much other travel information for every European country plus Israel, Egypt and Turkey. 128pp. 3½ x 5¼.   T260 Paperbound **60¢**

MONEY CONVERTER AND TIPPING GUIDE FOR TRAVEL IN THE AMERICAS (including the United States and Canada), **C. Vomacka.** The information you need for informed and confident travel in the Americas: money conversion tables, tipping guide, postal, telephone rates, etc. 128pp. 3½ x 5¼.   T261 Paperbound **65¢**

DUTCH-ENGLISH, ENGLISH-DUTCH DICTIONARY, F. G. Renier. The most convenient, practical Dutch-English dictionary on the market. New orthography. More than 60,000 entries: idioms, compounds, technical terms, etc. Gender of nouns indicated. xviii + 571pp. 5½ x 6¼.   T224 Clothbound **$2.50**

LEARN DUTCH!, F. G. Renier. The most satisfactory and easily-used grammar of modern Dutch. Used and recommended by the Fulbright Committee in the Netherlands. Over 1200 simple exercises lead to mastery of spoken and written Dutch. Dutch-English, English-Dutch vocabularies. 181pp. 4¼ x 7¼.   T441 Clothbound **$1.75**

PHRASE AND SENTENCE DICTIONARY OF SPOKEN RUSSIAN, English-Russian, Russian-English. Based on phrases and complete sentences, rather than isolated words; recognized as one of the best methods of learning the idiomatic speech of a country. Over 11,500 entries, indexed by single words, with more than 32,000 English and Russian sentences and phrases, in immediately usable form. Probably the largest list ever published. Shows accent changes in conjugation and declension; irregular forms listed in both alphabetical place and under main form of word. 15,000 word introduction covering Russian sounds, writing, grammar, syntax. 15-page appendix of geographical names, money, important signs, given names, foods, special Soviet terms, etc. Travellers, businessmen, students, government employees have found this their best source for Russian expressions. Originally published as U.S. Government Technical Manual TM 30-944. iv + 573pp. 5⅝ x 8⅜.   T496 Paperbound **$2.75**

PHRASE AND SENTENCE DICTIONARY OF SPOKEN SPANISH, Spanish-English, English-Spanish. Compiled from spoken Spanish, emphasizing idiom and colloquial usage in both Castilian and Latin-American. More than 16,000 entries containing over 25,000 idioms—the largest list of idiomatic constructions ever published. Complete sentences given, indexed under single words —language in immediately usable form, for travellers, businessmen, students, etc. 25-page introduction provides rapid survey of sounds, grammar, syntax, with full consideration of irregular verbs. Especially apt in modern treatment of phrases and structure. 17-page glossary gives translations of geographical names, money values, numbers, national holidays, important street signs, useful expressions of high frequency, plus unique 7-page glossary of Spanish and Spanish-American foods and dishes. Originally published as U.S. Government Technical Manual TM 30-900. iv + 513pp. 5⅝ x 8⅜.   T495 Paperbound **$1.75**

SAY IT language phrase books

"SAY IT" in the foreign language of your choice! We have sold over ½ million copies of these popular, useful language books. They will not make you an expert linguist overnight, but they do cover most practical matters of everyday life abroad.

Over 1000 useful phrases, expressions, with additional variants, substitutions.

Modern! Useful! Hundreds of phrases not available in other texts: "Nylon," "air-conditioned," etc.

The ONLY inexpensive phrase book **completely indexed.** Everything is available at a flip of your finger, ready for use.

Prepared by native linguists, travel experts.

Based on years of travel experience abroad.

This handy phrase book may be used by itself, or it may supplement any other text or course; it provides a living element. Used by many colleges and institutions: Hunter College; Barnard College; Army Ordnance School, Aberdeen; and many others.

Available, 1 book per language:

Danish (T818) 75¢
Dutch T(817) 75¢
English (for German-speaking people) (T801) 60¢
English (for Italian-speaking people) (T816) 60¢
English (for Spanish-speaking people) (T802) 60¢
Esperanto (T820) 75¢
French (T803) 60¢
German (T804) 60¢
Modern Greek (T813) 75¢
Hebrew (T805) 60¢

Italian (T806) 60¢
Japanese (T807) 60¢
Norwegian (T814) 75¢
Russian (T810) 75¢
Spanish (T811) 60¢
Turkish (T821) 75¢
Yiddish (T815) 75¢
Swedish (T812) 75¢
Polish (T808) 75¢
Portuguese (T809) 75¢

LISTEN & LEARN language record sets

LISTEN & LEARN is the only language record course designed especially to meet your travel needs, or help you learn essential foreign language quickly by yourself, or in conjunction with any school course, by means of the automatic association method. Each set contains three 33⅓ rpm long- playing records — 1½ hours of recorded speech by eminent native speakers who are professors at Columbia, N.Y.U., Queens College and other leading universities. The sets are priced far below other sets of similar quality, yet they contain many special features not found in other record sets:

* Over 800 selected phrases and sentences, a basic vocabulary of over 3200 words.
* Both English and foreign language recorded; with a pause for your repetition.
* Designed for persons with limited time; no time wasted on material you cannot use immediately.
* Living, modern expressions that answer modern needs: drugstore items, "air-conditioned," etc.
* 128-196 page manuals contain everything on the records, plus simple pronunciation guides.
* Manual is fully indexed; find the phrase you want instantly.
* High fidelity recording—equal to any records costing up to $6 each.

The phrases on these records cover 41 different categories useful to the traveller or student interested in learning the living, spoken language: greetings, introductions, making yourself understood, passing customs, planes, trains, boats, buses, taxis, nightclubs, restaurants, menu items, sports, concerts, cameras, automobile travel, repairs, drugstores, doctors, dentists, medicines, barber shops, beauty parlors, laundries, many, many more.

"Excellent . . . among the very best on the market," Prof. Mario Pei, Dept. of Romance Languages, Columbia University. "Inexpensive and well-done . . . an ideal present," CHICAGO SUNDAY TRIBUNE. "More genuinely helpful than anything of its kind which I have previously encountered," Sidney Clark, well-known author of "ALL THE BEST" travel books. Each set contains 3 33⅓ rpm pure vinyl records, 128- 196 page with full record text, and album. One language per set. LISTEN & LEARN record sets are now available in—

FRENCH the set $4.95
ITALIAN the set $4.95
RUSSIAN the set $5.95

GERMAN the set $4.95
SPANISH the set $4.95
JAPANESE * the set $5.95

* Available Sept. 1, 1959

UNCONDITIONAL GUARANTEE: Dover Publications stands behind every Listen and Learn record set. If you are dissatisfied with these sets for any reason whatever, return them within 10 days and your money will be refunded in full.

ART HISTORY

STICKS AND STONES, Lewis Mumford. An examination of forces influencing American architecture: the medieval tradition in early New England, the classical influence in Jefferson's time, the Brown Decades, the imperial facade, the machine age, etc. "A truly remarkable book," SAT. REV. OF LITERATURE. 2nd revised edition. 21 illus. xvii + 228pp. 5⅜ x 8.
T202 Paperbound **$1.60**

THE AUTOBIOGRAPHY OF AN IDEA, Louis Sullivan. The architect whom Frank Lloyd Wright called "the master," records the development of the theories that revolutionized America's skyline. 34 full-page plates of Sullivan's finest work. New introduction by R. M. Line. xiv + 335pp. 5⅜ x 8.
T281 Paperbound **$1.85**

THE MATERIALS AND TECHNIQUES OF MEDIEVAL PAINTING, D. V. Thompson. An invaluable study of carriers and grounds, binding media, pigments, metals used in painting, al fresco and al secco techniques, burnishing, etc. used by the medieval masters. Preface by Bernard Berenson. 239pp. 5⅜ x 8.
T327 Paperbound **$1.85**

PRINCIPLES OF ART HISTORY, H. Wölfflin. This remarkably instructive work demonstrates the tremendous change in artistic conception from the 14th to the 18th centuries, by analyzing 164 works by Botticelli, Dürer, Hobbema, Holbein, Hals, Titian, Rembrandt, Vermeer, etc., and pointing out exactly what is meant by "baroque," "classic," "primitive," "picturesque," and other basic terms of art history and criticism. "A remarkable lesson in the art of seeing," SAT. REV. OF LITERATURE. Translated from the 7th German edition. 150 illus. 254pp. 6⅛ x 9¼.
T276 Paperbound **$2.00**

FOUNDATIONS OF MODERN ART, A. Ozenfant. Stimulating discussion of human creativity from paleolithic cave painting to modern painting, architecture, decorative arts. Fully illustrated with works of Gris, Lipchitz, Leger, Picasso, primitive, modern artifacts, architecture, industrial art, much more. 226 illustrations. 368pp. 6⅛ x 9¼.
T215 Paperbound **$1.95**

HANDICRAFTS, APPLIED ART, ART SOURCES, ETC.

WILD FOWL DECOYS, J. Barber. The standard work on this fascinating branch of folk art, ranging from Indian mud and grass devices to realistic wooden decoys. Discusses styles, types, periods; gives full information on how to make decoys. 140 illustrations (including 14 new plates) show decoys and provide full sets of plans for handicrafters, artists, hunters, and students of folk art. 281pp. 7⅞ x 10¾. Deluxe edition.
T11 Clothbound **$8.50**

METALWORK AND ENAMELLING, H. Maryon. Probably the best book ever written on the subject. Tells everything necessary for the home manufacture of jewelry, rings, ear pendants, bowls, etc. Covers materials, tools, soldering, filigree, setting stones, raising patterns, repoussé work, damascening, niello, cloisonné, polishing, assaying, casting, and dozens of other techniques. The best substitute for apprenticeship to a master metalworker. 363 photos and figures. 374pp. 5½ x 8½.
T183 Clothbound **$7.50**

SHAKER FURNITURE, E. D. and F. Andrews. The most illuminating study of Shaker furniture ever written. Covers chronology, craftsmanship, houses, shops, etc. Includes over 200 photographs of chairs, tables, clocks, beds, benches, etc. "Mr. & Mrs. Andrews know all there is to know about Shaker furniture," Mark Van Doren, NATION. 48 full-page plates. 192pp. Deluxe cloth binding. 7⅞ x 10¾.
T7 Clothbound **$6.00**

PRIMITIVE ART, Franz Boas. A great American anthropologist covers theory, technical virtuosity, styles, symbolism, patterns, etc. of primitive art. The more than 900 illustrations will interest artists, designers, craftworkers. Over 900 illustrations. 376pp. 5⅜ x 8.
T25 Paperbound **$1.95**

ON THE LAWS OF JAPANESE PAINTING, H. Bowie. The best possible substitute for lessons from an oriental master. Treats both spirit and technique; exercises for control of the brush; inks, brushes, colors; use of dots, lines to express whole moods, etc. 220 illus. 132pp. 6⅛ x 9¼.
T30 Paperbound **$1.95**

HANDBOOK OF ORNAMENT, F. S. Meyer. One of the largest collections of copyright-free traditional art: over 3300 line cuts of Greek, Roman, Medieval, Renaissance, Baroque, 18th and 19th century art motifs (tracery, geometric elements, flower and animal motifs, etc.) and decorated objects (chairs, thrones, weapons, vases, jewelry, armor, etc.). Full text. 3300 illustrations. 562pp. 5⅜ x 8.
T302 Paperbound **$2.00**

THREE CLASSICS OF ITALIAN CALLIGRAPHY. Oscar Ogg, ed. Exact reproductions of three famous Renaissance calligraphic works: Arrighi's OPERINA and IL MODO, Tagliente's LO PRESENTE LIBRO, and Palatino's LIBRO NUOVO. More than 200 complete alphabets, thousands of lettered specimens, in Papal Chancery and other beautiful, ornate handwriting. Introduction by Oscar Ogg. 245 plates. 282pp. 6⅛ x 9¼.
T212 Paperbound **$1.95**

THE HISTORY AND TECHNIQUES OF LETTERING, A. Nesbitt. A thorough history of lettering from the ancient Egyptians to the present, and a 65-page course in lettering for artists. Every major development in lettering history is illustrated by a complete alphabet. Fully analyzes such masters as Caslon, Koch, Garamont, Jenson, and many more. 89 alphabets, 165 other specimens. 317pp. 5⅜ x 8.
T427 Paperbound **$2.00**

LETTERING AND ALPHABETS, J. A. Cavanagh. An unabridged reissue of "Lettering," containing the full discussion, analysis, illustration of 89 basic hand lettering tyles based on Caslon, Bodoni, Gothic, many other types. Hundreds of technical hints on construction, strokes, pens, brushes, etc. 89 alphabets, 72 lettered specimens, which may be reproduced permission-free. 121pp. 9¾ x 8. **T53 Paperbound $1.25**

THE HUMAN FIGURE IN MOTION, Eadweard Muybridge. The largest collection in print of Muybridge's famous high-speed action photos. 4789 photographs in more than 500 action-strip-sequences (at shutter speeds up to 1/6000th of a second) illustrate men, women, children—mostly undraped—performing such actions as walking, running, getting up, lying down, carrying objects, throwing, etc. "An unparalleled dictionary of action for all artists," AMERICAN ARTIST. 390 full-page plates, with 4789 photographs. Heavy glossy stock, reinforced binding with headbands. 7⅞ x 10¾. **T204 Clothbound $10.00**

ANIMALS IN MOTION, Eadweard Muybridge. The largest collection of animal action photos in print. 34 different animals (horses, mules, oxen, goats, camels, pigs, cats, lions, gnus, deer, monkeys, eagles—and 22 others) in 132 characteristic actions. All 3919 photographs are taken in series at speeds up to 1/1600th of a second, offering artists, biologists, cartoonists a remarkable opportunity to see exactly how an ostrich's head bobs when running, how a lion puts his foot down, how an elephant's knee bends, how a bird flaps his wings, thousands of other hard-to-catch details. "A really marvelous series of plates," NATURE. 380 full-pages of plates. Heavy glossy stock, reinforced binding with headbands. 7⅞ x10¾. **T203 Clothbound $10.00**

THE BOOK OF SIGNS, R. Koch. 493 symbols—crosses, monograms, astrological, biological symbols, runes, etc.—from ancient manuscripts, cathedrals, coins, catacombs, pottery. May be reproduced permission-free. 493 illustrations by Fritz Kredel. 104pp. 6⅛ x 9¼. **T162 Paperbound $1.00**

A HANDBOOK OF EARLY ADVERTISING ART, C. P. Hornung. The largest collection of copyright-free early advertising art ever compiled. Vol. I: 2,000 illustrations of animals, old automobiles, buildings, allegorical figures, fire engines, Indians, ships, trains, more than 33 other categories! Vol II: Over 4,000 typographical specimens; 600 Roman, Gothic, Barnum, Old English faces; 630 ornamental type faces; hundreds of scrolls, initials, flourishes, etc. "A remarkable collection," PRINTERS' INK.

Vol. I: Pictorial Volume. Over 2000 illustrations. 256pp. 9 x 12. **T122 Clothbound $10.00**
Vol. II: Typographical Volume. Over 4000 speciments. 319pp. 9 x 12. **T123 Clothbound $10.00**
Two volume set, Clothbound, only **$18.50**

DESIGN FOR ARTISTS AND CRAFTSMEN, L. Wolchonok. The most thorough course on the creation of art motifs and designs. Shows you step-by-step, with hundreds of examples and 113 detailed exercises, how to create original designs from geometric patterns, plants, birds, animals, humans, and man-made objects. "A great contribution to the field of design and crafts," N. Y. SOCIETY OF CRAFTSMEN. More than 1300 entirely new illustrations. xv + 207pp. 7⅞ x 10¾. **T274 Clothbound $4.95**

HANDBOOK OF DESIGNS AND DEVICES, C. P. Hornung. A remarkable working collection of 1836 basic designs and variations, all copyright-free. Variations of circle, line, cross, diamond, swastika, star, scroll, shield, many more. Notes on symbolism. "A necessity to every designer who would be original without having to labor heavily," ARTIST and ADVERTISER. 204 plates. 240pp. 5⅜ x 8.

T125 Paperbound $1.90

THE UNIVERSAL PENMAN, George Bickham. Exact reproduction of beautiful 18th century book of handwriting. 22 complete alphabets in finest English roundhand, other scripts, over 2000 elaborate flourishes, 122 calligraphic illustrations, etc. Material is copyright-free. "An essential part of any art library, and a book of permanent value," AMERICAN ARTIST. 212 plates. 224pp. 9 x 13¾. **T20 Clothbound $10.00**

AN ATLAS OF ANATOMY FOR ARTISTS, F. Schider. This standard work contains 189 full-page plates, more than 647 illustrations of all aspects of the human skeleton, musculature, cutaway portions of the body, each part of the anatomy, hand forms, eyelids, breasts, location of muscles under the flesh, etc. 59 plates illustrate how Michelangelo, da Vinci, Goya, 15 others, drew human anatomy. New 3rd edition enlarged by 52 new illustrations by Cloquet, Barcsay. "The standard reference tool," AMERICAN LIBRARY ASSOCIATION. "Excellent," AMERICAN ARTIST. 189 plates, 647 illustrations. xxvi + 192pp. 7⅞ x 10⅝. **T241 Clothbound $6.00**

AN ATLAS OF ANIMAL ANATOMY FOR ARTISTS, W. Ellenberger, H. Baum, H. Dittrich. The largest, richest animal anatomy for artists in English. Form, musculature, tendons, bone structure, expression, detailed cross sections of head, other features, of the horse, lion, dog, cat, deer, seal, kangaroo, cow, bull, goat, monkey, hare, many other animals. "Highly recommended," DESIGN. Second, revised, enlarged edition with new plates from Cuvier, Stubbs, etc. 288 illustrations. 153pp. 11⅜ x 9. **T82 Clothbound $6.00**

ANIMAL DRAWING: ANATOMY AND ACTION FOR ARTISTS, C. R. Knight. 158 studies, with full accompanying text, of such animals as the gorilla, bear, bison, dromedary, camel, vulture, pelican, iguana, shark, etc., by one of the greatest modern masters of animal drawing. Innumerable tips on how to get life expression into your work. "An excellent reference work,' SAN FRANCISCO CHRONICLE. 158 illustrations. 156pp. 10½ x 8½.
T426 Paperbound $2.00

THE CRAFTSMAN'S HANDBOOK, Cennino Cennini. The finest English translation of IL LIBRO DELL' ARTE, the 15th century introduction to art technique that is both a mirror of Quatrocento life and a source of many useful but ·nearly forgotten facets of the painter's art. 4 illustrations. xxvii + 142pp. D. V. Thompson, translator. 6⅛ x 9¼.   T54 Paperbound **$1.50**

THE BROWN DECADES, Lewis Mumford. A picture of the "buried renaissance" of the post-Civil War period, and the founding of modern architecture (Sullivan, Richardson, Root, Roebling), landscape development (Marsh, Olmstead, Eliot), and the graphic arts (Homer, Eakins, Ryder). 2nd revised, enlarged edition. Bibliography. 12 illustrations. xiv + 266 pp. 5⅜ x 8.   T200 Paperbound **$1.65**

STIEGEL GLASS, F. W. Hunter. The story of the most highly esteemed early American glassware, fully illustrated. How a German adventurer, "Baron" Stiegel, founded a glass empire; detailed accounts of individual glasswork. "This pioneer work is reprinted in an edition even more beautiful than the original," ANTIQUES DEALER. New introduction by Helen McKearin. 171 illustrations, 12 in full color. xxii + 338pp. 7⅞ x 10¾.   T128 Clothbound **$10.00**

THE HUMAN FIGURE, J. H. Vanderpoel. Not just a picture book, but a complete course by a famous figure artist. Extensive text, illustrated by 430 pencil and charcoal drawings of both male and female anatomy. 2nd enlarged edition. Foreword. 430 illus. 143pp. 6⅛ x 9¼.   T432 Paperbound **$1.45**

PINE FURNITURE OF EARLY NEW ENGLAND, R. H. Kettell. Over 400 illustrations, over 50 working drawings of early New England chairs, benches, beds cupboards, mirrors, shelves, tables, other furniture esteemed for simple beauty and character. "Rich store of illustrations . . . emphasizes the individuality and varied design," ANTIQUES. 413 illustrations, 55 working drawings. 475pp. 8 x 10¾.   T145 Clothbound **$10.00**

BASIC BOOKBINDING, A. W. Lewis. Enables both beginners and experts to rebind old books or bind paperbacks in hard covers. Treats materials, tools; gives step-by-step instruction in how to collate a book, sew it, back it, make boards, etc. 261 illus. Appendices. 155pp. 5⅜ x 8.   T169 Paperbound **$1.35**

DESIGN MOTIFS OF ANCIENT MEXICO, J. Enciso. Nearly 90% of these 766 superb designs from Aztec, Olmec, Totonac, Maya, and Toltec origins are unobtainable elsewhere! Contains plumed serpents, wind gods, animals, demons, dancers, monsters, etc. Excellent applied design source. Originally $17.50. 766 illustrations, thousands of motifs. 192pp. 6⅛ x 9¼.   T84 Paperbound **$1.85**

AFRICAN SCULPTURE, Ladislas Segy. 163 full-page plates illustrating masks, fertility figures, ceremonial objects, etc., of 50 West and Central African tribes—95% never before illustrated. 34-page introduction to African sculpture. "Mr. Segy is one of its top authorities," NEW YORKER. 164 full-page photographic plates. Introduction. Bibliography. 244pp. 6⅛ x 9¼.   T396 Paperbound **$2.00**

THE PROCESSES OF GRAPHIC REPRODUCTION IN PRINTING, H. Curwen. A thorough and practical survey of wood, linoleum, and rubber engraving; copper engraving; drypoint, mezzotint, etching, aquatint, steel engraving, die sinking, stenciling, lithography (extensively); photographic reproduction utilizing line, continuous tone, photoengravure, collotype; every other process in general use. Note on color reproduction. Section on bookbinding. Over 200 illustrations, 25 in color. 143pp. 5½ x 8½.   T512 Clothbound **$4.00**

CALLIGRAPHY, J. G. Schwandner. First reprinting in 200 years of this legendary book of beautiful handwriting. Over 300 ornamental initials, 12 complete calligraphic alphabets, over 150 ornate frames and panels, 75 calligraphic pictures of cherubs, stags, lions, etc., thousands of flourishes, scrolls, etc., by the greatest 18th century masters. All material can be copied or adapted without permission. Historical introduction. 158 full-page plates. 368pp. 9 x 13.   T475 Clothbound **$10.00**

* * *

A DIDEROT PICTORIAL ENCYCLOPEDIA OF TRADES AND INDUSTRY, Manufacturing and the Technical Arts in Plates Selected from "L'Encyclopédie ou Dictionnaire Raisonné des Sciences, des Arts, et des Métiers," of Denis Diderot, edited with text by C. Gillispie. Over 2000 illustrations on 485 full-page plates. Magnificent 18th century engravings of men, women, and children working at such trades as milling flour, cheesemaking, charcoal burning, mining, silverplating, shoeing horses, making fine glass, printing, hundreds more, showing details of machinery, different steps. in sequence, etc. A remarkable art work, but also the largest collection of working figures in print, copyright-free, for art directors, designers, etc. Two vols. 920pp. 9 x 12. Heavy library cloth.   T421 Two volume set **$18.50**

* * *

SILK SCREEN TECHNIQUES, J. Biegeleisen, M. Cohn. A practical step-by-step home course in one of the most versatile, least expensive graphic arts processes. How to build an inexpensive silk screen, prepare stencils, print, achieve special textures, use color, etc. Every step explained, diagrammed. 149 illustrations, 8 in color. 201pp. 6⅛ x 9¼.   T433 Paperbound **$1.45**

PUZZLES, GAMES, AND ENTERTAINMENTS

MATHEMATICS, MAGIC AND MYSTERY, Martin Gardner. Astonishing feats of mind reading, mystifying "magic" tricks, are often based on mathematical principles anyone can learn. This book shows you how to perform scores of tricks with cards, dice, coins, knots, numbers, etc., by using simple principles from set theory, theory of numbers, topology, other areas of mathematics, fascinating in themselves. No special knowledge required. 135 illus. 186pp. 5⅜ x 8.
T335 Paperbound **$1.00**

MATHEMATICAL PUZZLES FOR BEGINNERS AND ENTHUSIASTS, G. Mott-Smith. Test your problem-solving techniques and powers of inference on 188 challenging, amusing puzzles based on algebra, dissection of plane figures, permutations, probabilities, etc. Appendix of primes, square roots, etc. 135 illus. 2nd revised edition. 248pp. 5⅜ x 8.
T198 Paperbound **$1.00**

LEARN CHESS FROM THE MASTERS, F. Reinfeld. Play 10 games against Marshall, Bronstein, Najdorf, other masters, and grade yourself on each move. Detailed annotations reveal principles of play, strategy, etc. as you proceed. An excellent way to get a real insight into the game. Formerly titled, "Chess by Yourself." 91 diagrams. vii + 144pp. 5⅜ x 8.
T362 Paperbound **$1.00**

REINFELD ON THE END GAME IN CHESS, F. Reinfeld. 62 end games of Alekhine, Tarrasch, Morphy, other masters, are carefully analyzed with emphasis on transition from middle game to end play. Tempo moves, queen endings, weak squares, other basic principles clearly illustrated. Excellent for understanding why some moves are weak or incorrect, how to avoid errors. Formerly titled, "Practical End-game Play." 62 diagrams. vi + 177pp. 5⅜ x 8.
T417 Paperbound **$1.25**

101 PUZZLES IN THOUGHT AND LOGIC, C. R. Wylie, Jr. Brand new puzzles you need no special knowledge to solve! Each one is a gem of ingenuity that will really challenge your problem-solving technique. Introduction with simplified explanation of scientic puzzle solving. 128pp. 5.⅜ x 8.
T167 Paperbound **$1.00**

THE COMPLETE NONSENSE OF EDWARD LEAR. The only complete edition of this master of gentle madness at a popular price. The Dong with the Luminous Nose, The Jumblies, The Owl and the Pussycat, hundreds of other bits of wonderful nonsense. 214 limericks, 3 sets of Nonsense Botany, 5 Nonsense Alphabets, 546 fantastic drawings, much more. 320pp. 5⅜ x 8.
T167 Paperbound **$1.00**

28 SCIENCE FICTION STORIES OF H. G. WELLS. Two complete novels, "Men Like Gods" and "Star Begotten," plus 26 short stories by the master science-fiction writer of all time. Stories of space, time, future adventure that are among the all-time classics of science fiction. 928pp. 5⅜ x 8.
T265 Clothbound **$3.95**

SEVEN SCIENCE FICTION NOVELS, H. G. Wells. Unabridged texts of "The Time Machine," "The Island of Dr. Moreau," "First Men in the Moon," "The Invisible Man," "The War of the Worlds," "The Food of the Gods," "In the Days of the Comet." "One will have to go far to match this for entertainment, excitement, and sheer pleasure," N. Y. TIMES. 1015pp. 5⅜ x 8.
T264 Clothbound **$3.95**

MATHEMAGIC, MAGIC PUZZLES, AND GAMES WITH NUMBERS, R. V. Heath. More than 60 new puzzles and stunts based on number properties: multiplying large numbers mentally, finding the date of any day in the year, etc. Edited by J. S. Meyer. 76 illus. 129pp. 5⅜ x 8.
T110 Paperbound **$1.00**

FIVE ADVENTURE NOVELS OF H. RIDER HAGGARD. The master story-teller's five best tales of mystery and adventure set against authentic African backgrounds: "She," "King Solomon's Mines," "Allan Quatermain," "Allan's Wife," "Maiwa's Revenge." 821pp. 5⅜ x 8.
T108 Clothbound **$3.95**

WIN AT CHECKERS, M. Hopper. (Formerly "Checkers.") The former World's Unrestricted Checker Champion gives you valuable lessons in openings, traps, end games, ways to draw when you are behind, etc. More than 100 questions and answers anticipate your problems. Appendix. 75 problems diagrammed, solved. 79 figures. xi + 107pp. 5⅜ x 8.
T363 Paperbound **$1.00**

CRYPTOGRAPHY, L. D. Smith. Excellent introductory work on ciphers and their solution, history of secret writing, techniques, etc. Appendices on Japanese methods, the Baconian cipher, frequency tables. Bibliography. Over 150 problems, solutions. 160pp. 5⅜ x 8.
T247 Paperbound **$1.00**

CRYPTANALYSIS, H. F. Gaines. (Formerly, "Elementary Cryptanalysis.") The best book available on cryptograms and how to solve them. Contains all major techniques: substitution, transposition, mixed alphabets, multafid, Kasiski and Vignere methods, etc. Word frequency appendix. 167 problems, solutions. 173 figures. 236pp. 5⅜ x 8.
T97 Paperbound **$1.95**

FLATLAND, E. A. Abbot. The science-fiction classic of life in a 2-dimensional world that is considered a first-rate introduction to relativity and hyperspace, as well as a scathing satire on society, politics and religion. 7th edition. 16 illus. 128pp. 5⅜ x 8.
T1 Paperbound **$1.00**

DOVER BOOKS

HOW TO FORCE CHECKMATE, F. Reinfeld. (Formerly "Challenge to Chessplayers.") No board needed to sharpen your checkmate skill on 300 checkmate situations. Learn to plan up to 3 moves ahead and play a superior end game. 300 situations diagrammed; notes and full solutions. 111pp. 5⅜ x 8. T439 Paperbound **$1.25**

MORPHY'S GAMES OF CHESS, P. W. Sergeant, ed. Play forcefully by following the techniques used by one of the greatest chess champions. 300 of Morphy's games carefully annotated to reveal principles. Bibliography. New introduction by F. Reinfeld. 235 diagrams. x + 352pp. 5⅜ x 8. T386 Paperbound **$1.75**

MATHEMATICAL RECREATIONS, M. Kraitchik. Hundreds of unusual mathematical puzzlers and odd bypaths of math, elementary and advanced. Greek, Medieval, Arabic, Hindu problems; figurate numbers, Fermat numbers, primes; magic, Euler, Latin squares; fairy chess, latruncles, reversi, jinx, ruma, tetrachrome other positional and permutational games. Rigorous solutions. Revised second edition. 181 illus. 330pp. 5⅜ x 8. T163 Paperbound **$1.75**

MATHEMATICAL EXCURSIONS, H. A. Merrill. Revealing stimulating insights into elementary math, not usually taught in school. 90 problems demonstrate Russian peasant multiplication, memory systems for pi, magic squares, dyadic systems, division by inspection, many more. Solutions to difficult problems. 50 illus. 5⅜ x 8. T350 Paperbound **$1.00**

MAGIC TRICKS & CARD TRICKS, W. Jonson. Best introduction to tricks with coins, bills, eggs, ribbons, slates, cards, easily performed without elaborate equipment. Professional routines, tips on presentation, misdirection, etc. Two books bound as one: 52 tricks with cards, 37 tricks with common objects. 106 figures. 224pp. 5⅜ x 8. T909 Paperbound **$1.00**

MATHEMATICAL PUZZLES OF SAM LOYD, selected and edited by **M. Gardner.** 177 most ingenious mathematical puzzles of America's greatest puzzle originator, based on arithmetic, algebra, game theory, dissection, route tracing, operations research, probability, etc. 120 drawings, diagrams. Solutions. 187pp. 5⅜ x 8. T498 Paperbound **$1.00**

THE ART OF CHESS, J. Mason. The most famous general study of chess ever written. More than 90 openings, middle game, end game, how to attack, sacrifice, defend, exchange, form general strategy. Supplement on "How Do You Play Chess?" by F. Reinfeld. 448 diagrams. 356pp. 5⅜ x 8. T463 Paperbound **$1.85**

HYPERMODERN CHESS as Developed in the Games of its Greatest Exponent, ARON NIMZOVICH, F. Reinfeld, ed. Learn how the game's greatest innovator defeated Alekhine, Lasker, and many others; and use these methods in your own game. 180 diagrams. 228pp. 5⅜ x 8. T448 Paperbound **$1.35**

A TREASURY OF CHESS LORE, F. Reinfeld, ed. Hundreds of fascinating stories by and about the masters, accounts of tournaments and famous games, aphorisms, word portraits, little known incidents, photographs, etc., that will delight the chess enthusiast, captivate the beginner. 49 photographs (14 full-page plates), 12 diagrams. 315pp. 5⅜ x 8. T458 Paperbound **$1.75**

A NONSENSE ANTHOLOGY, collected by **Carolyn Wells.** 245 of the best nonsense verses ever written: nonsense puns, absurd arguments, mock epics, nonsense ballads, "sick" verses, dog-Latin verses, French nonsense verses, limericks. Lear, Carroll, Belloc, Burgess, nearly 100 other writers. Introduction by Carolyn Wells. 3 indices: Title, Author, First Lines. xxxiii + 279pp. 5⅜ x 8. T499 Paperbound **$1.25**

SYMBOLIC LOGIC and THE GAME OF LOGIC, Lewis Carroll. Two delightful puzzle books by the author of "Alice," bound as one. Both works concern the symbolic representation of traditional logic and together contain more than 500 ingenious, amusing and instructive syllogistic puzzlers. Total of 326pp. 5⅜ x 8. T492 Paperbound **$1.50**

PILLOW PROBLEMS and A TANGLED TALE, Lewis Carroll. Two of Carroll's rare puzzle works bound as one. "Pillow Problems" contain 72 original math puzzles. The puzzles in "A Tangled Tale" are given in delightful story form. Total of 291pp. 5⅜ x 8. T493 Paperbound **$1.50**

PECK'S BAD BOY AND HIS PA, G. W. Peck. Both volumes of one of the most widely read of all American humor books. A classic of American folk humor, also invaluable as a portrait of an age. 100 original illustrations. Introduction by E. Bleiler. 347pp. 5⅜ x 8. T497 Paperbound **$1.35**

Dover publishes books on art, music, philosophy, literature, languages, history, social sciences, psychology, handcrafts, orientalia, puzzles and entertainments, chess, pets and gardens, books explaining science, intermediate and higher mathematics mathematical physics, engineering, biological sciences, earth sciences, classics of science, etc. Write to:

Dept. catrr.
Dover Publications, Inc.
180 Varick Street, N. Y. 14, N. Y.